FREE TRADE NATION

Frank Trentmann is Professor of History at Birkbeck College, University of London. Born in Hamburg, Germany, he was educated at Harvard and the London School of Economics, before teaching at Princeton. He has published widely on modern history, and was Director of the £5 million Cultures of Consumption research programme.

Praise for *Free Trade Nation*

'Here we have 'a human history of Free Trade' that is at once a delight to read and a cause of profound intellectual stimulation. It graphically brings alive ... the popular passions and prejudices of a world that suddenly ended during the First World War ... This is a book imbued with fine scholarship ... that deserves a wide readership.'
Peter Clarke, *Times Literary Supplement*

'brilliant'
Sunday Telegraph

'This is terrific history that will inspire economists to remember their subject really can arouse passion.'
Evan Davis, BBC

'... an inspired history ... Trentmann's book unfolds a dramatic story ... gripping'
Neue Zuercher Zeitung

'Thoughtful and well-researched'
The Independent

'[A] lucid history of free trade in Britain'
Sunday Express

'a landmark in economic history and the history of ideas'
La Vie des Idées

'fascinating'
Il Riformista

FREE TRADE NATION

COMMERCE, CONSUMPTION, AND CIVIL SOCIETY IN MODERN BRITAIN

FRANK TRENTMANN

OXFORD

UNIVERSITY PRESS

OXFORD
UNIVERSITY PRESS

Great Clarendon Street, Oxford OX2 6DP

Oxford University Press is a department of the University of Oxford.
It furthers the University's objective of excellence in research, scholarship,
and education by publishing worldwide in

Oxford New York

Auckland Cape Town Dar es Salaam Hong Kong Karachi
Kuala Lumpur Madrid Melbourne Mexico City Nairobi
New Delhi Shanghai Taipei Toronto

With offices in

Argentina Austria Brazil Chile Czech Republic France Greece
Guatemala Hungary Italy Japan Poland Portugal Singapore
South Korea Switzerland Thailand Turkey Ukraine Vietnam

Oxford is a registered trade mark of Oxford University Press
in the UK and in certain other countries

Published in the United States
by Oxford University Press Inc., New York

© Frank Trentmann 2008

British Library Cataloguing in Publication Data

Data available

Library of Congress Cataloging in Publication Data

Data available

Typeset by Laserwords Private Limited, Chennai, India
Printed in Great Britain
on acid-free paper by
MPG Books Group in the UK

ISBN 978-0-19-920920-0 (Hbk.)   978-0-19-956732-4 (Pbk.)

1 3 5 7 9 10 8 6 4 2

Contents

Acknowledgements

Whether openness and free exchange or support and shelter better assist a nation's development is one of the oldest controversies in history. In writing this book I have been fortunate to benefit from both.

A wide network of intellectual exchange has provided me with a flow of ideas, stimulation, and points of debate. From the outset, I was lucky to have the encouragement of a group of outstanding scholars, whose support and own work have done much to guide me in mine: Peter Clarke, Tony Howe, Charles Maier, David Starkey, and John Turner. The seeds of this book probably lie in Hamburg, the 'gate to the world', where I grew up. More immediately, the book has been the product of several transatlantic exchanges. Princeton University and Birkbeck College have been wonderfully creative and supportive homes. Intellectual products are social creatures, and this book owes a good deal to my colleagues, past and present, in these two unique places. Sue Marchand, Jeremy Adelman, Shel Garon, Mark Mazower, Joanna Bourke, and Lucy Riall helped me work out the more general historical relevance of the Free Trade story, and stopped me whenever necessary from retreating into the inward-looking, specialist realm that is all too common in British history. In 2002 I benefited from a further breath of comparative fresh air when invited to a visiting professorship at Bielefeld University, which gave me a chance to explore new directions in political history with Gerhard Haupt and colleagues. The Centre for History and Economics at King's College, Cambridge, too, kindly gave me a fellowship, and I am especially grateful to the directors, Emma Rothschild and Gareth Stedman Jones. In thinking about the longer history of commerce, power, and social order, I have drawn much additional inspiration from friends and scholars working on earlier periods: James Livesey, Patrick O'Brien, Steve Pincus, and Donald Winch. For many years now I have been privileged to have the wisdom and advice of three superior intellects, Martin Daunton, David Feldman, and John

Hall. I sincerely thank them and my agent David Godwin for reading the final manuscript, and for always asking the right questions.

Several grants and fellowships provided invaluable infant industry support for a young academic. I am grateful to the Leverhulme Trust, the Scoloudi Foundation/Institute of Historical Research, and the British Academy. The Economic and Social Research Council kindly provided a small grant to assist with the production of maps, expertly drawn by Catherine D'alton, to whom I am very grateful, as to Jon Wilson, for help with editing pictures, to Alan Forth, for always coming to the aid of my computers, and to Stefan Schwarzkopf and Vanessa Taylor for research assistance. More recently, as director of the ESRC–AHRC Cultures of Consumption research programme I have accumulated a whole host of additional debts, many stimulating new contacts in the social sciences and arts and humanities, and, especially, invaluable administrative support from Stefanie Nixon. I am grateful to Matthew Cotton, Christopher Wheeler, the readers and everyone at Oxford University Press, and to Laura Bevir for the index. I also thank sincerely the many archivists and librarians who have helped me in my research, and the persons and institutions who gave permission to reproduce images.

Various parts of this book were first tried out at seminars and international conferences and I should like to thank collectively convenors, commentators, and audiences for helping me to crystallize my ideas at Cambridge University, Harvard University, the Institute of Historical Research (London), Newcastle University, Oxford University, Göttingen University, the Zentrum für Vergleichende Geschichte Europas and Humboldt University in Berlin, the Anglo-American Conference of Historians, the Cobden Bicentenary conference, and the North American Conference on British Studies. I am also grateful to many friends and colleagues for offering comments on earlier drafts and other kinds of help: Mark Bevir, Eugenio Biagini, Kevin Cramer, Jim Cronin, James Epstein, Tony Grafton, Catherine Hall, Peter Hall, Peter Hennessy, Matthew Hilton, Peter Lake, Peter Marsh, Susan Pedersen, Andrew Porter, Barry Supple, Miles Taylor, Duncan Tanner, Philip Williamson, and James Vernon.

With their combined happiness, creativity, and love, Oscar and Julia, my children, have given the book, and its author, the energy and focus they needed. Lumpi was one of the first canines to once again enjoy the benefits of international free trade after Britain reformed its quarantine regulations, a classic non-tariff barrier, and has been a reliable catalyst of fresh ideas in walks on both sides of the Atlantic. For their help with dog migration, thanks must also go to Roland Klemp and to Robert Crews and Margaret Sena. But my final thanks go to my wife, Lizza Ruddick, who has been a loving partner and mother, and the finest mind and editor any author could wish for. The book is dedicated to her with all my love and thanks.

London   Frank Trentmann
April 2007

List of Figures

List of Plates

Introduction
Free Trade and Political Culture

In early June 1904 ten thousand people gathered at Alexandra Palace in north London. They had come to commemorate Richard Cobden's centenary and to confirm their faith in Britain's global destiny as a Free Trade nation. Sixty years earlier the textile manufacturer Cobden had led a successful campaign against the protectionist Corn Laws. Now Britain was the only country in the world left championing Free Trade, a lonely island in a rising sea of tariffs. Even at home tariff supporters were mobilizing. The immense meeting at the 'Palace on the Northern heights' brought together two future British leaders who would shape the twentieth century: Lloyd George and Winston Churchill. The audience stretched from Liberal and Conservative MPs and members of the Peace Society to a large overflow meeting including women's groups, members of the cooperative consumer movement, workers, and radicals. From the moment the choir of Dr Clifford's church struck up the hymn 'God Save the People' the crowd knew what was at stake. 'We stand to-day at the parting of the ways', Henry Campbell-Bannerman, the Liberal leader and future Prime Minister, told them. 'One road—a broad and easy one—leads to Protection, to conscription, to the reducing of free institutions to a mere name. ... And the other road leads to the consolidation of liberty and the development of equity at home, and to treaties of arbitration and amity, with their natural sequences in the arrest and ultimate reduction of armaments, and the lightening of taxation, which presses upon our trade and grinds the faces of the poor.' As darkness fell, Campbell-Bannerman left, flanked by a guard of honour including three hundred torchbearers.[1]

Britain gave Free Trade to the world. It was the closest modern Britain ever came to a national ideology, as important as parliamentary liberty. The repeal of the Corn Laws in 1846 marked the adoption of liberal trade policies, but it was in the late nineteenth and early twentieth centuries that Free Trade grew into a genuine national and democratic culture, reaching all classes and regions, mobilizing men, women, and children, and cutting across party political divides. The meeting at Alexandra Palace was part of a dramatic and unprecedented mobilization of Free Trade into a powerful democratic movement. In tens of thousands of meetings, Free Trade brought together liberal Conservatives, like the young Winston Churchill, with anarchists, like Peter Kropotkin, business tycoons like Alfred Mond with workers, internationalists, and consumers. Free Trade Britain did far more than withstand the protectionist challenges abroad and at home. The battle with Joseph Chamberlain's imperial Tariff Reform crusade—the so-called 'fiscal controversy' that dominated Edwardian politics—also injected Free Trade with new energy and meaning. More than ever before or since, Free Trade occupied the centre of the political imagination, defining people's identity and shaping political communication. The defence of cheap food and open markets was linked to a popular narrative of a vibrant civil society unfolding in Britain thanks to Free Trade, a national story of liberty and freedom that was contrasted with the militarist path of protectionist countries like Imperial Germany.

Globally, Free Trade was Britain's civilizing mission of peace and progress. Domestically, it safeguarded the 'purity of politics' against vested interests. Groups without the vote, especially women, rallied to Free Trade as a form of citizenship. It included them in the political nation. Free Trade was widely embraced as a moral project, a medium for raising the civic-mindedness of all members of society, for creating international trust and understanding, and for civilizing markets—inoculating Britain against the evils of materialism and prejudice. Tariffs threatened Britons' national character and the survival of civil society, not just material interests. For many, the very 'purity and intensity of public spirit' depended on it; as the young Bertrand Russell put it, he felt 'inclined to cut my throat' if tariffs won.[2] Free Trade created a new sense of identity and interest, that of the 'citizen-consumer'. Alongside the citizen as voter, it developed the ideal of the consumer as someone who contributed to the democratic vitality of associational life and who, as a shopper thinking about the welfare of others, would raise the ethical tone of commercial society. For the first time in history consumers were expressly recognized as representing the national interest.

This book is about how Free Trade became so uniquely central to democratic culture and national identity in Britain, and how it lost that centrality during and after the First World War. It offers a historical reflection on a dilemma for all human societies, including our own: a choice between openness and protection. Should we live in an open commercial society and gain from exchanging freely with the rest of the world? Should we have free and equal access to all the goods and markets of the world, or should we have the right to protect our community against global forces? Are we and the world enriched by having free access to cheap goods, or does cheapness threaten welfare? These questions concern ethics as much as economics. And they relate problems of international order to those of democracy and welfare at home. In recent years, especially since the collapse of communism in the late 1980s, a new wave of globalization has given these questions fresh significance and urgency. But while the share of trade as part of the world economy may be unprecedented and new institutional mechanisms have emerged, like the World Trade Organization, the questions at the heart of the current debate about globalization have a longer history. It was in the late nineteenth and early twentieth centuries that the battle for Free Trade reached its peak, and nowhere more so than in Great Britain.

There was a major difference, however, between this earlier wave of globalization and our present one, and this is the central concern of this book. Unlike today, Free Trade was the popular ticket in Britain at the time. People rallied to the defence of Free Trade as the keystone of democracy, peace, and prosperity. This book tells the story of how Free Trade managed to build this democratic culture, and how it fell apart. It follows consumers and businessmen, statesmen and internationalists, women and workers, and looks at how they navigated their way through the challenge of globalization. All these people had material interests, of course, but, as this book shows, their view of the world economy was intimately tied up with passionate ideas about democracy and social justice, international understanding and national identity.

The Edwardian period was the high-water mark of popular political economy. In the decade before the First World War, Free Trade offered

a popular political education. It informed Britons' views of civil society
and economic interests, and of their national mission and place in the
world, at a time when knowledge still remained primarily local. Through
plays, magic lantern shows, and public exhibits, Free Trade entertained
and instructed millions in towns and villages, large and small. Free Trade
entered children's books and discussion circles for young men and women.
Cities were covered in square miles of posters. Political economy was
adapted for the demands of commercial mass politics. It is difficult not
to be sensationalist about the outburst of energy and the level of political
communication mobilized by Free Trade. One group alone organized
over five thousand meetings between the two elections of 1910. Free
Trade was political life. It was ubiquitous. Even tourists and day-trippers at
seaside resorts became engulfed by Free Trade ideas, demonstrations, and
entertainment.

During the course of the First World War and the 1920s, this political
culture came apart, never to be restored. It is tempting to pin the blame
for the problems of Free Trade on protectionist interests or the economic
depression. This is a mistake, this book argues. In modern history, Free
Trade's fate was not just determined by vested interests or a few vocal
groups who lost out in the process of globalization. Nor was it just a
question of institutional openness, or the access of lobbies to the political
process. In modern democracies, what mattered was Free Trade's own
cultural and political strength, its ability to tap into popular sentiment and
mobilize support. How Free Trade lost that ability, and how the ideas and
social groups that had been woven into a Free Trade nation unravelled, is
a central part of our story.

The world depression (1929–31) and electoral battles raised the stakes
for Free Trade, but ultimately its decline was already under way. It was
a longer erosion that reflected deeper moral–intellectual undercurrents
and can be traced to the First World War. Former Free Traders were
confronted with new challenges in domestic politics and international
relations as well as with new pressures of managing the economy. The
war sparked debates over subjects from consumer rights to international
governance. Many thinkers, social movements, and politicians began to
rearrange the relationship between commerce, consumption, and civil
society. As they moved towards a more active role for the state in
protecting consumer interests and towards ideas of trade regulation and
coordination, the earlier Free Trade vision lost its broader appeal. Instead

of giving it a separate economic treatment, I am keen to return the story
of Free Trade to the history of this larger political transformation. There
is a tendency to see Free Trade as a victim or hapless bystander. But Free
Traders were actively involved both in building a Free Trade Nation and
in pulling it down. It was in debates over commerce that many former Free
Traders moved to a new home, developing a new internationalism and a
new social democratic politics of consumption. The formal death of Free
Trade in 1931 was preceded, indeed prepared for, by the retreat of Free
Trade in the political mind.

Here lies the main significance of *Free Trade Nation* for our current
concerns about globalization: it charts the unmooring of civil society and
democratic politics from Free Trade. This book tells the story of how *Free
Trade* (in capital letters), a project that once managed to unite commerce
with ideas of citizenship, consumption, and civil society, became reduced
to *free trade* (in lower case), still, perhaps, a respectable trade theory and
policy goal for liberal economists and technocrats, but now no longer
inspiring widespread public support.

The history of free trade in the modern world can loosely be divided into
four phases. The late seventeenth and eighteenth centuries saw a growing
critique of mercantilism, a system that looked to economic nationalism
as the foundation of a powerful state. In the hands of Francis Hutcheson
and Adam Smith, this critique developed into a moral vision of free trade.
The economic argument—that unhampered exchange raised the level of
wealth for all by encouraging specialization and the most efficient use of
resources—became tied to a more general enlightenment project. Free
trade would put an end to the corrupting influence of aristocratic rule and
monopoly and foster instead the higher moral development of individuals
and nations. The *douceur* of commerce—its benign mild spirit—would
soften the unruly passions that fuelled war and antagonism.[3]

The end of the Napoleonic wars (1815) to the 1870s marks a second phase,
one distinguished by advancing trade liberalization. Liberalization was
particularly pronounced in Great Britain—initiated by William Huskisson
in his budgets in the 1820s and triumphing with Robert Peel's repeal of
the Corn Laws in 1846, the abolition of the Navigation Acts, and William
Gladstone's Free Trade budget of 1860. The switch from protection to
Free Trade was facilitated by the lobbying of the middle-class Anti-Corn
Law League in the 1840s and the influence of evangelical ideas about

Free Trade as God's design. For the political elite, Free Trade became a governing philosophy shared by Whigs and Liberals alike.[4] But the mid-nineteenth-century swing towards freer trade was a broadly shared European phenomenon. The Great Exhibition of 1851 advertized the greatness of Free Trade and stimulated its international reception across the continent. In terms of support and organization, the Anti-Corn Law League outnumbered its continental friends, but Free Trade enjoyed support amongst liberal middle-class groups and reform-minded aristocrats across Europe, stretching from Hamburg to Bordeaux and Milan. The Cobden–Chevalier treaty of 1860 was the diplomatic high point of this liberal moment. This Anglo-French treaty was a bilateral agreement, but via the most-favoured-nation clause it spawned a European-wide commercial treaty network. The mfn article committed the two countries that agreed to it to automatically extend to each other any benefits they gave to third countries: no country could end up with less favourable terms of trade than any other. Any advantages negotiated between France and Italy, for example, were also automatically granted to their other treaty partners, such as Britain.[5]

(3) The late nineteenth century brought a new reality. The Great Depression was followed by a new mercantilism, with demands for economic imperialism and more aggressive interest politics.[6] From the late 1870s governments abandoned low tariffs. A previously liberal atmosphere gave way to a conservative and protectionist climate—everywhere, that is, except in Britain. In this third phase, international convergence was replaced by dramatic divergence, in terms of policy, ideas, and culture more generally. On the Continent, states used tariffs especially to finance ambitious military and social policies.[7] In the British Empire, the white settler colonies such as Australia and Canada joined the protectionist drift. Whereas other societies strengthened and diversified their tariff regimes, however, Britain remained committed to unilateral and pure Free Trade. It was the era of 'insular Free Trade', in the image of Arthur Balfour, Conservative Prime Minister when the fiscal storm hit the nation in 1903.

Free Trade in Britain meant that there were no tariffs at all that discriminated against foreign imports in order to assist any branch of industry or agriculture. Customs duties were for revenue only. To prevent any protectionist effect, they were always matched by an excise tax on equivalent domestic goods. Britain stuck to Free Trade irrespective of the protectionist measures of other countries. In spite of being the most powerful empire and economy at the time, it did not engage in tariff bargaining or opt for reciprocity, where a special privilege granted by one party is only extended to those countries that reciprocate in kind. Moreover, rather than contracting, Free Trade in Edwardian Britain expanded from its earlier intellectual and social foundations into a genuinely popular democratic culture.

The First World War and the inter-war years witnessed the end of this third phase. Free Trade in Britain lost its doctrinal, quasi-religious status. As in other countries, it became one policy amongst others, an economic tool that, instead of inspiring profound cultural energy and dogmatic loyalty, could be modulated, revised, and complemented with subsidies or other forms of regulation. If necessary, it could be abandoned altogether.

Phase four, the final phase, stretches from the 1930s to the present. *Free Trade* has shrunk into *free trade*. The rules of multilateralism and non-discrimination have shaped the post-World War Two international order, following the Bretton Woods conference in 1944. But the habitat of free trade has been reduced to the more technical pages of economic theory and the diplomatic fineprint of international rules and negotiated tariff reductions under the umbrella of the General Agreement on Tariffs and Trade (GATT) after 1947 and the World Trade Organization (WTO), its successor since 1994. Popular sympathies and mass support are now on the side of 'Fair Trade', in favour of allowing developing countries some shelter against stronger competitors, and openly suspicious of free trade as a tool of global capital and unaccountable technocrats.

It is the third phase that is vital to this book. British Free Trade in the late nineteenth and early twentieth centuries did not differ only in degree from contemporary societies then or developments before or since. It differed in kind. Clearly, the four phases sketched above are not tight compartments. History is not that tidy. They contain overlapping waves of ideas, social movements, and political changes. Certain developments continue, some are revised, others, again, are cut short. Thus, it is possible, for example, to observe a radical appropriation of Adam Smith already in the writings of Tom Paine and Antoine-Nicolas de Condorcet in Britain and France in the 1780s and 1790s. Condorcet complemented Smith's belief in the progressive virtue of freedom of trade with a commitment to government intervention to ensure basic welfare for all citizens in the transition to a commercial society.[8] This vision fell victim to the reaction against the French Revolution. In Britain it was replaced by an evangelical and socially more conservative world view in which freedom of trade functioned as a divine instrument for stabilizing society.[9]

From a different ideological perspective, it is possible to point to existing neo-libertarian groups who continue to champion Free Trade pure today. Such instances, however, do not alter what is the main historical problem: why was Free Trade so central in Victorian and Edwardian Britain, and why did it erode? This centrality, as we shall see, was not created out of thin air, nor was it a simple economic reflex or echo of past ideas.

The real problem, therefore, is how Free Trade managed to generate such overwhelming support and become a secular religion in one context but not in others. Most commentators have focused on the mid-Victorian period, especially the repeal of the Corn Laws in 1846. But Edwardian Free Trade is a different problem, and it is important to put the difference between the two periods in perspective. The Anti-Corn Law League (ACLL) has received disproportionate attention. In part, this reflects its pioneering role as a lobbying group, something that has especially intrigued political scientists and economists eager to test models of public choice. But it never commanded a democratic popular culture. The repeal of the Corn Laws was masterminded by Robert Peel in a pre-democratic system.[10] The ACLL itself was largely middle-class and was viewed with suspicion as a bourgeois interest group. Popular alliances existed in a few towns but they were far outweighed by conflicts with Chartists elsewhere. Attempts to recruit urban operatives failed, while agricultural labourers feared Free Trade would mean lower incomes and higher unemployment. Most branches were concentrated in the industrial heartland of Lancashire and Yorkshire, while entire regions, including Wales, were virtually untouched by Free Trade.[11]

The dogmatic and popular force of Free Trade also sets Edwardian Britain categorically apart from other export-oriented economies, and highlights the limits of explanations invoking primarily economic factors, such as a country's involvement in international trade. The defeat of protectionism was absolute. Britain was a pure Free Trade nation, without any tariffs or subsidies. It is this fundamentalist stance that places Britain in its own category, and calls for our attention. Denmark and Sweden, for example, were societies that had a higher percentage of exports as part of GNP than Britain—28 per cent and 24 per cent, compared to Britain's 17 per cent. Yet they had tariffs on manufactures—14 per cent in the case of Denmark.[12] The United States, often seen to have taken up the mantle of free trade in the post-1945 era, still had a tariff of 12 per cent in 1962, subsidized the export of its wheat surpluses through its food aid programme, and has continued to rely on hundreds of countervailing duties, anti-dumping actions, and non-tariff barriers—practices that would have horrified the average Free Trade Briton before the First World War. The ease with which free trade policies are today qualified or complemented with subsidies or non-tariff barriers is a good illustration of how far Free Trade has fallen from its former ideological heights.

What is 'fair' trade and whether Free Trade is really 'free' are questions that have been hotly debated right up to the present day. Their meanings have shifted over time, bringing with them shifts in popular politics. This book is an attempt to think about how these competing terms changed their meaning and power in the public mind. In the historical period of the book, 'Fair Trade' first emerged as a movement of British producers who wanted to shelter their own trades against cheap imports coming into Britain freely. Other countries, it was said, were not playing fair, because producers were benefiting from cheap labour and operating behind the shelter of a tariff wall. 'Tariff Reform', its main successor in the decade before the First World War, was about an imperial sense of fairness—giving members of Britain's imperial family preferential treatment and using tariffs against those foreign countries which were not willing to lower their tariffs on British goods. By contrast, 'Fairtrade' today is about consumers in developed countries voluntarily helping distant producers in developing countries, such as small coffee farmers in Costa Rica or cotton farmers in Senegal. Fairtrade is a licensed logo reserved for products that offer producers a 'fair price', and most readers will be familiar with this concept, having sipped Fairtrade coffee or peeled Fairtrade bananas.[13] In social movements campaigning for trade justice, fair trade means allowing developing countries to assist their local producers and shelter them against more powerful competitors and trade liberalization. By contrast, many economists argue that far from promoting welfare and justice, Fairtrade merely aggravates the plight of poor producers by encouraging them to stay in markets already flooded with excess goods.[14] Progressive economists, led by Joseph Stiglitz, have proposed international reforms to make trade both free and fair. Freer trade, especially the rolling back of non-tariff barriers in developed countries, would be linked to a set of pro-development initiatives designed to give poor countries a fair chance to share in the benefits of free trade.[15]

For British Free Traders a century ago, fairness and freedom were one and the same. Free Trade for them meant that all groups in society were treated equally, without favours being given to particular industries or farmers. By the same token, Britain treated all foreign countries alike. In contrast to the multilateral Bretton Woods system after the Second World War, Britain's Free Trade system was unilateral. Britain kept its door wide open irrespective of whether other countries were building tariff walls, subsidizing their home industries, or dumping goods. Throughout this book I use the terms which the historical participants battled over so passionately: 'Tariff Reform', for the protectionist programme, 'Free Trade' for those who dogmatically defended an open door and were opposed to any kind of tariff, however small.

In spite of the libraries that have been written about trade, commercial policy, and interest group politics, the political culture of Edwardian Free Trade and its erosion has attracted little attention from either historians or social scientists. This is curious, especially from a purely economic point of view. The sheer size and passion of Free Trade politics at the time is at odds with the very marginal effects liberalization had on trade and growth. Industrial growth and GNP in Europe, in fact, increased faster in the protectionist period 1890–1913 than in the low-tariff mid-Victorian years. A few industries, like British cotton and French silk, benefited from the bilateral trade agreements initiated by the Anglo-French treaty of 1860, but overall the effect was slight. Some recent economists have even suggested that neither trade liberalization in the 1860s–70s nor the post-1945 multilateral GATT and its successor, the WTO, affected trade patterns at all.[16] Why then did Britons make such a fuss?

Few historians have failed to note the importance of Free Trade in Britain in our period, but this has hardly amounted to sustained attention, let alone explanation. The main focus has been on high politics: party political manoeuvres leading to the general elections of 1906, 1910, and 1923, where protectionism was defeated, and the formation of the National Government in 1931, which introduced the general tariff. With the exception of Anthony Howe, who has traced how the Whig and Liberal elite appropriated Free Trade as a governing formula after 1846,[17] most have tended to take its strength as given. They have concentrated their attention, instead, on the protectionist challenge and its devastating impact on the Conservative party. While we, therefore, have detailed insights into party leaders' strategies, the evolving imperial and social programme of Tariff

Reform, and its supporters,[18] we are ultimately left with a dilemma. These accounts are better equipped to explain the protectionist challenge than the successful defence of Free Trade. Without the latter, the former would have triumphed in Britain as it did in the rest of the world. All societies at the time generated protectionist pressures—and have continued to do so. What was peculiar in Britain and needs explanation was that they were rebuffed by a popular Free Trade army. Edwardian Free Trade overcame what political scientists call the costs of collective action. Consumers and the public were not steamrollered by more concentrated interest groups. Free Trade managed to mobilize quite diverse groups and diffuse interests into a national cause. It was a historic achievement of political energy and imagination, far from inevitable or natural. Quite the contrary, democratic politics have proved a difficult terrain for Free Trade. As recent American advocates have acknowledged, the limited progress of trade liberalization after 1945 stemmed in part from the difficulty of generating popular support.[19]

This book offers an alternative approach to the problem of Free Trade and of how to write about the economy in politics and culture more generally. So it is helpful to contrast it briefly with the three main explanations that have come to dominate. One views trade policy as an instrument of state power ('hegemony'). A second emphasizes the power of financial and mercantile groups with a strong interest in the global economy and access to government ('gentlemanly capitalism'). Finally, a third focuses on the rational interests of voters and sectors ('public choice'). These are not just academic models; their assumptions also inform the public discourse about globalization, where popular critics invariably present free trade as the result of either technocrats and institutional power (the WTO) or of organized capital, while its defenders blame the backlash against it on vested interests or small but vocal 'losers'. All these approaches are quite good at explaining the position of particular groups or sectors, as long as the question is one of economic costs and benefits. What they cannot explain is the reversal of fortune of Free Trade in democratic culture. For that we need a historical approach that places trade more fully within public life as a whole.

The 'hegemony' model, developed by scholars of international relations, views trade as 'determined by the interests and power of states acting to maximize national goals'.[20] Free trade comes about when there is a hegemonic state that can offer the rewards and punishments necessary to maintain an open world order—Britain in the nineteenth century, the United States after World War Two. This approach has the merit of recognizing the relative autonomy of the state, instead of seeing government as a mere vehicle of capitalist interests. But it also has historical weaknesses. Countries with similar positions in the world economy have adopted a range of different policies. Indeed, it fails to explain why the British state adopted unilateral Free Trade in the first place. In the mid-Victorian period, Britain enjoyed unrivalled power. Why did it not use its huge domestic market as a weapon, bargaining to maximize its wealth and power and drive down the tariffs of its competitors?[21] If Britannia was a hegemon, she clearly did not act as the model would predict. Again, it was Britain's stubborn unilateralism that in the 1880s and 1890s undermined French efforts to preserve the commercial treaty network.[22] Nor is it easy to explain why Britain did not modify its Free Trade position once it entered a stage of relative decline in the late nineteenth century. The state is not a uniform actor. Rather it was the site of a growing debate about what the national interest was and how best to protect it. This discussion included the fiscal capacity of the state in its relations both with taxpayers at home and with foreign countries and the Empire abroad.

The second approach is related. It links the interest of the state more directly to powerful groups with a stake in the global economy. Following Joseph Schumpeter a century ago, this is what some recent historians have rediscovered as 'gentlemanly capitalism'.[23] This thesis has the advantage of putting finance and trade back at the centre of Britain's imperial expansion. The City, the financial-mercantile centre, was of course materially involved in the running of the world economy, and benefited handsomely. What is less clear is how much weight should be attributed to 'gentlemanly capitalists' as a distinct group in the political driver's seat. Merchants and financiers were far more divided over trade policy in the 1840s and 1900s than is sometimes realized; so too were most industrial sectors.[24] Public politics ensured that Free Trade was more than just a trade policy, and this meant that gentlemanly capitalists adopted positions that were inevitably shaped by the broader ideas and anxieties of the political milieus they inhabited. In the final analysis, Britain's adherence to Free Trade was not brought about by a hegemonic state or the City but by the powerful mobilization of groups in civil society.

A final approach, largely favoured by economists and 'public choice' analysts, is to focus on the rational choice of voters and sectors. Individual outlooks and group interests are here determined by their position in the economy. Producers, merchants, workers, and so forth are rational actors who seek to maximize their utility through trade policy. The serious problem with this approach is that interests are viewed as prior to ideas. There is no space for the changing meaning and salience of an economic idea, the creation of knowledge, or the various beliefs and norms that guide human behaviour in the economy. Politics is reduced to a mechanical game that arranges pre-existing interests.[25]

Edwardians weighed the costs and benefits of Free Trade and Tariff Reform but this was not a purely individualist material calculation: it was also informed by a collective vision of social justice, democratic culture, peace, the national past and the future of civilization. Economists today would do well to recall what the founding father of their profession, Alfred Marshall, observed in the aftermath of the Edwardian elections where Free Trade defeated Tariff Reform: 'the division between the districts ... does not run with the interests of the population in T.R. or F.T'.[26] Political communication helped shape Britons' sense of their private and collective interest by moulding information about the standard of living, the national interest, and the world economy. Indeed, Free Trade culture played a decisive role in launching a whole new self-conscious interest: 'the consumer'. It was within and through this political culture, not outside it, that interests and trade policy were decided.

It would be gratuitous to rehearse all the problems of these approaches.[27] Two shared misunderstandings deserve emphasis because they have especially stood in the way of coming to grips with the making and unmaking of a democratic Free Trade culture. The first is the tendency to view Free Trade as a natural choice. This presumes that societies are best off with liberal trade, and will follow this course of action, as long as people have full knowledge of their rational interests and are not disadvantaged by a political system that favours the lobbying of more narrowminded interests. Obviously, trade theory has identified exceptions to this natural state of affairs, but the point remains that liberal textbook accounts presume that most people, given the choice, will choose free trade. As an idea, too, free trade is seen to reflect this higher rationality, steadily perfecting trade theory in the modern period as it sees off less sophisticated challenges.[28] From this view, the British Free Trade elections prove the soundness of economic theory.[29]

The second error is to separate ideas from interests. Free Trade is framed as a natural expression of rational interests, its rivals dismissed as products of prejudice, ideology, or vested interest. Free Trade, in short, is a lifeless calculation, free of ideology, passion, and culture. At best, beliefs and cultural practices become epiphenomena, a mere add-on to deeper material interests. Both these weaknesses ultimately result from an intuitive recourse to individualistic economic reasoning as a guide to what is normal and needs no explanation (free trade) and what is an aberration and needs explanation (protectionism). It obscures precisely what calls for investigation. The successful mobilization of Free Trade in Edwardian Britain was not the norm but the exception in the modern world. In spirit and practice it was closer to nationalism and socialism, the other two ideological churches and mass movements of the modern period, than to a simple material choice.

This book is a human history of Free Trade. It puts people, their ideas and values, their passions and prejudices, back into the picture. It offers a colour version of political economy. To explain how the Free Trade nation came together and fell apart, it follows Britons, their beliefs and hopes in freedom of trade, and their disillusionment. Instead of anchoring the analysis either in the market or the state, most of our story looks at the space between, that of civil society and popular politics. It was here that the energy and vision of a democratic Free Trade culture was generated, and lost. To prevent misunderstanding, this does not mean that developments within the economy or state can be ignored. Far from it, as the emphasis on the repercussions of the First World War for producers, consumers, and the state will show. But it is wise to recognize the gaps that exist between people's position in the economy, the way this position is known and understood, and the political beliefs and actions resulting from it. Interests, knowledge, and beliefs are socially created. Attention to the role of ideas, stories, and languages helps to explain why certain interpretations of material interests are formed (rather than others), and how they became important in political life. This does not mean that people are passive constructs of an enclosed discourse. Quite the contrary. Free Traders played an active role in shaping ideas of politics and the economy.[30]

At the centre of this story are the three C's that form the subtitle of this volume: commerce, consumption, and civil society. The survival of Free Trade before the First World War was the result of a novel convergence between these three C's—freedom of commerce became linked to a civil society of citizen-consumers. This combination would unravel during the war and inter-war years, resulting in the erosion of Free Trade.

Civil society plays a critical role in the story of Free Trade because it concerns both ideas of the appropriate relationship between state and citizens *and* the political action of social movements. The removal of tariffs in the mid-Victorian period helped soften people's earlier view of the state as a corrupt and exploitative instrument of the ruling class. It would be too simple, however, to see 'Free Trade finance' just as a 'technique by which market capitalism was justified to working men'. Free Trade not only 'permitted the relative autonomy and propriety of working-class politics',[31] it came to be viewed as an active nursery of democracy. While few people in the late nineteenth century any longer referred explicitly to 'civil society' in the language of the enlightenment, popular Free Trade envisaged the social as relatively autonomous from state and market. Groups like the Women's Cooperative Guild, the cooperative movement, and trade unions rallied to the defence of Free Trade as the natural habitat of a strong civil society.

The alliance of freedom of commerce and civil society rested on trust between governed and governors—trust that the state would treat its citizens fairly and not use taxes or tariffs to favour particular interest groups. Here Edwardian liberals inherited one favourable condition from the fiscal reforms initiated by Peel and completed by his pupil Gladstone: an image of the state as 'neutral'.[32] In addition, the alliance depended on a view that an open, unregulated market nurtured civil society, rather than spawning social division and moral decay. It is important to remember that the Free Trade nation was constructed against the backdrop of both growing reliance on foreign farmers and an expanding world of consumption. In fin-de-siècle Europe both developments brought anxieties about national dependence and the erosion of nation, culture, and social hierarchy by the commercial world. The period 1870–1914 saw the creation of an integrated global food system. This was the result mainly of technological advances in shipping, not trade policy. If in the late 1860s it cost 4s. 7½ d. to ship a quarter of wheat from New York to Liverpool, this had fallen to 11¼ d by 1902.[33] People became dependent for their daily bread on ever more distant producers. The British agricultural labour force declined dramatically: from 1.5 million in the late 1860s to just over 1 million on the eve of the First World War. This was far from atypical. Germany and the Low Countries became net importers of grain in this period. Everywhere protectionists voiced the same fear. Food might be cheaper if bought through the open market, but cheapness had a price: it sacrificed domestic producers, weakened the nation through emigration and depopulation, and left society at the mercy of foreign producers and the global economy, perhaps even risking mass starvation in times of crisis and war.

Politically, this was the winning argument—everywhere except in Britain. How was Free Trade able to withstand these nationalist panics? Partly, it revived an older internationalist ethics, in which Free Trade spread peace between societies. Partly it created its own national story of liberation in which Free Traders had led Britons from hunger and bondage to food and freedom. The willingness to live in an open world, rather than follow a beggar-thy-neighbour drift towards tariffs and greater self-sufficiency, also followed from a more positive, democratic embrace of the consumer. Instead of ignoring the consumer, or subordinating their interests to those of producers and states, the consumer emerged as a public interest not to be sacrificed.

The new civic persona of the consumer was crucial for completing the synergy between freedom of trade and civil society. The citizen-consumer gave Free Trade a democratic appeal in an age of mass politics. The idea of the consumer has become so ubiquitous in today's world that it may come as a surprise to hear how short its history is. At a time when one-third of male workers did not have the vote and organized women's movements were fighting for it,[34] it brought women and men, children and the elderly into public politics. Humans have of course always consumed, but for most of history this did not generate a shared sense of people as 'consumers' (rather than as citizens, workers, mothers, etc.). Before the late nineteenth century, the consumer had been very narrowly defined—someone who consumed or payed tax on resources like water and gas or foodstuffs like sugar—or carried negative connotations—an unproductive person, someone who used up or wasted resources.[35]

Free Trade put the consumer on the political map. This was in spite of the rapidly expanding commercial world of shopping, leisure, and material temptations, the sort of 'consumerism' that many contemporaries and observers since have held responsible for undermining public spirit and democratic culture. Free Trade, which was, after all, defending a policy of 'cheapness', managed to defuse the association between consumption, materialism, and self-centredness. Through a focus on 'necessities' or basic goods, cheapness became primarily a language of social justice, distracting from more selfish, acquisitive aspects of consumption. Consumers, in this view, were part of civic life—not just customers in a shop. Free Trade, it was hoped, would instil consumers with consideration for the rest of the community. Instead of a retreat from public life, consumption would foster civic participation and, over time, raise the quality of production.

With the 'cheap loaf' as a symbol of the right of all Britons to the cheapest goods available on the world market, Free Traders painted a picture of equity and social solidarity. This system was not egalitarian, but there was a strong belief that it kept the lid on extreme inequalities, both at the top of society and at the bottom. Millionaires and capitalist trusts, as well as hunger and social anarchy, in this view, were the products of protectionist societies abroad. As much as the power of the navy, it was the civic combination of the consumer and civil society that explains the remarkable public trust in Britain in an open market and the acceptance of dependence on others.

By turning private acts and choices into matters of public justice and action, Free Trade claimed the consumer for the political nation. There was nothing natural or inevitable about this. In most societies at the time, the consumer had not even made a political appearance. In Imperial Germany, where there was also agitation about the cost of living before the First World War, even liberal critics of tariffs looked at the consumer as a separate interest group, not the embodiment of the public interest.[36] In the United States, Simon Patten, one of the first thinkers to turn his attention to consumption, believed that selfish individuals would give way to a social age of abundance, yet supported tariffs as a way to reduce 'inefficient consumption' and preserve social balance and economic diversity.[37] In post-1945 Japan, social movements have embraced consumers as part of an organic interest of producers and nation, and promoted agricultural self-sufficiency.[38] More recently, consumer groups in West and East have rallied towards fair trade—not free trade. The historical significance of the Edwardians' democratic appeal to the citizen-consumer becomes clear when we compare it to the original vision of commercial society. In the eighteenth century this had developed in tandem with that of civil society, but had focused on the merchant, celebrating the public virtues of economic self-interest. This made Free Trade vulnerable in conditions of popular politics to the charge of being a hypocritical tool of selfish capitalists—charges with an impressive radical pedigree stretching from Chartists in the early Victorian period to today's movements for global civil society. The 'citizen-consumer' helped Edwardians build a democratic defence of Free Trade instead.

The First World War set in motion a process that unravelled the three C's woven together in Free Trade culture. The end of Free Trade in 1931 was not a temporary defeat, nor just the work of the world depression. It was the result of a more profound, ongoing erosion that began to gather momentum in the First World War and spread thereafter. The war disrupted the global trade and monetary system, restructured class relations, and created new forms of social identity and collective memory. Wartime challenges prompted a search for new ways of looking at society, the economy, and the world. Part II of this book follows people through this process. Organized consumers worried about the secure supply of foodstuffs at stable prices; internationalists were turning towards global governance and coordination; businessmen were concerned with organizing their trades to regain markets. What ultimately mattered were not the economic changes by themselves but how these groups made sense of their new material world and tried to order it. The old Free Trade model was subjected to doubts, disillusionment, revision, and rejection. Choice, cheapness, and competition lost their attraction. Stability and coordination of trade became the new gospel.

In the war and post-war years these groups would migrate to different ends of the political spectrum—the cooperatives and new internationalists as well as many progressive liberals moved to the Labour party, while businessmen and the middle classes moved further to the Conservatives. Underneath, however, there was a shared disillusionment with core Free Trade beliefs. Earlier assumptions about the autonomy of civil society from the state, about cheapness as the defender of the consumer interest, and about the ability of commerce to pacify international relations and stimulate wealth and welfare, all proved problematic. Organized consumers, once called into political existence, developed a life of their own. An emphasis on the consumer as citizen led to calls for greater state regulation to prevent scarcities and profiteering. International food trusts and price fluctuations showed how vulnerable consumers were, without some help from the state. The new knowledge of nutrition reinforced this momentum away from a Free Trade chorus of 'cheapness' to a more social democratic language of healthy food at stable prices for all. Stability, with the help of the state, also became a mantra for businessmen, who turned to tariffs not merely as a defence against unfair competitors but as an aid to modernization. Internationalists meanwhile recognized the power of states in the world economy. Instead of unilateral Free Trade, they looked towards international organizations to coordinate trade and to provide a new democratic bridge between the global and the local.

These processes happened in parallel and sometimes reinforced each other. If they all played a role in undermining Free Trade, however, they were not all of equal weight. How groups in civil society responded mattered more than bare economic facts or the interests of the state. It was from within civil society that Free Trade had been able to build its strongest bulwark before the First World War. And it was here that erosion would leave it most vulnerable when the world depression hit in the autumn of 1929. The doubts amongst organized consumers were particularly important. The critique of the international vision of Free Trade added to the damage. For it had been ideas about international peace and order that had kept many producers, business and labour alike, in the Free Trade camp before the First World War, in spite of serious economic doubts. When these broader links were broken, producers turned more easily towards trade regulation and protection. By the late 1920s, even some sections of the British state were warming to a more select, pragmatic use of tariffs; Board of Trade officials defended so-called safeguarding duties. In the final analysis, however, the main dynamics of erosion were coming from civil society, not business or the state. The general tariff, when it was finally introduced in the winter of 1931–2, was not the result of industrial lobbies or state actors. It was a revolution that was steered by politicians but only succeeded because Free Trade's public army of supporters had left the field.

This book is about more than Free Trade. It uses the case of Free Trade to write a new history of politics. The rise and fall of Free Trade illustrates how political sensibility and ideas changed from a liberal to a more social democratic order. But instead of sticking to a standard history of political ideas, I am keen to capture politics as a process, with its changing practices, rituals, passions, and conflict. There has been a tendency to overrationalize Free Trade, to emphasize its robustness as trade theory, and to invoke rational calculations. But Free Trade was also the stuff of riots, of entertainment, of fear and fantasy, of flying loaves and sausages, with mass meetings, parades, slide shows, and exhibits. Finally, the book is an attempt to reconnect domestic and global issues that have too often been put into separate containers.

When in January 1932 Neville Chamberlain, the Chancellor of the Exchequer in the national government, celebrated the introduction of the general tariff as the final triumph of the Tariff Reform crusade his father had launched three decades earlier, it was an act of filial piety. From this book, a more interesting and important story emerges. The battle between Free Trade and Tariff Reform that had dominated political life for generations had come to an end. Except for a diminishing minority of hardliners at the margins of politics, neither tariffs nor Free Trade was any longer an all-consuming subject. From the eighteenth century onwards, the idea of commercial society and freedom of commerce had been central to discussions of social development, global relations, and the relation between the two. Free Trade took on different meanings in different contexts. It could be tied to notions of the progressive unfolding of a commercial, civil society, to a vision of a more stationary, Christian society, or to popular democracy and social insurance—as in the Edwardian period. Yet, whatever form it took, freedom of trade had been the starting point for a more general discussion of the social and international order, the body politic and public morals, as well as of material wealth. The erosion of Free Trade during and after the First World War marked the historic end of this tradition of the modern imagination. People have, of course, continued to debate questions of social justice, wealth, political representation, and international peace. But freedom of trade ceased to be the shared frame of discussion, combining moral and political with economic subjects. In public life, political economy fragmented into a series of parallel discourses, ranging from employment, and the basket of the consumer, to trade figures, taxes, or monetary affairs. The central unifying frame had gone.

The erosion of Free Trade reveals the gradual realignment of a liberal vision of the world. This provides insights into the decline of the Liberal party, but it has broader implications for our understanding of modern politics. The rational picture of Free Trade has been supported by a frequent contrast in political styles between emotional conservatism and rational liberalism. This was a far cry from the reality of politics in our period. It needed political marketing to sell Free Trade ideas, Edwardian activists and politicians recognized. The rediscovery of their use of showmanship and advertising has implications for our picture of political culture in commercial societies and 'mass' democracies more generally. In intellectual traditions ranging as wide as communitarianism and the Frankfurt school, consumerism and citizenship tend to be viewed as polar opposites, locked in a zero-sum game.[39] With the expansion of mass media and commercial leisure, the late nineteenth and early twentieth centuries, in these views, witnessed the 'colonization' or absorption of deliberative democracy by commercial styles and imperatives. Yet Free Trade in fact produced a counter-narrative—that of the civic consumer—and manipulated commercial forms of communication—shopping, advertising, print—for the purposes of democratic politics.

The story of Free Trade also illuminates the changing flow between local and global ideas of equity and mutual obligation. Histories of citizenship have been overwhelmingly written in the shadow of the mid-twentieth-century welfare state and through traditions of the nation-state. These have mainly been domestic (some followers of Michel Foucault would say domesticating) stories: citizenship has been a saga of the changing relationship between individual and state defined in terms of voting rights, military service, social insurance, or governing the self. Free Trade was an essential part of the liberal compact that ruled Britain before the First World War, combining openness to the world with old age pensions and unemployment benefits at home. But while these social reforms and their genesis have received ample attention, we know far less about the role of Free Trade in people's lives. Putting Free Trade back at the centre of the story changes the chronological markers of this history. Edwardian politics were not only a milestone on the road to 1945 and the rise of the welfare state; they also connect with our current era of globalization and renewed concern about how to reconcile openness, fairness, and civil society.

Discussions of democratic inclusion and social justice took place in conjunction with debates about the international order and Britons' place in it. Free Trade held out a symmetrical image of peace and equity, an ethical link between a just and peaceful domestic order and a pacific and prosperous global order. The relationship between the place of citizens in their own state and in the world is, of course, a complex one, and we must not romanticize the Free Trade vision, forgetting the ambivalent social and ethical realities of freedom of trade in practice. In *Late Victorian Holocausts*, Mike Davis has vividly shown how imperial Free Trade policies spread famine and death in the late nineteenth century and helped create the Third World.[40] The precise impact of this liberal trade regime can be debated, as can the fairness and efficiency of earlier trade networks. But clearly we need to know more about the moral as well as material sources of support for policies that had major global consequences. How were 'nice people', like radicals, progressive liberals, and women's movements, able to support Free Trade? In recent years we have made significant progress in appreciating how imperial and metropolitan societies were intertwined.[41] Following the defence and erosion of Free Trade culture offers a further way to explore the dynamic between ideas of democratic inclusion and global order. Before the First World War, the Free Trade debate was a major channel through which Britons acquired a sense of the world. International peace and democracy at home were symbiotic in the Free Trade vision. But, in general, there was a political division of labour between the local and the global. Citizenship was a domestic matter internal to states. Internationally, it was freedom of commerce that would spin a web of peaceful and wealth-creating connections across the globe. Famine and war, in this view, were the result of bad government, artificial interference in a benign natural order, the fault of Oriental despotism or Western feudal elites.

The years after 1914 saw an intellectual and ethical rearrangement of the global and the domestic. As internationalists rediscovered politics and institutional modes of global coordination, they were forced to rethink the domestic foundations of democracy as well. They looked beyond the nation-state to new forms of international governance, while at the same time questioning the fusion of citizenship and nationality within societies. Civic identities needed to be expanded across local and global political spheres. Concerns for global justice, as well as international stability, suggested that consumers needed to care about distant producers, and vice versa. Here were essential parts of a new political imagination and international ethics that came to the fore in the 1930s–40s, shaping the outlook of early international organizations as well as the global civic understanding of social movements, like the cooperatives. The changing conception of famine and world hunger illustrates this shift. Hunger was no longer a foreign phenomenon, caused by internal problems. It was a world problem. Fighting world hunger became a shared political project. Citizenship at home, in this view, was coupled with a sense of belonging to a global order with global civic duties—fair trade, not free trade.

In a speech in Geneva in 2004, Anne Krueger, managing director of the International Monetary Fund (IMF), praised trade liberalization for accelerating growth and reducing poverty. Yet protectionism, she noted, remained remarkably successful. The success of future talks at the WTO would depend on generating more popular support for free trade. Krueger held up modern Britain as a historical example.[42]

Trade and global civil society, poverty, and social justice have once again moved to the top of the political agenda. The next few years will show to what degree a popular base for free trade can be rebuilt. The WTO's last round of negotiations, the Doha talks, stalled in 2006. Most of the pressure for trade liberalization has come from a ministerial level, from negotiators in developed nations, especially the European Union and the United States, while developing nations have resisted opening up their economies further. In society more generally, the supporters of free trade are few and far between. At the time of writing, the most dogmatic supporters of free trade are libertarian networks and anarcho-capitalist groups in America and Europe who view the WTO and any form of state interference as a sign of an expanding 'fascist' state.[43] Activists protesting at G8 and other meetings of the world's leading nations also detest the WTO, but for the opposite reason: it is seen as an undemocratic agent of multinational capital. Looking at broader sections of civil society and popular politics, it is clear that most social reform and consumer movements, progressive and environmentalist non-governmental organizations view free trade pure with suspicion. They advocate, instead, trade justice or fair trade, giving developing countries a chance to build up their own industries and shield their producers from the world market.

This book is not an economic argument about which side is right. Rather it offers a historical perspective on how people in the past tackled the challenge of balancing openness, democracy, and social justice. It retrieves important elements that have got lost in the current debate. For either side in the current battle over trade liberalization, it is timely to understand how Free Trade a century ago managed to build a democratic base, and why it came apart. For here lie the origins of our current predicament of how to combine commerce, consumption, and civil society.

PART
I

Building
a Free Trade Nation

Prologue

At 8.45 on Saturday morning 14 March 1903, the hull of the incoming liner *Norman* suddenly emerged out of the haze outside Southampton's Ocean Quay. On shore, groups had gathered around a colourfully decorated reception stand to welcome home 'Britain's Empire Statesman'. Slowly, the *Norman* was hauled alongside and great cheers erupted from the shore and neighbouring ships as Joseph Chamberlain and his wife came into full view. After travelling more than 16,000 miles, the colonial secretary had finally returned from his tour of South Africa. The sun broke through the clouds. 'The whole moving scene was upon us in a moment, for all the world', *The Times* correspondent wrote, 'as if a curtain had been raised.'[1]

What did the world behind this curtain hold for Britain and its Empire? Much recent writing has rediscovered the decade before the First World War as a golden age of globalization, an era marked by the gold standard and expanding transnational networks of cultural and commercial exchange. For contemporaries the picture was far less clear. Unlike the hull of the *Norman*, Britain never fully escaped the surrounding haze in the early twentieth century. The Boer War in South Africa, which Chamberlain's secret diplomacy had helped trigger, had shaken confidence in the future of the Empire. Well might the formal address welcoming the statesman praise his successes in 'welding together in one indissoluble whole of Great Britain and her colonies', and in speeding 'the steps of civilization' and advancing 'our commerce'. Yet, in fact, commerce, colonies, and civilization all faced a doubtful future.

Unemployment had been rising since the turn of the century, exceeding 8 per cent amongst industrial workers in 1904−5. As wages fell, prices were steadily rising, by over 4 per cent between 1900 and 1904. With her exports suffering from competition from newly industrializing great powers, Britain increasingly relied on earnings from services like shipping and overseas investment. These 'invisible exports' filled the gap in Britain's balance of payments; imports exceeded regular exports by over £100 million pounds. Anticipating more recent debates, contemporaries asked what the impact of global capital exports would be on employment. Capital was more mobile than labour and might migrate behind tariff barriers with a great sucking sound. This might produce earnings for financiers, but also cost jobs at home. Or, to put this anxiety in Edwardian terms: was Britain becoming a nation of rentiers rather than makers?

The international climate was no brighter. Free Trade Britain faced a host of mercantilist challenges. Since the 1870s there had been a global drift towards ever higher trade barriers, economic imperialism, and tariff wars. Moderate tariffs were raised to offer more effective protection in the 1890s and 1900s, in France (1892), Italy (1895), Germany (1902), repeatedly in Russia, as well as in Argentina and, indeed, in the white settler colonies of the British Empire. On the European continent, the 1890s saw a series of tariff wars. Overseas, the United States was expanding its sphere of influence in the Caribbean and the Philippines. In 1902 nominal tariff rates on manufactures stood at a phenomenal 131 per cent in Russia, 73 per cent in the United States, 34 per cent in France, and 25 per cent in Germany.[2] In February 1903, Russia and Austria-Hungary proposed what were clearly *tarifs de combat*, higher tariffs to allow for bargaining and retaliation. Britain, the most powerful empire in living history, was a powerless bystander in this new game. Adherence to unilateral free trade and a rigid version of the most-favoured-nation clause required Britain to treat countries strictly equally, without favours or discrimination, offering an open market to even the most aggressive protectionist competitor. There was a growing sentiment within the commercial community as well as sections of the Foreign Office that Britain was entering a new era of international rivalry with one arm tied behind its back. Moreover, Britain was shrinking—net emigration had been 71,888 in 1900, rising to 147,036 in 1903, far higher than that from its major European rival, Germany.

Within the Empire, the white-settler dominions were aiming at greater freedom in international affairs. Canada had become embroiled in a tariff war with Germany, which, not unreasonably, saw the Canadian granting of a preference to Britain as a breach of its trade treaty. For an imperial statesman like Chamberlain, for whom the Dominions were just as much a part of the Empire as Yorkshire, this was a frightening development. Germany's withdrawal of most-favoured-nation treatment from Canada appeared a denial of imperial sovereignty, an act of commercial warfare against Britain. Chamberlain had hoped to use a small duty on corn, which the Conservative government had introduced in 1900 to raise additional revenue to fight the Boer War, as an instrument to bind the units of the Empire closer together through a network of preferences. The Liberal leader of the opposition, Campbell-Bannerman, had feared that Chamberlain's return from South Africa would be like Caesar's from Egypt. But Britain was not Rome. Chamberlain's Free Trade colleagues in the Conservative government had used his absence from cabinet to threaten resignation, and, on his return, outmanoeuvred him. By April 1903 the corn duty was repealed.

Yet if Chamberlain had returned from South Africa thinner and exhausted, he was also emboldened in his imperial vision and optimistic about the domestic conditions favouring a political change of course. On 15 May 1903, he proclaimed the need for imperial Tariff Reform—a declaration of war on the liberal system of Free Trade that had defined British politics for half a century. His supporters likened the momentous speech to Luther nailing his ninety-five theses to the church door at Wittenberg. Chamberlain demanded a 2s. duty on foreign corn with preferential treatment for the members of the British Empire. By September Chamberlain had resigned from the cabinet and launched the Tariff Reform crusade. Quickly his programme developed into a broad tariff package that held out an additional prospect of social reform. A general tariff would protect home industries, offer preferential duties to the colonies on agricultural imports, allow for tariff bargaining, and raise revenue for old age pensions.

Free Traders were terrified—and with good reason. Not only was the social and economic health of the nation uncertain, public support for Free Trade was also in doubt. A Liberal party agent from Manchester of all places, the heartland of Cobden and Free Trade, reported an 'unprecedented state of apathy and inertia, amounting to paralysis' in many constituencies. It was difficult to get speakers. Audiences were 'extremely thin and indifferent'. Partly, the agent suggested along conventional liberal lines, this resulted from 'war fever' brought on by the Boer War: 'War invariably materialises and brutalises a people.' And brute instincts made them susceptible to the culture of imperial protectionism. But, he emphasized, Free Trade was a victim of its own success: 'the condition of the labouring and wage-earning classes had been so much improved, that a well-fed and easy-going and satisfied feeling had come over the people, lulling them into a state of political slumber'. Other Free Traders feared that the middle classes had become corrupted by imperialism, ready to drift into Chamberlain's arms.[3]

Whatever the reason, in the autumn and winter of 1903–4, Free Traders within the state as well as in the Liberal opposition realized that the momentum was with the protectionists. Chamberlain was winning by-elections, first at Ludlow, then at Lewisham. Free Trade was being overpowered by the protectionist campaign, the Liberal whip Herbert Gladstone diagnosed.[4] Lewisham, significantly, was one of the many growing suburbs in south London that attracted the middle and lower middle classes. Many voters here worked as clerks or in the service sector, a world far removed from industrial regions, like Birmingham, that produced for the home market and were more expected to support tariffs. The electorate had more than doubled in this suburban constituency since the franchise reform of 1884. The liberal *Daily News,* tellingly if grudgingly, explained the defeat at Lewisham precisely as the result of this new popular element, consisting mainly of the 'black-coated proletariat', having undermined Free Trade.[5] New, more democratic mass politics meant an unknown future for older liberal policies. As with clerks, so with manufacturing interests and highly paid artisans. Radical industrialists, like John Brunner of Brunner, Mond & Co. recognized the growing discontent amongst the manufacturing classes. Tariff Reform made progress in the East End of London, then experiencing a slowdown in the docks and foundries. Retaliation, in particular—the prospect of hitting back at foreign protectionist countries and forcing them to lower their own trade barriers—tapped the popular mood. But even in mercantile and financial circles, there was growing disquiet about the wisdom of following dogmatically the path of pure, unilateral Free Trade. Leading financiers like Natty Rothschild and Ernest Cassel were taken by Chamberlain's proposals. To Viscount Goschen, a well-connected former Chancellor of the Exchequer, the City seemed 'shaky' and 'deeply infected' with Chamberlainism, and displaying a fair bit of anti-German sentiment.[6] Foreign powers, like Imperial Germany, were bracing themselves for a protectionist victory. At the Treasury, Edward Hamilton, the opera-loving top civil servant and evangelist of Gladstonian finance, felt Chamberlain's was the winning side. Chamberlain's crusade, he feared, was making progress even among the 'consuming classes'.[7]

While the storm of the fiscal controversy swept across the country, the Conservative Prime Minister Arthur Balfour nonetheless managed to hang on to power. By November 1905, just over two-and-a-half years after Chamberlain pinned his flag to the mast of Tariff Reform, however, even Balfour's rare combination of philosophical skill and political acumen had run its course. On 1 December 1905 Edward VII accepted his resignation. The Liberals returned to power and called for a general election. By now the fortunes of Tariff Reform and Free Trade had dramatically reversed. The

1906 election was a landslide victory for Free Trade. It produced the largest swing at the polls since 1832. The Liberals returned 377 MPs, more than doubling their numbers. The Conservatives were decimated, reduced to a pitiful 157 seats; Balfour, the outgoing Prime Minister, was swept from his old seat at Manchester East. The young Labour party managed 53, the Irish nationalists 83 seats. Turnout had been a huge 83 per cent, at an election in which Free Trade versus Tariff Reform was the dominant issue. Free Trade won back voters in rural counties as well as in urban industrial areas.

In July 1906, Joseph Chamberlain suffered a stroke. But neither the decisive result of the 1906 election, nor his disability, put an end to the fiscal controversy. The battle between Free Trade and Tariff Reform was the most hotly contested issue of the Edwardian era. In the general elections of January 1910 and December 1910 fought over the Liberals' People's Budget and the constitutional position of the House of Lords, the question of Free Trade was a critical ingredient. Protectionists had promised social reform in exchange for tariffs. Liberals now held out an alternative compact of Free Trade and national insurance, made possible by redistributing income. Free Trade and the People's Budget were allied against peers and protectionists. The 1910 elections returned a more even balance between the two main parties—both with just over 270 seats, with the Liberals continuing in government thanks to additional support from Labour and Irish Nationalists. But they once again also brought to light the decisive popular support Free Trade managed to generate.

Foreigners who visited Britain regularly at the time were stunned by the extraordinary success of Free Trade culture. Italo Svevo, the Italian novelist who pioneered the use of psychoanalysis in the *Confessions of Zeno*, lived in Charlton, south London, for several months at a time in 1903, 1908, and again in 1910, working as a representative of an Italian paint manufacturer. At first the promise of 'seeing unemployment reduced and getting revenge (retaliation) against foreign countries that closed their borders to English products was received with enthusiasm', he recalled. Tariffs appeared bound to win. Then the Free Trade revival began: 'novels and short stories were neglected' as people turned to political economy. On his return in 1910, Free Trade had become unquestionable, a popular belief and common sense wisdom. 'People are still doing their sums', Svevo now found, 'but you couldn't repeat the idea [of a tariff] there without being booed.' 'I ... do not believe that free trade can ever be abolished in England. Years ago I thought otherwise.'[8]

It is the cultural and political resources that made Britain a Free Trade nation that are the themes of the following chapters. The unique survival of Free Trade as a policy in Britain was made possible by a social and ideological mobilization of unprecedented proportions. In the years 1903–10 Free Trade unleashed a fresh energy that simultaneously expanded political communication and enriched the meanings of freedom of trade. Free Trade became a master language for citizens and consumers, as well as addressing questions of wealth and commerce. Democracy, peace, and justice all depended on it.

I

Free Trade Stories

'Tis a fight 'gainst cold greed and self interest,
On our VOTE 'twill depend bond or free!
But we'll still trust the old well-tried BANNER
FREE TRADE for the ISLE of the SEA.
We dread those dark days of PROTECTION,
When want gaunt and fierce stalked the land,
When grim death claimed its toll of the children,
Nor Woman nor Man could withstand.
When no work could be found for the worker,
When oppression they had to endure,
When the workhouse could scarce give its shelter
To the hungry, the starving, or poor.

Free Trade Campaign Song, 1904[1]

He that withholdeth corn, the people shall curse him.

Proverbs 11: 26, quoted by Charles Fenwick, Liberal MP, at the annual
picnic of Northumberland miners, 1903[2]

The consumer ... is the whole nation.

Treasury memorandum, 1903[3]

In 1909 Free Traders took to the stage. With a touch of dramatic inspiration, the Free Trade Union adapted Charles Dickens' *A Christmas Carol* for the epic battle against tariffs.[4] *A Message from the Forties*, 'most successfully performed both in London and the provinces',[5] casts Scrooge as a mouthpiece of protectionist ignorance and selfishness, his nephew as the informed and civic-minded Free Trader. When Scrooge praises the Tariff Reform plan for broadening the bases of taxation, the nephew reminds him that 'taxes are paid by people, not by the articles'. Scrooge falls asleep and is visited by the ghost of Richard Cobden. Clinking his chains, the ghost explains that these 'are the chains that were forged by the Bread Tax, link by link and yard by yard girded around the people of England, and which I, after years of toil, yea, even persecution, struck from off the fettered limbs of the poor'. Scrooge has forgotten these lessons of history. His selfishness threatens to plunge the country back into those 'dark days of the past'. The stage goes dark. A magic lantern now projects the course of history since the repeal of the Corn Laws in 1846, throwing up images from Robert Peel to later Free Trade chancellors of the exchequer, and from the starving families in the 1852 Stockport riots to contemporary riots by the unemployed in Berlin. Cobden's ghost reminds Scrooge that one is never too old to learn from history: Free Trade brings 'peace and good-will among men, purity in public life'. Scrooge awakes, cured of his protectionist folly. As the play comes to a close, children appear and sing the liberal campaign tune 'Stamp, Stamp, Stamp upon Protection'. Scrooge shouts after them, wishing them a merry Christmas and to 'go home to your untaxed dinners, and thank God England is still Free Trade'.

A Message from the Forties was one of a whole host of stories about the 'Hungry Forties' created in the Free Trade campaign, in newspapers and public meetings, in popular books and in oral testimony by octogenarians. Free Traders and protectionists wove accounts of past, present, and future which gave Britons' immediate decision over trade policy an epochal significance. As the fiscal controversy unfolded, Protectionists increasingly looked to the future, while Free Traders invoked the past. The choice over trade policy became situated in rival versions of modernity and national history.

These stories were more than just vehicles for attracting supporters. They also shaped the main ideas and identities that would dominate the political debate. Social movements need stories, as well as funds and committees. In what was the richest society in Europe at the time, Free Traders turned to stories of hunger and starvation, bread and sugar. They created a populist saga of emancipation in which the repeal of the Corn Laws in 1846 set the people free. Food and freedom were one. These stories were linked to a larger vision of civil society and democracy. Free Trade created a virtuous atmosphere for public life. Consumers would become citizens.

The Hungry Forties

There were perhaps few people in Britain further removed from poverty than Violet Florence Mond, the author of *The Message of the Hungry Forties*.

Mrs Mond had written the play at the invitation of the Women's Free Trade Union, a campaigning body which coordinated plays, speeches, public meetings, canvassing, and leafleting, in Welsh and English. A merchant's daughter, she was married to the leading chemical industrialist and liberal Alfred Mond, the managing director of Brunner Mond & Co., and future founder of Imperial Chemical Industries (ICI). The Monds were not just rich: they were super-rich. Alfred's father, Ludwig, the son of a German Jewish merchant, had moved to Britain in the 1860s and established the chemical industry on a large scale. By the time of his death in 1909 he had assembled a stunning art collection, including Raphael's *Crucifixion* and Bellini's *Pietà*, which he left to the National Gallery in London. He also left £5,000 a year to his daughter-in-law.[6]

Nor did Mrs Mond's audience live in conditions of hunger, let alone starvation. Edwardian Britain was not an egalitarian society, but neither was it a particularly poor one. Today's readers may understandably be shocked by pictures of a society bereft of many of our own comforts, conveniences, and social services. For contemporaries, however, Britain stood out as the society with the highest standard of living in Europe at the time; only people in the United States and Australia were better off. Britain had long escaped the cycles of famine and mass starvation that continued to plague Italy, Spain, and Russia in the early twentieth century. The standard of living had improved vastly since the 1870s, thanks especially to the dramatic fall in the cost of food made possible by the technological advances in shipping and the integration of a global food system. A generation after the 1846 repeal of the Corn Laws, Londoners would still pay over 8d. for their four-pound loaf. By the late 1880s they paid a mere $5\frac{1}{2}d$.[7] The decline in prices of many basic articles disproportionately benefited the working classes. In 1904 an inquiry by the Board of Trade found that in the last quarter-century the average cost of articles of clothing had fallen by 5 per cent, of articles preferred by workers, by 15 per cent.[8] Contemporaries argued over the extent to which the corn duty introduced during the Boer War had driven up prices, but in most large towns other than London the price of bread in the spring of 1903 was exactly the same as a year earlier.[9]

Of course, hardship and poverty were far from eliminated. The spread of social surveys and inquiries into nutritional deficiencies at the time gave poverty a new visibility, a problem that could be measured, tabulated, and governed.[10] Industrial labourers still spent an average of 50 per cent of their budget on food.[11] They highlighted the significant proportion of the very poor and elderly untouched by the general increase in national wealth; 10 per cent of the population lived in 'primary' poverty, another 18 per cent in 'secondary' poverty according to Seebohm Rowntree in his contemporary survey of York. And academics since have debated whether real wages slightly fell after 1899 or continued to rise very slowly.[12] Clearly, not all groups in society followed the same trends—female workers in the clothing industry were losers in the Edwardian period, while men in iron and steel on average gained. But there can be no debate about the overall improvement of material life in the late Victorian period. The British people in 1900 enjoyed a standard of living and rich diet, with more meat and sugar, that would have astonished their parents and grandparents.

If there was a European society, then, which should have cared less about the threat of starvation and the price of bread it was Britain. On the eve of the Tariff Reform debate, the Board of Trade concluded in a confidential memorandum on bread supply in time of war that 'the ability of the working classes to sustain a large rise in the price of necessaries [like bread] has been greatly under-rated'. It found 'sufficient disproof' of the allegation that a large proportion of the working classes were either on the margin of subsistence or would be reduced to starvation, even by a 'large increase' in the price of basic foodstuffs.[13] In the second half of the nineteenth century, Britons had become less and less dependent on bread for their basic diet.[14] Tellingly, even relatively poorer societies at the time focused their political energy on higher-quality, more expensive foodstuffs, like the thousands of Germans who agitated against high meat prices. And yet, Edwardian Britain saw the mobilization on a grand, unprecedented scale of a popular battle against hunger and in defence of the 'cheap loaf'.

Already in 1902 about 20,000 people had protested in Hyde Park against the 'bread tax'. The following years brought together a chorus of liberal and radical voices stretching from members of the upper class to workers' movements and women cooperators—from Violet Mond with the £5,000 a year she received from her father-in-law alone to the typical skilled working-class family getting by on £200 a year. In December 1903, Campbell-Bannerman, the Liberal leader, warned crowds in Newport that there were twelve million people in Britain existing on the verge of starvation—a number that would escalate if Free Trade were abandoned. In recent years, hunger had developed into a new political weapon of the oppressed, the hunger strike used by colonial nationalists and anarchists confronting imperial power in various parts of the world. In Britain in 1901, there had been a hunger march by the unemployed.[15] Now Liberals seized on hunger not to challenge but to buttress the ruling power of Free Trade. Images and memories of hunger and suffering proliferated and became the main narrative thread in the battle over Free Trade. They were represented in posters, cartoons, and lantern slide shows in town halls and schools, invoked by old labourers and radicals at public meetings, dramatized in the radical press and liberal popular editions of 'the hungry forties'.

For Liberals to point to the sheer size of real, existing poverty was a strategy not without risks. The resilience of poverty, Tariff Reformers were quick to argue, was an indictment of Free Trade. But the Liberal fixation with hunger had strategic as well as cultural attractions. The potentially most popular and dangerous ingredient of Chamberlain's protectionist cocktail, Liberals recognized, was its call for retaliation. Tariffs would give Britain a weapon to hit back at protectionist countries which did not play 'fairly' and took advantage of Britain's open market by dumping cheap exports on a defenceless society. From south Wales, the Liberal Lewis 'Loulou' Harcourt warned that dumping was causing a great deal of disquiet amongst the iron men: 'I think you should steer as clear of this subject as you can manage.'[16] Tariff bargaining was also the one potential bridge between Chamberlain's more ambitious protectionism and the more moderate revision of Free Trade favoured by Balfour, the Unionist Prime Minister, and his Conservative supporters. The imperial appeal of Tariff Reform might be limited—'the Britisher takes his Colonialism with qualifications, and is a little tired of having our "over-sea kinsmen" trotted out to overawe him', Campbell-Bannerman noted. But retaliation was a real danger, as the Liberal leader clearly saw. It:

(a) cultivates the ingrained fallacy that imports are an evil;

(b) captures the Chamber of Commerce sort of man by appealing to his self interest;

(c) plays up to our pugnacity;

(d) has the air of an innocent compromise, and is a relief to the Free Trader who cannot swallow Joe's plan, but does not wish to break with the Protectionists altogether.[17]

There was a small but senior group of Unionist Free Traders with about fifty MPs who held the balance in Parliament. Liberals at this stage did not feel they could dispense with them altogether. A focus on the food tax and an impending threat of starvation neatly simplified the political landscape. It promised to turn the debate into a black-and-white choice: either Free Trade pure or comprehensive Tariff Reform threatening the food of the people.

The next decade saw a seemingly never-ending flood of memories of the 'hungry forties' and images of famine. Liberals at party headquarters and in their constituencies actively solicited hunger memories. Some Free Traders turned to the past as a conscious attempt to stir 'our contemporary public, grown fat and perhaps forgetful on cheap food'. In the early Victorian period, a genre of hunger literature had invoked fears of cannibalism and the racial degeneration of Britons to the level of the Irish. Edwardians revived the harrowing images of suffering, loss of human fellowship, and death in the poetry of Ebenezer Elliott, the early Victorian 'Corn Law Rhymer': 'I bought his coffin with my bed ... I pawned my mother's ring for bread', a widow declares in one of his poems.[18] At the Northumberland Miners' Picnic in July 1903, the editor of the radical newspaper *Reynolds's* drew a 'graphic picture' of the distress under protection from contemporary accounts. That summer, in a meeting in South Dorset, the senior Liberal William Harcourt found in his audience an old man who recalled how he had got three times as many loaves after repeal as before for the same amount of money. Harcourt urged fellow Free Traders to focus single-mindedly on cheap food: otherwise the Free Trade message stood in danger of being lost in a cry about the foreigner.[19] Free Traders started to publicize exchanges with old people who expressed fears that Chamberlain's policies would bring back 'the old days of perpetual hunger and suffering of the poor'.[20] Liberal women, like Mrs. E. O. Fordham in schoolrooms in Royston, gave lantern slide lectures on the times under protection when agricultural labourers were 'on the verge of starvation'. Conservative Free Fooders, like George Hamilton, who had resigned from the Cabinet in 1903 after eight years at the India Office, urged audiences to read Disraeli's *Sybil* to remember the horrors of 'the hungry forties'. 'A Truthful Picture of the Hungry Forties' occupied a prominent place in Chiozza Money's '100 Points for Free Trade', the most widely used guide for speakers.[21]

The use of history by Free Traders was not something new. In 1853, Alexander Somerville wrote a mystical-historical paean to the Anti-Corn Law league. In it he traced the 'biographic history of the pioneers of freedom of opinion, commercial enterprise & civilisation in Britain' from the earliest forms of exchange between 'Wassa', 'a naked savage' and

'Waub', a cannibal, all the way to mid-Victorian Liberals.[22] The Cobden Club, founded in 1866, a year after Cobden's death, had mobilized the past before, too, circulating a worker's memory of the high price of bread under protection in the general election of 1885, and 8,000 copies of Augustus Mongredien's *History of the Free Trade Movement* two years later.[23]

The Edwardian campaign produced a politics of memory of altogether new historic proportions. Its single most influential vehicle was *The Hungry Forties*, a collection of labourers' memories of past suffering, a project initiated and edited by Cobden's daughter, Jane Cobden Unwin. Published in 1904, *The Hungry Forties* assembled letters from old witnesses, who had responded to advertisements for recollections of hunger under protection in a variety of newspapers, ranging from *Reynolds's* to *The Christian World*. Testimonies and conversations were printed as spoken, giving them an air of authenticity and historical immediacy by following regional speech patterns, such as 'taters' instead of 'potatoes'. They 'have not been edited', Cobden Unwin stressed. They brought to life past sufferings 'almost incredible to us in these days of comfort and good eating', women liberal campaigners noted.[24]

The narrative of the 'hungry forties' turned personal suffering into national trauma, and provided Free Traders with a popular movement history. Collectively the accounts painted a picture of a people in semi-starvation, pushed outside the bounds of civilized life, driven to theft, and living in permanent fear of death because of protection. 'Life was a fearful thing in those days', a farmer's wife recalled from East Anglia. At night men would go and steal turnips for their children. Others remembered how men often went to work 'without a bit of bread... obliged to relieve the gnawings of hunger by eating some of the pig pease and horse beans he was threshing'. Diet reflected the barbarizing effects of tariffs on society. White bread, a symbol of civilized life for a century, was 'a great luxury'. Mark Moore, 'a man apparently of eighty years of age' described rye bread so doughy and poor that 'when the people put their bread into a basin of milk it would sink to the bottom like lead'. Children were 'half-starved', reduced to eating swedes for breakfast. '[T]ea-drinking was out of the question', sugar a luxury. Except for some pork on Sundays, meat was beyond the means of the people.[25]

The 'hungry forties' established a unifying collective storyline out of what were rather diverse, even contradictory individual recollections. Some, like the 88-year-old Lucy Buckland of Essex, did pinpoint the establishment of Free Trade as the time when 'the price of all things came down'.[26] Yet many memories dealt with the decade *after* the repeal of the Corn Laws in 1846, such as Edward Cook's recollection of a starvation diet of cabbage stalks. Other witnesses were not born until the mid-1840s or recalled how '[p]hysically and intellectually we dwelt next door to destitution' in the 1850s. The memorialization of hunger thus moved beyond the precise chronological marker of the repeal of the Corn Laws to make high prices and suffering more broadly synonymous with protection. The political opportunities from this stretching of the past were not lost on Free Traders. A party agent urged speakers to make the most of lantern slides showing 'the starvation prices of the old protectionist days. ... When I get to the time of the Crimean war [1853-6], I generally find that someone in the room remembers what they had to pay for the four pound loaf in those days.'[27]

As a history of the conditions of the British people *The Hungry Forties* was a dubious enterprise. The cost of living had in fact declined between 1842 and 1846, before the repeal of the Corn Laws. The book primarily gathered memories from rural England, with hardly any from the south of England, Wales, and Scotland; Ireland, where there was famine, interestingly did not feature prominently either in the book or in the Edwardian Free Trade campaign more generally. Of course, some people went hungry, but overall, the 1840s were no worse than the previous decades or for that matter the 1850s-60s. In England, 1838–41 had been bad years, but they were a small dip in the overall improvement of consumption levels in the decades after 1821.[28] At the time, the leading Evangelical Free Trader Thomas Chalmers had in fact contrasted the Irish famine of 1845–7 with the ' "jollity and abundance" ' in England where people enjoyed ' "all sorts of luxurious and even riotous indulgence" '.[29] In vain did Edwardian Tariff Reformers like the economic historian William Cunningham point out that the price of bread remained high after Repeal, during the Crimean war and into the early 1870s, and that the dramatic drop in prices thereafter had to do with the revolution in global shipping and transport, not with fiscal policy.[30]

Whatever its failings as history, *The Hungry Forties* constructed a successful popular narrative of the past, in which Free Trade had liberated the British people from oppression and enslavement. In the concluding chapter the labourite F. J. Shaw, writing under the pseudonym Brougham Villiers, provided a master interpretation of radical progress. From the French revolutionary wars until Repeal, Britain had lived in a 'state of semi-siege'. But Free Trade had not only freed 'the people' from decades of starvation. It brought to an end centuries of subordination. The Reformation had started a downward spiral of coercion leading all the way to the poor law, robbing the 'common people' of their freedom and 'their democratic organisations'. Free Trade was a triumph of biblical proportions, Villiers told readers: it delivered the people from 'an Egyptian bondage'.[31]

This story of the people's emancipation carried echoes of earlier radical narratives in which the poor overcame dispossession. It further elaborated the role of 'the people' in the progress of liberty, a central thread in popular Gladstonian liberalism.[32] Earlier points of conflict and violence between middle-class Free Traders and working-class radicals were air-brushed from this popular liberal saga. Many Chartists and early trade unionists had viewed foreign trade as a source of evil leading to starvation in the midst of plenty.[33] Such alternative radical trajectories disappeared in the 'Hungry Forties'. Historical memory is as much about selective amnesia as about remembrance.

The influence of *The Hungry Forties* on political discourse was enormous. *The Hungry Forties* was issued in a 'people's edition' in 1905 and reprinted in 1906 for 6d; for the 1910 elections an abridged edition was sold for a mere 1d. By 1912 the 1d. edition had sold 110,000 copies, the bound version another 100,000. The 'liberality' of the publisher Fisher Unwin helped its mass circulation—the publisher and the Cobden Club gave away 150,000 copies in 1912–13.[34] Excerpts from the book were widely used in public speeches and lectures, sometimes in combination with lantern slides based on F. C. Gould's cartoon 'The Good Old Days'. At Reigate's Central Hall in October 1905, Mrs Freeman Thomas spoke, drawing directly on 'examples of poverty and suffering which were selected from Mrs. Cobden Unwin's book [and] strongly emphasised the arguments against Protection': the lecture was 'warmly applauded'.[35] Public lectures on 'Richard Cobden and his Times' and on the 'hungry forties' were a staple of the liberal lecture circuit, especially those organized by the Women's Liberal Association.[36] The Free Trade Union and the North of England Free Trade Association distributed leaflets showing the level of starvation, unemployment, and child labour in 'England under Protection'. They made selective use of Victorian histories of England, by the women's rights' supporter and popularizer of political economy Harriet Martineau and by the historian Spencer Walpole, and cited from speeches by the

Whig T. B. Macaulay and the Irish nationalist Daniel O'Connell.[37] *The Daily News*, the leading liberal daily in terms of circulation, the radical *Reynolds's*, the *Westminster Gazette*, and liberal magazines and leaflets kept octogenarians' memories of hunger steadily in the public eye, aided by local newspapers and agents.[38]

Free Traders never monopolized the past, but the intense and widely popularized version of a dark age of barbaric conditions under tariffs narrowed opportunities for Tariff Reformers considerably. A rare attempt to rival Free Traders' horrific images of the 'hungry forties' was J. W. Welsford's lantern slide lecture on the French Revolution, circulated by the Women's Unionist and Tariff Reform Association; Welsford died in 1909 after months of illness, unable to complete his study of *The Strength of England*, which told the history of England from Saxon times. His lecture on the 'Reign of Terror' illuminated the dangerous foreign origins of Free Trade with the help of 45 lantern slides bringing to light the rule of the Parisian mob in 1789, the execution of the King and the slaughter of workmen at Lyons in 1793. 'What I am going to show you to-night', audiences were told, 'is how Free Trade so weakened the French that Great Britain, in spite of her small population compared with that of France, was able to win at Trafalgar and Waterloo, and thus gain sea-power and world-empire.' Free Trade here emerged as the product of 'French Socialist madness', in contrast to the 'old British remedy of protecting the labour of the British poor ... which made Britain great'. It led to 'predatory socialism', anarchy, and violence, in the process eroding national power.[39]

W. J. Ashley, W. Cunningham, and W. A. S. Hewins were the respectable proponents of historical economics. Instead of the universal principles of the new science of economics, with its emphasis on individual motivation and demand and supply, these men understood the economy as the product of historical growth, inextricably intertwined with the evolution of political institutions, morals, and power. Rather than debating current prices, they turned to the rise and fall of nations for guidance. The decline of Holland in the late seventeenth and eighteenth centuries in particular was a warning of what happened when strength was sacrificed for wealth. Just when Holland should have focused on production and protection it moved towards Free Trade. And was not British wealth itself the result of earlier state expansion and empire, rather than of market forces? The political lesson was simple: if Britain wanted to avoid decline it needed to return to its former method of imperial union which had laid the foundations of its greatness.[40]

In popular politics and discourse, however, Tariff Reform largely evacuated the past for the future. It was a future dystopia, a glimpse into an approaching abyss that inspired protectionist images and speeches. By projecting current problems into the future, they were made to look like systemic problems: today the loss of one industry, tomorrow an entire empire. Typical posters, for example, showed a sleeping British worker, behind whose back an immigrant was sneaking into the country, warning: 'It is not what you have now, but the question is: How long shall we keep it, and how much shall we keep of it.'[41]

The Tariff Reform campaign aligned protection with visions of the future. Protectionist modernity was represented by the motor car, symbol of a new era of speed and sensibility. Far from experiencing a 'sublime immobility', as some postmodernists have suggested, contemporaries reported on the intensely physical and sensory relationship with the new moving machine.[42] Tariff Reformers used the modern car to mock the supposedly universal and timeless principles of Free Trade. New means of transport reflected the shift from the outdated political economy of Free Trade to cutting-edge protectionism. In one colourful Tariff Reform poster, Britannia's '1846 Free Trade coach' was overtaken by the automobile 'Protection', in which Uncle Sam, a German officer, and other foreigners were driving happily on the road to prosperity (Colour Plate I). 'It's rather lonely in here all by myself,' Britannia complains, 'but the others are bound to join me soon', a line mocking Cobden's prophecy in 1846 that all European countries would follow Britain within five years of the adoption of Free Trade. In the general election of December 1910, Conservatives, dressed as footmen, carried a sedan chair through the streets of Manchester with the message 'In Cobden's Days we went to the poll like this. Now we have to alter the pace.'[43] The first massive use of motor cars by Conservatives in the Edwardian elections, then, was not simply a way of getting voters to the poll, but part of a symbolic performance, representing modernity more generally.

Free Traders won the politics of time by successfully presenting the past as the predictor of the future. Memories of past hunger were reminders of collective suffering and heroic liberation, but they also suggested how fragile historical progress was. History might reverse itself at any moment. Pictures warned of Chamberlain sowing 'famine' or of a new Egyptian

THE SPIRIT OF TORYISM.

"FAMINE."
(After J. C. Dollman, in the Royal Academy.)

Figure 1. Famine: the spectre of 'protection', bringing in its train slavery, war, conscription, and muddle. A radical cartoon from 1904.

plague with skeletons in the desert.[44] *Reynolds's News* turned *famine*, a grim snowscape with Death, wolves, and crows by the animal painter John Charles Dollman displayed at the Royal Academy in spring 1904, into a political allegory of 'the spirit of Toryism', with Death/Protection leading 'slavery', 'war', and 'conscription' (see Figure 1 above).[45] The most affluent and liberal market society in Europe mobilized an iconography of famine conventionally associated with an earlier 'moral economy', such as images of bleeding famine draped in sackcloth that women fighting for a fair price of bread had used a century before.[46] Again and again, Liberals and Radicals warned that Tariff Reform would be 'turning back the hand on the dial of civilisation', as the leading free-thinking Liberal J. M. Robertson put it.[47] Accounts of when the people 'starved under Protection' made audiences 'very fearful that history will repeat itself'.[48] Jane Cobden Unwin saw her oral history as an 'effective antidote to the raging, tearing campaign' of protectionists 'who would…bring England back to the times of the Hungry Forties'.[49]

It is on this sense of reversibility of history that speeches and political drama played, such as when *A Message from the Forties* placed riots and starvation in early Victorian Britain alongside riots and suffering in present-day protectionist Germany.[50] At Great Grimsby, where Liberals defeated protectionists in the January 1910 election, the simple slogan was displayed 'Will you go back: Remember the Hungry Forties', next to a bust of Richard Cobden.[51]

This public retelling of a national hunger story arguably reinforced what recent psychologists have identified as 'recall bias'; that is, the retrospective distortion that takes place as people revise their recollections of the past in accordance with present concerns.[52] It certainly was effective in containing the protectionist advance in what was potentially the most vulnerable segment of the electorate: labourers in agricultural districts. Agricultural labourers were a prime target of protectionists in late nineteenth-century Europe—a protected home market held out the promise of sustained employment and higher wages that could offset the higher cost of living that a tariff would bring. Protectionism in Germany was not a simple alliance between 'iron and rye', big industry and big landowners, but also had support from small farming communities.[53] In Britain, the collective memory of starvation, which was heavily biased towards memories from rural areas, inoculated labourers against protectionism. In a rural division like Suffolk North-East, for example, Conservatives were disheartened by the little progress they managed to make in the 1910 elections. A Conservative inquiry into the prospects of winning over agricultural labourers yielded an unambiguous response: 'We cannot get them to believe that Colonial Preference would ultimately benefit them.' The memory of their forefathers 'eating turnips' proved too strong. As one respondent summed up: rural labourers 'cannot and will not see Colonial Preference—[they] think "the Hungry Forties" will return'.[54]

Civil Society

Free Trade created a unifying vision of the British past. For social movements fighting for inclusion and recognition, especially for the cooperatives and the radical and liberal women's movements, these stories took on a deeper significance: the 'hungry forties' became part of their understanding of their own heroic role in the unfolding of freedom. Their own growth and autonomy testified to the positive relationship between freedom of trade and civil society. Free Trade, they believed, had allowed social groups to breathe and grow without interference by the state or oppression by privileged interests.

Such has been the dramatic decline of the cooperatives in Britain and most other European societies over the past half-century, that it is worth recalling just how strong and sizeable this movement once was. At the turn of the twentieth century, over 1.7 million Britons belonged to 1,439 non-profit retail cooperative societies. By the time of the First World War membership exceeded three million.[55] Membership was especially concentrated in the industrial north-west and north-east, and overwhelmingly from the better-off sections of the working classes. A Women's Cooperative Guild was founded in 1883 and, by the time of the 1906 election, could lay claim to being the largest independent women's organization. The English Co-operative Wholesale Society (CWS) ranked amongst the largest companies in the world; bigger than Lever's soap empire or the chemical giant Brunner Mond in terms of capital.[56] Most members joined the cooperative movement with a greater interest in the 'divi' or dividend, a kind of early customer loyalty scheme pioneered by the cooperatives, than in direct political activism. And formally the movement was non-partisan until the First World War, when it moved into alliance with Labour. Yet such formal definitions of political engagement can be misleading, for the cooperatives provided a world of everyday politics that would feed directly into the Free Trade revival.

The 'free breakfast table' was central to the cooperatives. In 1902 the Co-operative Wholesale Society paid £1.2 million on food duties, 16 per cent of its total turnover; almost £500,000 was paid on sugar duties alone.[57] It was not necessarily clear, however, how much energy members would devote to a political battle against the taxation of foodstuffs beyond formal declarations at annual conventions. When the Women's Cooperative Guild urged action against the proposed sugar duty in 1901, the parliamentary committee of the Co-operative Congress advised against it. An appeal to member societies to campaign against duties on corn and sugar in 1902 produced a depressing result—not even 50 of 1,500 societies even bothered to reply. 'It is evident', the committee concluded, 'that the majority of the societies took no action whatever in the matter.'[58]

Chamberlain's Tariff Reform challenge provoked a very different re-sponse. The feverish activism it generated tells us as much about the cooperatives' ideal of civil society under Free Trade as about their suspicion, even hatred, of the charismatic Chamberlain. At first, some cooperators expressed unease about collaboration with liberal bodies, such as the Cobden Club or the Free Trade Union. 'The Cobden Club stood for vested capitalist interests as well as Mr. Chamberlain', one cooperator argued at the 1904 congress.[59] Instead of celebrating progress under Free Trade, they should focus on the millions still living in poverty, unemployment, and overcrowding. In the past, cooperators had spoken out against the 'evils of competition', and the 'immoralities of greed' associated with the Free Trade motto of 'buy in the cheapest market and sell in the dearest'.[60] At the 1904 Co-operative Congress, the Revd Propert of west London warned against being drawn into a liberal choice between 'free trade' versus 'protection'. 'Why', he asked, 'need [there] be any excitement immediately Free Trade was mentioned?' Were not the many cooperators who were trade unionists also pursuing 'in principle Protection'?

These voices, however, were quickly drowned out in a mass mobilization in defence of Free Trade. The parliamentary committee endorsed cooperation with the Cobden Club, and even with the Unionist Free Food League. Leading cooperators, like Henry Vivian and J. C. Grey, also sat on Free Trade bodies and acted as brokers of collaboration with Harold Cox, the dynamic if controversial secretary of the Cobden Club. Cox's own experiments with cooperative farming made him a more acceptable go-between than the regular Liberal politician; he 'has been useful in keeping us in touch with the bodies cooperative which will not look at... anything akin to Liberal organization', even Lord Welby, the chairman of the Cobden Club and one of Cox's critics, acknowledged.[61] Regional sections co-organized demonstrations and conferences in autumn 1903, from Cardiff to Newcastle. These regional meetings were attended by over 3,000 delegates from cooperative societies, representing a total of over 1.6 million members. Individual societies made their halls available to Free Trade meetings, contributed to printing costs, and helped circulate literature, most importantly the 'Working Class Leaders' National Protest Against Preferential Tariffs', signed by representatives of leading trade unions and labour organizations.

For the cooperative movement, the battle between Free Trade and Protection quickly acquired the proportions of a life-and-death struggle for its very autonomy and existence. This vision drew on the popular liberal alliance that since the 1860s had come to replace the earlier (frequently violent) antagonism between radicals and liberals during the Chartist era. Few personified this rapprochement better than George Holyoake.

Here was a man who recalled his memories of the First Reform Act of 1832 and the repeal of the Corn Laws in 1846 on platforms up and down the country until his death in 1906. Born in 1817, the son of a printer and horn-button maker, he was converted to atheism and Owenite socialism in the 1840s and became a leading Victorian exponent of freedom of thought, without interference from state or church. A prophet of self-help, Holyoake emerged as the most influential mouthpiece of cooperation and co-partnership. He was the quintessential radical liberal of his time, supporting electoral reform at home and republican nationalists like Garibaldi abroad; he collected pressed flowers from a garden where Garibaldi used to sit.[62] Free Trade helped integrate radicals like Holyoake into popular liberalism. Tellingly, it was the Cobden Club that first elected him as an honorary member in 1884, a year when the National Liberal Club still chose to reject him, much to the distress of his supporter John Morley, the biographer of Cobden and Gladstone; he was finally elected in 1893.[63]

Already in 1897, at the annual meeting of the Cobden Club, Holyoake hammered home that '[s]o far as his intercourse with the working classes was concerned', Free Trade was vulnerable. It needed to recruit new members and remind people, 'particularly the younger generation', of the dangers of protection.[64] When Chamberlain launched the tariff campaign in 1903, therefore, Holyoake, now President of the Democratic League, was a natural first point of call for Liberals keen to rally popular support. H. W. Massingham, a correspondent for the *Daily News* and the future editor of the liberal weekly *The Nation*, planned a volume on *Labour and Protection* and asked Holyoake for an account of 'the condition of the workmen in England before Free Trade and the changes you have observed since'. Rather than follow the brief and focus on 'the increase in the purchasing power of their wages', however, Holyoake produced a set piece of radical collective memory, which was also serialized in the radical press.[65]

Holyoake's 'Days of Protection' offered a compressed history of civil society in which voluntary associations and freedom became directly linked to Repeal. Before Free Trade, workers were slaves, exploited by capitalism, with neither space for self-organization nor the opportunity to develop their self and autonomy. The rich flowering of clubs and associations in the seventeenth and eighteenth centuries—by 1815 over 8 per cent of the entire population belonged to friendly societies, including several female friendly societies[66]—was altogether erased in this story of Free Trade as the birthplace of democracy and social freedom. It was Free Trade, Holyoake wrote, that made possible the autonomy of social institutions, leading to the recognition that workers had 'rights which should be respected ... [and] interests which should be consulted'.[67]

Free Trade, in short, had not only brought wealth: it had enlarged 'the domain of freedom', in the image frequently used by Lloyd George in the Edwardian campaign.[68] It became central to the identity and memory of the cooperative movement. The repeal of the Corn Laws represented the beginning of 'the progress of the people' when cooperatives, trade unions, and friendly societies began to cultivate social independence, solidarity, and trust. The 'hungry forties' turned into the success story of the cooperative movement.[69]

Free Trade and civil society went hand in hand, in this view, because Free Trade secured distance between state and social groups or interests. Free Trade was linked to attacks on landed aristocrats and the capitalist 'trust monger'. The state was not expected to express or advance the ethos or welfare of the community. This was the job of self-governing social institutions. Holyoake put this view neatly in a formula widely repeated in the cooperative movement. Cooperation 'took no man's fortune, it sought no plunder ... it gave no trouble to statesmen ... it subverted no order ... it asked no favour, it kept no terms with the idle, and it would break no faith with the industrious. It meant self-help, self-dependence.'[70] Instead of social war, it promoted toleration and trust. The growth of thrift organizations and working-class saving was seen as testifying to the success of Free Trade in helping the working classes help themselves.[71]

At a time when women (and a third of men) still lacked the national vote, Free Trade forged a link to democratic culture for those groups formally excluded from political life. At the Free Trade Hall in Manchester in November 1903, in what was claimed to be the 'biggest and best demonstration' ever held under its banner, Mrs Bury, the vice-president of the Women's Cooperative Guild and a tireless speaker for the Women's Free Trade Union, reminded a crowded audience that 'Cooperation and Free Trade started together, and they had jogged along successfully.'[72] Thanks to the non-interference of the state, social groups were able to develop their own institutions and acquire the democratic talents that prepared them for eventual citizenship.

The cooperator Rosalind Nash captured this democratic self-understanding in her defence of Free Trade from the perspective of the cooperative housewife. After stressing the tight budget of the poor and praising the cooperative bakeries and flour mills as 'the most formidable defensive works of the Free Trade position', she turned to questions of democracy. 'Cooperation', she wrote,

> is in fact democracy in action, and apart from its economic achievements it forms a training-ground in the democratic qualities which the ballot-box demands—disinterestedness, forbearance, confidence, the capacity for responsible action and judgment. Can anything be more valuable to a democratic State than a movement which guarantees to a great mass of the people some share, at any rate, in every economic advance, and which amply repays its successive gains by political and municipal service, and by an extension of its missionary work amongst the poor, not to speak of the larger and happier range of life, and the gain to character which it brings to the individual?[73]

Cooperatives brought women together from the isolation of their homes into public life. They were 'nurseries of democracy', to borrow de Tocqueville's famous image from *Democracy in America*.

The role of the cooperatives in strengthening community and moralizing capitalism had been a prominent thread amongst advanced liberals from John Stuart Mill to idealists and 'new liberals' active in the late Victorian and Edwardian period, like D. G. Ritchie and L. T. Hobhouse, who briefly served as secretary of the Free Trade Union. Drawing on evolutionary theories of society as an organic body, these progressives targeted individualism and laissez-faire liberalism as selfish, brutal, and out of step with 'modern' science, morality, and politics. Instead of seeing individual and state as opposing forces, this organic vision of society stressed their natural interdependence. Cooperatives and trade unions were crucial vehicles in the creation of a stronger sense of community and social ethics in which citizens became ever more aware of their duties to each other. Some, like Ritchie, merely believed that competition between individuals would give way to competition between ideas. But others, following Hobhouse, saw a more general shift from competitive individualism to a communal spirit. Suspicion and class antagonism would give way to social harmony: mutual help would become the basis of the economy. Such a progressive interpretation of society's evolution from a selfish competitive muddle to a higher, organic community based on cooperation, trust, and morality had implications for politics—and policies. The state was more than a night-watchman establishing safety and order. It could (indeed should) intervene in the economy to eliminate waste and advance the welfare and moral good of the community as a whole, for example through a graduated income tax, land reform, or the public takeover of industries. In fact, for many new liberals the state ceased to have a separate existence: it was merely the political association of society and an instrument of the community.[74]

Much has been made of the 'new liberal' contribution to social reform in the Edwardian period. Yet in the campaign for Free Trade—far more popular and extensive than agitation for particular social reforms—older radical and liberal visions continued to be dominant. True, in the battle over the people's budget in 1910, social reform was grafted onto Free Trade. Colourful posters showed Asquith holding out cheap sugar for children with one hand, and pensions to an elderly couple with the other.[75] But the main body of Free Trade did not stand on the foundations of the new liberalism. Instead of an organic fusion of state and society, popular Free Trade before the First World War continued to draw on an ideal of social groups in separation from the state. Even in the politics of social insurance, voluntary associations remained more important than older, more state-centred accounts allowed.

We Plead for the Women and Children

Free Trade offered a virtual space of political inclusion—a kind of free civic training course that prepared the excluded for full citizenship, in the interim protecting the interests of housewives by ruling out protectionist taxes. Yet not all women who rallied to Free Trade were happy with the role of citizen-in-waiting. Middle-class women had been an effective support group in the early Victorian Anti-Corn Law Leagues, organizing fund-raising bazaars and tea parties, and going from house to house to solicit subscriptions, in a manner similar to missionary societies; 2,000 women met at the Hanover Square rooms in London in 1845. They did much to provide the Anti-Corn Law League with the moral, humanitarian clout of a 'women's mission', above party and commercial interests.[76] Women would play a more prominent and assertive role in the Edwardian campaign, drawing on working-class as well as middle-and upper-class support, giving speeches and lectures and helping with grassroots organizing, canvassing, and the distribution of literature.

Rejecting the image of women's apolitical 'moral purity' that spread after the First Reform Act (1832), women now turned to their role as housewives and tax-paying consumers to claim recognition as citizens.

Women were more affected than other groups by tariff proposals. They were the 'women with the basket', as the Women's Cooperative Guild referred to its working-class members, but the argument extended to women of all classes. The campaign strategy of the Women's Liberal Association was at all meetings to 'call attention to the injustice of tax-ing the food of unenfranchised women'.[77] For many Liberal women, support for Free Trade went with support for women's suffrage, indeed demanded it. The Liberal party would help itself by giving women the vote, Caroline Trevelyan argued: women understood best how protection-ist duties affected them.[78] Women were 'the housekeepers of the nation'.[79] They were 'the chancellors of the exchequer', Mrs Mond reminded the Women's National Liberal Association at their annual convention in 1909.[80] '[T]here never was an election which appealed so much to women because they were the great buyers of the nation', Lady Norman told an audience at South Wolverhampton during the January 1910 general election. Men 'were called the breadwinners, but what they won was not bread. It was pieces of gold and silver which it was the woman's duty to turn into food, warmth, clothing, and all that made of the happiness of a home.'[81]

The home and family life emerged as a symbolic battleground between Free Trade and Tariff Reform. More than one party could play on fears of the collapse of the home, however. Tariff Reformers produced a whole string of cartoons, posters, and plays that dwelled on the 'poverty, hunger, and dirt' that remained after sixty years of Free Trade, showing an exhausted woman, alone in a barely furnished room, stitching her absent husband's shirt by candlelight (see Figure 2).[82]

Plays by women Tariff Reformers dramatized the plight of 'Miss Homeless', 'Miss Artizan', and 'Mrs. Farmer' whose husbands faced un-employment and emigration, and how they roused Britannia from the evil influence of a Germanic 'Miss Foreigner' who confesses her 'lofe' for 'der goot frient of mine, Miss Free Trade ... who gifs me all der trade, so I get rich'.[83] Not surprisingly, given the expressly masculine culture of popular conservatism,[84] emasculation, the loss of a man's ability to be a man and provide for his family, was a prominent theme in protectionist propaganda. Posters showed the British workman, with half-broken shoes and a ragged jacket, the victim of cheap foreign imports, feeling the draught of the 'open door' that brought despair to his wife and children sitting crying around an empty kitchen table (Colour Plate II).[85] Tariff Reform would return the

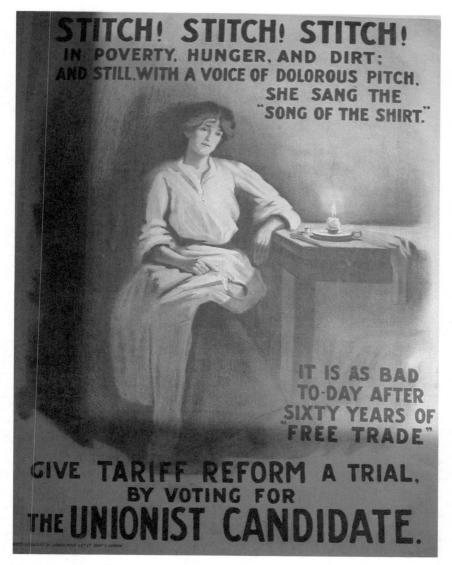

Figure 2. A Tariff Reform challenge to the myth of 'the hungry forties' and progress under Free Trade. A Conservative poster, *c.*1905.

Figure 3. 'Free Trade undermines the nation's racial strength.' A protectionist cartoon, 1904.

slouching British worker to his upright position, complete with pipe, and cheerful wife and children seeing him off to work.[86] Protectionist warnings of the export of capital and labour, on the one hand, and the threat of an alien invasion of inferior human stock, on the other, inevitably put the male worker centre stage. The contrast between 'the man we import' and 'the man we export' exploited anti-Semitism while at the same time appealing to Britons' sense of dignity and charity (see Figure 3). 'You would always be ready to help a man in distress, whatever his nationality', read the accompanying text. But 'unfair foreign competition' led to unemployment, lower wages, and emigration.[87] Posters carried 'The Wife's Appeal' in bold red colours (Colour Plate III). Others urged voters to 'keep your manhood at home by supporting tariff reform', as John Bull helplessly watched ocean liners depart a Britain lying in 'Free Trade Ruin' for a modern and booming new world.

In the early Victorian period, roles had been reversed, and it had been the Anti-Corn Law League that had warned middle-class women about how tariffs tore apart their families. Tariffs 'make husbands anxious and careworn, [and] drive sons and brothers to Australia or Canada'. The condition of the domestic sphere had long served as a marker of civilization and Christian life. Stable family life was the bedrock of civil society, and references to the freedom of social life and organizations effortlessly connected with contrasting images of families driven to despair by tariffs. Could there be a worse threat to status and respectability than their daughters having to 'go out as governesses or dressmakers' or wives having to adopt 'those painful and pinching economies which so grievously interfere with the comfort of everyday domestic life'?[88]

By the Edwardian period this earlier Free Trade concern for middle-class respectability was displaced by extreme and harrowing images of the poor living at the sharp end of civilization. 'Necessities', not comfort, moved to the centre, symbolized by the cheap loaf and the lump of sugar, and the security of these for the most vulnerable groups in society: poor women and children. Pale, emaciated mothers, with hollow cheeks, holding on to their babies and a crust of bread became a stock-in-trade of Free Trade representations of social injustice, sometimes contrasted directly with the rich capitalist trustmonger and the aristocrat, as in Robert Morley's depiction of the 'Hungry Forties' which won the first prize of the National Liberal Club (Colour Plate IV).[89] For Liberal activists, memories of the 'good old days of Protection' brought the suffering of mothers and children especially to life; 'as one read of the privations, we could hear the cries of the children for bread and the moans of the mothers at their inability to give it', Mrs Bury told a gathering of liberal women in 1904.[90]

In the play 'Saturday Night', two families experienced 'a dream of tariff reform'—a 'clever and entertaining' play in one act which was 'much appreciated by the audience' after the regular series of speeches and songs. Gone was the comfortable artisan's home, with tea and cake on the table, and cheerful children buzzing about. Instead Jane, the mason's wife, was 'plainly dressed and careworn', with an empty purse, unable to buy new boots for her children. Tariffs posed a direct threat to marriage and family life. Her friends, George and Milly, a haberdasher and dressmaker, in love and prospering under Free Trade, turned sad and struggling under Tariff Reform. The increase in the price of food meant customers had less money to spend on collars and lace in George's shop. Their marriage plans lay in ruins.[91]

All children would be the victims of Tariff Reform, the better-off as well as the very poor. One colourful Free Trade poster showed Conservatives waiting in ambush to attack neatly dressed Little Red Riding Hood and tax her shoes, clothes, and bread (Colour Plate V). But especially Conservatives wanted to tax one of the few pleasures the poor could afford, a leader in *Reynolds's* warned: 'the slum child is to have the treacle upon his bread taxed'.[92] Liberals had abolished the sugar duty in 1875. By the time the Conservatives restored the sugar duty in 1901, Britons consumed an extraordinary 90 lb. per head per year—three times more than the French or Germans. The consuming interest included the sugar-consuming industries in the confectionery trade. Sugar had become a democratic necessity, from the cradle to the grave. It was an 'excellent nutritive article of diet' and a 'most valuable substitute' especially for families who could not afford milk.[93] 'It is the first joy of the infant and the last comfort of the aged', opponents of the sugar tax emphasized.[94] In 'The Morning After', a typical liberal leaflet, Mrs Bull turned to John Bull decrying the suffering of children at the rise in the prices of sweets. Other images put Conservatives' lack of care for orphans squarely next to their threat to raise the tax on sugar further.[95]

At a time of lively concern about national fitness and undernourished children, Free Trade intersected with a more general liberal project seeking to reform and discipline the lives of families and children, by providing school meals and maternal care more generally. 'Poverty' had become ever more visible and intriguing as a project of identity for social reformers in the late Victorian period. It offered a new form of philantrophic hedonism, even an outlet for suppressed sexual desires. Charity was 'a kind of passion', the American novelist Henry James aptly put it.[96] Here was a society which saw the poor as an exotic tribe living at the margins of civilization or altogether beyond it. Countless stories and inquiries into slum life produced 'harrowing pictures of nearly nude folk, young and old', whose very poverty and shame kept them out of public life.[97] 'Who that has seen the starved children of East London, and think of the 100,000 of them who go hungry to morning school … [could] juggle himself into thinking that taxing is legitimate trading', asked one Liberal.[98]

These anxieties captured the imagination of children as well as adult investigators and reformers. In the early 1970s, an oral history project interviewed surviving Edwardians. These interviews give a sense of the impact Free Trade had on children, on their excitement at election times, their participation in political life, and the mark Free Trade left on their memories. Elizabeth Eade was about ten years of age at the time, the fourth of seven children in a poor family in Oxfordshire. 'I was a biggish school girl', she recalled seventy years later. She wanted to know what 'free trade and protection...was all about and some girl at school said she was rather down on the Tories because they could afford food, you see, good food. Well she said for us poor people, she said, it's too expensive, and if we have free trade we shall get our currants and sultanas cheaper.'[99] The two girls raced all the way to Hook Norton to get the election result, shouting as loud as they could.

To tax food would push the people out of civilization into barbarism and social anarchy. Free Traders were convinced that the corn duty had led to a rise in vagrancy and crimes against property—a rather simplistic and problematic correlation, and strongly rejected at the time by Tariff Reform experts, like the economist W. J. Ashley.[100] However exaggerated, what mattered was that Free Traders held a strong, even obsessive view that a duty, however moderate, would unravel the fabric of society. Protection undermined the very basis of family life, morality, and civil society. Biblical references and Christian prayers, especially 'Our Father' and 'The Sermon on the Mount', resonated with Anglicans and nonconformists alike. As a moral rather than a party political issue, Free Trade thus continued to tap into a hinterland of support. The Bishop of Lincoln readily joined the Free Trade Union even though it was all but Liberal in name. 'I am resolved not to join any society or union that avows political party aims,' he stressed, 'but I feel bound to declare myself on questions of moral and social importance ...[and it was] morally and socially wrong to tax the bread of the poor.'[101]

The Purity of Politics

Private interests, public benefits—from Mandeville's *Fable of the Bees* in the early eighteenth century to the present day, one liberal tradition has argued that the invisible hand of the market will generate public benefits from private interests, whatever a person's motivation. The defence of Free Trade in the pre-war years was founded on a different world view, one in which individual and public morality reinforced each other. Free Trade, in this view, secured boundaries between the private and the public. It kept the arm of the state out of private homes. 'Stop Thief!', a Liberal postcard exclaimed, as the hand of Tariff Reform reached through the window to 'rob' the family cupboard (Colour Plate VI).[102] Free Trade likewise insulated government against private interests and preserved 'the purity of politics'. For A. V. Dicey, the leading constitutional expert of the period, 'the worst danger of Protection' was precisely that it would lead to 'the confusion between public interest and private interest'.[103] Free Trade held out a mutually convenient if idealized concordat: politics kept out of business, and business kept out of politics.

In an abstract world, it might be possible to conceive of some special circumstances in which a 'perfectly wise Government' might use a tariff to some public benefit, but in the real world tariffs always corrupted politics.[104] It was this conception of politics, as much as trade theory, that brought out a group of eminent economists, including A. C. Pigou, Edwin Cannan, and F. Y. Edgworth, to warn the public in August 1903 of the 'evils which Protection brings in its train—the loss of purity in politics, the unfair advantage given to those who wield the powers of jobbery and corruption, and the growth of "sinister interest" '.[105]

But Free Trade did more than avoid the corrupting influence of tariffs. Its unselfishness and impartiality actively fostered private and public morality. A 'nation's greatness does not depend upon its wealth,' Mrs Bury told liberal women, 'but upon the healthy bodies, sound minds, and pure morals of its people'. Free Trade had done much to elevate these, making 'English men and women ... proud of our politics and their purity as compared with other nations'.[106]

The tariff challenge hit a deep nerve in a political system in flux. The electorate had dramatically expanded following the 1867 and 1884 Reform Acts to include most urban and rural workers. More than two-thirds of all men now had the vote. Older parties, like the Liberals and Conservatives, moved towards greater centralization, giving birth to the 'caucus'; the National Liberal Federation was born in 1877. New parties, like the Labour party, emerged on the horizon. Media, organization, and finance—all these forces assumed increasing importance in political life. Although the grip of central party organizations on localities was far from complete, their growing strength certainly fuelled anxieties.

Whatever the particular differences in electoral constitution and political system, there was soul-searching across Europe and America about the changing nature of politics in a modern age marked by ever more urban, industrializing, and mobile societies. Was the Anglo-Saxon liberal model of politics compatible with modern mass democracy? To some, the strengthening of party organization inevitably meant the domination of the elected over the electors—what the German sociologist Robert Michels called the 'iron law of oligarchy'. To the leading British Liberal and historian James Bryce, parties were necessary evils that enabled the representation of new social groups and interests. Moisei Ostrogorski, a Russian who had observed political trends in Britain and the United States first hand in the 1880s and 1890s, produced what remains the most famous account of the 'dwindling of individuality and the growth of formalism in political life'. People were released into a state of democracy, only to immediately become slaves, manipulated by the caucus, party bosses, wirepullers, and mass agitators. The middle class was:

> too faint-hearted to face the masses and it preferred to circumvent them by devices of management. Withholding from them the plain truth and offering them only the bait of gratification of self-love and vanity, it enervated and disgusted a good many of the best set to such an extent as to fling them into the sectarian but honest fanaticism of the Independent Labour parties, into the wild ideas of Utopiamongers and collectivist agitators.[107]

The liberal politics of reason, it seemed, was falling victim to a mix of fanaticism and apathy.

Not everyone, of course, agreed with these pessimistic accounts. Liberal public intellectuals like Graham Wallas rejected the assumption that there ever had been such a thing as rational individuals making for rational democracy, or that people in modernity merged subconsciously into a herd, easily manipulated by leaders, as Gustave Le Bon had suggested in his theory of mass psychology. Parties generated emotions and loyalties, Wallas argued. Politics would be better off recognizing the emotional side of human nature, instead of pursuing outdated notions of 'free reason'.[108]

Chamberlain and Tariff Reform became a lightning rod for these growing fears about the collapse of public life. John Burns, President of the Local Government Board in the Liberal government and the first working man ever to attain cabinet rank, had a 'serious talk' with

Gardiner of the liberal *Daily News* in 1909. He lamented the 'vulgarising of public life, Americanising of Peers, and the materialising of politics'.[109] Similarly, for older Conservatives, like Hugh Cecil, it was not the particular issue but Tariff Reformers' 'whole attitude...towards politics which is intolerable'—the sensationalism, the showmanship, their disregard for local constituencies.[110] Not until Margaret Thatcher would a British politician again attract such an extreme mix of enthusiasm and visceral hatred as Joseph Chamberlain, the energetic and outspoken leader of the Liberal Unionists. Chamberlain's rise from metal manufacturer to Birmingham mayor to colonial secretary symbolized a new style of politics. In an age of bearded radicals, he introduced a clean-shaven and youthful look. And, from his home in Birmingham he created a personal organizational base and mass following. The subject of unprecedented media exposure, Chamberlain became a celebrity in an expanding political mass market, a phenomenon well reflected in the hundreds of thousands of Edwardian picture postcards bearing his trademark image, wearing a monocle and button-hole orchid.

To his supporters, 'good ol' Joe' was the greatest prime minister Britain never had. To his enemies he was the worst example of that dangerous new specimen, the demagogue and megalomaniac. Chamberlain had been with the Gladstonian Liberal Party until he broke away over proposed Home Rule for Ireland in 1886. He went on to develop his own Liberal Unionist power base and entered into coalition with the Conservatives, leaving deep scars and an image of untrustworthiness. He was a 'fanatical charlatan', observed the young John Maynard Keynes, who was baptized into public politics during the fiscal controversy as secretary of the Cambridge Free Trade Association.[111] The Liberal Robert Spencer was 'really appalled' by the 'awful untruths...and vulgarity of the tone of J. Chamberlain's speeches' and worried about 'the degradation of public life'.[112] Chamberlain's whole style of politics lowered the standard of life—'a more deadly evil...even than Jingoism itself', Campbell-Bannerman felt, because it was 'more chronic in its effect'.[113] Whether in his earlier radical land reform programme of 'three acres and a cow', his annexation of gold fields in South Africa, or now with his promise of more work under Tariff Reform, it was always the same with Chamberlain: he 'plays up to the vulgarity and cupidity and other ignoble passions...; and he uses the foolishness of the fool and the vices of the vicious to overwhelm the sane and wise and sober'.[114]

His business background did not help. Not only was he seen as an upstart from the provinces, but many suspected that a new business style was invading politics. Writing at the height of the Boer war, Shaw Lefevre, who could look back on a long string of ministerial positions in Liberal governments since the late 1860s, thought that Chamberlain 'has shown himself totally unfit for the higher spheres of politics. He thought he could carry on the game in the same manner as that by which he succeeded in his screw business by bluffing his competitors in trade and establishing a monopoly. There ought to be no mincing of words with regard to him.'[115]

Chamberlain's adoption of Tariff Reform on the heels of the Boer war confirmed a longstanding radical analysis of the causal connection between war, protectionism, and oligarchy. The pursuit of war led to higher taxes which elites off-loaded onto the people. Protectionism and imperialism were the natural reflexes of the party of reaction and monopoly. This radical diagnosis had been famously updated by the journalist J. A. Hobson in his *Imperialism* in 1902, where he exposed the collaboration between financial interests, jingoist press, and imperialist policy leading to the Boer war. At the time Chamberlain was widely (and rightly) suspected of having given Cecil Rhodes' men a base from which to launch the invasion that started the war in the Transvaal in 1895. Now, his Tariff Reform crusade appeared the automatic domestic follow-up to imperialist adventures abroad. The combined offer of protection and old age pensions mixed jingoism with bribery. Harold Cox spoke for all Free Traders when he warned that Tariff Reform would replace honest public debate with the 'underhand machinations of secret agents corrupting the electorate by lying promises and debauching the constituencies with shameless bribes'.[116] Chamberlain, in short, threatened to turn the noble art of politics into a ruthless scramble for class and socio-economic advantage.

Tariff Reform also challenged the balance of powers between executive and the House of Commons by moving control over matters of taxation (such as bargaining tariffs) from the lower house to the government. It would be wrong, however, to see Chamberlain's failure to rally more support within the state or in Balfour's cabinet in 1903 as a simple clash between visions of a strong protectionist state and a weak Free Trade state. Rather, it was a conflict between different conceptions of what a strong state was. At one end was the Treasury, with its Gladstonian view of Free Trade and balanced budgets. For its leading officials, the Treasury was the guardian of a state whose strength derived from its legitimacy in the public eye as fair, equitable, and efficient. If it limited state power, Free Trade also ensured that it was as effective as possible, by preventing private interests from hijacking the state, limiting the room for corruption, and ensuring people paid their taxes. Free Trade, in this view, was essential to the trust between governors and governed. A surplus was as dangerous as a deficit, creating a 'great temptation to wasteful expenditure'.[117] The cardinal rule was that the sole purpose of taxation should be to raise revenue. Any other taxes would create an avalanche of interest groups demanding more and more from the state. Where the Treasury supported new taxation, as it initially did with the corn duty of 1902, it was in part as an instrument of moral discipline: people needed to feel the cost of war.[118] Once Chamberlain proposed to extend the corn duty into a system of colonial preference, the Treasury dug its heels in, and successfully pressed for the removal of the duty.

Nor did Tariff Reform find much support among groups in government and Whitehall keen to expand the scope and power of the state. For Arthur Balfour, the Prime Minister, the state was something bigger than the sum of individuals living at any given time. The state's interest transcended the creation of wealth and was no longer adequately served by a dogmatic adherence to the never-changing principles of Free Trade.[119] At the Foreign Office and the Board of Trade, Lord Lansdowne and Gerald Balfour, the Prime Minister's brother, also looked favourably on fiscal reform, and continued to do so after Chamberlain had resigned. A moderate revenue duty promised to return to government the power and freedom to tax for purposes other than that of raising revenue. It could give the executive greater elbow room in foreign and commercial affairs, allowing for the threat of retaliation or anti-dumping measures. Unlike senior colleagues at the Treasury, the heads of Customs beavered away with plans to broaden the base of taxation by £13 million, with a small food tax to make Britain more self-sufficient and offer some colonial preference, and a tax on silk as a democratic luxury tax.[120]

The problem with Chamberlain's scheme was that it threatened to weaken, not strengthen the government. A general tariff would mean a House of Commons full of sectional interests and infighting. Government would be deluged by lobbies and find it hard to push through its own programme. It had cost the German *Reichstag* a whole session to pass their new tariff in 1904, Gerald Balfour reminded colleagues, and even then it was eventually only carried by 'something approaching a Parliamentary coup d'État'.[121]

In the final analysis, it was the protection of special interests that created an unbridgeable gulf between Chamberlain's Tariff Reform and Lansdowne and the Balfour brothers. The old Free Trade doctrine needed to go, Lansdowne agreed. 'We want to make terms with foreign countries, to meet our colonies, so far as circumstances permit us, and to tap new sources of revenue. But this does not mean a high all round tariff, and an attempt to outbid the radicals by using the proceeds of the new taxes to corrupt the working classes.'[122] It proved impossible to square the circle between industrial protection and considerations of social equity and state legitimacy. In November 1905, one month before resigning, Arthur Balfour once more spelled out why. Even if it raised revenue, an industrial tariff would advantage manufacturers at the expense of, for example, agricultural customers. Of course, government could use the proceeds of the tariff to relieve their rates, but this was going 'very near to Joe's methods of bribing each class of the community in turn'.[123] He would have no truck with it.

The identification of Free Trade with the purity of politics was linked to a more general moral crusade against wealth and selfishness. Such has been the association of free trade policies with materialism and corporate interests in recent decades, that Edwardian Free Traders' ambivalent even anti-materialist self-understanding about wealth may be surprising. 'We have in all things three great enemies', according to the Liberal leader Campbell-Bannerman: '(1) devotion to material prosperity, national and individual; (2) love of sport and gambling in all forms; (3) apathy.'[124] Protectionism would exacerbate all three—appealing to people's selfish interests, inserting a kind of gambling spirit into matters of national interest through tariff bargaining, and thus accelerating a disengagement from public life.

In the battle with Chamberlain, Free Traders managed to occupy the moral high ground, distancing themselves from an association with selfish materialism that became stuck to protectionists instead. Chamberlain's tariff proposals were a 'wholesale ... and insidious appeal to human selfishness', the rising Welsh Radical star Lloyd George told the New Reform Club to thundering applause in 1904. 'Mr. Chamberlain proposed to reorganise society on a principle of universal loot.' He was fomenting 'that spirit of rapacity which seemed to possess the age ... for electioneering purposes. ... Mr Chamberlain's rallying cry was: "Down with freedom! Long live King Greed!"'[125] When the People's League Against Protection was founded in

December 1903, the democratic air of Free Trade was typically contrasted with the type of 'Park-lane millionaires' and 'wire-pullers of Trusts' who supported tariff reform.[126]

Free Trade, by contrast, acted as a benign moderating force on the potential excesses of materialism in a commercial society. It promoted thrift, independence, and civic-mindedness. Competitiveness raised the moral properties of independent citizens as well as the national income. 'Competition', Free Traders explained, 'acts on our selfishness, like the automatic governor of the steam engine acts on the steam, regulating it to the ever changing needs of the society. Remove your governor (competition) and the steam (selfishness) soon jars your body politic to pieces.'[127] Unregulated, selfishness was 'the motive power of the rave'. Tariffs therefore increased the 'robber or barbaric element' in societies. They were like opium, leading to addiction and dependence amongst depressed industries and the poor. They created a nation of beggars, according to Lloyd George. 'The real policy was to take him by the hand, pull him up, give him freedom, let him walk straight and erect, make him a man and not a beggar.'[128] Tariffs would also cultivate a hedonistic lifestyle, an emotive issue for many, like the Conservative Robert Cecil who saw 'nocturnal amusements' and 'idleness' as far greater national dangers than foreign competition.[129]

At the international level, too, Free Trade was believed to promote harmony, not greed and exploitation. Echoing eighteenth-century notions of the sweet *douceur* of commerce, Free Traders argued that trade wore down prejudice and animosity, and induced more peaceful, civil behaviour. Whereas enlightenment thinkers had mainly focused on the merchant as a peaceful man spreading an atmosphere of civil intercourse, Liberals now saw civilizing influences at work in an entire social system. Living in a Free Trade society made people more peaceful and other-regarding both at home and abroad. Early Victorian campaigners against the Corn Laws had presented the earth as 'diversified by an Almighty hand, each soil hath its productions, every land its capabilities', so that people traded with each other.[130] Edwardians continued to dwell on Britons' special role in this divine plan. Their holy mission, Lloyd George told a great demonstration at Aberdeen in 1903, was 'to open up through our national market-place a path for the nations to tread to the Temple of Concord'. Chamberlain's tariff proposals, by contrast, were 'a stirring of the evil passions', exciting 'international jealousy, rage, envy, anger, greed'.[131]

Direct contrasts with the materialist excess and decline of public life in protectionist America reinforced this moral message. Popular radicals joined liberal industrialists to decry the evil of American wealth. Chamberlain's wife Mary was American and on her mother's side connected to the Boston Brahmin Peabody family and Morgan, the bankers. America was proof of the unbridled materialism that naturally followed on tariffs. The real profits and social inequality in a Free Trade system faded from view. So did Americans' higher standard of living.

Free Trade has often been seen as a sharp break from an older culture, replacing a 'moral economy' with the 'modern' economics of the market.[132] In fact, it gave older moral traditions a new lease of life. Free Traders invoked notions of just profits. The problem with Tariff Reformers was that they were not satisfied with 'ordinary profits', Lloyd George told a crowd in Perth, Scotland, in 1904: 'they wish to become millionaires'.[133] The American trustmongers, the Rockefellers and Carnegies, now took their place alongside the earlier villains, the aristocratic landowners. Exploitation and inequality followed from bad fiscal policies—not commerce as such. America became a showcase for the new kind of 'financial politics' run by organized capitalist interest groups. The deterioration of public morality and government followed on trusts and rings, which themselves were the automatic products of tariffs. A few Free Traders, like J. A. Hobson, warned against simply tracing new forms of capitalist organization back to tariff policies and pointed out that they were part of a more general shift from competition to combination. In the case of trusts like the Standard Oil Co. or the Carnegie Steel Co., for example, it was railroads that had enabled financiers to extend their control over transport and industries[134] But these were isolated voices, muted by a large chorus proclaiming tariffs as 'the Mother of Trusts' and 'Foster-Mother of Monopoly'.[135]

Cartoons and lantern slides in the general elections showed John Bull, blindfolded, walking the plank 'Protection', while 'Monopoly' sharks circled underneath.[136] Leaflets provided voters with a 'Voice from America', with short reports from American governors and the assurance 'Free Trade Means Freedom from Trusts'—a position shared by Chamberlain's brother, Arthur, much to the embarrassment of Tariff Reformers.[137] St Loe Strachey, the editor of the *Spectator*, received regular updates from Earl Grey in Canada about how protection had tainted the Republican party in the United States with 'the arrogant ostentation of great wealth and with shameless political corruption'.[138] There was nothing in the Great Republic that appealed to

Hugh Bell. 'I do not desire to have a crop of millionaires ... 'I do not wish for a population striving for wealth at any cost', this not exactly poor Free Trader announced.[139]

The New Yorker Franklin Pierce offered a gripping story of the evil influence of American tariffs at the international Free Trade Congress in London in August 1908. Afterwards he toured Unionist Free Trade clubs. Free Traders made much of his account of how American tariff laws had led to a proliferation of trusts, 'parasites', and corruption. Lord Cromer wished Pierce's work would be read by everyone in the country, and it was widely quoted in popular propaganda. Because of tariffs, the 'plainer virtues'—thrift, rectitude, industry—had gone out of fashion, Pierce argued. A 'feverish, speculative, unscrupulous spirit' was sapping young American manhood. Selfish interests had taken hold of government.[140] For Strachey, America was proof of the 'deadly perils of the temptations of materialism'.[141]

There was nothing extraordinary as such about bashing America's materialism, as the global career of anti-Americanism in the twentieth century would show again and again. What is interesting is that this critique came not from a socialist or nationalist corner, nor from the margins of the world economy, but from what was the dominant Empire and centre of the global economy. The critique of American capitalism provided Free Trade with a human face. It disguised its own role in the creation of vast fortunes, social inequality, and imperial exploitation. It made it possible for the social reformer and supporter of the suffragettes Pethick Lawrence to attack Tariff Reform as part of a larger scheme to 'place free men and women more surely under the heel of capitalist domination'.[142] Adding a colonial voice, Bhupendranath Basu, on his way to become president of the Indian National Congress, congratulated Free Traders at the annual Cobden Club dinner in 1911 for not having forgotten India: 'We who don't belong to the capitalist class don't want India to be exploited as America is being exploited by its great capitalists.'[143] This was an extraordinary endorsement coming from a colony which had seen its textile industry destroyed by Free Trade.

When it came to stories of American wealth and corruption, Unionist Free Traders were a particularly receptive audience. After resigning from Balfour's government in the autumn of 1903, the Duke of Devonshire and Lord Balfour of Burleigh led a small group of Unionists in the battle against tariffs—although 'leading' may give an unduly active impression of years of indecision, infighting, and muted action. The Unionist Free Trade Club was a gentleman's club in an age of increasingly heated mass politics—and most members were keen to keep it that way. What this small group lacked in popular support and institutional muscle, however, it more than made up for with a passionate, dogmatic conviction about the general decay of politics. The achievements of the Glorious Revolution of 1688 were under threat and could only be defended by independent men, like themselves, whose moderation placed them above party and self-interest. In parliamentary speeches and articles Arthur Elliot, the editor of the *Edinburgh Review*, railed against the declining character of MPs and the fall in standards and procedures in the House of Commons.[144]

For Lord Cromer, just back from Egypt as Proconsul, protectionism would mean the 'probable democratisation of our public life', the rule of the mob and private interests.[145] Members of the old elite, like Robert Cecil, prided themselves on representing a constituency—not a party. The strategy of Tariff Reform confederates to target and oust such moderate men from their constituencies struck at 'the root of all electoral independence'. It was 'unconstitutional', a denial of the very principles on which 'true representation' and parliamentary sovereignty were based—Cromer denounced confederates as 'political Jack the Rippers' at the Unionist Free Trade Club in 1909.[146] Instead of being an exponent of the national will, providing a space for deliberative reason among men of 'high character', Parliament was becoming a mere mechanical instrument for advancing Cabinet policy and private interests. The death in 1907 of Viscount Goschen, the former Chancellor of the Exchequer (1887–92) and a staunch defender of laissez-faire in the battle against democracy and egalitarianism, produced an outpouring of nostalgia for a golden age when morality, truth, and loyalty to an idealized public kept self-interest and party in check. Some wondered openly whether even the absolutist Charles I or James II ever wielded as much power as the Liberal and Conservative parties.[147]

Such an idealized vision of parliamentary politics initially worked in favour of Free Trade. Once Liberals returned to power and began to marry social reform and progressive taxation to freedom of trade in 1909–11, however, this fixation with political purity was easily turned against the Free Trade government. Unionist Free Traders split into those to whom the defeat of tariffs remained the uppermost task, and a vocal camp to whom the greater evil was the state 'socialism' of the Liberal government. The defence of liberty now required the sacrifice of a Liberal Free Trade ministry which, with its policies of old age pensions and unemployment benefits, had turned out to be worse than Tariff Reform. It had become imperative to get 'rid of this Lloyd George and Winston [Churchill]-ridden Government', Strachey in 1909 told Harold Cox, who had decided to stand as an independent: 'Nothing will ever persuade me that predatory socialism plus demagoguery of the most reckless and unscrupulous description are not worse than tariff reform.' There were still 'a great many ditches and hedges and other obstacles to be got over before we have Protection' but the rot and 'demoralisation' spread by growing state expenditure and intervention were already seeping in.[148] Social reform was undermining Free Trade and its benign effect on personal and public morals. There would be a vicious cycle of rising taxes and escalating demands on the state by all sorts of groups and interests which, sooner or later, would kill Free Trade itself. The Liberal government was creating a dangerous culture of dependence, threatening a sense of individuals' duty to themselves and to the state. Pauperism should be looked upon as a crime, not as a problem deserving public support, Dicey wrote in 1910: it amounted to a 'failure to perform one's full duty to the State'.[149] For men like Cox, the importance of self-reliance was such that it developed after the war into support for eugenic schemes of sterilizing 'the unfit'; artisans and the middle classes were lowering their birth rate while the poor were rapidly increasing, leaving the slum child a burden on the rest of society and weakening the nation.[150]

Politically, this rear-guard campaign by champions of individual liberty was a solid failure. Neither was the Liberal government ousted, nor was the long-term trend of state expansion and welfarism halted. If the 1906 election had already reduced the 48-strong contingent of Unionist Free Traders to a mere 16, the January 1910 election annihilated them.[151] Only Hugh Cecil hung on for Oxford University, unopposed. Cox came bottom in Preston, never to return to Parliament. Free Fooders who survived (like Peel or Bentinck) did so by swallowing hard and standing as Tariff Reformers. The Unionist Free Trade Club dissolved. But intellectually, this group had done much to crystallize a libertarian definition of Free Trade, linked to a minimalist state, that would become its dominant meaning as the twentieth century went on.

Citizen–Consumers

Public morality, social justice, civic-mindedness—it was the 'consumer' who held moral and material concerns together. For contemporaries, consumers came to embody the public interest. Free Trade advanced into the first bill of consumer rights in history. It protected consumers against vested interests and unfair taxation. By giving attention to the consumer as a civic person as well as a customer, the defence of Free Trade planted 'the consumer' solidly on the map of modern politics. Consumers acquired a sense of belonging to a shared interest whose voice should be heard and whose interests should receive public recognition. As the campaign developed, there was a growing defence of the consumer as a universal, human interest. 'Tariff Reform... always takes it for granted that the consumer is a person who does not count', an article on 'the common sense of Free Trade' put it in the spring of 1910: 'We are all consumers; we have, most of us, dependent upon us other consumers who cannot be producers—women and children.' Tariff Reform might promise benefits to 'us [as] producers' but essentially this would always also be 'at the expense of ourselves as consumers and of our families'.[152]

Of course, humans have consumed goods and resources throughout history. But this does not mean they have naturally tended to see themselves (or others) as 'consumers', with a shared sense of rights and interests. The seventeenth and eighteenth centuries witnessed an unprecedented expansion of commercial life, goods, luxuries and shopping in western Europe and North America, as well as in parts of Asia. People shopped and debated the impact of luxury on public life. Adam Smith highlighted the place of consumption—'the sole end of all production'—in the *Wealth of Nations* (1776), but he and the next few generations of economists had surprisingly little to say about the consumer. Merchants and commerce, industrialists and agriculture were the focus of attention in the nineteenth century. Where consumers featured at all, they were treated as sectional interests, subordinate to the larger, more national interests of producers and landowners, and condemned for their wasteful, unproductive behaviour. A rare consideration of consumers in the 1820s, by the early cooperator William Thompson, neatly captured their low reputation: 'The consumer (monkey, king or bishop) devours the fruits without return.'[153]

In the mid- and late Victorian era, cities like London were booming centres of consumption, from the dance platform at the Cremorne Gardens

and new department stores in the West End, such as Selfridges and
Whiteleys, to the worlds of mass leisure and temptation in music halls.
These sites did much to open up public spaces for women, and in this sense
enlarged the sphere of citizenship.[154] At the same time, economists, like
Jevons and Marshall, put the maximizing behaviour of 'rational' individual
consumers at the centre of economic analysis. The so-called 'marginal
revolution' laid the foundations for liberal economics as we know it, with
a mathematical and psychological focus on measuring 'the utility'—the
pleasure and pain—of individual choices.

Significantly, however, it was neither the hedonistic shopper nor the
rational economic individual who would drive the growing appeal of the
consumer in public discourse. Rather, 'the consumer' matured in the political realm over questions of ethics, community, and citizenship. Boycotts
of slave-grown sugar in the early nineteenth century explicitly appealed
to consumers' human sensibility and social responsibility. Consumers also
began to flex their muscle in local battles over taxes and representation in
the mid- and late-Victorian period, especially in fights over gas and water
which gave rise to the first consumer defence leagues.[155]

The achievement of Free Trade was to invent a much more generalized
language of the consumer as a public, national interest. The consumer
became tied to the citizen, providing Liberal politics with a new base
of support in an age of mass democratic politics. The distance travelled
becomes apparent when we compare the early Victorian campaign against
the Corn Laws with the language of Edwardian Free Trade. The consumer
already appeared in a handful of places in Richard Cobden's speeches, but
mainly as the person paying a tax on specific imports (like sugar). In the
1870s and 1880s, popular editions of the *Sophisms* and *Essays on Political
Economy* by the French Free Trader Frédéric Bastiat helped circulate in
England the idea of the consumer as the embodiment of humanity.[156]
Gladstone could thus present the interests of the mercantile community
as 'represent[ing] the consumer, that is to say the world'.[157] If Gladstone's
voluminous diaries are any indicator, however, such references were still
exceedingly rare. By the Edwardian period, by contrast, the consumer was
ubiquitous, an umbrella concept denoting the legitimate public interest
as a whole.

Liberals' focus on people's 'necessities' and basic needs produced an
extensive campaign that addressed the consumer directly as the victim of
food duties.[158] The language of the consumer gave particular attention

to those without a direct voice in public politics—the poor, women, and children. It also had a unifying appeal that was contrasted with a protectionist community divided by particular interests. Posters compared the prosperous Free Trade shop with Chamberlain's abandoned Tariff Reform shop, and showed a typical working-class cooperative 'woman with the basket' alongside well-dressed middle-class ladies (Colour Plate VII). Importantly, and in spite of the preoccupation with the suffering of poor children and mothers, the appeal to the consumer was also open to middle-class men. A leaflet from 1909 shows the well-healed middle-class consumer in black top-hat outside a shop wondering about the effects of tariffs on gloves and shoes (see Figure 4, overleaf).

The democratic image of the consumer fostered by Free Trade in Britain at the turn of the twentieth century stands in interesting contrast to Europe and America at the time. In the transatlantic network of buyers' leagues it was middle-class women and men who saw themselves as 'consumers' whose ethical considerations would improve the conditions of working-class 'producers'. In Imperial Germany, consumers were seen as a narrow interest group; even liberal critics of protectionism avoided the term for fear of being seen as a specialist lobby of clerks and alienating the rest of their bourgeois supporters.[159] In Britain, by contrast, Free Trade extended the language of the consumer from disenfranchised men and women to the public as a whole.

Nowhere did the consumer as a general interest enjoy more support within the political system than in the Treasury. It fitted perfectly the Treasury's own sense of itself as shielding state and public against excessive taxation and the influence of vested interests. Free Trade, Treasury control, and the consumer interest mutually supported each other. For Edward Hamilton, its financial secretary, Free Trade had been an epochal shift in power. 'In days of protection, producers were more powerful than consumers. Nowadays consumers are the more powerful and will remain so.'[160] At a time when there was no consumer representation, indeed no formal consumer rights or regulatory oversight, Free Trade functioned as a virtual form of consumer empowerment. The Treasury did not distinguish between different groups of users and purchasers. Consumers were lumped together as the payers of indirect taxes, contrasted with payers of direct taxes. And it was the balance or equity of taxation between these 'two attractive sisters', in Gladstone's image, that deserved the utmost consideration. A preferential duty would place an unfair burden on British consumers for

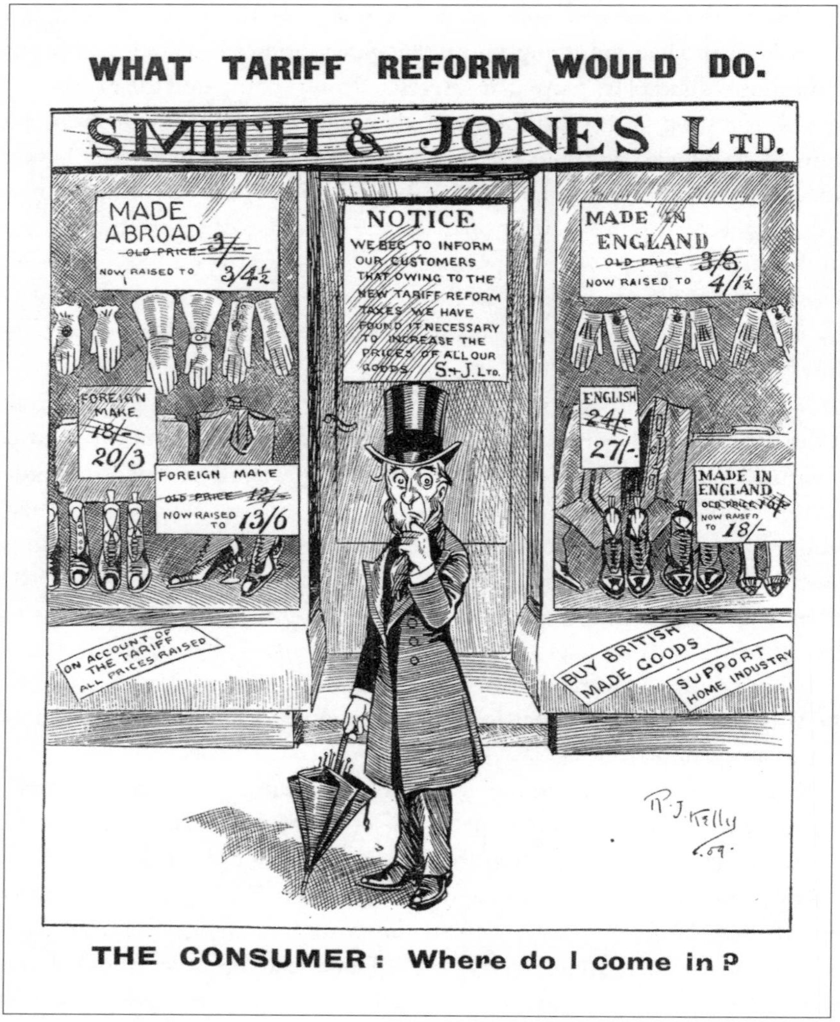

Figure 4. A well-to-do man ponders the consequences of tariffs, in a Free Trade Union leaflet from 1909. The tariff had raised prices of British goods as well as of foreign articles by making all imported materials more expensive.

the sake of colonial producers.[161] In vain did Conservatives point out that there could be a difference between consumers' immediate and permanent interests. Well might G. Ryder at the Board of Customs or William Hewins, the Tariff Reform economist, object that consumers would also in the long term benefit from a stronger, expanding colonial market.[162] Nor did Free Trade in practice treat consumers equitably. Food taxes fell on basic rather than superior foods, on sugar rather than salmon. This meant the poor paid a much higher share of their budget on food taxes than the middle class.[163] For the Treasury the point remained that tariffs would upset a fair balance between indirect and direct taxation and expose the state to the charge that it was penalizing the consumer more than it was benefiting the Exchequer. The interests of the state and of the consuming public complemented each other.

It was this view of the consumer as the silent majority that also kept most so-called neo-classical economists firmly on the side of Free Trade. They looked back to Adam Smith's authoritative critique of mercantilism, rather than to the new mathematical analysis of individual consumer preferences. 'The old tradition that the economist is generally on the side of the consumer as against the producer was mistaken in form', Alfred Marshall acknowledged. '[F]or everyone is a producer or the dependent of a producer, and everyone is a consumer.' Still, he felt, 'that tradition bears some resemblance to the facts of the case ... because economists have aimed at holding the balance fairly between the unvocal many who consume the products of a particular industry and the vocal few who urge its claims for favourable treatment'.[164]

Free Traders' dual fixation with the consumer and 'cheapness' took precedence even over the smooth working of the market. Sugar in the late Victorian period was what butter mountains and agricultural subsidies have been more recently. Since the 1870s central and eastern European countries had developed their beet sugar industries through an ever more elaborate system of subsidies and export bounties. The world sugar market suffered from overproduction and cycles, hitting especially Caribbean producers in the British Empire. Consumers benefited from falling prices, while producers faced instability and dislocation. Free Traders were passionate in their opposition to international agreements which sought to stabilize the market by reducing subsidies, such as the Brussels Sugar Convention of 1902.[165] British consumers had a right to benefit from cheap subsidized sugar exports—if foreign governments wanted to use export bounties that was entirely up to them. Free Trade meant free imports, not the global spread of free markets.

This was also the approach to the sensitive subject of dumping, shared by old and new Liberals and Treasury officials alike. It showed how the consumer interest could be extended to include industries as well as private shoppers. When foreigners 'dumped' surplus stock, like iron or sugar, Free Traders argued, this was a cause for celebration, not for alarm. Rather than driving out British competition, as Tariff Reformers argued, 'dumping' was a good thing, raising people's purchasing power and giving British industries extra cheap imports to turn into competitive products for the world market, such as steel or jam. And as the trusts and cartels behind these policies were seen as unsustainable, pathological outgrowths of protection in the first place, there was nothing to fear from putting the consumer first instead of regulating 'dumping' and related interferences with market forces.[166] This was the very reverse of the double-barrelled approach that has been so damaging to the reputation of the European Union and free trade more generally in recent years. Instead of pressing other countries to open their markets while creating an internal fortress of subsidies and price guarantees for European sugar and agriculture, Britain left other countries to their own devices and offered its own open market to foreign subsidized exports.

Liberals at the time stressed the prior consideration due to the consumer. 'Take care of the consumer and the producer will take care of himself', Free Trade women reminded audiences.[167] For Cox, the precedence of the consumer was rooted deep in the 'eternal facts of human nature'. 'The consumer gives the order; the producer only has to obey.' No 'Governmental contrivance' could ever change this.[168] This privileged position, though, was not limited to the private shopper. In the Victorian period shopkeepers and small businesses had sometimes combined to defend their interests as consumers, for instance regarding the provision of gas to light their shops. Free Traders broadened the consumer interest to include industrial consumers more generally. Alfred Mond embraced the 'British consumer, who is after all the most important person' in his defence of Free Trade from the point of view of the alkali industry; the commercial and private users of dyes, bleach, and alkaline chlorides would all suffer from a duty on imports.[169] When Free Traders contrasted consumers and producers, they meant the public versus a small self-interested class of the rich. 'The combatants were the producer and the consumer', Lord James of Hereford, a leading Unionist Free Fooder, told a demonstration in 1910. 'He would willingly, under all circumstances, range himself on the side of the consumers.' Not only were they 'the more numerous; but also … the producers, or one class of producers, represented wealth, to which he did not care to add'.[170] The emphasis was on 'one class of producers'.

Tariff Reformers worked hard to position themselves as a national alliance of producer interests pitched against a Free Trade camp of consumers interested in cheapness at any price. Leopold Maxse, the hot-headed editor of the *National Review*, went as far as to suggest in 1904 that it was protectionists, not Cobdenites, who carried on Cobden's true principles. Cobden, in this view was 'first and foremost, a Free Exporter', a practical man to whom the national interest lay in 'prosperous production'. It was Liberals who had perverted this tradition into a fanatical school of 'Free Importers', subordinating everything to consumption and cheapness. Tariff Reform would return the country to a productive system where one 'buys for the sake of selling', instead of the spendthrift Free Trader policy where 'one buys for buying's sake'.[171]

But Britain depended just as much on imported raw materials and semi-manufactured goods as it did on imported food, and Free Traders responded that manufacturers were consumers too. Older Liberals like John Morley, Cobden's biographer, reminded audiences of the 'great principle' on which Free Trade rested: 'that the most important interest, that of the consuming public, is entirely reconcilable with the interests of the aggregate producers of the country'.[172] Liberals of the next generation emphasized that industrialists were consumers too. These 'great consumers', Churchill told the inaugural meeting of the Free Trade League in Manchester in 1904, would have to pay more for their raw materials, and lose their competitive edge and independence: the 'small manufacturer…will find himself bought out—absorbed, like in America and Germany, in some vast syndicate—no longer his own master and an independent man, but the salaried servant of a great combine'.[173]

Since the eighteenth century the honest, jovial, beef-eating John Bull had been the symbol of British strength and liberty. The ideal Free Trade consumer, by contrast, was modest, concerned with access to basic goods like bread, and a responsible housewife as much as a contented man. Stories of 'the hungry forties' presented older Britons as akin to starving, root-eating, and oppressed Frenchmen, but their progress under Free Trade did not steer towards the jolly, well-fed John Bull. It was the Tories who initially exploited a more unrestrained version of popular consumption, a 'cakes and ale' conservatism high on manliness, sport, and drink.[174] This bullish version provided an antidote to the more sober nonconformist liberal culture in many towns in the late nineteenth century—and continues to do so. But it failed to generate a rival political language of the consumer. Tariff Reform's emphasis on 'the producer' as the most important national and imperial interest derailed what could have been a very different political history of the consumer. While protectionists argued that tariffs would increase employment and real wages, their denunciation of Free Trade's cult of 'cheapness' sidelined the older conservative celebration of true Englishmen indulging freely in occasional binges. Tariff Reform employers, like Mr Charteris, the head of the Rosefield Tweed Mills in Dumfries, asked workers at their annual social meeting in December 1903 to 'bear in mind that they were producers before they were consumers, and their interests as producers far exceeded their interest as consumers'.[175] Cheap goods and freedom to choose were bad for workers and bad for the nation. 'Free Trade means cheapness, especially cheap labour, cheap men', the Tariff Reform League told voters in January 1910.[176] The Conservative 'consumer' was stillborn—and would not find a significant political voice until the battle against rationing after the Second World War.

Instead 'the consumer' became the monopoly of Free Traders. Free Traders created a consumer associated with independent character, public morals, and social responsibility rather than luxury, selfishness, or the erosion of public life. At a time when there was grave concern amongst the elite and middle classes whether individuals could be safely left to choose in the political as well as the commercial market place, with moral panics about working-class gambling, excessive spending and debt, this was a considerable achievement. It depended on a distinction between different forms of consumption, rather than invoking a more neutral, indiscriminate use of 'demand' or favouring unlimited choice and consumerist hedonism. Free Trade offered a defence of the good consumer against flashy, morally doubtful or socially irresponsible forms of private behaviour. It was Chamberlain's programme that was portrayed by Liberals as appealing to 'speculators and loafers' and to 'fine ladies and "swells" more generally'.[177]

The distancing of the civic consumer and Free Trade from the socially and morally ambiguous world of a market society in full swing reached its apotheosis in the 'citizen-consumer', especially in the writings of the radical public intellectual J. A. Hobson. A genuinely heretical thinker, Hobson emerged as one of the most brilliant and prolific voices of the new liberalism. He mixed a good dose of Ruskin's ethical critique of commercial wealth with a controversial analysis of 'underconsumption'. The modern machine age, he argued, accelerated wasteful overproduction and set off violent economic cycles. There was a widening gulf between over-investment and society's ability to consume. Unless wealth was redistributed to boost consumption, capitalist society would self-destruct. Tariffs were doubly dangerous. Economically, they exacerbated the underconsumptionist crisis by shifting wealth further from the poor to the rich. The cultural repercussions were no less frightening. Unreformed capitalism, Hobson was convinced, promoted commercialization, bureaucratization, and the standardization of the human mind. It eroded the organic bonds of society, separating individual from community, family from labour, home from work. The music-hall, shopping, and cheap sensationalist media spread 'anti-social feelings' and weakened 'the bonds of moral cohesion between individuals'.[178] Civil society would be swept away by mass society.

A hallmark of this uncontrolled modernity was the growth of 'stimulants and drugs ... bad literature, art and recreations, the services of prostitutes and flunkeys'. Advertising and the spread of goods without 'survival value' were steadily weakening the natural instinct for healthy and creative pastimes. This was especially true amongst the lower middle and working classes, 'where a growing susceptibility to new desires is accompanied by no intelligent checks upon the play of interested suggestion as to the modes of satisfying these desires'. Worse, this transmitted the 'barbarian standards of values' of an old social order and its aristocratic elites. Modern leisure, epitomized by commercial sport, led to a 'lower leisure class' aping the leisured elite. It exhibited 'the same sex licence and joviality of manners' and adopted the life-style of the 'race course ... the club smoke-room, or of the flash music-hall'. Haunting this new pleasure economy were 'gypsies, tramps, poachers and other vagabonds, casual workers, professional or amateur thieves and prostitutes, street-sellers, cornermen, kept husbands, and other parasites'. Commercial leisure lessened class division, but any 'apparent gain in humanity' was outweighed by the damage done to social ethics and international solidarity. It put personal pleasure over social care. Honour displaced honesty, superstition reason. It encouraged uncritical conformity. And it fed into an imperialist sense of white superiority and a global racist division between Western leisure and colonial work.[179]

Hobson's critique, however idiosyncratic in parts, partook of the widespread unease about consumerist modernity on both sides of the Atlantic. Hobson exchanged ideas with the American Thorstein Veblen, whose seminal *The Theory of the Leisure Class* criticized the social waste from 'conspicuous consumption', as well as engaging with Le Bon's ideas of mass psychology. What was distinctive was that he also turned to the consumer as an answer to the problem of mass culture. Society could be regenerated by cultivating 'higher' forms of consumption. 'Everything in human progress will be found to depend upon a progressive realisation of the nature of good "consumption"', Hobson wrote in his *Evolution of Modern Capitalism* in 1897.[180] For Hobson, marrying Free Trade to the new liberalism would reverse what he saw as the ruinous producer-bias of earlier liberal economists for whom production simply and automatically created its own demand. In place of the increasingly numb consumer of standardized mass production, Free Trade and the redistribution of wealth would educate the people and raise the quality of their consumption.

The task was to turn people from passive shoppers into active citizens, to train what Hobson called a 'citizen-consumer'. 'Higher' consumption would reunite work and leisure. To genuinely enjoy goods, one needed to know how to make them. 'A true connoisseur of pictures must, in training and study, be a good deal of an artist: the exquisite *gourmet* must be something of a cook.' Gardening, painting, reading, and carpentry would lift the quality of consumption.

There was a pronounced gender division of labour in this vision; factory life was inconsistent with the position of a 'good mother', 'good wife' and homemaker: the promotion of quality consumption, Hobson believed, would also return 'female' caring qualities to the home. In general, the 'spirit of machinery' would give way to 'individual thought, feeling, [and] effort'. Free Trade was a favourable environment for this project of civic and cultural renewal. Not only did it provide material opportunities, but it also encouraged a civic outlook in which people acquired an interest in their neighbours. The citizen-consumer would show an 'increased regard for quality of life'. This included a concern for the conditions of workers who produced consumer goods, gradually raising the social and ethical standards of capitalist society. Selfishness in a competitive market would be transformed into 'generous rivalry in co-operation'. Hobson eventually extended this model to the level of global relations. 'It is through consumption', he argued, 'that the co-operative nature and value of commerce is realized. Production divides, consumption unites.'[181]

In Britain, Free Trade established a system of beliefs and values that was able to inspire loyalty and passion akin to that inspired by nationalism and socialism elsewhere. The successful revival of Free Trade was not based on a uniform ideology—some groups looked forward to a cooperative commonwealth while others were quite happy with a liberal market society of competing individuals. Rather, the strength of Free Trade culture came from its flexibility in building up a set of shared core assumptions about what was legitimate politics, and what not, about the public interest, and about national identity. This consensus was built from the bottom up as well as from the top down. Free Traders were able to recycle older liberal ideals of politics, such as the independence of political deliberation and parliamentary autonomy from vested interests, by adapting them to confront a modern cast of enemies, like protectionist trust-mongers and millionaires. But success also came from the creative promotion of new collective identities capable of inspiring mass loyalties. The 'hungry forties' was a narrative of the people's inclusion in an evolving democratic culture. What military triumphs and sleeping medieval kings were to newly unified countries on the European continent, the repeal of the Corn Laws became to many Britons. Free Trade was a saga of internal unification. Like all founding stories, it is more interesting for what it reveals about the internal belief system of a society than about the actual past. Free Trade Britain was not free of social polarization, inequality, and exploitation—far from it. But its powerful vision of civil society and its new public language of the consumer provided a sense of inclusion and legitimacy that allowed it to avoid the simple association of Free Trade with wealth and selfish capitalists so widespread today. Fairness and equity focused on consumers. By ensuring cheapness, Free Trade guaranteed a fair price for basic goods for the people, especially groups formally excluded from politics, like the poor, women, and children. 'The poor people hereabouts look upon Free Trade as we do upon Trial by Jury,' a Conservative concluded in Yorkshire in 1912, ' i.e. as an absolute fundamental right, to buy eatables as cheaply as circumstances will allow.'[182] The Free Trade consumer became a way of imagining a socially responsible form of capitalism, one that reconciled

considerations of social justice and public morality with the material interests
of importing trades and consuming industries. Free Trade culture was not
so much about the virtues of the market as about a remarkable trust in
civil society, its ability to thrive in an open economy, to raise civic-minded
consumers, and to escape the dreaded materialism and selfishness associated
with protectionist societies.

2

Bread and Circuses

This time the spread of enlightenment has reached the masses.

Alfred Mond, industrialist and Liberal politician, 1912[1]

Vote For Branch, and Don't Eat Doggy.

A Liberal in Enfield turns his dog into a walking political advert, exploiting
stories of dogmeat consumption in protectionist Germany, January 1910[2]

Since nobody can think statistically in millions, and only students can think
diagrammatically, the ordinary man must be helped to think by contrasts,
and in pictures.

G. Wallace Carter, secretary of the Free Trade Union, on the
principles of propaganda, 1910[3]

The trouble started on Friday. Just as a final group of men was
proceeding through the centre of High Wycombe, a small town
in south Buckinghamshire just west of London, to cast their vote in
the January 1910 general election, mayhem broke out. Amidst cheering
and jostling from Free Trade and Tariff Reform supporters, a stone was
suddenly thrown, shattering the screen of a motor car. Then, as the town
clock struck 8 p.m., 'a section of the crowd' made an attack on the Penny
Bazaar, the committee rooms of the protectionist candidate, Alfred Cripps,
smashing several windows. The police beat back the crowd, but not for
long. Free Traders now charged on Oxford Street, with the rallying cry
of 'Dump! Dump! Dump!' Protectionists had opened a 'Dump Shop'
there the week before with a shop-window display of cheap foreign goods
that were undercutting honest British labour. Free Trade supporters had
already threatened the Dump Shop in the previous days, and eventually
protectionists had boarded it up at the advice of Chief Constable Sparling.
Undeterred, the crowd now tore down the boards and knocked in the

windows. A helpless policeman was pushed through the window of a neighbouring shop. More stones began to fly. The police fought running street battles with a 'band of rowdy youths'. Officers drew their truncheons, only infuriating 'the mob' more. The crowd then made a final assault on the Dump Shop. Overwhelmed, the Chief Constable withdrew his men and allowed the shop to meet its fate.[4]

Within minutes the Dump Shop was demolished from top to bottom, including windows, gas fixtures, and its exhibits. More than one barrow-load of stones needed to be cleared away from inside it the next day. With loud cheers, the attackers threw the contents of the shop into the street. 'The chairs were smashed to atoms on the pavement', a local reporter observed, with 'many of the onlookers picking up pieces as mementoes of what they declared to be the "insult" perpetrated on the staple industry of the town'; High Wycombe was home to the furnishing trade. One woman was struggling with a carpet, others walked off with a bed. But most items were piled high in the street and set on fire 'by means of rockets and otherwise'. When the Mayor, Alderman Birch, finally arrived on the scene, the fire had grown large enough to threaten neighbouring houses and the fire brigade had to be called.

Friday was only a taste of things to come. After the disturbances on 21 January 1910, the nineteen members of the local police force were augmented by eighty men from the Bucks Constabulary, seven mounted. On Saturday, the whole force paraded in front of the Guildhall as the votes were counted and the election result declared. Cripps, the Tariff Reformer, had won, reversing the Free Trade victory of 1906. The town was quiet—until about 8.30 in the evening. Witness accounts and subsequent court testimony would later differ about what exactly ignited the violence and who was responsible, but they all agreed about the speed with which it spread. Groups began by charging the homes of local protectionists and smashing more windows. By the time the pubs closed at eleven o'clock, the crowd had swelled to over 6,000, singing Liberal songs and challenging the increasingly exhausted police. A local reporter who stayed close to the police denied rumours that the crowd threw bottles or pricked the police horses with hat pins, but there was certainly a growing scent of violence in the air. By midnight, fearful of a return of the events of the previous evening and urged on by the Chief Constable, the Mayor finally read the Riot Act and called on the people to disperse, but not before another massive chant of 'Dump!, Dump!, Dump!' erupted from the crowd.

Most people in High Wycombe that Saturday night either failed to realize the seriousness of the situation or were unable to hear the reading of the Riot Act. Suddenly, after waiting ten minutes for the crowd to disperse, the police, standing two deep in a line, drew their batons and rushed on the crowd. Even the local newspaper, which rejected many reports as exaggerated fabrications, was in no doubt about the gravity of what followed. 'It was an extraordinary scene, such as the streets of the ancient Borough of Wycombe had never before witnessed.' The Mayor was besieged by an 'angry throng'; 'some of the women present actually spat in his face!' The police bludgeoned the crowd 'unmercifully'. Innocent people got trampled and knocked unconscious, as the police chased them to the outskirts of town. It was 1.30 on Sunday morning before the police finally retired, leaving the streets of High Wycombe deserted, and over thirty wounded in the care of the local doctors, Dr Fleck and Dr Bell.

The next few days bore witness to the severity of the clashes. Across town there were signs of splattered blood. Young men walked around with hands in slings, their heads covered in bandages. Ten days later the inhabitants of High Wycombe would gather at an overflow town meeting to condemn the decision to read the Riot Act. Amidst cries of 'shame', many accused the police of unnecessary brutality. They had been like 'demons' let loose, knocking down men and women, even children. The reading of the Riot Act had trampled upon their English liberties, 'which had been bought by their forefathers with great treasure and blood'. 'Are we in Russia, or are we in good old England?', the chairman of the meeting, James Holland, wanted to know.

It was no accident that the Conservative Dump Shop was in the early line of fire, and that the crowd was swelled by the chant 'Dump!, Dump!, Dump!' As a constituency, High Wycombe was like a doughnut. The area surrounding the town had a residential population with Conservative leanings. The town itself, however, had a Liberal core. Before going to the Liberals in 1906, the constituency had been consistently Conservative, and in January 1910 swung back, to elect a Tariff Reformer with a majority of 2,556. There was heated debate about the Conservatives' decision to open a Dump Shop in the centre of the town. For many Liberals it was a deliberate provocation. Even to many who worked in the local chair-making industries facing foreign competition, the display of cheap dumped goods was like rubbing salt in open wounds. Rather than demonstrating the social costs of free imports, as Tariff Reformers had hoped, it mocked their proud British workmanship. The Dump Shop was like 'the holding of a red rag to a bull', said Councillor Forward.

Conservatives, in turn, insisted on their right to political expression and called for compensation; the Conservative owner eventually received only £52 for damages of almost three times that amount. Their Dump Shop was a novel but 'perfectly proper and legitimate' form of politics, they argued. It contained 'nothing to offend the common sense of anyone: it is simply an exhibition of articles in common use imported into this country, duty free, which might quite as well be made at home'. And, anyhow, they had followed the law every step of the way, even boarding up the shop before polling day when urged to do so by the police. '[Y]ou know quite well that the animosity the Dump Shop aroused was caused by its success in converting the electors from the fallacies of so-called Free Trade', leading Tariff Reformers told the editor of the local paper. Recalling an earlier attack on Conservative offices in the 1906 election, Tariff Reformers put the blame squarely on Free Trade Radicals, 'who, judging by their offensive posters and literature, have no consideration for the feelings of their opponents'.

The ringleaders behind the demolition of the Dump Shop were never identified. Subsequent hearings at the police court suggested that the mayhem probably resulted from a fairly spontaneous, pent-up popular irritation with protectionist propaganda. Some who had challenged Conservative supporters in the streets had been intoxicated; others were young men 15–18 years old. Those who were charged with destruction of property, throwing missiles, or endangering public safety, however, were respectable workers and small businessmen. One such was Frederic James, a local chairmaker, who together with a man known as 'Cheshire Cheese', asked others to join in as they made for the Dump Shop, armed with a hammer and sticks. James got off lightly, with a fine of £1 or 14 days' prison, though the Magistrate found it hard to believe that he simply happened to have his hammer in his pocket when he left his workplace. The carrier William Hoskins certainly did his bit to add to the commotion outside the Dump Shop as it was torn to pieces and its goods burnt in the street. Sober but excited at the time, Hoskins was charged with driving his cart and pony at great speed—no less than 16 miles an hour, according to a policeman—through the crowd, not just once but three times, knocking down Captain Butler of the Fire Brigade and interfering with the police. There was laughter in the courtroom when Hoskins rather ingeniously suggested that his actions had been nothing but a well-intentioned attempt to assist the police: he had hoped his driving would frighten the crowd and make it go away. It was £1 4s. 6d. for Hoskins.[5]

The wild scenes in Wycombe in January 1910 show us the emotion and energy unleashed in the conflict between Free Trade and Tariff Reform. The riots at High Wycombe may have been exceptional—though there was also violence in some other towns such as Droitwich[6]—but they point to the cultural, material, and indeed physical dynamics of political communication at work. Free Trade set people and objects in motion, in a battle over the meaning and representation of things. It generated passions all but lost in the more rational, institutionalized climate of today's advocates of trade liberalization. Feverish enthusiasm, emotional politics, and, indeed, urban riots and vandalism have become associated with movements opposed to free trade and globalization. Historically, however, there has not always been a simple divide between the reasonable atmosphere of Free Trade and the inflamed, passionate ideology of its critics. Far from being a sober calculation of economic costs and benefits, Free Trade in the past could be a warm-blooded creature. Wycombe combined new ways of communicating politics—the shop-window display of goods embodying the impact of globalization—with an older drama of popular protests.

What happened at High Wycombe runs counter to conventional accounts of Free Trade that have tried to explain its success in terms of its superior economic reasoning and material calculation. For liberal economists the strength of Free Trade is rooted in its superior theory of trade.[7] For liberal historians, too, its success has been related to its supposedly distinct and superior form of reasoning. Liberalism, in this view, promoted a culture of reasoned argument in public meetings which favoured the scientifically superior case of Free Trade. Free Traders won because they were able to dictate the terms of engagement, forcing Tariff Reformers to present their case 'rationalistically and publicly', and exposing the deficiencies and inconsistencies of the protectionist programme.[8] In brief, there has been a tendency to imagine a divide between two political cultures: sober public deliberation and scientific truth (Free Trade liberalism) versus beer, prejudice, and passion (popular Conservatism). The events at High Wycombe suggest we need to look at the two as a pair, playing at the same pitch of popular politics, responding to, observing, and emulating each other as the game developed.

The riots at Wycombe are an invitation to ask what Free Trade looked like in practice, in the world of everyday politics and public life, beyond the clean and sober pages of economic textbooks. For most people (past and present), 'the economy' is far more of an elusive riddle than most economists or historians have allowed. On the eve of the First World War, the Treasury economist Ralph Hawtrey penned a long 'Afterthought on Protectionism' in which he criticized Free Traders and Tariff Reformers alike for popularizing and simplifying their mantras. Yet Hawtrey had the good sense to realize that 'philosophers are not kings'. Politics followed a logic different from that of scholarly inquiry: 'arguments are no use in political controversy ... [if they] are too refined for the comprehension of the electorate or of the average politician'.[9] Nor was ignorance the preserve of the masses. At the Treasury, the staunch Free Trader Francis Mowatt was literally in despair in 1903 during the cabinet crisis over Chamberlain's proposals: half the cabinet did not appear to understand basic economics.[10]

Yet the increasingly violent nature of the disagreement over trade policy resulted from more than simple ignorance. Protectionists and Free Traders had different starting points and were asking different questions. Supporters of Free Trade pointed to the absolute increase in the volume and value of trade, while protectionists were worried about trends and degrees—the gradual decline of British trade relative to foreign competitors who were becoming increasingly self-sufficient, shielded by trade barriers and subsidies. To the latter, the future lay with imperial and home markets and it was worth sacrificing a share of foreign trade to foster them. Liberals viewed free imports as wealth flowing into the country; protectionists worried that they displaced British jobs and led to the emigration of capital and manpower. In the midst of the campaign in 1903, for example, the Ebbw Vale Steel company, undercut by cheaper foreign competition, closed plants with a loss of 3,000 jobs. To Liberals this was merely part of the natural and benign process of competitive adjustment and efficiency gains from trade, giving other British industries the cheap materials they needed to stay competitive in a tough world market. To protectionists, by contrast, it was the frightening sign of a jobless future to come.

Was the decrease in wages which preceded the 1906 election and the elections in 1910 a case for sticking to the old liberal policy or for ditching it? Food cost 15 per cent more in 1911 than in 1899 while wages rose only an average of 6 per cent.[11] Was this evidence of the failure of Free Trade or of it being more indispensable than ever before? Free Traders were quick to pull Chamberlain's figures to pieces—his picture of Britain's decline was based on the abnormal years of 1872 and 1902. Tariff Reformers in turn stressed the questionable methods used by Free Traders, especially in comparing the conditions of workers in Germany and Britain with data that was based on different wage structures and unemployment statistics. Liberals and historians since have pointed to the expansion of trade and returns from shipping and foreign investments as evidence of the superiority of Free Trade, but the burst of growth on the eve of the First World War only began in the winter of 1909–1910, after two years of depression and high unemployment. In fact, real wages continued to fall until 1911. For people going to the polls in the two elections of January and December 1910, it was a time of uncertainty.

For groups caught in the middle between these competing projections of Britain's future it was not immediately self-evident which side had the better argument, what counted as a fact, or indeed what measure to use. Was wealth more important than employment? Was secure employment worth a rise in the cost of living? For most Britons at the time, knowledge remained local, barely stretching beyond one's town or surrounding district unless the subject was sport.[12] Free Traders realized that Tariff Reform would not be defeated by statistics alone. Facts and good arguments do not win by themselves. They were also acutely aware that they faced a more difficult task than Tariff Reformers in communicating their programme. A tariff promises immediate, direct benefits for particular industries. This makes it easy to organize strong, concentrated support. For Free Trade it is harder to organize collective action: with the exception of trades like the cotton industry, which depended on cheap imported raw material, the benefits are more diffuse and indirect, spread out across society as a whole. It affects most people slightly rather than a few people greatly.

Free Traders faced two related challenges: they had to create and communicate a picture of the economy that was meaningful to people, and they needed to do so in a way that was entertaining as well as educational. Politics did not inhabit a distinct planet. The battle over Free Trade developed within a competitive and changing world of communication and leisure. The late Victorian and Edwardian period saw an explosion of commercial consumer culture. There were seemingly never-ending new opportunities for distraction and entertainment, from an evening out in a music hall or a bank holiday at the seaside to shopping at one of the new department stores, from reading one of the many new penny magazines to watching visual tricks on the screen. In addition to competing with each other, then, Free Trade and Tariff Reform also had to respond to this visually rich commercial and technological incursion into public space and time. Today it is often this expanding commercial sphere that is blamed for a decline in voting and political participation. But historically it offered fresh opportunities for political engagement, as well as challenges and distractions.

What had begun as an argument over the cost of a small tariff in 1903 had grown by 1910 into a vast political circus. With regiments of supporters, Free Trade and Tariff Reform organized tens of thousands of meetings, plastered millions of posters on town walls, and held picture shows and exhibitions, up and down the country. Far from declining, turnout shot up to extraordinary heights—87 per cent in the January 1910 election, unrivalled since. Political economy was revitalized by a new kind of politics of emotion, a politics that fused entertainment and education and entered into dialogue with commercial culture. Free Trade changed itself—and transformed political life in the process.

White Loaves, Black Bread, and Horseflesh

The single most popular icon in the Edwardian campaign was the Free Trade 'cheap loaf'. Everywhere cartoons, posters, and postcards offered visual contrasts between the large Free Trade loaf and the smaller 'protectionist loaf', between a British regime of cheap free imports and a foreign world of trade barriers, expensive food, and hunger. Supporters paraded the two loaves in the streets, some even dressed up as the cheap loaf in processions. The loaf was displayed on sticks, in shop windows, and worn as a badge. Liberal speakers threw loaves into their audiences.[13] It offered a tangible yet flexible way to communicate political economy to the people. The loaf revolutionized the sensibilities of consumers and provided a new barometer for the standard of living. It was the first time that actual goods were used to illustrate the effects of government policies on people's household budget, a role that has become familiar over the past few decades through politicians' use of the shopping basket, especially in debates over the European Community in the 1970s. But the loaf was much more than a register of prices. It expressed broad ideas about culture, society, and national identity. As the campaign developed, so did the symbolic use of the cheap loaf. Information about prices and the standard of living became linked to increasingly nationalist representations of the superiority of British civilization.

Most Britons had begun to prefer white bread already in the late eighteenth century, although oatmeal remained popular in Scotland and northern parts of England, and some regions retained distinct types of bread into the early twentieth century, including 'lava bread' made of seaweed in some Welsh towns. Whatever later generations of nutritionists would say, most Victorian people and social reformers were convinced that the shift from the coarser grains of the brown loaf to the white loaf followed naturally on the shift from hard outdoor labour to more sedentary work in towns and factories. Nineteenth-century experiments found that switching workers back to a coarser loaf increased their problems with digestion and led to a decline in morale and performance.[14] By the turn of the twentieth century, bread had been displaced by meat as the single largest item in the food budget of the working classes (25–32 per cent) but bread and flour still accounted for 20–25 per cent.

As a political symbol, the loaf was already deployed in the battle leading up to the repeal of the Corn Laws in 1846. Alongside the central image of the wheat sheaf that proclaimed 'Our Bread untaxed, our commerce free' on drawings and pottery, the Anti-Corn Law League adopted the loaf as a symbol in 1841. *The Anti-Bread Tax Circular* showed three loaves in different sizes to make a point about how Britons were less well fed than Poles and Frenchmen. On a few occasions, the League even used the loaves as stage props at meetings, suspending a large Polish, medium French, and small British loaf from the ceiling. Large French and small English loaves also made an appearance at Chartist meetings.[15] In Bristol, in the 1852 election, Liberals used the loaf to caricature and stigmatize Conservatives who had supported Free Trade in corn but whose interests in the West Indies now made them stop short at sugar. A large, smiling, and well-dressed loaf-man fronts the successful Liberal candidates on the hustings next to the grumpy, small loaf of the Conservative candidate.[16]

The Edwardian campaign made the cheap loaf its central symbol. It was a simple and entertaining shorthand that both appealed to common wisdom about the price of food and crystallized a single, clear picture out of the ever-expanding and much more complex data and arguments about the economy. Yet ironically, it was protectionists who first drew wide attention to this icon. In one of the defining moments of the campaign, on 4 November 1903, Chamberlain dramatically produced for his Birmingham audience one Free Trade loaf and one protectionist loaf, barely

Figure 5. 'A Sporting Question': Joseph Chamberlain displays two virtually identical loaves on this political postcard, re-enacting his stunt in Birmingham, 1903.

distinguishable in size. Conservative postcards quickly reproduced images of the 'actual loaves' shown by Chamberlain (see Figure 5). Chamberlain's point was simple: the 2s. duty he proposed was so small that it made effectively no difference. In response, the liberal *Daily News* promptly baked its own two loaves based on the statistics of the government's recent blue book and displayed a big Free Trade loaf next to a smaller protectionist one in its London offices. What, then, was the correct size of these competing loaves? Which factors should be taken into consideration for comparison—prices, or also different wages and living conditions more generally? And whose figures could be trusted?

Liberal cartoonists seized the opportunity to contrast the common sense of British workers who knew their loaf with the abstract promises of Tariff Reformers. 'Spectacular Deception' was one of F. C. Gould's many influential cartoons for the *Westminster Gazette*, and widely used in posters, lantern lectures, leaflets, and postcards. Chamberlain here appeared as a con-artist on a soap-box, with a tiny loaf in the palm of his hand trying to persuade two passing workers to look at the loaf through his 'patent Imperial Protection double magnifying spectacles'. The workers reject this trick and remind Chamberlain that 'we want to Eat the loaf, not to look at it'.[17] Chamberlain's stunt was a public relations disaster. It reinforced popular suspicions of his untrustworthiness. And instead of demolishing the Free Trade icon, it encouraged a much broader use of the loaf to represent the condition of entire societies.

The late nineteenth century ushered in a revolution in statistical knowledge and social surveys. Governments knew ever more about the economy in ever greater detail. The Board of Trade had started an index of a number of retail prices in 1896. The government blue book of 1903 compared conditions in Free Trade Britain with those in protectionist countries. This new wealth of information provided Liberal and Conservative rivals with endless material for debate and refutation, but it was also far too voluminous and detailed for popular politics. The big loaf and the little loaf were attractive symbols for embodying complex economic relations. In the 1906 election, Liberals used handbills showing a photograph of candidates next to the two loaves, with information from the blue book about wages, hours of work, and prices in Germany and Britain. The loaves' respective size did not try to capture the price of flour but to reflect working conditions more generally: 'Half an hours skilled labour in England purchases 3 times as much Bread as half an hours skilled labour in Germany.' (Colour Plate VIII.) An argument about price had expanded into one about purchasing power and social conditions.

Whatever the statistical merit of the comparison—Tariff Reformers complained that the blue book figures unfairly ignored higher wages for unskilled labour in Germany and that Liberal pictures presumed that the entire wage was spent on bread—it was this visual image of the Free Trade loaf three times the size of the protected loaf that won out. Often numbers disappeared altogether, and the loaves were left to speak for themselves, as in the posters sponsored by the *Daily News*: 'We Plead for the Women & Children' (Colour Plate IX).[18] In Bradford in 1906, a man dressed up as the big loaf led a children's procession in support of the local Liberal candidate.[19] Dudley Ward's 'The Storm Cloud. Wake Up! Your Children's Bread is in Danger' draws on fairy tales and shows the loaf 'Prosperity' running away from a tornado with the face of Chamberlain seeking to carve it with the knife 'Taxation'. The household loaf's irregular shape lent itself well to broad cultural claims based only loosely on actual numbers and prices; the image of a sliced loaf, which could represent economic differences more precisely, was exceedingly rare.[20]

Tariff Reformers tried to argue away the cheap loaf and shift concerns to wages and employment, but in the process they only reinforced the centrality of the liberal icon. 'Yes, lass, the bread may have gone up a farthin', a British workman explains to his plump wife in a Conservative picture, but it was nothing to worry about since his wages had increased, and other taxes had been lowered. At the same time, his wife was serving a loaf.[21] Other Conservative postcards illustrated the British lion's 'Obvious Preference' for a 'preference loaf made of colonial and home grown wheat' over a Free Trade loaf. Tariff Reform efforts merely helped to keep the loaf in the public eye. [22]

In the new medium of film, Lewin Fitzhamon, a pioneer of the moving image, was a director with strong protectionist convictions—his horse, which acted in many of his films, was called 'Tariff'. Famous for the hugely popular animal drama *Rescued by Rover* (1905) and social comedies like *What*

Figure 6. John Bull triumphs over the Free Trade witch, on his left, with the Fair Trade fairy and a saved working-class couple, on his right, with Britannia presiding. Note the two loaves on display on the table. A still from 'The International Exchange', 1905, one of the earliest political propaganda films, directed by Lewin Fitzhamon and produced by Hepworth.

the Curate Really Did (1905), 'Fitz' also teamed up with Cecil Hepworth to make *International Exchange* in 1905, one of two pioneering political films championing protection. In the short film John Bull is freed from the spell of the ugly Free Trade witch by the charm of a fairy maiden 'Fair Trade'. Yet, again, the loaf is a central and ambiguous image on the screen: John Bull leaves a Free Trade witch holding a large loaf for a fairy with a smaller loaf (see Figure 6).[23]

There was a remarkable failure by Tariff Reformers to develop their own images of political economy. The figure of the 'dumper', recognizable by his German cap and pipe, or of 'Herr Schmit', the German shopkeeper who had infiltrated the open British market as an agent of foreign producers, were the closest protectionists came to developing a rival image. Yet even these never entirely managed to escape the magnetic pull of the loaf. The pictures by Huskinson, the gifted chief cartoonist of the Tariff Reform League,

FOUND!

THE RÖNTGEN RAYS AND THE LARGE LOAF.

Figure 7. With the help of modern scientific technology, Tariff Reformers expose the German dumper hiding in the Free Trade loaf. A protectionist cartoon, 1904.

show the dilemma. X-rays expose the scheming German 'dumper' hiding in a large loaf (see Figure 7, above). Elsewhere, the loaf is used to block John Bull's binoculars as he tries to scan the seas for British traders in difficulties.[24]

Many of these representations developed a life of their own. Cartoonists and politicians closely followed each other's images, emulating and undercutting each other. So it was perhaps no accident that the contrast of the big loaf and the little loaf eventually found its way back into the Tariff Reform campaign. Harry Furniss, the fat and restless illustrator who had caricatured politicians for *Punch* since the 1880s and whose humorous

Figure 8. The sun is rising over a plentiful future under Joseph Chamberlain, next to the bleak present under Free Trade.

weekly *Lika Joka* had sold 140,000 copies on its first day of publication in 1894, turned his brush to political cartoons for the Conservative weekly, *The People*. Furniss shows Chamberlain still holding out two similarly sized loafs, but now he is standing proudly on a heap of gigantic loaves, brightly illuminated by the rising sun. 'If "Joe" succeeds Bread will be Plentiful.' Next to Chamberlain, against the backdrop of a gloomy, grey industrial horizon, a lonely, miniscule loaf sits on a placard which explains: 'This is all the bread working men can afford to buy while foreigners rob us of our trade and English works are closed.'[25] (see Figure 8.)

The cheap loaf was a powerful symbol of prosperity under Free Trade—as long as prices were low and steady. Once prices starting rising in 1908–10 it ran into difficulties. 'Where is that Radical Cheap Loaf?', Conservative posters asked, showing Asquith, the Liberal Prime Minister, serving the regular $4\frac{1}{2}$ lb loaf at an increased price of 6d.[26] Price became a deeply ideological issue.[27] In response, the Free Trade campaign shifted its focus from quantity to quality, played out in increasingly stark contrasts between civilized life in Free Trade Britain and barbaric conditions in Germany. The large white Free Trade loaf and the smaller protectionist white loaf were now joined by coarse black bread, typical, it was said, of the subhuman diet that tariffs forced upon Germans, driven to eat even horses and dogs.

From the beginning of the campaign in 1903 some Liberals had produced black bread to entertain audiences and remind them of Britain's higher civilization embodied in the white Free Trade loaf. Loulou Harcourt proudly told his father, Gladstone's last Chancellor, how he had held up in the course of a speech 'two loaves of German black rye bread to show what protection had done for the German peasant—and there was nearly a riot afterwards to get hold of pieces of the loaves!'.[28] Lloyd George, who knew how to whip up a crowd, told audiences that Chamberlain was a 'new Joshua' who asked them to proceed 'to a land, not flowing with milk and honey, but rolling with black bread and German sausages'.[29] Radicals and Liberal Unionists voiced fears that a tariff would drive British workers to a diet of horseflesh, as in protectionist Germany.

Horses figured prominently in Horatio Bottomley's election campaign in South Hackney, in the heart of London's East End, in 1906. Bottomley was a self-styled 'born champion of the people', Holyoake's nephew and president of the Workman's Anti-Sugar Tax Association. He was also a well-known sportsman and knew about horses. His horse Wargrave won the Cesarewitch, the famous flat handicap race for thoroughbreds at Newmarket, named in honour of the future Tsar Alexander II. Bottomley's propaganda made much of the testimony of a dealer in worn-out horses at a recent county court hearing in Newcastle. In the last ten months he had exported 1,500 horses to be sold as butcher's meat abroad.[30]

By 1910 horrifying examples of life under protection were everywhere. Britons were deluged with figures of German horse consumption; the daily slaughter of sixty horses in Breslau alone fed 24,000 people, leaflets by the Free Trade Union reported. There were photographic reproductions taken directly from German newspapers, like the Chemnitz *Volksstimme*, in which a butcher advertised his horseflesh for its nutritious qualities. Horseflesh steaks and sausages were exhibited alongside black bread in shops and market displays in many towns, from York and Hull to Brighton. Following Lloyd George's witty challenge to those members of the House of Lords who opposed the Liberal budget to go and try the horseflesh sausage that came with tariffs, Liberal Club windows displayed pictures of a couple of German sausages next to two peers.

Britons were treated to sensationalist accounts of what happened to horses in Germany. When a drayman's horse fell and died, German crowds dragged it to a meadow, skinned it, and within minutes 'cut away all the flesh from the bones' before the police could intervene. In the 1910 elections, Free Traders paraded with placards of sausages and old mares. As late as 1912, in a by-election in Bolton, Liberals paraded through the streets a broken-down pony labelled 'Horseflesh for Germany'.[31] Worse, protection drove hungry Germans to eat even man's best friend. Seven thousand dogs a year were killed for human consumption according to official German statistics eagerly circulated by Free Traders. In suburban Enfield, just outside London, a Liberal had the ingenious idea of giving his dog a run with a card round its neck pleading 'Vote for Branch, and don't eat Doggy'.[32]

With their dietary propaganda Free Traders fanned the flames of Anglo-German rivalry—Tariff Reformers responded by publicizing the outrage expressed by conservative German papers at the jingoistic tone of radical propaganda with its ' "fairy-tales about German workers subsisting on sour black bread, horse sausage, and dog's flesh" '.[33] But it was also part of a new and dynamic stage in the production of knowledge about foreign societies, and its manipulation for a popular audience at home. The average British worker had little awareness of the colonies, let alone of protectionist countries like Germany. In addition to tapping into a tradition of national caricatures like Uncle Sam and John Bull, revived by economic nationalism on both sides of the Atlantic, the battle over Free Trade unleashed an unprecedented flow of information (and prejudice) about an unknown world of life and labour. It accelerated and popularized the international distribution of news, in print and increasingly also through photos. Previously *terra incognita*, distant places like Düsseldorf, Breslau, and Bocholt entered the everyday life of British politics.

It was Tariff Reformers who first set this wave of foreign reporting in motion with a new kind of educational tourism. In the autumn of 1908 the Yorkshire newspaper editor Rayner Roberts together with the Conservative candidate for Dewsbury, W. B. Boyd Carpenter, organized a trip to Germany for a small group of working men from the local heavy woollen industry. By the summer of 1910, Conservatives had financed some five hundred of these 'Tariff Trippers'. They returned with vivid reports of the favourable conditions of life in Germany: German workers had respectable homes, social insurance, and labour exchanges. Germany was living proof of the Tariff Reform vision of high wages and social welfare buttressed by protection. Progressive Liberals had their own social reform schemes, but at a time of high unemployment it was far from clear whether they could compete with the Conservative picture of well-paid Germans who worked securely behind the shelter of a tariff. For the first time since the battle began, Tariff Reformers had an effective challenge to the cheap loaf.

Free Traders were under pressure to present an alternative dystopian vision of life under protection. Once again, they made food their central theme. Excerpts from the foreign press, especially social democratic papers in Germany and Austria-Hungary, became a staple of local and national politics in Britain. Liberal candidates read to audiences from German newspapers about clerks' protests at high prices. The *Free Trader* reproduced photographs of protests against meat prices in Vienna. Reports critical of the tariff system by the British consul-general in Germany, Francis Oppenheimer, were disseminated through leaflets, pamphlets, and local newspapers.[34] Some who had deserted from the Tariff Trippers, like Edward Baker of Limehouse, spoke of the bribery and duplicity involved in the protectionist tours. It was impossible to find a single loaf of white bread anywhere, Baker told readers; German sausages 'struck me as having been designed for cow diet'.[35] Free Traders' own investigations reached their climax when Ramsay MacDonald, the Labour leader and future

Prime Minister, travelled to Düsseldorf, Nuremberg, and Bocholt in 1910. His report on the 'true conditions' of German workers in an influential series of newspaper articles sold at one penny. MacDonald acknowledged that Germany had been getting richer. But this was in spite not because of tariffs; it was the result of education, organization, and social reform, especially an effective system of unemployment relief. Germany emerged as a text-book illustration of the horrors of protection. Horsemeat could be found in any butcher's shop. He bought bread only to find it 'rough, heavy, unpalatable'. He tried to buy tea and was unable to find any. The 'stories about horseflesh, dogflesh, and black bread are perfectly true', MacDonald reported.[36]

Tariff Reformers pointed out in vain that it was nonsense to collapse diet, living conditions, and culture into one inevitable result of protectionism. Not only did Germany have a low tariff by international standards. A darker bread was popular with most people in Germany, and 'eaten by the same class of people which here in London dined at the Ritz and the Savoy'.[37] It did not reflect either poverty or tariffs. Holland, the country on the continent closest to free trade, also had a preference for rye bread. Debunking the supersize Free Trade loaf versus the small German loaf, Tariff Reformers pointed to Board of Trade statistics which showed that the price of the typical household loaf in Berlin in 1908 was identical to that in London, and even less than in Edinburgh and Dublin. Conservative papers printed letters by Britons who had spent some time in Germany and praised the taste and nutritious qualities of rye bread. Was there better proof than the absence in Germany of the British craze for patent pills? Even *The Lancet*, the authoritative voice of medical science, was dragged into the debate to prove that black bread was not famine food, nor nutritionally inferior to the white loaf. Queen Alexandra herself was a keen consumer of black bread, Conservatives stressed, reproducing the royal warrant held by a local baker.[38]

Not surprisingly, the reality behind the stories of horseflesh and dogmeat was more complex than in Free Trade accounts. German protests against meat prices had at least as much to do with rising expectations as with the direct effects of a tariff. German meat prices, in fact, fell in 1906 and stayed constant until the autumn of 1910, until well after the British horseflesh drama had unfolded. The German standard of living had improved sharply in the late nineteenth century. This created a pronounced sense of relative deprivation once the general price of food began to rise after 1900, in Germany as elsewhere. The typical German worker now expected a piece of meat for lunch. In fact, German workers ate as much meat as civil servants. And as workers began to eat more expensive, higher quality meats, so their sensitivity to prices increased. In Chemnitz, several restaurants served raw dog. But consumption of horseflesh and dogmeat reflected not poverty but distinct regional cultures, as the Board of Trade acknowledged in its inquiry into industrial conditions in Germany in 1908. Almost all of the 6,000–7,000 dogs killed in Germany per year met their end in slaughterhouses in Saxony and Silesia, an area with a high number of Polish immigrants who saw in dog flesh an antidote to tuberculosis.[39] In rich areas like the Rhineland more than twenty times as many horses were slaughtered as in poorer areas like Posen. *Chevaline* was, and remains, a perfectly acceptable food in France and Italy, and could be had in the 1980s in the Harvard Faculty Club, not especially known as a canteen of the poor.

Whatever its accuracy, however, there can be little doubt about the success of the Free Trade campaign. Conservatives wrote in despair to their party central office for guidance as stories appeared in their local papers about tariffs driving Germans to eat dogs; the most 'effective' point which the information department was able to suggest to speakers was to remind meetings that 'the German does not live on dog meat nor on horseflesh'.[40] Free Trade tapped into broader national stereotypes and cultural sensitivities. Victorian campaigns against vivisection and cruelty towards animals had left behind a new humane sentiment.[41] The dog was a social animal, capable of trust and loyalty. In mid-Victorian Britain, The Society for the Propagation of Horse Flesh sought to advertise the nutritious benefits of horsemeat, but its campaign only reinforced a sense that this was really a pagan, foreign custom. A civilized nation did not consume horse or dog. In truth, butchers continued to sell horseflesh in the poorer districts of the East End and in Camden, where many Belgians settled. In 1910 medical officers even believed that some cat meat 'may in fact be used for human consumption'.[42] But at the popular level, accounts of dietary customs abroad corroborated a view that protection meant barbarism. When the general secretary of the Union of Blastfurnacemen, P. Walls, was asked in a Board of Trade inquiry during the First World War whether the living conditions of German workers would not be an inducement for British workers to support a tariff, the answer was simple: 'I think the standard of living for the workers in Germany requires no discussion: we do not use any horseflesh here.'[43]

Free Trade now seemed at the root of a very British form of civilization. The difference between Free Trade and tariffs was not one of degree. Protection did not simply lead to slightly higher prices, shifting supply and demand curves, as economists might see it. Rather, as Free Traders returning from Germany amplified again and again in 1909–10, tariffs had produced a fundamentally different culture. It was impossible to find tea or jam. 'The German working classes do not know the pleasure of sitting down to a roast joint, large or small of beef, mutton, or pork ... not one in fifty has the knowledge which the English average working-class housewife has of cooking.'[44]

This wholesale attack on German 'barbarity' was shared even by those advanced Liberals who looked to Germany for inspiration in the realm of social insurance. No one was more active in condemning German culture at the time than Lloyd George, who has been mainly remembered as a modernizer inspired by Bismarck's welfare system.[45] Up and down the country, Lloyd George rallied supporters with stories of German horseflesh. 'Three months of blackbread diet and the most juicy horseflesh rump steaks' would make the peers pass the Liberal budget before three days were out, he assured voters in the January 1910 election.[46] He 'was not afraid of the Germany navy; he was not afraid of German trade competition; but he had a real dread of the German sausage. (Cheers and laughter) ... Tariff Reform had brought people to poverty in Germany and to food which we here would not give tramps.'[47] 'If this country wanted German tariffs', he told a meeting at York, 'it must have German wages ... German militarism, and German sausages.'[48] Free Trade had become a cultural question. Stark comparisons with Germany now required Liberals to backtrack from earlier warnings of the millions of starving Britons to whom a tariff was a matter of life and death: Britons were much better off.[49] Positive observations, such as Germans' much-noted cleanliness, were explained away as a mere reflection of the authoritarian atmosphere bred by tariffs. Germans only appeared to be cleaner. In reality, tidiness was the sign of a police state. Fear of authority meant poverty was hidden from public sight. In Britain, by contrast, the air of liberty meant the poor were not ashamed to go out in rags.[50]

Crusading Armies

When Chamberlain christened his campaign for tariff reform a 'crusade', he captured the zeal and manpower that would be unleashed on the political landscape. In the first half of the nineteenth century, the campaigns against slavery and for the repeal of the Corn Laws had introduced a new kind of pressure group politics. Edwardian politics gave birth to their own variety of lobbies and pressure groups, from the Navy League to Single Taxers. But the battle over Free Trade inspired mobilization on an altogether different scale. In the Ludlow by-election in December 1903, Tariff Reform dispatched an unprecedented 18 agents to this small agricultural constituency in Shropshire, and won.[51] Liberals were stunned. Over the next few years, the Tariff Reform League and Free Trade Union swelled into veritable mass armies. Between January 1909 and the January 1910 election, the Tariff Reform League held 7,763 meetings, distributed 53 million leaflets and pamphlets and organized 161 Dump Shops, motor omnibuses, and caravans; 900,000 copies of the cartoon *Fiscal Facts* were sent out and 166,000 posters were issued in the election alone.[52] Its main rival, the Free Trade Union, expanded from a small committee in 1903 into a vast organization of permanent campaigning. By 1908 it sponsored 2,943 meetings, by 1909 over 5,000. In 1910, a year with two general elections, it held no fewer than 12,471 meetings.

The activities of local branches give a sense of the size of the operation. The Free Trade Union branch in Middlesex and North and West London had a central office at Caledonian Road with branch offices in Hornsey, Teddington, Ealing, North Kensington, Wembley, and Fulham. Henry Nettleship here headed a staff of 29 speakers, 3 messengers, 1 typist, 2 errand boys and another 32 voluntary workers. They organized no fewer than 190 meetings in the January 1910 election.[53] In that election, the volume of printed material sent out across the country had increased by more than half over 1906, including 660,000 Free Trade coloured pictures and posters and one million *Liberal Song Sheets*.[54]

The agitation is impressive for the sheer numbers of people involved, but equally for the new forms of political marketing it pioneered. 'Chamberlain shows us how to do it', concluded Herbert Gladstone, the organizational mastermind and whip of the Liberal party, after the early by-election battles in the winter of 1903–4. The Tariff Reform League was an active organizing force, enlisting 'heaps of men who are not paid'.[55] The Free Trade defence, by contrast, started out as a loose alliance of campaigning bodies without a general headquarters. Free Trade initiatives ranged from the Whiggish and exclusive Unionist Free Trade Club to Sheridan Jones' People's League Against Protection, which rallied Trade Union leaders and Labourites, from the donnish Oxford Free Trade League to Miss Birch's private, non-party Free Trade organization which sought to bring together Free Trade speakers across the political spectrum, from the Conservative Arthur Elliot to advanced Liberals like L.T. Hobhouse and Bertrand Russell.[56] Much energy was wasted in attempting to recruit Conservative and Liberal Unionist allies, even though to most of them the prospect of appearing with Radicals on the same platform was as distasteful as Tariff Reform itself. They were 'fine weather free traders', Elliot despaired. The Cobden Club was likewise considered unsuited for a 'strong agitation'. It was too small, with an ageing membership, and widely viewed as a partisan body.[57] It was the Liberal-dominated Free Trade Union and its auxiliary regiments that became the main fighting force of the campaign.

The Free Trade Union underwent a remarkable evolution from its birth in the summer of 1903 to its full fighting strength in 1910. Its birth was not uncomplicated. It displayed the classic symptoms of a pressure group, with competing egos of overzealous organizers and diverging strategic priorities. Chiozza Money, the Liberals' statistical brain, felt snubbed at having to work in a subordinate position to L. T. Hobhouse, the sociologist, and first secretary of the Union. Some Liberals like Herbert Gladstone and Hobhouse wanted to build a popular organization of activists with Free Trade bodies all over the country. The majority of the organizing committee, by contrast, wanted to focus on instant propaganda to respond to the protectionist avalanche and prepare for a general election that they feared would be called at any moment.[58] Initially, the Free Trade Union did not recruit grassroot members but acted mainly as a leafleting and information bureau. By Christmas 1903, 15 million leaflets had already been distributed. Loulou Harcourt single-handedly raised money to hire 37 lecturers on his own initiative, but overall the Union operated on a shoestring. In the autumn of 1903 it had one overburdened researcher who prepared information on particular industries, like potteries.[59] A year later its funds were near exhaustion.

The 1906 election landslide victory turned out to be a mixed blessing for the Free Trade Union. On the one hand, it demonstrated its ability to strengthen the sinews of war: money. Publicly, Free Traders tried hard to position themselves as a movement supported by small people and toilers, in contrast to Tariff Reform millionaires. Notwithstanding many small contributions, however, most of the work of the Union was made possible thanks to large donations from rich Liberals and businessmen, such as J. B. Robinson's £2,000 or the £1,000 donation by the oil and engineering tycoon Weetman Pearson in the summer of 1903, only the first in a series of generous gifts.[60] In addition to millions of leaflets targetting voters, the Union was also a vital source of information for candidates and speakers. It supplied them with much-needed ammunition in the form of updated, trade-specific figures, and concise primers, such as the *ABC Fiscal Handbook*, penny books like *Look at Germany*, and *101 Points against Tariff Reform*. On the other hand, such was the historic size of the Liberal triumph that an air of easy complacency began to spread. When the Tariff Reform League resumed its crusade in 1907, colonizing the Unionist party, Free Traders were caught napping. Tariff Reform tactics became more aggressive and ruthless. Working from Unionist committee rooms, protectionists 'import[ed] large numbers of alleged "unemployed" who had lost their occupation owing to Free Trade', and freely adjusted their proposals to the particular make-up of different constituencies.[61]

It was now that the Free Trade campaign began to undergo its metamorphosis. By the time of the 1910 elections the Free Trade Union and its auxiliary bodies had grown into a nationwide network of 400 branches, supported by an army of 'missionary volunteers'. Already in 1909, a non-election year, the Union held over 5,000 public meetings, almost double that in 1908.[62] While leafleting continued at an ever greater rate (over 16 million leaflets and pamphlets in 1909), the style of politics now shifted towards new forms of engagement in mass meetings and spectacles: education via entertainment. Not much has been known about this new political world, simply because the later unravelling of Free Trade culture led to the decline and disappearance of these organizations, and with them their records. Fortunately, records have survived, hidden away in Churchill's papers, from one main auxiliary of the Free Trade Union: the National Free Trade Lectures and Exhibitions. This important set of sources makes it possible to not only reconstruct the size of the campaign but, even more importantly, to watch how Free Trade became embedded in a new style of mass politics.[63]

The world was fundamentally different after 1906, the Free Trade organizer G. Wallace Carter explained two years later. Before 1906 the Tariff Reform League on average sent between six and twelve workers into constituencies during a by-election, now they sent one hundred.[64] This huge jump in the scale of the opposition aggravated Free Trade's growing problems in maintaining public support. Here, again, Free Trade was in part a victim of its own success. The huge expansion of statistical information and economic literature generated in the battle over tariffs created dilemmas of its own. In the domain of popular politics, statistics proved to be like the many-headed hydra of Greek mythology. The moment one head was cut off, another appeared. While statistics gave Free Traders factual ammunition to challenge Tariff Reform prophecies of doom, they also offered Tariff Reformers endless fresh opportunities to draw people's attention to yet another dying local industry. For Free Traders, this partly raised questions of resources, but it also became more than that. Simply put, they faced a communication problem of the highest order. There was a mismatch between Free Trade, the economic idea, and the dynamic nature of democratic politics. The world of economic knowledge was becoming ever more complex and specialized at the very time that politics had come to rely more than ever before on mass support, rather than experts or authorities. And, to add to the pressure, Free Traders faced a marketing problem, having to rally support, again and again, over the course of a decade, for what was effectively the same basic article.

To meet these challenges the Free Trade campaign developed two somewhat contradictory strategies. The first one expanded the efforts to provide speakers and voters with short statistical information on particular industries. By the time of the general election in January 1910, the Free Trade Union operated an Information Bureau together with sixty local offices with no less than fifty permanent agents who trained local speakers and workers. The country was divided into districts according to their industries. As R. B. Dack, the Free Trade Union agent for Stirling, explained, the campaign work 'will be more telling and effective if the speaker grasps the conditions of local industries'. General speakers were easily embarrassed by protectionist opponents and hecklers who cited specific trades harmed by 'dumping'. The division into districts boosted speakers' local knowledge, enabling them 'to dispose of such [protectionist] "fairy tales" as that the Cambusbarron Mills have been ruined by Free Trade'.[65] Yet such specialization by region and industry also carried a potential problem. After all, Free Traders' identity and reputation rested on speaking on behalf of the public interest, not the more particular interests favoured by Tariff Reformers. Hence the appeal of unifying national stories and symbols in the campaign.

The work of the National Free Trade Lectures and Exhibitions organization, NFTLE for short, shows how much the particular, industry-oriented aspect of the campaign was subordinated to more general types of communication. The NFTLE was financed by J. K. Caird, a leading Dundee jute industrialist, then seventy years of age, without wife or children. To Caird, who employed almost 2,000 men and attributed his own success to Free Trade, the fact that the 'well to do Classes' had to a 'great extent [become] heterodox' on this great principle was deeply disconcerting.[66] He gave £13,500 to the cause, a huge donation, though not unusually large by the standards of this benefactor; in 1914 he sent the explorer Edward Shackleton a cheque worth £24,000 in support of his Antarctic expedition, and Shackleton duly named his 23-foot whaler after Caird. But by the standards of political campaigning, this made all the difference. The Free Trade Union had a fighting fund of only £12,000 at the time, having spent £27,168 in the first half of 1910, while the Tariff Reform League managed to raise £30,000 in the course of the year.[67] The Free Trade campaign is often thought of as the poorer cousin, but this picture changes considerably, indeed is even reversed, once the funding and level of activity of associated bodies like the NFTLE are taken into account. The body was run by G. Wallace Carter, the secretary of the Free Trade Union, and the former private secretary to the chief whip. Carter reported directly to Winston Churchill, who had taken refuge in Dundee as Liberal MP after his famous by-election defeat in Manchester in 1908, and who took a lively interest in putting Caird's money to effective use.

Between May and early December 1910, that is, not counting the election campaign of December 1910, the NFTLE organized an extraordinary 5,460 meetings (Colour Plate X). Of these, only 87 were targeted specifically at business groups, 37 at trade unions and cooperatives, and 6 at farmers' clubs and agricultural societies; 863 of the public lectures were aimed at rural audiences, 106 at women. The largest group, 4,361 meetings and lectures, was for general audiences. Over 370 general lecturers were at work. To put this in perspective, the prominent Congo-reform campaign managed only 300 lectures and 43 town meetings in 1906–7. At its peak in 1840, the Anti-Corn Law League had employed 15 speakers, giving 800 lectures. The NFTLE managed to double the campaign volume of the Free Trade Union, which itself was responsible for a not insignificant 2,558 meetings during the December election, outdoing the Tariff Reform League (2,127).[68] In other words, the NFTLE altogether erased the comparative advantage the

Tariff Reform League had previously enjoyed. As these numbers show, most of that fresh activity went into the pursuit of public audiences, not specialized groups, and most occurred during the regular year, not the election fight.

The sheer size of the campaign transformed the challenge of recruiting and training a new generation of volunteers. Bodies like the Cobden Club had offered prize essay competitions in the past but these attracted mainly aspiring young intellectuals, such as F. W. Hirst, who became editor of *The Economist*, or the economist A. C. Pigou. They were hardly designed to produce the army of informed speakers and organizers required by a mass movement. One purpose of the massive campaign in the summer and autumn of 1910 was to recruit 'progressive helpers' and 'new and permanent auxiliaries of Free Trade work', Wallace Carter stressed. Audiences were not just listeners, they were potential members. The Liberal party dispatched 'live' agents to meetings to 'spot the right man' for recruitment.[69] Seaside gatherings offered a particularly good opportunity to draw interested members of the audience into 'yeoman service', helping distribute literature and posters or, even better, returning to their home town to found a new branch of the Free Trade Union. By 1910 a network of several hundred local branches had emerged. Where most of the activity of the early Victorian Anti-Corn Law League had centred on the manufacturing towns of Lancashire, Cheshire, and Yorkshire, the Edwardian movement was a genuinely British one, with branches in small towns like Totton in the New Forest or the Fenland village of Wimblington, alongside those in Bournemouth and Swansea.[70]

The mass campaign created fresh opportunities for women activists especially. In London, the Free Trade Union's chief organizer was the effective and attractive Miss Ivy Pretious, who was pursued by more than one Liberal minister. 'A perfect woman, nobly planned... with something of an angel's light', was how the staff of the Union, reciting Wordsworth, congratulated her on her wedding.[71] The schedule of women speakers and organizers like Miss McLaren Ramsay gives an indication of the intense level of activity. After taking part in the by-election in the New Forest in early December 1905, she went to North Dorset to set up three new branches for the Women's Liberal Association (WLA) in ten days. She then went to work in Rutland until 30 December, then off to Lincoln, where she took charge of a committee room leading up to the poll on

15 January 1906, back to Mid Hertfordshire for the poll on 17 January, then by night train to Carlisle to work until the end of the month in Cumberland and North Westmorland.[72] By 1910 the WLA had amassed over 120,000 members. In the Home Counties, Miss Isabel Edwards organized 104 associations for 1,850 'Crusaders', visiting an estimated 52,000 homes each month.[73] In the first half of 1910 The Women's Free Trade Union campaigned in 52 constituencies and six by-elections, holding another 86 special meetings and distributing half a million leaflets.[74] Speakers included educated middle-class ladies like Dorothy Hunter but also women like Jessie Richardson, 'a Cockney of the most delightful type' who 'is quite at home with the roughest audience' and 'has a most happy knack in her addresses of intertwining humour with pathos' one organizer remembered (see Figure 9).[75] Enthusiasm even spilled over to the children who were often recruited to sing. In North Staffordshire, children 'took possession of a shed and made it their own committee room, where they learnt Liberal songs and organised processions'.[76]

The engine of political education went into top gear. If there was considerable distrust of women's analytical and statistical intelligence at the

Figure 9. A woman speaking on Free Trade during the Reading by-election, 1913.

outset—the Free Trade MP Thomas Lough started a typical speech to a women's audience in 1903 warning that the subject was a difficult one 'since figures were trying subjects for women'[77]—the campaign quickly enabled women to prove themselves as students, teachers, and speakers. There were prize essay competitions for women; in 1910 Miss Muriel Parker, the honorary secretary of the Mildenhall WLA, collected the first prize worth £2 2s. for an essay showing how a tariff diminished imports. She cited a wide range of sources, from established British texts like Brassey's *Fifty Years of Progress* to evidence given by Mr Rotch of the US Commission on Merchant Shipping 1904 on the deplorable state of the American mercantile marine.[78]

By 1910 the mass campaign developed an infrastructure of teacher-training. Local Liberal associations set up study circles. In Birmingham, Charles Fellows of the Free Trade Union taught a weekly class for 'young people (of both sexes)' on the 'Principles ... Fruits ... Ethics and The Opposition to Free Trade'.[79] For self-improving 'young men', there were the classes sponsored by the Lancashire and Cheshire branch of the FTU, designed along the lines of the economic lectures of the university extension programme. From 60 to 200 pupils, 'all earnest young men of the right type' would listen to lecturers like F. Bower Alcock (MA, Pembroke College, Oxford), a senior extension lecturer at Ruskin College, the Oxford college for the working classes. Students wrote weekly essays and submitted their final papers to the Manchester committee for examination.[80] By September 1910, the Free Trade Union was promoting private classes 'in all sorts of houses, from cottages to mansions' supported by trained lecturers with a simple promise: 'Make yourselves masters of the question.' W. Wilkins (MA) provided 'Our Study Circle Page', which outlined study plans on general subjects like Land, Labour, and Capital, and recommended readings, ranging from the more academic, like Fawcett's and Cannan's introductions to political economy, to the more journalistic, like Bastiat's 'Things Seen and Things Not Seen'.[81]

'Fifty students are more valuable to the cause of Free Trade than five hundred men in an average audience', Wallace Carter argued. Study circles for men and women would prepare a new generation of speakers with the knowledge and skill to withstand hecklers and inspire audiences. They would support candidates often out of their depth on the particularities of the Free Trade question. 'We have had Tariff Reform meetings "captured" by Free Trade students', Carter noted proudly. By the spring of 1911, Carter was drawing up plans for a kind of popular university of Free Trade, a national network of 'Free Trade Instruction Classes' in 200 doubtful constituencies, complete with examinations, public demonstration, and prizes. Twenty to fifty students per constituency would meet fortnightly or monthly for three terms with a fully qualified lead lecturer. Caird gave his 'enthusiastic approval' and happily funded 114 study centres, of which he wanted to see 80 in London. In the autumn of 1911, the Liberal MP Eliot Crawshay-Williams took over from Carter to complete the scheme, arranging for the supply of textbooks (G.W. Gough's *Fifteen Fiscal Fallacies*), examinations and national competitions for gold, silver, and bronze medals, and prize money. The elite of Free Traders, including J. M. Robertson, Fred Maddison, Captain Wedgwood, and Henry Vivian, chaired the inaugural session and gave lead lectures.[82] How many students passed through these classes, and what were their backgrounds? Unfortunately, we do not know. But, together with the nationwide campaign and educational activities by movements like the cooperatives—books on Free Trade and Morley's biography of Cobden were a staple of cooperative libraries and courses—these classes played some role in the broad popular resurgence of interest in political economy in the Edwardian period, a phenomenon that may help explain the remarkable 52 per cent of classes in 1913 run by the Workers Educational Association on economics or economic history, a proportion that has steadily declined ever since.[83]

On the Beaches

By the end of the summer of 1910 the Free Trade campaign had swelled into a wave of unprecedented size and force, crashing into areas previously untouched by politics at a time of year normally considered a 'close season' for political agitation. Most seaside resorts had by-laws protecting their towns and visitors from partisan agitations to preserve an air of leisured political neutrality. The seaside campaign of July–September 1910 opened up these virgin lands. Free Traders invaded the sands and piers, competing with ice-cream vendors, fortune tellers, and minstrel singers for the attention of the perambulating tourist.[84] Free Traders now fought the enemy across the entire country, in market towns, in rural villages, and on the beaches.

Wallace Carter had experimented with a few seaside meetings in the summer of 1909 in Blackpool and Brighton and found them 'a great success'.[85] In the spring of 1910, Caird's cheque provided the opportunity to turn the experiment into a nationwide campaign that would send an army of hundreds of lecturers across the entire English, Welsh, and western Scottish seaside. Carter was fortunate to have the backing of a Liberal leader with an instinctive appreciation of strategy and military-style campaigning, Winston Churchill.[86] For not all Liberals were convinced by Carter's ideas of modern political communication. Montagu complained to Asquith about the 'odious and useless Carter' who was left in charge of the Free Trade Union in 1909 with the impending marriage and departure of Ivy Pretious.[87] Wallace Carter may have lacked his predecessor's charm, but he certainly had a feel for the shifting rules of political engagement. Caird, himself on the way to Karlsbad to take the waters, thought Carter's seaside scheme excellent, as did Churchill. Already by the end of April 1910, Carter had selected fifty seaside towns and secured permission to hold meetings in another twelve. Where political activity was formally banned, Carter planned to have a large yacht cruise up and down the coast, with speakers on deck, and 'Free Trade' in bold letters emblazoned on its sails. Even the sudden death of King Edward VII on 6 May 1910 did not put a brake on the massive campaign. By early June Carter had engaged sixty-seven speakers, at a cost of £1,550, to hold a planned 1,500 meetings in fifty-six resort areas. By the end of the summer, more than 1,343 lectures had taken place, ranging from 87 meetings in Brighton to 5 on the Isle of Wight, and from 85 in the west of Scotland to over a hundred in Devon and north Cornwall. Such was the success of the seaside invasion that the yacht proved superfluous.[88] (Colour Plate XI.)

In Morecambe the campaign began on 2 August. It was led by Alfred Smith, who was assisted by Mr. C. F. Lamble from London, and by Mrs Fletcher from nearby Oldham. At first these Free Trade speakers set up their pitch at Sandylands just outside the Morecambe boundary, to circumvent the town's by-laws against political meetings. After a fortnight of being 'exposed to every wind that blew [such that it] required as great an effort to speak as it did to listen', they changed tactics. On Monday afternoon, 15 August, they moved into Morecambe itself and held a meeting near the old pier in defiance of the town council. Given free advertising in a local newspaper, the story ensured 'a fine audience' the following evening. A day later the Free Traders had secured the town's permission to hold meetings on the beach, right opposite the Winter Garden—'an admirable pitch' for three meetings a day, 'whenever the weather was favourable'. Altogether, they held 45 meetings with an attendance of 10,500, Mr Smith calculated.[89]

The appeal of this 'novelty' was not lost on local tourists. The 'wonderful melange' of Free Trade politics, *The Lancaster Guardian* mused, made an interesting addition to the 'cosmopolitan' attractions that normally greeted the visitor, who 'may have his thirst quenched by vendours of mysterious compounds... have his fortune told by palmists' or his cravings 'for the refined and elevating [satisfied]... by the grotesque antics of men with blackened faces'.[90] Morecambe was mainly, though not exclusively, a middle-class resort, and attracted amongst others businessmen from the wool, cotton, and lace trades. The decision to target such upmarket resorts as well as seaside towns popular with working-class day-trippers, like Blackpool, is revealing. In thinking about the effects of commercial leisure on political life, it has been customary to focus on the 'affluent worker' who withdraws from public life into a world of private pleasure. The seaside campaign shows that for Free Traders it was as important to pull the middle classes back into the political domain as to educate the working classes. Caird's frustration with the apathy of the middle classes chimed with the experience of Free Trade activists. Wallace Carter had found it increasingly difficult to engage the middle-class voter at home, where he was 'pressed with the affairs of his work or business'. The seaside campaign was designed to reach him where he was easy prey for political persuasion. 'The average middle class man', Wallace Carter told Churchill, 'soon tires of the usual sea shore attractions, and is very glad to listen to Free Trade speeches as a sort of intellectual exercise.' On 'his holiday his mind is in a more receptive condition'.[91] For campaigners beginning to think about voters as people outside constituency boundaries, seaside resorts, with their playfulness and social mixing across class and geographical background, offered particularly fertile ground.

As in Morecambe, so along the entire British coast. Free Traders were remarkably successful in planting themselves on beaches and promenades, overcoming by-laws, and pulling crowds away from rival amusements. In north Wales, the authorities gradually gave in to the public interest in the meetings and tolerated speeches, although the distribution of political literature remained prohibited. Only in parts of Norfolk did local corporations stick to a ban, limiting Free Traders to Yarmouth and Lowestoft.

On the Isle of Man alone Free Traders held 46 meetings with an estimated attendance of 37,500, the largest open-air meetings there in living memory. Across the country, 90 per cent of the overall planned 1,500 meetings were held, reaching almost one million people.[92]

The 'novelty' character was aimed especially at 'people who did not often attend open-air meetings'.[93] It reflected more generally how far Free Traders had moved away from the ideal of the reasoning, informed, independent male citizen. Entertainment, in the form of bazaars, balls, and concerts, had of course been a long-standing feature of political culture. What was distinctive about Free Trade was that it self-consciously turned entertainment and spectacle into an integral part of political communication. In many ways, it was a mode of politics that put into practice Graham Wallas' warning against over-intellectualizing political behaviour: politics should not be divorced from instincts and impulses. Wallas' 1908 *Human Nature in Politics* spoke to the heart of that growing professional body, the political agent, who did much of the organizing, canvassing, and speaking in the localities, and who were always on the look out for new ways of engaging people. The professional magazine *The Liberal Agent* cited Wallas approvingly about the emotional needs of politics. A party was 'something which can be loved and trusted'. Party colours and songs were important for triggering 'emotional associations'. It was from Wallas that agents learnt how advertisers had discovered the importance of variety: 'Our nervous system shows itself intolerant of repeated sensations and emotions.'[94] The seaside campaign aimed to fuse reason and emotion, and win support by playing on excitement, thrill, and group feeling.

Seaside meetings were a lively mix of questions and heckling, often with a hint of physical confrontation in the air. Heckling and interference by 'roughs' were widespread. Disturbances were not the preserve of Tariff Reformers. Free Traders, too, found themselves fined for disrupting political meetings with 'beastly noises' under the 1908 Public Meetings Act.[95] On Brighton Beach, the 'political cockpit of Sussex' where 'unquestionably the best seaside meetings are held' according to *The Free Trader*, keen hecklers from both sides would form an 'inner circle' around which 'huge crowds' gathered.[96] The local Tariff Reform League would send their entire staff to heckle. There was a party of men who travelled from Hull to Scarborough specifically to go to Liberal meetings. On Rhyl sands in north Wales, there was the farmer from Stourbridge who reportedly 'became so interested in the meetings that he prolonged his holidays for a week for the express purpose of being able to continue his attendance at the meetings'.[97]

Heckling and verbal sparring combined entertainment with education. At Morecambe, for example, after a good deal of heckling and laughter from the audience, Mr Smith invited a gentleman to the stage who kept insisting that imports were paid for in money, and not by exports, as Free Traders were keen to point out. They then had several turns of ten minutes each.[98] Such exchanges were new opportunities for Free Traders to cite statistics in their favour or to challenge protectionist arguments about imports as the cause of unemployment. Free Traders delighted at teasing protectionists about their contradictions and fallacies and recounted with joy how their opponents had been reduced to rowdyism and personal abuse as a last resort.

Yet Free Traders were far from innocent themselves. They too con-tributed to the 'effective spiciness' and 'fun' of the meetings. On the Isle of Man, speakers managed to draw groups away from the various 'religious platforms and amusements on the beach' for meetings lasting 'sometimes as long as $2\frac{1}{2}$ or 3 hours'. When one Tariff Reform 'gentleman' called for three cheers for ' "Free Trade, the workhouse, and thieving" ', the meeting spun out of control. It immediately raised the 'most hostile demonstrations' against him. If the Tariff Reformer had not been 'surrounded by his few supporters and escorted with them as a bodyguard to his hotel', the *Free Trader* reported, he would have suffered a 'forcible dip' in the sea.[99]

Accounts of these meetings suggest not only that Free Traders were right about the attraction of 'novelty' but also that they had good reason to worry about the level of public knowledge. Activists, of course, have a natural self-interest in presenting their audiences as ignorant and in need of instruction, but, read carefully, reports by speakers and local newspapers offer some intriguing insights into the limits of public understanding. After millions of leaflets and pamphlets setting out the case for Free Trade, there remained a large gulf between the worlds of professional knowledge and local knowledge. In Yarmouth, agents were struck by the 'paucity of questions, and the elementary character of most of them'. Across holiday resorts, *The Free Trader* found that even where there were 'intelligent questions', they revealed 'that the questioners were making their first real acquaintance with Free Trade arguments'.[100] For *The Lancaster Guardian* the meetings at Morecambe afforded 'abundant evidence of the necessity for propaganda work on the part of the supporters of Free Trade'. 'It is remarkable that after all that has been said and written and notwithstanding the admissions of leaders of the Tariff Reform movement, there should still exist people who claim that our imports are paid for in hard cash.'[101]

Some historians have argued that the triumph of a liberal democratic order in nineteenth-century Britain came with a decline in public and open-air meetings and a shift to a more restrictive and regulated form of politics.[102] On the contrary, the Edwardian period is proof of a re-energized political culture, interactive and face-to-face. The controlling power of the printed word, or for that matter of government statistics, is easily exaggerated. 'A pamphlet is a poor substitute for a personality', the editor of the *Liberal Agent* noted in 1910. Democratic politics made the public meeting more, not less important. 'The keen and instructed politician may be satisfied by papers and pamphlets, not the average elector.' People were too exhausted after a day's work to spend a lot of effort on obtaining political information. 'At the close of a day of heavy toil the mental application necessary to master a pamphlet involves weariness to his flesh.' 'Listening to a lively speaker he will certainly be exhilarated.' Words were more easily remembered. Above all, the 'spoken word of the magnetic personality' would generate 'enthusiasm' and the 'courage' to become politically active. Agents stressed the importance of cultivating a 'living voice'.[103]

The growing number of professional agents at the same time responded to and reinforced this fresh emphasis on public meetings. One borough agent considered 'outdoor meetings in summer [as] by far the best means of imparting political information to the public', especially since there was 'a class of electors who never went to a Liberal meeting of any kind'.[104] Another recalled how he had spoken in 1908 in 127 indoor meetings in south-east Cornwall, 28 open air, and another 17 in other constituencies. It was his 'settled practice' to address a public meeting the week after any Tariff Reform speaker.[105] On 4 January, a single day in the 1910 general election, the Speakers' Bureau estimated that there were 4,000 political meetings and speeches, the bulk addressed by 'men who never thought of oratory much a year or two ago'.[106]

Speeches were about personal magnetism, exhilaration, and accessibility. They were also about authenticity. Drawing on personal experiences, speakers endowed Free Trade with a personal authority that economic experts were never able to command. From the outset of the battle, Tariff Reformers had ridiculed Free Trade as an antiquated theory out of touch with the everyday reality of 'dumped' goods and unemployed men. Professor Alfred Marshall, the leading liberal economist of the era who had defended Free Trade in a long and characteristically complex analytical fashion, was mocked in protectionist cartoons, lecturing John Bull about the 'truth' that imports did not displace labour but merely redirected employment, just as a long line of displaced workers passed by, reduced to earn their living as sandwich men advertising 'continental novelties on sale at Dumper & Co'.[107] In the political debate, economic theory easily became a handicap. The fact that economists themselves were divided did not help.[108] What mattered most was practical knowledge. In March 1909, Asquith, the Prime Minister, proudly told a large meeting with representatives from over 170 constituencies that he had 'never even produced a pamphlet (laughter and cheers) about the theory of free trade'. The idea that Free Traders were sitting in a study with blinds drawn, a bust of Cobden on the mantelpiece and Bastiat's writings open on the desk, was ludicrous. They were not 'unworldly doctrinaires' but practical men from the world of business, administration, and work, men like Lord Avebury, the Banker, or statesmen like Lord Goschen and Lord Balfour of Burleigh.[109] The seaside campaign was one opportunity to draw on such knowledge at a local level, for example in Morecambe, where speakers pulled in members of the audience to testify to their own experience, enabling other tourists to hear from men in the textile industries.

Speakers played a vital role in bringing the 'real world' to life. The vivid accounts of past suffering by old speakers authenticated the 'hungry forties' in popular memory. In the case of W. H. Chadwick, the last survivor of the Manchester Chartists imprisoned in 1848, neither deafness nor eccentricity—he also worked as a clairvoyant and organizers despaired at his unreliability—lessened the impact of his 'fine, far-reaching, resonant bass voice' giving a dramatic 'delineation of angry scenes, such as groups of wild-eyed, starving men parading the streets of towns with passionate cries of "Bread or Blood"', as one agent would later recall.[110] Public meetings were excellent opportunities for old people to step forward—sometimes pushed forward by local Liberals—to add their personal memories to the case against tariffs. An ounce of practical knowledge was worth a ton of theory, as Liberal posters and stories of the old instructing the young never failed to point out. The Glasgow *Daily Record* reported with pride how 'an old-white haired, white-bearded man [told] a youth, who seemed to think that he was the repository of all the economics in the world, his experience of the "hungry forties"'.[111] One Edwardian would recall in the 1970s how his grandfather—'a great man for politics'—'loved to stand in Market Street [in Guildford] and harangue the crowd': 'he talked to them excitedly about the…hungry forties or whatever he called them'. On several occasions he had to be moved on by the police for blocking the traffic.[112]

The discovery of Germany in 1909–10 placed a new premium on travelling speakers who could recreate the reality of life under protection through eyewitness accounts, such as Edward Baker, of ' "German Trip" fame' who had deserted the protectionist 'tariff trippers'. Wallace Carter even hired a fully paid German speaker, Franz Wendel, at £59 10s. for four months in 1910. Since much of the debate was fought out over the everyday realities of household and family life, women lecturers played a crucial role. Mrs King, 'a lady who has lived on the Continent for the greater part of her life' toured the south-west of England and gave 'most interesting' accounts of her life in Germany.[113] Annie Esplin, of the Women's Free Trade Union, was despatched to Berlin and Paris to bring back photographs and information for the campaign. And for £10 she was commissioned to produce a lantern lecture for use by other speakers on housekeeping in protectionist countries. Sadly, these lectures do not survive. But agents' reports leave little doubt about their importance in bringing knowledge about everyday life in Berlin and Frankfurt to Britons living in places as far away as Devon, Somerset, and Wales. Esplin's lantern lecture proved 'very popular' in the December 1910 general election. Baker told audiences 'night by night…the plain, unvarnished tale of his experiences' and attracted the largest outdoor meeting ever held in East Dorset.[114]

Shop-window Politics

Novelty and authenticity reached a new fusion in the Dump Shops and Free Trade Shops that sprang up all over Britain in 1909–10. By the end of 1910, there were more than two hundred of these shops exhibiting foreign and British goods and prices (Colour Plate XII). The prototype of these exhibits was the Dumping Van. The Dumping Van was a motorized adaptation of the horse-drawn van pioneered by travelling Conservative speakers in the 1890s.[115] A shop on wheels, the van carried samples of freely imported, 'dumped' goods and displayed them alongside political posters. Some vans doubled as travelling theatres. In Chatham and the Midlands, John Bull was pushed from his 'British-Isles' van by men dressed as 'foreigners' in the national costumes popularized by the stage, such as Uncle Sam. The shop window had been integral in protectionist iconography from the beginning, illustrating the costs of cheapness to the British worker in pictures of 'Herr Schmitt' or 'Von Kraus' with their shops full of cheap, foreign wares. Tariff Reform posters showed haggard British workers passing by grumbling that they would rather work themselves than give work to foreigners. The Dump Shop gave a physical presence to these anxieties by placing foreign imports directly in front of spectators. It enabled 'the working-man whose employment is gone or menaced [the chance] to apply the test of his own eyes to the often faked statistics of the Cobden Club', as conservative newspapers put it.[116]

In 1910, Tariff Reformers fitted out over 160 of these Dump Shops, starting in Chamberlain's heartland Birmingham and then expanding to London. Activists from as far as Glasgow and Eastbourne went to London's Old Kent Road to study the shops and their effects. The Dump Shop soon spread to provincial cities, from Hull to Brighton and from Plymouth to St Helen's. Located in working-class districts or thoroughfares used by workers, some shops combined the display of foreign articles with evidence of the rising cost of living under Free Trade. The shop window in Sheffield's Howard Street, for example, exhibited bread and butter in 'size today' and 'size four years ago'. A shop in Paignton displayed a picture of 'Free Trade' in a frame made from American oak, Belgian glass, and German nails.[117]

Whatever the particular local layout, all Dump Shops displayed generic foreign articles in everyday use alongside those raising particular anxieties for local industries. In Colchester, home to several engineering works, a passer-by would see a chaff-cutter next to boots marked 'Made in America' and a tea-service 'Made in Japan'. In Hull, domestic tinware and undergarments from Germany were on show next to the cotton-cake for cattle (from Egypt) which competed with local factories. In Walworth Road, one of the London Dump Shops, carpets and ironmongery were joined by window frames and doors made abroad, a warning to the joiners and carpenters in the area. Prominent in almost all shops were cheap Swedish doors and coffins, which greeted viewers at the entrance and reminded them that Free Trade spelt death for the British worker (Colour Plate XIII). Ten per cent of joiners and carpenters were unemployed in 1909, while Britain imported over 30,000 doors a month. A Swedish four-panelled door sold in Britain at 5s. 6d., basically the same as a British carpenter would have to pay for the wood alone, Tariff Reformers pointed out.[118] How, under Free Trade conditions, could British workers possibly hope to compete?

'There is no doubt that the Tariff Reformers' "Dump" shops exercised considerable influence at the Election', Wallace Carter told Churchill in March 1910. Like Carter, Churchill was alarmed by their 'remarkable effect'.[119] Dump Shops drew crowds and led to discussions in the streets about the costs of Free Trade: what is the good of a cheap imported article if men were thrown out of work and had no money to pay for it, people asked.[120] Taken by surprise, Free Traders initially responded with a variety of tactics. In Newport and Swansea, Liberals paraded a column of sandwich men with Free Trade posters in front of the Dump Shops, simply blocking the view. In Sittingbourne in Kent, they questioned the price listed for a Swedish coffin, only to be pelted with rotten eggs. In Leeds, four Free Trade-minded employees of the Post Office's travelling department used their spare time to descend on the Dump Shop near the Corn exchange, attracting a considerable crowd as they challenged the genuineness of article after article on display. Elsewhere, local tradesmen opened their own 'anti-dump' shops. Some local offices of the Free Trade Union began to exhibit items of food and clothing, others displayed export samples and statistics, yet others focused on locally manufactured items. Some of these were open to the public, others, as the one in Fleet Street, were private affairs arranged for the press. In Maidstone, Free Traders opened a shop and displayed a chair 'Made in Maidstone' from Kentish oak and elm to prove that British industries were thriving under Free Trade. In Brighton, the staff of the Free Trade Union put together an exhibition in which British manufactured exports, each listing the ratio of exports to imports, framed the centrepiece: 'a case of black bread and of horseflesh steaks and sausages'.[121]

However creative, these spontaneous local responses failed to add up to a coherent answer to the protectionist initiative. The earlier sensationalist appeal of German black bread and horseflesh sausages had begun to fade. '[P]eople have heard enough of these things', Wallace Carter found; 'and they are a nuisance to store.' The answer lay in adapting the Dump Shop to Free Trade purposes by organizing a standardized, travelling exhibition comparing British and German consumer goods. A standardized outfit offered economies of scale. And it conveyed a centrally planned message that could target especially doubtful constituencies. Exhibits could be sent out to any constituency at short notice, Wallace Carter explained, with 'no loophole for local blundering'. Caird loved the idea. He wanted the shops set up in 'the very best thoroughfares, well lighted and supplied with mechanical music'. Window displays were to be changed regularly to attract window shoppers, as in department stores. Churchill even wanted to shift the entire focus of the campaign to the Free Trade shop, away from lectures. In the end Wallace Carter dissuaded Caird from throwing his money away on shop windows in the West End;[122] rents were prohibitively high—up to £1,000 a year or twice as much as what the fifty standardized exhibits eventually cost.

But this reluctance to concentrate on the West End also reflected a working model that politics, while it might learn from the world of commerce, remained a distinct sphere, with its own characteristics, needs, and modes of behaviour. Political engagement and persuasion was about more than selling and buying. It was not like window-shopping. Unlike Selfridges on Oxford Street, catering for the affluent citizens of the metropole, the Free Trade campaign needed to reach millions of voters from different classes across the country. Shops needed to fit in on the provincial high street, not emulate fancy developments amongst West End retailers. The Free Trade shops found their way into a remarkable cross-section of Britain, from Oxford's Queen Street to Renfield Street in Glasgow, and the Grand Parade in Brighton to the cotton town of Hyde and other towns throughout the country.

The Free Trade shops appealed to a much broader identity of the consumer than in earlier campaigns. Instead of the cheap loaf and the spectre of hunger, the 50 travelling exhibits looked beyond 'necessity' to include the trappings of a comfortable home. Shop displays included branded goods, as well as articles of clothing that would have been worn by the more affluent working classes and lower middle classes. There was everything from Lea and Perrins sauce and Quaker Oats to an artisan's cap and the bowler hat of the professional and clerical classes. On Wallace Carter's instructions, the Free Trade Union sent a representative to Berlin, accompanied by a German workman, to buy a standardized set of items from the department store in Wertheim, situated in a working-class district. Together with a sworn declaration from German officials verifying their retail prices as authentic, the items were then displayed next to goods with London prices. In Oxford, the shop in Queen Street showed Quaker Oats selling at 3d. in London and $4\frac{3}{4}$d. in Berlin. A suit bought in Berlin was over 24s., that made up by the firm of John Barran in Leeds merely 17s. 11d. In Leeds, N. G. Morrison returned from Germany with a bagful of pricey branded goods, including tins of Nestlé's Swiss milk and Colman's mustard, a jar of Keiller's marmalade and some of Huntley and Palmer's 'superior cracknel biscuits'. '[N]one of these articles enumerated are needful for the subsistence of the people', the *Leeds Mercury* admitted: still, they exposed the general trend of prices in a 'tariff-ridden country'.[123]

As bread prices were rising in 1908–10, the 'cheap loaf' ceased to be an easy rebuttal of Tariff Reformers' claims that living conditions were better in protectionist countries. In place of the earlier threat of starvation, the Free Trade campaign now produced an ever-longer list of domestic goods that would become more expensive under tariffs, from sewing and washing machines to carpets and cutlery.[124] This more diverse and prosperous basket of consumer goods became especially important as knowledge of high-wage America began to interfere with the black-and-white contrast between Britain and Germany. Protectionist propaganda publicizing the Board of Trade's report on the cost of living in American towns proved a considerable headache for Free Traders. The report found that workers in America enjoyed wages that were 130 per cent higher than those in Britain, while they only paid 52 per cent more on rent and food.[125] Much to the distress of British Liberals, the report's narrow focus on food omitted many other articles, like clothing, where tariffs pinched American pockets. The image of the consumer expanded accordingly. Alongside the poor mother with barely a crust of bread to feed her baby, American middle-class ladies appeared, lamenting tariffs on hat pins, lace collars, and silk lingerie.[126] In the summer of 1910 Wallace Carter went to New York and Dowding, his assistant, even planned an 'Anglo-American Exhibition' to show the impact of tariffs on a full range of goods, especially clothing—a scheme that was aborted once the Tariff Reform crusade began to disintegrate in the course of 1911.[127]

Exhibitions had become such a regular feature of public life that by the turn of the twentieth century many people complained of exhibition fatigue. Already in 1851 at the Crystal Palace, some of the organizers saw the display of British manufactured goods as a demonstration of the superiority of Free Trade, and world exhibitions in the next decade disseminated the ideal of free exchange.[128] When Edwardians finally appropriated the technique of the exhibit in their shops, they kept spectators interested by incorporating elements of the fairground and the music hall. In the shop in Camberwell, Thomas Macnamara, the Liberal candidate well known across London for his 'hard-hitting speeches spiced with good stories' and for having the 'slimness and the energy of an athlete', theatrically dressed up in flimsy German clothes—a 'really excellent method of propaganda' according to Wallace Carter and one reason for including suits and shirts in the standardized exhibits. The clothes 'would lend themselves to dressing up two members of the audience to represent the Briton and the German and to contrast their cost of living, their wages and hours, etc.'.[129]

Free Trade shops were not safe from Tariff Reform attacks—in Blackburn, Tariff Reformers painted thick blue paint over the shop window the day before polling, while in Camberwell, local Conservatives occupied the floor above the Free Trade shop and hung out a banner 'Radical Swank, Look Below and Laugh'.[130] Yet, in general, they were remarkably effective combinations of entertainment and politics. The display of goods silenced critics and allowed organizers to draw sceptics into the shop to let the articles demonstrate the superiority of Free Trade. When challenged about the origin or price of goods, speakers produced invoices 'to the delight of crowds'. The shop in Glasgow proved the 'most popular form of propaganda', according to W. E. Dowding. Local organizers praised the exhibits for attracting thousands of people on their way home from work in the large cities. Others found them 'most satisfactory' in smaller towns. We do not have oral testimonies to tell us what spectators made of these shows. What we do know is that passers-by engaged with these shops as political audiences rather than as window shoppers flitting through the landscape of consumption, sometimes seen to typify new modern sensibilities. In Exeter, the shop was surrounded by crowds from 9 o'clock in the morning to midnight. J. Howard Wilson, who was in charge of the travelling shop in North East Derbyshire and Chesterfield, confirmed its 'great success'. 'The only criticism I have to make is that the same people stayed too long.' People were so interested, 'it was almost impossible to get near the window day or night'.[131]

Picture Politics

The battle over Free Trade produced the first multi-media campaign in modern politics. More than ever before, politics was visualized and brought into mass circulation via an array of different artistic genres combining old and new technologies. The use of the moving image of film was still in its infancy—although Tariff Reformers like Fitzhamon and Hepworth experimented with short political films and so-called vivaphone shorts which produced synchronized images of Conservative leaders miming to pre-recorded sound.[132] Champions of the new film technology thought it a great pity that our 'old friend, the optical lantern, and its first cousin, the kinematograph' were yet so rarely used together, as they were in the United States.[133] But this does not mean Edwardians were idle when it came to experimenting with emerging technologies or creatively manipulating established ones. A typical meeting like the divisional tea of the Bedford Women's Liberal Association in October 1903 would include an 'excellent address on "Free Trade Principles"', followed by a gramophone and a cinematograph—'much enjoyed' by the audience—and conclude with a singing of the National Anthem.[134] Liberal agents like W. Ford, who lectured in rural areas, emphasized the importance of song and new technology in attracting audiences. Free Traders had just as much right to hear and play songs as the Primrose League, the large Conservative women's association. He even built into his meetings the display of new recording devices, such as the graphophone, an early dictaphone developed by the American inventor Charles Tainter in the late 1880s. The graphophone was used to sing songs as well as to show off the marvels of this new technology capable of recording and replaying the human voice on the spot.[135] Tariff Reformers and Free Traders sometimes fixed a gramophone to the top of their vans. In the metropole, Free Trade speakers in North Paddington and Enfield even attached a screen to a pantechnicon van and drove right through these constituencies, 'attracting large crowds and securing meetings which were in some cases phenomenally large'.[136]

The most popular and influential types of visual technology were the lantern and the colour poster. The magic lantern had its origin in the mid-seventeenth century but it was in the Victorian period that it became widespread. It offered entertainment and instruction in phantasmagoria shows, panoramic spectacles, and missionary displays.[137] By the 1890s automatic lanterns had been developed that were illuminated by electric light and capable of showing fifty slides in less than two minutes. They were a springboard for future producers of moving images. They also became a favourite medium for speakers and agents in the political mass market. Already in the 1890s the Conservative Primrose League had used the lantern for shows of images of the Empire, the navy, and landmarks of history.[138] With Free Trade the lantern became a more direct weapon of political campaigning. It was only in the 'last few years that its possibilities as an engine for political warfare have been discovered', J. Wigley, a Free Trade organizer from Manchester, noted in 1903. The lantern was inappropriate in certain contexts, Wigley acknowledged, such as when a cabinet minister came to give a speech. 'But, as every political organiser knows, elections are not won by big meetings, big speeches, or big men, but by steady, persistent, and systematic "spade work" among the great mass of voters. And it is in work of this kind that the value of the lantern as a means of interesting people in politics, and impressing elementary political principles on their minds, becomes apparent.'[139]

One of the Liberal pioneers of the lantern was James Martin. Since first experimenting with a lantern in politics in 1890, Martin, the agent for Ipswich, had given hundreds of shows in small towns and villages and advised fellow Free Traders on how to make the lantern a success. Martin approached schools to use their rooms for free and, in exchange, would offer children a lantern entertainment without charge. He would give the children a short story such as Dick and his Donkey, illustrated by 24 slides to teach 'truthfulness, honesty, and perseverance', making sure to put in well-known hymns and 'plenty of singing'. The schoolmaster would then hand out a flyer for the children to take home, advertising a lantern lecture on politics with upwards of 50 slides plus entertainment for children with 'laughable sketches'. The children invariably returned with their parents in tow.[140]

Martin was convinced that 'no other agency is so well adapted to reach the masses and so successfully educate them ... as the lantern'. It 'secures the attendance of those who otherwise would never be persuaded to attend a political meeting'. The use of the lantern in Free Trade stage plays, such as the masque A Message from the Forties, in combination with shadow play, new lighting techniques, and the dramatic conjuring of Cobden's ghost, borrowed from an existing body of magical theatrical performances. In the Victorian period, places like the Royal Polytechnic Institution had enthralled audiences with shows that mixed lantern slide shows with visual illusions, shadow play, or supernatural appearances. Comic panoramic slides were also popular. Free Trade lantern shows especially capitalized on the images by the outstanding cartoonist of his generation, F. Carruthers Gould of the *Westminster Gazette*, the first cartoonist to draw for the front page of a political newspaper. Via lantern slides, handbills, and postcards, Gould's cartoons linked the worlds of high and low politics, connecting the 20,000 readers of the *Westminster Gazette* with a political mass market; speakers were able to obtain Gould slides from the newspaper at 1s. 3d. each (his cartoon leaflets cost 41s. per thousand); a cheaper supply of fiscal cartoons was available through the *Morning Leader*, a Liberal halfpenny daily, which mailed sets of twelve post free at 8s.[141] 'As long as F.C.G. can hold a pencil,' one county agent wrote, 'Liberals are missing a fine opportunity, if, in the more remote and outlying places, they do not bring the lantern into operation.'[142] Cartoons from *Reynolds's*, too, were considered especially effective in villages, where readers of that radical newspaper would 'often recognise one of the pictures thrown on the screen as an old acquaintance'.[143]

Slides and cartoons helped build a new working model of political persuasion. Colourful cartoons and posters became central to popular Free Trade politics. Their commercial design and print stood in contrast to the older tradition of handmade political banners as well as to contemporary arts and crafts design, hand printing, and needlework developed by the suffragettes, who had their own Suffrage Atelier.[144] The lantern's projection of colourful images enabled speakers 'through the eye to reach the heart', Martin explained, because what people 'see enables them to think over what they hear, and when an Englishman begins to think there is some hope of success'.[145] Symbols and pictures made complex realities accessible and entertaining. Churchill, who personally oversaw the national lecture and exhibition campaign, saw lantern slides and pictures as essential for 'setting out in simple and attractive diagrams those statistics which are so important and yet so difficult for the impatient man to grasp'.[146] Where speakers quoted figures these needed to be accompanied by simple 'pictorial diagrams', such as large and small ships illustrating the superiority of British trade. Wallace Carter based the Free Trade Union's propaganda work on the assumption that 'since nobody can think statistically in millions, and only students can think diagrammatically, the ordinary man must be helped to think by contrasts, and in pictures'.[147] The lantern reinforced the presentation of stark contrasts. Lantern lectures illuminated the gulf between past and present, between the big loaf and the small loaf, between living conditions in Britain and Germany. In schoolrooms and town halls up and down the country, the Free Trade Union and the Women's Free Trade Union organized 'most instructive' shows of lantern slides which contrasted the hungry forties with the present under Free Trade and offered simple diagrams of progress.[148] When Free Traders introduced standardized lectures written by leading Liberals like J. M. Robertson for their battalion of general speakers, Churchill insisted that each lecturer should be accompanied by a lantern operator: 'special attention should be given to making the lecture not merely convincing but also picturesque and entertaining'.[149]

From the windows of their branch offices, Free Traders projected lantern slides onto the walls of the buildings opposite. Free Trade vans operated as travelling shows with a sheet 'stretched tight across the back end of the van' and with gas cylinders lighting a lantern inside. In January 1910, Mr Mitchell, who travelled with a van in rural Sussex, gave 20 meetings in 16 days 'in spite of occasional bad weather'.[150] The National Free Trade Lecture campaign offered political entertainment for large crowds in cities and country alike, including at night. In north London, lantern shows attracted 'enormous audiences' in 1910. In Yorkshire, audiences were treated to eight 'beautiful coloured lantern lectures' in village schoolrooms and on village greens. In Honiton, a small market town in Devon, slides were shown for ten nights in open-air meetings: 'Huge crowds watched them for hours in the rain.' In nearby Exeter, 'huge crowds loudly cheered the appearance of almost every picture', so much so that in the words of one agent it barely required a lecturer: 'There was no need to explain to them; the crowd did their own explanation!'[151]

The colourful poster was the second prominent form of this dynamic visual politics. Like the lantern shows, the political poster evolved in a hybrid sphere between the worlds of politics and commerce. Several advertisers lent lantern slides to mechanics' institutes and similar bodies without charge in exchange for advertising pictures shown at the end of the entertainment.[152] Colour printing by lithography had become cheap and widespread by the mid-Victorian period and new technologies like the photo-zinc process further boosted the production of cartoons, handbills, and posters. In the Maldon division of Essex, for example, 15,000 handbills

Figure 10. The Free Trade Union office in Clarence Chambers, Plymouth, in 1910, showing a multitude of campaign posters, with local organizers at the door.

found their way into the hands of villagers in 1904. In the January 1910 general election, the billposters Walter Hill and Co. estimated that posters coming from London alone would cover 2 million square feet of wall space. Posters ranged from the modest double crown sheet (30 × 20 inches) to the gigantic 32-sheet version covering a space of 240 × 160 inches. Crewe was the only constituency where candidates agreed not to have posters. Billposting was increasingly recognized as a vital part of political advertising (see Figure 10). It kept a candidate's name and cause 'continually before the electors', one agent noted in 1905, and attracted 'the attention of the non-politician or doubtful voter, who is so often the deciding factor at an election, and who so frequently "goes with the crowd"'.[153] Many of the leading artists like John Hassall and F. C. Gould were involved in commercial as well as political art and advertising. Advertisers like S. H. Benson and billposters like David Allen & Sons, the largest billposting firm in the world, served both political and commercial masters.[154]

Political and commercial posters also shared many icons and reference points, such as John Bull or the coach, widely used in the new brands of food and drink.[155] Yet it would be a mistake to think that political communication was simply taken over by commercial marketing. Artists, activists, and audiences continued to expect different things from a political poster than from a commercial advert. In 1909, at the height of the political poster craze, *The Daily Graphic* observed that it was not easy to define what made for a successful political poster. The 'funny posters' by Reed and Hassall were singled out. One portrayed a German and American at an Englishman's counter with a long dialogue between them; 'Hier you can everydings buy and more goot and much more sheap as England', the German observes.[156]

The continued mix of images and dialogue in political posters ran directly counter to the principles driving commercial advertising. For John Hassall, the 'king of posters' who in 1905 founded the New Art School and School of Poster Design (the John Hassall School), the commercial advert was all about responding to a new society in motion. 'The poster artist has to design an advertisement, not for those who *cannot* read,' he explained, 'but for those who have not *time* to read. The man on the omnibus, the tram, or the suburban train has no time to solve the riddle of a poster charged with letterpress: he must catch the message at a glance.'[157] Hassall's golden rule was that the poster 'should hit the passer-by right in the eye-ball' with 'a huge splash of one colour, which should dominate the whole picture'. For Hassall, the simple political cartoon was a model for the commercial poster. But many political posters continued to mix colours and gave extensive commentary. Instead of eliminating figures and text so that one dominant image could catch the 'momentary glimpse' of the mobile modern citizen, they used familiar images as props for additional figures or political stories. Political symbols and posters were designed to trigger an emotional memory in viewers but also presumed they would stop, think, and listen, as they did around the Free Trade shops and vans, which displayed slides and posters. The imagined gaze of the citizen was still longer and more reflective than that of the shopper.

The most successful political poster of the period was T. B. Kennington's 'Free Trade', a Conservative poster produced by David Allen and Sons (Colour Plate XIV). No picture could possibly have been further removed from the single splash of bright colour that dominated successful commercial advertisements like those for Coleman's Mustard. Kennington, a member of the Royal Society of Portrait Painters and vice-president of the Royal Institute of Oil Painters, made a name for himself with scenes of upper-class mothers and children. In 1889 he had exhibited a street scene, 'The Pinch of Poverty', at the Royal Academy, today hanging at the Foundling Hospital in Brunswick Square, London. Whereas here at least the flowergirl's red lips and yellow daffodils lent some colour and hope to the surrounding misery, his protectionist campaign poster 'Free Trade' was a thoroughly gloomy brownish depiction of a working-class family in despair. His cap and tool-bag thrown down by his side, a worker sits defeated in a barren room, his wife with her head bent on the table, his daughter holding a baby and looking sullenly to the unemployed breadwinner. The table has no tablecloth, the teapot a broken handle. Some clothes are hanging out of the washtub, unwashed. The scene starkly inverted the familiar Victorian image of middle-class domestic harmony popularized by Millais and others. Kennington's was the most widely displayed and controversial poster of the period; 11,000 alone were printed for the January 1910 election, and the image was widely reproduced in the provincial press and on countless handbills and postcards. Handbills used the reverse of the picture to spell out the connection between foreign imports, poverty, and unemployment. Some quoted in bold letters socialists like Philip Snowden, that ' "Free Trade" has not brought prosperity to the Masses.'[158]

Instead of the bold and simple contours of the political cartoon, Kennington's poster impressed because of its almost photographic quality—Tariff Reformers were at the forefront of camera advertising, introducing photos of German conditions and of dumped goods, like manufactured doors, in lantern shows and handbills.[159] Liberals were furious at Kennington's portrayal of working-class life, especially of the position assigned to the mother. 'It is a pitiable libel upon the women of Britain', *The Cambria Daily Leader* complained. Instead of cheering up her husband, 'the wife, a slattern of the worst type … has set herself out apparently to deepen his gloom'. 'It is the abiding place—to call it a home would be a misnomer—of an untidy, shiftless, comfortless creature, who is an obvious failure both as wife and mother.' The poster proved just how ignorant Tariff Reformers were of the true conditions of the people. The 'party which keeps it on the walls is simply insulting the wives of the workers'.[160] It even prompted a parliamentary debate. On 23 February 1910, Ramsay MacDonald vented his anger. 'Free Trade' was a 'magnificent poster, full of human sympathy' but it was a cheap tactic for Conservatives to exploit the real misery of unemployed people for their cause. The 'picture could be reproduced in France and in Germany, and with emphasis and added darkness in America',

MacDonald insisted. They had had no right to use it.[161] So effective was the poster that Free Traders were driven to caricature it, replacing the original heads of the family with those of Balfour and other Tariff Reformers.[162]

If the battle over Free Trade intensified the role of commercial entertainment and advertising in political life, this did not mean politics became a standardized commercial product or followed the logic of the marketplace. The Free Trade campaign, with its general as opposed to specialized meetings and its self-representation as a public not sectional cause, ran counter to any strategy of market segmentation. There were attempts to centralize and streamline political activities, such as by sending out standardized Free Trade lectures, but speakers could ignore these and audiences often preferred spontaneity and authenticity; instead of sticking to the pre-arranged script, Mrs King, for example, gave her 'own experiences which were most interesting'.[163] There remained plenty of room for improvisation. In addition to plays, Free Traders organized pageants in which participants dressed up as industries. At carnival, boys appeared with Tariff Reform costumes stitched together from cartoons, and topped with a loaf-shaped hat.[164] Hundreds joined in children's processions, carrying locally assembled posters and banners; in Stirling such a protest against the taxation of food and toys was 'the most interesting incident' in the election, according to *The Free Trader*. It 'came as a dramatic surprise to the bulk of the citizens, and the children were enthusiastically cheered'.[165] In the West Country market town of Tavistock, Fred Ford contributed a large linen poster 'Vote for the Tories who tax food and vote against Old Age Pensions! Why we mus' be mazed', considered a 'remarkably fine piece of work'.[166] Another poster adapted Nestlé's Milk original advert contrasting a well-fed, healthy girl with a skinny, small boy into a political message about the health benefits of Free Trade.[167] Commercially produced political posters were easily manipulated. Their text and image could be altered by political enemies to undercut the message, an early example of adbusting, the art of subverting adverts that today has become the weapon of critics of free trade and consumerism. In Bradford, a leading Liberal, H. H. Spencer, was fined 20s. plus costs for cutting 'Free Trade' out from Kennington's poster and sticking on printed 'Tariff Reform' slips instead.[168]

New technologies and forms of entertainment reshaped civic culture in the decades before the First World War. They opened up new political spaces, as well as cutting into older ones. The lantern, the seaside, and the shop window were joined by film. At the Peckham election in 1908, for example, audiences enjoyed 'Singing Pictures' alongside political speeches. The Chronomegaphone show brought together an estimated forty thousand people one night. And the audience did not only enjoy the novelty of the Singing Pictures. 'Interspersed amidst the crowd were various political enthuasists ... and their audiences were enabled to realise the unique situation of listening to heated discussions on Cheap beer and dear bread ... and at the same time to be entertained by the Arab on his Steed singing his Bedouin Love Song ... and several other more modern airs, among which were Zuyder Zee, and Waltz me round again Willie.'[169] Politics invaded the music hall too. In London, the 'Oxford' and the 'Pavillon' performed plays caricaturing Liberals, which the *Daily Chronicle* decried as 'bad business' as well as 'bad taste'.[170]

Often it was the world of commerce which copied politics. The popularity of the Free Trade question did not escape the attention of advertisers of food brands like Bovril, which created posters of Chamberlain drinking Bovril—'Protection Against Colds & Chills Means Free Trade in Bovril'—and of a horned Balfour taking the place of the life-strengthening bull (Colour Plate XV). Local advertisers, too, tried to cash in on the excitement generated by politics. On especially wide screens, lantern slides were used to show commercial and political adverts side by side, a feat that sometimes exceeded the skill of the two operators in charge of running the slides synchronously and left 'startled spectators' with combined messages like 'Palmer's Spring Bedsteads ... Deserves the Working Man's Vote'.[171]

The popular campaign for Free Trade paid off. At the level of electoral politics, it limited the swing to the Conservatives. The Liberal Free Trade government was able to hang on with the slenderest of majorities—274 Liberals plus 40 Labourites against 272 Conservative MPs in January 1910; 272 Liberals plus 42 Labourites against 271 Conservatives in December 1910. Free Trade was not the only issue, but it rallied the troops and voters. The January 1910 election demonstrated the advance of tariff reform in the south, in London and in most English rural areas. Free Trade activism was an attempt to contain the Conservative invasion of England, to retain crucial sections of middle-class support, especially in the north of England, and to target marginals and areas of remaining Liberal support like Cornwall and Norfolk. It is impossible to measure the electoral influence precisely—not least because the massive seaside campaign was not constituency-oriented. However, comparing cases where the Free Trade movement was particularly active and welcomed by local Liberals with open arms with areas that were distinctly cool to outside agitators suggests some correlation between the degree of activism and electoral success.

In the first place, the campaign kept the issue of Free Trade before the eyes of voters, especially once the Conservative party sought to shift attention to the constitutional question of the House of Lords by pledging to postpone tariffs until after a future referendum. Activists brought much-needed additional manpower and resources, giving several speeches a day, dealing with hecklers, writing letters to the local press, helping with the electoral campaign, and, not insignificantly, reducing the pressure on local candidates and agents to respond to Tariff Reform arguments. But, more generally, campaigners mobilized Liberal voters, and nowhere more so than in doubtful and marginal seats. Where Free Traders were especially active, they helped win back several marginals in December 1910, such as Coventry and Cricklade, where Liberals won by 523 and 128 votes, respectively. Their efforts also paid off in London and in parts of the East Midlands where they reversed Conservative gains; in London, Liberals enjoyed a net gain of three seats. Elsewhere it helped them hang onto seats in traditionally Conservative areas won in the 1906 landslide, as in Somerset North or in Romford, the largest county constituency, with a sizeable middle class, where Liberals even increased their majority between the January and December 1910 elections. Cheltenham and Radnorshire were gained, Tottenham retained. Here local Liberals were grateful for the help from Free Trade speakers and volunteers. In Gloucester, where Free Trade activists praised the 'cordial' reception and the 'plenty of local help & enthusiasm', the protectionist majority was reduced to four.[172]

In Lancashire and Cheshire the story was very different. Here the offer of outside help was largely declined. In many constituencies, Conservatives pledged themselves to a referendum on tariffs, making the issue of Free Trade less urgent. At the same time the Tariff Reform League kept up its propaganda work. Free Trade was left largely undefended at the December 1910 election, and Conservatives increased their share of the vote; in Eastern Lancastria there was a 3.3 per cent swing to the Conservatives. 'It is impossible to maintain Free Trade majorities where such tactics are adopted', Wallace Carter fumed: 'people imagine that Free Traders have given up their case!'[173] Similarly, in parts of Wales where Free Trade lecturers received little encouragement, as in Montgomery, where relations with local Liberals were 'not at all cordial', the seat was lost in the December election.

Without the popular Free Trade revival the Conservative party would have won in 1910, and Britain would have adopted some sort of tariff regime. The survival of the Liberal government and its programme of social reforms, such as the National Insurance Act, depended in material terms on popular Free Trade. The political impact of the campaign, however, went far beyond the realm of elections. The thousands of meetings and lectures had turned an electoral issue into a more permanent, ongoing feature of public life. There was a new cross-fertilization between politics and commercial spectacle. Free Trade survived because it understood how to mobilize passions as well as to appeal to self-interest or reason, making use of a wide repertoire of entertainment. Some of this pointed ahead to strategies of political marketing to come. But it also carried forward and enriched a colourful tapestry of political culture associated with the seventeenth and eighteenth centuries, with its processions, pageants, spicy rhetoric, and riots.

In the battle over Free Trade, political economy reached people through ever-expanding channels of communication and entertainment, spilling over into the most ordinary and intimate aspects of private as well as public life. No medium typified this better than the political postcard. There was a deluge of postcards after the postal monopoly was abolished in 1903. In 1910, 866 million cards were sent through the post. Beginning in Germany and Japan, the initial craze was for touristic, patriotic, and sometimes erotic images. It was the conflict over Free Trade that rang in the golden age of the political postcard. In the election of January 1910 alone, several million Free Trade and Tariff Reform postcards were produced; even 'music cards' were introduced.[174] Many postcards were reproductions of cartoons from newspapers and posters. Others showed leading politicians or advertised local candidates. But as telling as the image is the use to which contemporaries put them. Some used the postcards to add their political opinion—'poor old Joe! [Chamberlain]'. For others they satisfied the growing appetite of the hobby collector. Yet others used the cards for private communication, informing friends or families of when they would arrive at the local station or inquiring about their health. 'I know you are really longing for a moonlight stroll on the Esplanade, aren't you', one woman wrote to another. 'You must think I am a horrid girl not to have sent you a card before.'[175] Did the two women ever meet for their walk? We do not know, nor whether they would have talked about the figure of John Bull with his historic liking for the big loaf gracing the front of the postcard. What we do know is that Free Trade had become ubiquitous, flowing almost effortlessly between public and private spheres.

3

Uneasy Globalizers

The days are for great Empires and not for little States. The question for this generation is whether we are to be numbered amongst the great Empires or the little States.

> Joseph Chamberlain, 16 May 1902[1]

The British Empire is held together by moral not by material forces. It has grown up in liberty and silence. It is not preserved by restriction and vulgar brag.

> Winston Churchill at the inaugural meeting of the Free Trade League, Manchester, 19 February 1904[2]

Free Trade was a hardy tree, indigenous to British soil; it had grown till its branches covered the whole earth and yielded to us the fruits of every clime.

> William Angus, president of the National Liberal Federation[3]

This idea of the Free Trade Party to leave things to take their natural course has resulted in the production of a submerged tenth which cannot be equalled in any other country in Europe. Our people have been driven from the land to herd in the great cities, robbed of the opportunity of working for their own livelihood till they could find a market. The harrying wind of Free Trade Radicalism has swept over the nation and destroyed all that is most beautiful in our nature.

> Keir Hardie, founder of the Labour Party, Manchester, 28 February 1909

Anniversaries are a time for stock-taking. Richard Cobden's centenary in 1904 provided Edwardians with a chance to reassess his legacy in the light of the new realities of globalization. Like no other nineteenth-century figure, Cobden symbolized the liberal vision of a peaceful, prosperous global order held together by the benign forces of Free Trade. But as a popular hero, Cobden had always sat uneasily alongside other great figures like

Bismarck or Garibaldi, commemorated in super-human monuments on the continent. If Cobden's adult life had been marked by an open international atmosphere in which ideas, goods, and people came to flow more freely, by the time of his death in 1865, nationalism was in the ascendant. Whatever the efforts by the Cobden Club to preserve Cobden's memory, the late nineteenth century was an inhospitable time for an 'international man'. Free movement became constrained by national barriers, symbolized by the passport. As with people, so with goods and politics. Cobden's legacy was the liberal commercial treaty system of which he had laid the foundation with Chevalier in 1860. In an era of economic nationalism it was unravelling fast. As with globalization today, the advancing integration of financial and commodity markets in the late nineteenth century was fractured by increasingly complex trade barriers, subsidies, cartels, and monopolies.

The Cobden centenary in 1904, then, was not just a celebration but a defence of the Cobdenite global project in an age of new imperialism and mercantilism. The successful defence of Free Trade, as we have seen, depended on democracy, consumers, and civil society. Invariably in a battle over trade, these were related to perceptions of empire and international order. While popular liberals and conservative Free Traders clung to Cobden's vision of unfettered global exchange, weaving bonds of peace and prosperity between peoples, other circles openly wondered about its ongoing relevance. Amongst socialists and the young Labour party, it had never been entirely forgotten how Cobdenites had opposed social and factory reforms and attacked the Chartists in the 1840s; 'Cobden, the Chartist breaker', was how some remembered him.[4] But the critique of Cobden went beyond the actions of the man himself to prompt a more general reassessment of Britain's place in a changing world. Looking at the general drift towards self-sufficiency amongst other industrializing nations, Philip Snowden, one of the leaders of the Labour party, freely declared that the 'idea of the Manchester School that we should devote ourselves to building up a foreign trade, that England should be the workshop of the world, was a mistake'.[5] Soon there would be no foreign markets left for British goods, as other countries developed their own industries behind the shelter of tariffs. What was needed was self-sufficiency, not an open door.

Few people in the British state or business went quite as far as Snowden. But here too, the liberal vision of comparative advantage and an international division of labour began to seem out of synch with the shifting realities of geopolitics. Together with the arrival of new industrial competitors, first and foremost Germany, the imperial expansion of the United States in the Caribbean and of Russia in Asia raised doubts about unilateral Free Trade and about Britain's foreign policy of splendid isolation more generally. In the 1880s, a National Fair Trade League began to attack what it called 'one-sided free trade', and, in 1887, it even managed to win a Conservative party resolution in favour of retaliation, that is of hitting back at foreign tariffs. A new 'commercial Barbarossa' was poised to invade a sleeping Albion.[6] In 1898 the Trades Union Congress extended its opposition to immigration and the import of 'sweated' prison-made goods to an attack on the 'obnoxious bounties' used by other nations to boost exports.

These anxieties may have been exaggerated in purely economic terms— there was no concerted attack by protectionist countries on the British market, although British exports to Germany and to the United States declined. But they drew strength from parallel developments in imperial and international relations, especially the use of new tariffs favouring one's own colonies and possessions, a practice perfected by the United States and France at the turn of the twentieth century. Was a dogmatic adherence to unilateral Free Trade and the most-favoured-nation clause the most effective policy in a world of tariff bargaining, economic imperialism, and cartels? Perhaps it was time for the British lion to show his teeth in the field of economic statecraft? After all, was Britain not still the most powerful empire on the planet and the largest single market in the world?

Such calls were articulated in a new language of geopolitics. Instead of an image of mutually beneficial relations, the 1890s saw growing talk of 'living' and 'dying nations', engaged in a Darwinian struggle for survival. These ideas circulated across the political spectrum all over Europe, deep into the corridors of power. Fears in Britain about the carve-up of the world by the new powers of the United States, Germany, and Russia echoed continental ideas of three emerging empires, the so-called *Dreiweltreichtheorie*. Lord Salisbury, the Prime Minister, spoke in 1898 of 'living nations' struggling for control over 'dying nations'. War itself served as a mechanism for securing the survival of the fittest, as Benjamin Kidd argued in his *Social Evolution* in 1894, a book that sold a phenomenal 250,000 copies in the first five years after publication.[7]

What made the debate between Free Trade and tariffs so passionate, then, was that it was the battleground over a reordering of domestic, imperial, and global relations. Talk of national struggle and organized power blurred the distinctions between politics and markets, between social and international policy, between states and firms. Tariffs not only steered the flow of goods. They were a weapon of international power and imperial consolidation. They provided revenue for state projects. And they could be a tool for ordering society, building social alliances and organizing national strength. In the rest of Europe, the spread of tariffs in the 1880s–1900s had come not only with a shift in commercial policy but with a more corporatist style of politics, organized interest groups, and experiments in social imperialism. Chamberlain's Tariff Reform programme offered a British version of such *Sammlungspolitik*, an alliance of productive forces in industry and labour.[8] For advanced Tariff Reformers, the so-called 'coefficients' around W. A. S. Hewins and Leo Amery, the Empire was the lynchpin of this programme: social stability and political power alike hinged on creating a new solidarity of imperial interests. Tariffs, in this view, were not a return to old-fashioned mercantilism: they were modern instruments of a new 'constructive imperialism'.

The debate about Free Trade, however, was not a simple choice between embracing globalization or fleeing from it. In this earlier moment of globalization, as in today's, the battle lines were rarely that simple. Supporters and critics of Free Trade do not conveniently map onto cosmopolitanism versus imperialism. An imperial Zollverein and Free Trade internationalism were merely two poles on a broad spectrum of opinion. Empire and Free Trade were never mutually exclusive. Cobdenite internationalism was challenged from several quarters, including liberal imperialists. Many groups in the British state, business community, and labour movement came to see Free Trade as a straitjacket. Approaches to international relations were no straightforward reflection of material interests—far from it. They were also shaped by a sense of state power, imperial trust, and international ethics.

In Search of a Revolver

'Canada is the greatest, the most prosperous, of our self-governing colonies', Chamberlain proclaimed in his great speech at Birmingham on 15 May 1903, which launched the Tariff Reform crusade. Canada may have been the 'most backward' when it came to contributing to imperial defence—Laurier had declined to share the costs of imperial wars at the

1902 Colonial Conference—but, Chamberlain claimed, it has been 'the most forward in endeavouring to unite the Empire ... by strengthening our commercial relations'.[9] In fact, Canada showed how Britain's mission to spread Free Trade across the world had been a failure even within her own colonies. While Britain and her protectorates and non-white colonies were a free trade zone, the self-governing colonies like Canada and Australia were strongly protectionist. Canada's tariff in 1858 had already raised duties to over 20 per cent on British manufactures. The Fielding tariff in 1897 raised duties further, especially on cotton and leather goods. Here was a classic case of protection being used as a shelter for infant industries. At the same time, Canada combined harsh protectionist realities with a nod towards imperial patriotism. In 1898 she gave imports from the mother country preferential treatment of 25 per cent. In 1900 this was raised to 33.33 per cent.

From an economic point of view, the gains were minimal. But politically it was an explosive step that opened a Pandora's box of questions about Britain's international and imperial trade system. For Canada's favour to Britain was a violation of Britain's most-favoured-nation treaty with Germany. Unable to convince Canada to reconsider, the Salisbury government was forced to withdraw from the commercial treaty with Germany. Germany, after a series of protests about being deprived of the right to equal treatment in Canadian markets, retaliated against Canadian exports. Canada, in turn, hit back with an extra penalty, an additional surtax on German goods. Germany made it clear that it would suspend most-favoured-nation treatment to any other colony that was to follow Canada's example. Without any aggression on its part, Free Trade Britain faced the prospect of a tariff war spreading through the Empire.

The Canadian–German tariff war captured the tension between Free Trade and empire in a nutshell. To think of empire as a family, whose strength and survival depended on its organic unity, was to deny that its members had an existence as separate countries with separate commercial policies. Canada's generosity, Chamberlain insisted, 'was a matter of family arrangement, concerning nobody else. But, unfortunately Germany thinks otherwise.'[10] Legally, Germany was right, as British experts recognized. The British commercial treaty with Prussia and the German Zollverein in 1865 had clearly stated that all stipulations concerning most-favoured-nation treatment also extended to British colonies.[11] What was worse, and this was what Chamberlain failed to fully appreciate, Canada's forward policy in commercial affairs signalled her own ambitions for national development and sovereignty. Canada and the United Kingdom had always insisted that they were autonomous in fiscal matters, with their own customs systems. Canada's preference may have been a generous recognition of imperial sentiment, but it was also one step in the direction of greater autonomy for the Dominions that took off with Canada's 'National Policy' in 1876. 'Canada is for the Canadians', in Macdonald's phrase, sat uneasily with an ideal of an imperial family composed of a metropolitan patriarch and colonial children. Indeed, from the British government's point of view, one problem with the Canadian–German dispute was precisely that Canada, rather than working through the Foreign Office, used the opportunity to assert its autonomy and dealt directly with Berlin.

For Britain, Canada's action highlighted a whole series of dilemmas. The future relations between colonies and metropole were in doubt. Chamberlain's insistence on the 'domestic character' of imperial relations was, in part, a response to centrifugal dynamics in the self-governing white settler colonies. Rising tariffs in the Dominions reflected a growing sense of distinct identity and demands for economic self-determination. Why should Canada want a tariff that would close mills in Canada for the benefit of some industrialist in Yorkshire, the Canadian Conservative leader Robert Borden asked in 1902.[12] Then, there was the prospect of Canada falling under the influence of its increasingly powerful neighbour, the United States. Plans for regional reciprocity, a kind of North American trading zone, spelled imperial disintegration. Free Traders pointed out that Canada's preference was an empty gesture since her tariff wall as a whole had been rising, and most of all on manufactured items in which Britain specialized.[13] For imperial reformers, by contrast, the question was not one of immediate benefit but of seizing a historic chance to switch the colonies onto a track of closer imperial union. Plans for a commercial union had been floated at colonial conferences for the last two decades, in vain. Here, at last, was a practical step.

Canada's action certainly put pressure on the Conservative government. Ernest Williams, who a few years before had raised the alarm about a deluge of goods *Made in Germany*, wrote of 'The Sacrifice of Canada', even asserting (wrongly) that Canada had been excluded from most-favoured-nation treatment with the assent of the British government.[14] It was not necessary to be a doomsayer, however, to be swayed by Canada's gesture. In the spring of 1897, Henry Birchenough, active in the silk industry and soon to join the commercial intelligence department at the Board of Trade, publicly rejected fears of Britain's decline as vastly exaggerated. He emphasized her competitiveness in spite of foreign tariffs. Yet by July he wrote of the Canadian preference as marking 'an epoch in the history of development': 'Canada has made the first move; it is for the mother country to meet her at least halfway.'[15] Chamberlain's plan for a preferential treatment of colonial wheat would do this.

The Canadian problem also brought to the fore questions about Britain's commercial policy towards other nations. In the Free Trade system the relationship between foreign commercial policy and imperial relations had effectively been a non-question. Britain did not discriminate between foreign countries and her colonies. The European commercial treaty network of the 1860s, which established the practice of most-favoured-nation treatment, put an end to 'favour for favour' policies. It eliminated the need for state intervention, a considerable bonus in the eyes of Victorian Free Traders deeply suspicious of the feudal and militaristic culture of the state. The most-favoured-nation clause ensured that any favour between two countries would automatically be extended to Britain. That was the theory. The introduction of preferences by protectionist colonies and the use of retaliatory tariffs by foreign countries pointed to a different reality. Canadian farmers and fishermen were being punished by a rival great power while other colonies were warned to think twice before turning imperial sentiment into commercial preference. Could a British government afford to sit silently along the sidelines?

At the Foreign Office, Salisbury's eldest son Cranborne recognized the danger. It might 'be thought in the Colonies that we hardly rise to the patriotic occasion', he noted in 1901. Perhaps it was time to be more assertive. 'I understand Germany is much afraid of the possibility of a British Zollverein', Cranborne told Lansdowne, the Foreign Secretary. Germany might be warned 'not to press us too far by refusing to recognise the domestic character of our fiscal arrangements with our Colonies'. That was 'the larger question ... no doubt to be faced', Lansdowne agreed, but not quite yet.[16]

The conflict between Canada and Germany crystallized more general doubts about the inadequacy of the mid-Victorian settlement. The 1865 treaty with Germany was a result of 'Manchester delusions' at their peak, and completely out of touch with the new demands of a 'United Empire', Birchenough wrote. 'We are too hesitating, too timid in our commercial policy. We cling to the protection of treaties, as if we had no weapons of our own to fight with.'[17] What good were treaties that were obstacles to imperial consolidation? And did the most-favoured-nation treatment policy really secure Britain's commercial and imperial interests?

Trade never takes place on a level playing field. Participants arrive with different degrees of power. The degree to which Free Trade is an imperialist strategy has been a subject of long-standing debate. How 'free' was Free Trade really? In the mid-nineteenth century, there had been a widespread critique of Free Trade for favouring powerful advanced societies like Britain over those seeking to catch up, a critique popularized by the national liberal economist Friedrich List. Far from free or equal, freedom of trade disguised the inequalities of wealth and power at play. Free Trade could be portrayed as an instrument of imperialism by other means. It forced open markets, allowing more developed British industries and financial interests to drive out less developed, indigenous competitors. Already during the first Opium War in the early 1840s, Chartists had attacked the Anti-Corn Law League for standing for Free Trade by peace if possible, by force if necessary. This argument would be revitalized in the mid-twentieth century at a time of colonial struggles for independence and American super-power. Britain, in Robinson and Gallagher's famous account, did not swing from an anti-imperialist Free Trade project in the mid-Victorian period to an imperialist programme in the late Victorian period. Rather imperialism was a continuum, merely changing its *modus operandum* from informal to formal means.[18]

Few historians today fail to recognize the strength of imperial culture and expansion in the mid-nineteenth century, in places from New Zealand and Hong Kong to Natal and the Punjab. Free Trade and imperial power could be symbiotic, especially in the early Victorian period. Manchester supported an imperial policy of developing India through public works and communication.[19] John Bowring led a one-man foreign PR campaign for Free Trade in the 1830s–50s from Europe to China and did not hesitate to call for imperial force to put the higher 'civil' idea into practice. A Unitarian, friend of Bentham, and autodidact, who had taught himself a dozen languages, it was Bowring who was in Karl Marx's line of fire in 1849 as a 'shameless hypocrite' for publicly exclaiming that ' "Jesus Christ is Free Trade, and Free Trade is Jesus Christ" '. Bowring did not want territorial dominion—Britain had to avoid Rome's error. But he called in the navy in 1855 nonetheless, to enforce the commercial opening of China.

Britain needed to ' "strike boldly at the head,—the heart,—and not trifle merely with the extremities of these great empires" ' in China and Japan. ' "We have been trifled with—,—tantalised too long." '[20]

More generally, however, the 'imperialism of Free Trade', remains open to question. Measuring 'informal' imperial power has proved difficult. In the mid-nineteenth century, in areas like Latin America, the Levant, and China, British merchants and industry found it difficult to establish a foothold, let alone dominate. Most of these areas had little to offer by way of a profitable return trade, and (outside cotton) indigenous craftsmen and producers remained surprisingly strong. The idea that Britain was able 'to command those economies which could be made to fit best into her own' through a combination of commercial penetration and political influence is debatable.[21] Until the 1870s investors, manufacturers, and merchants were largely indifferent to distant markets, and businessmen and state alike accepted the limited role of government intervention.[22]

The thesis of Free Trade imperialism is equally problematic for the late nineteenth century. Analogies between the British Empire and the United States post-1945 can be misleading. America secured its global influence through international institutions and multilateral agreements (Bretton Woods, GATT). It was also a 'market empire' in which state, civil society, and business were working together to export a civic ideal of a dynamic, classless consumer society.[23] Free Trade, Victorian style, was a very different beast. From the mid-nineteenth century British Free Traders prided themselves on their unilateralism. International institutions that might have forced freedom of trade on less developed societies were actively resisted. The tariff-reducing momentum of the 1860s was the result of bilateral treaties extending most-favoured-nation treatment to third parties. For Cobden and Gladstone the loss of bargaining power in foreign affairs that came with this regime was one of its principal attractions: it avoided huckstering and interference.[24] In the Foreign Office, unilateral Free Trade was also considered to have the distinct advantage of 'soft power': it made foreign powers less apprehensive of British supremacy than if they faced the hard force of protectionism, as Eyre Crowe stressed in his 1907 Foreign Office memorandum.[25]

In fact, Britain might well have benefited from a more aggressive use of its economic clout to secure better conditions of trade, especially in the mid-nineteenth century when its industrial supremacy was unrivalled.[26] Arguably, too, Britain's refusal to play an active role in the commercial treaty system during the Great Depression in the 1870s–80s was one reason for the rise of tariffs.[27] Britain refused to act as a 'hegemon', using its power to provide free exchange as one of the 'public goods' for a liberal international order. It counted on other nations driving down trade barriers in negotiations with each other and then extending them to the rest of the world via the most-favoured-nation clause. The 1870s–1900s revealed this as a serious miscalculation. The virtuous circle in which the most-favoured-nation clause extended the benefits of bilateral negotiations to the rest of the world turned into a vicious cycle of higher trade barriers as foreign nations progressively adopted 'beggar-thy-neighbour' strategies. The Russian and Italian tariffs of 1877 and 1878 were followed by rising protection in Germany (1879, 1887, 1902), France (1882, 1892), and the United States (1890, 1897). In addition to the German–Canadian tariff spat, there were major tariff wars in Europe, especially those between Germany and Russia (1892–4) and France and Italy (1887–98).

If the test of informal power is the capacity to get your way without having to use force, Free Trade Britain failed the test. 'Open door' treaties with several developing countries in Latin America, China, and Turkey often required military pressure. Britain could do little to strip its main trading partners and geo-political rivals in the late nineteenth century of their neo-mercantilist strategies. Trade was, indeed, not a level playing field, but it was increasingly Britain which was finding itself at the lower end. And, from the 1890s, the naval supremacy which had supported Britain's Free Trade empire was being threatened by foreign gunboats and submarines.

The conflict between Canada and Germany left a sense in the Colonial Office that the 'days of simple m-f-n treatment treaties seem to be doomed, though they die hard'.[28] The Foreign Office, too, began to reassess its traditional approach. In 1900, the head of the Foreign Office's commercial department, H. G. Bergne, highlighted how 'it is becoming more and more difficult to conclude satisfactory Commercial Treaties with foreign countries'.[29] There were three clusters of problems. For one, it had become difficult to come to arrangements that suited both Free Trade Britain and her protectionist colonies. Then, there was the problem that Free Trade paralysed Britain at the bargaining table, leaving her unable to retaliate or to offer concessions.

Above all, there was the proliferation of tariffs and non-tariff barriers. The problem was no longer just their height. Germany, France, and other powers introduced complex discriminatory schemes. So-called minimum and maximum tariffs made it possible to reward friend and punish foe by placing different articles in different tariff brackets. They combined a protectionist tariff with a bargaining tariff. The dilemma for Britain was that countries engaged in tariff negotiations focused on those goods that they exported themselves, goods that might play little part in British exports. As the Foreign Office realized, 'even if Great Britain gets nominal most-favoured-nation treatment, it is often not so in reality, as the incidence of duties is so fixed as to favour the particular commodities exported by countries other than Great Britain'.[30]

Export bounties posed a second threat. The classic Free Trade position was that these were costly and counterproductive for the countries that used them, diminishing the gains from an international division of labour and overall efficiency and growth—in the long run, such policies were bound to fail since they were based on 'the negation of economic laws', as the Treasury put it.[31] From the perspective of the Foreign Office, however, this was a liberal delusion. 'Unsound as the system of bounties and protection may be in theory', Bergne concluded, 'it is impossible to ignore the fact that several states are gradually by these means acquiring a commercial supremacy of very great extent.' The United States was surpassing Britain in iron and steel. Russia, too, was progressing. Germany was on the brink of becoming the greatest manufacturing country in Europe; some of her steamship lines were already bigger than Britain's. Britain's excess of imports and her poor performance in industrial exports 'cannot be viewed without some apprehension as to our future prosperity as a manufacturing State'.[32]

Anxieties about being shut out of European markets were reinforced by the emergence of a new imperial power overseas, the United States. In May and June 1900, two years after defeating Spain, the United States introduced preferential tariffs in its new possessions of Cuba and Puerto Rico. Hawaii was incorporated as a customs district, and the Philippines appeared the next target of American mercantilism. The United States' colonial policy was a blow to British shipping interests; the carrying trade between Puerto Rico and the United States was reserved for American ships. And in Cuba, Britain was rapidly losing ground to its European competitors. In the second half of the 1890s, Cuban imports from Britain and her colonies increased by only 5.2 per cent, compared to 150 per cent from France and 122 per cent from Germany. 'I do not know any more discouraging figures than these, to British pride, nor ... a more pessimistic view of our progress now and in the future in the internecine strife of commerce which is going on in the world', the head of the Board of Customs told the Foreign Office.[33]

Cuba, moreover, occupied an important position in imperial trade. The Liverpool Indian rice trade to Cuba was 'the backbone of the whole rice trade, and had done more than anything else to develop Burmah', Lansdowne told the Cabinet.[34] A reciprocity treaty between the United States and Cuba would be felt as far away as Calcutta and Rangoon. Liverpool feared for its steamship service, which every year carried about 150,000 tons of freight to Cuba. British exports of machinery and sugar bags were equally threatened. The chambers of commerce of Liverpool, London, Manchester, Glasgow, and Sheffield warned the British government that without action the bulk of their trade would be lost. When the feared reciprocity treaty came into effect in 1903, the British West Indies were especially hard hit, shut out from the American sugar market.

Free Trade was impotent. 'Great Britain can expostulate' as much as she liked, but, Lansdowne emphasized, 'expostulations without the power of doing something serve no useful purpose'.[35] American policy was particularly irritating because it undermined the entire most-favoured-nation clause system. Unlike Britain, the United States preferred a conditional version of mfn treatment. Instead of extending all benefits negotiated to the rest of the world, the mfn clause American style was about reciprocity: it limited favours to the negotiating partners directly involved. If two countries negotiated a certain concession, the mfn clause only extended that concession to third countries if they offered equivalent concessions in turn. And either party also retained the right to object to the other lowering duties to a third country. In other words, under the US–Cuban reciprocity treaty, even if Cuba had wanted to lower trade barriers on British goods, it could have been penalized by the United States. US policy, therefore, involved 'grave questions of principle', the Board of Trade recognized.[36] It set a dangerous precedent, not least for Canada, which was suspected of falling under the spell of the US version of the mfn clause. The Americas were moving towards a commercial system of their own; in 1904 the United States was granted preferential treatment by Brazil, with which Britain did not even have a commercial treaty.[37]

The Cuban case showed how a more combative spirit was gaining ground in Britain as well. Calls for negotiation and retaliation were growing within the state and the business community. At the Board of Trade, even a progressive liberal like Hubert Llewellyn Smith felt his way towards a more assertive policy. When in January 1904 the President of Cuba was authorized to increase existing tariff rates by another 30 per cent, the Board of Trade urged the Foreign Secretary to make use of the few weapons Britain had at its disposal: threatening to raise customs duties on fine tobacco and cigars.[38]

The transformation of the global trading system in the late nineteenth century, then, does not easily fit the 'imperialism of Free Trade' thesis. Within the British state—in the Foreign Office and the Board of Trade as well as in the Colonial Office—the recognition grew that unilateral Free Trade did little to make other countries offer Britain concessions in return for free access to the largest market in the world. Few became converts to genuine protectionism. But questions of trade policy encouraged a reassessment of the role of the state. Trade negotiations were intimately tied to customs duties and thus to revenue. Should the state preserve its autonomy and neutrality by limiting taxation to revenue purposes only? Or should it be allowed to use and adjust taxes to gain concessions for its subjects in foreign markets? Under Gladstone, unilateral Free Trade had helped seal a new social contract between government and people around a self-limiting state. After Gladstone, this remained the dominant view in the Treasury. Other departments of state, however, began to question this self-denying ordinance.

The dilemma for the British state was perhaps nowhere more apparent than in the case of smaller, lesser powers, like Spain and Portugal, which did not even grant Britain most-favoured-nation treatment. In 1891 the convention between Spain and Britain lapsed. A new minimum–maximum tariff went into effect, raising duties on some goods by 200 per cent. The following three years exposed the rifts in the British state. Britain's wine duties provided a potential weapon to force Spain to lower her trade barriers. The Foreign Office asked the Treasury whether the wine duties might be lowered if Spain lowered her duties in return. The Treasury refused. The Foreign Office then asked the Treasury to back a threat to raise the duties. They declined. Finally, the Foreign Office asked for a promise not to raise the duties in the future. Again, the Treasury rejected the idea. The Treasury's absolute stance was helped by division within the Board of Trade. Here some members supported tariff treaties as more effective than the conventional most-favoured-nation policy. But Robert Giffen, the head of the Board of Trade and a fervent Free Trader, would have none of it. He joined with the Treasury in a policy of 'no surrender': tariff bargains were 'a commercial sin'. Eventually, the Board of Trade agreed to use the threat of higher wine duties, but the Treasury remained adamant in its refusal. In the end, in 1894, Britain only managed to obtain a *modus vivendi* which granted temporary mfn treatment, but failed to lower Spain's tariff.[39]

Relations with Portugal were, if anything, more frustrating. Portugal had renounced its commercial treaty with Britain in 1892. Since then, Britain was not only without a formal most-favoured-nation arrangement. Portugal levied higher duties on some British imports than on her competitors. When Giffen retired in 1897, the Board of Trade now joined the Foreign Office in calls for a tougher attitude. It was not possible to be pushed around by Portugal. Portugal's demand for preferential treatment—it asked Britain to lower her wine duties, if she wanted mfn treatment—was outrageous. To be fair, Portugal was uniquely affected by Britain's particularly high customs duties on strong wines and ports—a concession from Liberals to their temperance supporters. It was a classic case of a seemingly impartial duty that in fact discriminated against a particular country of origin; such hidden barriers to trade have been struck down repeatedly by the European Union in recent years. The official line at the time, however, was that Britain had an 'equitable claim' to mfn treatment in exchange for her policy of Free Trade. It was 'not their practice to pay for such treatment' by offering additional, specific concessions. But the Board of Trade was nonetheless willing to revise the wine duties in exchange for Portugal lowering her duties on British manufactures. Britain was Portugal's best customer. The wine trade depended on British drinkers. It should have been possible to come to an agreement.[40] Again, it was the Treasury which fought such negotiations tooth and nail. To give the Board of Trade 'exercise of their talents for negotiation' was dangerous. Chamberlain's Tariff Reform challenge only encouraged the Treasury to hold the line in the winter of 1905–6. By turning the Free Trade system to retaliatory use, Hamilton reminded Asquith, the Chancellor of the Exchequer in the new Liberal government: 'we lay ourselves open to the retort from Tariff Reformers of "how much better off you would be if you had more duties to retaliate with than you have now"!'[41]

These attempts at a more active commercial policy were part of a more general rapprochement between state and business. While formally the official mind remained opposed to intervention on behalf of particular businesses, the state began to expand its capacity for intelligence and development. The new infrastructure stretched the very framework of Free Trade. With Chamberlain at the Colonial Office, the state became more directly involved in developing its colonial estates, with the help of public funds and projects like the Uganda railway. Under the Cobdenite treaty network, commercial intelligence had been all but abandoned; by the early 1870s the commercial department of the Board of Trade consisted of one assistant secretary and four clerks who did not even have a full day's work.[42] The 1890s brought a reversal of this trend. Commercial intelligence was rationalized, in part due to pressure from leading Chambers of Commerce like Manchester. The borders between state and commerce became more porous.

In May 1900 a new Advisory Committee on Commercial Intelligence was set up at the Board of Trade, bringing together business leaders and members of state departments. Trade commissioners and commercial attaches were investigating the strength (and often weakness) of British trade in foreign and imperial markets. Unlike rival great powers, the British state did not actively promote trade, nor did most traders want a genuinely interventionist state. And many of these initiatives revealed the haphazard, uninformed, or passive approach to the world of commerce among consular staff overseas. But the Advisory Committee provided a new umbrella for the world of business, the Board of Trade and Foreign Office. It was a clearing house for information. More than that, it was a place for the discussion of trade policy and an outlet for interests and grievances. Commercial intelligence about foreign tariff schemes was passed confidentially to Chambers of Commerce. In exchange, Chambers of Commerce voiced their anxieties about 'unfair' treatment, foreign tariffs and subsidies, and the risk to local industries.

The appointment of the Advisory Committee was in itself an attempt to outflank more ambitious demands from the business community for a departmental committee to renegotiate commercial treaties.[43] In April 1900, the Association of Chambers of Commerce had contemplated the denunciation of some treaties. Calls for 'fair trade' had been heard from sections of the business community since the late 1870s. The spread of min–max tariffs and tariff wars since then had considerably heightened sensibilities. The world economy had become like a billiard game. Bargaining tariffs created a dynamic where one country's tariff increases set off a whole series of tariff rises. All eyes were on the imminent new German tariff; commercial intelligence in 1901 warned that it threatened to increase duties from 25 per cent to 100 per cent, and would further subdivide tariff schedules from 900 to 1,400 heads. At their annual meeting in September 1901, and notwithstanding the presidency of Lord Avebury, the Free Trade banker, the Associated Chambers of Commerce urged the Foreign Secretary to do more to make the German government reduce its tariff. Talk of a tariff war was in the air.[44]

Trades particularly affected by rising continental trade barriers—like iron and steel, wool, and machinery—were alarmed and reluctant to rely any longer on the bargaining power of other countries to attain reductions for British exports. The punitively high Swiss and Romanian tariffs of 1904, for example, were a direct response to the German tariff. Many Chambers complained that their exports would be badly hit. Free Trade had failed them: official protests were useless unless the government could back them up 'by holding out the prospect either of concessions or reprisals'.[45]

As Chamberlain and the Tariff Reform commission would learn, most trades were divided, politically as well as economically; genuine support for comprehensive protectionism remained muted outside certain key strongholds, like the metal industries of the Midlands, Chamberlain's base. Some Chambers, led by Manchester, remained largely loyal to Cobdenism. Others, like Glasgow and Oldham, felt that lobbying within foreign countries was likely to be more effective than external diplomatic pressure.[46] But opposition to Tariff Reform was not necessarily support for Free Trade. There were only two Chambers (Manchester and Newcastle) in clear favour of Free Trade. The majority were feeling their way towards reciprocity, bargaining, and retaliation. The London Chamber of Commerce reflected the new current. Some, like the Liberal Unionist Avebury, would only accept retaliation as a legitimate last resort 'provided it would be effective'. The dominant line was tougher. J. Innes Rogers, the London Chamber's chairman, maintained that the mfn clause was 'not an equitable return' for Britain's open market and urged the government to negotiate 'special Tariff Conventions'.[47] Even in Manchester, cracks were appearing in the Cobdenite consensus. The Bleachers' Association, one of the four largest textile amalgamations in Britain, urged the government to consider retaliation if Portugal continued to turn a deaf ear to quiet diplomacy.[48]

This shift in opinion, away from a unilateral open door towards some kind of *quid pro quo*, was not confined to particular sectors or regions. Most Chambers and trades (even individual firms) were internally divided, and by 1903 were increasingly swaying towards retaliation. Ideas of an underlying divide between City and Industry, or between internationally oriented Free Trade sectors and domestically oriented protectionists, have been exposed as myths.[49] Both finance and industry were fluid and amorphous, economically, socially, and culturally; Arthur Keen, for example, who supported tariffs, both had a major interest in iron and steel and was chairman of the London, City and Midland bank. Few British trades benefited as much from an open world economy as shipping, and, indeed, with the exception of Alfred Jones, shipping remained opposed to Tariff Reform. At the same time, even here Free Trade pure was being diluted by mercantilist sentiment. The United States had extended its coastal laws to define trips from New York around Cape Horn to San Francisco as coastal voyages to be conducted in American ships only. The Chamber of Shipping appealed to the Foreign Office to prevent British shipping from being 'gradually shut out from the trade of one half of the world'. British coastal and inter-imperial trade should become the monopoly of imperial tonnage.[50] Even in cotton, the export industry *par excellence*, there was probably one fiscal reformer for every two Free Traders.[51]

The City, too, was divided. There were those, like Felix Schuster of the Union Bank, a leading clearing-banker with a strong role in transatlantic finance, who felt that for banking the defence of Free Trade was a matter of life and death. But next to the Schusters and Aveburys, there were prominent merchant bankers such as Eric Hambro and Herbert Gibbs who rather liked a modest tariff as a step towards a lower income tax. The stock-broker Faithfull Begg warned that under Free Trade Britain was creating commercial rivals who eventually 'would be attacking her with their ships and destroying her commerce'.[52] The chairman of Martin's Bank, too, wondered whether in a world of trade barriers the future of London as the centre of the global money market did not eventually depend on Britain's industrial strength and its ability to control foreign tariffs.

Overall, Chamberlain's plans for a general tariff went too far for most in the City. But as George Sandeman, a former deputy-governor at the Bank of England, put it succinctly in 1903 'many were free traders who were not free importers'.[53] Letting foreign goods enter the home market freely did not stop British goods being shut out of foreign markets. Retaliation could be justified as a step towards freer trade. There was considerable support for a mild version of fiscal reform, a mix of a bargaining and revenue tariff, favoured by Balfour, who became an MP for the City in 1906. Lloyd George's 'socialist budget' in 1909 made a revenue tariff even more palatable in the City.

The main reason for these internal divisions was politics: trade policy went to the core of political identities and allegiances. Political milieus shaped the sense of economic interest, rather than the other way around. This was partly a matter of party loyalty but it also expressed broader beliefs about international relations. Might carrots and sticks reopen markets and establish a more level playing field for British traders? Or would retaliation end in tariff wars abroad and political corruption at home?

However futile in the end, demands for bargaining and retaliation show that there was a growing momentum in the state and business community towards reforming the Free Trade system. It was against this background that Balfour and Lansdowne began to move towards reciprocity. Attempts to redefine Free Trade to no longer mean free imports were more than just verbal acrobatics, a 'philosopher's romance' and 'farce', as Chamberlain cynically put it.[54] Reciprocity was neither just a reaction to Chamberlain's challenge nor simply a high political strategy by Balfour to retain control in the Cabinet crisis of 1903.[55] Calls for a new trade policy had a logic of their own, as leading statesmen, businessmen, and civil servants tried to come to terms with the changing world around them. Free Trade began to feel like a straitjacket.

The Foreign Office view was put clearly to cabinet in June 1901. They saw the 'necessity of modifying our fiscal policy so far as to admit the principal of retaliation'. Free Trade had made Britain 'powerless' in the face of Germany's punishment of Canada. It threatened Britain's imperial and global position more generally. Without a change in policy, Britain would have to discourage Australia or any other colony from giving imperial preferences—'it would be the greatest national blunder since we lost America', Cranborne warned. Then there were imperial rivals like France which simply ignored mfn principles and subjected virtually all British colonies to a maximum tariff. Again, 'we are impotent to help our Colonies, and in the case of Crown Colonies our acquiescence in this treatment is almost in the nature of a breach of trust, as well as a danger to our Imperial position'. Foreign industrial trusts, too, were becoming a danger to British industries and colonial producers. The Treasury dismissed trusts and cartels as costly mistakes, doomed to collapse under their own weight. But the Board of Trade took a more pragmatic view. Trusts were neither inherently bad nor good. They were permanent fixtures in modern capitalism to which governments had to respond. Retaliation could put a stop to orchestrated 'dumping' policies. Even American trusts, the Foreign Office mused, would not be 'rich enough to defy retaliation ... if the whole British Empire could be induced to retaliate together'.[56]

In government, Prime Minister Balfour and his brother Gerald, the President of the Board of Trade, led the campaign for retaliation against 'unfair' competition. Gerald Balfour devised a plan for a 5–10 per cent industrial tariff—enough to allow powers of bargaining and defeat dumping, too little to offer protective shelter. This, he admitted, would leave Britain 'comparatively helpless' to deal with the United States and Russia, which mainly exported food and raw materials. In the case of Germany, Belgium, and Italy, on the other hand, it would provide a lever to gain concessions for British exports. The mfn clause would be amended, to allow both for imperial preferences and for the use of measures to counteract foreign subsidies or bounties, so-called countervailing duties. Even the prospect of a tariff war became acceptable: 'we must be prepared to retaliate [and] ... hit as hard as we can with the least damage to ourselves'. Britain, in this view, had fighting strength as long as a low revenue tariff was complemented with the power to impose prohibitively high duties on select key imports.[57]

Retaliation was attractive because it promised to increase state power without sacrificing state autonomy. There would be no vested interests—it was a strategic weapon that would not afford long-term protection. Retaliation could also be tied to a low revenue tariff that would help fund the rapidly rising costs of war and defence.[58] And it complemented a shift in Britain's overall foreign policy.

The swing in opinion away from unilateral Free Trade to reciprocal trade diplomacy coincided with a major transition from a policy of 'splendid isolation' to one of foreign alliances. From 1901 Lansdowne steered foreign policy away from Salisbury's dislike of alliances. And, significantly, it was the Foreign Secretary who also emerged as an ardent advocate of tariff negotiations. In 1902 Lansdowne had concluded a settlement with the United States and an Anglo-Japanese alliance, after plans for an alliance with Germany had failed. Alliances would preserve Britain's naval power, new trade treaties defend her commercial power.

The Canadian–German tariff drama whetted Lansdowne's appetite for new agreements. The Foreign Office had already called the bluff of the German government, which had initially threatened to withhold mfn treatment to Great Britain herself if other colonies followed Canada's example. The threat of retaliation did the trick.[59] Lansdowne knew that the British market was far more important to Germany than vice versa. This was the background to Lansdowne's open call in the House of Lords on 15 June 1903 for arming the government with 'a revolver'. The world was not a peaceful marketplace. It was like the Wild West:

> We seem to be in the position of a man who in some lawless country entered a room in which every one else was armed with a revolver in his pocket; the man without a revolver is not likely to be very considerately treated. If we take the opportunity of supplying ourselves with a revolver, and let it be seen by everybody that … it is a rather larger revolver than everybody else's, my own impression is that we shall find ourselves carefully let alone.[60]

Britain's big market was a big weapon. Part of this speech was for internal party consumption. But part of it was also directed at audiences abroad.

Lansdowne knew that Germany was ready to negotiate a new commercial treaty with Britain. He even took the initiative, without authorization from Cabinet, to raise this possibility with the German ambassador.[61] The German commercial treaties with Russia, Italy, Austria, Switzerland, and Belgium could all be denounced at twelve months' notice, and these countries had been preparing 'tarifs de combat' to brace themselves for this scenario. Free Trade and mfn clauses would not serve British interests if tariffs went up all round. 'Speaking generally,' he told colleagues, 'we should be safer with commercial treaties of our own than under the most-favoured-nation clause.' It was the right moment for a forward policy. To achieve concessions, Britain could threaten retaliation, promise a reduction of existing duties, or offer a guarantee to not raise duties in the immediate future. Given foreign countries' dependence on the British market, even the last measure should yield results, Lansdowne believed. France, for example, sent Britain silks, gloves, and fancy goods worth £14 million a year, all free of duty. French wines, meanwhile, were facing competition from other countries. A British offer of a slight reduction of duties on French wines, Lansdowne felt, should 'certainly bring about the desired result' of inducing France to lower its duties on British textiles.[62]

Lansdowne's instincts about Britain's relative position of strength were not off the mark. The German government was fully aware of the importance of the British market and of the growing support for retaliation which came with anti-German sentiment. In 1902 German exports to Britain were worth 958 million Marks, almost twice its imports from Britain. If 'our relations worsened or if we entered a tariff war,' the German ambassador, Metternich, concluded, 'we would lose more than Britain'. Count von Bülow, the German Chancellor, agreed.[63] Even Conservative ministers who supported retaliation, however, were not prepared to let Lansdowne overhaul British trade policy without an election. In an age of advancing democratic expectations, it would be political suicide for the executive to introduce such a major policy shift without a popular mandate. Such a mandate, moreover, would put more bullets into Britain's revolver.[64] The defeat of the Balfour government in 1905 and the on-going ideological polarization into rival Tariff Reform and Free Trade camps meant that—with the exception of a treaty with Roumania—plans for commercial negotiations fell victim to history.

Sweet Power

Retaliation was not just a strategy of an 'eye for an eye'. It involved fundamental questions of principle, about the true meaning of Free Trade, about global governance, state sovereignty, and how to balance the interests of consumers and producers. It was sugar which crystallized these larger questions, questions which continue to haunt today's champions of 'fair trade' versus 'free trade'. Was true freedom of trade about laissez-faire and non-interference, even if that meant the import of goods artificially cheapened by subsidies or bounties? Or did it permit interference to create fairer market conditions and protect the weak against the strong?

Sugar underwent an unprecedented transformation during the course of the nineteenth century. At the beginning of the century, sugar was a tropical product. By the end, tropical cane sugar had been overtaken by beet sugar. There were already some three hundred beet sugar factories in Europe at the end of the Napoleonic wars, but the big shift came in the last quarter of the nineteenth century, as temperate countries led by Russia, Austria-Hungary, and Germany expanded their sugar production with an ever more elaborate system of subsidies and export bounties. A mere

8 per cent of world production in 1840, beet sugar made up 65 per cent
of the world's sugar in 1900. And, increasingly, most of it was for export;
in 1870 only 26 per cent of German beet sugar was exported, by 1900,
61 per cent.[65] It was a historic moment in the globalization of food—'the
first important seizure by temperate agriculture of what were previously
the productive capacities of a tropical region.'[66] It also mounted a historic
challenge to the liberal Free Trade system.

The classic argument for Free Trade, made by enlightenment thinkers
and popularized in the Victorian period, was that it made the best of the
diverse endowments of the world by encouraging the most efficient use of
each country's particular resources. Arguably, there were few places better
suited by nature to produce cheap and plentiful sugar than the West Indies.
Yet in the 1870s–90s tropical cane sugar producers were struggling for
survival. With the help of subsidies and export incentives, beet sugar had
grown into a powerful industrial rival, driving down world prices. There
was a glut of artificially cheapened sugar. In the 1890s the price of unrefined
sugar fell by over 20 per cent, that of refined sugar by 30 per cent. By
1900 consumers were able to buy five times as much sugar for what it had
cost them in 1841. In the tropics, the large producing islands like Barbados
and Jamaica were particularly hard hit. Here good soil and cheap labour
had discouraged mechanization—central mills and factories only became
widespread after the First World War. In the 1890s Jamaica and Trinidad
suffered a 60 per cent drop in exports.[67]

The diverging fortunes of cane sugar and beet sugar came to symbolize
rival systems of trade. Instead of nurturing development, wealth, and
efficiency, critics argued, Britain's version of Free Trade had permitted
ruinous over-production and social dislocation. Caribbean producers were
collapsing while beet sugar was thriving with the support of states and
powerful cartels. Central European governments supported beet sugar in
order to prop up rural elites and counteract migration from country to
city. At first, it had also been a welcome additional source of tax revenue.
This changed with the increasingly aggressive use of export bounties and
the arrival of cartels of sugar exporters in the 1890s. 'Natural' market
competition disappeared from the world sugar trade. British consumers
were the principal beneficiaries of this export bounty system. Their sugar
consumption doubled between 1860 and 1900. More than 80 per cent
of Britain's sugar imports now came in the form of beet sugar, with 65
per cent coming from Germany alone.[68] Some of it found its way into

the manufacture of jam, sweets, and drink, but two-thirds was for private consumption. The question was not only what these bountied exports did to producers in the colonies and to imperial merchants and sugar barons, but also what the long-term impact of overproduction and dumping would be for consumers and industrial users of sugar. Once beet sugar cartels had driven Caribbean competitors into bankruptcy, would they not then exercise their monopoly power and drive up prices?

Sugar 'furnishes a complete object-lesson of the fallacies which underlie some of our most cherished economic theories, and of the injuries which may be inflicted on consumers as well as on producers by any device which destroys freedom of competition', argued George Martineau, a passionate critic of the bounty system and spokesman for West Indian planters.[69] Liberal Free Traders countered that the benefits from cheap sugar to British sweet manufacturers outweighed the costs to imperial planters. The challenge, however, went much further. The bounty system encouraged gluts, price fluctuations, and, above all, cartels. It could be seen as symptomatic of a new world order, in which organized capitalism broke down the natural divide between state and market, and between domestic and international affairs, challenging national sovereignty. Perhaps export cartels were more than just the problem of the country where they were based. The search began for a new, more active role for the state in global governance. And in that search, Britain's willingness to modify its Free Trade system would be decisive.

International attempts to reform the bounty system had a history almost as long as that of the sugar subsidies themselves. A first abortive convention was held in 1864. It was followed twenty-five years later by the London Convention, which agreed to a 'penal clause' but collapsed when the House of Commons failed to support it. Britain was by far the world's largest sugar consumer, and any international attempt to eliminate bounties and subsidies was bound to fail as long as Britain kept its doors open to artificially cheapened sugar. Committed Free Traders fought such international conventions tooth and nail in the 1880s. In the opinion of the government law officers, countervailing duties were an infraction of the mfn clause. To popular Free Traders they were a violation of the people's right to the cheapest goods, irrespective of their origins or mode of production.

Advancing cartelization, rising export bounties, and a global glut began to change political sensibilities in Britain and abroad. Holland and

Belgium were the first to argue that bounties were an international problem that called for an international solution. Even within the Cobden
Club, there were some who leaned towards intervention as a way to
liberalize trade.[70] Within the British state, too, international cooperation
gathered support. Export bounties had spiralled out of control and were
extremely burdensome to beet sugar countries. France and Russia were
sitting on the fence, but most producing countries wanted the bounty
system to end. Yet, as long as Britain was an open market, no producing
country would be foolish enough to abandon its subsidies, the Foreign
Office recognized. Competitors would simply capture the British market
by dumping their own sugar below cost price. If Britain joined an international trade agreement, however, then France and Russia might soon fall
into line.

In 1900 the Association of Chambers of Commerce swung around
from earlier opposition to support prohibiting the import of bountied
sugar. India, with Britain's approval, even imposed differential duties on all
imported bounty-fed sugar. With other countries moving towards more
conditional, reciprocal versions of the mfn clause, it was difficult to see how
countervailing duties by Britain could any longer be seen as an infringement
of the mfn principle. For the Foreign Office, prohibition or countervailing
was 'reasonable and justifiable on the true principles of Free Trade'.[71] The
shift in British opinion had the desired effect: France began to look for a
deal with Germany and Austria-Hungary to slash export bounties.

The successful negotiations that followed and led to the Brussels Sugar
Convention of 1902 showed this new spirit in action. For British ministers,
Brussels was a new international instrument responding to a new world.[72]
Britain joined nine other countries in a pioneering experiment in global
governance. Member states formed a commission to investigate export
bounties and decide on penalties. Of all the main beet sugar producers, only
Russia and Argentina abstained. It was Russia, not any longer the British
government, which rejected Brussels as an interference in internal matters.
For Lansdowne, the negotiations at Brussels demonstrated how much
bargaining power Britain possessed. The British threat of countervailing
duties and, at one stage, possible subsidies to the West Indies, gave the
negotiations much-needed teeth. Austria-Hungary decided to join the
convention rather than lose the British market. A general agreement was
hammered out to phase out export bounties, while Britain agreed to
prohibit the import of subsidized sugar.[73]

On the international stage, the Brussels experiment was a remarkable success. It brought together ten governments with vastly different political and economic systems and enabled them to work harmoniously together; most decisions were unanimous.[74] They created a fairer, more balanced trade environment. The decline of cane sugar and the growing dependence on beet sugar had caused violent price fluctuations by making world markets more vulnerable to poor harvests in regions of beet cultivation. Now prices stabilized. Nor did consumers suffer as alarmist liberals had prophesied. The price of standard sugar in the decade after the Brussels convention was hardly any different from that before—a mere increase from 10s. 1d. to 10s. 5d., below the average increase in world prices in this period. Continental Europeans developed a taste for cheaper sugar that made a return to the bounty system all but impossible politically. Beet sugar producers began to sell more in their own markets and dumped less on the world market. On the eve of the First World War, the entire system of export bounties had been abandoned by all countries but Russia. Brussels also threw a lifeline to Caribbean sugar estates. British imports of cane sugar from her colonies in 1904–10 were 60 per cent greater than immediately prior to the Brussels convention (1897–1903).[75] Total production increased only slightly in the Empire, but at a moment when the reciprocity treaty between the United States and Cuba shut out colonial sugar from that market, the Brussels convention kept open other markets for colonial cane sugar producers.

Yet international success did not translate into domestic popularity. British Free Trade was too dogmatic, even fanatical, for that. From the outset Liberals had spread dark prophecies of higher prices, robbing British consumers of millions of pounds. Most of these contentions were 'either great exaggerations or wholly unsound', as the Board of Trade recognized, based on 'most fallacious and contradictory conclusions ... produced by selective statistics',[76] in other words, exactly what Free Traders accused protectionists of. Still, as we saw earlier, sugar was an especially sensitive commodity on which to experiment with duties. It was widely regarded as one of the 'prime necessaries of life' and it topped the list in radical demands for the 'free breakfast table'. Sugar was the 'most essential among the articles of food of our people', Herbert Gladstone told audiences: the Brussels Convention put the British people at the mercy of foreign speculators.[77] It would disproportionately hurt consuming industries like the confectionery industry. And it would not even help people in the colonies. It merely subordinated the interests of British consumers to those of West Indian planters, who have 'the tradition of the old slave drivers', according to the radical newspaper *Reynolds's*.

British Free Trade was commercially internationalist but politically isolationist. It was the polar opposite of the post-1945 era associated with American free trade, with its international agreements and organizations. In spite of the imperialist civilizing fervour of many Victorian Liberals, British Free Trade never spawned a similar mission to export its way of life; this was left to civil society and small international networks of Cobdenites. Change had to come from within societies, not from without. To Liberal MPs, by joining Brussels Britain was trying to shield protectionist countries from the results of their own stupidity. They should be left to learn from their own mistakes. Cartels and export bounties were artificial, self-defeating, and unsustainable. Could there be any 'better lesson in free trade than the money which the German nation has to pay for these bounties'?[78] And why should British consumers be deprived of cheap sugar, only because foreign countries were foolish enough to subsidize it? This line of reasoning ignored the fact that without the Brussels convention, cane sugar producers would have been driven out of the market, leaving a powerful central European cartel to dictate prices. Only with the abolition of export bounties could a level playing field be restored.

As with bread, so with sugar: the Free Trade defence of the consumer was clothed in a language of constitutional patriotism. Cheapness, consumer democracy, and parliamentary sovereignty became one. The Women's Liberal Federation protested against the Brussels convention for placing 'our fiscal arrangements under the control of foreign nations'.[79] *Reynolds's* talked of a 'foreign syndicate'. Liberal propaganda presented Brussels as a 'stupendous piece of folly', not only for involving a loss of over £8 million to the country, but for undermining historical principles of taxation and liberty. Instead of taxes requiring the consent of the House of Commons, Brussels—this 'monstrous Convention'—bound Great Britain to a tax determined by an international commission: 'On this Commission there will be One Englishman and Nine Foreigners.'[80] With Brussels, the Liberal leader Campbell-Bannerman told a Cobden Club banquet, 'we subside into the tenth part of a foreign Vehmgericht', invoking the ghost of medieval feudalism. Getting involved in an international trade commission would expose Britain to the virus of tariffs, militarism, and autocracy. Britain should instead stand apart, a little island of liberty and sanity surrounded by 'struggling and groaning' nations 'caught in an inexorable chain' of protectionism.[81]

The whole idea of using pressure or penalties to open up foreign markets or lower trade barriers was distasteful. 'We did not conceive it to be any part of our business to start a crusade at the expense of the consumers of this country for the purpose of ramming our doctrines down the throats of other nations', as one critic put it.[82] Unilateral Free Trade was built on a strict view that Britain should do what it thought best, and let other nations do the same.

Sugar, then, was a powerful precedent for all sides in the conflict over Free Trade. For moderate reformers, the sugar controversy legitimated a more active role for the state in securing equal conditions of trade. If sugar proved the danger of cartels and the merit of international action, why not also support a small general tariff which, in addition to bringing in revenue, could counteract other forms of subsidies abroad, such as cheap railway rates, as Gerald Balfour speculated?[83] This was exactly what the vast majority of Free Traders feared, even after the Liberal government had triumphantly returned to power in December 1905. For them the Brussels convention remained a stain on the conscience of Liberal Britain. In 1908, the government tried to compromise. Asquith slashed the sugar duty by 50 per cent. Britain would keep its seat on the Brussels commission but stop penalizing bounty-fed sugar. Subsidized Russian sugar was allowed to enter freely again.

Many Free Traders were not satisfied. For anti-collectivists, Brussels demonstrated the need to fight all forms of state intervention. The Cobden Club in 1908 condemned the Liberal government's renewal of the convention. Strachey called on it to defend more generally the true spirit of Free Trade against the eight-hour bill and old age pensions.[84] For Unionist Free Traders, the sugar policy raised 'a very grave constitutional question' about the shift in power from parliament to executive. Ministers, Gibson Bowles warned in 1908, could by the mere exercise of their prerogative, limit the export of sugar from Russian ports: 'If they may do it with sugar, they may do it with corn, or with anything.'[85]

These were voices from the sidelines of politics but they were soon joined by the bulk of Liberal MPs. Sugar prices were rising in the first half of 1908 following droughts in the Caribbean and India. In July 1908, 210 Liberal MPs signed a memorial condemning the renewal of the convention. On 15 July 1908, a deputation of 210 Liberal MPs went to see Asquith, the Prime Minister, in his private rooms at the House of Commons. The group brought together the captains of the Free Trade campaign, including Alfred Mond, J. M. Robertson, and H. Vivian. Ernest Villiers, who introduced the deputation, charged the government with having betrayed the principles of Free Trade and infringed the rights of the House of Commons. It had 'violated the Constitution'. It was, perhaps, unwise to start a constitutional wrangle with Asquith, one of the top lawyers of his generation; Asquith reminded the deputation that it was not customary for the government to go to Parliament for assent in their exercise of the treaty-making powers of the Crown. In matters of policy, he emphasized, the Liberal government had effectively returned to Free Trade principles: Britain had decided to stay at Brussels to enable Russia to adhere to the convention but had refused to support any restriction of Russian subsidized exports.[86]

After 1908 Britain managed to maintain the right to export sugar and sugared products to the continent in spite of being permitted to import bounty-fed sugar. In fact, the success of the sugar convention had eventually made it possible for the British government to withdraw without having to fear the return of monopolies. None of this did much to change Free Traders' conviction that the Brussels convention was a dangerous foreign combination. Popular Free Trade had doomed the Brussels convention from the outset. Its demise was only a question of time. In 1912 that time had come. The beet sugar crop had been disappointing, threatening to force up prices. The British government demanded an ambitious 150 per cent increase in the quota for cheap, subsidized Russian sugar. The members of the convention refused. Britain returned to a dogmatic defence of cheapness. Instead of working towards a diplomatic solution, the Liberal government formally denounced the convention.

Friends of Empire

Chamberlain's crusade for a *Zollverein* followed on the heels of a more aggressive imperialism in the late nineteenth century. Ironically, this imperial culture proved more of a stumbling block than a stepping stone. Chamberlain's problem was not with cosmopolitan critics of empire—these were lost to him anyhow—but with the many imperialists whose vision of imperial power, history, and trusteeship had no room for Tariff Reform. Today Free Trade is often associated with liberal commercial internationalism but the importance of empire for its earlier survival deserves emphasis. Free Trade culture envisioned an imperial community held together by trust and morals, free of material interests. In the light of ever-increasing tariffs in the self-governing colonies, and their introduction of preferential treatment in the 1890s, this was remarkable. The language of 'the spirit of empire' versus 'the spirit of commerce' propped up an ideal of imperial harmony that had long been disrupted by the realities of economic nationalism and imperial force.

The advancing polarization between Chamberlain's protectionism and the Liberals' dogmatic Free Trade response again eliminated any middle ground. Chamberlain thus had to face not only the 'Limps', or Liberal Imperialists, around Asquith, Grey, and Haldane,[87] but also Conservative imperialists and members of the imperial ruling class. Far from being committed Cobdenites, many Conservative 'Free Fooders' supported retaliation and revenue tariffs. It was Chamberlain's fusion of colonial preferences and food taxes which proved incompatible with their sense of imperial solidarity. Free Trade was the beneficiary of this reaction. It absorbed and recycled a language of imperial trust and patriotism that insulated it against charges of either cosmopolitan 'Manchesterism' or Little Englandism.

In part, the problem for Tariff Reformers lay in the unique size and diversity of the British Empire. It was a heterogeneous amalgam of colonies and possessions, as different from each other economically as they were politically, culturally, and ethnically. Not only had Canada, Australia, and South Africa adopted protectionism, but the flow of trade between them and Britain was highly uneven. The future Dominions sent three-fifths of all their exports to Britain, but the mother country only sent one-fifth of its exports to them. Preferences might give Canadian wheat a competitive advantage over foreign wheat in the British market, but the reciprocal benefits were doubtful. Foreign competition was not the principal threat to British trade in the self-governing colonies. British exports to Canada either had a virtual monopoly or were facing competition from heavily protected Canadian industries; in fact, Canada was more protectionist against British goods (the average tariff here was 18 per cent) than against goods from the United States (12 per cent). Canadian preferences did not add up to much.

When ministers from the colonies called on Britain to impose a small duty on foreign goods—the South African Hofmeyr pitched 2 per cent in 1887, the Canadian Denison went as far as 5–10 per cent at the colonial conference of 1902—to allow for preferential treatment for the colonies, the response in the British state was one of disbelief, even ridicule. The 'colonials' were out of touch with reality, 'not well informed' and 'crying for the moon', Giffen at the Board of Trade wrote. Britain depended on foreign, not colonial, markets. The burden of colonial preference would thus be borne disproportionately by British export industries and British taxpayers; adjusting for their populations, Giffen calculated that each Briton would pay four times more for preferential duties than people in the self-governing colonies. It would be an 'infinite disaster' for Britain. Preferences also raised complex technical issues of how to prevent foreign goods that entered Britain via the colonies from enjoying preferential treatment. The prospect of an expanding bureaucracy and monitoring devices like certificates of origin filled the Board of Customs with horror. In short, the uneven balance of trade between mother country and colonies meant Tariff Reform was a 'specially stupid and mischievous form of attempted protection'.[88] Edwardian protectionists were confronted by the same point Lord Ripon, the Liberal colonial secretary, had made to the colonies in 1895: preferences involved too unequal a sacrifice.

Worse, trade was uneven not only between Britain and the self-governing colonies but between colonies as well. Some colonies, like the sugar-producing West Indies, were veritable monocultures, while others, like South Africa, had a mix of minerals, wool, and wine. Any attempt to give preferences raised the question: preferences on what? As taxing the raw materials of British industry was ruled out, this left major food stuffs. A duty and colonial preference on corn appealed to Tariff Reformers eager to make Britain less dependent on foreign wheat in case of war and to build up a loyal agrarian hinterland. From an intra-imperial point of view, it was extremely divisive. The Empire was not one vast field of corn. Canadian farmers would benefit, but what about Indian rice producers or Australian sheep farmers? And what about the different tariff levels across the Empire? Constructing a preferential tariff scheme that was reciprocal both in sacrifice and benefit was like squaring a circle. Chamberlain floundered where earlier champions of imperial preferences and federation had failed in the 1880s and 1890s.

Within the self-governing colonies, too, reactions to Chamberlain's tariff scheme were ambivalent. This only reinforced anxieties about imperial divisions. Imperial Tariff Reform was attractive in a colony like New Zealand where closer imperial federation promised to contain the 'Asian peril'. Elsewhere even leaders who backed Chamberlain, like Deakin in Australia, knew that domestic support was fragile. Tariff reform offered little to colonial governments, Labour parties, industrial interests, and even key agricultural groups, like Australian sheep farmers.[89] The dream of an Anglo-Saxon imperial premier league took no account of the Empire's ethnic diversity, including French–Canadian settlers.

In the colonies tariffs were the main source of revenue—over 90 per cent in Australia; there might be an interest in raising tariffs on foreign goods, but little in lowering them on British imports. As the Canadian Laurier told the new Conservative leader Bonar Law in 1911, it was madness to think that Canadian manufacturers would 'be willing to abate one jot of their protection against British manufactured goods'.[90]

From an imperial perspective, Tariff Reform was never a modernizing programme. The point of Tariff Reform was to preserve the status quo between an industrial centre and an agrarian hinterland, not to assist colonial development. As Chamberlain told a large audience in Newcastle on 20 October 1903, colonies in the future should revise their tariffs 'in order not to start industries in competition with those which are already in existence in the Mother Country'.[91] Chamberlain's supporters subsequently erased this particular passage from his published speeches, but it was never fully erased from the mind of industrialists and businessmen in the white settler colonies eager to move up the ladder of economic development.

Empires are, by definition, systems of great inequalities of power and wealth. They have not held back from exploiting such inequalities with the help of mercantilist measures. What made the British Empire hesitate in this case? One answer has been to look at the price tag of Tariff Reform. Tariffs would have interfered with the free flow of cheap foreign food on which Britons depended; the Board of Trade estimated that it would take over forty years for Canada to expand wheat production enough to replace British imports from the United States.[92] It is clear that for Britain, foreign trade and investment were more profitable than trade with the Empire. A preferential tariff would have come at a price. Arguably, however, a Free Trade Empire was itself a drain, steering money and innovation away from investment at home in education, new technologies and infrastructures, and reinforcing social inequalities. From a cost/benefit analysis, Britain might have been best off not only without Tariff Reform but without Empire altogether.[93]

To explain the opposition to Tariff Reform at the time, however, such counterfactual calculations are of limited value. Costs are always relative and subjective. Most Free Traders were committed to Empire and accepted its costs, not least the burden of imperial defence. Many supported imperial federation and other forms of assistance, such as subsidized steam services between Britain and the colonies. Tariff reform was not unacceptable because of its cost, but because colonial preferences on corn clashed head on with a rival model of empire based on trust, fairness, and freedom. We have become accustomed to see empire and freedom, free trade and fair trade as mutually exclusive. In a historical perspective, however, imperialist support for Free Trade can be seen as a pioneering stage in the evolution of an idea of 'fair trade' as an ethical alternative to self-interested commercial exchange.

The Free Trade system, as it was established in the 1840s and early 1850s, was a hybrid, bringing together Cobdenite critics of empire, evangelicals, Peelites, and a Whig ruling elite. The Whig government grafted Free Trade onto a reformed Empire which did away with mercantilist vestiges such as the navigation laws and sugar preferences. It saw the Free Trade empire as a common economic union.[94] But the imperial culture of Free Trade spread beyond the high aristocratic world of Whig ministers. Victorian Free Trade absorbed a powerful mix of protestant nationalism and evangelical religion.[95] Britain was Israel, an elect nation. Its civilizing mission was an article of faith to Liberal imperialists and critics of empire alike.

There had been a generous overlap of ideas and membership between Free Trade and the anti-slave trade movement and missionary societies in the first half of the nineteenth century. At the same time as it was critical of aspects of the old Empire, like the East India Company, this humanitarian community blended freedom of trade and the conversion of 'heathens' into a single civilizing mission. Commerce fostered initiative, enterprise, and autonomy and liberated natives from superstition, corruption, and dependence. Free Trade created a fertile ground for missionaries to do Christ's work.[96] Conversely, Britain's ability to fulfil her Christian mission depended on her credibility as a Free Trade nation. Amidst deafening cheers, George Thompson, radical MP and veteran anti-slaver, reminded an interdenominational conference in Manchester in 1841 that the Corn Laws were sabotaging Britain's divine work. It was good to send missionaries with the book to the 'barbarous nations' to preach to them how God had made provisions for every human being, and to pray together 'Give us this day our daily bread.' But what, Thompson asked, if the native finally asked the missionary 'from what blessed land he has brought him these glad tidings'? The missionary would tell him of the land where Christianity ruled supreme and 'where the gospel shines brightest'. The native would enthuse 'O Happy land ... just on the verge of heaven; would I were there', until the sudden news of millions of Britons starving under the Corn Laws reached the 'unsophisticated convert'. Without Free Trade at home, Thomson concluded, the British would face the 'scorn of the barbarian' abroad.[97]

In the Edwardian period there were still those, like Lloyd George, who echoed the older idea of the *douceur* of commerce and divine providence. Lloyd George was virtually unable to give a speech about Free Trade without falling into a eulogy about how providence had selected Britain for this global civilizing mission, even reciting Cardinal Newman—

> Providence has selected the people ... inhabiting these islands from amongst the people of the earth to carry through the victory of this one idea, the banner of freedom in commerce, brotherhood through commerce, and good will through commerce ... If we have the courage ... of our ancestors, we will prove ... that we are worthy of the leadership of the human race upwards, along the path which ascends 'O'er moor and fen, o'er crag and torrent, till the night is gone'.[98]

For many Edwardians, however, especially Conservative Free Traders, commerce was morally suspect. The Indian Mutiny and Rebellion of 1857, disappointment at the failure of freed slave economies to take off, and an increasingly biological form of racism,[99] had combined to erode earlier optimism about the civilizing magic of commerce. The imperial case for Free Trade shifted, presenting it as the moral framework for imperial trust and sentiment, as if untainted by money. 'The British Empire is held together by moral not by material forces', Winston Churchill told the inaugural meeting of the Free Trade League in 1904. 'It has grown up in liberty and silence.'[100]

Of course, the Empire was nothing of the sort. It was violent, vocal, and greedy. Churchill himself had recently returned from the Boer War, only the latest in a string of colonial wars that, in part, were fuelled by a competition for land, labour, and resources. Yet this was not just a rhetorical ploy to disguise deeper interests. The moral vision endowed Free Trade with a sense of imperial purpose and legitimacy. It moved the goalposts of the debate, away from questions of material costs and benefits, to ones of imperial duty and sentiment. And this imperial self-understanding holds some clues as to how a Free Trade regime managed to distance itself from the dislocation and famine it brought to many parts of the Empire.

Few Free Traders were as influential in propagating a divide between 'the spirit of Empire' and 'the spirit of commerce' as Robert Cecil, the third son of Lord Salisbury. Cecil was a leading conservative 'Free Fooder' and backbencher, who fused his father's moral conservatism with a commitment to ethical and progressive causes, including women's suffrage and industrial co-partnership. The 'spirit of Commerce and the spirit of Empire are essentially divergent', Cecil believed. 'Commerce depends on competition, the trader seeks to enrich himself, to get the best of the bargain. His maxims are, "Business is business" and "Each man for himself and the devil take the hindmost".' For Cecil it was impossible that any broader social values could arise out of the pursuit of self-interest. 'Self interest in a word is essential to commerce. It is fatal to Empire.'[101]

From this perspective it was Tariff Reformers, not Free Traders, who appealed to commercial self-interest. Social values like imperial duty and sentiment needed to be shielded from such commercial considerations. By turning the Empire into a marketplace of colonies competing for concessions, Tariff Reform would erode, not cement imperial solidarity. Colonies with the highest tariffs would obtain greater concessions than those with lower duties, a point already made by the Board of Trade in the 1890s.[102] And the new bargaining spirit would dissolve further the ties between Britain and the large protectionist white settler colonies such as Canada, Cecil added. Tariff reformers were encouraging Canada to consider the Empire as a 'business proposition'. This would only accelerate Canada's much-feared drift into the orbit of the United States.

Such fears of materialist threats to 'corporate values' were reinforced by a widespread sense that the Empire had come together under Free Trade. Tariff reform was threatening to repeat the mercantilist mistakes that had led to the revolt of the American colonies in the 1760s–70s and the loss of half the Empire.[103] John Burns, the liberal labour leader, saw Chamberlain as 'the greatest enemy the Empire has had since George lost America'.[104] Chamberlain's cabinet colleagues predicted that they would have tea in Boston harbour if they did not take care.[105]

For democratic imperialists, Tariff Reform dangerously combined bureaucracy and mercantilism. Tariff Reformers suffered from a 'Prussian' mindset that inclined them to think of people in the third person and put excessive confidence in bureaucratic bodies, like the Tariff Commission, remarked the young Alfred Zimmern, who would emerge as a leading new internationalist during the First World War. Protectionists forgot 'that there had been a French Revolution between the Navigation Acts and Mr. Chamberlain'. To survive, the Empire had to become a union of self-governing units sharing a democratic imperial patriotism which might some day even evolve into 'planetary patriotism'.[106] In a speech to the Cambridge Union, the young John Maynard Keynes presented Chamberlain's scheme as 'Napoleonic', alien to the spirit of empire, 'replacing freedom by uniformity ... [and] a machine-like interdependence'. Its underlying vision of empire was completely defective, Keynes argued. Again, the contrast was between the true Free Trade view of empire as bound together by 'sentiment and community of ideals' and an alien protectionist one favouring 'common forms of government and an interdependence of commerce'.[107]

For moderate fiscal reformers as well as for convinced Free Traders, colonial preferences were dangerous because they openly brought issues of money into the Empire. Colonial preferences would weaken what they were designed to strengthen.[108] They would destabilize relations between metropole and colony, and even worse, undermine the imperial spirit within the metropole. Without a popular consensus in Britain in favour of imperial preferences, Gerald Balfour told cabinet colleagues in 1902, 'the result ... would simply be to bring the Colonies back into English politics [and] to rekindle the spirit of Little Englandism'.[109] Rosebery, a Liberal Imperialist, painted a dark picture of workers turning against the empire:

> It will be a bad day for Great Britain—it will be a worse day for the Empire at large—when the artisan returning to a stinted meal—stinted by taxation—may say to his family, 'Ah, things would have been very different had it not been for this Empire, for the preservation of which we are now so heavily taxed.'[110]

Racial ideas severely restricted the humanitarian project of freedom of trade. Africans were viewed as an agricultural race immune to the logic of commercial development.[111] In its emphasis on trusteeship, this imperial vision echoed an older eighteenth-century concern with the obligations that came with power. In 1783, in a famous speech attacking the East India Company for tyranny and corruption, Edmund Burke had argued that the rights and privileges of empire were a 'trust' to be discharged for the benefit of native societies. More than a century later, faced with Chamberlain's new mercantilism, imperialists rallied to the defence of a Free Trade Empire of liberty and justice.

India continued to sit uneasily in a Free Trade Empire. In 1877, at a time of famine, strict adherence to free trade principles dictated the export of surplus wheat, with tremendous human suffering.[112] India's tax system breached the pure liberal model. General duties had been abolished in 1882, but, to fix a hole in the budget, Britain revived a general tariff in 1894. The 5 per cent Indian tariff violated core principles—there were duties on raw materials for industry, and for many articles it meant a lot of interference for little revenue.[113] Parliamentary lobbying by Lancashire cotton interests secured a lower 3.5 per cent tariff on their finished articles. At the same time, to preserve the Free Trade principle of 'no favours', an equivalent excise or consumption duty of 3.5 per cent was imposed on Indian cotton manufactures. Here was an uneven playing field if ever there was one.

Instead of avoiding the issue of India, however, Free Traders exploited it. Partly this hinged on political and economic self-interest. Chamberlain's imperial vision was dominated by white settler colonies. India occupied a subordinate, unclear place. In the cabinet crisis of 1903, Lord George Hamilton resigned as secretary of state for India over this question. Significantly, Hamilton sympathized with the case for retaliation, and had himself imposed countervailing duties on sugar in India. However, with Tariff Reform in Britain, he warned, it would be all but impossible to deny India the right to impose industrial tariffs as well. And, as he told conservative Free Trade audiences, Tariff Reform would seriously undermine the interests of Indian finance and imperial stockholders. India imported far more from Britain than she exported. India paid for this trade deficit by sending large exports to Germany, France, and Belgium. Britain, in turn, received imports from these countries which paid for a considerable percentage of the annual interest due to British holders of Indian stocks. A British tariff, and likely foreign retaliation against Indian and other imperial exports, would break this financial circle.[114]

Trust in the humanizing and supposedly non-materialist workings of Free Trade continued to blind popular liberals to the links between British policy and Indian suffering. In Bristol, in 1904, for example, Mrs Gray traced the history of political economy for an audience of liberal women, presenting the famines of India as an automatic result of 'correct principles discarded'. It was vital to recognize 'our interdependence', she concluded, and this meant to 'break down all barriers, military, monetary, fiscal and otherwise to attain prosperity'.[115]

Lancashire, the industrial sector which had gained most from Free Trade at the expense of the Indian cotton industry, nonetheless condemned Tariff Reformers' lack of humanity. In July 1909, W. A. S. Hewins went to Manchester charged with the uphill task of selling protectionism to three hundred cotton spinners, manufacturers, and merchants: irrespective of their dependence on foreign markets and access to cheap raw material, they would benefit from the stimulus that tariffs would give to the buying power of British society as a whole.[116] The reaction was prompt and predictable. Local newspapers and pamphlets noted the vagueness of the proposals. Worse, the 'humanitarian side' had been left out entirely. To 'bribe Lancashire with the promise of Preference in India', showed a frightening lack of 'human element', according to 'A Lancashire Man's Reply'. 'I think to suggest that they [Indians] should be taxed for the preference of Lancashire cotton manufacturers and workmen was most vicious.' Hewins' speech was an 'insult' to Lancashire men's 'humane feelings'.[117]

Robert Cecil epitomized the faith in the civilizing anti-materialistic mission of a Free Trade Empire. In India, the 'whole land was at the mercy of every famine and every pestilence', Robert Cecil wrote in 1912, 'and its people were sunk in ignorance and barbarism'. Much remained to be done, 'but we have at least established throughout India order and security. We have given to the humblest peasant the protection of British justice.' If anything, Britain had given 'him perhaps too lavishly education and enlightenment. And we have granted him such political liberty as he is able to enjoy.' By making the Empire look like a business proposition, Chamberlain distracted from its essential ideal and purpose. The reply to citizens asking 'what advantage to them is the Empire', was a humanitarian one: 'a great opportunity and a great responsibility'.[118]

Chamberlain's plea for material sacrifice failed not because of domestic indifference to empire but because it clashed with a non-materialist ideal of fairness and shared imperial sentiment. This was an ideal that lived in denial of the commercial and social realities of empire, but it corresponded with the idealized history of the Free Trade nation. Elements of Whig history were mixed with radical and conservative stories of liberty and solidarity. In this picture, the stability and legitimacy of the British Empire mirrored that of the British state after the repeal of the Corn Laws. A shared commitment to fair, equal treatment would nurture a sense of interdependence between groups in the Empire as it had in Britain itself.

In the final analysis, it was not the cost of imperial reform but its uneven distribution that threatened the imperial concordat. Colonial preferences would pitch winners against losers and create an atmosphere of distrust that would erode imperial patriotism. Just as Free Trade supposedly immunized society and politics at home against vested interests and social extremes, so it would prevent the Empire from fragmenting into competing blocks of strong protectionist colonies currying favours at the expense of weaker dependencies. And just as tariffs would bring in their train millionaires and materialism, so they would corrupt imperial ideals of justice and equity with haggling over money and preferences.[119] At home, Free Trade warded off socialism, in the Empire colonial nationalism. Concern for the poor, mothers, and children were matched by a sense of trusteeship and parental care for Britain's imperial 'children' and Indian peasants. Even the stories of liberation from hunger and autocracy complemented each other. Free Trade had liberated the British people from 'the hungry forties' and political enslavement. It saw itself as liberating the Indian peasant from centuries of corruption, ignorance, and famine.

Internationalists

Defenders of Empire were not the only Free Traders to question the virtue of international commerce. Progressive internationalists and social reformers also began to have doubts. Travelling across Europe in the mid-nineteenth century, Cobden had dreamt of a network of interdependent civil societies at different levels of development.[120] Brought together by commercial exchange untainted by political power, nations would have no need for foreign policy. According to the leading new liberal J. A. Hobson, the modern world looked very different. The older picture of the harmonious exchange of goods and services between an infinite number of small, competing firms, merchants, and consumers was belied by the growing collision over markets between organized business and between nations. Hobson had been moving away from orthodox economics for a decade when in 1899 he was sent to South Africa to report on the Boer War for the *Manchester Guardian*. That visit sharpened his sense of the political power of sectional interests and made him one of the most influential observers of the changing face of global capitalism. As Hobson explained in *Imperialism* (1902) and a string of books and articles,[121] the world was dominated by several industrial countries locked in heated competition for foreign markets. Instead of Cobden's world of individuals, big combinations, trusts, and financial groups had emerged, pressing for expansion. It was a fallacy to believe that only feudal elites were militaristic and that the industrious classes were naturally peaceful. Economic interests and political power were inseparable.

This 'new imperialism' had domestic roots. Older liberals, Hobson wrote, had focused on the overall gains from trade between societies, ignoring the unjust distribution of these benefits within societies. Free Trade had not eliminated sectional interests. Rather, the maldistribution of income had led to 'underconsumption' at home and triggered a feverish search among financiers and traders for new and often dangerous places for their 'surplus' capital and goods abroad. Here was what Hobson famously called the 'economic taproot' of imperialism. 'If the consuming public in this country raised its standard of consumption to keep pace with every rise of productive powers,' he wrote, 'there could be no excess of goods or capital clamorous to use Imperialism in order to find markets.'[122]

Free Trade, in this new liberal analysis, was no longer the panacea it had been for many older radicals. International trade, in fact, accelerated the growth of organized capital and the social and political problems arising from it. Laissez-faire and competition, Hobson argued, led to wasteful overproduction, violent trade cycles, and a widening gap between productive power and consumer welfare.

> Full free trade would supply, quicken, and facilitate the operation of those large economic forces…the tendency of capital to gravitate into larger and fewer masses,…a growing keenness on antagonism as the mass of the business-unit is larger, and an increased expenditure of productive power upon aggressive commercial warfare: the growth of monopolies springing from natural, social, or economic sources.

On its own, freer trade 'has no power whatever to abate the activity of these forces, and would only serve to bring their operation into more signal and startling prominence'. The new imperialism was a response to unresolved questions of social democracy in Western societies. And, in turn, the undemocratic tendencies created by expansionist policies would flow back and reinforce sectional interests and an undemocratic culture at home.

To break this vicious cycle required social reform. This would reduce underconsumption and oversaving and ease the pressure on investors to find new markets and opportunities abroad. Ruthless competition abroad would give way to a more harmonious and balanced relationship between consumption and production at home.

In the long term, this analysis pointed towards the erosion of Free Trade's cultural status in the twentieth century.[123] But Hobson's ideas also gave Free Trade a new lease on life. It was a much-needed liberal self-critique that recognized that the Free Trade project had not been completed by Cobdenism. Sectional interests, speculative finance, and trustmongers were new challenges to be answered by a progressive movement. Hobson attuned the conception of trade to a more organic vision of society characteristic of the new liberalism. Instead of reducing trade to rational self-interest, the organic approach lifted genuine Free Trade to a plane above material transactions between individuals.

From a purely economic point of view, Hobson upgraded the importance of the home market at the expense of foreign trade. Home trade, he argued in the late 1890s, was 'a more solid and substantial basis of industrial prosperity than foreign trade'. It insulated a country against fluctuations beyond its control. And, he heretically suggested, the gain from home trade was 'double instead of single', as the benefits from exchange were kept within the nation.[124] The pressure to find foreign markets, he repeatedly emphasized, was 'not based on any natural economic necessity. There is no natural limit to the quantity of wealth which can be produced, exchanged, and consumed within Great Britain except the limits imposed by restricted natural resources and the actual condition of the arts of industry.'[125] Except for a small 'surplus' of manufactured goods to pay for food imports, most trade could be absorbed by a dynamic home market once wealth was more evenly distributed. If stimulated, home consumption would keep pace with any increase in 'producing power'. It was never entirely clear how this shift from international to domestic goods and markets would occur in a Free Trade society. Why would a more prosperous, discerning public not want tasteful, high-quality foreign goods? What was so bad about British consumers buying French clothes or German musical instruments? A higher level of domestic consumption would not by itself invalidate the benefits of an international division of labour.

In the late 1920s Keynes would rediscover the idea of underconsumption, but the implications of Hobson's argument were already clear to Cobdenites at the time. Leonard Courtney, an old radical and leading internationalist, praised Hobson for his exposure of imperialism as 'a vain and costly delusion', but strongly refuted the idea that the gain from international trade was so small that it could easily be replaced by expanding domestic consumption. 'We could all of us easily extend our consumption of the commodities and services of others.' The problem, Courtney pointed out, was: could we as 'easily satisfy these others by producing and giving them something they are content to take in exchange'? Trade made this more likely. It made for a more efficient use of resources to satisfy human wants. Hobson's was a dangerous fallacy, not least 'because it could easily be used by those who hanker after protection in support of their propositions'.[126]

Hobson never altogether resolved the tensions between the domestic and international priorities of the new liberal programme. On the one hand, he defended the benefits of an open economy. On the other, he warned how unregulated trade gave power to sectional interests and capitalist combinations and sowed the seeds of international friction. His distinction between 'ordinary commerce' and 'illegitimate and speculators' imperialistic commerce' was convenient, but where exactly one began and the other ended remained unclear.[127] Hobson even granted that certain tariffs could help combat unemployment, foreign monopolies, and 'aggressive dumping'. The problem was politics, not principle. Tariffs would be 'clumsy and ineffectual weapons' in 'the hands of imperfectly wise officials'.[128]

In the decade running up to the First World War, Hobson increasingly emphasized the positive role of foreign trade and investment, but this did not reflect an overall conceptual shift.[129] Hobson was a progressive first and theorist second, and what changed after 1903 was not so much his theoretical position as the political context. His critique of speculative finance and trade in the 1890s had targeted the rising imperial mood within the Liberal party in favour of an aggressive 'open door' policy. Chamberlain was a more dangerous enemy and his declaration for Tariff Reform in 1903 changed the implications of Hobson's critique. Tariff reform was far worse than laissez-faire liberalism. Cobdenites might have been blind to the uneven distribution of wealth, but protectionists would exacerbate 'underconsumption' and openly encourage a militaristic culture at home and imperialism abroad.

Hobson had not attacked Free Trade as such, but its 'speculative' and imperialist pathology as opposed to 'ordinary' and legitimate commerce.

Chamberlain's challenge made him re-emphasize the positive qualities of genuine Free Trade. Free Trade plus social reform would make trade and finance genuinely 'international'. They would not be driven by artificial 'national' pressures to find outlets for 'surplus' capital abroad. Hobson now dressed the eighteenth-century *douceur* of commerce in new liberal clothes. Trade might indeed provoke rivalry and friction, but that was because it had been deformed and misdirected by base competitive rivalries within societies. International and colonial conflict and class conflict fed off each other. With the help of a more even distribution of wealth, it would be possible to purify trade and make it a virtuous conduit of higher reason, social solidarity, peace, and human advancement. In fact, without it, the prospects for social reform and democracy in any one society were slim—sectional interests would degrade public life.

The new liberal idea of humanity as a social organism strengthened rather than weakened a commitment to freedom of trade. If humans were 'social beings' not individuals, and society was an organism, this meant that feelings and sympathy were strongest within the family and community. Hobson was aware of the lengthening of the food chain and the growing distance between producers and consumers that came with the era of globalization in which he lived. Trade would bridge that distance, extending human sympathy and international instincts and preventing communities from becoming inward-looking, nationalist, and barbaric. Far worse than the economic damage of protectionism, he told the Quaker Society of Friends, would be the 'moral and intellectual injury involved in a loosening of the bonds of [human] intercourse'. Trade provided an important first rung on the ladder of civilization and reason. It bound 'the members of foreign lands to one another by kindling the first sparks of a sentiment of humanity, transcending the more primitive limits of the city or the nation'. It prepared humans for 'the common purpose of higher life', first in science, arts, and morals, but increasingly also in international justice and international institutions.[130] The ethical and political case in favour of Free Trade trumped whatever disagreements old and new liberals had about social policy and economics.

More generally, Free Trade internationalism and the peace movement were inseparable. The international Free Trade Congress and the Universal Peace Congress were both held in London in 1908. The Cobden Club promoted an International Free Trade League. At the Free Trade Congress, Churchill fought off repeated interruptions by women suffragettes to reiterate that peace and Free Trade went hand in hand. He even cited Diderot to show how commerce had made societies more interdependent—the 'central current of the modern world'.[131] Enlightenment ideas of the humanizing *douceur* of commerce continued to circulate through popular Free Trade, sometimes reinforced by Christian lessons from the New Testament. Free Trade might not guarantee peace, but it made for more peaceful societies. It 'remains one of the best promoters of good temper and of good-will', Courtney emphasized: 'if we could instil in the minds of the statesmen of the world broader conceptions of mutual intercourse in place of the petty jealousies which now make the nations the slaves of sectional interests, most of the bickerings which disturb international relations would disappear'.[132]

While not all Free Traders were members of the peace movement, peace campaigners were invariably fervent supporters of Free Trade. J. M. Robertson, president of the secular Rational Peace Society, was a vocal defender of the ethics of Free Trade, as was Bertrand Russell. Courtney presided at the Universal Peace Congress and was president of the National Peace Council, a federation of peace bodies formed in 1908. Its secretary was H. G. Perris, a former secretary of the Cobden Club. Hobson and Hobhouse were old friends of Perris' since the days of the International Arbitration and Peace Association in the late 1890s.[133]

The popular Free Trade revival did not necessarily mean a commitment to Cobdenite principles of non-interference, however. The new liberal critique of individualism within society extended to international relations. In an interdependent world, the autonomy of nations was obsolete. Free exchange was a joint global project to raise the moral and material level of humanity. Colonial peoples did not have a right to close themselves off and deny the rest of the world access to their resources, Hobson argued. The future lay not with laissez-faire or imperial control but with international government. It would give 'civilised powers' equal access to global resources while protecting 'lower races' against private forms of commercial 'despotism'.[134] Hobson did not yet make the same demands on the 'civilised powers' that were themselves shutting out the world economy.

The story of internationalism ended with a twist just before the First World War. Angellism, the movement sparked by Norman Angell's best-selling *The Great Illusion* (1910), reconstructed the older Cobdenite vision of the benign force of economic self-interest.[135] Pointing to the thickening global web of modern finance and communication, Angell argued that war had become irrational (though not impossible). In a globalized world, older mercantilist strategies of capturing trade or fighting wars of economic conquest no longer worked: they would bankrupt conqueror and conquered alike. Grafting Herbert Spencer's ideas of social evolution onto liberal individualism, Angell produced a straight biological line of human development: economic exchange invariably fostered peaceful sentiment and reduced international conflict. The problem was not economic interests, but that ideas lagged behind their 'real' interests; his earlier encounters abroad, reporting on the Dreyfus affair in France and seeing the mismatch in America between farmers' support for tariffs and their 'natural' interest in Free Trade, had moved Angell to look to 'psycho-politics' for answers.[136] Peace required the education of both publics and statesmen about globalization—foreign policies, he criticized, were still 'framed according to the principles dating back to an age when the locomotive and the steam ship had not yet been invented, and when international trade had hardly begun'.[137] By 1913 there were over fifty clubs, study groups, and exchange programmes spreading Angell's gospel.[138]

Some progressive Free Traders and peace campaigners were skeptical of Angell's appeal to self-interest. Would economic motives be enough to prevent war in times of crisis, without a strong moral commitment to peace as well? Perris, Hobson, and the socialist radical H. N. Brailsford pointed out that war might not pay nations, but it might still benefit powerful groups within them.[139] Angell rallied to a defence of Cobden's ideal of 'buying cheap and selling dear': 'I challenge most absolutely the whole premise that the consideration of one's interest is immoral.' Morality was not based on collective interest or self-sacrifice. It progressed as individuals gained greater consciousness, revealing to them their enlightened self-interest and 'the ideal motive'.[140] The spread of Angellism showed how vibrant and attractive portions of the older idea of Free Trade still were on the eve of the First World War.

Worlds of Labour

In the labour movement and on the left, opposition to Chamberlain's Tariff Reform was immediate and virtually unanimous. In May and June 1903 Keir Hardie, Ramsay MacDonald, and other leaders of the Labour party joined a democratic phalanx stretching from the socialist Edward Carpenter to the old Owenite George Holyoake, all condemning Chamberlain's scheme as unjust, unfeasible, and undemocratic. In September, Trade Union leaders joined the protest almost to a man. Chamberlain's belief that a tariff, by strengthening domestic industry, would result in higher wages cut little ice with labour leaders, who knew that greater profits did not automatically translate into better pay. George Barnes, of the Amalgamated Society of Engineers, simply denounced the idea as 'Rubbish!'[141] Support for the Trade Union Tariff Reform Association was confined to a handful of heterodox labourites, such as Henry Henshall, who was expelled from the Independent Labour Party (ILP) in Stockport in 1909, and a few marginal industries, such as glass and paper.[142]

But opposition to Tariff Reform was not the same as support for Free Trade. Protectionists, naturally, were quick to dismiss Labour as the paid servant of the Cobden Club, and later historians, too, have portrayed a harmonious union between like-minded Liberals and Labourites. Chamberlain simply awoke 'all the slumbering Free Trade principles of British working-class leaders'.[143] In fact, many Labour leaders had had a crisis of faith over these principles and were actively exploring alternatives.

Labour leaders had to manoeuvre between two more powerful political antagonists. Opposing Tariff Reform for raising the cost of living and promoting imperialism was straightforward. But Labour was a new party, barely three years old and keen to establish its socialist credentials with proposals for a national minimum wage and the right to work. It was equally important to highlight the poverty and suffering under Free Trade. 'Free Trade was a capitalist warcry; protection was a landlord warcry', as the Federation of Trades and Labour Councils put it. Labour's duty was to show that 'national prosperity, and the prosperity of the working classes, are dependent on deeper economic causes'.[144] Labour promptly denounced the tariff question as a 'red herring', distracting from the real issues of poverty and unemployment, which only socialist reforms could remedy. This was good rhetoric, but in the real world it was the two big players, Chamberlain and his Liberal adversaries, who were shaping the contours of politics. In this sense, the Labour party and socialist groups found themselves in a similar position to that of Balfour's Conservatives who, as the fiscal campaign gathered momentum, had to respond to the flow of a political game controlled by others.

Cracks had appeared in the radical Free Trade façade already in the 1880s. While agricultural trade unionists and railwaymen absorbed popular liberal sentiment, others revived an older attack on cheap imports as the twin of cheap wages. Unemployment fuelled fears of imported 'sweated goods' and an influx of unskilled foreign labour. In 1886, protectionist Fair Traders actively sought to exploit such anxieties in the famous 'Red Flag' meeting in Trafalgar Square. 'There can be no doubt whatever,' Henry Champion, one of the Labour martyrs imprisoned after the demonstration, emphasized the same year, 'that under what is called Free Trade ... the market of the world will confer its custom on those countries where ... labour is cheapest.'[145] British workers would soon have to accept the low wages of Italians or face unemployment. Nor was the critique of Free Trade necessarily the preserve of the unskilled poor around the ports and slums of east London. Skilled mechanics, too, were overheard to speak in favour of protection.[146] Even the Trades Union Congress asserted the need to 'protect ourselves' against foreign bounties in 1898.[147] Opposition to food taxes did not rule out penalizing sweated imports, a frequent demand of the Labour party in the Edwardian period.

For most in the Labour movement, Free Trade was a lesser evil than tariffs, but discussion rarely stopped there. In April 1904, for example, members of trade unions, friendly societies, and cooperatives met in west London. Fred Maddison, the Lib–Lab leader, attacked preferential tariffs for increasing the cost of living and promoting international conflict. A heated debate followed, which led to a critique of capitalism and demands for public ownership on a cooperative basis. The meeting concluded with a joyful chorus of the Red Flag.[148]

For leaders in the ILP like Hardie, Snowden, and John Paton, the tariff question was in the first place an opportunity to put their distinct case for socialism and explain the inherent limits of Free Trade. Tariff Reform meetings, Paton recalled, were 'magnificent opportunities for socialist propaganda'; after earlier heckling, local Tariff Reformers would stand down voluntarily to let Labour activists address their audiences.[149] Instead of leading to improved living conditions, they pointed out that Free Trade had brought a decline in real wages. At a time of rising prices and when labour's share of the national income was shrinking, this was a forceful argument. *The Labour Leader*, the party's paper, ridiculed the *Hungry Forties* and its idea that the progress of the people could be traced to Cobden's triumph.[150] Hardie echoed Hobson, arguing that Free Trade capitalism led to underconsumption and a mad scramble for markets. Soon, he predicted in 1903, 'each country will be more and more driven back upon itself for the consumpt[ion] of its own produce'. Tariffs were a last ditch attempt by capitalists to escape the inescapable, by promoting greed and distracting workers from 'better ways of supplying themselves with the necessaries of life' than through commerce. [151]

Liberal trade and an open world economy were unsustainable. This was the essence of Labour's position and fully shared by men like Snowden, still far removed from the stubborn Gladstonianism that would guide him as Chancellor of the Exchequer in the first two Labour governments and that has coloured (and destroyed) his historical reputation. In the Edwardian years, he prophesied that the 'tendency all over the world is for manufactures to settle down where the raw material is grown. Each country must devote itself to developing its natural resources. This is the new policy we must adopt.'[152] The global picture was bleak. Trade drained nations of their resources. Demand was inherently limited: 'there was not one manufacturing trade in this country which was capable of any further expansion'. At best, he gave the export of manufactures 'another twenty-years lease of life'.[153]

British Labour leaders were not Marxists, but there were overtones of Marx's famous speech on Free Trade in 1848. Capital accumulation, Marx explained, increased productive forces, and this accelerated the concentration of capital. Production began to outpace demand. The greater the productive capital, the greater the competition amongst workers. Free Trade inevitably drove down wages. Unlike Marx, however, British Labourites imagined change as evolution, not dialectics. As capitalism was evolving into ever more efficient productive units, cartels, and trusts emerged. This process prepared the coming of socialism. Free Trade had not insulated Britain against trusts.[154]

There were echoes, too, of the anarchist prince Peter Kropotkin. Snowden had met Kropotkin in Aberdeen in 1889 and absorbed his *Fields, Factories and Workshops*; socialists are not immune to plagiarism. Future welfare demanded the integration of industry and agriculture, not specialization. Land reform was more than a matter of social justice, it was the precondition for national survival. The 'only possibility of national salvation', Snowden proclaimed, was to nationalize land and make 'our nation a self-sustaining nation'.[155]

Labour was ambivalent about modernity. As MacDonald put it in 1907 in Labour's official view on empire, fiscal preferences would make 'the Imperial fabric a gross erection of the commercial spirit—a kind of United States sky-scraper ... —and such erections do not stand the test of time'.[156] Such anxieties about globalization set British Labour aside not only from Liberals but from colleagues on the continent, like the revisionist social democrat Eduard Bernstein, who believed that the world market was unlimited.

Immiseration, overproduction, and the imminent fragmentation of the world into rival national and imperial blocs were prophesied across the Left. H. M. Hyndman and the Social Democratic Federation felt that Britain's commercial system was 'played-out'. It was impossible for Britain to maintain its 'supremacy in competition with the nations, African and Asiatic, which are now entering the field of production, tariffs or no tariffs'.[157]

Liberal appeals to a public consumer interest fell flat with the Labour party, the SDF, and *Clarion* socialists. 'Cheapness' might be in the interests of consumers, but not all consumers were producers. The *Clarion*, by far the best-selling leftist paper, with sales of over one million, warned again and again that the cult of cheapness led to social waste and cheap labour. The consumer interest disguised the parasitical interest of financiers and rentiers who were devouring the nation. In pamphlets and articles R. B. Suthers mobilized an older national iconography and showed 'Doctor Socialism' visiting John Bull paralysed by 'Starvation Sores, Unemployed Congestion, Divident Tumours [and] Smart Set Boils'.[158] The ILP caricatured the cheap loaf as a rentier's sham: workers created the 'big loaf of wealth' but received only its crust, while its bulk in rent and profit went to the 'idle and leisured class' (see Figure II overleaf). Labour party leaders like MacDonald emphasized that the producer interest might clash with that of the consumer: the producer's came first. Labour's policy was, indeed, that of 'buying in the best market', but 'the idea of the best must include some consideration of the circumstances under which the produce on the market has been made'.[159] Interfering with trade—even prohibiting imports—was legitimate, if imports had been produced under inferior or 'sweated' conditions.

The Fabians did not share the fatalistic view of trade, but they too argued that Free Trade, without a minimum wage and other social reforms, was leading Britain and the world down a spiral of decline, inefficiency, and exploitation. Capital would move wherever labour was cheapest. Instead of a world in which each community devoted itself to what it could do best, the Webbs predicted already in 1897 in their *Industrial Democracy*, 'we should get ... a world in which each community did that which reduced its people to the lowest degradation'.[160]

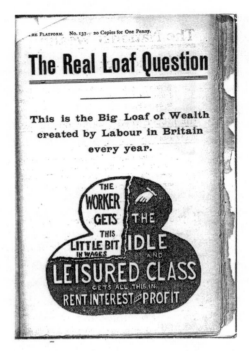

Figure 11. The big loaf used to illustrate social inequality, in a 1904 Labour leaflet.

Chamberlain's Tariff Reform crusade split the Fabian Society. Some, like Graham Wallas, resigned in protest against the majority report which recognized bounties and shipping preferences as acceptable means for developing imperial trade and resources. Those less squeamish about imperial organization and international intervention, like George Bernard Shaw, campaigned for 'preferential socialism'. Shaw had drawn up the Fabian report on Empire in 1900, which asserted the right to intervene in other parts of the world, like China, if their institutions stood in the way of the commercial interests of 'the civilised world'. He now censured Sydney Webb for ' "behaving on every public occasion as if you were up for examination at the Birkbeck [college] and had to get marks from [the Cobdenite] Henry Fawcett" '.[161] Beatrice Webb confided to her diary that Chamberlain 'has hit on a fundamentally right idea, which he ignorantly and rashly spoils by plunging on an impracticable device'.[162] Still, she had hopes of combining conservative tariffs with social reforms as late as 1910.

Such rapprochement was unthinkable for the Labour party. For all the shared analysis of a world committing commercial suicide, the Labour party took a radically different political path from the *Clarion*, the SDF, and most Fabians. It was one thing, in Hardie's image, to attack 'Commercialism, [which] like some fabled monster, having devoured its own offspring, can only now exist by preying upon its own vitals'.[163] It was quite another to jeopardize social reforms by sabotaging the Free Trade campaign and letting protectionists win. Already before the 1906 'progressive alliance' between Labour and Liberals, the Labour party leadership adopted a line of sympathetic neutrality towards the Free Trade campaign. While it refused to give official support to Liberal candidates in by-elections or to provide speakers requested by bodies like the Free Trade League, it did not bar individual speakers from appearing on the League's platform. Snowden attended several League meetings in 1905. At the 1905 Labour party conference such involvement was officially outlawed, but it never ceased in practice.

The SDF, by contrast, pursued a more confrontational 'class war' strategy. Personal biographies played their role—Hyndman was a socialist with a Tory background and fought a long-standing battle over empire and defence with the Cobden Club and its secretary, Harold Cox. Clearly, too, the progressive rapprochement over social reform between Labour and new Liberals offset differences over political economy. But, ultimately, it was the rival ethics of internationalism and nationalism that channelled Labour and the socialist Left in opposite directions.

For Labour party leaders, as for Free Trade imperialists, ethics trumped economics. They did not apply a straightforward economic calculus of costs and benefits but were guided by political traditions and international morals. Hardie and MacDonald were prominent peace activists. In 1903 they led a group of workers to Paris to promote Anglo-French friendship and the international brotherhood of man. MacDonald was a supporter of the International Arbitration and Peace Association, and Hardie, in 1910, organized a campaign for arms reduction.[164] Whatever their analysis of capitalist overproduction, it was this revisionism of the heart that built a bridge to Free Trade liberal internationalists, like Robertson, Perris, Hobson, and Hirst. Unlike for Hyndman and the SDF or Blatchford and the *Clarion*, there was no fusion of political and economic nationalism. Hyndman's insistence that a 'nation in order to obtain a full outlet for its own economic development may be compelled to make war against an oppressing nation'[165] was emotionally repulsive to Labour leaders. Even Snowden, never a pacifist, argued in 1913 that a German invasion was preferable to further arms spending.[166]

Traders were condemned as non-productive parasites in the home economy, but when it came to the global sphere older internationalist sentiment shone through. When some Labourites attacked Cobden in 1903 for having acted out of the lowest possible motive, a desire for commercial gain, Hardie leapt to his defence. Trade was not the 'highest conceivable form' of human intercourse, but it is 'the one form open to us as things are'. He painted a picture of the *douceur* of commerce that neither Montesquieu nor Cobden himself could have bettered. Merchants were 'great missionaries of a brighter day ... majestically coming and going with their freights of barter, teaching the nations the much-needed lesson of their mutual dependence one upon the other'. Commerce promoted peace:

> Despite the keeness of the commerical struggle there comes a time when on each side there grows up a feeling that underneath the hard bargaining ... there is a human element on both sides which, despite superficial differences of creed and colour and tongue, begins to make itself felt, and ... the dykes which separate man from man are broken down, and the waters of their common humanity begin to intermix and commingle.[167]

Across Europe, labour movements had to come to terms with globalization and new mercantilist regimes. Cheap grain on the one hand, and imperialist and protectionist struggles for markets on the other, made the tariff question a central issue for labour party identities and their strategy towards governments, agrarian elites, and industrial producers. In the mid-1880s, the Belgian Workers' Party (POB) switched to Free Trade. For the Catholic governments which, with popular rural support, ruled until the end of the First World War, free trade in food was one thing, industrial goods another; Belgium retained a tariff on manufactures of an average of 9 per cent. The POB, under Vandervelde's lead, wanted to go further: an open economy that combined growth with a social insurance scheme for those harmed by change.[168] In Germany, the mass Social Democratic party was divided. From the late 1890s, there was a growing popular agitation against agricultural tariffs and the rise in the cost of living; already in 1902 the SPD organized a petition with over three million signatures against the 'Hunger-tariff'. The campaign against high meat prices never generated a solid Free

Trade culture, but it set limits on protectionism. Some revisionists, like Bernstein, who knew MacDonald well, favoured Free Trade internationalism. But there were also others, like Max Schippel, who wanted a free hand with regard to industrial protection and imperial expansion.[169]

What was distinctive about the Labour party in Britain was not some worn-out inherited Cobdenism, nor a simple calculation that, in an export-oriented nation, globalization and social welfare went hand in hand. Labour leaders were deeply sceptical about globalization, indeed fearful of an imminent collapse of the global order into rival blocs. Much more so than popular Liberals, they had recognized that cartels and trusts were changing the capitalist order. What set them apart was an ethical internationalism which could draw on broader support in radical culture. If, as far as Labour was concerned, Free Trade was increasingly standing only on this internationalist leg, it was a strong and healthy leg nonetheless.

Chamberlain was the best thing that could have happened to Free Trade. At the turn of the nineteenth to the twentieth century, confidence in an open and peaceful global trading system was steadily diminishing. Within the state and new social movements, and across industrial and commercial sectors, there was a search for more flexible instruments to respond to foreign tariffs, trusts, and subsidies. Free Trade's days looked numbered. Proposals for reciprocity offered the best of both worlds: a state that would be more assertive in securing markets abroad but that did not touch the people's food. Chamberlain's Tariff Reform crusade completely transformed the stakes. Tariff Reform polarized the political world. The demand for an all-out general tariff with imperial preferences, on the one hand, and the popular Free Trade cheap loaf, on the other, eliminated the space for moderate reforms and ideas of a third way. Political choices were fenced in, and the fence cut right across the middle ground. Statesmen and businessmen toying with bargaining tariffs and Labourites dreaming of greater self-sufficiency were forced to settle on one side. Balfour's problem was that he tried to stand with one foot on either side. Free Trade had some cosmopolitan supporters, but it would be misleading to see its survival as a sign of Britain's embrace of globalization. Free Trade derived its strength from its ability to accommodate both imperialist sentiments and an older radical internationalism. Ethics mattered more than economics.

PART II

Unravelling

Prologue

In 1913 history seemed on the side of Free Trade. The year 'was more satisfactory to the Free Trade movement throughout the world than any in the history of the Cobden Club', its members were told.[1] At home, Imperial Tariff Reform formally conceded defeat, when Bonar Law dropped the food tax from the Conservative programme in December 1912. The Edwardian boom was in full swing. Internationally, too, the wind was blowing in a liberal direction. In Holland, tariffs were defeated at the polls, and the United States adopted the Underwood tariff, lowering its trade barriers to the lowest level for half a century. In Germany and Austria, people were protesting in the streets against agrarian tariffs and high food prices. At last, Cobden's prophecy appeared fulfilled: as other countries began to approach Britain's level of civilization and development, they were following its Free Trade lead.[2]

A year later the world was at war. When peace returned in 1918, the global trade system lay in tatters. The political and commercial landscape of Europe had been transformed. The break-up of the continental empires left behind a new multitude of states. Goods had to cross 7,000 additional miles of customs barriers. For old and new nations alike, the war demonstrated the importance of controlling their own economic destiny. Commercial treaties became shorter and more complex to enhance bargaining power. The world's pre-eminent trading and lending nation at the beginning of the war, Britain at the end was weaker and poorer. Foreign assets had been liquidated to pay for the war. Markets abroad were falling to the rising powers in the West and East, the United States and Japan.

The war shook the foundations of British society and politics. Liberals had entered the war united, with an unquestioned faith in the combined programme of Free Trade and social reform. They left the war divided, split over personalities, principles, and politics. Formally, the parties adhered to a 'tariff truce', burying the great ideological divide over trade for the sake of a war coalition. But, inevitably, the war put pressure on the Free Trade nation. Victorian and Edwardian liberals and radicals had upheld Free Trade as the bearer of democracy and peace. Now trading partners were at war with each other. For consumers, war brought shortages and inflation, and with them questions about the Free Trade ideal of 'cheapness' as an instrument of social justice. Producers and the state, in turn, were confronted with the limitations of a competitive system based on small individual firms and free exchange. When peace returned, the state would retreat from controlling the economy, but the broader erosion of pre-war beliefs and assumptions continued. The connections between commerce, civil society, and consumption that had created the Free Trade nation had begun to fray.

4

Consumers Divided

Yes, we know there is a war on! Have we not sent our sons, brothers, and husbands to fight for the King.... But we also know that we are being robbed right and left by the profiteer, and that every halfpenny of war bonus that is doled out to us with the right hand is snatched back with the left. We know that our children are suffering from filthy scabs caused by the war food.... Even a semblance of equity in the distribution of foodstuffs would have satisfied us; but when a Government ... fails, after three-and-a-half years, to grapple with the problem of the people's food, it is time for us to raise our voices and demand that the same despatch and thoroughness that was brought to bear in raising and equipping the army shall now be used in organising an equitable distribution of food.

Eleanor Cuddeford, a woman from Salford, January 1918.[1]

The period of free trade and freedom of competition ... had passed away, never to return. Competition among traders could no longer be regarded as any real protection to the consumer.

Charles McCurdy, parliamentary secretary to the Ministry of Food, in a speech at Northampton, 24 February 1920.[2]

Eat an Empire apple a day and help to keep the dole away.

Conservative women's magazine, July 1925.[3]

P eace was not yet one year old when on Sunday, 21 September 1919, thousands of men, women, and children descended on London's Hyde Park. They had come not to play but to protest against high prices. At lunchtime, ten processions of Labour and cooperative marchers set out from across the metropolitan area with bands, banners, fife, and drum. Estimates of the number of demonstrators stretched from 100,000 to 250,000; Labour's *Daily Herald* even went as high as 500,000. In spite of the unseasonably 'cold and nippy' air, this was one of the largest popular demonstrations since the twentieth century began. The procession took forty minutes

just to pass through Trafalgar Square. In Hyde Park, sixty speakers on
ten platforms attacked high prices, profiteers, and capitalist trusts. One of
them, Jack Jones, a Labour MP, urged protesters to unite to 'knock a nail
in the coffin of Capitalism and give it a decent funeral'. Another—Bob
Williams—called on people to give three cheers for the International
Socialist Revolution, inspiring a 'response of the great gathering [that]
spoke volumes for their vocal powers'.

The crowd was angry about the price of food, especially the price
of milk. Marion Phillips, Labour's leading woman organizer, denounced
the recent price hikes. More than any other food, milk had come to
illustrate the injustice of the current system. Mrs Barton of the Women's
Cooperative Guild spoke of the day-to-day realities of milk profiteering:
dealers were selfishly driving up prices, robbing the people of that most
necessary food. The mass demonstration culminated in a series of joint
resolutions, read simultaneously from the ten platforms at 5.15 pm, calling
for a fight against capitalist trusts and profiteers. The free market had failed.
Only regulation and public controls could free the public from the tentacles
of trusts.[4]

There would be no revolution in Britain, and Britons were spared
the extremes of privation that ravaged the rest of Europe. Nonetheless,
London and Glasgow, as much as Barcelona, Paris, and Berlin, witnessed
food protests and consumer activism. The war opened a Pandora's box of
questions about the rights and duties of consumers. Inflation and shortages,
market failure and profiteering taught a crash course in popular economics.
If Britain managed to escape the mortal crisis of legitimacy that pulled
down Germany and her allies, the war still cracked the foundations of
popular Free Trade.

From the outset of war, consumption was handled differently in Britain
than in enemy countries. Britain declared war as a Free Trade country.
Whereas in Germany and Austria-Hungary governments were quick to seek
out consumers and organize them into committees to promote rationing
and fight waste, the British state saw consumers as represented by market
and civil society. It was suspicious of granting them any official status in
the running of the war. The war, however, soon brought bottlenecks and
inflation, and with it explosive questions about fairness. Were loyal patriotic
consumers entitled to food, and if so to how much and at what price?
And who had the right and power to decide what was a 'fair' price and
share?

The divergence in their approach to managing the economy in the first half of the war left Britain and Germany with opposite cycles of expectations and conflict in the second half. Germany introduced rationing early to achieve equity based on need. But this egalitarian ambition also meant that, with the spread of black markets and hunger in 1916–18, anger was quickly directed at the regime itself for failing to deliver on its promises. The German state collapsed because it had raised expectations of social justice that proved impossible to satisfy.[5] Britain, meanwhile, resisted rationing. The British state ignored demands by workers and consumers for the control of food. In the opening two years of the war, this laissez-faire policy arguably helped to defuse grievances. As the war entered its third and fourth years, however—especially after Germany resumed unrestricted submarine warfare in February 1917—soaring prices and precarious food supplies made it increasingly dangerous to ignore consumers.

That milk was the centre of attention in the Hyde Park demonstration of September 1919 was no accident. Milk was about nutrition and healthy mothers and children, but it was about far more than that. It was the liquid successor to the cheap white loaf, illustrating the workings of the economy and where consumers stood in relation to state and civil society.[6] Profiteering and shortages prompted a new, social democratic vision of the consumer. Instead of cheapness and an open market, this new vision looked to democratic entitlements, fair shares, and regulated, stable supplies and prices. That fairness was more important than cheapness was a motto that also attracted a consumer movement with a quite different social and ideological complexion, centred on more middle-class and imperialist Conservative women. Buying food, they argued, should be an expression of caring for their imperial brothers and sisters. A rival Conservative model of the citizen consumer was gaining ground, fighting state regulation but shopping for Empire.

Queuing Up

The labour movement had demanded the public control of food from the outset of war. During the July crisis Labour leaders joined together in a War Emergency Workers' National Committee to speak with one voice against the threat of war. When over one hundred delegates finally met on 5 August 1914, war had broken out. The National Committee brought together leaders from the Labour party, trade unions, the Women's Labour

League, and the cooperative societies. Already at its first meeting it called for a Consumers Council to protect the people against exploitation, for fixed maximum prices, and for the government to take over the purchase and distribution of food. A month later, in September 1914, it urged the commandeering of the national wheat supply. Demands for state control of freights, the municipal control of milk, and free milk for nursing mothers soon followed.[7]

The National Committee had to perform a difficult balancing act between offering patriotic support for the war effort and defending working-class men and women against the consequences of government policies. Inevitably, this patriotic imperative limited its power with the government, which in the first two years of the war simply ignored the labour and cooperative movements. The popular mood was equally unresponsive. Nationwide campaigns for food control met with apathy in major towns from Bradford to Cardiff in January and February 1915. The 'people did not care a button' about the Committee's efforts, one cooperator reluctantly concluded.[8]

All this changed in the course of 1916 and 1917. The increase in prices in the first four months of the war had been relatively mild (16 per cent) and many people had compensated for it by working overtime. But the rise in food prices did not stop. By the summer of 1916 they stood at 161 per cent of pre-war prices. A year later, they had risen to 204 per cent. British prices for beef, bread, butter, and milk rose faster between 1914 and 1917 than in any other country at war, except Austria.[9] For most foods, prices continued to rise slowly after the winter of 1917–18, reaching their peak in 1920 (291 per cent).

The government's initial response was to appeal to voluntarism and patriotic sacrifice. Already in October 1914 a National Food Economy League had been formed to fight waste. In London, some eighty speakers worked with the London County Council to teach school children how to get more out of their food by eating more slowly. The government threw its weight behind a campaign for frugality. Films promoting thrift and food economy were produced for the Treasury and the Ministry of Food. The first Food Controller, Lord Davenport, launched a programme of 'voluntary rationing'. In spring 1917, the campaign began for a 'National Lent'. Britons were urged to follow the King's example, eat 25 per cent less bread and reduce their overall consumption by one-quarter. Such heroic sacrifices would merit a metal badge announcing 'on voluntary rations'; the initial response was so enthusiastic that the Ministry of Munitions had to step in to protect scarce metal supplies. The badge was replaced by a 'very small bow' and purple ribbon more 'suitable' for women. By February 1918, the Ministry of Food estimated that an average of five million people saw moving pictures or lantern slides about the food problem every week. Domestic economy teachers were touring the country, training some 3,000 fellow teachers. Arthur Yapp's League of National Safety, which campaigned for food economy across the country, claimed over three million members.[10]

These numbers were impressive, their practical effect less so. Experts on the Royal Society's Food Committee were in despair. The official 'voluntary rations' ignored the very basics of nutrition, only allowing for half the required calories.[11] They were also out of touch with the everyday constraints faced by most working people. People who had to turn over every penny several times to afford basic foods like milk, tea, and butter had little use for cookery demonstrations and exhortations to cut back on bread and eat more fish and game. To many it felt 'something like impertinence' to be lectured by people 'from a higher stratum of society' about how best to economize.[12]

The government's initial response was to try and woo consumers and producers alike, by extending food controls and introducing maximum prices. In August 1914 it had set up a first commission to buy and sell sugar and regulate its supply. But much more was to come in the last months of 1916. In October it set up a Wheat Commission, a government trading concern with the power to purchase, sell, and distribute wheat and flour. The Price of Milk Order of 1916 further interfered with the laws of supply and demand.

By 1917, the government was forced to reverse its earlier opposition to rationing and its arms-length, even patronizing treatment of organized consumers. Inflation, shortages, and unrest could no longer be ignored. Meat, tea, bacon, and cheese were becoming scarce. A 'Monstre [sic] Protest Meeting' at the old Pudsey Street Stadium in Liverpool in August 1916 signalled a new, aggressive tone: 'Workers! Come in Your Thousands and Bring Your Wives'.[13]

Queues began to disrupt vital munitions work. Men and women began to campaign for food control. In towns like Huddersfield, handbills about the 'Dear Food Scandal' were circulating in May 1917. In the same month, workers in Coventry downed their tools because of food shortages.

Food prices threatened to undermine the war effort. High prices and the unequal distribution of food were a major source of conflict in the summer of 1917, the Commissioners on Industrial Unrest reported. August 1917 had seen demonstrations in most large cities, from London to York and Plymouth. Some of these were violent. In Sheffield women threatened to raid shops. The language at labour demonstrations, too, became more ominous. A convention on the national food supply in December 1917, organized by the main labour bodies, warned the government 'very gravely' that 'organised workmen will not tamely endure either government inefficiency in its primary function of assuring the Food Supply, still less any favour to private food-dealers or to the well-to-do classes'.[14] In Manchester in January 1918, men and women in munitions factories stopped work for several hours to demand rationing to guarantee equal distribution of food for all. At the Vickers' plant, workers took the morning off to help with the family shopping. In Brighton, railway workers, women, and children 'a thousand strong' demonstrated in front of the local food committee and threatened to stop work if food supplies were not increased.

Queuing for food was getting in the way of working for victory.[15] There was a growing sense that working people were the victims of daylight robbery. Why else were queues widespread only in working-class districts? The snake-like profiteer and monopolist became ubiquitous images. Soldiers, it seemed, were being betrayed on the home front: 'Whilst the Soldier risks his life, the Monopolists robs the wife', as a leaflet by the *Daily Citizen* summed it up.[16]

The government realized it needed to play more to consumers to contain unrest. If the Free Trade revival in the Edwardian period had been built around a solid phalanx of radical liberals and cooperators, the early years of the war saw widening rifts between the Liberal-led coalition government and the organized consumer movement. The cooperatives were responsible for 10 per cent of the retail trade and had three million members. Yet the state refused to draw on this vast machinery to address the food problem. Worse, the government included the co-ops in the general excess profits tax. This not only challenged their very self-identity as a not-for-profit social enterprise, it cost them dearly—nearly £1 million in 1916 and 1917.[17] Tellingly, the Ministry of Food was set up in early 1917 without cooperative representatives. Later that summer, local Food Committees were introduced to tackle problems of distribution, register retailers, and to turn central policy into local reality. Two thousand of these Food

Committees were eventually set up—'the most important single decision' in the career of the Ministry, as William Beveridge, the architect of Britain's rationing scheme, would recall.[18] Yet, at first, cooperators were equally missing from these local committees.

This was a confrontational course. As one local cooperative society in a Glasgow suburb advertised: 'Parliament refuses to save you. Join Kinning Park Co-op. now and save yourself.'[19] This was precisely what more and more people did. The movement mushroomed during the war from three to four million members. And, abandoning Free Trade wisdom, it concluded that the state was no longer neutral. To defend their interests, cooperators needed political representation. The Cooperative party was born.

The appointment in June 1917 of Lord Rhondda, the second Food Controller in charge of the Ministry of Food, set a new tone. From the outset, Rhondda presented himself as a man of the people. Much was made of his initial plebeian background as the 'son of a grocer'—he was the fifteenth of seventeen children (only five survived) of a Welsh shopkeeper who rose to become a powerful coal owner and a strong supporter of trades union rights. Rhondda set out with a public relations campaign to defuse the growing agitation about profiteers. The popular belief that profiteering was widespread was undermining the legitimacy of the state. The main cause of the food problem, Rhondda explained in September 1917, was not profiteers but world scarcity and high freight charges. They were beyond the government's control. The answer was not to take over businesses and eliminate all profit, but to protect the consumer by fixing prices and allowing only reasonable profit.

Rhondda also turned the Ministry of Food into a major arm of the state. Staff increased tenfold. Controls increased in leaps and bounds. In spring 1917, farmers and farm labourers were guaranteed prices and wages in an attempt to boost production. The nine-penny loaf was introduced in September, supported by a £50 million flour subsidy. The same month brought controls of the meat retail price. By the end of the war 94 per cent of all food consumed in the UK was subject to ceiling or maximum prices.[20] The 'predatory middleman', the Ministry proclaimed, 'has been almost wholly eliminated'.[21] Fines for violators were doubled at the end of the year, and the Ministry publicized its tough action against irresponsible citizens, such as Miss Caroline Stiff, who was fined £5 for feeding bread and milk to her dogs for breakfast. Between June 1917 and April 1918 there were 7,000 prosecutions with 6,000 convictions for profiteering and fraudulent declarations.[22]

By the end of 1917 the government was seeking to contain increasingly assertive and rebellious consumers by co-opting them. Consumers were no longer mere victims of the food situation, they would be part of the solution. The 'fundamental fact', the Ministry of Food emphasized, was that 'it is the consumer who provides the motive force for the producing organisation, and that, therefore, it rests very largely with the individual how far the rise in prices may be checked and the existing supplies of commodities equitably distributed'. Instead of just leaving it to voluntary action, however, the government now recognized the contribution an organized consumer interest could make. Forgetting the many earlier snubs, Rhondda announced that the government would work hand-in-hand with the cooperative societies. Since they 'represent consumer's interests', their inclusion was the first priority.[23]

In January 1918, the government institutionalized this strategy of coop-tation by creating a Consumers' Council. It was composed of six members from the Cooperative Congress, six from the Trades Union Congress and the War Workers Emergency Committee, and three from women's indus-trial organizations. The women's representatives included Marion Phillips and Mrs M. Cottrell from the Women's Cooperative Guild, a Birmingham city councillor and the first woman director of the Cooperative Wholesale Society. Together, these women and men represented movements with six million members. In addition, there were three members representing 'un-organised consumers', including the Countess of Selborne, the conservative suffragist and daughter of Lord Salisbury. Formally only an advisory body, the Consumers' Council played a vital role in connecting the Ministry of Food to consumer and labour groups across the country. Its role was to investigate prices and shortages and consult with the government. In return, it would give the state's food policies a much-needed air of legitimacy. If there was to be rationing, fixed prices, and controls, consumers would be made to share the responsibility.

Organized consumers reacted ambivalently to this new role. Since 1914, labour and cooperatives had pressed for the representation of the consumer interest. Powerful unions like the Dockers' Union even called for a Consumers' League. Now, many in the labour movement suspected (rightly) that for Rhondda one purpose of the Council was to take the heat off government by persuading people that better supplies and prices were simply impossible. Robert Smillie, the miners' union leader and a staunch opponent of the war, and H. J. May, the cooperator, had both rejected Lloyd George's invitations to serve as Food Controller precisely because they did not want to be implicated in government policy. They would have wanted powers to hang profiteers and eliminate private traders, not just to fix prices and then justify them to the public. The Consumers' Council was a poisoned chalice. The Workers' National Committee felt 'very much like a fire brigade called up after the blaze has got going', facing an almost hopeless task.[24] Robert Williams of the National Transport Workers' Federation accepted his nomination with reluctance, feeling that the Council was little more than a government 'screen' to cover up past failures.[25] But there were also those, who, although feeling the U-turn in policy came dangerously late, saw the Council as an opportunity to create at last a consumer watchdog and steer policy in the direction of controls and fair shares. This group included J. R. Clynes, the Labour leader at the Ministry of Food who would chair the Consumers' Council, and cooperators and Labour women like Phillips.[26]

The Consumers' Council held its first meetings in January 1918 just as queues and demands for the complete control of foodstuffs were reaching their peak. In the winter of 1917–18 unprecedented queues emerged across the country—more than half a million people were stuck in queues in London on Saturdays in late January and February 1918.[27] In Bristol, the Cooperative Wholesale Society was demanding compulsory rationing. 'Sensible women' were urged not to riot but to express their anger peacefully. At a conference in Battersea, Labour, trade unions, and cooperatives called on the government to immediately control all necessaries of life.[28]

From the outset, the Consumers' Council made it clear it would be no simple mouthpiece of government policy. Rhondda emboldened them. The Food Controller told the Council at their first meeting that old liberal principles had ceased to work: 'they had put political economy on the shelf'. 'Free competition had its chance for three years': all it had brought was price rises and shortages.[29] Meat rationing was finally introduced in February 1918 in London and extended to the rest of the country in April. By July, a general food rationing system was in place. Queues disappeared. The rapid increase in prices was checked. Yet the new Consumers' Council was not satisfied with short-term material improvements. It strove to turn its limited advisory powers to maximum effect, initiating inquiries into profits, prices, and distribution, and demanding greater state controls. If the crisis of provision went away, the new knowledge and political ambition of consumers did not go with it.

Liquid Politics

In January 1918, readers opened *The Co-operative News* to learn of a coming 'world shortage of food', a new era in which 'national life will wither' for those nations unable to subsist on the food grown on their own soil. The war had shown that traders could unite against the cooperatives. For 'the people's economic improvement, for their social improvement, for their education, for their liberty from the thraldom of profiteer and diplomatic caste', consumers needed to organize and carry the 'fight for the people's livelihood' to Parliament.[30] To this call for action, the events of 1918 added the painful day-to-day realities of food shortages.

More than anything, it was the 'milk famine' which stirred emotions and provided a popular vocabulary for the increasingly heated debate about fairness and the rights of consumers. The Consumers' Council provided a new outlet for consumer frustration through its inquiries into milk pricing, distribution, and profiteering. Consumers, it found, had been right to complain about milk being too expensive or too hard to come by in working-class districts. Milk was scarce, overpriced, and dirty because the market was chaotic. Just as the 'cheap loaf' had symbolized a liberal vision of social equity and inclusion before the war, so the milk crisis now showed how unregulated trade led to unfairness and exclusion. The milk crisis cast a shadow over the entire liberal system of markets and trade that had ruled before the war.

Serious problems in the supply, distribution, and pricing of milk gathered pace during the war, culminating in 'milk famines' in the winters of 1917–18 and 1918–19. Cities like Paris and The Hague also experienced milk scarcities during the war,[31] but the situation in Britain was especially grim. In the mid-winter of 1919, Britons had to make do with 25 per cent less milk than normal, and 15 per cent less than in 1918. Britain's cows had failed to keep up with the growth of her human population in the late nineteenth and early twentieth centuries. By the time war broke out, Britain had only about 2.8 million milch cows, fewer per person than the other European powers.

Wartime policy made things worse. The government's trust in markets in the early stages of the war had catastrophic consequences. Milch cow herds need to be raised over time. For many of the first calf heifers in 1915 the 'invisible hand' of the market worked with deadly efficiency. Farmers slaughtered their heifers to cash in on high meat prices, rather than invest in future milk production. *The Statist* noted how the number of cattle reared for beef in the United Kingdom increased during the war by 200,000, while milch cows declined by at least 80,000.[32] Figures from the Ministry of Food were more optimistic, suggesting even an increase of 100,000 in the dairy herd. But, ultimately, what mattered was not just the number of cows but how much milk they gave. And that was falling sharply. Milch cows had to do without hay, now requisitioned for the army. Shipping was moving men and munitions, leaving less room to import feedstuffs; the supply of linseed and cottonseed dropped by 50 per cent. Farmers had to do without skilled farm labour, and as anyone who has helped on a farm knows all too well, it needs an experienced hand to milk a cow properly. In an average year before the war, there were 1.23 billion gallons of liquid milk. By 1918 this had dropped to a mere 955 million.[33]

Uneven distribution turned this scarcity into 'famine' for most poorer and working-class consumers. The increased consumption of milk in army hospitals and munitions works meant that there was even less milk in the pail that made it down a residential street. In addition, there were the demands of industrial consumers, like the producers of cheese, chocolate, and condensed milk. The government eventually restricted the sale of cream and chocolate, and drastically reduced the manufacture of cheese and condensed milk. Even then, only 645 million gallons of milk out of a total of 955 were left for drinking. In winter, when cows produced less milk in the first place, this left not even a quarter of a pint per head per day.

Highly uneven social and regional patterns of distribution meant many people had access to even less than the quarter-pint. The problem was not simply that milk carts carried less milk, but that they seldom if ever found their way into many parts of the country. Local food control committees found that people in Inverness only consumed 0.10 pints per head per day, while Londoners enjoyed three times that much. Wartime scarcity exacerbated existing disparities. Britons on average drank less milk than Americans, Canadians, the French, or Danes—people in New York and Paris drank more than half a pint per person per day, twice as much as people in London. Even more striking was the divergence along class lines. In New York, consumption in the poorer quarters was 40 per cent higher than in wealthier districts. In British cities, by contrast, it was the poor who tasted little or no milk. In early Victorian Britain, skilled workers had drunk more milk than members of the gentry. By the early twentieth century, the opposite was true. In Bradford, for example, people drank

about 14,500 gallons of milk a day; two-thirds of this was still produced
within the city itself. But 22 per cent of homes never got any milk at all,
the local Health Committee estimated, leading in these areas to 'abnormal
malnutrition, infantile sickness, and unnecessary death'.[34] The milk system
was a postcode lottery of life and death: areas of poor supply were also areas
of high infant mortality.[35]

In April 1917, the government appointed a committee, chaired by Lord
Astor, to consider steps to boost milk supplies and ensure they reached
all sections of the community. As winter approached, protests against the
imminent 'milk famine' became ever harder to ignore. In Winsford there
was no milk because the local milk association refused to supply the Food
Committee at maximum prices set by the government. In Glasgow, there
was too much milk, but most consumers could not afford it. Elsewhere
producers and retailers were fined for selling milk above the maximum price
of 1s. 4d. per gallon. Local Food Control Committees had already secured
powers to give poor areas priority treatment. Now local councils added
pressure on government to subsidize milk for poor infants, children, and
mothers. In the House of Commons, Labour MPs pointed to working-
class areas where people could not find any milk at all. There were
parliamentary questions about London dairymen buying the best milking
cows and refusing to sell them back to the farmers, 'as it pays them better
to fatten them off for the butcher'.[36] When the Astor Committee's second
interim report appeared it confirmed what many had suspected: the existing
distribution system created enormous waste.

The government was trapped between a rock and a hard place. The
only way to keep dairy farmers milking their cows rather than selling
them for beef was to raise the price of milk. Farmers threatened to kill
their beasts unless they were allowed higher prices[37]—a threat that was
especially effective in winter, when 37 per cent of dairy cows were dry,
twice as many as in summer. In November 1917, the food controller
introduced a maximum price of 2s. 8d. per gallon—more than double
the peacetime price; this was raised further to 3s. 4d. the following year.
Raising prices too far, however, threatened a consumer rebellion and
charges of government-approved profiteering. If the government was to
walk this tightrope successfully, it needed to give its pricing policy an air of
democratic legitimacy. The Consumers' Council became an essential part
of this balancing act. It was given powers to investigate the milk situation,
including pricing and distribution.

London, more than any other place, came to symbolize the chaos of the market. On the one hand, the Consumers' Council found that milk was going to waste in some parts of the city, as numerous retailers fought over the same neighbourhoods. On the other, attempts to centralize distribution by the United Dairies, a combine founded in 1915, raised fears of a giant monopoly squeezing consumers. Milk travelled a long way from cow to consumer, which meant high prices and low quality, as milk easily went sour in transit. Once in the city, it was carted to various parts for treatment, rather than being treated centrally. And decentralized treatment and retailing meant that bottling and pasteurization lagged considerably behind France, Germany, and the United States. In Britain, pasteurization had mainly worked as a 'cloak' to hide poor treatment and disorganization, according to the Consumers' Council. Local medical officers of health renewed their pre-war efforts and told the Council of the 'large amount of cow-dung and other dirt' that polluted people's milk.[38]

The Astor Committee had already highlighted waste and reported in favour of war-time control. The Consumers' Council went much further. It called for permanent control, a government takeover of the milk trade, the introduction of grading to promote cleaner milk, centralized distribution, a national milk clearing house and subsidized milk for the poor, infants, and mothers.[39] Government policy went half way to meet these demands. A Milk Control Board was set up, which included Mrs Cottrell of the Consumers' Council, as well as producer interests; it looked at various aspects of distribution, from the improvement of churns to the simplification of transport. In 1918 the state was on the point of taking over the entire wholesale milk trade.

Trusts and Freedom

The coming of peace put the brakes on the momentum towards control. True, some reforms were carried forward. Milk grading, for example, was introduced to promote purer, healthier milk. The Milk (Mothers and Children) Orders of 1918 and 1919 expanded the power of local authorities to provide children and nursing and expectant mothers with milk for free or at less than cost price—$1\frac{1}{2}$ pints daily for children under 18 months, 1 pint daily for children between 18 months and 5 years, and as much milk to nursing mothers as the local health officer saw fit. But if this was a step forward, it fell short of the Consumers' Council demand for complete control of supply and distribution and for a fair price. The Mothers and Children Order was merely permissive legislation. Consumers remained at the mercy of their local government's ability or willingness to spend tax-payers' money to subsidize cheap milk.[40]

If consumers were increasingly identified as victims of a wasteful, chaotic, and dangerous commercial system, they were far from passive or silent. Local actions gave muscle to the Council's findings. In November 1918, housewives in Chertsey organized a 'silent strike', refusing to buy fresh milk for a week in protest against high prices. In Staines, women started a 'muddling strike', buying a lot of milk one day and nothing the next to upset the plans of 'profiteers'. In both towns, these strategies were effective: traders reduced the price of milk from 1s. a quart to 10d.

This was a new kind of mass consumer politics. Boycotts and buycotts had been the weapon of choice amongst mainly middle-class consumer leagues on both sides of the Atlantic in the generation before the war. Now they became the tools of grassroots activism. There were mass demonstrations. The Women's Cooperative Guild organized protests across the country against the high price of milk. Fifty of its branches took some form of direct action about the price and supply of milk; some even stepped in and distributed milk themselves when the 'milk interests declined to deliver'. In London, there were demonstrations at Charing Cross. In Bristol, a thousand women marched to the council house shouting 'We Want Cheaper Milk' and 'God Save the Babies'.[41]

Yet milk was not just an issue for women and children. The National Federation of Discharged and Demobilized Sailors and Soldiers added their voice to the protests against the high price of milk.[42] The inquiries by the Consumers' Council raised fundamental questions about consumer rights, social justice, and political legitimacy. In September 1919, for example, delegates from Food Committees in the south west of England met at Exeter to discuss policy. James Owen, mayor of Exeter, argued that they needed to give more voice to the consumer and the retailer, and less to the producer—the only voice parliament and politicians seemed to hear. Dr Winter of Torquay found refuge in metaphors, comparing politicians to an orange: 'the more they squeezed them the more they would give away. But, unlike the orange, they did not give away of their own, but gave away the rights of the community by further taxing the community.' He was greeted with applause when he insisted that 'as consumers', they all had a right to know the findings of the Consumers' Council travelling commission that had investigated prices. 'Milk was an essential food, and it was wicked to put up the price beyond the figure that it legitimately should be put to.' The meeting ended by condemning price increases.[43] In south Wales 'much unrest' was caused by the high price of milk, and feeling became so 'intense' in December 1919 that all the food committees in south Wales threatened to resign unless they were given separate powers to force a lower price on producers.[44]

In November 1919, Charles McCurdy, the parliamentary secretary at the Ministry of Food and one of the Lloyd George Liberals favouring tougher regulation, faced uncomfortable questions in Parliament. Milk, it was said, was being fed to pigs instead of to starving children.[45] Such images of starvation in the midst of plenty would become a dominant way of talking about world hunger in the twentieth century. They captured a sense of an ethical and economic mismatch between supply and needs, overproduction and underconsumption. Scarcities, high prices and distributional crises no longer seemed to be temporary glitches that could be quickly corrected by short-term paternalistic intervention. They appeared inherent in a commercial world. Regulation and the empowerment of consumers were the only answer. Here was an important difference to an older 'moral economy'. Milk was a stepping stone towards a more ambitious reform of the food system. By 1919–20, the Consumers' Council was demanding the democratic control of the purchase and distribution of all essential foodstuffs. Consumers were no longer protected by Free Trade: they needed a direct voice in government.

All of these plans for consumer representation and controls hinged on the surival of the Ministry of Food. A year after the war, the government announced plans to abolish it. The Consumers' Council urged instead that the Ministry be strengthened and made permanent. Only a Ministry with control over food imports and exports and with powers to purchase food would be strong enough to stem the influence of 'national and international food profiteering Trusts'. This was more than just an economic argument. In his report on the machinery of government, Lord Haldane had emphasized that government needed to avail itself of advisory bodies if it wanted to retain public confidence. The Consumers' Council went one step further. 'The continuance of a democratic, elected body on the lines of the Consumers' Council is essential', it argued. It was the only way to 'check policies favourable to sectional interests though detrimental to the community at large'.[46]

For Clynes, Labour's first chairman of the Consumers' Council, the Council was part of a democratic revolution. Consumers could not as easily look after themselves as producers could, yet most people were consumers rather than producers. In the existing system of liberal representative democracy, 'those whose duty it is to cater for the public at large' had not always held 'consumers' rights in … due regard'. 'Present and future government', Clynes insisted, 'must be less and less of a secret service.'[47] The Consumers' Council was a first step towards greater democratic transparency and accountability. Clynes continued to preach the gospel of government control and consumer representation when he succeeded Rhondda as Food Controller in July 1918. Addressing the fifth Labour Conference at Grosvenor House in September that year, he presented the Council as clear evidence that the Ministry of Food aimed to 'practice the doctrine of democracy'. Partly this was a rhetorical attempt to contain frustration with the recent increase in the price of milk. But it also reflected a genuine belief that democracy and active citizenship needed consumer representation. 'Democratic government must bring the governed into closer touch with those who governed them.' Bodies like the Consumers' Council gave expression to 'the wishes of the governed in the desire they had to take a personal part in their own internal affairs'.[48]

Organized consumers agreed. *The Co-operative News* praised the food card as 'an Agent of Reconstruction' and predicted that workers would embrace its democratizing qualities. Only 'plutocrats' would want to go back to the pre-war system. The food card meant 'dining a la carte' for all citizens and would drive 'the nation gradually to democratic conditions'.[49]

The conflict over milk, then, raised profound questions about entitlements and who had the right to decide what a 'fair price' was for 'essential' foodstuffs. The cooperative movement appealed to 'women as food controllers'. Drawing on the Hammonds' popular social history of the *Village Labourer*, it reminded consumers of earlier food crises like the one in 1795, when women seized grain and formed a public committee to regulate prices.[50] But the call for collective action now went further. Milk attracted so much attention precisely because investigations suggested that profiteering was endemic. Milk was a home product, undermining government propaganda that blamed higher prices on German submarines, costly shipping, and foreign markets—'those three great dopes that have served to keep the people quiet', in the words of the London Food Vigilance Committee, a coalition of Labour, cooperatives, and trade unionists. Profiteering was not limited to shipowners. It pinched the entire breakfast table. Cooperative dairy farms argued that commercial prices and wholesale traders' profit margins were too high. 'Upon whose evidence', the London Food Vigilance Committee asked, had it been decided that a 100 per cent increase in milk prices was justified? It amounted to *legalised profiteering*. Government was testing 'the claims of loyal citizenship'. How much longer would the people wait until they were going to 'demand and enforce by direct action, if necessary, that Commissions fixing prices should be public in their operation, and that the Co-operative and Labour Movements should have a majority represented upon all controlling and administrative authorities?'.[51]

None of this was to happen. A Profiteering Act was passed in 1919, but it only created powers to investigate. It fell far short of the Consumers' Council's demands for powers to set price ceilings, fix profits, and eliminate middlemen. As with milk, there would be no permanent state interference. Britain's approach was mild, particularly compared to Germany; in Britain in 1919 there were 21,698 prosecutions for profiteering in food, which included the illicit purchase and unlawful slaughtering of animals. In Germany in the middle of the war, the number of convictions had almost reached half a million, including 3,928 imprisonments.[52] Still, the growing agitation against profiteering left a deep and long-lasting imprint on the minds of consumers in the inter-war years, which the fall in prices after 1920 would not erase. The demand for 'fair prices' became tied to a demand for a redistribution of income through a 'conscription of riches' and a capital levy: stiff taxes would ensure that profiteers handed back what they had unfairly taken from consumers' pockets.

Attacks on profiteers became intertwined with fears of the growing power of trusts and combines. Before the war, liberals and radicals had trusted Free Trade to immunize Britain against trusts and cartels. The war exposed this as naive. Again, milk provided a test case. In 1915 the three leading wholesalers in London were amalgamated into the United Dairies. By the end of the following year it had a capital of £1 million. By 1920 it controlled 470 shops and 75 per cent of the London market.[53] The US-controlled meat trust posed a similar threat at a more global level. The meat trust controlled over 60 per cent of beef imports into Britain. Fearing that British consumers would end up in the grip of such international food trusts, the Consumers' Council even threatened to resign en masse in the summer of 1919 unless the government extended controls.[54]

The power and persistence of trusts undermined Free Trade's credibility. If combines and trusts could spring up in a Free Trade nation, then free exchange no longer guaranteed 'cheap prices'. Instead of protecting them, Free Trade left consumers at the mercy of mighty trusts. Women's pages in the cooperative press discussed the US Federal Trade Commission's investigation of the meat trust. 'We women are practically helpless victims of this evil system', caught 'in the tentacles of this huge trust monopoly'.[55] The ' "open market" is a fraudulent expression. How can there be an "open" market when so many sources of supply are controlled in the financial interests by various trusts and rings?', asked the *Co-operative News* in 1919.[56] In a front-page article in the *Co-operative News* in July 1919, T. W. Allen, the chairman of the parliamentary committee of the Cooperative Congress and knighted for his service on the Consumer Council, told readers that to 'talk of returning to pre-war conditions of trading is to "imagine a vain thing" '. Competition among traders no longer protected consumers. Instead it would only strengthen 'those great trade organisations which have come into being and are an open menace to the community'.[57]

Charles McCurdy, the Coalition Liberal who chaired the committee investigating trusts after the war, was especially attuned to the growing anxieties about American trusts and profiteers. He realized, he told the Consumer Council in the summer of 1919, that most Britons were more interested in high prices than in peace terms: 'a great many people would be willing to let off the Kaiser if they could hang a profiteer'. The 'really big offenders', however, were not the small profiteers but the big trusts. The local fishmonger who charged an extra penny was a 'drop in the ocean' compared to organized trusts. These had effectively brought 'the economic period of free competition to a close'. It did not matter what policy government chose: 'control of prices will certainly be no longer left to free play … but will be controlled by these trade organisations'. Britain was 'a kind of Alsatia amongst the countries of the world', McCurdy argued, the only major country which did not try to rein in trusts. It needed to follow the example of the United States, Canada, and Australia if it wanted to protect the consuming public against exploitation. Casting his eye back to the reign of Henry III, McCurdy mourned the abolition of medieval legislation against forestalling and engrossing in the 1840s, just at the time when Britain embraced Free Trade. 'It may be desirable to re-enact them (hear, hear).'[58]

Fears of world food shortages reinforced the alarmist tone. One year after the armistice, McCurdy warned that simply throwing open the doors to food imports would not resolve Britain's problems of food supply. The United States, South America, and all the resources of the British Empire were not sufficient for our 'future needs'. It was wrong to believe that 'a policy of free trade and laissez-faire will see us through. It will not.' European livestock had been reduced by a third, and the United States was expected to start importing meat. There would be a 'scramble for meat imports'. The meat trust would get away with 'speculative profiteering'. 'High prices are an evil, but fluctuating prices, prices that rapidly rise and fall, would be productive of far worse consequences to our national life.'[59] This was not an eccentric prophecy but part of the official statement of the Ministry of Food. Stable prices and secure supplies mattered more than cheapness.

Organized consumers agreed that they were no longer protected by Free Trade. What they could not agree on was what to put in its place. The Consumers' Council split in three directions. The majority embraced state control as the only effective democratic alternative to control by trust. A Labour conference in January 1920 praised the Ministry of Food as 'the most beneficient [department] of the Government'. To abolish it and 'allow the food of the people to be managed, controlled and manipulated by Trusts, Combines and Profiteers will precipitate a revolution in this country'. Without control, Marion Phillips prophesied, 'we go back not to the pre-war chaos with regard to food supplies, but to chaos infinitely worse'.[60] Most on the Council wanted permanent controls of all essential foods, food imports, and prices. This meant extending the scope of cooperative trade and continuing wartime experiments with international controls. As Golightly of the Cooperative Wholesale Society told the inter-allied cooperative conference at Paris in early 1919, 'he was just as heartily sick of the Manchester School ... as he was of Protection'.[61]

For a second group, however, state control threatened an older democratic tradition of civil society. This was especially true for the Women's Cooperative Guild, a body representing working-class and lower-middle-class consumers that had been at the forefront of democratic feminism. It had a particularly strong attachment to self-government and to keeping civil society apart from the state. Public bodies could not be trusted to monitor their own services for the benefit of consumers, Honora Enfield argued. Who would protect the consumer if a reactionary party gained the upper hand in local government? In times of industrial action, reactionary councils might even turn controls over milk and coal against the people. Full-blown national controls were even worse than local ones, since they would make government 'absolutely irresistible' and allow it to abuse its power in elections and public life. The answer for civil society-minded co-operators was not municipalization or nationalization but the independent growth of the cooperative movement.

At the time a cooperative takeover of the economy was not as unrealistic as it might sound today. The First World War had boosted membership from 2.9 million in 1913—one in ten of the British population—to 4.5 million in 1920. The cooperative milk trade expanded by leaps and bounds, from 1 per cent of the national market in 1910, to 6 per cent in 1925 and an impressive 26 per cent in 1939. One-fifth of groceries and provisions were in cooperative hands. In Leicester the cooperatives controlled 40 per cent of the milk trade in the early 1920s, in Derby even 60 per cent.[62] There were, then, good reasons to be optimistic about the coming of the cooperative commonwealth. Margaret Llewellyn Davies, who led the Women's Cooperative Guild for three decades until 1921, thought the war had proved the pre-eminence of consumption and cooperation over production and statism. The 'effects of the war have roused the consumer as never before and turned people's attention in the direction of Cooperation'. Amongst the cooperatives, profiteering was impossible. Here 'the consumer is accorded his rightful place in the social economy'. The consumer was the community. Consumption was the site of true power: 'The power of the basket is a greater one than the power of the loom or the vote.' And consumption distinguished civilization from barbarism. It was through international cooperation, not coordination between states, that a new world civilization would be built.[63]

This suspicion of the state drew on a powerful sense of pluralism. In any kind of society, 'capitalist or socialist', people had multiple identities, Honora Enfield explained. 'They are citizens in relation to other individuals; producers in relation to their work; consumers in relation to their food, clothes, and other possessions; learners in relation to their studies, and so on. The same individual may desire one thing as a citizen, another as a consumer, another as a producer.' To give the state power over all these 'sides of life' would suffocate freedom. 'The liberties of individuals and rights of minorities, even the wishes of the majority in regard to other aspects of life, may all be sacrificed to whichever interest is strongest at the moment.' This might be unavoidable in times of crisis, like war, but

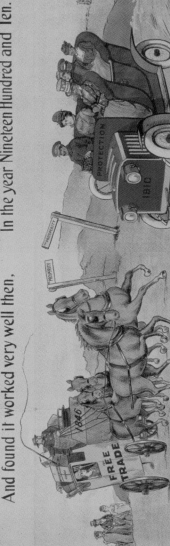

Plate 1 The modernity of protection versus the outdated vehicle of Free Trade, in a Conservative poster, c.1910.

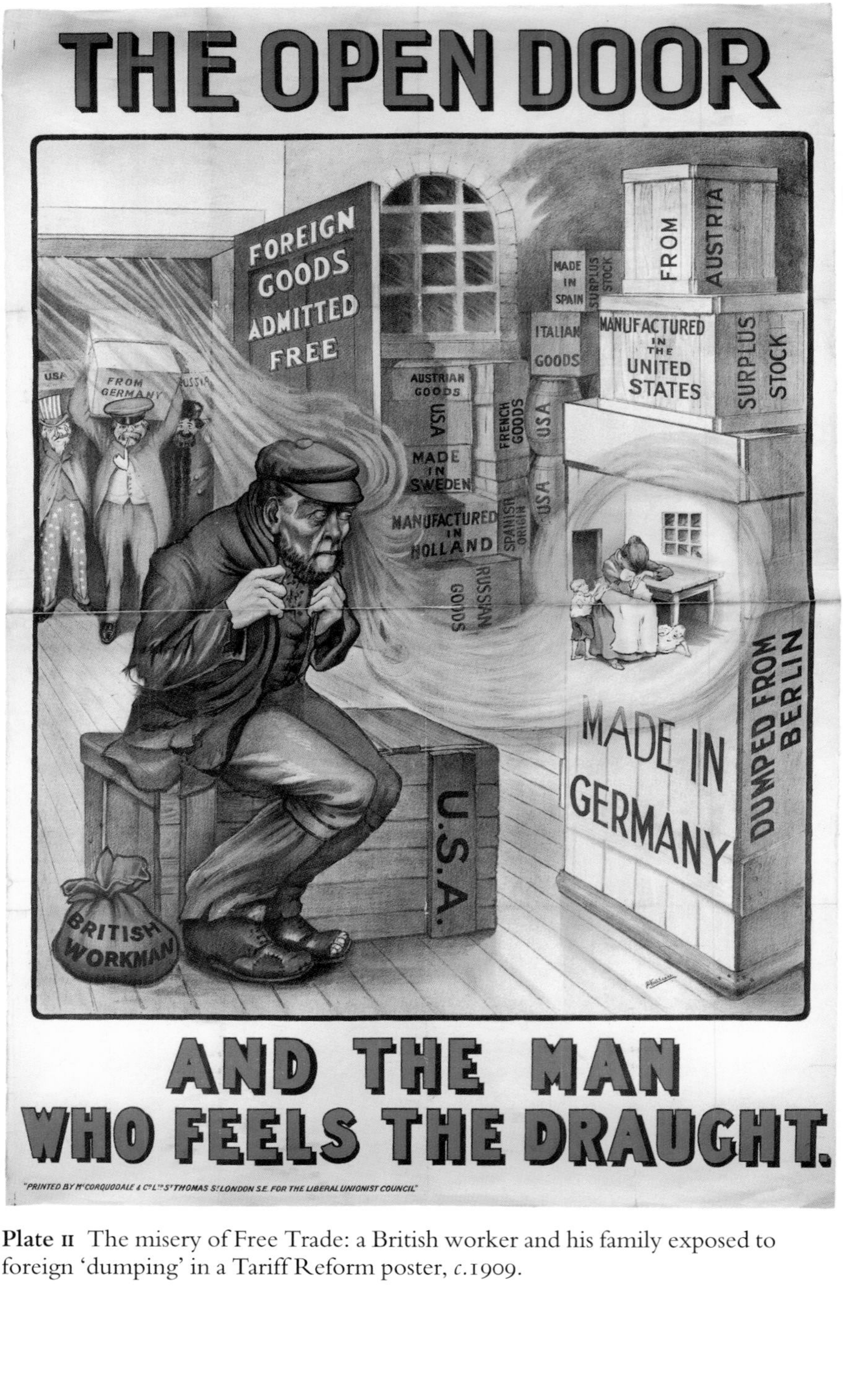

Plate II The misery of Free Trade: a British worker and his family exposed to foreign 'dumping' in a Tariff Reform poster, *c.*1909.

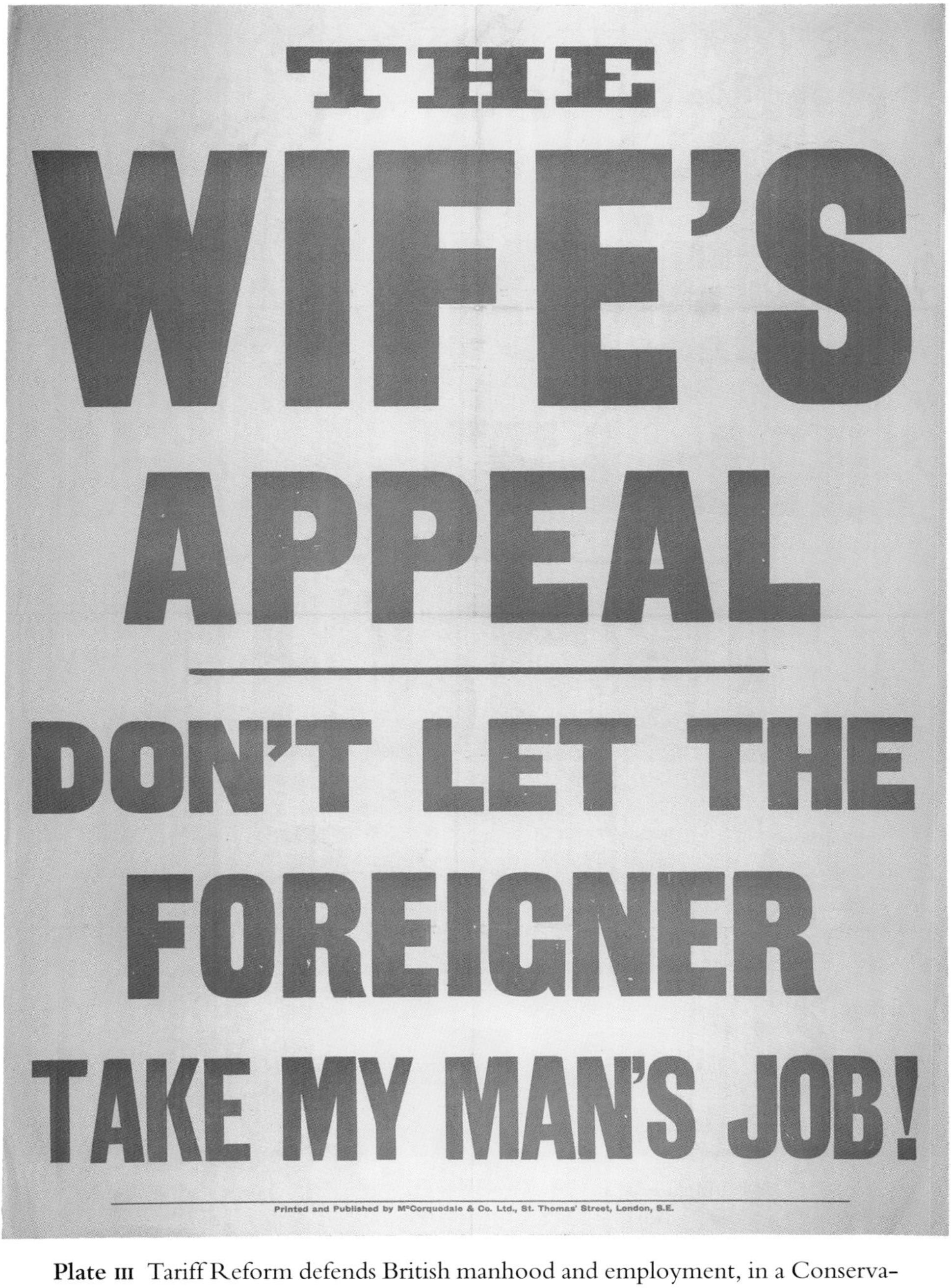

Plate III Tariff Reform defends British manhood and employment, in a Conservative poster, *c.*1905.

Plate IV 'The Hungry Forties', by Robert Morley, the Free Trade poster that won first prize from the National Liberal Club in 1905.

Plate v Conservatives waiting in ambush to attack Little Red Riding Hood with taxes. Free Trade poster, *c*.1909.

Plate VI Breaking into the home: protectionists are trying to get their hands on the Free Trade cupboard, in a Liberal postcard, *c.*1905.

Plate VII Women of all classes in a bustling Free Trade shop, while a poor shopkeeper, Joseph Chamberlain, is deserted in his overpriced and empty shop. Liberal poster, *c.*1905.

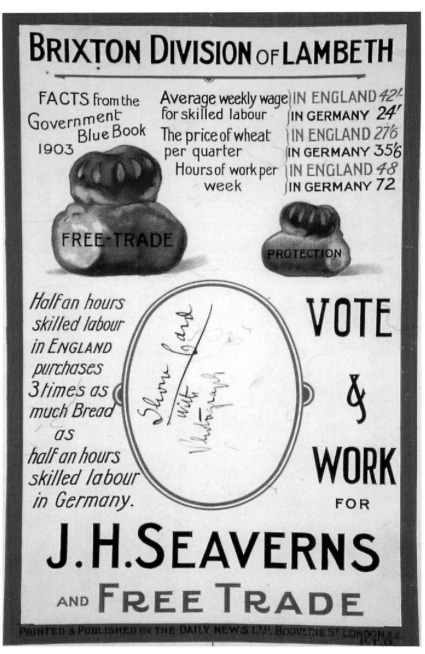

Plate VIII The big loaf and the small loaf as illustrations of the standard of living under Free Trade and protection, in a 1905 election card.

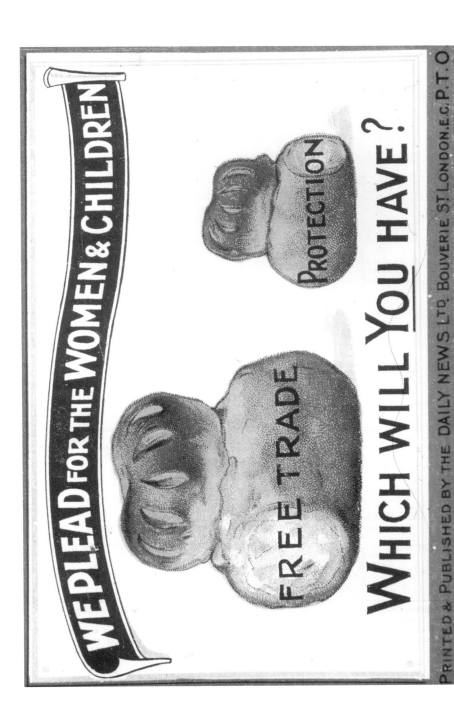

Plate IX Size speaks for itself: the big loaf and the small loaf in a 1905 election poster.

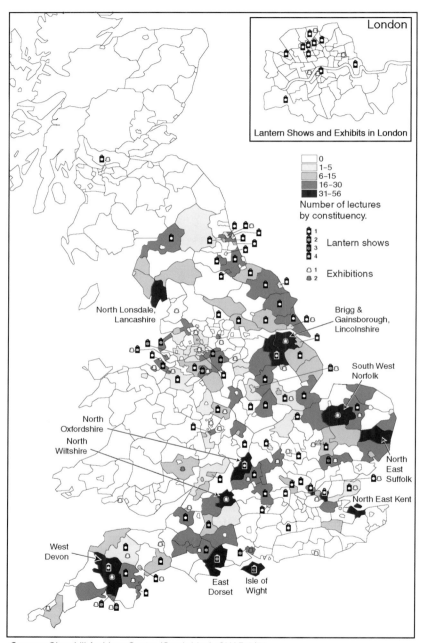

London

Lantern Shows and Exhibits in London

0
1–5
6–15
16–30
31–56

Number of lectures
by constituency.

1
2
3
4   Lantern shows

1
2   Exhibitions

North Lonsdale,
Lancashire

Brigg &
Gainsborough,
Lincolnshire

South West
Norfolk

North
Oxfordshire
North
Wiltshire

North
East
Suffolk

North East Kent

West
Devon

East
Dorset

Isle of
Wight

Source: Churchill Archives Centre (Cambridge), CHAR 2/54.

Plate xii Free Trade lectures, lantern shows, and exhibitions, in the run-up to the December 1910 election.

Plate XIII A rare photograph of a protectionist Dump Shop displaying cheap foreign goods; note the coffin at the entrance. The image was probably taken in Coventry, 1910.

Plate XIV A family driven to despair and destitution by Free Trade. T. B. Kennington's 1909 painting: the most widely disseminated picture in the Edwardian campaign.

Plate xv Mixing politics and advertising: Arthur Balfour with horns fighting Bannerman with the strength of Bovril, in an advert by S. H. Benson & Co., 1906.

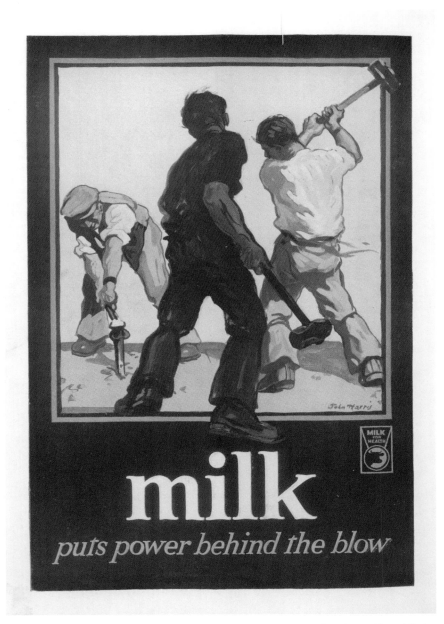

Plate xvi Milk as a source of industrial strength; a poster by the milk publicity campaign, 1923.

Plate XVII John Bull shops for the Empire: H. S. Williamson's poster for the Empire Marketing Board, 1928.

in general it was the dualism between state and society that promised to 'secure the largest and freest life for each individual and so the best possibility of progress for the community'.[64]

Above all, controls created growing resentment at the centre of the cooperatives as a business, the Cooperative Wholesale Society. Government controls interfered just as much in the day-to-day business of the CWS as they did in profit-making companies. Some wholesalers, like Allen, argued that cooperators needed to embrace the state if they wanted to survive the battle with organized capital. But what if state controls were strangling the cooperatives, others asked? Decontrol would give them back the freedom to purchase in the open market and a chance to fight trusts and combines head-on. The armour of the state, in this view, was really a straitjacket. This was the majority view, which narrowly captured the Cooperative Congress in December 1919.

The pressures for decontrol at home and the unravelling of international controls forced these viewpoints into direct confrontation. Amidst outcries against the 'waste' and 'inefficiency' of government controls, traders and grocers attacked the Consumers' Council as an unrepresentative kabal. Later, in 1919–20, as the campaign against government controls gathered pace, critical voices like *The Times* would attack the Consumers' Council as a 'mysterious body', a ragbag of London cooperators and socialists who 'represent themselves and not much beside', 'a pretentious excrescence' that was little more than 'a fussy hobby for a few of the illustrious obscure'.[65] This was powerful rhetoric, but unfair. The Council provided the most popular and democratic forum of consumer representation in British history, altogether representing six million families. The serious and sober *Statist* described it as 'fairly representative of the interests of the mass of the population'.[66]

The Manchester Chamber of Commerce complained that the Council would give the cooperatives a monopoly at the expense of other traders and destroy 'the principles of freedom of trade on which British commerce has hitherto been successfully conducted'.[67] The collapse of the interallied machinery of coordination further undermined the case for domestic controls. The Cooperative's Central Committee now backed the export trading side of the movement and opposed a permanent Food Ministry. In a capitalist society, government controls strengthened 'vested interests and their power over ministries while choking cooperative business'.[68] The government's treatment of the Consumers' Council in 1919–20 fed such ideas of a capitalist conspiracy. In August 1919 the Council had sent a deputation to Lloyd George urging that the Ministry of Food be made a permanent department. Half a year later, they were still waiting for a reply. The Ministry was not even represented in cabinet. State control was increasingly denounced as a 'sham' and 'mere mis-control'.[69] Perhaps the future of democracy lay with cooperative control, after all.

The showdown came on 19 February 1920, when the Consumers' Council met with representatives of its member organizations in Westminster. The old socialist Hyndman took the chair. He began by reminding members that the French Socialist Fourier had already a century earlier foreseen that competition always led to monopoly. The majority on the Council repeated their demand for ongoing controls and for a department of state to protect the consumer. Gallacher of the Cooperative Wholesale Society had no patience with the majority's thinking. It was out of touch with the practical effects of state control.

> We make butter in Ireland; we are not allowed to use our butter... We took over certain places as creameries, so that milk could be turned into butter or cheese, and were told "We do not want your butter or cheese, the milk must be disposed of as milk." We incurred a loss of many thousands of pounds as a result.

Government controls introduced new brokers between cooperatives trading with each other, government middlemen who were as wasteful as the profiteering middlemen cooperatives had fought since their birth. Control of milk meant 'dearer milk'. '[W]e certainly cannot afford much longer to go on along those lines.'

Gallacher rebuked Marion Phillips for speaking of chaos before the war: 'I do not think that anything was better done than the [sic] food distribution in pre-war days.' Clynes, the Labour MP who had served as Food Controller until January 1919, rallied to her defence. Britain had entered a new era of trusts and combines. It was these bodies and their high prices that were spreading 'revolutionary doctrines and... extreme discontent amongst the minds of the people'. Continued controls and price regulation were more urgent than ever before. Milk showed 'how much good work... for many years to come' controls could do.[70]

Few became more agitated by the CWS's reasoning than Fred Bramley. Bramley represented the parliamentary committee of the Trades Union Congress. Speaking as a 'consuming cooperator', Bramley was incensed by

Gallacher's 'profit-making opinion'. How could the CWS side with the recently founded Federation of British Industries? To decontrol to maximize profits was a producer view, not a consumer view. Others denounced Gallacher for adopting a 'buyers' view' rather than a 'consumers' view'. People were living in a 'fool's paradise' to think it was possible to go back to pre-war conditions, Jack Jones, the Labour MP, argued. Workers were consumers too. Watkins, a cooperator, reminded councillors of the lessons of the war: 'We have found that supplies and raw materials have come steadily into the hands of a few people in the countries from which they originate. ... [The] whole structure of trade and commerce has altered.' It was imperative to 'maintain this Food Ministry and this Council must be charged with the power to obtain supplies of food and distribute food equitably, and that distribution takes place at something like fair prices'.

In the end, eight members of the Council supported controls, three were opposed. The Labour groups and Cooperative Union were on one side, the CWS and the Parliamentary Committee of the Cooperative Congress on the other. The Women's Cooperative Guild abstained. The withdrawal of support from the large wholesale wing of the cooperatives was the coup de grace for the Consumers' Council and for control. The government continued its bonfire of controls—milk was decontrolled in January 1920, the bread subsidy ended in October 1920, and price support for cereal production was stopped in 1921. By 4 January 1921 even the staunchest supporters of the Consumers' Council acknowledged that its historic moment had passed. They resigned. The vision of a democratic Ministry of Food protecting the consumer lay shattered. Three months later the Ministry was disbanded. If at first the war had given rise to new levels of consumer mobilization, it ultimately divided consumers. It was this internal division, as much as external pressures from business or government, that ended the political power of new forms of consumer representation.

Food Values

The campaign for milk control and fair prices drew on a transformation in food values. Before the war, Free Trade culture had looked to white bread as a symbol of liberty and equity. The cheap loaf was the British people's guardian against the starvation and barbarism ravaging protectionist countries. In the 1920s, new nutritional politics would challenge the liberal

trinity of cheapness, whiteness, and civilization. This challenge came in
two parallel stages. Scientific knowledge and public awareness of vitamins
undermined the cheap white loaf, while milk was upgraded to an 'essential
food'. Talk of 'necessaries', so vital to the public appeal of Free Trade
in the Victorian and Edwardian period, now moved away from a liberal
defence of markets and cheapness to a more social-democratic focus on
public health. To be a citizen meant to have access to 'essential' food,
which states should provide at fair prices. Cheapness, in other words, no
longer prevented malnutrition.

   The Free Trade cult of cheapness fitted in well with the dominant British
diet of bread, sugar, and potatoes. Before the First World War, the average
working-class man spent between 50 and 60 per cent of his budget on
food and ate almost 7 pounds of bread a week. The war narrowed the
little choice there was and lowered quality as well. Working-class families
ate less sugar, butter, cheese, and meat, and relied even more on bread
and potatoes, and to a limited degree, milk. While infant mortality might
have declined, the conditions for older children probably deteriorated, and
rickets was on the rise.[71]

   From the 1880s, food reformers had attacked white bread as a threat to
national fitness. Flour was contaminated by bleaching and vital nutrients
were lost as the wheat berry was extracted in milling. A strong virile race
needed brown bread, they insisted. Brown bread nourished better teeth
and better nerves. In 1911, Northcliffe's half-penny *Daily Mail*, a tariff
reform paper, put its weight behind the campaign for brown bread. But
such campaigns foundered on the deep-seated popular association between
the white loaf, liberty, and comfort. Brown bread continued to stand for
poverty and dirt, as the *British Medical Journal* recognized.[72]

   The war and post-war years gave brown bread a boost, and gradually
diminished the cultural capital of the white loaf. In part this had to do with
changes in diet. Britons began to eat more of the new breakfast cereals
and less bread. And they spent less on cereals as part of their food budget
overall. Commercial developments assisted the rebranding of brown bread,
weakening the earlier association with dirt and poverty. Hovis was the
principal player here, giving 'wholemeal' bread a new image as 'hominis
vis'—the strength of man—with the help of advertising campaigns and
branded baking tins.[73]

   Above all, it was the combination of state power and consumer campaigns
that promoted brown bread at the expense of the cheap, white loaf. Before

the war, the pleas of the Bread and Food Reform League had fallen on deaf ears. The shipping crisis changed all that. The state's approach to the bread crisis was dilution rather than rationing. In the past, most of the wheat berry had been thrown out during the milling process and was fed as 'offals' to pigs and cows rather than finding its way into the belly of the consumer. In the winter of 1916–17, the government lengthened the extraction of flour, raising the percentage of wheat to be turned into flour from 70 to 78 per cent. By the beginning of 1918, 92 per cent of the wheat berry was used. Not surprisingly, in a nation raised on the white loaf, war bread had a mixed reception. Some consumers grumbled. One hospital patient even inquired whether her ovarian cyst had been caused by war bread.[74] But there was also a scientific and patriotic embrace of brown bread that began to undercut the public reputation of the Free Trade loaf.

In the final year of the war, the Royal Society's Food War Committee started experiments with 'special breads'. These were made of wheat flour of 80–90 per cent extraction with small additions of maize and rice. In carefully monitored trials, groups of chemical workers, laboratory attendants, children, and patients suffering from pulmonary tuberculosis were for two months given the 'pale yellow' and 'light brown' breads. Every morning their faeces were tested. The results were astonishing. Even children digested large quantities of the bread well. In fact, in 'certain cases health seemed to improve during its use'. The 'bread was stated by all to be palatable, and no one complained of becoming tired of it ... as was feared by some members of the Committee'. Patients with 'more or less impaired digestions' liked the brown bread so much they asked for future supplies. Indeed, the sixty-one employees of the West Riding Chemical Co. Ltd. composed a memorial in praise of brown bread. They asked for more wholemeal bread in the future from which 'we derived great benefit', 'as we do not wish to resume the use of the ordinary flour, which we are convinced contains deleterious materials'.[75]

The Bread and Food Reform League used these experiments to step up its campaign to put the white loaf on a blacklist of dangerous foods. New nutritional knowledge was now grafted onto an older concern with adulteration. Free Trade appeared a feeble guardian of the citizen-consumer. The state needed to protect future citizens, the League told the Lloyd George Coalition in 1919 and 1920. The wheat berry contained calcium phosphates, a vital constituent of teeth and bones that was being lost without state regulation, they explained.

In this new nutritional politics the cooperative movement played a leading role. The Women's Cooperative Guild began to promote 'Food Purity' in the 1920s. Unbleached flour in cooperative mills was contrasted with the bleached but inferior flour that caused dermatitis and was used by 'unscrupulous bakers'. Basic nutritional lessons introduced consumers to vitamins, first discovered in 1912. Pure white flour lacked the vitamins contained in the germ and outer skin of the grain, notably vitamin B, popularly known as the 'anti-neurotic vitamin' because it aided the development of the nervous system. In advice books on *Food Values* and *Food Purity*, Florence Ranson gave housewives recipes for wholemeal scones and for salads with ground nuts accompanied by brown bread and butter. Cooperative wholemeal flour like 'Hermes' and 'Star', she explained, contained iodine and vitamins, 'one of the elements in which minute quantities has lately been discovered to be of great importance in human diet'. Her advice was to eat more wholemeal bread for the 'anti-rachitic' vitamin A.[76]

Towards the end of the war, the Ministry of Food proclaimed the 'Passing of the White Loaf', predicting that a 'good many of us have learned to prefer the taste of dark bread, and…that when we eagerly turn once more to white bread we shall find it flavourless'.[77] This was far too optimistic. Once the war was over, most Britons returned to the white loaf. A few people, especially pensioners and more affluent, educated groups, ate more brown bread, but as late as the early 1970s the white loaf still made up 80 per cent of bread consumption in Britain; in 1900, it had been 95 per cent. What had changed, however, was the symbolic status of the cheap white loaf. It could no longer easily be held up as an embodiment of the public interest. As Mrs Wilson, the wife of a London artisan, told the Royal Commission on Food Prices in 1925, she ate the cheaper white bread but felt brown bread was 'more nutritious to the children [and] I think it would be better if they had less pure white bread'.[78] Individual habits and public values were diverging. When the world depression hit in 1929, the remaining defenders of Free Trade found that they had lost their most valuable icon. Women cooperators confessed how difficult it had become to stir up public interest in 'the loaf'.[79]

If no single food was to take the place of the white loaf in modern political memory, pure and clean milk came close. It became the symbol of social citizenship. Mothers' milk has a long association with fertility and plenty. Milk has been seen as the nectar of life in a wide range of cultural contexts from the Celts, to whom it symbolized immortality, to the Sanskrit epic, the Ramayana. In ancient and Christian stories, suckling by a divine mother symbolizes adoption and knowledge; St Bernard was suckled by the Virgin Mary and thus became the brother of Christ.

Unfortunately, cow's milk was neither pure nor plentiful. British families faced a dilemma. Cow's milk was expensive—and rare or absent in many working-class areas; it was so dear that health clinics advised mothers to continue breast-feeding until their babies turned one.[80] Worse, most milk was also dirty or diseased, often carrying tuberculosis. Not being able to buy milk might stunt growth and development, but drinking it could kill. The distinct British taste for raw milk made things worse; the risk was lower abroad, where milk was boiled at home.[81] In Britain, some contemporaries suggested that 50 per cent of infant mortality resulted from digestive disorders. *The Lancet*, the voice of the medical profession, blamed a total of 95 outbreaks of epidemic disease between 1881 and 1896 on infected milk. Tuberculous milk was one of the biggest killers in this period—health reformers spoke of 'veiled infanticide' and the slaughter of the innocent—although the incidence of human tuberculosis caused by bovine infection can be exaggerated.[82]

Milk was first exposed as unsafe by doctors and medical health officers in the late nineteenth century. Bovine TB, it became clear, was contagious, not hereditary. Research revealed the cow as the source of infection, and that the bacillus could jump the species barrier. This was a genuinely transnational moment as new scientific knowledge circulated between societies. For British reformers, it was cities on the eastern seaboard of the United States that were the pole star. In 1909 Dr Eastwood was sent to America by the Local Government Board to study improvements in the control and supply of milk. A first project for certifying clean milk had been launched by the Medical Milk Commission in Newark in 1892. In New York, where an infants' milk depot had been set up as early as 1889, the city provided milk stations across town in 1911, offering wholesome milk and education to consumers. A year later, the city introduced grading, distinguishing milk with a low bacterial content fit for infant feeding (Grade A) from that only fit for cooking purposes (Grade C). International meetings, like the conference on infant mortality in London in 1913, facilitated such transnational knowledge transfer.

Unlike Scandinavia and continental neighbours, Free Trade Britain resisted regulation. Some individual towns took action to reduce the prevalence of the bacillus, but in general, the state was unwilling to pay for inspections or help modernize farms. The agricultural lobby, though small, vehemently opposed change. Few consumers were willing to pay extra to those farmers who introduced TB-free herds and quarantined infected cows. The powers of inspection that were introduced were rarely used, a problem not helped by the vast and diffuse network of small shops in the milk trade. By 1899 only 38 local authorities had even appointed a veterinarian. A bill prohibiting the sale of TB-infected milk only made it to Parliament in 1913, and was then postponed by the outbreak of war. Compared to the United States, France, or Sweden, inspections and pasteurization proceeded at a snail's pace in Britain. There was no state collaboration with dairies, and no state subsidy to eliminate TB. For the Board of Agriculture the milk question was one of commercial risk, not the responsibility of the state.[83]

This disappointing record, however, also reflected public apathy about milk. The debate was mainly fought in the arena of public health, bringing together doctors, veterinarians, medical health officers, and farmers. The maternalist campaign of the Women's Cooperative Guild was one of the few links between popular politics and medical debates. In 1913 the Guild had successfully fought to add maternity benefits to the National Insurance Act. In the campaign to improve the conditions of mothers during and after pregnancy, greater access to cheap, clean milk came to play a central role. In 1914 local government grants in aid were introduced for national maternity care.

It was the war that galvanized consumer power and sparked a more general debate about consumer rights, markets, and social justice. Mothers and babies were recognized as national assets. In 1915 the WCG shocked the public and the government with an exposé of the horrible conditions faced by working mothers. Graphic personal letters revealed the lack of fresh milk, food, and assistance, and its causal link with miscarriage, disease, and death.[84]

In 1915 a National Clean Milk Society was set up. Its chairman, the indefatigable Wilfred Buckley, pointed to the vast gulf between British and American standards. Milk in London contained ten times as many bacteria as even the lowest grade of milk in New York, he told the Consumers' Council. The dramatic fall in infant mortality in Cincinnati after municipal authorities began to supervise the milk trade showed what was possible. In Britain, by contrast, samples in 1916 and 1917 were shocking: not even one-quarter of the milk supplied to London hospitals and schools would have passed the bottom grade in the United States. In one London borough, the Ministry of Health found that 99 out of 100 samples contained traces of manure.[85]

Lantern lectures, pamphlets, and films reported the sickening state of this essential food. The National Clean Milk Society gave demonstrations on cooling, bottling, and storing milk. People, it argued, needed to appreciate the aesthetics and taste as well as the nutritional benefits of milk; Lord Plunkett, the president, urged firms to supply milk in more attractive bottles in Greek designs and asked 'ladies [to] turn their attention to designing covers such as those used for bringing champagne bottles to table, and thus give an artistic pleasure to a utilitarian beverage'.[86] From America, it imported films illustrating modern milk processing. In the immediate post-war years, Buckley lectured to 'crowded audiences' about the dangers of dirty milk. Posters, slides, and film put science and statistics into simple, visual form; 'Clean Milk Films' were watched by Labour conferences in the post-war years. There were posters of 'bacteria' and catchy illustrations of the dangers of pollution as milk travelled from cow to consumer, epitomized by the notorious 'small milkboy who was seen carefully straining milk through his pocket handkerchief on somebody's doorstep'.[87]

In spite of the ultimate failure of the wartime campaign for a government takeover of the milk trade, these educational efforts left their mark on a new political culture of food. For the Consumers' Council, knowledge of disease and dirt was further proof of the chaotic nature of the food system. The control of the milk supply—before the war the demand of a few reformers like James Beattie, a bacteriologist at Liverpool University—became the mantra of consumer politics. The Council's milk committee demanded a more effective system of pasteurization, cooling, and bottling. Inspectors and medical officers readily supplied evidence of how the unregulated milk trade victimized consumers. In Nottingham much of the milk arrived with a 'large amount of cow-dung and other dirt'. Elsewhere, milk carts were dirty and rusty.[88] Civic groups, like the Edinburgh Women's Citizen Association, sent a deputation of women doctors to the Food Commissioner to demand a government takeover of the milk supply, highlighting the need to educate consumers and protect them from disease.[89]

In the 1920s, the cooperative movement continued to draw a link between new nutritional knowledge and the social rights of consumers.

People needed to realize the 'value of milk as food', the Women's Cooperative Guild emphasized.[90] Milk was not any ordinary beverage but an essential food, with Vitamin A for bones, Vitamin B against 'nervous disorders', and Vitamin C to prevent scurvy. The Milk Order of 1923, which introduced four grades of milk, was a step in the right direction, but cleansing methods were still backwards. In one cooperative experiment, refuse removed from milk was thrown to a dozen hens: 'within twenty-four hours eight had died'. The cooperative milk campaign was meant to be the stepping stone to greater consumer power. It would simultaneously defeat the profiteer and raise quality and production. Twenty-eight cooperatives had already introduced pasteurization facilities by 1925; by 1930 a quarter of all milk was pasteurized or heat-treated. Some local societies introduced white overalls and peaked caps to promote cleanliness, others sponsored prize competitions for the best-kept milkcarts and ponies.

Together, the new nutritional knowledge about vitamins and the critique of markets and profiteering left milk with a very different public status from that of the cheap loaf. Not only did people have a right to milk as an essential food, but price had become subordinated to quality. The discovery of vitamins meant that the price of food was no longer an indicator of social welfare. A quart of milk was equal in value to almost a pound of lean beef or ten eggs, according to the Ministry of Health.[91] Free Trade had promised consumers equitable access to 'necessaries' by keeping food cheap. What mattered now was not so much what food cost, but what was in it.

All this moved food as a 'necessary' closer to public goods like water, away from other goods bought and sold in the market place. As Marion Phillips put it: 'Just as pure water is a national need, so is pure milk.'[92] By the 1920s, it was as improbable to die of starvation as to be hit by lightning. What the knowledge of vitamins and 'diseased' food did was to shift attention from starvation towards hidden hunger: malnutrition. The appeal to mothers and children, so central in pre-war liberal iconography was now given a social democratic expression: 'What the Babies Want: Healthy Mothers—strong bodies—clean milk—gardens to play in', as Labour leaflets put it.[93]

This new social democratic politics of rights and social service would finally come into its own during the Second World War, when welfare milk made up 20 per cent of all milk consumption. But the shift in values and sensibilities was well under way long before the introduction of universal free school milk by the Labour government in 1946. By 1931, 500,000

school children received free milk.[94] Equally important, the First World
War and immediate post-war years had spread a sense of entitlement to
basic 'food values'. Pure food and price control were the goal for Labour
and cooperative movements in the inter-war years. Children under 18
months of age needed one-and-a-half pints of milk a day, older children
one pint, the Ministry of Health noted in 1920. Milk become known as
the 'great body-builder'.[95] Experiments, such as John Boyd Orr's famous
study on milk consumption and growth of children in Scottish schools in
1926–7, validated the new awareness of malnutrition. Actual consumption
in Britain in the 1920s remained far from ideal; the average Briton still
drank only a quarter of a pint of milk a day, in many industrial regions it
was a mere one-tenth. Adulteration continued to be a problem into the
1930s. But the idea of minimum nutritional standards, which would be
popularized by the League of Nations in the 1930s, had been planted.

This shift from the cheap loaf to clean milk transformed a whole culture
of political ritual and symbolism. The white loaf, as we have seen, was
waved around, thrown about, and imagined in demonstrations, posters, and
exhibits as a marker of British liberty and civilization. It never recovered this
central role after the First World War. Instead, a new style of representation
emerged, which publicized the health-giving and beautifying properties
of milk. Alongside the cooperative milk campaign, it was especially the
National Milk Publicity Council which promoted the image of this new
'essential food'. Founded in February 1920, the NMPC brought together
milk producers, dairy farmers, medical officers, and the National Clean
Milk Society. It championed the Dairy Shorthorn as the 'general purpose
cow', a breed also favoured by the Prince of Wales. It pressed for school
milk. Its adverts rebranded milk as a source of strength, as vital for men as for
children and women—'Workers Need More Milk', its posters proclaimed,
and milk helped women to keep their looks (Colour Plate XVI). Children
visiting the British Empire Exhibition in 1924 received 'Drink More Milk'
puzzles. There were milk weeks, health weeks, and campaigns for milk
clubs in factories. The industry began to promote ice cream to boost
demand. Between August 1924 and August 1925, the Council gave 2,614
lectures to a quarter of a million people and distributed almost a million
leaflets. It even introduced cartoon films. All this was more than just a
commercial campaign. Milk Weeks reinforced a sense amongst the public
that milk was a national need and that the state needed to look after its
consuming citizens. Milk was the 'Backbone of Britain'.

A new way of representing food was emerging. In place of white loaves and black loaves, food was now shown with its constituent chemical parts. Borrowing an idea from America, the National Milk Publicity Council in 1928 entered the Lord Mayor's Show with a decorated car, pulled by four Suffolk Punches, displaying an enormous milk bottle. Around it stood children dressed as the 'food fairies', 'Violet Vitamin', and 'Peter Protein' (see Figure 12).[96]

Figure 12. The Vitamin 'Food Fairies' at a performance produced by the YWCA in Kent in 1925.

Undercurrents

Politics is not a canal carrying all vessels in the same direction with the same speed. There are tides and cross-currents. The 1923 general election gave Free Traders a brief hope that they had turned the tide of their decline. In October 1923, Stanley Baldwin, the Conservative Prime Minister, decided to call an early election and run on the tariff issue. Protection, he hoped, would strengthen his own authority, send a positive message to working-class voters at a time of unemployment, and reunite the Conservative party, driving a wedge between Lloyd George's Coalition Liberals and Coalition Conservatives. It was a mistake. His sudden move managed to reunite Lloyd George and Asquith's Liberals, and alienate leading Conservatives critical of tariffs, like Cecil, Devonshire, and Derby.[97] For Conservatives the election was a disaster. They lost 88 seats, leaving a mere 258 Conservative MPs in the Commons, a record low only surpassed in 1966. Labour gained 47 seats, making it the second largest party, with 191 seats. The reunited Liberals, too, added 43 seats, especially in rural and suburban areas, giving them a respectable parliamentary contingent of 158 MPs. Such was the size of the defeat, that Liberals saw 1923 as the 'annus mirabilis' of Free Trade.[98] But electoral fortunes can be deceptive, and the Liberal vote collapsed in 1924 and 1929.

Clearly, 1923 was a powerful vote *against* tariff reform, but to what degree was it also still a vote *for* Free Trade? The events of 1923 proved little more than a temporary whirlpool. Underneath the surface of Liberal reunion, undercurrents continued to wash away popular belief in Free Trade. Election battles between Liberals and Cooperative and Labour candidates revealed a widening chasm between an older all-encompassing ideal of Free Trade and a more ambivalent view of its place in the post-war world. In Sheffield in the Hillsborough division, for example, the Liberal E. Woodhead ran as an out-and-out Free Trader against A. V. Alexander, a leading candidate of the Cooperative party who enjoyed Labour support. To Woodhead, a newspaper owner and former international rugger player, Free Trade 'meant something more' than just sound economics: it was a 'moral question, a deep and real moral question'. It was 'sacred'. Alexander, too, attacked protection for raising prices, creating millionaires, and leading to international tensions. But, in a world of unemployment and high prices Free Trade was no longer a panacea, Alexander countered. From the Cooperative side, the call for a 'free breakfast table' now came with the complaint that the 'Liberals left you with higher food taxes than when they went in.' Free Trade and protection were a 'sham issue'. What was needed was public works and a capital levy.[99] Alexander won with a sizable majority of 6,718 votes. Woodhead came a poor third.

One of the keenest fights was in Paisley, where Asquith, the former Liberal Prime Minster, faced J. M. Biggar, the Labour and Cooperative

party candidate, for the second time. After being defeated in the 1918
general election, Asquith had returned to the Commons in 1920, winning
the Paisley by-election. Now, in December 1923 the two men met again.
Asquith had been in the front line of the campaign against tariff reform in
1903 and now, with genuine pride, produced the same speech on the ABC
of Free Trade against Baldwin that he had delivered twenty years earlier
against Chamberlain.

What delighted Liberals as a sign of the unchanging, universal truth
of Free Trade, however, appeared to a new generation of radicals as
mouldy politics out of step with the new realities of unemployment and
poor housing. Times had changed, a Labour speaker summed it up, and
Asquith's speeches were typical of outdated Liberals who should be out
of politics altogether. Liberal Free Trade was not innocent. It was part
of the problem. Biggar told audiences to remember 'the results which
had come to this country, particularly to the workers, by the Free Trade
policy. To-day, under Free Trade, they were living in the most abnormal
period of unemployment which the country had ever known.' Free Trade
had produced 'a C3 population, which meant ultimately a C3 nation'.
Forty-five per cent of children had 'some defect or another, and 5 per
cent had rickets'. Criticizing tariffs was no longer good enough. 'Mr.
Asquith ... must give them a reason why Free Trade could do no better
than it was doing or had done in the past.'[100] As another speaker, John
Elliot of the Scottish Horse and Motormen's Union, summed it up: 'For
the last 80 years they had been living under Free Trade, and all the wars, all
the unemployment of their time, and all the hardships they had suffered had
been under the banner of Free Trade.'[101] Biggar and others also attacked
Asquith and Liberals for adulterating the Free Trade system by introducing
higher food duties. Hands off people's food should mean no taxes at all.
What was wanted was a more active policy to give people work, better
housing, and a decent standard of living.

In the end, Asquith won, but only barely, with 9,723 votes to Biggar's
7,977. Asquith benefited from an internal split in the local Labour party,
although it is debatable whether that was decisive; Biggar had alienated
sections of the Left with his tough stance on evicting tenants—housing was
an explosive issue in Paisley as elsewhere—and a rival Labour candidate,
D. D. Cormack, a lawyer with a good track record of defending tenants'
rights, entered the field and took 1,746 votes. The Conservative party
would probably have abstained without the arrival of the leftist Cormack,

and so, in a straight fight with Biggar, Asquith might have attracted many Conservative anti-socialist voters.[102]

What ultimately mattered, however, was that the election signalled a clear reversal in the reputation of the two parties as friends of the people. The Liberals were not dead; their women's groups, for example, had expanded. But they had become the party of the establishment, promising to fight socialism and conservatism. The cry for Free Trade was now linked to an attack on government waste and high taxes. It was Labour and the Cooperative party which put unemployment, housing, and health at the forefront. Unlike Biggar, Asquith would not even meet a deputation of unemployed men, preferring to speak only on what he saw to be general matters affecting all classes. Liberal rhetoric was making Free Trade increasingly look like a distraction from the problems of everyday life. At the next election, ten months later, the old Liberal leader would be defeated.

Such scenes were played out in many constituencies across the country. Cooperative and Labour supporters were more and more ambivalent about Free Trade. Some still repeated that tariffs would plunge the nation back into the 'hungry forties'.[103] But just as widespread was talk of the failure of Free Trade. King's Norton saw a battle between Mrs Barton, the friend of cooperative families, and Mrs Cadbury, the 'rich employer's widow' and chocolate heiress, running for the Liberals. Tariff reform was no answer to unemployment, the *Co-operative News* argued, but neither was leaving society at the mercy of market forces which had 'screwed down wages to the lowest limit'.[104] No credit there for Free Trade as a source of high real wages.

Many Labour candidates did not even refer to Free Trade in their election addresses, and spoke, instead, of unemployment, public work schemes, and public health. Robert Murray was one of the Labour MPs involved in a scuffle in the House of Commons earlier in 1923 that had followed the singing of the Red Flag. After the speaker adjourned the House, Murray was hit by a Conservative member with an Order paper, and struck in return, hitting Walter Guinness, the undersecretary for war; struggling in front of the mace, the two men had to be separated by MacDonald and fellow Labourites.[105] It was Murray who noted how in many constituencies the debate had moved beyond the 'threadbare issue' of Free Trade. 'Tweedledum says, "Protection", so Tweedledee says "Free Trade"', the trades union paper told voters in Sheffield. The issue was 'utterly irrelevant' according to the local Labour candidate: 'Protection will make things worse; Free Trade cannot make them better.'[106]

The agitation against the profiteer provided good ammunition against protectionists—still branded as selfish millionaires—but some of it now also hit Free Trade targets. The president of the Trades and Labour Council in Sheffield, E. G. Rowlinson, appealed to trades unionists and their wives to vote Labour: 'We believe that under the present system the workers can be robbed by Free Trade and by Protection'—'more flagrantly, perhaps, by the latter', he added, but robbed by Free Trade nonetheless. Under Free Trade, workers and consumers bore a double burden: a high cost of living and high unemployment. In Parliament, Jack Jones objected to the 'christ of labour' being crucified between the two thieves of Free Trade and Tariff Reform.[107]

Many cooperative societies endorsed the International Committee to Promote Universal Free Trade, established in 1923 and run by the Cobden Club, but they did so with mounting reservations. Everyone in the cooperative movement pressed for the removal of 'artificial barriers' to trade, and some happily joined in the election song 'Free Trade and the People and the League'. Others, however, championed trade regulation and openly wondered about Free Trade's negative side-effects. Leading members of the Women's Cooperative Guild, like Mrs Harsent, a council member, gave public election addresses on 'War Against War' in which she explained how international trade and finance always led to war.[108] Cartoons in The Co-operative News labelled Free Trade a 'quack remedy' just as much as protection.[109]

In the 1923 election, cooperative voters were asked to put the abolition of the competitive system above all other considerations. Free Trade would be a safe policy within the framework of an international cooperative alliance. In its present liberal guise, however, it would only fuel international conflict. A special election supplement told voters: 'Competition in trade was at the bottom of the war with Germany.'[110]

The agitation against the high cost of living continued unabated after the defeat of tariffs in 1923. From 1920 on, governments had pursued a deflationary programme with the aim of restoring the gold standard. Prices dropped rapidly, from a peak of triple 1914 levels in November 1920 to just over one-and-a-half in February 1922. Deflation might have been designed to favour the professional and commercial middle classes of suburban England against industrial producers,[111] but it failed to satisfy consumers. Neither the sharp fall in prices nor high wages eradicated the sense that the cost of living was simply too high. In the 1920s Free Trade increasingly looked irrelevant to the routine extortion faced by consumers in their daily lives.

Baldwin's return to government in November 1924 did little to change the overall direction of policy. Deflation continued and Britain returned to the gold standard at the pre-war parity of $4.86 in 1925. A few small trades like pottery, enamelled ware, and motor tyres benefited from Safeguarding Duties, but any general tariff on food or major imported materials like iron and steel was ruled out. Like his predecessors, Baldwin refrained from tough actions against trusts and profiteers and offered little more than palliatives, in the shape of advisory agencies.

The Food Council, appointed by Baldwin in 1925, never had the power to open company books and punish profiteers. Nor could it control prices. It could merely investigate high profits and short measures, and publicize its findings. Where prices were too high, as in the bakery trade, it told consumers so, but then left it up to them to act accordingly. It was composed mainly of officials; consumers were all but absent. Its sheer existence, however, validated the idea that consumers had a right to fair prices, and that Free Trade no longer automatically brought cheap food. In the autumn of 1925 it investigated the high price of bread, setting off a reduction in the cost of the quartern loaf. A year later it found that the price of milk (7d. a quart instead of 6d.) was unjustifiably high. An inquiry into London beef prices revealed profit margins of 50–70 per cent to be routine. Another report revealed that 70 per cent of milk was sold in short measures. Markets and prices were neither efficient nor transparent. In many products, such as tea, investigations showed that the fall in wholesale prices never reached the consumer.

The 1925 Royal Commission on Food Prices similarly showed how consumers were affected by price cycles in wheat. Between 1921 and 1924 the world wheat price was low because of speculation and overproduction. Then in 1924–5 prices increased. Bakers and small retailers made a fortune at the expense of the consumer, critics charged—prices and profits were judged to be about 10 per cent above normal.[112] British consumers paid between £500 and £700 million pounds a year over the price of the same food sold at wholesale markets and ports of importation, according to Christopher Addison, a recent Labour convert from the Liberals. Schemes to stabilize prices by organized traders only reinforced these problems.[113]

In spite of formal Free Trade, there was no cheap loaf. What was needed instead were schemes to stabilize food price and organize trade, such as imperial and bulk state purchases, along the model of the Canadian wheat pool and the Danish milk board.

The banner of fair and stable prices was taken up by the fast-growing mass movement of labour women. Women gained the vote in 1918. The Women's section of the Labour party grew from 120,000 members in 1923 to 300,000 four years later. Much of this was due to the drive and skill of Marion Phillips, who had served on the consumers' Council. In most local Labour meetings, women now were the largest group. As it was incorporated in the more traditionally male-dominated culture and *Realpolitik* of the Labour party, working-class feminism softened. Demands for birth control and family allowances were abandoned.[114] But this was not the whole picture. Labour women subjected Free Trade and competitive markets to intense and sustained criticism. All the way through the deflationary 1920s in the Labour press and women's magazines, like *The Labour Woman*, they denounced butchers, bakers, and milkmen for combining against consumers.[115] Free Trade had failed to prevent the 'robbery of the housewife and the community' by profiteers and speculators, as one woman put it in 1928.[116] Consumers needed a Food Council with statutory powers to punish profiteers.

Internationally, too, there was a turn towards state intervention. Labour women attacked international trusts and unregulated commerce as leading to waste and famine. Liberals and Tories alike were condemned for supporting an un-Christian system of trade that put profits above human needs. Unregulated trade encouraged the wanton destruction of food by international combines. The best way to cut out the 'profiteer' was to bring consumers and producers closer together. Instead of the old chorus for Free Trade, there were routine calls at Labour women's conferences for bulk purchases from the Dominions and other producing nations, a national wheat board, and for an international organization to coordinate scarce resources.[117]

Empire and Choice

It was not, however, only progressive politics that eroded the older liberal Free Trade culture of cheapness and open markets. Free Trade was squeezed from both sides of the political spectrum. Before the war, the citizen-consumer had been the monopoly of popular liberalism. In the 1920s, consumer politics was in flux and parties were competing for new women voters. Conservatives began to develop their own contender: an imperial consumer. For newly enfranchized Conservative housewives, shopping became a test of imperial citizenship.

The Empire Shopping and 'Buy British' campaigns of the inter-war years transformed political culture in ways that would have repercussions for the rest of the century. Conservatives took the civic consumer from its liberal parents and gave it a Conservative pedigree. For Conservatives it was a major make-over. From the Fair Trade campaign in the 1880s to Chamberlain's tariff crusade, Conservatives had spoken for the producer. It was the manufacturer who needed to be protected against 'unfair' competition. It was the unemployed male worker who was being forced to emigrate. Where they featured at all, consumers were treated as passive dependents. The consumer imperialism of the 1920s redressed this balance. Consumers were no longer treated as second-class citizens. Instead, housewives with their shopping baskets held the key to the welfare of their husbands and the Empire as a whole. Demands for tariffs were complemented by a new appeal to consumer choice. Consumer imperialism was about educating consumers to choose wisely. We tend to associate the emphasis on the sovereign consumer and choice with Thatcherism or trace it to the campaign against rationing after the Second World War,[118] but this shift was under way in the 1920s.

Traces of consumer nationalism were already visible before the First World War. In March 1911, British and colonial goods were put on display in London in an 'All-British Shopping Week'; some shopkeepers in other parts of the country followed. But these were feeble, isolated efforts, organized by a group of retailers, without much public or commercial support. Many firms in the West End thought it was simply impossible to hold such a week, since such a small part of their turnover involved British products. Others felt it was mixing advertisement with fraud. Conservative Tariff Reform was conspicuous by its absence. The event was not repeated.[119]

It was the war which mobilized a Conservative-led patriotic consumerism. At first, this was an upper-class initiative, led by the British Women's Patriotic League, which numbered among its supporters the likes of the Countess of March, the Dowager Lady Nunburnholme, and Lady Cowan. Founded in 1908, the League's original mission had been to alert

the nation to the need for home defence, and to instil in children a sense
of duty and self-sacrifice. Its early meetings tried to stir up public interest
in national hygiene and sea power. It encouraged rifle clubs and sent boys
on the training ship *Warspite*. The war expanded the terrain of their activities to consumption and recycling. When household sugar became scarce,
the League campaigned against the use of sugar in decorated cakes and
expensive sweets. It worked with the National Salvage Council to rescue
valuable waste for munitions and clothing, and held economical cookery
demonstrations to teach thrift. It even distributed materials for women to
make shirts in War Clubs, though this did not prove 'satisfactory' and the
contract with the army clothing department was closed.[120]

After the war, it continued its campaign to promote sound imperial
consumption. It warned against the corrupting force of American mass
culture. In some 4,000 cinemas, young Britons were fed the dangerous
'mental food' of American films and their 'shocking travesty of life', with
scenes such as 'a man dressed half in the garb of a man and half in the garb
of a woman standing behind a screen, being kissed by an old gentleman'.
What 'impression are they going to get of life in general?' Indeed. What was
needed was Empire film and British history produced by British artists to
stop this rot. Without it, 'the younger generation' would 'base their lives on
American ideas of morals and on American ideas of life generally'.[121] This
sort of cultural protectionism prepared the way for the film quota in 1927.
For some Edwardian Liberals, most notably Henry Cowan, the businessman
whose wife led the League after the war, the League was one step in the
transition from Free Trade to Conservatism. Defeated as a National Liberal
in 1922, he supported tariffs and became a Conservative MP in 1923.

In 1922, the League pioneered the first Empire Shopping week to
celebrate Empire day (24 May). Within the space of a few years, Empire Shopping mushroomed into a mass movement. There were Empire
pageants and produce stalls, Empire dinners and pudding competitions.
Lantern lectures and travelling cinema vans broadcast the glory of Australian sultanas and New Zealand honey. Little imperialists played with
model Empire Grocery Stores. Across the country consumers were urged
to 'Buy British', meaning colonial as well as home goods. Rubber stamps advertised 'Buy British Goods and Reduce Unemployment and Taxation'.[122]
By 1930, the number of Empire Shopping weeks had passed the two
hundred mark in Britain alone, with additional events in Canada, Jamaica,
Trinidad, and Australia.

Empire Shopping and 'Buy British' campaigns drew on the publicity provided by the Empire Marketing Board. Defeat in the 1923 election had moved tariffs beyond the realm of practical politics. The Board was set up in 1925 as a small concession to imperial protectionists in the Conservative party, and led by the Dominions Secretary and staunch Tariff Reformer Leo Amery. Denied any formal powers of imperial preference, the Board turned to advertising and mass communication instead. In the twelve months before the world depression hit in 1929, it sponsored 2,438 lectures which reached half a million people. It displayed millions of posters and, with professional help, made the most of new advertising techniques, from night-time advertising in cities to the display of enormous banners at the 1927 Wembley Cup final. Over 25,000 schools received imperial literature. An estimated 12 million people saw the special appeal by Prime Minister MacDonald to Buy British shown in 1,000 cinemas in 1931.[123] Retailers, too, were finally persuaded to provide more organized support. The National Chamber of Trade joined the Buy Empire Goods campaign at the end of 1925 and, together with the Board, helped local traders with shopwindow displays.

Equally, if not more important, was the expanding grassroots movement. In the course of the 1920s, imperial consumerism became part of the every-day life of a vast network of middle-class Conservative women. Its hub, the Women's Unionist Organisation, had one million members by 1928; the women's National Liberal Federation, by comparison, was in decline with just over 70,000 members. *Home and Politics*, the Conservative women's magazine, reached an impressive circulation of 200,000.[124] Housewives were the footsoldiers of the movement, organizing Empire cake competitions, canvassing shopkeepers to stock and label Empire goods, and promoting 'surprise Empire boxes'—the 5s. box included peaches, currants, tea, and rice, as well as honey, salmon, spaghetti, sugar, pine slices, raisins, and prunes.[125] Between April 1925 and April 1926 alone, 4,807 of these boxes were sent out to all parts of England and Wales.[126] These women inhabited a different world from the high society that had made the Women's Patriotic League an extension of the London season. Their Conservatism was that of the middle-class suburb and Middle England, of Finchley, Burnley, and Oxford, not of Empire luncheons at the Dorchester or exclusive balls at the Hyde Park Hotel. Many of them did their own cooking and shopping. It was at middle-class housewives like them that cooking exhibits, Empire recipes, and Empire pudding competitions were aimed. It was a hands-on imperial consumer politics, the Conservative middle-class counterpart to cooperative culture.

Their imperial consumerism connected metropolitan leisure and novelties with respectable suburbia and provincial England. At the enormous Empire exhibit at Wembley in 1924–5 Empire products featured alongside an amusement park: 'bigger and more exciting than Coney Island and all the amusements sections of previous British exhibitions put together' without, the Conservative women's paper added, being 'flashy or tawdry'.[127] An estimated 30 million people saw the 'miniature Empire' at Wembley. In the Palace of Industry, a housewife could learn 'the right methods of thawing frozen meat from New Zealand, of soaking Australian dried fruits to make delicious summer dishes, and with many other interesting hints that will encourage her to introduce Empire dishes and Empire food into her own domestic programme'.[128] She could even familiarize herself with new gas cooking technologies. Conservative women brought such demonstrations from Wembley to the rest of England, making Empire teas for children and families, demonstrating how to handle dried fruit and unchill meat, and circulating recipies for imperial dishes, such as for Banana jelly made from Jamaican bananas and glacé cherries from South Africa.

There was a seemingly unstoppable competition for ever-bigger plum puddings made from Australian sultanas and other ingredients produced by 'British settlers'. The imperial Christmas pudding was the Conservative housewives' version of the 'cheap loaf'. Imperial consumerism was rapidly taking over the political space which had been carved out in the Edwardian fiscal controversy, with its bazaars, lantern performances, and shop-window politics of food. Some Conservative Empire fêtes and exhibits were small-scale, like the product displays at Wantage and Driffield or the Empire stalls put together with the help of local grocers at Alresford (see Figure 13 overleaf). Other activities were considerable affairs, such as the great demonstration and gala in Burnley on 28 August 1926, which attracted some 10,000 adults and 2,500 children, and boasted a 'Buy Empire Goods' float.[129] Alongside the posters of the Empire Marketing Board, there was a good deal of local creativity. One enterprising Conservative woman, Miss L. V. Sutton of Finchley in north London, even dressed up in a costume of imperial products, not quite, perhaps, matching the seductive charms of Carmen Miranda, but still good enough to win her three first prizes (see Figure 14 overleaf).[130]

As before the war, politics and entertainment were often inseparable. In addition to the usual shop-window displays, speeches, and guidebooks, the

Figure 13. An Empire produce stall in Yorkshire, 1925.

Empire Shopping Week in Walthamstow in November 1927 included a
weight-guessing competition and a 'Mystery Man', who appeared in the
streets distributing gifts and cinema tickets. Shopkeepers gave away 'spot
prizes'. Children were encouraged to write Empire essays during school
hours for a great prize competition. At the local Baths, over one thousand
members of the community came together to sing Empire songs. They
were conducted by Mr. T. P. Ratcliffe, who arrived in 'white flannels' and
'speedily put his audience in a good temper'. For others, there was a Carnival
Dance and an Empire Ball, where the Trade Commissioner of South Africa
presented a 'beautiful ostrich feather fan' for the best Empire costume.[131]

In Oxford, Empire Day in 1927 was celebrated with stalls for different
Dominions that personalized products and producers in ways that anticipate
what today is called 'emotional branding'. White farmers and products from

Figure 14. Miss L. V. Sutton, a Conservative Empire woman in her
prize-winning entry as 'Empire Products', 1926.

the Dominions were at the centre of attention. Canada's stall displayed
bread, flour, and grain; Australia's tinned food, as well as dried fruit. Kenya
had a coffee-making demonstration 'and sample cups of coffee were much
appreciated'. But native products were displayed, too. From India there
was brass and copper ware as well as foods, from Africa native hand-work,
beads, and trinkets. Here was an imperial precursor to the international
FairTrade movement that would spring up half a century later.[132]

More generally, though, caring for imperial producers meant helping
white farmers in Canada and Kenya, not Indian peasants or Caribbean
sugar cane workers. The 'Buy British' campaign gave an imperial twist to

the evolution of ethical consumerism. In the 1890s and 1900s middle-class consumer leagues had sprung up on both sides of the Atlantic, using their shopping power to drive up the social conditions of urban workers. Now, in the 1920s, the focus was on preserving the conditions of Anglo-Saxon kin in the Dominions.

Buying Empire products was an act of imperial caring, an extension of a mother's caring duty in the home. True Conservative consumers were not selfish, but knew how to reciprocate, Anne Chamberlain, the wife of Neville, the future Prime Minister, emphasized in 1924. '[E]very white person in South Africa' bought £3 5s. 11d. worth of British goods, but people in the United States only 10s. 9d. 'Are we to take all and give nothing?' Surely not. 'The idea of Empire service makes a more certain appeal to women than the selfish bluntness of a question that asks, "What has the Empire done for *me*?".'[133] As Conservatives kept pointing out, Britain bought more than two-thirds of its imports from foreign countries, while the Dominions disproportionately imported British goods. British consumers had the power to help producers, at home and in the white settler colonies. It was estimated that the average Britain ate 100 apples a year, of which only 27 came from the Empire, 25 from Britain, but 38 from the United States. By buying a Canadian apple, the British consumer set in motion a virtuous circle, increasing the purchasing power of people in the Dominions to order more British manufactures in turn. In 1928, the Empire Marketing Board sent some 10,000 posters to over 500 firms that exported goods to the Empire, exhorting their workers to remind their wives to buy Empire goods to keep the order books full.[134]

Conservative housewives, of course, argued that Empire goods were good value for money, but ultimately it was an argument about solidarity, not price. The Empire produce scheme sought to help 'our women to be Empire builders', 'to give them a feeling of kinship with the Empire through the practical help of their shopping baskets'.[135] In newspapers and travelling lectures, housewives were reminded of their common bond with British producers, local ex-soldiers, and women living thousands of miles away in Canada or Australia. Conservative 'wireless' vans carried speakers born and bred in the Dominions across the country. In between radio and gramophone programmes, they gave first-hand accounts of life in the Empire. Housewives, too, learnt of the service provided by 'empire enthusiasts' like Mrs R. H. Godwin in South Africa who 'can ride any horse either side or astride, use a gun or pistol, and speaks Dutch,

Kaffir, French and English. ... Her love for England and the Empire is intense'.[136]

Empire goods absorbed the language of Christian cleanliness and race. Empire products were pure and clean; Mediterranean products were dirty. Reports told consumers of the 'sweet, clean and carefully packed dried fruits of Australia and South Africa'. By comparison, Turkish sultanas were 'dirty' as ' "bare-footed workers coming and going with their baskets tramped freely over the fruit" '. ' "This brown man was very dirty. His feet had certainly not been washed for a long period." '[137]

Racist beliefs could be complemented with a hope that the Empire held the answer to international conflict. Strengthening the imperial economy would improve relations between races and nations, some argued. Empire Shopping even took on the mantle of Free Trade as a source of peace and goodwill. In Walthamstow in 1927, for example, much was made of the Empire Shopping week's contribution to peace and prosperity:

> The Walthamstow housewife buying Empire produce finds work for our kith and kin across the seas, and they thus obtain the means to purchase goods manufactured in Great Britain. Empire Shopping Week does not inculcate a spirit of antagonism towards nations outside the Empire. Rather, the increase of the purchasing power of the Empire will enable its peoples to render aid to less fortunate portions of the world, still reeling from the shock of the Great War.[138]

It would be wrong to see in this imperial consumerist spectacle little more than a second-best version of protectionism. True, it had little immediate effect on policy. Baldwin made sure to install the Free Trader Churchill at the Treasury to keep a tight leash on Amery and his Empire Marketing Board.[139] Studies at the time suggest that the campaign primarily influenced middle-class consumers for whom price mattered less. Yet, seen in a more global context, a more interesting picture emerges. The 'Buy British' campaign was part of a historical moment where a variety of movements across the globe turned to consumer nationalism. In China, there was a national products' campaign. In India, the swadeshi movement boycotted British cloth and favoured indigenous industries.[140] What all these had in common was the use of consumption as a political substitute for formal state power. Consumption was a flexible tool, mobilized as a form of informal imperialism (Britain), as well as by people challenging imperial power (India) or seeking to compensate for the lack of full sovereignty

(China). As the example of Conservative housewives in Britain shows, it would be wrong to equate consumer nationalism with anti-imperialism.

One consumer who used Empire goods whenever possible was Mrs Ada Wilson, the housewives' representative on the Food Council. Wilson's home epitomized the Conservative ideal. It was 'a comfortable house...at the end of a quiet street', *Home Politics* observed, with a tea-table full of 'delicious milk rolls, jam, and fruit cake made by Mrs. Wilson, for she does all her own cooking and jam making'. This female consumer was always a maker as well as a shopper, using her skills to turn food and textiles bought in the market place into something of superior, respectable quality. She even did 'all her own washing and cleaning', and it was with a sigh of regret that she had to sacrifice 'her own leisure time in which to rest or do needlework' to do her work on the Food Council: ' "I have to buy frocks now, instead of making them".'[141]

Mrs Wilson was held up as a model of the hard-working, skilful housewife who as a consumer had the power to bring down prices and create a competitive market. The government should not meddle with trade. Government controls produced waste and democratic unaccountability. This was the lesson of the war, Wilson argued, when the government had sold bread below its real cost, losing taxpayers £150 million. All the state needed to do was provide information and fight fraud by 'keeping a watchful eye on offenders'. The consumer was a better guardian of the public interest. After all, if prices were too high in one shop, consumers could take their business elsewhere. 'Personally...I feel the best way to bring prices down is to boycott some of the things and go without them entirely for a certain period, as the housewives do in Australia.' Housewives had to 'take a keener interest in their shopping', compare prices, and learn more about the qualities of the things they bought.[142]

It was this sort of reasoning that enabled Baldwin and the Conservative party to reposition themselves as the friend of the consumer after the election disaster of 1923. It also helped deflect from their association with protectionist producer interests and from the costs to the consumer of the safeguarding duties.

Baldwin's Food Council might have been weak institutionally and was received with a mix of cynicism and despair on the Left, but from the point of view of Conservative housewives that was its very attraction. Since profiteering was not endemic, they argued, there was no reason for government interference. The return to the gold standard in 1925 and the deflationary programme this required may have hurt industry but it also lowered prices. Under Labour, tea and sugar prices had gone up, while it was Baldwin's government that lowered the duty on sugar in 1925, Conservative women pointed out. Stealing the old slogan from their radical enemies, they even began to talk of 'Our Free Breakfast Table'.[143] In addition to reducing the sugar duty and abolishing the tea duty, Baldwin stressed before the 1929 election, the Conservative government had overseen a 10 per cent fall in the cost of living, the equivalent of £160,000,000 a year more purchasing power for insured wage earners alone.[144] For the one million out of work at this time, cheaper goods were little consolation, but for the majority in work or living on a pension, it meant a considerable improvement in their standard of living. Free Traders no longer held a monopoly on cheapness.

Conservatives began to appropriate the democratic image, likening the shopper to the voter, that had been so central in progressive women's politics before the war. As Leo Amery told a women's meeting in 1929, it was the 'purchaser who was the real employer of labour in the last resort... and [who] in every purchase cast a vote which definitely decided one way or another where that employment was going to begin'. Adam Smith could not have said it better. Indeed, Amery continued, even more than the political vote, 'it had its definite effect every time'.[145]

Conservative protectionism was becoming a hybrid of liberal consumer and protectionist producer politics. If Amery continued to press for imperial tariffs, Conservatism had also begun to absorb a liberal, market-based vision of the consumer. In this view, there was no necessary clash of interests between consumers and producers. Through their voluntary preferences, consumers could assist producers, at home and in the colonies. And consumers had the power to stop profiteers and ensure the smooth running of a competitive economy.

This new emphasis gave Conservatives a distinct voice as champions of the consuming public who nonetheless opposed state regulation. It was a Conservative alternative not only to Labour's Consumers' Council but to progressive anti-monopoly alliances between state and consumer groups, most notably the one that emerged in the United States in the mid-1930s, when New Deal agencies combined a system of price controls with a campaign mobilizing housewives to enforce 'fair' prices.[146]

This idealized Conservative version of the empowered consumer finally drew its strength from faith in modern marketing. The visual politics of Free

Trade and Tariff Reform had already made some use of advertisers before the war. The 1920s produced a tighter, more self-conscious association. In 1926 a Merchandise Marks Act was passed to distinguish British and imperial products from foreign articles. The branding of home and colonial goods, Conservatives believed, would benefit consumers and producers alike. A more secure home market would make it easier for national producers to join selling agencies and cut costs. This would mean cheaper goods for consumers.[147] The Buy Empire Goods campaign rigorously embraced modern marketing, in practice and philosophy. For the young advertising profession, the Empire Marketing Campaign was a golden opportunity to establish its legitimacy. For Conservatives it was a chance to make the most of the limited resources of the Empire Marketing Board. Amery portrayed advertising as a 'social service'. 'It enabled new ideas, new comforts, new reforms in the whole manner of living to be equally spread throughout the country.'

Such language was partly meant to ingratiate himself with advertising audiences. But it also expressed a genuine Conservative vision of a society in which both consumers and producers enjoyed the fruits of economic growth. Attacks on profiteers and calls for government controls during and after the First World War were part of a long-standing radical critique of middlemen, advertisers, and distributors as wasteful and responsible for high prices. Amery, by contrast, proclaimed their social utility. Adverts made possible a cheap press, the foundation of democratic culture. More directly, by staking 'his reputation on his branded goods', 'the modern advertiser' gave a personal guarantee of their value. This laid the basis of 'good will' between the producer and the consumer, 'who has learnt by experience to trust the maker's printed word'. It was wrong to think that advertising added to the cost of goods. It created trust, made distribution faster and more efficient, and informed consumers of the means available to satisfy their needs.[148] In a sense, advertisers took on a mediating role between producers and consumers comparable to that of the merchant, so central in earlier Enlightenment and liberal thought.

This Conservative vision operated at a higher social level of consumption than Free Trade's initial focus on 'necessaries', 'the cheap loaf', and the conquest of hunger. Still, it was a Conservative version of choice and cheapness—a promise of choice and a higher standard of living aimed perhaps more immediately at the middle classes than the poor, and expressed in terms of comfort rather than necessity, but a vision of choosing, empowered consumers nonetheless.

Free Trade had established the consumer as a political subject. Indeed, before the First World War, Free Trade had virtually owned the consumer. Free Trade, cheapness, and a civic-minded consumer seemed inseparable. By 1929, on the eve of the world depression, they had drifted apart. In progressive politics, in the Labour party as well as the cooperative movement, the war sparked a decade of rethinking. Free Trade, it appeared, had failed to protect consumers against trusts and monopolies. What was needed were price controls and regulation, not free exchange. Organized consumers discovered the state. Nutritional knowledge and demands for social citizenship deepened the estrangement between Free Trade and the citizen-consumer. The Victorian and Edwardian 'cheap loaf' was superseded by demands for healthy, clean milk for all citizens at stable, fair prices. At the same time, Conservatives developed their own competing appeal to consumers as imperial citizens. This process was a cultural as much as a political or economic one. In the place of Free Trade, with its iconography of the white loaf and horseflesh sausages, its seaside lectures and shop-window politics, there emerged a new more imperial landscape of Conservative consumers, of Christmas puddings and Empire Shopping weeks. Free Trade could no longer count on the support of the consuming public.

5

Visible Hands

As defence, however, is of much more importance than opulence, the act of navigation is, perhaps, the wisest of all the commercial regulations of England.

Adam Smith, *The Wealth of Nations*, 1776[1]

Free Trade ... is the real anchor of peace for the future.

J. M. Robertson, Liberal MP, House of Commons, 8 August 1918[2]

Economic activity uncontrolled, uncoordinated, unpoliticized, means chaos; for the indiscriminate jostling of private interests, whatever Cobden may have thought, will never lead automatically to the public good.

Alfred Zimmern in *The Spectator*, 23 November 1929[3]

Over the last weekend of September 1918, a small group of British wartime experts retreated from Whitehall to Oxford to prepare for 'the transition period'. There was little time to be wasted. In the previous week, the allies had led successful offensives in Macedonia and in Palestine. On the Western front, the German army was being driven back by British tanks in Flanders. The Central Powers were crumbling. While British officials sat in Balliol College thinking about the future of inter-allied economic policy, Generals Hindenburg and Ludendorff were demanding that the German government offer an immediate armistice.

The Oxford meeting brought together some of the best minds of a generation of progressive intellectuals. All had been recruited by the British state at war. Alongside John Maynard Keynes, the economist at the Treasury, there was Alfred E. Zimmern, the ancient historian and social reformer who advised the Foreign Office, C. Delisle Burns, the prolific publicist and social thinker at the Ministry of Reconstruction, E. F. Wise, who coordinated the allied purchasing of raw materials and,

in the 1920s, became a prominent spokesperson on the Labour Left, and
E. M. H. Lloyd from the Ministry of Food. Looking back at the growth
of inter-allied organizations since autumn 1915, they reached sweeping
conclusions. 'The old theory of national independence in economic policy
has been abandoned by the force of events.' The 'full Free Trade point of
view' was no longer useful. A quick return to free markets would bring
chaos. The market might indeed right itself in the long run, but, as Keynes
famously remarked later, in the long run we are all dead. In the meantime
there would be 'universal strikes and social disaster' and 'revolution in more
than one European country'. Competition would abandon people across
Europe to the mercy of international cartels.

The future lay with international controls. The war had produced inter-
allied controls of shipping, food, and raw materials. If these elements
had not yet 'logically developed into a coherent whole', they nonetheless
provided a blueprint for the post-war world. Parts of the new international
machinery could provide coordination for the transition period, others
should be retained permanently for the 'post-transition period, when
conditions will once more be normal'. It was 'worth considering', they
concluded, 'whether an international control arranged by the Governments
themselves was not better than [a] syndication of international capitalists'.[4]

When they returned to these topics the following week, the discussion
had been overtaken by events. On the night of 4 October 1918, the new
German government under Prince Max von Baden submitted its request
for an immediate armistice to President Wilson. At long last, the end
of the war was in sight. For the moment, general principles of post-war
international coordination were swept aside by practical concerns of how to
bring enemy ships and trade under inter-allied controls. The big question,
however, remained: was a new economic order emerging in which visible
hands needed to complement, even replace the invisible hand of the
market?

In the context of 'total war' this was a global debate, but it had special
significance for the one great power that had entered the war as a Free Trade
nation. Some of the debate was technical and concerned the measures best
suited to promote the interests of Britain, her Empire and her allies. Should
Britain give preferential treatment to the Empire and her allies, and, if so,
on what goods and for how long, and by means of subsidies, prohibition, or
even a customs union? Were there key raw materials and pivotal industries
that needed to be protected? Underneath lay fundamental questions about

the changing world order, about the appropriate relationship between government and commerce, and, indeed, about the essence of national sovereignty and citizenship. The war thus opened up a whole series of challenges for the Free Trade world view. Put at its simplest, the problem was this: did it still make sense to view trade as exchange conducted between individuals for their own benefit, or was it a political project, connected to war and national security? If the latter, was the Cobdenite instinct to trust commerce to create international harmony part of the problem, rather than the solution?

The war did not suddenly obliterate the divide between Free Trade and Tariff Reform that had defined the British political landscape. Both camps picked up their old banners and battle cries in 1915−16 at the prospect of a trade war. Even in wartime, Free Trade managed to muster some popular support as a project of ethics and peace. Yet these were not simple re-runs of earlier engagements. The terms of the debate were changing, moving beyond the old divide between Free Trade internationalism and Conservative protectionism. Some Free Traders were left behind, others joined the momentum towards a new internationalism.

The men who took part in the Oxford conference emerged as leaders of a new progressive generation of public intellectuals and international ad-ministrators. They would shape and popularize a new view of international relations in the era of the two world wars. To them, Free Trade looked increasingly naive, quaint, even irrelevant. Political institutions mattered, not just commerce. In a world of organized states and trusts, shortages and cycles, only international agencies with the power to coordinate trade could defuse explosive conflicts over markets and raw materials. New internationalists looked to the League of Nations and prepared the ground for what would become the United Nations. But this was not a purely cosmopolitan story. Empire and race shaped their ideological framework, as it had for many Free Traders before them. To some, the British Empire was an embryonic model of global governance.

The future of Free Trade was bound up with the future of democracy and the nation-state. During the First World War, conflict over military conscription and the power of the state polarized Liberals, separating individualists from those who saw people as part of an organic community.[5] The debate about internationalism accelerated the disintegration of Liberal culture. Before the war, Free Trade had held old and new Liberals together in spite of their different social philosophies. The war threw up new global challenges that neither markets nor individual nation-states were able to handle on their own, such as migration, international rivalry over scarce resources, and the power of international capital. Citizens were helpless. Parliamentary democracy itself seemed overburdened and distant from the concerns of citizens. The local and the global were drifting apart. The new internationalism was an attempt to bridge that gulf, to reconnect citizens with the global order that shaped their lives. The search for visible hands to coordinate trade was always also a search for a new democratic culture.

Power or Plenty

Few dictums were as widely quoted in Britain during the First World War as Adam Smith's observation that defence was more important than opulence. What Conservative writers had failed to accomplish in the Edwardian campaign, the war accomplished almost overnight. Smith was celebrated not as a classic liberal but as someone who understood that trade and wealth came second to national security and power. By July 1916, even Alfred Mond, still the secretary of the Free Trade Union, was attacking those Liberal colleagues whose ideas were so 'inelastic' that they failed to grasp Smith's insight. '[B]lood is thicker than money'. To survive, Mond argued, Britain needed to adopt a national policy of defence and development. This was different from selfish protectionism. It was foolish to think that trade was just between individuals pursuing their own advantage. The war showed how Germany had used it as a weapon of domination. Trade involved power and struggle.[6] Professor J. S. Nicholson argued that there was nothing for Free Traders to be ashamed of in coming round to Adam Smith's recognition of the national foundations of wealth.[7]

From the early stages of the war, growing alarm about Germany's 'peaceful penetration' put Free Trade on the defensive. In Britain, shortages of key materials like dyes, spelter, and optical instruments were taken as evidence of Germany's aggressive plans. Germany, it appeared, had used trade policy and corporations like the *Metallgesellschaft* to prepare for war, throttling her enemies and capturing the markets of her competitors. Trade to her was war by other means. Historians have long rejected that Germany went to war to capture trade, but to contemporaries the Hun's 'peaceful penetration' was a fact. Liberals and Conservatives disagreed not about whether Germany had used trade for purposes of war and domination but about how best to respond.

Asquith's coalition government, formed in May 1915, was an acrobatic effort to sidestep the question of Free Trade versus protectionism. A 'tariff truce' was vital to the coalition's running of the war. Bonar Law knew this as much as Asquith. The problem was not the leaders but their troops. Protectionist pressure groups felt that Bonar Law had sold out to Liberal ministers, and in the summer and autumn of 1915 began to press for a tariff. Free Traders outside the government, meanwhile, saw the coalition government as a protectionist plot to keep Free Traders muzzled while letting tariff reformers off the leash. Liberal ministers, it seemed, were coming under the dangerous influence of protectionist ideas, even taking the lead in dismantling pure Free Trade.

The Morning Post set the tone for the protectionist attack. Under Free Trade, it argued on 6 August 1915, Britons had forgotten that war was not just about arms but also about industry and commerce. This lesson had been relearnt painfully in the first year of war, establishing a new national consensus: 'a Free Trade party no longer exists in this country'. What Britain needed now was a double-decker tariff, with favourable terms for her Empire and allies and rising penalties against Germany, 5 per cent for every month more the war lasted.[8] Germany was already hatching schemes for a future trade war, and Britain needed to respond. Plans for an economic empire stretching from the North Sea to the gulf of Persia had been made by the Axis powers at the Vienna Conference in June 1915. Significantly, it was a former German critic of tariffs, Friedrich Naumann, who now led the crusade for *Mitteleuropa*. The mobilization for a trade war after the military war had begun.

In Britain, the political and business community was enthusiastically joining up. September 1915 saw the first formal breaks with the Free Trade system, when McKenna, the Liberal Chancellor, introduced a 33 per cent tariff on motor cars, musical instruments, and other luxuries. Three months later, John Pilter, of the British Chamber of Commerce in Paris, proposed an imperial, allied customs union with a high tariff against neutrals and enemies. Hewins, the veteran Tariff Reformer, joined Alfred Duche, the president of the French Chamber of Commerce, in calling for an economic union of the allies to establish supremacy after the war. One after another, Free Trade citadels began to fall, first the Cardiff Chamber of Commerce, then Leicester, Swansea, and Bradford. In February 1916, even Manchester's Chamber overthrew their Free Trade directors. Frustrated by Bonar Law's timidity, protectionists formed the Unionist Business

Committee to pressure Conservative ministers into action. Across the country, there was a growing feeling that Britain needed to hit Germany, hit her hard, and hit her everywhere.[9]

Liberals were caught up in the bellicose mood. An Edinburgh Liberal confessed to C. P. Scott, the editor of the *Manchester Guardian*, that even in Free Trade Scotland people disliked 'the idea that after the war the Germans should come in again on equal terms as beforehand'. There was 'a desire to safeguard … our raw materials, and a feeling that Colonial desires must be consulted'. When a Liberal official went to East Fife to raise funds he was told bluntly that 'they would subscribe willingly but no free trade for Germans after the war; otherwise they would not'.[10] In the House of Commons, Walter Runciman, the Liberal Minister of Trade, added his voice to the chorus: 'our object is to see that she [Germany] does not get her head up and carry on the same activities when the War is over'.[11]

In the end, it was pressure not at home but from France that forced the trade war onto the policy agenda. At the end of 1915 it was doubtful whether France would survive another war winter. France, it was feared, might even opt for a separate peace with Germany. Étienne Clémentel, the French minister of commerce, demanded an economic offensive. Clémentel was a cultured man—in his youth he had aspired to become a painter. He had also served as colonial secretary and could see the attractions of a more aggressive trade policy. If it was impossible to beat Germany on the battlefield, perhaps a trade war could bring her to her knees. An allied economic union would guard France against any future German stranglehold and commit Britain to help with France's recovery after the war. A customs union, however, was anathema to the British cabinet. Asquith and Grey had their reservations when the French proposed an economic conference; McKenna was altogether opposed. But clearly something needed to be done to support the French government. On 15 February 1916, the Germans launched the Verdun offensive. The next day, the British cabinet agreed to the allied conference.

The Paris conference of 14–17 June was designed as a show of allied solidarity. Together Britain and France were ready to crush a German *Mitteleuropa*. For the British government it was about politics rather than economics. It had more to do with stabilizing a fragile ally than with any significant revision of Free Trade. It was Runciman and the British Board of Trade, not Clémentel, who emerged as the architects of the Paris resolutions. Runciman, the son of a shipowner and a Liberal with impeccable Free Trade credentials, had met Clémentel at Chat Hill in Northumberland at the beginning of February 1916. The two men agreed on the general principles of uniting the allies' resources after the war to avoid dependence on Germany, but the price of this agreement was that any reference to a customs union or tariffs was dropped.[12] From that moment, it was Runciman who took charge of drafting the principal resolutions—not even the Foreign Office was consulted. More than anything, the Paris agreements reflected the evolving mindset of the British Board of Trade.

The main argument against an allied customs union was that it would inevitably hurt British trade with neutrals. The more German goods were excluded from Britain and her allies, the more they would be driven into neutral markets. Holland and Sweden would be pushed into the arms of Germany. It also threatened to further undermine Britain's position in Asia and Latin America, where the neutral United States was fast expanding at Britain's expense. Take the case of the Argentine, developed with British capital and enterprise. There might be good grounds for giving the Dominions preferential treatment over the Argentine, but, the Board of Trade stressed, 'there is no very obvious reason why that preference should be extended to Russian grain'. In view of the United States' ambitions it was crucial that 'nothing avoidable' should be done to weaken British trade with the Argentine.[13] Giving allied Russian corn preferential treatment against corn from the United States also risked provoking retaliation by America against British imports.

Runciman rejected any suggestion of a tariff. All it would do was 'deprive our consumers…of whatever advantage they can draw from German goods'.[14] Similarly, it would hurt British export industries that depended on cheap German materials, again putting British goods at a disadvantage in neutral markets. It was classic Free Trade reasoning. Supporters of a tariff urged Runciman not to forget that Britain's one big weakness had been her vulnerability to 'German raids' of the home market. Runicman brushed this aside. He did not believe Germany would be in a position to 'dump' its goods on Britain after the war.

A month before the Paris conference, Runciman told Clémentel he was generally opposed to state regulation. After the war, trade and industry needed to stand on their own as soon as possible. Transition methods had to be short.[15] In any case, as even Clémentel recognized, it was doubtful whether all the allies could be brought into a general scheme against Germany after the war. Italy and Russia might be military allies of Britain

and France but their economies had strongly depended on Germany before
the war. Russia had no interest in cutting itself off from a major market for
its grain. Japan, too, was lukewarm. Llewellyn Smith, the British veteran
at the Board of Trade, went to Paris expecting 'little practical result of a
concrete kind'.[16]

The Paris conference bore out these divisions. Ill-health prevented
Runciman from leading the British delegation, but W. M. Hughes, the
aggressively imperialist premier of Australia, fought tooth and nail against
any changes in the wording of the resolutions drafted by Britain. The
proposed exclusion of enemy ships was watered down, but otherwise Britain
pushed all her resolutions through. Two measures mattered especially to the
Board of Trade. One was an allied agreement to withhold most-favoured-
nation treatment from Germany after the war. This was a breach of an
important Free Trade principle, but it was more of a preventative, negative
measure than a positive step towards a trade war. No ally would enter into
a separate tariff treaty with Germany. Russia and Italy refused to commit
to a timetable and made the Paris conference scrap the proposed five-year
ban. Still, the suspension of most-favoured-nation treatment would leave its
mark on the Versailles treaty. The second measure was more constructive.
The allies agreed to preserve key materials like chemicals and other goods
vital for defence and security in the post-war period. For the Board of
Trade this was the 'most important of all resolutions from a practical point
of view'. Internally the Board leaned towards prohibiting the import of
dyes, spelter, and optical glass, though it left it entirely open to the different
allies how they would pursue greater self-sufficiency.[17]

What the allies agreed to at Paris were only recommendations. They
dealt with the allies' relations with the enemy, not with British trade policy
or, for that matter, allied policy in general. There was no commitment
to a tariff. The allies agreed to assist each other and to make each other
independent of Germany in essential materials, but the British negotiators
made sure that it would be left to the discretion of each country to decide
what specific measures to adopt.

As a general allied strategy, the Paris proposals never took off. In Britain,
the Balfour of Burleigh Committee, set up by Asquith to examine trade
policy in depth, reported largely in favour of protecting key industries
and punishing dumping. At the same time it seriously doubted whether
the allies would be able to act together. Russia, Italy, and Japan proved
stubborn. Russia insisted that it would modify the application of any Paris

measures that conflicted with its national interests. Italy made it clear that it would only participate if the allies found it new markets to compensate for the loss of German ones. It was unlikely that the allies would denounce their treaties with neutral countries. As Balfour of Burleigh concluded, a 'temporary community of political interests ... does not necessarily afford a secure basis for a commercial policy intended to be of a reasonably permanent character'.[18]

That political community was transformed overnight when the United States entered the war on 6 April 1917. From the outbreak of war, the United States had been worried that Europe was drifting into rival economic blocs. The Paris resolutions rang alarm bells in Washington. Congress gave the US president the power to retaliate against the allies if necessary. By the time America declared war on Germany, the prospects of the Paris resolutions had dimmed. On 3 April 1917, the British war cabinet expressed 'considerable doubts' about their expediency, not least because they gave the German government a propaganda tool to stiffen the resistance of the German people.[19] At the time of the Paris conference, British delegates considered it unlikely that Germany would be able to continue a trade war after the war and 'dump' cheap goods on allied markets. By the spring of 1917 it looked impossible. America's entry into the war drove the final nail into the coffin of the Paris project. Paris became irrelevant. Clémentel gave it one more go in the autumn, seeking to win over Wilson to an economic offensive that would force Germany to accept peace or face commercial punishment. Wilson was not interested in economic war, but in laying the foundations for peace by removing discrimination. Equality of trade conditions was the third of his Fourteen Points.[20]

In hindsight it is easy to see the Paris resolutions as doomed from the outset. For contemporaries, however, they were a momentous step. Paris was ambitious in scope. In addition to plans for pooling resources and punishing Germany for the duration of the war, the allies adopted resolutions covering the transition period and beyond. The problem was that the resolutions were so broad that they confirmed the hopes and fears of all sides. For convinced Tariff Reformers, the Paris conference was the first brick in the wall of a general tariff, establishing the principle of preferential treatment; Hewins heralded it as 'the most important economic consultation that has ever taken place in the modern world'.[21] For Snowden, by contrast, Paris would be 'fatal to the future welfare of this country, to the future of international relations and to the future of world peace'.[22] Others, including

Conservatives, found it difficult to understand the Paris resolution at all.[23] Asquith avoided giving a government statement until 2 August. The Paris resolutions, he finally claimed, did not involve any breach of Free Trade principles.

For Free Traders, the Paris conference was a defining episode in what they came to see as a plot to establish a general tariff. First there had been the McKenna duties, then Paris, then the government placed a tax on palm kernel exports to markets outside the British empire, and in March 1917, it let India raise her cotton duties. All of these policies had their internal logic. McKenna was hoping to support sterling and preserve shipping space by cutting back on the import of cars and musical instruments. The increase in the Indian cotton duties from 3½ to 7½ per cent was in part a revenue measure for the service of a loan; India had agreed to contribute £100 million pounds to the cost of the war. For committed Free Traders, however, these were all pieces of what Hobson in the summer of 1916 labelled 'the new protectionism'.

Hobson resigned from the Liberal party at the time of the Paris conference. It was Liberals who had compromised Free Trade principles. All these measures were carried through by Liberal ministers and overseen by Liberal prime ministers, first Asquith, then from December 1916 Lloyd George; they probably would have faced much tougher opposition if they had been introduced by Conservatives. They poisoned the political atmosphere. Paris was an important chapter in the widening split in the Liberal movement that, together with the controversies over military conscription and the running of the war, led to Asquith's fall and a new coalition government under Lloyd George in December 1916.

If Paris divided the Liberals, it also gave the Free Trade rump a welcome impetus to regroup. After the self-imposed silence of the 'tariff truce', Free Trade came back into the open. On 6 April 1916, Hugh Bell, the old steelmaster, presided over a dinner for the 'Manchester martyrs', the Free Trade directors who had recently been ousted from the Manchester chamber of commerce. Over the next two months, the *Manchester Guardian* published a series of articles by Hobson and others attacking the new protectionism, culminating in a Free Trade manifesto on 6 July 1916. The following day, Lord Beauchamp, who had taken over the presidency of the Free Trade Union in April, formed a parliamentary committee for the defence of Free Trade. Paris had also woken the Cobden Club and the Free Trade Union from their slumber.[24]

In Parliament, the defence of Free Trade was led by John Simon and Philip Snowden. Simon, who had resigned from the Home Office over conscription earlier that year, put the Liberal argument for Free Trade. Free Trade had been crucial for Britain's war effort. Unlike her protectionist allies, who all faced financial ruin, Britain had been able to raise enormous sums (£300 million) to beat the enemy. The Paris resolutions would be commercial suicide. To stop Britons buying German goods would hurt British interests as much as German ones. It would make it more difficult for British traders to compete with German firms in the markets of the world. Yes, Germany needed to be brought to her knees, but this could only be achieved by beating her in the field.[25]

From the Labour benches, Snowden joined in the attack on the Asquith government. The only thing Asquith had not surrendered was his office; Snowden urged him to go. Paris had pushed aside any reservations Snowden had had about Free Trade. He was a more ardent Free Trader than ever. Alliances were fragile and did not last. Competition after the war would be stiff, and industry needed lower not higher burdens. Above all, the Paris resolutions endangered any future peace. They would unleash an 'explosion of hate' and commit international relations to 'the idea that hate and enmity are to be permanent'.[26]

In the country, the Paris proposals produced a wave of protests from liberal and radical groups. None of these rivalled the popular Edwardian movement, but the mini-campaign by the Cobden Club, the Women's Liberal Association, and the Union of Democratic Control demonstrated just how deep-rooted and hardy a plant Free Trade was in some quarters. The war had brought with it a harsh climate, but it had not altogether killed off Free Trade sentiment.

The voice of radical dissent was the Union of Democratic Control. The UDC was the home of the great and the good of radical internationalism, stretching from E. D. Morel and Angell to Courtney and Hobson. C. P. Trevelyan, its founder, had resigned from the Liberal government at the declaration of war, and would join Labour at its end. From the outbreak of war the Union had challenged the government's foreign policy and pressed for a lasting peace. It offered a typical radical denunciation of the twin evils of tariff and reaction: there was a 'close kinship between Imperialism, conscription, and tariffs, just as there is a natural association between peace, free trade, and good will among nations'.[27]

In the spring and summer of 1916, the Union held meetings denouncing a trade war in many towns and cities, from Birmingham and Bolton to Warrington and Leicester. Some of these discussions found a home in Quaker and humanitarian societies like the Hampstead Ethical Institute Debating Society. Others drew support from labour organizations which opposed the Paris resolutions, such as the 100,000 strong Glasgow Trades Council. The Trades Union Congress rallied to Free Trade in September, although keen to exclude sweated goods. In Hammersmith and Chiswick record numbers turned out to hear Hobson.[28] An economic war after the shooting war threatened the Union's plans for a future League of Nations. The campaign against Paris led the Union to add a fifth to its four cardinal points: 'British Policy shall be directed towards promoting free commercial intercourse between all nations and the preservation and extension of the principle of the Open Door.'[29]

On the more traditional Liberal side, Hugh Bell and the free-thinker J. M. Robertson led the defence of Free Trade. They joined together with Beauchamp, the new president of the Free Trade Union, and F. W. Hirst, who in 1917 laid down the editorship of the *Economist* and threw himself into the battle to save Britain from tariffs and state intervention. The fundamental principles of political economy were timeless, Bell insisted—the war had not changed that. Exports paid for imports. All other countries had been forced by war to overthrow their existing tax system. Free Trade Britain alone was financially sound. Even talk of protecting key industries was exaggerated. Most key industries were extremely small—Britain only imported £1.9 million worth of dyestuffs before the war. It was surely foolish, Bell argued, to favour a few small industries at the expense of the many competitive trades.[30] Hirst further feared the Paris resolutions would divert financial business from the City to Copenhagen and Zurich.[31]

Ethics and economics remained inseparable in the popular campaign, which rehearsed familiar arguments about the reciprocal nature of trade, its mutual benefits, and its contribution to peace and civilization. Robertson warned against applying 'war temper' to commercial questions. The widespread feeling of 'I do not want to buy German goods' was understandable. He, too, was repulsed by Hun atrocities. The problem was that the Paris proposals were 'extremely obscure and ... self-contradictory'. A few individuals might gain from a trade war, but Britain as a whole would suffer. How would it be possible to indemnify Belgium and Serbia if Britain destroyed Germany? Yes, Robertson acknowledged, Germans were brutes—'a menacing aggregate of racial egotists'. But this made it even more urgent to help them become civilized beings, a slow process that needed the growth of trade and democracy.[32] In fact, Robertson was convinced that Germany's future lay with Free Trade. The war had taught the German people a lesson. They were casting off authoritarian oppression and walking towards the light of liberalism. Britain should help free them from the Junkers, not push them back into the arms of a militaristic ruler, Robertson warned prophetically. A tariff in these circumstances would be suicidal: 'Free trade in Germany against a tariff-ruled Great Britain means the commercial overthrow of Great Britain.'[33]

As before the war, it was especially Liberal women who acted as popular defenders of the faith. Robertson's pamphlet 'Fiscal Policy after the War', for example, was sent to every branch of the 70,000-strong Women's Liberal Federation, together with a syllabus and a call to set up study circles. In June 1917 the Federation received Robertson and F. J. Shaw from the Cobden Club to discuss further action. For Shaw, the WFL newsletter became a convenient forum to warn women of the dangers of the new protectionism. 'Free Trade had been a triumphant success', Shaw exclaimed. It was the true patriotic policy. It had given Britain an unrivalled position of financial strength and allowed her to help protectionist allies and Dominions. In fact, 'Free Trade has done a great part in saving the world from Prussian militarism.'[34] Tariffs would ruin the chance of future peace. They also threatened peace at home. Shaw reminded Liberal housewives of the bread riots and threats of revolution that followed the Napoleonic wars to illustrate what it would mean to maintain war prices in peace time.

We know little about the local meetings on international trade addressed by Liberal women themselves, but the calendar of events points to a wave of speeches in 1916 and 1917. Amongst Liberal women, none were more active than Miss McLaren Ramsay and Caroline Trevelyan, C. P. Trevelyan's wife. The two addressed meetings on 'international trade relations after the war' in towns from Sittingbourne to Northampton. At her lectures McLaren Ramsay distributed Shaw's leaflets for the Cobden Club on 'Can We trade with Germany after the War?'[35] Liberal women also protested against the Indian cotton duty. They reaffirmed their 'adherence to the principles of Free Trade', convinced that 'their practical application both to internal and external trade is essential to the interests of our country and to the well-being of consumers'.[36]

The reaction against the Paris resolution looked like the beginning of a popular Free Trade revival, but it turned out to be just a blip. By 1918 and 1919, international trade had all but disappeared from the weekly topics of Liberal women's meetings. Unlike Asquith's, Lloyd George's coalition government with Bonar Law came to involve an acceptance of certain select measures of protection, including the principle of colonial preference, though Lloyd George was careful to stay clear of new food taxes. In the 1918 election, Lloyd George and his Coalition Liberals pledged their support for anti-dumping measures, and soon thereafter introduced duties to safeguard key industries. There were no Free Trade mass meetings in protest. The Free Trade Union still had its officers and a few thousand pounds in its coffers, but, as Beauchamp confessed to McKenna in 1919, 'I am afraid there is not much interest in the subject at present.'[37] Two years later sympathetic observers found the Free Trade Union reduced to a 'small organisation whose best days…are done'.[38] Tellingly, the call for an international Free Trade Congress after the war came from Holland, Switzerland, and Austria, not from Britain. The Cobden Club haemorrhaged members. The surviving subscription book shows a large number of resignations in 1921−2. Many coalition Liberals were moving away from Free Trade, prepared to support selective safeguarding, subsidies and a more active state.

Liberals reunited to fight the 1923 election, but this could not reverse the downward spiral. One Liberal found in 1928 that the 'Cobden Club has almost ceased to function' and that it was now better known abroad than in the motherland of Free Trade.[39] A generation gap opened up. Once the home of leading politicians and economists, from Gladstone to J. S. Mill, indeed the young Chamberlain, the Cobden Club found it impossible to recruit fresh blood. Young, cutting-edge thinkers and ambitious politicians looked elsewhere. John Maynard Keynes, the most influential liberal economist of his generation, resigned in 1924.[40]

Asquith's followers never forgave Lloyd George for taking over the government in December 1916. Lloyd George's support for colonial preference in principle and the introduction of safeguarding duties confirmed to Independent Liberals that Lloyd George and his Coalition Liberals could not be trusted. The question of Free Trade became a lightning rod for more general fears of the dangerous statist temperament of Lloyd George and Co. For many, their Free Trade conscience made it impossible to accept Coalition Liberals as members of the Liberal party.[41] Conveniently, attacks on

Lloyd George distracted attention from the fact that it had been Asquith's helpers, Runciman and McKenna, who had violated liberal purity in the first place, as Lloyd George kept pointing out. After being manoeuvred out of Downing Street, Asquith never regained the vision and energy necessary to direct a Free Trade campaign. When the Indian cotton duties were introduced, he was unwilling to lead. When Beauchamp pressed for more activism by the Free Trade Union in 1917, he was called off by Runciman and McKenna.

Hirst's editorials in *Common Sense*, the new house journal of disaffected Cobdenites, give a sense of the dilemma. There was little to choose from between Lloyd George and Asquith, Hirst argued. Lloyd George was holding office at the pleasure of the Protectionists. But so had Asquith. It was impossible to rely on this 'Old Gang of official Liberals' who had sacrificed the core of liberalism in a 'miserable hunt for offices and titles', 'in order to please their Protectionist colleagues and remain in office'.[42] When Hirst drew up his blueprint for a government to pursue a negotiated peace in January 1918 (the Lansdowne scheme) he did not see it necessary to include either Asquith or his allies at all. Of course, this paper ministry was pure fantasy, but the idea of a Lansdowne government with key positions filled by old-fashioned Liberals like Lord Loreburn, a former Lord Chancellor, and Richard Holt, an archetypal shipowner and critic of government controls, shows how out of touch committed Free Traders were. And it revealed the dearth of talent considered worthy upholders of true Free Trade. If Free Trade had not yet sunk, it had been cast adrift without a strong helmsman in an ever more turbulent sea.

Underlying this lack of leadership was a deeper disengagement from the realities of politics. For Hirst, Bell, and Holt, their cause was synonymous with a battle against state spending and intervention. Free imports were a way of smashing bureaucratic controls. Behind interference with trade lurked socialism. Such fears had already circulated before 1914, but the Russian revolution and the growth of the Labour party gave them an altogether new meaning. For Hirst and friends, to combine Free Trade and social reform was to sup with the Devil. The fight for Free Trade had to be a fight against all forms of state assistance. Liberals like Runciman joined this anti-statist platform after the war.

This line of reasoning was about more than philosophical principles. It had implications for trust and social alliances: some groups could be trusted to defend sound finance and free exchange and some could not. Gladstone's achievement had been to use Free Trade to build trust between the middle and the working classes about the role of government. Gordon Harvey was the Liberal MP for Cobden's old constituency of Rochdale. For Harvey, the war and the rise of Labour had shattered this bond. His 'reading of these men' was that they were only Free Traders 'so long as they thought that Protection would help the "Private Employer" '. The 'rank and file of the [Labour] Party are perhaps the most narrow minded of all sections of the community': ' "to H—l with the foreigner", is the motto of too many of our working folk in their moments of candour'.[43]

The campaign for 'economy' and for rolling back the state would receive a big push with the world depression in 1929, but many older Liberals had already switched to that track by the end of the First World War. At a time of industrial decline and unemployment, this anti-statist outlook was unlikely to be an attractive platform for a new popular Free Trade movement. Amongst middle-class voters, on the other hand, it merely reinforced fears of socialism and the bankruptcy of the state. As these fears grew, Free Trade came to seem less important than retrenchment.

Free Trade had always attracted a libertarian, laissez-faire wing, but its success before the war had never depended on any one definition. Its strength had come from multiple radical, progressive, and conservative meanings that managed to muster support across social classes and political traditions. Now its meanings and networks of support were shrinking. Many radicals who continued to denounce tariffs were warming to other forms of regulating trade. The most obvious rift was with progressives like Christopher Addison and Chiozza Money, who emerged as champions of state trade in foodstuffs. Addison had been Lloyd George's minister of health and would join Labour in 1923. Chiozza Money had been the statistical factotum of the Free Trade movement before the war. Finance and numbers were his bread and butter. There were few MPs better qualified to speak on trade and finance, and, as a speaker for the Free Trade Union, his fees had tided him over hard times in 1910. In August 1916, in the parliamentary debate about Paris, it was Money who turned against old Liberal colleagues with their outmoded Free Trade ideas. 'I totally disagree with those Free Traders who say that because an article is imported at any particular time that that is a reason why we should go on importing it, or that the importation itself is a proof that we ought to import it.' Britain was not as financially secure as Free Traders would have people believe. The nation was struggling to pay for magnetos from Sweden, machinery from the

United States, and margarine from Holland. Britain should never have allowed these industries to drift abroad. Refashioning himself as a 'modern Free Trader', Money called on the state to develop national and imperial resources, with a range of measures from the support of key industries and the public control of agriculture to the coordination of imperial resources.[44]

There was a growing disagreement about how 'free' Free Trade really was and how much of it was good for peace. Those opposed to a trade war shared a negative view that tariffs were evil, but now began to disagree with the positive view about the benign and peaceful spirit of trade as such. Free Traders like Robertson had trouble answering those who pointed out that trade could be a source of conflict and that for many countries it was about political power and independence. Trade, they simply repeated, 'is not war. Trade is the negation of war. Trade is the beginning of human civilisation as against war.'[45] For many in the Union of Democratic Control this was a far too rosy picture. A good case in point is Goldsworthy Lowes Dickinson, a Cambridge Apostle and one of the intellectual founding fathers of the League of Nations. Raised by a Gladstonian father, Dickinson first rebelled by becoming a socialist Tory, then was seduced by Fabianism. 'Goldie', as friends called him, had taught himself German reading Heine with a dictionary in Heidelberg. As for so many Victorians with close ties to German culture, the outbreak of war had been a personal tragedy for Dickinson. He threw himself into the campaign to stop future wars and became one of the most active members of the UDC. In his widely read *European Anarchy* (1916) he traced the causes of the war to an anarchic state system. And it was Dickinson who wrote the UDC's pamphlet on *Economic War after the War*—distributed in over a hundred thousand copies.[46]

Like Robertson, Dickinson warned that Paris was about more than economic policy. It threatened the 'whole future of civilisation'. To cast Germany as a 'mad-dog' nation would destroy a 'durable peace'. It was foolish to believe that a nation could use war to take trade away from another. So far this was a standard pre-war argument with echoes of Angell. But he also went further. 'Trade and commerce, carried on as it is now carried on in the modern world, must always be a source of friction, simply because it is competitive.' It was 'Utopian' to presume that nations would embrace universal free trade. Instead, Dickinson looked to a lower common denominator: the abolition of discriminatory duties. The problem was not protection as such; countries had the right to protect their industries against outsiders. It was discrimination that was the root cause of international friction, especially where empires sealed off their colonial markets or gave preferential treatment. The answer to this problem was an international federation with a set of rules to outlaw 'unfair' practices. Dickinson envisaged an international body with the power of commercial boycott to penalize offenders, something altogether alien, even distasteful to Free Traders brought up on a view of commerce as a politics-free zone.

To Hobson, Paris was just another example of old 'protectionist-imperialist-militarist interests'. He now looked to the League to secure an 'equitable distribution of wheat, cotton, timber, oil and copper'.[47] The benign workings of Free Trade were similarly questioned by Morel and others in the UDC. Trade, they argued, needed to be regulated to prevent combines from crushing native producers. Left to its own devices, trade led to the exploitation of colonial races, as Europeans scrambled to gain control of their raw materials. This was the lesson of the Congo.[48]

This acceptance of regulation came with a politically more realistic view of protection. Instead of condemning protection all-round, Dickinson appreciated that nations, especially 'undeveloped nations' like China, Turkey, and Persia, had a right to protect their societies against any form of exploitation that was 'predatory and unjust or incompatible with the principles of their social order'.[49] It was less universal Free Trade British-style and more an 'open door' in the American mode. Wilson's third point was full equality of trade conditions, be it in a low- or high-tariff country. Significantly, the demand for equality of access to markets came from a rising protectionist world power. The Paris peace conference of 1919 never considered removing trade barriers. Wilson's goal was to stop the kind of discriminatory policies lambasted by Dickinson. This was a new internationalism, where markets were not completely free but regulated by international rules and institutions.

New Order

In April 1919 Lord Loreburn confessed that 'the old doctrines of Cobden are a part of my mental equipment of which I cannot divest myself even if I wanted to do so'.[50] Born in 1846, the year of the Repeal of the Corn Laws, Loreburn was one of the names in Hirst's fictive cabinet of peace, retrenchment, and reform. Most younger men who entered public service during the war had few qualms about refurbishing their liberal inheritance. Some mental furniture was rearranged, some bits and pieces thrown out altogether as no longer fit for purpose. In the process, a new order emerged, both in the realm of ideas and in the world of international relations. There was an intellectual climate change in state and civil society. The future of Free Trade was not simply a topic of debate amongst Liberal MPs and radical commentators. It also involved those actively running the war, civil servants and expert advisers, and many intellectuals of a progressive persuasion, who tried to apply its lessons to a post-war order. At first practical questions dominated, such as how to deal with bottlenecks in shipping, but soon a more ambitious vision of global governance began to take shape. Instead of keeping trade and politics at arms' length, they were reconnected. For Free Trade as a fixture of political culture, the problem was not that the Liberal party had stopped being interested in it. Rather, it was that outside it the public debate was moving on rapidly, rearranging the grand design between politics, trade, and institutions.

The shipping crisis of 1917 was the decisive impetus towards the new order. In the spring of 1917 Germany had resumed its submarine campaign. In April alone 373 British, allied, and neutral ships were sunk, destroying over 800,000 tons. By autumn, the war had wiped out 17 million tons of the world's shipping. Together, Britain, France, and Italy had at their command a commercial fleet that had lost one-quarter of its pre-war strength.

In late November 1917, the allies agreed to plans for a more coordinated and efficient allocation of the ships that were left. National programmes for food and raw materials, too, had to be adjusted to fit the shrinking room to ship them in. Two inter-allied bodies were set up. One was the Allied Maritime Transport Council (AMTC); this was composed of ministers of the allied governments. Alongside it was the Allied Maritime Transport Executive (AMTE) staffed by top civil servants. The allies had already set up a Wheat Executive earlier in 1917 to help them plan general requirements and to use everyone's ships to the best advantage of the allies as a whole. The allied maritime bodies extended this joint mode of operation to shipping in general, and, thus, to practically all traded goods and materials. It was a milestone on the road to international coordination.

The AMTC and AMTE represented an administrative and mental revolution. By the end of the war, they controlled 90 per cent of the world's tonnage. They supervised the Belgian relief effort and coordinated the flow of food and raw materials between the allies. If Italy or Britain needed food or coal, it was the AMTC that decided whose ships were best placed to deliver it, not their own national governments. Partnership now meant pooling. What mattered was what best met allied purposes, not what national flag a vessel was flying. National control and market forces were suspended simultaneously. It was a fundamental break with the principles of national sovereignty, and nowhere more so than for the nation that controlled most of the shipping: Britain. The wartime advisers meeting at Oxford in September 1918 fully recognized this shift. Whereas Britain once had control over her own imports, 'now all the Allies had a claim to an equal share in all commodities'.[51]

This new body offered a prototype for the post-war order. To the experts at Oxford, it was 'the germ of any future international organisation'.[52] The AMTC, it was hoped, would foster a supreme economic council, fully integrating the United States. Robert Cecil, the assistant secretary of state for foreign affairs, was in charge of the blockade and emerged as a fervent supporter of a League of Nations. Already in August 1918 he called for the pooling of allied resources. On 13 November 1918, two days after the armistice, the British cabinet extended such ideas to the problem of European reconstruction, proposing a general economic council that would distribute essential commodities.[53] Such hopes were dashed by American opposition. The United States wanted to see war institutions scrapped as soon as possible. The AMTC was discontinued in April 1919 and merged into the short-lived Supreme Economic Council. The AMTE was terminated one year later.

For internationalists in Britain, however, these two bodies remained a defining experience, the seeds of a new international order. Inter-allied controls seemed to be the natural response to the crisis of the nation-state. The Allied Maritime Transport Council and Executive offered a model of cooperation between nation-states too centralized and over-stretched to deal with complex international problems. This was the vision developed by Arthur Salter in his book on shipping control for the Carnegie Endowment for International Peace. Salter himself had served as the chairman of the Executive and after the war became the proselytizer of coordination as the heart and soul of a new world order. For internationalists, Salter's was a seminal text.[54] It was not just a wishful intellectual proposal, but a vision based on hard practical experience.

The genius of these new international bodies, according to Salter, was that they created supranational powers without formally violating state sovereignty. The AMTC had no independent executive power.

Rather international and national spheres overlapped. Ministers and civil servants had one foot in an international body, the other in their national governments. This made it possible to come to international decisions, which were then passed back to national governments for approval. It 'solved the problem of controlling the action, without displacing the authority, of national Governments', as Salter put it.[55]

But this was much more than an administrative solution. National experts and ministers were 'linked together from within'.[56] Sitting together in such an international body and having to tackle shared problems would teach decision-makers to see the world from an international perspective, rising above the self-centred concerns of any particular nation. The Belgian relief scheme and allied food programmes suggested how international coordination could address problems which sovereign nation-states were incapable of handling on their own. Salter looked forward to a time when 'no Minister will frame a tariff affecting the trade of other countries without previous consultation with the countries which it affects'. He would then have to defend it to an international council on grounds which he could justify 'before the whole world, to whom their discussions are known'.[57] International government would one day be checked by an international public.

'Coordination' became the new paradigm of international relations. It gave internationalists a fresh sense of identity and democratic legitimacy. The war and the League of Nations system created a new network of international administrators, advisers, and public intellectuals. Arthur Salter, Alfred Zimmern, E. F. Wise, and E. M. H. Lloyd typified this new generation. After the war, their careers would diverge. Salter moved to Geneva, where he became director of the Economic and Finance Section at the League. Zimmern, who had prepared the Foreign Office memorandum for a League, helped found the Institute of International Affairs (Chatham House) and headed the League's Institute of Intellectual Co-operation. After 1945, he led its successor, UNESCO, the United Nations' Educational, Scientific and Cultural Organization, although the top job at the United Nations eluded him. Wise moved further to the left, resigning from the civil service after a trip to Moscow in 1923 to study Soviet export plans, to emerge as a prominent spokesperson on international trade for the Independent Labour party. Finally, there was Lloyd, who first moved from the Ministry of Food to the League's Economic and Finance Section, then to the Empire Marketing Board, before returning to international

organizations in the 1940s, when he directed the United Nations' Relief
and Rehabilitation Agency's efforts in the Balkans.

These men did not form a single party, but they shared a core belief: the
war had been caused by a system of nation-states and the pathological
growth of central government. Nation-states had become top-heavy.
They suffered, in Salter's words, from 'over-concentration'. They were
neurotic and self-destructive, with an 'abnormally and dangerously sensitive'
'controlling brain'. Most problems were beyond them. It 'is important that
the nation should begin to realize how relatively unimportant and parochial
is the range of problems which can satisfactorily be dealt with by a national
Parliament', Lloyd told readers of the *Nation and Athenaeum* in 1922.[58]
The world needed a new system of international coordination, staffed by
people who had broken free of the self-centred outlook of the nation.
In short, it needed a new type of international men like themselves. This
was more than a self-serving rationale of bureaucrats. New internationalists
were not advocating a world-state. International coordination was 'a great
effort of decentralisation', in Salter's phrase. It was the antidote to the
overconcentration of power that had led to war and chaos. Coordination
would shift power 'from the few overstrained centres of excessive power,
and … base it boldly and broadly on the general wishes and will of the
peoples of the world'.[59] It connected the international machinery of
government directly with local civil societies. This was the promise of the
League of Nations.

What gave the vision of coordination additional force was its potential
to forge a new economic order. New internationalists disdained economic
nationalism, but they no longer embraced Free Trade as a remedy. The
war had shown just how explosive trade could be, especially when it
came to access to materials essential for national survival. This was the
lesson of the blockade, a theme developed especially by Zimmern in his
writings and speeches, most notably in *The Economic Weapon in the War
Against Germany*, published in the last year of the war. The blockade,
Zimmern told working-class organizations in Birmingham in 1917, had
brought 'statesmen face to face with a situation in which all the old
landmarks of capitalist economics and fiscal controversy are submerged'.[60]
Governments would be unlikely to leave essential raw materials like coal
at the mercy of market forces. Other resources, like petrol, were already
in the hands of mighty bodies like Standard Oil and the Anglo-Dutch
Petroleum Combination.

That 'war did not pay' had been the credo of Angell and Edwardian internationalists. The blockade exposed the idea of keeping business out of politics as a great illusion. 'The true moral to be drawn from the fact that war is bad business,' Zimmern continued, 'is not that Governments should eschew business for fear of burning their fingers at it, but that Governments should go into business in a spirit calculated to maintain the world's peace.'[61] *Mitteleuropa* and Paris were 'wrong applications of right principles', as Brailsford put it in a League of Nations prize essay.[62] Commerce had to be supported, at times even checked, by an international machinery of coordination. New internationalists sought to build on these lessons. Keynes, in his *Economic Consequences of the Peace* in 1919, favoured a regional customs union under League auspices covering Germany, Poland, Mandates, and the states of the former Habsburg and Turkish empires, a scheme that came rather close to Naumann's *Mitteleuropa*.[63]

In Labour circles, it was Leonard Woolf who pushed the new approach most strongly. Free Trade, he argued, had been a 'mainly negative' policy. It was opposed to tariffs, but had little positive to offer to create international cooperation. This task required interventionist policies and international organizations. The inter-allied organizations of the war showed the way. They had avoided the ruinous scramble for money, food, ships, and finance that came with the 'ordinary rules of competition and the theory of international rivalry', and, instead, apportioned them according to national need 'and on the principle that the economic strength of one nation is a gain to all the other nations'. Woolf called for an economic council of the League to maintain credit and allocate supplies fairly and, through cooperative channels, distribute food according to need.[64]

Such reasoning went to the heart of the British Free Trade project. That project had been based on unilateralism and a principled defence of national sovereignty: what Britain did in her trade policy was Britain's business, what other countries did was theirs. Governments were not to interfere with international trade but leave it to merchants to conduct mutually beneficial exchange. As far as new internationalists were concerned, by contrast, unilateral Free Trade was part of the problem rather than the solution.

It was foolish to pretend that Britain's interest lay in splendid isolation, Wise argued in the summer of 1919. Wise was the delegate of the British Food Controller to the Supreme Economic Council of the League.

Instability in other European countries, like France and Italy, where the cost of living was escalating, inevitably had international repercussions. Such problems exceeded the capacity of individual nation-states and called for international coordination. Political order and social stability depended on it, if European societies did not want to follow Russia down the path of revolution. Wise suggested giving the League an Economic Council of ministers who would supervise economic organization and be directly responsible to its Supreme Council.[65] Lloyd went even further and called for the regulation of international monopolies and of petrol, oil, coal, and other key raw materials.[66]

Before the war, progressives had broadly succeeded in detaching Cobden's Free Trade vision from charges of laissez-faire liberalism. Now the critique of his international outlook caught up with the earlier new liberal critique of his individualist view of social relations. Half a year into the war, Ernest Barker, the Oxford theorist, concluded in his *Political Thought in England* that 'the Cobdenite interpretation of life was rather economic than moral. Everything was made to hinge on the economic sentiment of the individual;... there was little conception of any national duty to intervene either internally on behalf of depressed classes, or externally on behalf of struggling causes.'[67] The Liberal journalist Harold Wright followed the same year with a paper at the progressive Rainbow circle, wondering aloud whether Cobdenite non-intervention would ever again be a sufficient strategy. In the ensuing discussion, the opinion was aired 'that the peaceful influence of trade is perhaps something of a delusion and that trade has in fact been one cause of the present war.'[68]

An Introduction to the Study of International Relations, published in 1916, became a key text for new internationalists. The discussion of international economic relations was by Arthur Greenwood. After the war, Greenwood would embark on a political career, and eventually rise to become Labour's minister of health and deputy party leader. Then, he was secretary to the Council for the Study of International Relations and a civil servant at the Ministry of Reconstruction. Greenwood offered an alternative narrative of international relations. There was no automatic connection between trade and peace. History showed that economic interdependence sometimes encouraged peace, but at other times had been the 'cause of international unrest and hostility', especially over raw materials like iron, copper, oil, and rubber. Unilateral Free Trade was a kind of global class politics. It limited the freedom of the weak, who, 'crushed and trembling under the fear of aggression, are unlikely to participate fully in that complex life of the world which is richer and fuller than a self-contained national life can ever be'.[69]

The root problem, according to Greenwood, was that the modern world had seen a divergence of economic and political forces. The economy had moved towards ever greater interdependence—what we now call globalization. Yet there was no parallel trend towards political unification. Politics was caged in national or imperial units. Economic globalization had outpaced political globalization. Neither the British option of Free Trade plus imperial sea power nor foreign protectionism would enable an interdependent world of commerce and finance to develop peacefully. Instead, Greenwood looked to a world where political institutions would catch up with the global economy, with international controls over crucial resources under the direction of an international political body. 'Economic internationalism', he concluded, 'will perform its real function in the world only when it is politically controlled in the wider interests of humanity.'[70]

This was a new world view. Together, Greenwood and Zimmern would flesh it out for the public in a series of long articles on internationalism, published anonymously in *The Athenaeum* between October 1917 and December 1918. The series was a head-on attack on Free Trade internationalism. Experience had demolished its 'two cardinal beliefs' in the beneficient influence of trade. The breaking-down of tariff barriers had not led to universal peace. Nor had the rest of the world followed Britain's Free Trade example. Free Trade theory did not match political reality. 'Young nationalities' had consciously embraced economic nationalism. The feeling behind Swadeshi and Polish boycotts had to be taken seriously. Protectionism did not arise only out of ignorance, vested interests or selfish plans to shelter national industries from foreign competition. The case of the British Dominions showed it was also popular because it offered 'the most convenient instrument for controlling and directing the social development of the country'. The real threat was no longer protectionism but the 'shortsighted' and 'shallow' mindset of Victorians like Cobden. Politics needed to be put into international economic relations, not taken out. A future world order depended on international organizations, building on inter-allied councils, that would protect the common interest and foster a more political view of internationalism where 'conscious public service' took the place of 'individual ambition and the pursuit of personal profit'.[71]

For a few, Cobden continued to be an attractive model in the fight against great power diplomacy after the First World War. Most noteworthy were two attempts to revive Cobden's teachings: *Richard Cobden: The International Man* by Hobson in 1919 and *Richard Cobden and Foreign Policy* by W. H. Dawson in 1926.[72] Hobson tried to reposition Cobden as an internationalist first and foremost and so to extend his sell-by date for progressive politics—'to rescue the memory of Cobden from the narrow misinterpretations to which it has of late been subjected, by giving stronger emphasis to his international work'.[73] Cobden's true essence, he argued, had been obscured by laissez-faire Cobdenism. For Dawson, Cobden's internationalism offered a blueprint for attacking foreign policy makers after the war. Non-interventionism was the best strategy in the 1920s, just as it had been in Cobden's days. Its superiority was timeless.

Historians have long been fascinated by Hobson and his persistent, if not always intellectually consistent, attempts to reinvent the radical tradition, fusing a critique of imperialism with his analysis of underconsumption.[74] Contemporaries were less impressed. Cobden was indeed 'a great man', Greenwood wrote in *The Athenaeum* in 1919, 'but not "an international man"'. It was foolish to try to separate his individualist mindset from his views on foreign policy and Free Trade. They were one and the same. Cobden's internationalism was just as defective as his democratic imagination. His dislike of Palmerston's gun boat diplomacy was purely the 'reflection of an individualist domestic policy'. '[E]conomic democracy remained outside the range of his speculations, and international democracy was a conception he did not grasp.'[75] The *Journal of Political Economy* similarly took Hobson to task. The flaws of the book were summed up in its title: 'there is nothing in these letters that even so much as hints that Cobden was in sympathy with the current positive propaganda of international cooperation, or would be were he alive today'.[76]

Dawson suffered a similar fate. He was attacked for demonizing British and French foreign policy. Chatham House found his presentation of mid-Victorian politics naive and biased, the proposals for non-interventionism blind to the realities of international affairs since the First World War.[77] The *Economic Journal* complained that Dawson 'turned the reader from fruitful study of Cobden to mere distrust of his panegyrist'.[78] Leonard Woolf summed up the main objection: 'a policy of complete non-intervention, in Mr. Dawson's sense, which would be a policy of splendid isolation, is simply incompatible with membership of the League'.[79]

Cobden looked increasingly outmoded and irrelevant, even a danger to international democracy. In 1927, for example, the *Nation and Athenaeum* defended Cobden against the charge of standing just for laissez-faire and low taxes, but only to swiftly expose the flaws of his internationalism. History had proved Cobden wrong: 'the growth of international commerce, if it has not made for war, has done disappointingly little to make for peace'. Cobden's doctrine of a general harmony of interests ignored the many sources of conflict between them. His non-interventionism may have been a useful 'protest' against Palmerstonianism but it was 'no solution' for international politics. 'We must organize peace if we are to secure it; and the League of Nations represents our attempt to do so.'[80]

Between Manchester and Moscow

Not cheapness and freedom of exchange, but stability and coordination were the new watchwords. Already towards the end of the war, Lloyd was beginning to assemble the building blocks of trade regulation. Concerned about the precariousness of food supplies after the war, he took the old orthodoxy head on. To the standard liberal objection that an international body coordinating exports 'would kill private enterprise and initiative', Lloyd proposed 'Answer—it would foster them among producers by giving security.' To the critique that it would stop 'progress and tend to stereotype methods', Lloyd had the 'Answer—with the abolition of speculation and insecurity, the science of distribution... would be developed.' In short, even consumers would benefit from trade regulation. It would guarantee regular supplies and stalibize the cost of living.

Here, in a nutshell, was the argument Lloyd began to popularize in the 1920s, in his books on *Stabilisation* (1923) and *Experiments in State Control* (1924). Some of these ideas found their way directly into the Independent Labour Party and its 'Living Wage policy'.[81] But they also attained wider public circulation, especially through his articles for the *Nation and Athenaeum*, the *New Statesman*, and the *New Republic*. Lloyd wrote against a backdrop of uncertainty. The world economy was suffering from a decline in production and cyclical prices. In 1922 the six main cotton-producing countries exported one-third less than in 1913. To leave this malaise to 'blind economic forces' was madness. It would result in 'poverty competition' with nations and classes racing to the bottom.[82] Like Cassel and other critics at the time, Lloyd condemned extreme deflation and attempts to lower wages as a sure road to social unrest. But while monetary stabilization was good it did not go far enough in his view. The root of instability in exchanges was the instability of internal purchasing power, which meant budget deficits and governments printing money to stay afloat. Some of this could be helped by disarmament, which would allow tax cuts, and by a Central Bank regulating the purchasing power of gold, something that the Brussels international conference of 1920 had rejected. But it was equally important to stabilize commodity prices through international action, such as wheat pools or purchasing schemes.

For Lloyd, the war demonstrated what coordination could achieve: 'There was less destitution, less unemployment, less pauperism and less crime than there are at the present time.' Allied controls had worked. Now they needed to be extended in peace time. The years after the war saw inflation followed by slump. Speculation and profiteering had spread unchecked. Trade had turned into a series of 'commercial cyclones that go sweeping over the world, leaving ruin and destitution in their wake'.[83] In addition to bringing uncertainty, unemployment, and conflict over wages, these trade cycles damaged democratic culture. Politics became overheated. Producers demanded action against high wages one year, consumers pressed the government to bring down prices the next. Fluctuations threatened the 'foundations of civilised life' everywhere.

The diagnosis of the systemic dangers of fluctuations was an important blow to Free Trade orthodoxy. Cheapness had been a key selling point of popular Free Traders: it benefited consumers and forced producers to stay competitive and efficient. But what if cheapness was just one half of an unhealthy cycle, inevitably followed by inflation and speculation? In the past, Free Traders had been able to brush aside the protectionist call for stability as benefiting merely a few vested producer interests, outweighed by the interests of all consumers in cheap imports and open markets. The novelty of Lloyd's writings was that they showed consumers had an interest in stability too. Consumers and producers were floating on the same sea. Both had an interest in sailing smoothly, instead of being rocked by giant waves. *Stabilisation* bore the subtitle: *An Economic Policy for Producers and Consumers*. Price stabilization offered 'compulsory insurance against bad times'.[84] Stable prices would help producers to plan and invest, and over time enhance productivity; it would especially shield farmers against serious miscalculations and violent changes in the global market price. Farmers could not be expected to suddenly switch from growing wheat to raising cattle. But consumers would benefit equally. Not in the direct sense that stability would lower overall prices—Lloyd doubted it would. Rather, stabilization protected the public against an inflationary spiral, and the social dislocation and pressure to lower wages that followed. The 'friction and discontent caused by a rise in the cost of the loaf is not lessened or compensated by the benefit of subsequent falls'.[85] The gospel of cheapness, in other words, was an illusion.

Here was a different way of viewing commerce, but the contrast between the new view and the old was not only about ideas. It had practical implications for international politics, perhaps nowhere better illustrated than in the competing strategies for increasing world trade in 1926–7. The mid-1920s were a period of relative stability. By 1925 European food production had returned to its pre-war level; world raw material production had even exceeded it. What was sluggish was world trade, and especially European trade—in 1913 Europe had 56 per cent of world trade, in 1926 48 per cent. Following international financial conferences at Brussels and Genoa in 1920 and 1922, governments, banks, and the League had worked hard to get inflation under control. But trade barriers proved more stubborn. The creation of many new states after the war, especially in central Europe, added to a climate of economic nationalism, favouring what contemporaries called a beggar-thy-neighbour approach to trade. Commercial treaties were becoming shorter and shorter—on average less than a year, compared to over ten years before the war—and bargaining tariffs were becoming more widespread. The French tariff of 1910, for example, had a 50 per cent difference between minimum and maximum duties. After the war it was 400 per cent for many items.[86] Almost everywhere, tariff levels were rising—including in Britain, with its safeguarding duties. In Germany, tariffs were 22 per cent higher in 1927 than before the war, in Italy 12 per cent, in Bulgaria almost 300 per cent. If anything, these figures are conservative estimates, taking into account revenue tariffs, but underestimating the impact of truly protectionist tariffs.[87]

One strategy for trade liberalization was to take a leaf out of Cobden's book and preach the gospel of Free Trade abroad, relying on liberal opinion to challenge protectionism from within. After the repeal of the Corn Laws in 1846, Cobden had travelled across Europe evangelizing Free Trade. Now, in 1926, George Paish set out on another European mission, encouraged by the chairman of the Cobden Club, Hugh Bell, and the Free Trade banker Henry Bell. Paish was a financial journalist and had been adviser to Lloyd George. In a memorandum circulated among British ministers in 1917, he had concluded that domestic welfare politics would inevitably rule out raising indirect taxes and thus compel other European nations to move towards Free Trade.

In fact, the reverse happened. In central Europe, democracy led to a pressure-group politics that made governments more, not less, vulnerable to demands for protection. At home, Paish's attempts to enter parliament as a Liberal fell flat. The early 1920s saw a few Cobdenite initiatives to stem the tide. In 1921, a Free Trade congress met in Amsterdam. Two years later an International Committee to Promote Universal Free Trade was set up. It was a body run by the leaders of the Cobden Club, Wedgwood Benn, Hugh Bell, and F. J. Shaw, and had affiliate members from Free Trade cells in continental Europe and the United States. Supported by the cooperatives, the Committee called on all countries to unilaterally abolish all protectionist duties—to little effect.[88]

Paish was undeterred. In 1926 he embarked on his European tour, which took him from Paris to Rome and from Bucharest to Oslo. In Rome, he urged Mussolini to form a Free Trade committee; the Duce politely said he might consider it. Meetings in Belgrade were no more productive. In Hungary, a small Cobden Club survived, and in Prague there was a new Free Trade league, which made for a more encouraging visit, but Germany revealed the limits of Free Trade as *Realpolitik*. The German chancellor reminded Paish of the fiscal pressures of Germany's reparation payments. In Poland and Scandinavia, the final stop of his tour, Paish was not able to elicit any official interest in Free Trade at all. Altogether, the trip was a failure. 'The results of my visit were practically nil', Paish accepted with an air of resignation.[89]

New internationalists, by contrast, looked to international governance to coordinate trade. Trade liberalization was at the top of the agenda of the World Economic Conference in Geneva in 1927. Twenty-seven countries signed up to its recommendations. Some representatives of the British Empire were willing to move away from the traditional British view that tariffs were a subject for domestic policy, not international agreements. Walter Layton agreed with the French that tariffs were international matters that called for international attention. An international body should monitor tariffs and interfere if they threatened international relations.[90]

The 1927 conference had only limited success. More trade treaties were extended, fewer tariffs were subject to endless revision. Real trade liberalization, however, proved more elusive. France and Britain were at loggerheads about the appropriate interpretation of most-favoured-nation treatment; France pressed for a conditional mfn clause and for reciprocity, Britain defended the full unconditional version. In a world of high trade barriers, it was difficult to ask individual countries to lead by example and lower their own. The United States had surrounded itself with a high-tariff wall to shield its producers from European competitors but at the same time pressed into the European market. Understandably, most countries felt it was to their disadvantage to extend automatically and unreservedly full most-favoured-nation treatment to a high-tariff country like the United States. As the late 1920s would abundantly make clear, collective action to lower trade barriers was enormously complicated by the fact that most countries drew up their tariffs as a balance of commodities: they were unwilling to make concessions in one area without a gain in another.

Such a quid pro quo mindset was still anathema to the country closest to the Free Trade ideal, Britain. The Board of Trade simply refused to enter into reciprocal guarantees or to consider giving up the few tariffs in its arsenal, like the protection of the dye industry.[91] This principled refusal to negotiate was also one of the biggest obstacles to bilateral progress. Daniel Serruys, France's negotiator, even argued that the unconditional mfn clause had contributed to the rise in tariff barriers: smaller nations, disadvantaged by their size, were compelled to set tariffs as high as those of their bigger competitors.[92] For Britain's protectionist neighbours it simply did not make sense to exchange 'an open door for a closed door', as Serruys put it.[93]

Alongside the failure to put trade liberalization into practice, however, the Geneva conference also showed an imaginative expansion of the terrain of commercial diplomacy. International trusts and combines were invited to be partners in stabilizing trade. Instead of denouncing international cartels as vested interests or tariff mongers, the World Economic Conference stressed their constructive potential.

Cartels were not inherently 'good or bad', the final report found. It depended on their 'spirit'. In many cases, they helped trade. They promised to 'act as a check on uneconomic competition and reduce the evils resulting from fluctuations in industrial activity'.[94] Big capital might succeed where governments had failed. Of course, not everyone agreed. Cassel worried that encouraging cartels might leave the world at the mercy of monopolies. Still, the broad drift of new international opinion was clear. At the League, Salter, Alexander Loveday, and Pietro Stoppani warmed to industrial ententes as a force for good. After the war, it was difficult to keep up the Edwardian belief that trusts and cartels were the artificial products of fallacious tariff regimes. Industrial combinations had come to stay. If they could not be driven away, they should be harnessed to the internationalist project.

This turn-around was, in part, borne out of a cool sense of realism that unilateral Free Trade had failed. But internationalists also joined in the more general fascination with 'rationalisation' that characterized the inter-war years. Industrial ententes promoted standardization and eliminated waste. They exchanged information and, by centralizing purchase and streamlining production from raw material to finished product, lowered prices. Rationalization would take up where inter-allied controls had left off. It adjusted supply and demand across national boundaries, steadying the fluctuations that rocked the boat of the world economy. In the run up to the Geneva conference, inquiries into producer agreements confirmed new internationalists' belief that cartels helped to stabilize prices and lessen unemployment, benefiting consumers and producers alike.[95] What was true for the meat trade, in the hands of the US meat trust, was true for cartels and trusts more generally. 'Tariffs and free trade are alike unimportant' in such a world, Lloyd argued. The question was no longer for or against private trusts. Their potential benefits were clear. 'You can control a Trust, but you cannot control a chaos', Lloyd wrote in *The Nation* in 1922. The issue was how to get them to work in the public interest: were private trusts to be 'owned by hundreds of thousands of irresponsible shareholders and controlled by a few powerful trust magnates, or by a business-like combination representing producer and consumer interests, financially guaranteed by the Governments of the Empire and administered by patriotic businessmen'.[96]

For new internationalists, the task ahead was to reap the full benefits of industrial ententes. They were greeted as a sign that the world economy was becoming more conscious of itself. This was their message in-house at the League but they also broadcast it more widely to the new social movement of internationalists such as the League of Nations Union. The League had a historic opportunity to guide this development and to 'save the rest of the world from many of the rather disastrous mistakes that were made in the early stages of the trust movement in America'[97], Salter told the summer school at the Geneva Institute of International Relations in 1927. In a world divided by war, international cartels brought rival groups together. Fordism required big markets—something the United

States had, but Europe did not. Efforts to curb protectionism at the Brussels and Genoa conferences in 1920 and 1922 had failed. Balkanization might instead be overcome through industrial and market agreements, such as the one proposed by Austria and Hungary in the mid-1920s. At the same time, producers and merchants needed to see themselves as more than capitalists. The view at the League was that production 'involves obligations, not only to the possessor of the factors of production, labour, landowner and the capitalist, but also to the public'.[98]

This rapprochement between internationalists and cartels demanded a different approach from that which had governed the tough anti-trust legislation in the United States. The Geneva conference in 1927 recommended giving industrial ententes proper legal status, and empowering the League to oversee their international activities. Public service required openness; ruthless prosecution, by contrast, bred secrecy. The Labour party and the Trades Union Congress agreed: 'the economic growth of the world has outstripped the growth of political and social institutions', it reported to the League in 1927. Labour wanted international organizations to control trusts in the interests of the 'peoples of the world'. The League should become a tribunal, investigating cases where nations felt their citizens were being treated unfairly and arbitrating between governments and economic bodies.[99] Cartels, Salter hoped, would provide 'a vital constituent element in a General World Economic Council'.[100]

This was no longer an authentic Free Trade project. Salter had no problem with tariffs, as long as they were reasonable and introduced for social purposes, such as to stop dumping and protect living standards. Nations had a right to protect their economies. Internationalists had to learn to work with economic nationalism rather than against it. The problem started when tariff systems became excessive and chaotic, designed not with a view to the national interest but with an ear to the demands of vested interests. By stabilizing trade, cartels would curb the worst evils of tariffs, especially tariff mongering. International cartels would shield politicians from the lobbying of local interests. Trade barriers would be lowered by trade regulation. This was not socialism, but nor was it any longer the global competitive market championed by Victorian Free Traders. Geneva lay halfway between Manchester and Moscow, as Loveday, the head of the League's financial section, neatly put it. It believed 'not in free, but in "freer trade"'.[101]

Zimmern's World

Trade talks can sound dry and technical, so it is important to remember that, just as with the debate about fair trade today, they formed part of a broader democratic movement. New internationalists saw themselves as pursuing a dual project of civic renewal and global peace. Free Trade, in their view, had failed both. At a time of closer ties between big business and governments, its minimalist view of politics was outdated. It had tried to take politics out of international relations, expecting commerce to produce global harmony between nation-states of emancipated peoples. Free Trade and the nation-state, in this view, were symbiotic. The First World War saw both in ruins. New internationalists made a self-conscious break with their liberal inheritance and set out to redefine citizenship, commerce, and nationality. Free Trade, then, was not only confronted by particular problems in the arena of trade and diplomacy. It also suffered by association from liberalism's failure to foresee militant nationalism and check international anarchy.

For new internationalists, trade was part and parcel of a search for a new democratic order. One man at the forefront of this movement was Alfred Eckhart Zimmern. Today all but forgotten, his public stature in the 1920s was considerable; journalists at the time labelled him 'the ideal Prime Minister'.[102] True, Zimmern was not a wholly original thinker—few public intellectuals are. What he did have, however, in the words of his student Alfred Toynbee, was a powerful 'psychic antenna'[103] that enabled him to pick up major currents of opinion and broadcast them to wider audiences. His speeches, writings, and activities in Britain, Europe, and the United States give an especially clear insight into the changing democratic mind during and after the First World War.

By background and education, few new internationalists were better equipped to navigate European and transatlantic opinion, to act as a go-between for international reformers and social movements, and to reflect on what it meant to be a citizen of a country instead of a member of a national culture or ethnic group. Zimmern was born in 1879 in Surbiton, that quintessential English commuter town, just a few miles from London. His mother's family was Huguenot by background; his father, an East India and China merchant, came from a family of liberal German Jewish bankers who had moved to Britain after German unification and converted to Anglicanism. At ease with European languages, Zimmern went to New

College, Oxford, then the centre of Greek studies, first as a student then as a fellow. In 1911 *The Greek Commonwealth* established him as one of the brightest and most widely read ancient historians of his generation at a time when ancient empires were a popular prism for projecting the future of the British Empire. Now largely forgotten except by a handful of experts, the book had an enormous impact at the time. Lewis Mumford, the American writer, ranked it alongside Emerson's *Journals* and Plato's *Republic*; Zimmern was 'one of the heroes of my adolescence'.[104] *The Greek Commonwealth* showed what wealth and imperial expansion did to a civic community. As with his contemporaries, Zimmern's interest in empire was complemented by an interest in social reform—he was active in Toynbee Hall, the Workers' Educational Association, and, via Jane Addams, the founder of the settlement house movement in the United States, in a broad transatlantic network of social reformers.

Ancient history and philosophy came in handy in discussions about citizenship and empire, but the First World War effectively marked the end of Zimmern's career as a classical scholar and his rise to fame as a new internationalist. Zimmern served first in the Ministry of Reconstruction, before moving to the political intelligence department of the Foreign Office in 1918. An early advocate of the League, he was a founding member of the Institute of International Affairs, better known as Chatham House, in 1920. Ten years later he became the first Montague Burton professor of international relations at Oxford. Zimmern's career, however, was always more in the public domain than in academia, and European and transatlantic as much as British. In the second half of the 1920s, he acted as the deputy director of the League's Institute of Intellectual Cooperation, based in Paris, and ran summer schools on international relations in Geneva. All of this he combined with a feverish schedule of writing books and newspaper articles, and giving public lectures to everyone from working-class audiences in Wales to civic groups in New York.

Zimmern's driving concern was to show that citizenship needed to be divorced from nationality. Both were important and needed to be stimulated if civilization was to escape the two evils of virulent nationalism and cultural globalization. But fusing political membership and cultural identity in nation-states had been disastrous. To Zimmern, Liberals' fixation with nationality exhibited the same defect as their cult of Free Trade. Cobden and Bright's belief in universal Free Trade, Zimmern argued, and their 'enthusiasm' for the cause of nationality were based on 'the same philosophy of self-interest'. Just as they believed that, under Free Trade, individual traders would benefit their nation by pursuing their own interest, so they thought that in a world of independent nations, 'every nation would pursue its own self-interest, and that calculations of profit would determine the adoption of a Free Trade policy'. They saw ' "the economic nation," as a complement to the familiar "economic man" '.[105] Nations simply did not behave like this. In international relations, power and independence often mattered more than plenty.

It was also a narrowly materialist view of people as citizens. For Zimmern, Cobden, Marx, and Spencer had constructed the biggest single cul-de-sac in modern history. They had advanced 'theories of Progress without the glow of movement, theories of Society without an interest in the affairs of ordinary life, theories of Humanity without an interest in human beings'.[106] Zimmern urged 'old style socialists and old style liberals' alike to shed their 'shibboleths from the eighteen-forties' and to 'join forces in a new movement which, going back behind Marx and Cobden to the broader and more truly prophetic gospel of Mazzini, will unite the social and national streams that for the last two generations have flowed in separate channels'.[107] Strictly speaking, it had been the Kaiser 'who pulled the trigger'. Yet, ultimately, it was commercial capitalism, Zimmern insisted, with its 'philosophy of self-interest' which had nurtured 'the atmosphere of selfishness and domination which made the war possible'.[108]

Zimmern's alternative programme developed in three complementary parts. The first concerned civic life itself: citizenship needed to be set upon a spiritual basis of shared social motives, shielded from materialism. The second part concerned a healthy regard for nationality as a form of collective memory and identity but separate from political community. Finally, there was the sphere of international relations, where decentralized forms of coordination would establish new connections above and below an over-burdened nation-state, linking international organizations with social movements.

Commercial life needed to be subordinated once more to social ethics. Never one to shy away from grand historical narratives, Zimmern saw an opportunity for modern society to bridge a divide he traced back all the way to ancient Greece. In the *Greek Commonwealth* he had vividly portrayed a great divergence between freedom and civic life, on the one hand, and progress and riches on the other. The first half of the fifth century, according to Zimmern, had been a 'wonderful half century' for

Athenians. A sense of social duty and fellowship blossomed. In Zimmern's hands, Athenian society became a canvas on which to paint a picture of an organic community with an idealist brush.[109] 'Politics and Morality had moved forward hand in hand towards a common ideal, the perfect citizen in the perfect state. All the things in human life seemed to lie along that road: ' "Freedom, Law, and Progress; Truth and Beauty; Knowledge and Virtue; Humanity and Religion" '. Contemporary society paled beside this ancient model. Instead of 'our senseless greed for more', a luxury fever for 'yachts and motor-cars', Athenians pursued wealth in order to build a higher civilization, 'a refined and many-sided and effort-loving society'. The Peloponnesian war destroyed this organic unity, splitting freedom and community from wealth and empire.

The coming of the First World War made this account seem prophetic. Zimmern seized the opportunity to put classical ideals of citizenship to use in the propaganda battle against Germany. The war, in this view, was about much more than land and markets. It was a battle between two rival forms of civilization and government, between *Kultur* and Commonwealth. The English were the heirs of the Greeks. For them as for Aristotle, the state meant community, Zimmern told working-class groups at Ruskin College. The state was not some separate species but of the same type as parties, social movements, and cricket clubs: simply the 'highest of all forms of association'. The English had carried on the Greek tradition of associational life. Zimmern singled out the working classes, who, unlike the commercially minded middle classes, had kept alive 'the instinct and habit of association' with their chapels, cooperatives, and trade unions—'even the factory is sometimes a kind of college', he mused. This was a romantic picture, which ignored the role of merchants, professionals, and shopkeepers in the evolution of civil society, but it did serve his broader goal of fusing economy and democracy once again: material life was itself a branch of social association. This was what progress in government was all about: 'the deepening and extension of man's duty towards his neighbour'.[110] Without it, the pursuit of wealth led to imperialism and the eventual collapse of state and civilization.

If the English were the Greeks of the modern world, the Germans were the Romans. Prussianism had turned community into a 'military and economic unity, a barracks and a plantation', where social life and government were subordinated to the General Staff.[111] Ethics and associational life had been forced out of politics. German 'Kultur' was a 'State product'. It was cultivated by the state for the state. That is what made it so dangerous. The state lost its moral personality. The 'inevitable atrophy of moral action in its citizens means a corresponding decline in their moral freedom'. Britain, by contrast, was a commonwealth. A strong state and strong social associations were mutually dependent, held together by moral reciprocity. Unlike in German *Kultur*, in Britain 'education *is* fellowship, *is* citizenship'. Government based on association offered a chance to cultivate citizenship and social service, to make Britain immune to extreme nationalism and selfish materialism alike.[112]

Coming from a son of German immigrants in the heat of war, such patriotic exclamations may not look surprising, but, in fact, Zimmern did little to hide his national roots—far from it. In the same breath as he denounced German authoritarianism, he publicly acknowledged 'the debt I owe to the heritage with which I am connected by blood and tradition'. Reaching manhood, he realized that 'I was not an Englishman in the deeper side of my nature.'[113] Zimmern presented himself as living proof that citizenship and nationality did not need to be one and the same. At a time of anti-German riots and revelations of 'Hun atrocities', this took courage. It also reflected the importance of 'nationality' for Zimmern and new internationalists.

New internationalists were not cosmopolitans. They did not want, as Bertrand Russell put it in *The Atlantic Monthly* in 1917, a cosmopolitanism of 'couriers, *wagon-lit* attendants, and others, who have had everything distinctive obliterated by multiple and trivial contacts with men of every civilized country'.[114] True internationalism added to the love of one's country. What had made nationalism false and dangerous in the past, Zimmern argued, had been its political ambition. Nation-states had not brought universal emancipation and freedom but often intolerance and persecution. Nation, state, and representative democracy were not co-extensive, as John Stuart Mill had believed. In a world of big organizations, Zimmern wrote, small nations were 'relics of a vanished past'. Nineteenth-century Liberals had misunderstand the essence of nationality. Nationality was a spiritual force, giving people 'character' and a connection to the communal past. It was not a means of political emancipation.

Zimmern's attack on Mill, like his bashing of Cobden, was emblematic of the self-conscious way in which new internationalists sought to break with their liberal forefathers. Mill's ideas on nationality were, to be fair, more nuanced than Zimmern and more recent commentators have allowed. Mill did not believe common nationality and language were necessary for stable democracy. Nor did he view the progress of civilization simply as a story of energetic majorities absorbing backward minorities; he had no desire to see big nations like Russia expand. In other contexts, like the position of French Canadians, he favoured constitutional patriotism rather than nationalist assimilation.[115]

In taking on Mill, Zimmern turned to Lord Acton, one of Mill's earliest critics, who already in 1862 had described the nation-state as potentially the worst 'retrograde step in history'. But Zimmern went further. For Acton, nationality was an atavistic identity, at the lower and more instinctive stage of human development. It would retreat as civilization advanced. For Zimmern, by contrast, nationality became more, not less important with modernity. Nationality 'recalls an atmosphere of precious memories, of vanished parents and friends, of old custom, of reverence, of home, and a sense of the brief span of human life as a link between immemorial generations, spreading backwards and forwards'. It was a 'school of character and self-respect'.

Globalization made this spiritual reservoir ever more important. It was in multi-national bodies like the United States and the British Empire that the joint pressures of globalization and migration were most manifest, and answers to problems of diversity and integration might be glimpsed. Europe, by contrast, was a 'stuffy little world'—'the most backward of the continents'. Zimmern shared Victorian imperialists' fascination with America as a successful experiment. To supporters of a federal Greater Britain like J. R. Seeley, the United States had found the answer to the problem ancient empires had failed to solve: how to expand territorially without losing liberty.[116]

But Zimmern's visits to America also left with him a powerful sense of the dehumanizing effects of mass migration. Immigrants arrived at Ellis Island 'sad, bewildered, and hopelessly ignorant', he recalled. America to them meant an 'earthly Paradise', but it was 'only an abstract ideal', for they had 'no knowledge and no power to weave it into the textures of their lives'. Without nationality as a cultural refuge and source of self-respect and independence, 'primitive' peasants stood no chance against the 'steam-roller of American industrialism', which turned them into the cheap 'raw material of labour for some remorseless business enterprise'.[117] Zimmern supported new national communities, but ultimately he was concerned with preserving diverse national ways of eating, celebrating, and remembering, not establishing group rights based on language or regional autonomy.[118] In a political community, he argued, there was no danger if English inhabitants loved toast while Greek immigrants ate olives. Multi-national communities would keep cosmopolitan capitalism in check at the human level, just as coordination would keep trade in check at the level of international relations. Nationality placed a 'sling in the hands of weak undeveloped peoples against the Goliath of material progress'.[119] The free flow of goods, so heralded by Cobden and his followers for weaving together people in a world of harmony, now appeared to destroy humanity, blending cultural identities into a 'drab cosmopolitanism'.

Such anxieties about cosmopolitanism drew on ideas about race, class, and empire. Zimmern pointed to the 'spiritual degeneration' in the Levant, where traditional culture had been traded in for ugly Western clothes and poorly understood Western concepts. The battle between cosmopolitanism and nationality, however, was not confined to the Orient or the United States. All societies where their members abandoned their 'natural' cultural habitat were at risk. Britain, too, was afflicted by rootlessness. Classes, like nations, had distinct patterns of thought, Zimmern argued. Individuals lost their true personality if they tried to change them like a piece of clothing. The working-class scholarship boy who put on Oxford airs was in this respect no different from 'the ambitious young Boston Jew from a Russian ghetto [who] ape[s] the manners and customs of New England, or the nimble-witted Bengali student [who] adopt[s] the facile phrases and opinions of Macaulay and Mill'. Cosmopolitans, like snobs, were fakes: in trying to be something they were not, they became like 'shorn Samsons, full of noble purposes, but devoid of the strength to carry them out... helpless and foolish', 'parasites', 'pale ghosts of their former selves'.[120]

The answer to cosmopolitanism and assimilation was multinational communities. For liberals like Murray and Zimmern, the war triggered a crisis of racial and political confidence.[121] Colonial peoples were challenging white empires. Europe no longer was the undisputed centre of political gravity. The liberal answer was not to extend the principle of national self-determination—racial ideas ran too deep for this; sovereignty was reserved for white 'adult' nations. Rather it was to upgrade empire and Western multinational states morally and present them as organisms capable of inter-racial harmony. Zimmern praised American commentators who favoured the political integration of former slaves yet at the same time saw their racial culture as distinctive. For him, America was a political melting

pot, not a cultural one. 'If Nationality can help America' to integrate the
descendants of slaves into the 'American citizen body', he told social service
unions in 1915, 'it can help us British citizens also ... in dealing with native
races in our Empire'.[122] The British Empire had exposed native races to
commerce and Anglicized culture. Together, this 'process of unregulated
contact and ill-assimilated education' had produced 'poor invertebrate and
unamiable characters', 'miserable specimens of civilisation ... in place of the
young robust barbarians or heathens which they were before the Goddess
of Progress laid her seductive hand upon them'.[123] This picture of a
golden age of authentic culture before the arrival of Empire was, of course,
historical nonsense. At the time, however, it helped Zimmern tie his non-
political ideal of nationality to contemporary critiques of empire associated
with the shift towards 'indirect rule' and trusteeship. The 'white man's
burden' school of empire had been wrong. The mission of empire was
not to Anglicize and lift up 'backward' people to the level of metropolitan
civilization, but to preserve and deepen the cultural diversity in its midst.
This would boost their cultural immune system against the disease of
cultural and commercial globalization.

Stripped of its association with Anglicization and commercial power,
empire would be the germ of a new international order. The First World
War had produced a 'Third British Empire', to use Zimmern's term.
Unlike the First mercantilist version of the eighteenth century or the
Second type of the nineteenth, the Third British Empire for Zimmern was
a genuine commonwealth built on cooperation and mutual service. Instead
of material ties, what held the Third British Empire together were spiritual
ties and political traditions. It anticipated and prepared the ground for the
League of Nations. The principle of trusteeship, the peaceful settlement
of disputes, and the deployment of an international police force, all these
were pioneered within the British Empire. Under the pressure of war,
the Empire had begun to move away from central control; the white
settler Dominions were admitted to the imperial war cabinet in 1917,
and three years later to the League, finally achieving equality of status in
1926. 'The League', Zimmern argued, 'is the *deus ex machina* of the British
Commonwealth.'[124]

The commonwealth was a microcosm of the spirit of cooperation,
mutual dependence, and decentralized politics that Zimmern saw as the
logic guiding history more generally. The Third British Empire was no
longer isolated or self-sufficient. Like other countries, it depended on a

global society of nations. Empires had been superseded by the League. By the late 1920s, Zimmern had become convinced that for members of the Empire there were hardly any interests left that were distinctly imperial: interests had become international. This was why the Empire had failed to match the expansion of institutions and activities of the young League. It was 'not that the peoples of the British Empire do not wish to co-operate ... [but] that there is nothing particular for them to co-operate together about'. The Third Empire was dependent on 'a co-operative system safeguarded by the League of Nations'.[125]

Inevitably, the disentangling of state and nation, alongside the critique of commerce and cosmopolitanism, meant that Free Trade lost much of its value in the years after the First World War. Zimmern, for example, had no problem with a small country seeking to protect its producers against foreign 'dumping'.[126] Attention to the importance of key raw materials especially put a big dent in the self-image of Britain as a Free Trade nation. Zimmern recognized that a world in which 'the greatest trading nation ... holds a controlling interest ... in one of the most important oilfields [Burma], and shares with two of its Dominions the ownership of a valuable phosphates deposit—not to speak of its controlling interest in a Dyestuffs Combine—is not a world which is moving towards Free Trade in Cobden's sense of the word'.[127]

New internationalists agreed with Wilson. The main source of international tension was not protection but those tariffs that discriminated between friends and foes. It was the desire for exclusive markets that caused wars. This is what made imperial preference, however small, so unacceptable. To maintain peace, free trade between developed societies was less important than an open door in their dependencies.

The sharp extremes of the pre-war debate had softened. It was no longer a stark choice between freedom of trade on the one hand, and imperial tariff reform on the other. It was about the right kind of international trade coordination. New internationalists had no qualms about taking a leaf out of the Conservative book for their own purposes. In 1925, for example, Zimmern discussed Baldwin's safeguarding policy for the *Daily Herald*. Instead of simply rejecting it outright as just another protectionist ploy, Zimmern emphasized its constructive potential for the scientific control of key industries. In progressive hands, safeguarding could be part of an international control of foreign trade. What took the place of commerce as a force of peace and civil society was coordination and public opinion.

New internationalists like Zimmern and Salter were opposed to schemes of world government. This would turn the League into a 'cockpit of contending national interests'.[128] What was needed, instead, was an international body in which different national governments were linked from within, and which was open to groups from civil society. Globalization had destroyed a political system based on self-contained units with concentrated power and created a 'world of interdependent groups' and a 'system of distributed power'. What 'sovereignty' had been to the old order, 'co-operation' was to the new.[129] Whereas 'sovereignty faces inward and marshals its forces against "the foreigner"', Zimmern argued, '[c]o-operation looks outward, and transforms what has been strange and "foreign" into elements of working collaboration for recognised common interests'.[130]

This system no longer functioned as government by command but by the free flow of ideas and sentiment. The League was an attractive framework for transmitting this public opinion. It would connect public opinion above and below the level of the centralized nation-state. For all its failings, the League did succeed in creating a circle of non-governmental organizations that expanded the debate about social welfare and human rights.[131] For new internationalists, this was a step towards democratic renewal. Centralized states had become deaf to their citizens. Commercial capitalism threatened to make people interested in their private rather than public life. 'If we want to have really efficient international government,' Zimmern told the British Cooperative Congress in 1931, 'we must build it up from international voluntary societies, so that at every step voluntary associations watch over the work of the governments.'[132]

The First World War destroyed the global system of trade and finance. It is tempting to see the 1920s in mainly negative terms, a run-up to the world depression and the economic nationalism that would poison the world in the 1930s. But the impact of the war was not all destructive. Alongside growing customs barriers and beggar-thy-neighbour policies, the years after the war also saw the rise of a new, revitalized internationalism. It prompted a rediscovery of the political in international relations. Instead of relying on the automatic workings of commerce, liberals and progressives turned to ways of managing globalization and coordinating trade. These ideas gained ground initially within the state during the war. When peace returned and inter-allied controls were abolished, new internationalists took these ideas with them into the realm of public opinion and to the League of Nations. Older Cobdenite ideals of commerce and peace were increasingly crowded out. The new internationalism was a critique of both the market and the nation-state. Leaving commerce to itself spelled dangerous fluctuations and social dislocation and would put people at the mercy of international trusts. The nation-state was equally overburdened. New international institutions needed to regulate global developments. The intellectual seeds for a new global civil society had been planted.

6

Losing Interest

Abstract principles, in my opinion, are excellent servants but they are very bad masters.

Balfour of Burleigh, chairman of the Committee on Commercial and Industrial Policy, July 1916.[1]

It is not with me a political question; I do not want to call it Tariff Reform or anything else. I think we want to look at it in a commonsense way.

F. D. Moore, exporter of wool tops, October 1916.[2]

The wages in our exporting industries, if fixed by competition, must be controlled by the lowest wages paid for similar work in any part of the world. The skilful savage will determine the living conditions of the civilised British workers .... Civilisation, in self-preservation, must organise to destroy this system. Britain must choose now between an earthly heaven or an earthly hell.

John Wheatley, former Labour minister, 1927.[3]

'[I]n spite of my deep grained Toryism, I was an out and out unrepentant Free Trader, today I have no view at all', Milton S. Sharp confessed to a Board of Trade committee in the summer of 1916. As with many contemporaries, so with businessmen: the war unsettled deep-seated beliefs. Established truths lost their authority, a search for new principles began. '[A]fter the war I am going to try and be a little child again and learn my lessons anew. No view that I hold in regard to the fiscal question influences me in the least in expressing that opinion.'[4]

Sharp was a major player in the textile industry, the quintessential export trade whose fortunes had been tied to Free Trade and an open world economy. He was chairman of the Bradford Dyers' Association, formed in 1898, which controlled the bulk of the cotton piece dying in that part of

Yorkshire and owned some of the largest dying works in Lancashire. On the eve of the war, the Association had a capital of over £5 million, with 41 branches, including works in Germany and the United States. Sharp and his fellow firms dyed the cotton worn by the world.

The war was a shock to their business as much as to their convictions. Before the war, Free Trade guaranteed export industries cheapness and choice. Like private consumers, industrial consumers could count on having the cheapest imports the world market had to offer. These could then be worked up and exported at a profit. For industrialists like Sharp, the war disrupted that flow, and the economic reasoning based on it. Dying textiles required colours and chemicals as well as cotton; dyes were the 'lifeblood' of the cotton industry.[5] In 1913 three-quarters of the colours had come from Germany. One year after the outbreak of war that formidable proportion had shrunk to less than 1 per cent. For two-thirds of their colours, Bradford now had to look to domestic British suppliers; Switzerland provided the other third. If British dyes had increased in volume, the range of colour available had narrowed drastically: 65 per cent of it was Khaki, Sharp lamented. This made it difficult to hang on to foreign markets, where competitors were wasting no time in making the most of Britain's wartime problems. Even if the war were to stop tomorrow, Sharp estimated, the Association would only be able to execute 60 per cent of their orders from the dyes available.

The war threw up similar challenges across British industry. What dependence on foreign food was for consumers, dependence on 'key' products like chemicals, magnetos, and scientific instruments was for producers. Importing cheap chemicals from abroad might make sense in the short run, but what if in the long run it meant having no viable chemical industry and no trained scientists at all?

This dilemma was tied to a second, no less fundamental one, about the international orientation of Britain's economy. Victorian and Edwardian Britain had been the world's dominant trading and lending nation. The war changed all that. Many export markets were lost forever to American and Japanese competitors, especially in Latin America, India, and Asia. There had been inroads already before the war, but Britain's vast earnings from financial investment, shipping, and insurance had amply compensated for them. Now, the war also undermined Britain's status as global financial hegemon; one-tenth of Britain's foreign assets were liquidated to pay for it.

Some of these problems were beyond Britain's control. As the most internationally minded economy around, it would inevitably be hit hard by any shock to the global economy. Arguably, the dramatic expansion of world trade during the pre-war phase of globalization had been a mixed blessing. It had accentuated Britain's lopsided dependence on the big staple industries like cotton, iron and steel, and shipbuilding—all sectors in which second industrializing nations were catching up fast. The war boosted the capacities of the heavy industries like shipbuilding further; when the war ended, they were simply too large for peacetime demand. The global turn from coal to oil added to Britain's problems. New industries, like cars and electrical goods, were still too small to absorb the labour and capital shed by the declining industries. The return to the gold standard in 1925 only made things worse. How far, indeed whether, sterling was overvalued has been hotly debated, but the stubborn pursuit of the pre-war parity of $4.86 to the pound came with a policy of dear money that depressed industry further. Mass unemployment became the defining characteristic of the 1920s, sticking stubbornly around 10 per cent—the 'intractable million' as contemporaries called it.[6]

It would be wrong, however, to blame only finance and 'gentle-manly capitalists'. Industry suffered from its own internal weaknesses. In the Edwardian boom, these older export trades had still been successful, making profits, providing jobs, and finding foreign markets. Success had bred complacency, especially in the staple industries. The list of 'British deficiencies' was a long one. In the words of one iron and steel merchant, who knew German and American plants well, it ranged from 'lack of industrial courage ... narrowness in money matters, poor standard of education ... the one man theory of management ... want of cooperation amongst makers ... inefficient rolling mills', all the way to poor labour relations.[7] None of these flaws were insuperable or genetic. There was no reason to believe that the 'German character ... makes him a superman in colour production', as Milton Sharp put it.[8]

For contemporaries like Sharp the war therefore raised profound questions about the nature of the economy, Britain's place in the world, and the role of the state. For an ailing patient, was Free Trade still the best medicine for recovery, or had it become an addictive poison? What kind of society, and how open did Britain want to be? Should the government support certain trades and developments or was it better to trust market forces? Some of these questions paralleled the discussion amongst internationalists and consumers about the costs and benefits of cheapness versus coordination. But they were especially acute for producers, business and labour alike, struggling for survival.

The defence of Free Trade before the war had never rested on the shoulders of industry and finance. In the final analysis, it had been an achievement of democratic culture. Still, capital and labour played their part. Working-class support for Free Trade remained solid in the export industries, like cotton, in the Edwardian period. Business was more divided, as we have seen. Some traders, exporters, and financiers even toyed with bargaining tariffs, although the prospect of a genuine imperial tariff ultimately frightened many away from tariff reform. Politically, Free Trade benefited from its democratic reputation, its peaceful ideals, and its ties with civil society. But it was also an economic proposition and needed an economic case to support it. Before the war, Free Trade continued to have the upper hand in the debate. Those arguing for the benefits of mutual exchange and free imports could point to the rising number of ships and cotton exports. Free access to cheap imports maximized national wealth. The international monetary system was working, with Britain at its centre reaping the benefits.

The argument was about more than statistics. It was about what made a society modern and successful. Free Trade, in this view, went hand in hand with individual enterprise and private ownership. It symbolized a functioning market society. National wealth and personal liberty were inseparable. In business, just as in politics, Free Trade was held together by a web of mutually reinforcing ideas and interests. How well would this economic culture hold under the pressures of unemployment, industrial decline, and a fractured world economy?

The Business Mind

Milton Sharp was one of a thousand businessmen who gave evidence in the course of the war in what proved to be a comprehensive review of Britain's commercial system. These testimonies give a unique insight into the change of the business mind. The Board of Trade in 1916 set up a group of committees for all the main trades and industries, from textiles to iron and steel and shipbuilding. After the allied economic conference at Paris in June of that year, the government added an umbrella committee to advise on commercial and industrial policy, under the chairmanship of

Lord Balfour of Burleigh.[9] Free Traders might have met his appointment with a sigh of relief; Balfour of Burleigh had been one of the Conservative ministers whose uncompromising Free Trade stance led to his dismissal in the cabinet crisis of September 1903. He quickly disabused Liberals of any illusions. '[S]ome people might attribute to me an undue adherence to special fiscal doctrines', he told the committee at the first meeting on 25 July 1916. If they did, they were mistaken. Old dogmas about Free Trade and Tariff Reform needed to be cast aside. They had to take a fresh look at which industries were essential to the future safety of the nation, how best to recover trade, and how to develop imperial resources.[10]

The Balfour of Burleigh Committee failed to produce a blueprint for a new commercial policy. Hewins, the old Tariff Reformer on the committee, sought to relaunch an imperial tariff, but was sidelined. For most members, Free Trade was no longer good enough, but a general tariff went too far. They continued to worry about how to protect the public against vested interests. That 'the establishment of any protective tariff would give impetus to the formation of combinations for the purpose of exploiting the consumer' remained one of the main concerns for Balfour of Burleigh.[11] Without a clear direction from either Asquith's or Lloyd George's coalition governments, both equally unwilling to reignite the fiscal controversy, the committee became stuck in a political limbo.

Where the Balfour of Burleigh and the trade committees did succeed was in offering the business community a forum for testing, challenging, and rehearsing ideas and information about their trade, rival business models, and the future role of government. A new style of conversation about commerce developed. For the vast majority of traders and industrialists it was a conversation in which the old dogmatic voices of Free Trade and imperial Tariff Reform were silenced.

A few remained stubborn Free Traders. Pockets of loyalty were especially strong in the shipbuilding and cotton industries, opposed to any duties that would raise their costs of production. The two major combinations, the Fine Cotton Spinners' Association and the Calico Printers' Association, feared that any restrictions, even on enemy imports like German dyes, would be suicidal, giving competitors a chance to cut them out even further from foreign markets; the enemy countries had made up roughly 40 per cent of the fine spinners' customers before the war.[12] The Free Trade case was restated passionately by William Priestley, the Liberal MP for East Bradford, and himself a manufacturer and merchant in cotton, silk, and

woollen goods. If Bradford yarn manufacturers were protected, he would
be unable to buy his yarn in Roubaix and Rheims. His costs would increase,
and he would be priced out of the market. For a small island like Britain,
a tariff was a step in the wrong direction. Britain simply was not America.
Geography mattered: 'if you could turn the Atlantic into land, so that we
would be in the same position as the great West is today to the eastern
States of America, it would satisfy me for 200 years to go under protection.
But we are crowded; we are small; we must live on our reexport trade.'
Tariffs also had a tendency to grow like weeds. It 'might be very wise for
two or three years' to pick out a trade that might benefit, 'but you have
sown the seed and the plant will grow, and the bigger it gets the weaker we
shall get'.[13] Others were unashamed to stress their self-interest in resuming
trade with the enemy as soon as possible after the war, though few were as
explicit as Mark Oldroyd, a Dewsbury woollen manufacturer. Rather than
strangling Germany, he wanted her happy and prosperous, so Germany
could pay an indemnity and he could benefit from her wealth. 'I do not
think her commercial prosperity has been a menace to the world—I think
it has been an advantage.' To do business with Germans was in his own
interest: 'I should be cutting off my nose to spite my face if I refused to do
business with them on terms that are profitable to me.'[14]

The general shift of opinion, however, was all in the other direction. Even
the most archetypal export industries now made a case for selective protection. Priestley himself was prepared to fight dumping and safeguard key
industries.[15] One after another, businessmen expressed their change of faith.
In the wool industry, the women's dress trade called for a protective tariff,
men's goods for a bargaining tariff. J. E. Shaw was the chairman of directors
of a woollen and worsted manufacturing firm near Halifax. Before the war,
all of the company's directors had been in favour of Free Trade. The war
'had altered the whole aspect of things'.[16] In the London Chamber of Commerce, the textiles section came out solidly in favour of a tariff. Manufacturers and merchants of carpets, jute, lace, and silk followed suit. R. Edwards
of Drewry and Edwards Ltd, a Nottingham firm making cotton and wool
underwear, typified the exodus of businessmen from the Liberal milieu.

> I have been a Liberal all my life, and very much in favour of free trade,
> but I think to-day, in view of what we have learned during the last two
> years, that it is to our supreme interest to develop our own industries and
> to obtain, as far as possible, all that we require from our own manufac-
> turers.[17]

Cecil Cochrane, of the Cast Iron Pipe Founders' Association and Liberal MP for South Shields, aptly described his opinions as in 'the melting pot'.[18] Of the hundreds of businessmen giving evidence, there was only a single witness who had become impressed by the case for freedom of exchange: W. Watson, the managing director of Lister & Co., silk and cotton spinners, who now abandoned tariffs for Free Trade as the only way of holding onto foreign markets. As Watson acknowledged, however, this was merely his personal view, not that of his chairman or fellow directors.[19]

The electrical trades and iron and steel went furthest, demanding protectionist duties for the long term, that is, after the reconstruction period. The electrical engineering industry wanted tariffs ranging from 15 per cent on electrical machinery all the way to 50 per cent on component parts, like tungsten lamps, mass manufactured in Germany. The National Light Castings Ironfounders' Association enjoyed a total production value of over £5 million in 1913. A good quarter of this was exported. Before the war, more than 50 per cent of their members had been Free Traders, especially in Scotland. By the end of 1916, one witness confessed he knew of only one surviving Free Trader in the Association.[20] Wire-netting and other trades in the iron and steel sector tell a similar story.[21] In the chemical industry, William Pearce abandoned Free Trade to support the protection of select industries.[22]

In 1917, the Federation of British Industries, the first unified producer organization, surveyed its members about commercial policy. The result was unambiguous. It confirmed how much further business opinion had moved since the protectionist manifestos of many regional Chambers of Commerce in 1915–16. Of 352 firms and 56 Associations that replied, over 96 per cent wanted a change in Britain's economic system involving some form of trade barriers.[23]

Unsurprisingly, this sentiment was sharpened by patriotism and anti-German animus. To Alfred Herbert, a manufacturer and importer of machine tools, protection against Germany was 'the most important thing of the lot'. A tariff, he acknowledged, would interfere with his import business—he had had branches even in Germany—but he would rather see his income reduced by 50 per cent 'than that we should again be at the mercy of German competition'. Without it, he was convinced, the British steel trade would be destroyed. Germany had to be made to 'pay for what she has done now long after the war is over. That is the way to touch the German—in his pocket and his stomach; I think those are the

only two sensitive parts of his anatomy.'[24] John Corby headed a company
manufacturing and trading in dress goods. A 'very staunch Free Trader' in
the past, he had become convinced, like many in the textile trade, that if
nothing was done to stop German goods coming into Britain, Germany
would re-emerge as a more serious competitor than ever before. 'Therefore
I should like to make them, if I may put it in this way, our commercial
slaves, at any rate for a year or two.' A high tariff would be harmful,
but Corby had no problem with a moderate revenue tariff on neutrals as
well as enemies. This way, he believed, Britain would recoup some of the
profits competitors made out of the British market, a dubious proposition
in liberal economics if ever there was one.[25]

There were a few complementary exhortations to imperial solidarity;
Herbert wanted import duties against the entire rest of the world other
than the Dominions, India, and the allies. It might hurt his pocket, but it 'is
a wonderful opportunity for bringing the Empire together, and I think that
would help it more than anything else'.[26] What is perhaps more interesting
is how rare such sentiment was. A food tariff, so critical to developing a
system of imperial preferences, was virtually absent from the business mind.
Businessmen could see giving preferences on existing duties, but, with the
exception of old Tariff Reformers like Hewins, a tariff on food and imperial
economic union attracted little support. Wartime discussion was first and
foremost about industrial, not imperial protectionism. And here the focus
was as much on the United States, Japan, and neutral competitors as on
Germany. It even included the Dominions. Tariff proposals rarely meant
free trade with friends. Typically, the underwear manufacturer Edwards
wanted a 10 per cent tariff on hosiery from the Empire and the allies, as
well as 15 per cent on neutrals and 25 per cent on German goods.[27]

Free Trade had survived nationalist sentiment before, even at times
thrived on it. A more serious challenge was the growing sense that
the economy was not working the way Free Trade predicted. Three
developments stood out: Britain's dependence on 'key industries'; strategic
dumping; and the economic advantages of combination and integration.
It was their discussion that both generated new business knowledge and
introduced reservations about the old faith in choice, competition, and free
imports. The Edwardian fiscal controversy had been conducted between
the pure point and counterpoint of Free Trade and Tariff Reform. Now
the debate moved into a different key, fusing the old notes into new mixed
harmonies.

The importance of key industries for national security was the first and most immediate lesson of the war. Cut off from enemy supplies, Britain found itself lacking materials, plants, and technical expertise vital for military and economic defence, such as synthetic dyes, scientific instruments, optical glass, tungsten, and magnetos. Most of these were small industries themselves, but they had pivotal importance to many larger industries. In most of them, Britain had been almost completely dependent on German supplies. Magnetos, for example, were crucial for the ignition of internal combustion engines, military and commercial. Before the war, Britain had an annual demand for around 270,000 magnetos. Of these only 1,140 were produced in Britain itself, mainly of a small, simple type. Most of the rest came from Germany. Britain was literally in the hands of a Bosch monopoly.[28] The First World War was fought with steel. Hard steel required tungsten, both as metal powder and as ferro-tungsten, which gave it the strength and magnetism necessary in modern engineering with its twist drills, metal milling cutters, and engine valves. In 1916, Britain used 8,000 tons of such tungsten steels. Here the problem was not that Britain did not control the principal raw material—tungsten was made from wolfram ore, and almost half the world's known deposits were in Burma and other parts of the British Empire. Rather, the processing of wolfram into tungsten powder was controlled by Germany. At the outbreak of war, Britain had barely three months of tungsten left.[29]

How Britain managed to overcome this challenge is a complex story, the details of which lie beyond our scope—in 1915 the government took the lead in setting up a group of industrial consumers who would produce their own dyes. British Dyes Ltd was launched with government finance at a low rate of interest and an additional research grant. By 1916 some nine works were running producing tungsten, without government funds but on the clear understanding that the business would be supported by the state to make it permanent, 'not simply a War Time stop gap'.[30] These first children of protection, unsurprisingly, were soon pressing the government to continue safeguarding them after the war. Without protection, it was difficult to expect such new ventures to withstand established competitors or attract investors.

Here was a classic infant industry argument. It moved the goalposts of the debate, both for Free Traders and Tariff Reformers. In many cases, the industrial consumers of these key materials became their own suppliers. Lister of the M-L Magneto Syndicate, for example, entered the business because his firm made agricultural engines. Such interconnections undercut the old Free Trade warning about consumer exploitation. As far as Lister and fellow magneto makers were concerned, 'the protection of the consumer would be best secured by encouraging investment of capital in the industry', not by throwing the door open to cheap German and American products.[31] A small number of businessmen held on stubbornly to a solid Free Trade position and insisted that key industries, like dyes, needed to stand on their own feet.[32] Most, however, left the war having made their peace with some form of assistance. The question was now about the most effective method—bounty or tariff—and how to protect the interests of users, not about government assistance as such.

The recognition that 'essential' or 'key' industries potentially merited protection set off a scramble among industries to claim that special status. In a total war, virtually all industries were essential, including textiles, shipbuilding, and mining, as Alfred Mond pointed out to the Committee. Some wanted to include the entire steel industry, others only small industries vital to the national interest. In the end, the narrower definition won out. In a political compromise between former Free Traders and Tariff Reformers, Lloyd George committed the coalition government to safeguarding in the 1918 election. To protect a big industry might have still been repugnant for coalition Conservatives and Liberals like Churchill. They no longer, however, had scruples about targeted, selected protection. The 1921 Safeguarding Act introduced a $33\frac{1}{3}$ per cent duty on a long list of small key industries, ranging from optical glass to synthetic chemicals and magnetos.

If safeguarding was less than what true protectionists wanted, it nonetheless marked a significant shift in perspective. In the Edwardian debate, the focus had all been on finished goods. Tariff Reformers wanted a tariff on finished manufactures. Free Traders countered that such a tariff was impossible: the finished article of one industry was the raw material of another. Framed in these terms, a duty on raw materials was politically unpalatable. The debate on key industries now turned a losing into a winning argument. Protecting raw materials of finishing industries became a boon, not a loss. Modernizing industrialists, like Peter Rylands, a leading wire manufacturer who had given evidence to the Tariff Commission before the war, picked up on the sea change involved. 'Instead of thinking it desirable to protect our finished articles, we want to protect the foundations of our industry. I and those with whom I have discussed it in the trade all seem to take the view that that is the line, that the war has taught us the necessity of having the foundations of our industries secured.'[33] Free Trade had lost one of its strongest arguments with producers. The path lay open for a new solidarity between end-manufacturers and their suppliers.

The fate of key industries was intimately connected with a second problem that unsettled the Free Trade mindset: dumping. There was little debate that the German hold on essential chemicals, tungsten, and magnetos partly reflected a better integration of manufacturing, science, and research and development. Germany led the world in chemicals in 1913, with 180,000 workers in an industry worth £120 million. In Britain, by contrast, only one university even had a chair in organic chemistry (Manchester); when Chaim Weizman, the Zionist chemist who would contribute to the Balfour declaration, arrived there in 1905 he found the laboratory in a ' "dingy basement room which had evidently not been used for many months" '.[34] These disparities had been recognized in Britain ever since the late Victorian 'efficiency' movement. But now businessmen and the Board of Trade also blamed dumping for the harsh climate facing British industries. Unsurprisingly, the makers of magnetos were terrified that established German and American competitors would do everything possible to crush them and regain the British market after the war. They wanted protection against a flood of imports.[35]

It is easy to vilify 'dumping', much harder to agree on what it is. Dumping is in the eye of the beholder. Are goods 'dumped' if they are cheap by the standards of the importing country or by those of the foreign producer? Are they goods sold below cost price, or also goods that just happen to be cheaper because of other advantages, such as low wages or poor labour conditions? It tends to be evil competitors who are the dumpers, never oneself. Yet, as one British cotton trader reminded the Textile Committee in 1916: Lancashire was one of the biggest dumpers of all.[36] Three concepts came to dominate. The first concerned strategic dumping. This had happened in the case of tungsten, for example, where German firms nipped in the bud attempts by British producers to enter the market before the war. Another fear was about systematic dumping, a regular flood of cheap imports from foreign producers who benefited from 'unfair' advantages, such as cheap labour, low taxes or a depreciated currency. This was perhaps closest both to the Edwardian caricature of the German dumper and to the fears of 'sweated imports' threatening good jobs and wages that persist to this day. Finally, there was a third type. Here, cheap exports were not part of an intentional strategy for destroying competitors, but reflected dual pricing, where a higher home price supported a lower export price.

Before the war, the defence of free imports had been a dogmatic, non-negotiable part of Free Trade; this was what killed attempts to eliminate export bounties in sugar. Cheap imports, the argument went, benefited industrial and private consumers alike and maximized national wealth. Dumping was good. If foreign countries wanted to pay a bounty to artificially lower the price of exports, such as steel shafts, Britain would be foolish to interfere, since British engineers could then produce and export their own machinery and locomotives more cheaply. Cheapness and costs of production were all relative. Different countries had different wage levels, social conditions, and environmental characteristics. To stop the dumping of cheap foreign toys because their workers were paid less than those at home might benefit domestic toy-makers, but hurt society as a whole. Letting trade flow freely encouraged countries to pursue those trades that were to their greatest comparative advantage, a law central to trade theory since Torrens and Ricardo in the early nineteenth century.

Businessmen and politicians did not stick hard and fast to any particular definition of dumping—these could shade into each other—but the movement away from a Free Trade defence of cheap imports was clearly discernible across the board. On the Balfour of Burleigh Committee, Hugh Bell, the iron and steel master, now in his seventies, pitched once more all the classic arguments for Free Trade: if, after the war, a large number of goods flooded into the British market it would simply be because it was to 'the benefit of the buyers'.[37] But Bell was now in a clear minority—his place was 'not on a Committee but in a museum', as the protectionist *Morning Post* uncharitably put it.[38]

Right, left, and centre, merchants and export trades included, former Free Traders demanded anti-dumping measures. 'Whatever my opinions as a Free Trader were in the past', the London merchant Charles Henry was now clear in his mind that the disadvantages of dumping outweighed its advantages. None other than the secretary of the Free Trade Union, Alfred Mond, pointed out the collective costs of dumping: a few trades might benefit, but the national economy was dislocated. Harold Raylton Dixon, a shipbuilder, proposed a graduated import duty to prevent dumping by any foreign country, not just enemies. Shipbuilders, understandably, were still opposed to a general duty on iron and steel, but they recognized that the industry had been vulnerable to the periodic influx of German shafts and forgings dumped at unprofitable prices; German makers 'did cut right into their charges and right down to their labour, and sometimes even into the cost of material and labour'.[39]

Free Trade was a beautiful theory, in the words of Peter Rylands, 'a very good theory, but when the ingenuity of man was brought to bear you could get the whole of that upset'. International trade did not flow from a natural allocation of resources but was steered by human intervention. Development was directed by state action and organized business. Germany might not be better suited for certain industries, theoretically, but in reality it had managed to build them up with the help of protection and dumping. Rylands knew what he was talking about. In 1906 he had signed a price and quota agreement to prevent dumping with the German counterpart of the Wire Netting Association, the *Verband Deutscher Drahtgeflecht-Fabrikanten*. The two agreed to stop a price-war and not to undersell each other in most other European markets. Any breach was to be punished by a fine of up to one-third of the net invoice value of the order.[40] It was one of a growing number of price and market-sharing agreements with which British businesses sought to contain dumping by German cartels in the Edwardian period.

In essence, Rylands' point was, of course, what nationalist critics of Free Trade had argued for a century, most famously Friedrich List in *Das Nationale System der Politischen Oekonomie*.[41] Yet, this argument had been made for industrial late-comers trying to build their own infant industries and get a foot on the ladder of economic development. Britain was the first industrial nation, not a member of the second or third generation. What Rylands and fellow businessmen—many merchants as well as industrialists—saw was that protection and dumping could benefit even developed industries. It was a kind of mature industry protection to keep them fit as they advanced in age. Protection made dumping possible by providing a secure shelter. It was necessity, however, not the desire to eliminate competitors, that drove it. Dumping enabled German cartels to keep their plants running full time, instead of stopping works when foreign orders fell. Overall, this created greater productivity and economies of scale. The sheer growth of industrial capacity required dumping. Sales, therefore, were in part dictated by the productive machine rather than by the market. The domestic market absorbed as much as it could at regular prices; excess production was then off-loaded at a lower price on foreign markets. Rather than a sign of weakness, dumping was a recipe for growth and productivity.

The model was the German steel syndicate, the *Stahlwerksverband*, founded in 1904. More than any other organization, it was this German cartel that opened British eyes to the dynamics of productivity, combination, and dumping. One of the witnesses who gave confidential evidence on the *Verband* in 1916 was J. H. Pearce, of the Wolverhampton Corrugated Iron Company. Few knew the ins and outs of that German cartel better than Pearce. Before moving back to Britain, he had worked for the Differdingen Works in Luxembourg, which were amalgamated with the Union Works in Dortmund. For three years he worked as the English correspondent for the Verband's export department. In 1907 he took charge of the department. Initially, the Verband was designed to prevent price fluctuations for semi-manufactured goods like blooms, ingots, and rails. But soon the cartel extended its tentacles. It offered export bounties, pooled orders, organized the home market and extended its trade spheres abroad. It used its combined force to obtain rebates from Dutch and Belgian railways; according to Pearce, German producers enjoyed a rate per ton per mile that was 40 per cent of what a British firm had to pay. Above all, it encouraged combination. Firms became vertically integrated, absorbing every stage of production under their control. Thyssen owned coal mines, blast furnaces, steel plants, and rolling mills, and even had its own fleet of steamers.[42]

Derided as inefficient, sclerotic, and unworkable in the Edwardian debate, combines, cartels, and associations now appeared as the essence of a future productivist order. Before the war, the magic of ownership with its entrepreneurial ideal of the independent head of a family firm had been at the heart of a shared competitive ethos. Even most protectionists had seen little need to put their own houses in order. They had wanted self-defence, not modernization. 'We do not believe the combinations lead to any economy in production', one iron company put it in 1904.[43] British firms were efficient. All that was needed was protection against unfair competition. Foreign 'tariffs are themselves a testimony to the excellence of our production. There is not a nation in the world that dare meet us on equal terms', one member of Chamberlain's Tariff Commission boasted.[44]

The war shook such self-confidence. Combination, not individualism, became the watchword. The 'average German', Pearce concluded, '—speaking merely in a commercial sense—is not better than the average

Englishman, who for sheer business instinct, has few equals, yet the results prove that individual effort is no proper match for organized cooperation'.[45] Industrialists directed some of their frustration at banks and the state for not providing sufficient support. But there was also genuine soul-searching about the wastefulness within industry and the 'desperate individualism' of manufacturers.[46] The point was put strongly by Birchenough, the silk industrialist on the Balfour of Burleigh committee and a long-standing critic of Free Trade. Britain suffered from excessive individualism. Lancashire was fighting Lancashire. Lancashire was fighting the Midlands. Both were fighting the railways. In a world of organized competition, this was no longer good enough. Most of the evils that had befallen the nation were due 'to our small view, to the fact that each man has cultivated his own plot and has avoided combination'. Combination was the only way for industry to survive, and 'the only one way to avoid Government interference'.[47]

With the partial exception of the cotton industry, the war produced a veritable chorus in favour of combination. That 'competition is becoming increasingly wasteful' was the slogan at meetings of the new Federation of British Industries.[48] Businessmen looked to German syndicates, like the *Verband*, as a middle way between the competitive individualism of Free Trade and the overcapitalized and overconcentrated giant enterprises in the United States, such as the US Steel Corporation. New trade associations mushroomed, such as the Steam Engine Maker's Association, or that of the Boilermakers. The government's need to plan and direct resources reinforced this trend, but it also sprang from a change in the business mind. H. Pilling, the general manager of a Manchester firm of boiler and engine makers who had been instrumental in setting up the two Associations just mentioned, explained: 'We have been like a gas molecule split apart, and we are now trying to liquify ourselves and cohere.' Associations tried partly to maintain prices, partly to build up confidence and 'friendly relationships amongst ourselves [so] that when a difficulty arises we shall put our heads together and consider what is to be done, instead of each firm endeavouring to work itself up to its full capacity when there really is not a trade for everybody'. The Boilermakers Association did not yet fix minimum prices or control the export trade, but it had introduced a pooling arrangement for domestic orders: 'any firm taking an order puts something into the pool which is distributed, and that has had a curiously steadying effect'.[49]

A tariff was no longer just a defensive weapon, it was a precondition for industrial reorganization. Steady markets would be the first step towards pooling resources. For the iron and steel committee, this meant that industrialists needed to form a common selling organization to distribute orders and encourage combinations. This would lead to more integrated, modern plants and cheaper mass production. The Board of Trade began to ponder how the state might assist the creation of combinations for marketing abroad.[50] In the new landscape of organized business, the family firm and individual initiative looked increasingly out of place. As the managing director of the Siemens Dynamo Works in Britain put it, a businessman of the old type 'lives on his business and probably lives well, keeps motor cars, goes to the theatre, and looks after his children, and all that sort of thing, and he will not feel inclined suddenly to dump down £100,000 for a new thing which his father did not need'. The corporate firm, by contrast, was run by trained managers, who took a longterm view of what was best for the trade as a whole and who had an interest in the stability necessary for modernization. 'I do not want the fiddling competition of thirty or forty little people, ironmongers for instance who make dynamos in their backyard and ruin the trade. It is the small man who makes the price, not the big one. The public is better served by strong concerns without a monopoly.'[51]

For producers, as for consumers, the spread of cartels and combinations destroyed a significant part of the aura of Free Trade. Cheapness was no longer a virtue. It could be temporary, followed by high prices and economic dislocation. Longterm stability outweighed the momentary advantage of cheap iron or chemical imports. Industrial arguments corresponded to some of the arguments made by new internationalists and organized consumers for stabilizing food prices.

It was equally difficult to present Free Trade as an insurance policy against cartels. Just as consumers and internationalists pointed to meat trusts and milk combines, producers realized that combinations had sprung up everywhere. The iron and steel merchant H. J. Skelton neatly summed up the fallacy: 'It is useless for the ordinary free-trader to argue that it would not do to institute a system of protective duties because of the system of Rings and Trusts that would grow up behind such a barrier. We have a large number of Rings and Trusts under our existing conditions in various trades in this country.' In any case, the economies of scale in integrated works in protectionist countries like the United States and

Germany, made it 'useless to pretend any longer that "Free Trade" ensures low prices'.[52]

If the war hastened the movement towards combinations and associations, it also reinforced the trend towards greater vertical integration first apparent in the final years of peace. It was no coincidence that producers like Rylands preached protecting business from the bottom up, streamlining production from the raw material stage to the final product. Rylands had been a driving force behind the amalgamation of large enterprises in Edwardian Britain. His wire-making business had merged with the iron and coal company of Pearson and Knowles, and, on the eve of the war, they had started their own steelworks.

Combination, stability, and rationalization—these were the watchwords of a new business politics. New organizations were formed: first and foremost, the Federation of British Industries in 1916, of which Rylands was a co-founder, together with that other big businessman and 'trade warrior', Dudley Docker, who ran a leading rolling-stock company and had a conglomerate of industrial interests stretching from Vickers to the Midland Bank. Much more so than in Chamberlain's movement, protection for these men was part and parcel of a 'politics of productivity', an outlook that would reach its apogee in the United States in the mid-twentieth century.[53] Tariffs, in their view, secured a larger home market, allowing for economies of scale, which encouraged investment, which in turn led to greater productivity, greater sales, and more secure employment. Industrial peace hinged on productivity.

Developing a productivist vision was one thing, turning it into political reality another. The post-war years only saw limited concessions in the direction of protection. The government retained the McKenna duties, which provided the motorcar industry with some shelter (and the Treasury with some revenue), and continued the effective protection of dyestuffs. An integrated system of regulating imports, however, failed. In 1919, the imports and exports regulation bill, one of the worst drafted bills in history, fell victim to cries of bureaucratic control and anti-democratic conspiracy. Two years later, the Safeguarding of Industries Act offered what is best described as scattered protection. Several thousand 'key' items were now protected. It also contained provisions against dumping—both against 'abnormal' imports and against currency depreciation. This was a departure from the pure Free Trade position that had governed Britain since the middle of the nineteenth century. It reflected some of the new points of view that had come to the fore during the war. All in all, these measures never affected more than 3 per cent of Britain's trade in the 1920s. How significant or small a change it was depended on one's point of view. For surviving hard-line Free Traders it was a dangerous, revolutionary breach of principle; for most businessmen and protectionists, it was far less than what they had wanted.

Why did the erosion of Free Trade sentiment in the business community not produce more tangible results? In part, the answer lies with party politics. Lloyd George and Bonar Law had managed to create a united front amongst Conservatives and Coalition Liberals around the protection of key industries and anti-dumping. Big industries, like iron and steel, were not included in this compromise, and Baldwin's loss in the 1923 election ensured they would not be eligible for safeguarding for the rest of the 1920s. Enforcing some of the protectionist provisions, too, proved difficult. It was easy to decry dumping, much harder to prove it or do anything about it. Rumours that Germany was stockpiling supplies for a festival of dumping after the war proved wildly exaggerated; some of them, in fact, were deliberately spread by German merchants seeking to attract foreign buyers.[54] As British intelligence had predicted, Germany ended the war with a shortage of key supplies and skilled labour, not an abundance.

Businessmen also disagreed about the respective merits of different anti-dumping policies abroad. Many engineering and textile firms looked to the United States, which had a policy of prohibition, something better equipped to stop systematic dumping. Others, however, like Mond or the steelmaker Scoby-Smith, preferred the Canadian approach of levying up to 15 per cent on dumped goods on top of its tariff. The Canadian Customs Tariff Act of 1907 defined dumping as exporting an article at a price less than the 'fair market value' of the same article when sold for home consumption; this was also the interpretation favoured by the Board of Trade. Still, as the Board of Trade recognized, it would be vastly more complicated to administer the Canadian anti-dumping policy without also having the machinery of Canada's general tariff; it might need over a thousand additional customs officers.[55]

In the end, the anti-dumping provisions of the Safeguarding policy were a mixed bag. One part targeted the dumping of articles sold below their cost of production. The other focused on currency dumping; that is, instances where British producers were unfairly disadvantaged by the depreciated currency of their foreign competitors. Potentially it was a

major protectionist advance. In practice, it produced little. Many former
Free Traders had softened in their principles but only within certain limits.
Lloyd George tried hard to pitch anti-dumping measures as an act of
self-defence. Keeping out cheap German goods, he told a deputation of
cotton manufacturers, should be understood 'not as a tariff, but as a wall
against a deluge which has come from quite an exceptional storm'.[56] Half
the Coalition Liberals were in open rebellion and managed to put the
burden of proof that dumping was happening on the British manufacturer.
The divide hastened the end of the Lloyd George coalition government
in October 1922.[57] Winston Churchill and Edwin Montagu had no
problem with tackling regular dumping or protecting key industries but
were opposed to blocking goods from countries suffering from collapsed
exchanges. To keep depreciated German goods out was counterproductive.
How was Germany to pay its reparations and earn the money to buy British
goods without export markets? Dumping, Churchill argued, would also
have a welcome disciplinary effect on 'the uneconomic demands of labour'
and help bring down British wages.[58]

British anti-dumping policies proved a bleak register of unfulfilled
protectionism. The Board of Trade received nine applications under the
main anti-dumping terms. They were all rejected, some because producers
failed to document that imports were sold below the cost of production,
as in the case of glass bottles from Holland, others for failing to even
make out a *prima-facie* case. Protection against currency dumping proved
even more difficult. Currencies depreciate in the short run, and often
suddenly, but to be effective, a tariff needs to give suffering industries
longterm security. Moreover, by 1923, it was not only former enemy
countries whose exchanges were collapsing but also France and Belgium.
In the end, action was limited to keeping out a few offending articles
from Germany and Czechoslovakia: fabric gloves, gas mantles, domestic
and illuminating glassware, and enamelled hollow-ware. When it came to
allies, the policy was ignored. At the beginning of 1923 the British lace
industry was suffering from 15 per cent unemployment. In the previous
year alone, its exports had dropped by two-thirds. Nottingham producers
wanted to shield their home market against lace from France, Belgium,
and Italy, all rivals whose exports had soared thanks to their depreciated
currencies. In cabinet, passionate Tariff Reformers like Amery wanted to
see the treaties with Belgium and Italy denounced to 'free our hands for
the general application of the Act the better'. In 1923 this was fantasy,

not politics. The Foreign Office felt that France would shy away from an open quarrel with Britain—it had just occupied the German Ruhr. Still, it deferred to the judgement of the Board of Trade, which worried France might withdraw most-favoured-nation treatment if French lace was subjected to anti-dumping measures. The potential losses far outweighed the uncertain and shortlived benefit to one declining British industry.[59]

The feeble progress of protection reflected the new pragmatism of business politics. In Britain, the war did not establish a continental-style corporatist politics.[60] It lacked the ideological and institutional conditions favouring corporatism. As the evolution of the Federation of British Industries showed, few businessmen were interested in organizing themselves into an independent political force. They had no desire to challenge, let alone supersede, parliamentary politics. By June 1917, one year into its existence, the FBI had grown from 80 to over 400 members. Initially dominated by the heavy and armament industries, it expanded across all sectors. This growth spurt quickly created problems of identity. Docker had wanted a 'business parliament', loosely modelled on the Belgian superior council of industry and commerce. Others, like Rylands, did not want the FBI to become an industrialists' party. Inevitably, if it wanted to grow into the representative voice of industry, the FBI needed to accommodate a small number of Free Traders. Fearful of internal splits, the FBI adopted a position of silence on the tariff question. This was about more than concern over membership, however. Indeed, such was the overwhelming support for some measure of protection that an open declaration for tariffs might have boosted the number of subscribers. Free Traders were never more than a small if sometimes vocal minority, probably no more than a quarter.[61]

Ultimately, the FBI was held back by two things: a recognition of the rules of democratic politics and a sense that tariffs were a matter for business, not ideology. The two were complementary. The new business politics was about maintaining a division of labour between government and business. Government needed to listen to businessmen where policies affected them directly, but stay out of their affairs. The aim was to prevent a return to Liberal social and tax policies before and government interference during the war. Businessmen worried that trade and industry would end up 'a sort of political shuttlecock'.[62] Business, in turn, would leave policy to parties and Parliament.

In the 1918 election, the British Commonwealth Union ran its own campaign and managed to install an eighteen-member 'Industrial Party' in the House of Commons, but such direct efforts at political organizing were shortlived.[63] In practice, policy helped some groups more than others, but political success in a pluralistic democratic culture with established parties depended on making a broad appeal across classes and sectors. Business leaders understood and accepted this. For the FBI to run a protectionist campaign after the war would have looked selfish and sectarian. At a time of industrial tension, it might have backfired. Here was, perhaps, one of the more indirect, long-lasting legacies of Free Trade on political culture: ideals of the purity of politics had left behind a suspicion of organized interest groups. Tariffs needed national support and could not be pushed through the backdoor. Even a protectionist like Docker doubted the wisdom of Baldwin's call for tariffs in 1923. It was, he told fellow business leaders, bound to generate 'distrust, suspicion and uncertainty among the industrial community'.[64]

The war had made most businessmen more distrustful of party politicians than ever before. High taxes and bad patent laws and industrial policies, all of these were the fault of politicians who did not understand the real world of business. Sharp, the Bradford dyer, spoke for many when he heaped scorn on politicians: 'All Governments, of whatever party, have one idea and one only, and that is vote-catching.'[65] The problem in the past had been that politicians had turned the whole subject of trade policy into an ideological fetish.

This critique cut both ways, undermining Tariff Reform as well as Free Trade. The debate over trade needed to be brought down to earth from the loftier planes of ideology. Chamberlains' Tariff Reform campaign had been a self-styled crusade. The more modest goal of the post-war years was 'safeguarding'. The spread of trade associations and international cartel agreements was already taking some of the heat out of tariff politics—market sharing, pooling, and price agreements were a substitute protectionism all arranged by businessmen themselves. 'One of the reasons why you do not see anything like as much about tariff reform today as ten years ago', the secretary of the Cable-Makers' Association explained in 1916, was that these Associations had consolidated industries, 'enabling them by threats and even by paying blackmail sometimes to ward off unlimited competition from abroad'.[66] There was a general sense that politics had failed business, and understandably so: with its fixation on Empire and food duties the Tariff Reform movement had helped destroy the chances for a compromise over industrial protection. Instead 'Tariff Reform must be solved by competent people and no longer as a party political question', insisted the British engineers' association, a body representing £100 million of capital. Industry needed its own ministry 'free from party political element', the association argued in vain.[67] By 1921 the Tariff Reform League was moribund, out of funds and members. The Empire Industries Association was set up as a successor but never managed to recharge the ideological energy of Tariff Reform. Trade policy was becoming a business proposition.

Genuine policy changes were in the end modest and selective. More important in the long run, however, was the fragmentation of older world views and political milieus that made these changes possible. By the early 1920s, Free Trade had been reduced to a minority view, feeble and mostly silent. The overwhelming mood was for some form of industrial protection. There was hardly any principled opposition to the safeguarding policies; even the Manchester Chamber of Commerce's Board of Directors rejected safeguarding in 1921 by only twelve votes to eleven, and only to favour subsidies instead.[68] With the exception of the cotton industry, resistance came almost exclusively from directly affected merchants; and while fine cotton spinners opposed tariffs on fabric gloves, fearing retaliation and the loss of their German markets (Saxon glove-makers used yarn spun in Lancashire), they no longer spurned other forms of state assistance.[69]

As far as business was concerned, Free Trade was not yet completely finished, but it no longer brought the blood to boil either. The lack of a united front amongst its critics and Baldwin's defeat in the 1923 election gave it one last breath, but it now had few defenders left of its own. Most businessmen were like the iron and steel merchant H. J. Skelton, who felt the time had come for a middle way. 'Protection, in my judgement, is 50 years out of date, and Free Trade is probably 25 years out of date. You want something that is neither one nor the other quite—some kind of variation if you like, which, without giving away the whole Free Trade position, will get you the advantage which the Protectionist countries have.'[70]

The Loaf and the Plough

What raw material was to business, food and agriculture were to Labour. That domestic agriculture and the regulation of food imports became increasingly important to the Labour party in the 1920s may at first appear surprising. After all, Britain's agricultural sector was miniscule. Already by 1870 only one in five men worked in agriculture. Under Free Trade, more and more arable land fell out of cultivation, as cheap foreign food flooded into the country. On the eve of the First World War, home agriculture contributed a mere 21 per cent of the total supply of wheat and flour in the United Kingdom.[71] This sharp decline in agriculture, political scientists and historians have long argued, strengthened Free Trade in Britain. It reduced the potential for an agrarian protectionist lobby so visible on the continent and at the same time expanded the number of urban consumers with an interest in cheap food. In a society that exported its manufactures and imported its food, an open economy could appear naturally identical with the interests of Labour. Yet, the disappearance of arable fields could also provoke a radically different reaction. To some, frightened by the fact that Britain could no longer feed itself, there was a greater need than ever to reverse Britain's dependence on international trade and to regulate food imports. Far from having resolved the agricultural question, Free Trade exacerbated it, pushing it back to the centre of politics.

In the aftermath of a world war, a dramatic boom and bust, and at a time when British industries were losing export markets, neither of these two perspectives was inherently more convincing. Indeed, the Labour Party in the 1920s tried to be a home to both. This was its dilemma. Opposition to tariffs continued to provide a shared platform, at least until the world depression, but it could not disguise the growing tensions about what a positive policy on food and trade might look like. As for businessmen so for many Labourites, Free Trade was becoming subject to doubts and dilution.

Labour emerged from the war a mass party officially committed to Free Trade. Many leaders had been internationalists before they had become socialists. As in the Edwardian era, their internationalism made protection and preferences distasteful. Tariffs were denounced in standard radical language for hindering the growth of international peace and communication, for hurting Britain's export industries, and for being unfair. 'We believe that nations are in no way damaged by each other's economic prosperity or commercial progress', *Labour and the New Social Order*, the party's 1918 vision for reconstruction, proclaimed: 'on the contrary ... they are actually themselves mutually enriched thereby.'[72] The 'very definite teachings of economic science should no longer be disregarded', it urged. The ubiquitous figure of the wartime profiteer reinforced a sense of social injustice. The war had left behind a mountain of debt, and the government appeared to be set on shifting that burden onto working men and women. For Labour leaders, the McKenna duties, safeguarding, and preferences on the few existing food duties were proof of the government's underhandedness. 'They were getting protection', Snowden told delegates at the party conference in 1919, 'not in a fair, straight, and honourable way, but by sneaking, backstairs methods which were far more sinister than any open attempt to impose protection upon the country.'[73]

If the Labour party refused to enter a joint campaign with the Free Trade Union in 1919, there was a manifest proximity to Cobdenites. Radical internationalists like Hobson and Woolf sat on the party's advisory committee on trade. Indeed, Labour paid the Cobden Club's secretary, F. J. Shaw, £10 to draft the party's formal position on *Tariffs and the Worker* in 1919. Shaw's background lay in the socialism of the 1890s, but there was little in his Labour pamphlet that would have worried a classic Liberal. Goods paid for goods. Imports were good not bad. From 1877 to 1912, unemployment had been highest when imports were lowest. Free Trade was no cure for unemployment, but in protectionist countries it was worse. And tariffs caused international friction. Through Free Trade, by contrast, peace and welfare advanced hand in hand. The 'direct and righteous aim of the Labour movement is the improvement of the standard of life for the masses of the people'. Raising the standard of living was 'an end in itself' and, hypothetically, might justify cutting into Britain's trade or her wealth.[74] In the real world, however, protection offered no such means: it would lose Britain her neutral markets and lower the purchasing power of the people.

Among party leaders, it was Philip Snowden who emerged as the staunchest defender of this liberal international version of social democracy. The war put an end to his ambivalence about the workings of inter-national trade. Free Trade, peace, equity, and welfare were inseparable. As Chancellor of the Exchequer in the first two Labour governments of 1924 and 1929–31, Snowden was Labour's Gladstone, fighting ever more vehemently the growing number of challenges to fiscal orthodoxy. The leitmotif was taxation for revenue purposes only. The first Labour budget in history was a paean to the radical pledge of a 'Free Breakfast Table'. Snowden slashed the duties on sugar, tea, tobacco, and coffee. The McKenna duties, too, were phased out; the Conservatives would restore them when they returned to government in November 1924.

Snowden, however, did not own trade policy. His stalwart defence of Free Trade could not stop a steady stream of attacks from within the party.

Not only did the Labour government introduce an agricultural subsidy and continue the protection of the dye industry, but also broader demands for a 'Living Wage' and import boards were spreading from the left of the party.

Labour came to power in January 1924 in the midst of a prolonged agricultural crisis. Formally, the economic depression only began on Black Tuesday, 29 October 1929, but for cereal farmers it had arrived early, with the collapse of prices in 1921–2. From summer 1921, with the abolition of the Corn Production Act, British farms were once again at the mercy of the market. And the world market was flooded with cheap wheat and foodstuffs. For British consumers this meant less expensive food. For British farmers, already suffering from high labour costs, it meant arable farming was a losing proposition. In wartime, the government had encouraged farmers to grow cereals and arable cultivation went up by 10 per cent. Now, the market sent the opposite signal: move from cereal to livestock. In 1918, 12.4 million acres were under the plough. By 1929 it was less than 10 million—1 million acres less even than in 1913. The rapid decline spoke of rural poverty, unemployed farm workers, dilapidated buildings, foreclosures, and abandoned fields.[75]

This was the backdrop to the beet sugar subsidy, one of the few achievements of the shortlived first Labour government. Beet sugar was the wonder crop of the nineteenth century. Britain had been alone among the European powers in not developing a beet sugar industry by a variety of bounties and incentives. Beet was a multi-purpose crop. It was a substitute for cane sugar and provided an industrial basis for rural areas in the form of beet sugar factories. The pulp that came back from the factory could be used as fodder. It was also a useful cleaning crop. Ploughed back into the land, its leaves boosted the yield of wheat or barley cultivated in the next rotation. And its cultivation was closely allied to scientific research and development.

It is noteworthy that of all the branches of agriculture, Labour selected beet sugar for a subsidy. For the sugar question had been one of the flashpoints in the ideological conflict over Free Trade. If foreign countries were prepared to spend their tax-payers' precious moneys on developing an artificial industry to compete with cheaper, plentiful Caribbean cane sugar, that was their mistake. For Britain, the principles of Free Trade ruled out such special incentives. The war and the boom and bust that followed reversed the balance of argument. Britain had Europe's sweet tooth, but, unlike her rivals, had no domestic sugar supplies to feed it with.

If Britain had developed its own beet sugar industry, it was now argued, there would have been no wartime sugar shortage. After the failure of the one operative beet sugar factory in the country, at Cantley in Norfolk, the Lloyd George coalition injected government funds in a new venture at Kelham in Nottingham in 1919. The difficulty was how to attract investment and develop a new industry once prices began to tumble from the winter of 1921–2.

Labour's answer to the sugar question in 1924 captures its Janus-faced outlook. One side looked towards Free Trade. Snowden lowered the duty on sugar. The other side offered beet sugar farmers a subsidy. The 'Free Breakfast Table' now came with hidden charges. Not surprisingly, Conservatives greeted his policy with cries of 'protection' in the Commons.[76] The classic Free Trade position was that, to prevent discrimination, a duty on imports had to be accompanied by a corresponding excise duty on the same kind of goods. Without it, a duty would not just be for revenue but would give protection to a domestic industry. Snowden's dilemma was that beet sugar had been exempt from such an excise duty. When Snowden reduced the general duty on sugar, therefore, he also diminished the comparative advantage enjoyed by British beet sugar producers; effectively the preference went down with the duty, from 25s. per cwt. to 11s. per cwt. An Edwardian Free Trader would have stopped there, defending the interests of the consuming public against the vested interests of a few, uncompetitive firms. Snowden, after initial doubts, did not. He made up for their lost preference by handing them a subsidy—19s. a cwt.—and a pledge to assist the industry for the next decade.

It was the Conservative government which, with the Sugar Act of 1925, would see this policy through. But it was the child of the first Labour government. For Labour, beet sugar offered hope to farm-workers and smallholders alike, containing the flight from the land and the decline of arable farming, especially in East Anglia. Labour's Minister of Agriculture, Noel Buxton, a recent Liberal convert with a Norfolk constituency to worry about, brushed aside conventional Free Trade objections in cabinet in May 1924. 'It may be asked why the sugar industry cannot establish itself under ordinary conditions.' The answer was that this industry depended on reforming 'another industry of exceptional conservatism, viz. agriculture, into which a novel standard of skill has to be introduced'. Only government assistance could provide the security needed for progress and investment. 'The example of Holland shows that assistance was the road to a free trade industry.'[77] Free Trade now was an eventual outcome, not a starting point.

By the time the world depression hit, the beet sugar industry had grown from the isolated and abortive experiments of the early 1920s into a substantial sector with eighteen factories handling the yield of close to 350,000 acres, a fifteen-fold increase. For every three acres of potato there were two growing sugar beet. One-quarter of Britain's sugar consumption came from homegrown beet sugar. Some 40,000 growers, many of them smallholders, cultivated the crop. For three months a year, it gave seasonal employment to 30,000 casual workers. The factories employed an additional 8,500 workers.[78] Like the protection of key industries, the sugar subsidy was a significant breach of Free Trade principle. It also came with a considerable price tag: between 1924 and 1929, the government paid £12 million in subsidies, effectively giving the factories their beet sugar for free. It was a kind of mini common agricultural policy for East Anglia. A subsidy was not as unfair as a straightforward tariff, an indirect tax that disproportionately hit consumers. But it committed the state to nurse certain trades up to a competitive level, at public expense.

Formally, the Labour party remained vehemently opposed to tariffs throughout the 1920s. Its election manifesto in 1923 attacked tariffs as:

> an impediment to the free interchange of goods and services upon which civilised society rests. They foster a spirit of profiteering, materialism and selfishness, poison the life of nations, lead to corruption in politics, promote trusts and monopolies, and impoverish the people. They perpetuate inequalities in the distribution of the world's wealth won by the labour of hands and brain.[79]

This was classic radical stuff. As far as it went, however, it was a negative argument against tariffs. To what degree did freedom of trade also continue to appeal as a positive programme? On the left of the party, in the Independent Labour Party (ILP), an increasingly vocal and assertive group began to look beyond Free Trade to trade controls and import boards to achieve 'Socialism in Our Time'.

The mid-1920s were the golden years of the ILP. Its membership soared to over 50,000, and the growth in circulation of the *New Leader* made it one of the most influential progressive magazines of its times. Forty-five of its sponsored candidates were returned at the 1923 election. In addition to pre-war leaders like MacDonald and Snowden, the first Labour cabinet included ILPers like John Wheatley at Health and Fred Jowett as first commissioner of works, two fiery socialists who refused to wear top hat and morning dress when receiving their seals of office from the King. The next generation, including Clement Attlee, held junior positions. More than numbers, however, the ILP was about brains. It was an early 'socialist think tank' that sought to steer the amalgam of different working-class and socialist milieus that was the Labour party.[80]

Doubts about the future of Britain's export trade had been a fixture of party pamphlets in the past. Labour's arrival in power gave the discussion about trade a new political context. Labour needed policies, not mere conference resolutions. It was this that the ILP sought to provide, most notably with its blueprint for a 'Living Wage' in 1926.

Disquiet with unregulated Free Trade came from different quarters in the ILP, but they all boiled down to a view that Britain was too much at the mercy of the international economy, and too little in control of her own resources and future. The tendency to look to the world economy and European recovery for salvation was part of the problem, not the answer. At the ILP conference in 1923, John Wheatley, a red Clydesider who had already criticized Free Trade at the 1922 election, railed against those who were looking abroad for the source of Britain's problems. Yes, the French occupation of the Ruhr ought to be condemned, he agreed. It was wrong, however, to think that 'the ruin of Europe was responsible for the unemployment and misery in Great Britain. The cause was British competitive capitalism. The enemy was not beyond the sea; it was here at home.' It was not that Britain could not get goods from abroad—'the repositories were bulging with goods'. The problem was 'the shortage of purchasing power in the pockets of the workers'. Free Trade was anti-socialist. Not everyone agreed with Wheatley. An old Lancashire cotton worker and a Welsh delegate from Abercynon near the shipping city of Cardiff pointed the finger at the poverty of the world and doubted that a more home-oriented policy was the answer.[81] But the momentum was swinging towards schemes for reducing Britain's dependence on a fractured world economy.

For socialists, in Britain as abroad, the war was an object lesson in trade regulation. Ernest Hunter, the chairman of the ILP's agriculture committee, ran study courses in praise of new internationalists like Salter and of experiments with bulk buying.[82] Wartime shortages had crowded out the historical memory of 'the hungry forties' and advancing freedom. Clement

Attlee, the future prime minister, portrayed 1846 as a simple transfer of power from one gang of exploiters to another. It had been about cheap labour, not democratic emancipation.[83]

Above all, the war highlighted Britain's precarious dependence on foreign food. In 'The Loaf and the Plough', published on the eve of the 1923 election, H. N. Brailsford, the trenchant editor of the *New Leader*, spelled out the link between agricultural change and trade regulation. Victorian and Edwardian Britain had become 'an over-industrialised society, raising its children in mean streets under a smoke cloud' while importing half its food. The concentration on industry and exports had been reckless. There could be no return to this 'perilous' state of affairs. 'The simple plan of exporting cotton and importing wheat begins to look like the most precarious scheme on which any nation could build its economics.'

Brailsford accepted that Britain did not need to grow all its food at home. Isolation was not the aim. He reasserted a 'belief in international cooperation'. But the 'anarchy of the market' was unlikely to stimulate British farms to become more like their efficient, modern Danish neighbours. Like business leaders and new internationalists, Brailsford diagnosed fluctuations as a major obstacle to modernization. They turned millers into gamblers. Farmers were discouraged from longterm investment. 'Thus fluctuations mean anarchy: they reduce production; they lessen the farmer's earnings; they increase the consumer's costs.' Where businessmen looked to combination, Brailsford proposed nationalization, starting with the wholesale trade in the main foodstuffs such as wheat, meat, and milk.[84]

This became the *Socialist Policy for Agriculture*, adopted by the ILP in 1924. Imports would be state-controlled, as during the war. Import boards would enter into long-term contracts with farmers overseas and build up reserves. There might come a time when staple foods and raw materials would come under international control. In 'the meantime, we must proceed on a national basis'. Significantly, it was E. F. Wise, one of the internationalists with personal experience of wartime controls, who emerged as the champion of import boards on the Left, unperturbed by critics who thought such schemes impracticable. For Wise, Britain's dependence on American and Russian farmers was no longer a reason for taking advantage of free imports, but for regulating them. 'Three-quarters of our wheat supply had to be imported', he told the 1924 ILP conference, 'and under these circumstances the English farmer was at the mercy of world forces against which he could not protect himself and with which he could not grapple'. A tariff or general subsidy was out of the question—Labour could not take 'the money out of the meagre resources of the town people'. The solution was import boards. They would stabilize prices for the long-term benefit of farmers and consumers alike.[85]

Working together with Hobson and Wise, Brailsford developed these ideas into *The Living Wage* programme in the course of 1926. The programme began with a nod to Hobson, who had long stressed 'underconsumption'. Lack of purchasing power at home was recognized as 'amongst the most potent causes' of unemployment. But from here *The Living Wage* proceeded in new directions. Over-production was the root cause, not under-consumption and over-saving. A full solution required several fundamental changes: redistribution of the national income, higher wages, and increased output of essential goods and services.

Few in the Labour movement would have quibbled with these general aims. What set *The Living Wage* apart was its focus on specific intermediary policies to pave the way for 'socialism in our time'. First and foremost was the abolition of the trade cycle, or at least reducing it to 'harmless and barely perceptible oscillations'. Monetary policy would stabilize prices, but the 'chief instrument' was import boards. These, it was hoped, would maintain the real value of the living wage. 'A living wage implies what one may call a "living price".'[86] Taking food and raw materials out of the marketplace would stabilize prices and create a favourable environment for reorganization. It would protect consumers against middlemen, profiteers, and inflationary price-hikes, just as it would protect workers against sudden cycles and attacks on their wages.

The idea of a national purchasing board had its imperial supporters. The Australian Prime Minister Stanley Bruce, to Brailsford's delight, pitched it at the imperial conference in 1923 as a way of linking the interests of British consumers and Dominion farmers through longterm future contracts.[87] More directly, this line of thinking had been pioneered by new internationalists like Lloyd whose influence was palpable throughout.[88] Social democrats were absorbing some of the key ideas of the new internationalism.

At the same time, however, *The Living Wage* also looked to the home market, and away from international trade. 'If we can distil our oil from coal, and raise more butter, cheese and meat on the land, we may import less and need therefore export less.' Some pure export trades, like cotton, would be helped by import boards, which would deliver cheaper raw materials by cutting out middlemen. However, 'few "export" trades, if any, work solely for the foreign market. Our policy will expand their home market, increase their total output, and so reduce the overhead charges which each article must bear.'[89] Here, in the focus on boosting purchasing power at home, was a new idea of how to fight depression and unemployment. In the ingenious hands of Keynes, it would develop into the new orthodoxy in the 1930s, albeit with a different method and theory. Interestingly, too, it was not altogether different from what productivist businessmen were saying. The economy had to be ordered from the bottom up, beginning with the control of raw materials; it also needed shelter, to make economies of scale and reorganization possible.

It was never likely that *The Living Wage* would become government policy. With its rival milieus, traditions, and personalities, the Labour party was too heterogeneous to be captured by its socialist wing. MacDonald's personal dislike of Brailsford did not help—he thought he had become 'cranky'.[90] *The Living Wage* was a challenge to the party leadership and its more evolutionary approach to social change. It suggested that socialism could be created here and now, if only leaders introduced a better trade and credit policy. For MacDonald and Snowden, this was the irresponsible prattle of utopian intellectuals, out of touch with the realities of power and the complexities of the world economy. Labour was suffering from mass unemployment and defeat in the general strike in 1926. It was no time for confrontation or experimentation. The tensions proved insuperable. Snowden resigned from the ILP in 1927, and MacDonald followed three years later. When he formed his second cabinet in 1929, MacDonald did not call back any leading ILP members.

Still, the ILP had succeeded in planting the seeds of trade regulation. On the eve of the world depression, there was now in the labour movement a positive set of measures that superseded a simple defence of Free Trade. In spite of the declining fortunes of the ILP, it was one that many Labourites, from Leonard Woolf to Harold Laski, found increasingly attractive. Bulk buying of food imports, through longterm arrangements with the colonies, offered an alternative to the preferences favoured by Tariff Reformers.[91] In fact, it was one of the few practical alternatives that Labour had to offer. At trade union, Labour party, and Labour women's conferences, there were now standard calls for import boards to secure 'stable prices to the producer and a fair price to the consumer'.[92] Labour members on the Royal Commission on Food Prices recommended bulk purchases. At the

1929 election, the party programme *Labour and the Land* included import boards. Yes, food taxes needed to be reduced and abolished, but the only way to protect working-class families against exploitation and profiteering was through national bulk purchases. The radical 'Free Breakfast Table' would be set without freedom of exchange.

The End of Laissez-Faire

Governments govern best when they govern least. This dictum had been at the heart of a general predisposition towards laissez-faire ever since the eighteenth century. Individual initiative, unfettered by the state, would create wealth and liberty. This suspicion of collective action, John Maynard Keynes recognized in 1926 in his essay on 'The End of Laissez-Faire', had its roots in a broad universe of beliefs and opinions—a belief in natural liberty, Darwinism, and a love of money—rather than in economics. Indeed, John Stuart Mill, J. E. Cairnes and Alfred Marshall had attacked laissez-faire as unscientific and focused on areas where the pursuit of private interest and the interests of society were in conflict. 'Nevertheless, the guarded and undogmatic attitude of the best economists has not prevailed against the general opinion that an individualistic laissez-faire is both what they ought to teach and what in fact they do teach.'[93]

Society, it was believed, had an in-built tendency towards harmony. It was best achieved by leaving the individual members of society free to do with their money, time, and initiative what they thought fit. Assistance and interference, by the government or other corporate actors, whatever their intentions, disrupted these harmonizing forces.

But what if this harmonic model was wrong? In 1920s Britain specifically, what if wages proved 'sticky' and could not be reduced to make industry competitive? Keynes was not yet ready to disavow Free Trade, the 'most fervent expression' of the doctrine of laissez-faire. Still, he was busy chipping away at the doctrine's core beliefs. Some of this came in technical language, especially in his *Tract on Monetary Reform* (1923) and his critique of Britain's return to the gold standard. He was also, however, developing a new understanding of how society worked, and what could be done to make it work better. Self-interest was not always in the public interest, nor necessarily enlightened, Keynes pointed out. Leaving things to 'natural' forces could have disastrous social costs, like the havoc wrought by price fluctuations. A liberal system required management and maintenance.

This shifted the appropriate balance between private individuals and collective actors. Private initiative had to be complemented by the 'directive intelligence' of society, managing problems beyond the reach of individual action. Keynes singled out three instances: the central control of credit and currency; the balance of savings and foreign investment; and population policy. Exactly how the 'coordinated act of intelligent judgement' would emerge in these sensitive areas Keynes left unclear. What was clear, however, was that the market and private individuals could no longer claim a monopoly on the intelligent ordering of society.

Keynes' reflections are a useful reminder that, to be understood, the rise and fall of economic precepts needs to be placed in the broad environment of beliefs and values that nourish and sustain them. Keynes' own call for a 'new set of convictions' did not yet include a departure from Free Trade; it was not until 1930 that he pointed out that Free Trade and the gold standard shared a mistaken reliance on automatic adjustment.[94] But his own critique of laissez-faire reflects the more general shift in intellectual atmosphere away from many of the unspoken assumptions that had supported freedom of trade.

The 1920s are today mainly remembered for Britain's costly return to the gold standard and for the stubborn orthodoxy of the 'Treasury view'. Following the 'bonfire' of wartime controls, however, the state also gradually expanded its role in trade and credit, with a host of duties, subsidies, and financial supports. Alongside the safeguarding of key industries, the state had continued to shelter the dyestuffs industry. The choice now lay between effective protection of the dyes industry and a market share arrangement with the superior German cartel, the *Interessengemeinschaft*. Users in the cotton industry disliked the former, but, from a political point of view, the latter was the greater evil. The British government had a significant share in the Dyestuffs Corporation and could not be seen to enter into an alliance with a German cartel. It fell to the Labour government in 1924 to veto the cartel arrangement and extend what was effectively protection.[95] A year later, the Conservative government provided the struggling coal industry with a £23 million subsidy. The state also assisted traders by underwriting approved risks in overseas markets. After a slow initial take-up and some modification, over £4 million were guaranteed under the Export Credits Guarantee scheme in 1928–9.[96]

On its own, none of these measures was particularly large, nor much of a cure for mass unemployment. Together, they signalled a move towards a

more active state. The Board of Trade adapted to the new mood. Selective
protection was accepted, even defended. It brushed aside the Free Trade
critique that safeguarding made no sense since it was impossible to know
what articles would be 'key' in a future war. The nation had a duty to neglect
'no reasonable precaution'. The Board of Trade included articles that were
not even made in the United Kingdom at the time, such as tartaric acid and
citric acid. Safeguarding was a forward-looking industrial policy. Particular
key articles might change, but the future importance of the chemical
industry was beyond doubt. Safeguarding protected 'great national assets',
vital for industrial efficiency and research and development. The Board of
Trade rejected the claim that firms had raised their prices since protection.[97]

From a Free Trade point of view, this was pure heresy. Protection
became a self-fulfilling prophecy. It was invoked for failing industries, but
then also justified as a reward for the very trades thriving behind a shelter.
A defensive policy was turning into a more general policy of building new
industries. In general, civil servants and scientists wholeheartedly supported
the extension of safeguarding when industries came up for renewal of their
'key' status in the mid-1920s. Infant industry protection had come to stay.

For the state, revenue made protection additionally attractive. At a time
of mounting debt, duties brought much-needed revenue into state coffers.
This was especially true for the McKenna duties on cars and pianos. These
had been introduced as emergency measures in 1915, partly to save shipping
space, partly to bring in extra revenue and offer a little bit of protection.
Unsurprisingly, automobile makers like Herbert Austin and William Morris
fought hard to see them continued in peacetime. The Labour government
briefly suspended them in 1924, but the need for revenue paved the
way for their prompt reintroduction by the Conservative government the
following year.

The national debt made the wartime emergency a permanent fiscal
one. It was a disincentive for dropping existing duties. Indeed, it could
be used to justify new ones. Churchill, now Chancellor of the Exchequer, remained instinctively opposed to general protection, but he
no longer had any scruples about using a few tariffs to bring in revenue. At a time when the national debt stood at £7,545 million, the
McKenna duties brought in almost £3 million a year. Churchill even
made a joke out of violating Free Trade principles. 'To some', he
told the Commons amidst loud laughter in his 1925 budget speech,
the McKenna duties 'are a relish, to others they are a target, and

to me a revenue.' Churchill completed his 'fortification of the revenue' with new duties on natural and artificial silk, raising another £5.6 million a year. These duties had a protectionist effect, of course. As Churchill knew, however, silk stockings were not loaves of bread. Consumers did not absolutely need them, and if they had to have them, then they should have no difficulty in paying that little bit extra. Churchill defended them as a sumptuary tax.[98]

What Churchill took from consumers, he gave back to middle- and high-income tax-payers, who benefited from substantial deductions. Snowden condemned the 1925 budget as a 'rich man's budget'. The parties had come to loggerheads over the appropriate balance between indirect and direct taxation before the war. Now the mounting national debt and the rise of Labour sharpened class divisions, eroding the liberal middle of British politics.[99] This process ate deep into the propertied middle-class milieu of Free Trade: better a tariff than socialism and high income tax, was their new mantra.

Persistent high unemployment and rising social expenditure in the late 1920s would accelerate the momentum towards a revenue tariff, but the signs were already visible earlier in the decade. Even as tariffs were defeated at the 1923 election, cracks appeared in the liberal milieu. 'Nothing can immediately repair the waste caused by the war, but Tariff Reform has the appearance of proving a palliative for our troubles,' in the words of Harold Crawford, a solicitor and former honorary secretary of the Liberal Federation in Leeds.[100] The spectre of a socialist 'capital levy' drove many middle-class liberals to vote Conservative, tariffs and all. For the first time, not a single Liberal MP was returned in Leeds.

The poor economic climate of these years further eroded Free Trade opinion in the business community. The 1920s were like the English weather, in the words of Gilbert Vyle, head of the Birmingham Chamber of Commerce: occasional sunny intervals, otherwise dull and grey.[101] Decline affected new and old industries alike. One of the hardest hit was iron and steel. In 1925 unemployment stood at 25 per cent, twice the national average. The industry was suffering from backward technology, especially outdated furnaces, as well as from increased capacity amongst foreign producers who flooded the British market. Before the war Britain's exports of iron and steel had exceeded its imports by almost 3 million tonnes; by the late 1920s this had fallen below 1 million. Britain produced 29 per cent less pig iron in 1924 than in 1913. Steel was doing better but even here the industry only ran at 70 per cent capacity.[102]

Free Trade had survived bad economic weather in the past, such as the Great Depression of the last quarter of the nineteenth century, or the early years of the twentieth century that gave rise to Chamberlain's tariff reform crusade. Then, the wider associations with democracy, social justice, cheapness, and Britain's civilizing mission had contained protectionist pressure. With those supporting beliefs eroding, more and more businessmen shed earlier reservations and became outspoken in their demand for a tariff, especially in the iron and steel industries.

Measured simply in terms of policy, the iron and steel industry's campaign for protection was a failure. Safeguarding iron and steel would have had major consequences for most other industries and made a sham of Baldwin's pledge not to use safeguarding as a vehicle for general protection. At the same time, it revealed how flexible many industrial consumers were becoming on the Free Trade question. Heavy users of iron and steel, like the engineering and motor trades, supported the industry's renewed application for safeguarding in 1928; a poll in the Sheffield Chamber of Commerce recorded a vote of 11 to 1. The Association of the British Chambers of Commerce, too, abandoned its neutrality and openly called for an extension of safeguarding. Resistance to protection was confined to re-rollers of steel, who depended on cheap semi-finished steel from abroad. Even here there were now voices for a tariff or export subsidies.[103] Many shipowners, too, were abandoning the liberal fleet, calling on the government to retaliate against foreign shipping in British ports by doubling their tonnage fees. As Cunliffe-Lister, the President of the Board of Trade, remarked to his cabinet colleagues in October 1925, the 'Free Trade conscience is developing a convenient elasticity'.[104]

There were also growing signs of rebellion in the labour movement. In the past, Free Trade had offered an attractive programme of cheap food and high wages. It promised prosperity through openness, making the most of what the world economy had to offer Britain and vice versa. Welfare would be maximized through international specialization. Working-class consumers were already criticizing the consumption side of this model, questioning whether Free Trade actually guaranteed low prices. The stubborn fact of mass unemployment added a critique from the production end.

Britain's return to gold in 1925 sharpened the reaction against Free Trade. The Free Trade model presumed flexibility, the smooth flow of labour and capital from less into more productive channels of employment. In reality, the economy was 'jammed'. Wages proved inflexible, out of step with the fall in prices in the 1920s. Neither unemployment nor Labour's defeat in the 1926 general strike unblocked the pipes. Recapturing foreign markets, economic historians have confirmed, would have required a significantly more flexible labour market.[105] To some in the Labour movement, the home market now became an attractive alternative to the global economy: managing credit and domestic demand would compensate for the loss of foreign trade. Oswald Mosley, a recent Labour recruit, openly railed against the 'fetish worship' of the export trade and urged a planned policy of credit expansion to boost domestic demand.[106] His 'Birmingham proposals', supported by the local Labour party, did not yet feature tariffs, but, like the ILP's *Living Wage*, they included import boards to steady prices and prevent speculators from cornering commodities. Mosley sneered at 'gold standard socialists'. A good socialist took control, instead of leaving the community at the mercy of distant forces.

Some looked to the Empire. In 1925 twenty Labour MPs voted for imperial preferences. Red Clydesiders like Tom Johnston wanted to consolidate and socialize the Empire, not smash it. A handful of imperial Labourites around the maverick MP Haden Guest even put out feelers to the Empire Industries Association, the protectionist business pressure group.[107] If the abortive negotiations showed that general protection remained a stumbling bloc, it also pointed to the range of alternative measures that were becoming respectable, such as prohibition and non-tariff preferences.

The biggest challenge came from the big staple industries themselves, especially iron and steel, and wool. Trade union officials had already signalled a more flexible attitude to Free Trade during the war. In the discussions of trade policy in 1916–17, for example, John Hill of the Federation of Engineering and Shipbuilding Trades, a union representing 900,000 workers, opposed a tariff on iron and steel, but wanted to stop imports produced under inferior conditions. Before the war, 'sweating' had primarily referred to poor working conditions in Britain itself. In the 1920s, it acquired an international dimension, coming to play in the labour movement the role 'dumping' played in business politics. To trade union leaders in the iron and steel industry, what mattered was that real wages in Berlin and Paris were a mere 62 per cent and 71 per cent of those in London. Britain could not possibly compete. In 1925 Arthur Pugh of the Iron and Steel Trades' Confederation pressed MPs for immediate steps to prohibit imports from low-wage countries. This would create 100,000 jobs, he argued.[108]

For Free Trade, this was a devastating turn. Britain, after all, was a high-wage economy. Most other countries were by definition 'low-wage' competitors. In the liberal paradigm, trade was mutually beneficial. To keep out goods made by cheaper labour would hurt Britain as a whole. Trade was about comparative advantage; what mattered in theory was not the cost of production in any one country, but how relatively easy it was for countries to produce different goods. If iron and steel workers could justifiably ask for protection against 'sweating' from abroad, most other trades could too.

Not even the cooperative movement was immune to this way of thinking. 'Unless the European standard of wages is on a parity with our own, how are we to face competition on equal terms?', Thomas Allen, the prominent director of the Cooperative Wholesale Society asked in 1925. 'The ardent Free Trader as consumer inevitably becomes the rigid Protectionist as producer when his own industry and standard of living is threatened.' And there was nothing wrong with that. For Allen there was no difference between cheap immigrant labour pressing down wages in Britain and cheap imports made by cheap labour abroad. Unless everyone enjoyed the same high standard of living as Britons, 'Protection is the corollary of Socialism, just as Free Trade was the corollary of individualism.' Labour needed a new point of view. It was 'time to consider whether high prices with tariffs, PLUS higher wages, greater security of employment, better social conditions, and more of the general amenities of life, are not worth a trial'. For Free Traders like the Scottish cooperative wholesaler Gallagher, the answer remained 'No'. Allen, by contrast, looked to a general tariff with imperial preferences.[109]

By the late 1920s, workers in wool and lace had decided to follow the path of their brothers in steel. Wool was a major industry, with a quarter of a million workers. Its centre was in the West Riding of Yorkshire, the heartland of Liberal nonconformity. Bradford had in many ways been typical of the open, global atmosphere of Free Trade culture. While 'determinedly Yorkshire and provincial', it was also 'one of the most cosmopolitan of English provincial cities' at the beginning of the twentieth century. Some of 'its suburbs reached as far as Frankfort and Leipzig', J. B. Priestley would recall.[110] In the 1920s, it began to turn inward. Wool exports were declining. In 1925, 50 per cent of looms were idle. Loss of export markets made manufacturers naturally turn to the home market, but here, too, the industry was facing growing competition from cheap German, Italian, and French imports. Most employers were already abandoning Free Trade in 1923. Millowners were leaving the Yorkshire Liberal Council in despair. A majority in Bradford demanded safeguarding.[111] Trade unionists initially opposed tariffs as a selfish employers' policy. By 1928 their resistance had softened. Without the support of older ethical and social convictions that had elevated it into a whole system of justice, peace, and people power, Free Trade was reduced to a question of economic costs and benefits.

In November 1928 unemployment in the heavy woollen districts of Bradford and Huddersfield stood at 30 per cent. For employers the choice was simple: either wages had to come down or prices had to go up, with the help of a tariff. A wage agreement had already been terminated. The threat of lower wages brushed aside whatever Free Trade sentiment was left amongst the wool workers. In December 1928 a new application for safeguarding went forward, this time with trade union support. Tariff proposals were especially designed to assist women's dress goods. Only the fall of the Conservative government the following year stopped a tariff on wool. Even liberal-minded stalwarts at the Board of Trade like Hubert Llewellyn Smith now came around in support. It was impossible to compete with countries like Germany or France, where the hourly income was between a quarter and a half less than in Britain.[112]

The economic consequences of safeguarding are unclear. Between 1925 and 1928, 49 trades applied for safeguarding as a key industry, 9 successfully. Most safeguarding industries were small, like packing and wrapping paper or translucent pottery, and did not receive separate treatment in official statistics, making it impossible to compare protected with unprotected branches. There is some evidence that wrapping paper workers benefited from higher wages, and that production went up for gas mantles.[113] Evidence for what safeguarding did for prices and employment is conflicting. The price for fabric gloves, for instance, declined, but then the mid-1920s saw a general fall in prices. In the cutlery trade, employment grew to over 35,000 in the summer of 1926, but much of that increase had begun before the trade received protection. In the lace industry, safeguarding failed to stop the loss of jobs.[114]

The one industry that saw substantial growth was the car industry. The Edwardian car industry had been typical of the fragmented world of small firms so lambasted during the war; it produced 198 different models in

1913. After the war, sheltered behind the McKenna duties, the industry concentrated, rationalized, and grew. Austin built a mass car, the Austin 7, in continuous flow production. Austin's productivity increased five-fold. Together, British firms produced 180,000 cars in 1929, five times more than before the war, providing over a quarter of a million jobs. Free Traders argued that tariffs made the motor industry less efficient than it otherwise would have been, especially compared to American rivals. But we need to compare like with like. Austin and Morris had a smaller home market than Ford. It is fairer to compare them with French makers and to ask about their respective export performance. This yields a more favourable picture. Protection did not retard economies of scale. British cars even outpaced French cars in exports, notwithstanding a depreciated franc.[115]

Far more significant was the political impact of safeguarding. In the Edwardian Free Trade campaign, the cheap loaf had provided an effective rallying cry, an icon which communicated an entire moral and material world at stake. Baldwin, at the 1923 election, gave Liberals another chance to capitalize on the fears of a tax on food (see Figure 15). Safeguarding

Figure 15. 'Vote Liberal and keep the taxes off': a Liberal wagon in Devonport in the 1923 general election campaign.

changed the symbolic field of politics. It fragmented the debate about protection into a seemingly endless and increasingly specialized and time-consuming examination of special industries; the pottery application alone produced 136 hours of sittings in committee and 2,500 pages of shorthand notes.[116] The tariff question was moving from the open air of public politics into the back rooms of expert tribunals. Individual consumers were not even represented.

Goods have cultural values, and these differ. Liberals attacked safeguarding duties with the same arsenal of objections they had aimed at the protection of food: tariffs raised prices and diminished wealth and employment. But it is easier to generate passion about bread than about wrapping paper or translucent pottery. Safeguarding hit consumers of a range of little things, from coat buttons to fabric gloves. Other tariffs, like the McKenna duties on cars and the protection of artificial silk, touched goods that were still luxuries to most people. It was difficult to weave these into a moral drama about democracy, civilization, and national greatness. The closest Free Traders got was in deploring the duties on gas mantles as a tax on artificial light, 'an essential of life and industry' in 'modern civilisation'.[117]

The lead in public campaigning passed to the protectionists. In 1927, the Empire Industries Association introduced open-air meetings in London in support of safeguarding. In the following years, these were extended to industrial centres in Lancashire and Yorkshire. By 1929–30, the EIA was organizing a thousand meetings.[118] In Hyde Park, vans exhibited the benefits of tariffs for safeguarded trades and their workers (see Figure 16 overleaf). None of this rivalled the flair or magnitude of the Edwardian campaign. Like business politics, the protectionist campaign was operating in a narrower cultural terrain. It now displayed specific industrial products, rather than the broad canvass of imperial culture. The public fight over tariffs was becoming a more muted, one-sided show, with little Liberal resistance.

The liberal Free Trade milieu disintegrated. The Liberal camp split three ways. One group defected, to find refuge with the Conservatives or with Labour. A second, progressive group stayed with the Liberal party but hoped to steer it towards a more interventionist programme. For a third, the path of true liberalism pointed in the opposite direction: less state, not more. It was with this shrinking laissez-faire band and its battle against a tax-and-spend 'state socialism' that Free Trade increasingly found its home in the late 1920s.

Figure 16. 'The largest reel of wrapping paper ever made in Europe': a safeguarding van, with British paper bags and corrugated boxes, advertises a demonstration in Hyde Park in support of tariffs, c.1928.

Free Trade no longer faced just the old Conservative enemy but was now challenged by Liberal renegades like Addison and Mond, Coalition Liberals who joined Labour and the Conservatives, respectively. Indeed, it was Addison who, with his schemes for regulating food imports, planted the idea of an agricultural quota that would be reaped by Neville Chamberlain and the Conservatives in 1931. A Free Trade stalwart before the war, Mond gave mercantilist ideas new respectability in the 1920s, circulating a territorial vision of the world economy. The world was settling down into economic blocs. Flow and exchange were becoming irrelevant. Cartels provided the blueprint for a future international order. As Mond proclaimed in one of his many speeches in 1927, the 'logical consequences of the economic groupings of industries is the economic grouping of countries themselves.'[119]

As with the safeguarding duties themselves, the origins of this disenchantment with a liberal paradigm of markets and exchange can be traced back to the First World War.[120] Productivists like Docker were convinced that small firms would disappear like small nations. In cabinet, in 1917, Mond had pressed for Britain to develop her 'estates' in imperial language that echoed Joseph Chamberlain a generation earlier. Five years later he campaigned for a £100 million empire and development loan, including a state subsidy to help firms put the unemployed back to work. The benefits from cartelization were not as self-evident as Mond, the archpriest of rationalization, liked to suggest. In fact, in Mond's own Imperial Chemical Industries, a merger established in 1926, firms remained almost distinct units. For all the bellicose language, ICI had to make do with a small share in world market arrangements compared to the German IG Farben.[121] Still, at a time of mass unemployment when many foreign markets looked lost forever, Mond's campaign for rationalization and size made a territorial view of the economy look attractively modern. It opened the door for a rapprochement between business and the trade unions, the so-called Mond–Turner talks that began in 1927. Rationalization and imperial groupings would produce a new balance between agriculture and industry.

Within the Liberal party, too, plans emerged for public investment and development. *Britain's Industrial Future*, the Liberal Yellow Book, was published in February 1928. Sponsored by Lloyd George, it bore the imprint of the progressive wing of the liberal intelligentsia, first and foremost Keynes and his fellow economists H. D. Henderson and Walter Layton. Collective authorship ensured a long-winded document—'speaking when it has nothing say, as well as when it has', Keynes confessed to his wife, 'droning at intervals, "Liberals, Liberals all are we, gallant-hearted Liberals".'[122] It accommodated a conventional critique of tariffs—'nothing which has happened during and since the War serves to diminish the overwhelming force of the Free Trade argument'.[123] But the main thrust lay elsewhere, with 'a programme of national development' that would rehabilitate agriculture, build roads and houses and promote electrification. The national accounts would be reformed, creating a Capital Account that would work in close connection with a Board of National Investment. In short, the state would spend money to develop employment and demand in the home economy. How exactly such a Board would utilize savings for investment more effectively than the market, indeed how much weight should be attributed to 'frozen savings', so important to Keynes' follow-up *We Can Conquer Unemployment* in 1929, was something that had yet to be worked out.

What was clear was that the answer had to be sought outside the framework of laissez-faire. The Liberal Yellow Book took up where Keynes had left off in 'The End of Laissez-faire' two years before. A new economic order was emerging. Large industrial units were replacing the small firm. More and more large-scale industry was coming under social control. Liberals needed to steer a middle way between socialist control and individual competitive enterprise. International trade was not written off altogether, but it was certainly downgraded vis-à-vis home trades. 'It is a fallacy to assume that the national wealth is more truly increased if the fruits of British savings embodied in British labour are used to embellish the city of Rio de Janeiro than if they are employed to demolish the slums of South London or to build motor-roads through the Midlands.' Developing new trades might revive exports somewhat, but the future lay with the home economy. It was time to rebalance the economy. This had already been Keynes' advice to the Balfour Committee on Trade and Industry in the summer of 1925: a gradual transfer of labour from export trades to new home industries, assisted by 'a large programme of capital expenditure at home, which would absorb the savings that had previously found an outlet abroad'.[124] The Liberal Yellow Book openly questioned the wisdom of Britain's pre-war international orientation. It had depended on a vast export of capital. There was no reason 'why the national interest should require indefinitely the exportation of wealth on so great a scale'.[125] In fact, Keynes wanted a national board to limit foreign investment if necessary. It was a Liberal way of questioning what Mosley had more directly denounced as the 'export fetish'.

In the past, there had been a classic Free Trade defence of capital exports: capital exports stimulated the export of goods, and with it national employment and wealth. In March 1929 Keynes took this argument to pieces in an exchange with *The Economist*, the home of economic orthodoxy. True, foreign investment stimulated exports. Britain, however, was on the gold standard, and under conditions of dear money this process, far from smooth and benign, could only be accomplished at considerable social cost. 'If next time you applaud the tendency of foreign lending to stimulate exports, you will add the explanatory words "because it will make the maintenance of full employment impossible at the present level of wages, so that unemployment will continue until British wages are reduced".'[126]

How much any of these development schemes would have achieved is debatable—Keynes like Mond presumed spending in the order of £100 million a year. Treasury critics at the time warned that public works would simply 'crowd out' private sector spending. Recent simulations suggest a somewhat more positive picture, but even here government spending even of £500 million would only have provided work for 10–18 per cent of the unemployed.[127]

The political impact of these schemes, however, was undoubtedly to marginalize Free Trade further. Plans for state investment polarized the Liberal community. The most vocal defence of Free Trade came from Liberals dogmatically opposed to an active state. To men like F. W. Hirst, Hugh Bell and Ernest Benn, the publisher, the fight for Free Trade and the fight against state socialism were two sides of the same coin. Their home was the Individualist Bookshop, a meeting place for libertarians from 1926 onwards. In 1931 they would form the 'Friends of Economy'. Their answer to Britain's problems was to cut state spending by £100 million, not to raise it. This anti-protectionist, anti-socialist combination struck a chord in some sections of the flailing Liberal movement. Walter Runciman urged the Young Liberals to prevent socialism from destroying 'the very mainspring of social advancement': 'the impulse and thrift of the individual'.[128] A true Liberal accepted 'the whole Free Trade economic doctrine on its logical basis throughout', he told a meeting of the Free Trade Union in 1926. 'If you start compromising, you will land yourself in endless difficulties, and probably plunge into serious fiscal and industrial evils.'[129] Trade facilities, beet sugar subsidy, tariffs: they were all part of the same rot. The state ought not to put money into the pockets of favoured groups. Once the state began to dictate in one sphere of life, liberty and property everywhere were at risk. For one last time Free Trade was held out as a guide for the life of the nation. It was an increasingly narrow view of social life.

A few decades earlier, Free Trade had inspired mass support through a vision of civil society with active citizen-consumers. Now the vision was shrinking into one of libertarian individualism. In the context of the 1920s, this was nothing but a liability. The defence of Free Trade became tied up with a campaign to lower taxes and cut back social services. In part, this was a middle-class reaction to the redistribution of income since the war. The contemporary statistician Josiah Stamp drew attention to the reversal of fortunes that lay behind the middle classes' status anxieties. Lower paid, regularly employed workers were better off, benefiting from higher real wages, social insurance, and shorter working hours. The rich, however, had less money to play with; real income from real estate and foreign investments was down.[130] There was a growing sense among the middle classes that the working classes were having it too good, living off their income-tax-paying superiors.

Instead of class harmony, Free Trade now came with class politics. This made it difficult to maintain any meaningful Free Trade alliance between

Liberals and Labourites. Wedgwood Benn had carried the Liberal fight against safeguarding in the post-war years. By 1927, the 'very logic of the Individualists' convinced him that he was a 'socialist' and to join the Labour party.[131] It also left Free Trade vulnerable on a second front. The focus on 'economy' and cutting spending contributed to a general atmosphere of national crisis, and a sense among the middle classes that taxes had to come down at all costs. Ernest Benn naively presumed that the Tories could be dissuaded from protection and join with individualists in a 'big conglomerate party of the Right'.[132] Instead, with their anti-socialist language, the individualists ultimately played into the hands of their Conservative enemies. They presumed that retrenchment and Free Trade went hand in hand. What if it came to a political situation where to attain the former it became convenient to sacrifice the latter?

For producers as for consumers, the First World War was an eye-opening experience. It set in motion a re-examination of the fundamental beliefs and assumptions that had supported Free Trade as a policy and world view. Cheapness, competition, and the magic of ownership were being pushed aside by a new fascination with stability, coordination, and combination. Across all sectors, Free Trade was losing political support and ideological importance. Opposition to tariffs became tempered by calls for controlling imports and developing the home market. By the time the world depression hit Britain in late October 1929, Free Trade was more vulnerable than ever before. There were even signs of reorientation in parts of the British state like the Board of Trade. For the fate of Free Trade, however, what was most decisive was not the inroads into business and the machinery of government but the ebbing away of support in civil society. It had been the public culture of Free Trade and support from the British people and social movements that had been critical for keeping tariffs out in the past. Now doubts in the labour movement reinforced the disillusionment amongst consumers and internationalists with Free Trade as a way of life. In popular politics, Free Trade was increasingly looking like a dinosaur, a philosophy of individual liberty at a time of a growing state and disillusionment with laissez-faire. Even its shrinking band of ardent defenders recognized that the 'general public' had grown 'apathetic'.[133] The end of Free Trade had become a question of when and how, not if.

7
Final Days

When it was done, it was done quickly. On 17 November 1931, Walter Runciman, the Liberal at the helm of the Board of Trade in the new national coalition government, introduced measures to stop the flood of 'abnormal' imports of various manufactures, from cutlery and woollens to tyres, electric lamps, and cotton goods. A month later came stiff duties on fresh fruit, vegetables, and flowers. In February 1932, a general tariff was added. The tariff started at 10 per cent, but an Import Duties Advisory Committee had the power to raise duties further, and it soon did.[1] In a predictably emotional scene, Neville Chamberlain, the Conservative Chancellor of the Exchequer, told the House of Commons that his father's work at last was done.[2] Preferential trade agreements with the Dominions, negotiated at Ottawa in the summer of 1932, put the final nail in the coffin of Free Trade. Free Trade, for over four generations a defining feature of British policy, was finished.

How should we interpret the end of Free Trade? Most accounts, now and then, have focused on high political drama, ministerial manoeuvres, and the world depression. For the few surviving Free Traders their defeat was a conspiracy, a betrayal, and a constitutional revolution. A cabal of power-hungry politicians had used a national election to demand an unfettered 'doctor's mandate' to cure the crisis any way they saw fit. Never fairly put to the test of public opinion or economic reason, Free Trade was left defenceless in the face of a Conservative-dominated government and Liberal traitors. For F. W. Hirst, who headed the Free Trade Defence Committee for the shrinking band of Liberals outside parliament, Runciman was Judas. Instead of defending sound liberal principles, Runciman had engineered a 'Tariff of Abominations, the worst since Waterloo'. The national government, in this view, was a Conservative plot to smuggle in a general tariff behind the back of the people. The Ottawa agreements confirmed the whole unconstitutional spirit of the tariff. Britain's policy, Hirst emphasized, was no longer under the control of the British parliament but had become bound to that of the colonies. In fact, it was an 'inversion' of the dangerous policy of George III that had caused the loss of the American colonies in the 1760s: 'It is now the turn of the Colonies to control the mother country's taxes!'[3]

Political manoeuvres and the world depression both played their role.[4] Initially, in 1929–30, protectionist forces had been immobilized by internal division and personal conflict. In June 1929, the press baron Lord Beaverbrook launched a campaign for 'Empire Free Trade', a nice euphemism for a tariff on food. It was a direct challenge to Baldwin and his decision to keep the tariff question, so divisive and ruinous in the past, out of Conservative party politics. Fighting off this challenge invigorated Baldwin as leader and consolidated the Conservatives, creating the conditions for a new protectionist programme along the way. By the autumn of 1930 Neville Chamberlain had managed to steer Baldwin and his party towards a common platform: a tariff, wheat quotas, and powers to negotiate. The Labour government was brought down by its own split over tariffs in August 1931, paralysed between two unpalatable solutions to the budget crisis: a revenue tariff or severe cuts in unemployment benefits. A national government was formed, with the support of Snowden from Labour and Runciman and Samuel from the Liberals. This was a critical step in seeing through a tariff on the back of economy measures, as Neville Chamberlain was acutely aware. Responsibility for tough fiscal medicine and cuts in public spending would be shared between all parties. Instead of looking like a suspect partisan cause, a tariff could be justified as one part of a national programme to save the budget, sterling, and the country.

An ingenious 'agreement to differ' in January 1932 allowed the Free Trade-minded Snowden and Samuel to stay on in the cabinet whilst the government introduced the general tariff. Tellingly, only a minority of Liberal MPs voted against it. Snowden and Samuel almost had to be pushed out. In the end, it needed the imperial Ottawa agreements to make them resign.

The world depression hit a British economy that was already under the dark cloud of high unemployment. Britain now had to cope with the collapse of global trade and finance, in addition to her declining industries. In the year after the Wall Street crash in October 1929, unemployment rose from 1.5 to a staggering 2.5 million, over 20 per cent of insured workers. Britain's exports fell by almost half between 1929 and 1931.[5] In the first quarter of 1929, half the British shipbuilders did not have a single order.[6] This fall was not matched by a corresponding fall in imports. In fact, Britain sucked in 23 per cent more food in this period; the collapse of global food prices destroyed what was left of British agriculture. Earnings from foreign investments, too, were down. Britain was heading towards a balance of payments crisis. The collapse of the central European banking system added to the strain. Already by the summer of 1931, the Bank of England was haemorrhaging $2 million of gold a day. By comparison with the rest of Europe, Britain's finances were still relatively strong and, technically, it might have been possible to hang on. But, politically, the experience of ten years of high unemployment ruled out the harsh deflationary measures that might have defended the gold standard. On 21 September, Britain moved off gold.

With the pound no longer tied to the dollar, the case for a tariff acquired an additional argument. Runciman was opposed to the genuine industrial tariff favoured by many Conservatives, but he supported a 10 per cent tariff to stop the flight of capital and restore the balance of trade; in fact it was Runciman who pitched this idea to Neville Chamberlain and effectively sealed the fate of Free Trade.[7] Recovery needed confidence. A trade deficit undermined it. In a world depression, it is easier to improve the balance of trade by lowering imports than by stimulating exports. The cabinet committee on the balance of trade agreed with Chamberlain that they could not wait for trade to adjust itself automatically unless they were prepared to accept any sterling value, and a steady worsening of Britain's capital position.[8] A tariff now appealed as part of a confidence package, strengthening the balance of trade, sterling, and the economy as a whole.

Yet Free Trade's problems were not simply a function of the slump. It had easily weathered the great depression (1873–96), and successfully seen off the imperial tariff reform crusade in the Edwardian period. What was different in 1931 from 1910, 1906, or the 1880s was not only the size of the attack but the absence of a public defence. Free Trade was disappearing as a central feature of political language, belief, and behaviour. The year 1931 was not just a change in policy but a change in political culture. The decline of Free Trade as a secular religion was well under way when the depression hit Britain, and recovery, after 1932, did not bring it back.

Ramsay MacDonald described the economic depression as a blizzard. It was a blizzard that Free Trade was too weak to withstand. By 1929 it was a house with sinking cultural foundations. The internationalist roof was leaking, and several of the social supporting beams had cracked or fallen away. The moral atmosphere, previously pure and invigorating, had grown stale. Free Trade could still count on some stern and loyal residents like Philip Snowden, Labour's iron Chancellor, who fought tooth and nail against any major refurbishment. But many others, amongst the working classes and businessmen, internationalists and even consumers, had already moved out. In a society that was searching for various new designs of coordination, its architecture no longer looked fit for purpose. Worse, some former Liberal residents, the Monds and Addisons, now pelted the building from the outside. The depression accelerated the collapse of Free Trade. It did not set it in motion.

In the business community, defenders of Free Trade had already shrunk into a small, vocal minority when Black Tuesday plunged Wall Street into crisis on 29 October 1929. International resolutions for Free Trade had achieved disappointingly little. In October 1928, at the Association of the British Chambers of Commerce, there had been open attacks on the 'fetish' of the most-favoured-nation clause.[9] The following year, it voted solidly for protection. There was a growing feeling that Free Trade had ceased to be an effective response to economic nationalism. British business vehemently opposed Graham's attempts, in the Labour government, to negotiate a tariff truce. They wanted a bargaining tariff, not a truce which would merely stabilize the existing handicaps under which British industry laboured. Even traditionally liberal export sectors were irritated. The cotton exporters in Manchester joined the protest. Without support from the United States, a tariff truce never stood a realistic chance. Unimpressed by the pleas of one thousand economists, President Hoover backed the punitively high Hawley-Smoot tariff. A poll by the Manchester Chamber of Commerce at the same time, in May 1930, showed how deeply opinions had been shaken, even in the former citadel of Free Trade. Out of over 2,000 members voting, just over a quarter defended Free Trade. The rest demanded some form of protection.[10] By 1931, even shipbuilders and the steel-rollers, who had held out against a tariff on steel, abandoned Free Trade, afraid of becoming the next victims of cheap competition. The game became one of accommodation, of demanding subsidies or other concessions like drawbacks on exports to sweeten the protectionist pill.[11]

As the world economy closed down, the search began for regional groupings. On the continent, Aristide Briand looked towards a European union. In Britain, more and more sought refuge in the Empire from the balkanization of Europe. Mahatma Gandhi's challenge to British rule in India made an imperial economic union doubly appealing as a counter-strategy of integration. During the summer of 1930, the Trades Union Congress joined the Federation of British Industry in a call for 'Common-wealth economic machinery'. If the TUC sidestepped the question of a tariff for the moment, it had clearly turned its back on free exchange. The state needed to direct trade. Trading blocs were even hoped to lead to 'the elimination of most of the economic causes of conflict'. The Common-wealth was heralded as 'almost self-contained',[12] a rather stark exaggeration in the light of competing industries emerging in the Dominions. Walter Citrine, the TUC's general secretary, returned from his world tour in 1930, thinking it was 'absurd to try to build up Australian secondary industries behind tariffs'.[13]

Many industrial supporters of an imperial union were moving beyond a hierarchical vision of an advanced industrial core in the mother country complemented by agrarian, raw-material-producing Dominions. Roland Nugent, the FBI's first director general, urged a combination of protection and industrial development, raising imperial markets from 'the raw material-producing stage' to the 'sort of stage which the more highly developed countries in Europe ... have already reached, so that their demands shall be for an ever-increasing variety of goods'.[14] Here was a much more dynamic vision of the Empire than that of the founding fathers of tariff reform.

From the City came outspoken support for a general tariff. On 2 July 1930, a group of prominent bankers met at Hambros Bank and issued a resolution in favour of 'urgent measures for the promotion of inter-Imperial trade ... to secure and extend the market for British products both at home and through the export trade'. Amongst the signatories were Reginald McKenna of the Midland Bank, R. H. Tennant of the Westminster Bank, Beaumont Pease of Lloyds, Vivian Hugh Smith of Morgan Grenfell, and E. R. Peacock of Baring Brothers, who was also a director of the Bank of England. 'Bitter experience' had taught these men that efforts to bring down foreign tariffs had failed. Trade barriers had risen and 'the sales of surplus foreign products in the British markets have steadily grown'. Hope for free trade was relegated to some distant future. The bankers now called for reciprocal trade agreements with the Empire and 'duties on all imports' from foreign countries.[15] While the City had international interests, it also understood that were Britain's industrial base to sink, it would pull down finance with it. Industry's troubles in the 1920s had led to extended credits and banks' involvement in industrial affairs, leaving behind a greater degree of mutual dependence.[16]

Free Traders' attempt at a counter-manifesto was pitiful, drawing together a small and predictable group of Cobdenites, including Hugh Bell, Harold Cox, the journalist, and Ernest Benn, the libertarian publisher. They were the core of the 'Friends of Economy' who led the public campaign for retrenchment. They denounced 'the control of economic forces by political means' as 'un-English', violating 'every principle on which British prosperity was founded' and 'alien to the free instincts of the national character'.[17] Leading bankers were conspicuous by their complete absence, with the exception of Henry Bell of Lloyds. Free Trade had lost the City.

High wages made Britain uncompetitive. Either wages had to come down or prices had to go up. This was the crux of the matter. Most industrialists and bankers agreed with the 'Friends of Economy' that Britain was over-taxed. What divided them was a sense of political realism. In the pure textbook world, a drastic fall in wages might restore Britain's competitive edge. In a world of trade unions and with a Labour government in power, this was not going to happen. Even if it did, it would be slow and painful, risking social conflict in the interim. Tariffs were a lesser evil and promised more immediate effects. They would increase profits for manufacturers, attract capital and investment, and raise confidence, avoiding more direct taxes and public works. By 1930 this was the thinking guiding an increasing number of bankers, such as Felix Schuster, who had led the fight against tariff reform in the City before the war, and R. Holland Martin, the President of the Institute of Bankers.[18]

The 'Friends of Economy' fed a growing panic about the evil of 'socialist' taxation. By spring 1931 they ran demonstrations in 50 provincial towns.[19] The campaign involved a major miscalculation, however. Retrenchment created a joint platform for protectionists and liberals. For public audiences and middle-class voters 'economy' came to overshadow earlier partisan differences about trade. Free Trade became a subordinate issue in the larger battle over the national finances. It could be sacrificed if necessary. Instead of saving Free Trade, the economy campaign proved its own worst enemy.

In Liberal circles, individualists and progressives alike warmed to the idea of a revenue tariff. At a meeting organized by the National Campaign for Economy in March 1931, at the Free Trade Hall in Manchester of all places, John Simon urged all Liberals to put aside 'inherited free-trade traditions' and 'to ponder on the fiscal methods' necessary to tackle the budget deficit.[20] The Rubicon had been crossed. From here it was a small step to Simon's formation of a separate National Liberal group and their absorption into the national government.

The contractionist road was not the only one that brought Liberals to a tariff. Others, with Keynes in the lead, took a more social democratic, expansionist route. Theoretically, an expansionist policy of public works and public credit might increase purchasing power, boost the economy, and generate jobs. This was the cumulative effect that Keynes and his fellow economist Hubert Henderson had aimed for in their plans to cure unemployment in 1929. In a world slump, however, confronted with a growing deficit, rising unemployment, and lack of confidence all round, such a programme stood little political chance, as Keynes came to appreciate in the course of 1930. Free Traders typically denounced a tariff as an attack on real wages. It drove up prices. The world depression turned this problem upside down. The problem was not that prices were too high but that they were too low. A tariff was a good way to raise them. It was 'both a more expedient and a more just way' of lowering real wages than by reducing nominal wages. 'In so far as it raised the spirits of business men it would increase the readiness to invest in Great Britain ... and thus raise the equilibrium terms of trade.' To simply stand by and do nothing threatened a 'social catastrophe'.[21]

Without a tariff, the downward spiral would be unstoppable, Keynes elaborated to the Economic Advisory Council in the autumn of 1930. Advancing poverty would diminish saving. Wages would decline. Britain would have to do with fewer imports and be forced to be more self-sufficient: 'a point may come ... if we stick to laissez-faire long enough, when we shall grow our own vines'. The country would end up being richer with a tariff than without. It would save capital goods and foreign investments from destruction.

Keynes had hit on a crucial weakness in the Free Trade position. In normal conditions, the free flow of goods might lead to the most efficient use of a nation's resources. 'The trouble today is that we are violently out of equilibrium, and we cannot wait long enough for *laissez-faire* remedies to bring their reward.' Jobs and savings would be sacrificed while the economy again found its equilibrium. In any case, as Keynes highlighted again and again, it was unclear how Free Trade would work its magic of adjustment, since, in reality, wages and workers were not as mobile as the theory presumed. Free Trade 'assumes that if you throw men out of work in one direction you re-employ them in another. As soon as that link in the chain is broken the whole of the free trade argument breaks down.'[22]

Free Trade's problems, however, were not limited to temporary adjust-ment in an emergency. Keynes also pointed to a fundamental historical shift. The classic Free Trade case was that, by letting goods and services flow freely, it encouraged each country to specialize in what it did best. In the nineteenth century, Keynes agreed, this view 'in favour of specialisation as against stability may have been right, at any rate for Great Britain'. As more and more countries had industrialized, these gains from specialization had diminished. 'Any manufacturing country is probably just about as well fitted as any other to manufacture the great majority of articles.' Keynes was no longer worried that a tariff would lead Britain to produce the 'wrong things': 'I do not think that there are any wrong things, or at any rate not many.' Stability was becoming more important, and 'the price we should have to pay for it as a result of diminished specialisation a far smaller price'.[23] The 1920s had seen a range of arguments in favour of stability and coordination against cheapness and fluctuations. Here was another that went to the heart of Free Trade's general case about the benefits of international exchange.

At first these were arguments tested only in government committees, in an atmosphere of growing distrust between Keynes and Lionel Robbins, a fundamentalist Free Trader. In March 1931 Keynes went public. In an explosive piece, and to the delight of protectionists, he tied his colours to a general tariff. Britain, Keynes emphasized, faced an international crisis, no longer just a domestic one. Capital was edgy. 'It would not be wise to frighten the penguins and arouse these frigid creatures to flap away from our shores with their golden eggs inside them.' Keynes proposed an all-round tariff of 15 per cent on manufactured goods and 5 per cent on all foodstuffs and certain raw materials, low enough not to be genuinely protectionist and discriminatory, but widespread enough to boost revenue and confidence. He somewhat optimistically imagined at first £50, even £75 million revenue, later scaling it down to a more modest £40 million.

Such a tariff would relieve the pressure on the budget and restore the confidence necessary for Britain to lead the world out of the slump. It would also increase employment: Britain would make goods previously imported. Britain was not turning her back on the world, however. Rather, under the 'cover of the breathing space and the margin of financial strength', Britain would march 'to the assault against the spirit of contractionism and fear'. By reducing the pressure on the balance of trade, Keynes argued, tariffs would allow Britain both to pay for the additional imports which expansion would suck in and to finance loans to foreign debtor countries. In Keynes' hands, a tariff and a policy of expansion became a possible progressive combination. He even gave it internationalist credentials. Only 'fanatical free traders' were unable to see these benefits. Britain had reached a crossroads. Come with me on a progressive tariff road to international recovery, Keynes was saying to fellow liberals: the only other path was full-blown economic nationalism.[24]

The attention which the press accorded Keynes' volte-face reflected the changing balance between professional knowledge and popular knowledge in the debate about tariffs. In the Edwardian period, many economists had chipped in on both sides of the fiscal controversy, but the campaigns were carried by popular ideas (and prejudices), not academic arguments. With the popular culture of Free Trade fading away, what economists thought and said became relatively more important. A group of Free Trade economists, around Beveridge and Robbins, took up Keynes' challenge and subjected the case for a tariff to detailed cross-examination in August 1931. *Tariffs: the Case Examined* restated many classic objections. A tariff either kept out goods or it brought in revenue: it could not do both. It was a wasteful and not very flexible or predictable way of raising revenue.[25] Pure logic, however, could not make up for public apathy. The book was a failure; the publisher insisted on a hefty subsidy of £275 to cover its losses.[26]

Whatever the respective merits of these rival arguments, there was little doubt which side created the bigger splash. Since the days of Adam Smith, David Ricardo, and John Stuart Mill, Free Trade had been able to rely on the authority of liberal economists. Free Trade had the brains. It was the Conservatives who were ridiculed as the 'stupid party'. Now, the leading economist of his generation had come out in favour of a tariff. The cartoonist David Low captured the significance of the moment with characteristic brilliance. Low showed Keynes and E. D. Simon, who had previously floated a revenue tariff at the Liberal Summer School, hard at

Figure 17. 'Spring Renovations' by David Low, *Evening Standard*, 16 March 1931.

work in 'Spring renovations' outside the National Liberal Club, chipping away at the statue of Cobden the Clown (see Figure 17).[27]

As the association between Free Trade and extreme retrenchment tightened—the Friends of Economy wanted cuts of £100 million out of a budget of £800 million—the labour movement also began to adopt a more pragmatic attitude to tariffs. Encouraged by Keynes' critique of orthodoxy, Bevin, for the TUC, and Allen, for the cooperatives, signed the minority report of the Macmillan Committee on Finance and Industry. Ideally, they wanted state planning as a cure for unemployment, but failing that, would support tariffs as a last resort.[28]

For Bevin, unlike for Keynes, the emphasis remained firmly on devaluation, rather than a general tariff. But in the popular imagination, the gold standard and Free Trade were twinned, part of the same disappearing world. The failure of one inevitably reflected badly on the other. 'What is Free Trade?', Bevin asked trade unionists at the 1930 Congress. '2,000,000 unemployed is the Eldorado in the working of a Free Trade and monetary system.'[29] Head of the 300,000 strong Transport and General Workers' Union, Bevin gave voice to a growing army of sceptics in the labour movement marching towards open rebellion against Snowden. The two groups came to a showdown in August 1931 in the crisis that broke the Labour government. The cabinet was evenly split between ministers, led by MacDonald, Henderson, and Graham, supporting a revenue tariff to minimize cuts in unemployment benefits and those, led by Snowden, standing firmly behind Free Trade. When the cabinet met on 19 August, only six refused to contemplate protection. Fifteen preferred a revenue tariff; five were even prepared to consider a tariff on food.[30]

The events between 17 and 20 August 1931 have been some of the most closely studied in British history. They split the Labour leadership and party and set in train the process that would produce a national government, a decade of Conservative dominance, and the collapse of the Liberal party. The crisis was not a 'bankers' ramp', as Labour myth had it at the time. Politicians, not financiers, were in the driver's seat. [31] Labour ministers' willingness to sacrifice Free Trade was more than just a desperate bid to save unemployment benefits. As we have seen, disillusionment had become endemic long before the budget crisis and reflected more fundamental doubts, outside as well as inside the cabinet. Ernest Bevin had returned from the United States in 1927 convinced that peace and economic unity went hand in hand and that Britain's future, too, was with a larger regional union. All 'the old war cries are out of date', Lansbury had told cabinet colleagues already in November 1930. 'None of us are now Free Traders. Every Government—Liberal, Tory, and ourselves—in one way or another protects and helps Home and Dominions trade and industry.' This was 'all to the good, because the more we aid the more right we have to control'. Tariffs were dangerous where they created private monopolies. For more and more members of the Labour party, public controls eliminated that danger.[32]

Demands for the control of food spread across the Labour movement. In power, MacDonald's government was paralysed, unable to construct a majority for any of the agricultural policies on offer. Some supported a wheat quota, reserving a portion of wheat to British and imperial farmers, plans championed by Addison and Buxton. Others, especially Wise, wanted to go straight to an import board. Yet others wanted a state monopoly of the entire grain trade and flour industry. These schemes amounted to more than minor surgery. As one civil servant put it, an import board would be 'the greatest departure in the direction of the permanent substitution for private trading that has ever been adopted by this country'.[33] Several cabinet colleagues vigorously contested Snowden's rejection of quotas as 'wrong in principle'. 'In what respect is it wrong in principle that the British grower should have a fair share of the British market?', Addison asked.[34]

And why presume that consumers naturally benefited from leaving things to market forces? The depression was eliminating open competition around the world. Producer combinations were on the rise in Russia and the United States. Not protecting independent British farmers would leave consumers weaker and defenceless, too. Champions of quotas and import boards extended the arguments made by Lloyd and Wise in the 1920s. The slump, in this view, was not a temporary jam, but a continuation of a general trend towards controls. The growth of combines, selling schemes, and the international concentration of shipping and financial control 'have knocked the bottom out of the old arguments for Free Trade', Wise argued.[35] For Snowden to evoke the plight of those Britons depending on exports was 'all very interesting and picturesque, but very irrelevant' at a time when the staple industries were in crisis and two million unemployed. It was the business of politicians 'not merely to look at absolute figures alone, but at the tendencies'. This was, of course, precisely what Joseph Chamberlain had argued when he launched his crusade for tariff reform. Now, a quarter of a century later, there was a Labour alternative to tariffs. Free exchange had failed. Only the state was strong enough to rescue the economy through price regulation, import boards, and export marketing organizations.[36] Most Labourites remained opposed to a tariff, a measure that hit the poor more than the rich, but it makes little sense to see such protestations as signs of a more general 'reassertion of free trade'.[37]

The men and women in the labour movement were, of course, consumers as well as producers. During the war, consumers and internationalists had begun to prize stability over cheap imports. With the depression, the bottom fell out of the political value of cheapness. After all, it was the collapse of prices that was at the root of the world crisis and that left workers on the dole. Here and there, in the women's pages of the cooperative movement, the old cry of 'hands off the people's food' was heard. Far more common, however, were attacks on cheapness as unfair and short-sighted: 'low prices meant underpayment and keener competition, resulting in a lower standard of living'.[38] Why should you have cheap food at the expense of the farmer, one delegate asked at the Cooperative party conference at Blackpool in April 1931?[39] In any case, it was not clear that, under Free Trade, the benefits of low prices were passed on to the consumer: while the world's granaries were overflowing, the price of the loaf rose in early 1930, and again in February 1931.[40] Fairness required that consumers and producers join forces to regulate supplies and prices. In the cooperative mind, Free Trade was outshone by a fascination with Canadian wheat pools and bulk-buying arrangements. Even James Hudson, Snowden's parliamentary secretary who attacked tariffs in the cooperative pages, championed pooling and state assistance. In the words of J. T. Davies, a Free Trade director of the Cooperative Wholesale Society, 'even sane cooperators' were unintentionally assisting the 'march of Protection against the tax-free homes of the people' by revolting 'against everything, good or bad, formerly associated with the "musty shibboleths of Manchesterism" '.[41]

The Labour party conference in October 1931 met in Scarborough just as Parliament was dissolved for the general election. It showed how defenceless Free Trade had become, now that its main guardian, Snowden, had left the party for the national government. Graham, Labour's outgoing President of the Board of Trade, denounced protection but pleaded for a 'vigorous trade policy' involving import and export boards, public ownership, and control of prices. For many, even this did not go far enough. There were attacks from the floor: Graham was trying to have it both ways. 'Tell the electorate that you are free traders, and then tell them that you approve of the regulation of imports, and they will think you are either fools or knaves.' In Russia, 'the Socialist free trader is the polite bourgeois name for a lunatic'.[42] Free Trade had been a costly 'fetish'. Workers had not benefited from low prices. If Labour wanted to reorganize industry, it needed to control what came into the country. In the end, criticism of a tariff was replaced with a socialist plan to protect the standard of living.

When the election got under way in earnest in the second week of October 1931, Free Trade found itself exposed on all sides. The Conservatives campaigned for economy and tariffs. Baldwin's manifesto emphasized that Britain's departure from the gold standard and the devaluation of the pound were 'no valid substitute for a tariff'.[43] Protection was still the most effective weapon to reduce 'excess imports', protect Britain against dumping, strengthen the Empire, and compel other countries to lower their tariff walls. Labour opposed tariffs but pitched import and export boards and public controls instead. Simon's Liberal Nationals saw tariffs as unavoidable, Samuel's Liberals accepted them if necessary. For Liberals, the need for economy overshadowed any talk of Free Trade; only every

fifth Liberal candidate was pledged against a food tax.[44] Of all the political
leaders, only Lloyd George, who had suddenly rediscovered his old faith
in Free Trade in the course of the crisis, tried in vain to stem the tide. For
most Liberal voters the battle was between national stability and socialism.
Few were persuaded by Lloyd George to put the defeat of a tariff first and
vote Labour in constituencies without Liberal candidates.

Old Free Trade arguments found it ever more difficult to be heard.
There were only a few public speakers left like Mrs Beavan, who explained
to a cooperative audience in Lancashire how the last hundred years showed
how Free Trade made Britain rich. A few individual candidates still repeated
that tariffs meant war and corrupted public life.[45] More widely, Free Trade
was disappearing from historical memory. References to how Free Trade
had liberated Britons from 'the hungry forties' were rare and isolated.[46] The
Cooperative party even dumped Free Trade from its election manifesto
in an attempt to present itself as a constructive force for change—not
very successfully: seventeen of its eighteen candidates were defeated. The
cooperatives broadly accepted that Britain was too dependent on foreign
trade. Indeed, on the eve of the election, the cooperatives launched their
'Britain Re-Born' campaign urging people to 'Buy British'. The working
class now had their own version of the conservative Buy Empire Goods
movement. The latter, meanwhile, received a fresh boost in 1931 from
the 350,000 strong Tudor Rose organization founded by the imperialist
engineer Gilbert Vyle.[47]

The election was a landslide victory for the parties of the National
Government, and especially for the Conservatives, who now had 470 out
of the 615 seats in the Commons. Labour was almost wiped out, left with
a mere 46 of the 265 seats it had had. If the two main Liberal groups were
able to hang on to just over 30 MPs each, and Lloyd George managed 4,
their miserable share of the vote (10 per cent) and their internal divisions
confirmed that Liberalism as a major political force was dead.[48]

All this suggests that Free Trade was experiencing a far more fundamental
displacement from political culture than references to a 'protectionist ramp'
or the party political rivalries of the moment can explain. Tariff Reform
versus Free Trade was no longer an all-consuming topic. Free Traders'
attempts to mobilize public opinion were pitiful and easily contained by
protectionists, who headed off their few speakers in advance.[49] Hirst raised
barely £400 for the Liberal Free Trade Defence Group, which managed
to distribute a mere 100,000 pamphlets in the election, a miniscule number

compared to the many millions that rained on Britons before the war.[50]
Once the stuff of seaside resorts and popular exhibits, of visual entertainment
and mass rallies, the defence of Free Trade was reduced to manifestos and
letters to the struggling liberal press.

As the supporting network of Free Trade groups fell apart, it was Hirst
who tried to keep Cobden's legacy alive, almost single-handedly. He was
married to Cobden's great-niece, Helena. In 1927 the Richard Cobden
Memorial Association was set up, but it could not even match the support
offered by the Carnegie Endowment. By 1931 it was in such dire straits that
Hirst was forced to turn Dunford House, the Cobden family home, into
a guesthouse, begging American friends for donations.[51] The guestbook at
Dunford House shows the declining pull of Cobden's ideas and memory.
It records the names of a diminishing circle of ageing friends, consisting
of diehards like Snowden and old liberals like Bell, Paish, and Hirst
himself.[52]

Free Trade faced a general apathy that went far deeper than any short-
term doubts about the balance of trade. Organizers knocked in vain at
the doors of former donors, canvassers, and volunteers. Anxieties about
class and high taxes had led to a permanent cooling-off amongst the
middle classes. E. G. Brunker, an old war-horse with unrivalled campaign
experience stretching back to the years before the war, offered a sobering
analysis of the role of class sentiment more generally, and unemployment
benefits in particular. 'The inability of would-be employers... to obtain
domestic servants and unskilled labour, while they see the statistical record
of the participants in "the dole" mounting every week, is making a
formidable impression, particularly on the mind of the middle-class voter,
and especially of the women.' A tariff was no longer a problem, as long
as the dole was abolished and taxes lowered. There was a view, Brunker
reported, that ' "the worker is getting too uppish, and will have to be put
in his place" '.[53]

The rise of Labour since the war had fundamentally disturbed the more
organic and harmonious image of Free Trade as a programme of social
justice and inclusion. Class cooperation had been replaced by class conflict.
A decade of high unemployment and taxes washed away the genuine
concern about the poor that had characterized the Edwardian battle
against hunger and immiseration. Amongst staunch Free Traders there
was little sympathy for the unemployed poor. A Gladstonian concern for
retrenchment and balanced budgets outweighed all other considerations.

For Hirst and friends, the Labour party held the dangerous belief that
'[p]ublic waste and extravagance are good things ... at any rate for the
working classes': 'slackers' were thriving at the expense of the community
while wealth, enterprise, and personal responsibility were undercut.[54] It
was a dismal view of society and unlikely to make Free Trade many friends
amongst the working classes.

The campaign for tariffs in 1931 attracted greater support, but it, too,
could only generate a weak echo of its earlier fervour. The Empire
Industries Association organized some 2,600 meetings in 1930–1, especially
targeting working-class areas in the north of England—far less than what
the Tariff Reform League had managed in its heyday. Most propaganda
was now in industrial hands, run and financed directly by big manufacturers
like Morris, the car manufacturer. The FBI and the League of Industry
distributed over a million leaflets and 30,000 posters directly outside factory
gates. They set up exhibits of foreign goods indicating the lower wages
of their competitors.[55] The tariff movement had shrunk into a form of
industrial lobbying.

The switch to a general tariff in 1932 proved the final act in the battle
between Free Trade and protection. They then exited the centre stage of
public life. Economically, tariffs were of marginal significance. The Ottawa
conference showed the difficulties of using the tariff to drive bargains that
really mattered to Britain. Outside Canada, Britain already had a large share
of the Dominions' markets. Room for expansion was limited from the outset, handicapped further by the low incomes of primary producers. Britain
was more successful with Argentina and Sweden and Finland, but, overall,
trade agreements accomplished little. At home, the tariff probably slowed
rationalization, the opposite of what its champions set out to achieve.
The Import Duties Advisory Committee gave greater protection to trades
willing to shed excess capacity. This boosted mergers rather than productivity. Government advisers already suggested at the time what economic
historians have confirmed since: Britain's recovery was primarily fuelled by
cheap money, made possible by going off gold, not by tariff protection.[56]

Neville Chamberlain understandably introduced the general tariff in
Parliament as a paean to his father, a vindication of the historic significance
of tariffs in British life. With the benefit of hindsight, we can see that
the very opposite was true. Tariffs and Free Trade mattered less and less.
For most people, they were secondary, even tertiary issues. The political
landscape had changed forever. When the economic blizzard passed, Britons

did not move back into their old political quarters. Free Traders stayed in the political wilderness, but so did the old guard of authentic tariff reformers, like Amery.

Within the state, the growth of intervention and, especially, cheap money produced a new policy world. The departure from the gold standard had freed the government's hands. Civil servants who had been raised on Free Trade were unwilling to tie themselves down in old dogmas. The Import Duties Advisory Committee took the tariff question out of public politics and passed it into the hands of experts, a transfer already visible in the safeguarding inquiries of the late 1920s. Free Trade and the most-favoured-nation clause looked out of date in a world of managed currencies and trade agreements. The world economic conference in 1933 was a failure. Everywhere bilateralism was the new fashion, championed by everyone from Cordell Hull in the United States to Hjalmar Schacht in Nazi Germany. Liberal ministers like Runciman publicly criticized Gladstone for failing to develop any arms for bargaining and defended trade agreements as a legitimate new system, not just a temporary departure from Free Trade.[57] Lloyd George, too, came round to bargaining tariffs. And the mix of new policies spoiled any simple grand causal connection between trade policy and the state of the nation. Cheap money mattered more than cheap imports.

The 1930s completed the search for new visions of order and coordination that had their origins in the First World War and that, in the course of the 1920s, were unravelling the strands of commerce, civil society, and consumption that had given Free Trade culture its democratic strength. Once upheld as the guardian of public life, political purity, peace, and progress, Free Trade, in capital letters, now shrank into free trade, in lower case. It was no longer a solid philosophy of life, a defining part of political culture and national identity. It was just a policy tool, something that could be bent and twisted, even discarded if necessary.

In a broadcast for the BBC at the end of 1932, Keynes registered the softening of the old ideologies. The arguments of Free Traders and protectionists alike were no longer valid, Keynes told listeners. Free Traders had 'greatly overvalued the social advantage of mere market cheapness'. Tariff Reformers, on the other hand, while often using bad economics, 'sometimes had a truer sense of the complicated balances and harmonies and qualities of a sound national economic life'. 'National protection had its idealistic side, too.' Keynes still acknowledged the 'peace and truth and international fair-dealing of free trade', but it no longer made up a comprehensive world view. Instead, it could now be comfortably complemented with a 'well-balanced national economic policy' of tariffs.[58]

This shift in climate swept across the entire political landscape. For Labour, the future lay with the public control of industry and banking; the national organization of trade via export and import boards would be stepping-stones on the road to socialist management. Labour housewives concluded that 'fiscal policy is not going to solve the problems of poverty and injustice'.[59] For other progressive groups favouring a middle way, like the Next Five Years group, tariffs became an acceptable component in a mixed system of planning. The memory of the 'hungry forties' was overshadowed by that of the 'unemployed thirties'. New plays of the 'hungry forties' found inspiration in Chartism, not Free Trade. Friedrich Engels made an appearance, not Richard Cobden.[60] For Clement Attlee and a new generation of Labour leaders there was nothing noble about Cobdenism. The idea that trade was harmonious, beneficial, and peaceful suited capitalists 'but necessarily failed to enlist the support of the exploited', he told young internationalists at Geneva.

At the League, and then the United Nations, new internationalists put together the final building blocs for a global regulatory framework, with ambitious plans for a world food board distributing food according to need. In internationalist circles, as much as in domestic ones, plans to advance social welfare and improve nutrition looked towards coordinated, not free, trade. As the League recognized, commercial policy had become an integral part of an expansionist social programme to maintain work and raise the standard of living.[61]

The few remaining Free Traders were ever more isolated. Dunford House provided a British point of contact in a small international network of libertarians and economic liberals, like William Rappard, Wilhelm Roepke, and Friedrich Hayek.[62] By the mid-1930s Hirst and his Liberal Free Trade Committee fought not only Conservatives and Labour but also the 'socialistic' Liberal party. By the time they formally broke away, in 1944, Liberals had conceived the Beveridge plan, a commitment to full employment and social security. When Hirst asked Liberal Headquarters for Free Trade literature, they had none to offer.[63] In the 1945 election, S. W. Alexander stood as a lonely Free Trade candidate in the City, denouncing all forms of state interference for fostering a servile mentality.[64] Economists continued to advocate the theoretical wisdom of free trade, but as a public language it was all but extinct.

Epilogue

On 1 July 2001, globalization came to the small town of Mugron in south-west France. Two hundred years earlier, the Free Trade apostle Frédéric Bastiat had been born, and now a small group of libertarians were gathering in his home town to celebrate his bicentennial. As a new plaque on Bastiat's statue was being dedicated, local activists from the international network Attac descended on the town square. Shouting 'the world is not for sale', they glued toy money all over Bastiat's statue.[1]

The events in Mugron are a long way from where we started in this book, almost a century earlier, when the centennial of Cobden's birth sparked popular celebrations. Mugron is a sign of our times. Disillusionment with freedom of trade has spread far and wide. At certain moments, it has even erupted into violence, most memorably at the bloody G-8 summit in Genoa in 2001. In government and international organizations, economists and trade negotiators have time and again rallied to keep rounds of trade liberalization alive. In civil society, however, defenders of free trade are lonely figures, like the two hundred odd representatives of the International Society for Individual Liberty who came to celebrate Bastiat. They are a small drop in an ocean of general scepticism, even outright opposition. Free trade supporters have nothing to match the hard core of 100,000 globalization critics organized in Attac, let alone the ten million people from over seventy countries who come together in marches and festivities during trade justice and fair trade weeks each spring.[2] Fair trade, not free trade, is cool and progressive, attracting film stars like Antonio Banderas and rock musicians like Chris Martin of Coldplay. Richard Cobden, by contrast, has long ceased to be a popular hero. He is virtually unknown outside small circles of academics and neoliberal think-tanks (see Figure 18 overleaf).[3]

Figure 18. Decayed and neglected, Richard Cobden today. The statue, on London's Camden High Street, was originally unveiled on 27 June 1868. It had been commissioned from W. & T. Wills and funded by public subscription, to which Napoleon III was principal contributor.

Once the preserve of farmers, nationalists, or workers in a threatened industry, the critique of free trade is now widespread, including everyone from environmental groups to Christian charities, from supporters of fair trade to the hundreds of thousands marching to end world poverty. Free trade has lost its moral association with justice, peace, and democracy. It is now vilified as an instrument of the rich exploiting the poor. Full freedom of trade is criticized as inherently unjust, never between equals, a source of global poverty, not its answer. Developed countries are accused of preaching free trade while practicing protectionism, maintaining unfair trade barriers against the developing world. They shirk their share of the costs of globalization. As the World Development Movement, a trade justice alliance based in Britain, neatly put it in its adbusting spoof of the famous Thatcherite anti-Labour poster: 'Free Trade is Not Working'.[4]

Few developments better illustrate the change in historical fortunes than the joint campaign by The Cooperative Bank ('consumer led, ethically guided') and Christian Aid in 2005. Core constituents of Free Trade a century ago, they now proclaim '[t]here's nothing free about free trade'. It is 'forced' onto the poor, as a condition of aid, leaving them powerless in the face of richer competitors. Trade liberalization widens the gulf between rich and poor. Instead of having their markets forced open, poor countries should have the right to protect and develop their farms and industries. Once it was called slavery, now it is called free trade: adverts showed two African hands shackled by a free trade chain.[5]

Liberal economists and trade negotiators have been perplexed by this popular backlash. After all, that societies benefit from freer trade is an idea as accepted in economics as the law of gravity. Trade liberalization, they point out, has brought tremendous gains in global wealth and welfare. Between 1947, when the General Agreement on Tariffs and Trade (GATT) started, and 1984, tariffs on manufactured goods fell from around 40 per cent to 5 per cent. Since then, the end of communism in eastern Europe and liberalization in India and China has fast accelerated this trend. Four billion people joined an ever more integrated world economy in these years. By the early twenty-first century, trade made up more than 20 per cent of the world's gross domestic product, compared to a mere 8 per cent in the earlier wave of globalization before World War One; as recently as 1990 it had been less than 15 per cent.[6] In 2005 the World Bank estimated that full trade liberalization would boost global income by $290 billion over the next ten years, especially benefiting developing countries.[7]

Liberalization has brought about major improvements in the lives of most people on the planet, the World Bank and leading economists emphasize. Between 1990 and 2004 the percentage of people in extreme poverty, living on less than $1 a day, has fallen from 29 per cent to 18 per cent. In China alone export-based growth has lifted three hundred million people out of poverty. Globally, life expectancy and infant mortality figures have improved. In the developing world, infant mortality fell from 107 per thousand in 1970 to 58 in 2000—a trend especially pronounced in fast-growing East Asia, but even in sub-Saharan Africa it declined from 116 to 91. Child labour, often held up as the symbol of an exploitative global trade system, fell by half in developing countries between 1980 and 2000. Globalization, economic commentators argue, gives parents the money to send their kids to school instead of to work; much of the child labour that remains produces for the domestic not the global market. Within most developing countries, income inequality has diminished. It is societies that embraced openness in the past few decades that have done well, like western Europe, the United States, and east Asia. Countries that refused to open themselves to trade, like Brazil and much of Africa, missed out.[8]

Globalization's overall balance sheet according to these commentators is clear. Freer trade has eased the misery of the many. Not everyone has shared equally in its benefits. Extreme poverty remains as high in sub-Saharan Africa today as it was two decades ago. However, to shelter local trades or to use 'fair trade' to artificially boost the income of farmers in markets already suffering from over-production is to give the patient the wrong economic medicine. Instead, there should be assistance for those losing out in the short run as the economy is opened up. What the world needs is more openness, not less. The problem is not with free trade but with other barriers to development and welfare, North and South.

Many regional trade agreements do discriminate against poor countries. In OECD countries, tariffs and subsidies to agriculture added up to a staggering $350 billion in 2004—more than three-quarters of it going straight into the pockets of producers. Real tariffs may have fallen, but non-tariff barriers have not disappeared. Anti-dumping measures and various forms of quality controls and import licenses are especially directed against developing producers. In Europe, sugar is the most notorious offender. In the early 1980s, the European Union was still a net importer of sugar, now it is a net exporter. The United States gives $3.1 billion in subsidies to cotton, almost twice the amount it gives as foreign aid to Africa.[9] For most economists, the task ahead is not to put a brake on trade liberalization but to make it work more smoothly and fairly. Joseph Stiglitz, the Nobel prize-winning economist, has developed an ambitious reform agenda for coordinating the different processes of globalization, including plans for more progressive income taxes, an international reserve currency and penal tariffs to get the United States to sign up to Kyoto.[10]

This book offers a historical perspective on today's battle over globalization. Trade shapes our lives. It is too important to be left to economists and campaigners. In addition to asking who is right or wrong and to listing costs and benefits, we need to place today's polarized debate in a longer historical context. Both sides are part of a larger transformation in modern history. Once standing shoulder to shoulder, freedom of trade and social justice have moved apart. Economists and the people no longer see eye to eye. This book has charted the source of this estrangement. It is also an attempt, by using the past, to imagine free trade in a richer, more open and morally complex way.

The main story of this book has been about how Free Trade managed to build a democratic culture in the late nineteenth and early twentieth centuries, and how it unravelled. This democratic moment has not received the attention it deserves in the current debate. Where historical antecedents matter at all, commentators tend to look either to the repeal of the Corn Laws in 1846 or to the world depression (1929–32) for lessons for the present. This book, by contrast, focuses on the period in between as a turning point in the history of Free Trade and democratic politics, one that is especially well suited to shed light on the democratic dilemma of globalization today. Cobden and his Anti-Corn Law League are well known to economists and political scientists as a modern—liberals would add heroic—lobbying group who took on vested interests. But this battle took place in a world before mass democratic politics. The world depression, by contrast, has been an important historical warning of the speed with which nationalist policies can undo global integration. From this perspective, free trade appears the victim of the insular forces of vested interests and prejudice. Our period, the centre of this book, is a reminder that Free Trade was once a vibrant and powerful democratic force.

The historical story of *Free Trade Nation* has implications for all sides. It prompts us to re-examine core assumptions. Above all, it is a reminder of the emotional, political, and moral underpinnings of liberal trade policy in the past. On both sides, there has been a temptation to produce a sanitized account of free trade with all the blood and guts taken out. Today's critics denounce it as a heartless instrument of rich states and corporations, while its defenders invoke its scientific credentials as a superior trade theory. From the perspective of the latter, the battle is between the forces of reason and prejudice, superior economic logic versus selfish lobbies and populist fallacies. To win, free trade needs to insulate institutions against pressure groups and defeat bad economics.

This book reveals the limits of this rationalist approach. Free Trade in Britain before the First World War derived its power from popular enthusiasm, from passion and morals, and from its connection with national identity and social emancipation, not from people's rational understanding of their self-interest or of the theory of comparative advantage. It appealed to the ethics of fairness and international understanding. It could also be imperialist, even anti-materialist, especially in the belief that a Free Trade Empire raised the moral tone of the world and diminished the influence of money. Free Trade was not the creature of economic textbooks. Entertainment, ideology, and mass politics were essential, as was a creative engagement with modern forms of mass communication. It was this broad democratic culture which helped Free Trade to overcome the costs of collective action and defeat the protectionist challenge. Instead of being a dispersed general interest, it stretched across parties, classes, and economic sectors.

The past fifty years have been dominated by a different, parallel politics of international trade. With the GATT in 1947, international diplomacy became the principal engine of trade liberalization. Trade was taken out of popular politics. International organizations never became the organic channel between local civil society and global governance that new internationalists had dreamt of. The new multinational regime insulated global trade against populist and nationalist pressures. At the same time, it created a hyper-world of economic and legal technocrats and ever more complex diplomatic fine print, increasingly removed from the people they sought to benefit. This divide can be traced back to the inter-war years. In part, it was a retreat from the pressure group politics of new mass democracies. States, too, used trade policy as a weapon for their own ambitions.[11] Without the erosion of popular Free Trade, however, the story might have been very different. National governments and international agencies were able to take trade out of democratic politics because the public had lost interest in free trade.

This book shows that the fate of free trade depends on its potential friends, not just its enemies. It introduces a different way of looking at trade politics and the challenges to globalization. It moves the emphasis from a concern with protectionist pressure groups and lobbies to the cultural meaning and political appeal of free trade itself. Today's champions of trade liberalization tend to focus on 'losers' as the main threat to an open world economy. Of course, globalization always brings in its train social dislocation for some. It is an inherent problem, well restated by Ben Bernanke, the chairman of the US Federal Reserve, in a recent speech to fellow bankers. The 'expansion of trade opportunities,' he emphasized:

> tends to change the mix of goods that each country produces and the relative returns to capital and labour. The resulting shifts in the structure of production impose costs on workers and business owners in some industries and thus create a constituency that opposes the process of economic integration.

Fears of cultural change and unjust enrichment further distract from the public benefits of globalization.[12]

This book suggests that there may be another conclusion from history. The relative strength of free trade is not determined only by the 'losers' of globalization, but also by its ability to muster the support of the 'winners'. Economic discontent and fears of change have been intrinsic to globalization for centuries, but they do not automatically prevail. Free Trade's ability to mobilize the people in Britain before the First World War contained these threats and stemmed the protectionist tide. It has been the loss of this democratic culture that leaves globalization so vulnerable today. The challenge is not only from textile workers in Europe and the United States or from farmers in Brazil or Ghana, that is from particular groups who have an interest in keeping cheaper imports out; trade liberalization has had popular support in Latin America, as did the North American Free Trade Agreement (NAFTA) in Mexico.[13] The broad reaction against free trade comes from people in the North who more than anyone have been its beneficiaries over the past two decades. In other words, it is not just concentrated losers who oppose liberalization, as conventional approaches would predict. The groundswell of opinion favouring fair trade over free trade brings together quite dispersed social groups and interests.

The public disillusionment with free trade has deeper historical roots than commentators have been able to see. It is not just the result of tempo-rary dislocation, of interest groups, or of the WTO becoming a convenient lightning rod for socialists and anarchists after the end of communism. Doubts and disillusionment run too deep to be easily overcome by a restatement of the liberal theory of trade. Free trade may still be a winning formula when it comes to growth, but it has lost its former distributional magic. Here the First World War and post-war years were a watershed. Before, freedom of trade appealed to liberal, radical, and excluded groups alike as a way of dispersing power by reining in the state and putting the interests of the consuming public above those of vested interests. Internationally, commerce was hoped to weave a web of exchange between the peoples of the world and supplant great power politics.

Even in its heyday, reality never fitted the ideal. Free Trade had imperialist as well as internationalist strands, and co-existed with extremes of wealth and poverty. We must resist the temptation to be nostalgic about Free Trade and see its defeat as a temporary aberration brought about by an economic crisis, leaving its basic virtues untouched, a project to be revived for later generations. Before the First World War, Free Trade had come with a strong view of civil society that ruled out not only tariffs but a whole range of alternative ways of governing the economy. It painted a highly optimistic picture of the peaceful coordinating powers of the market. It also denied consumers a more direct role in the state. The war and post-war years were not just destructive. They expanded the place of politics—in terms of policies but also in broadening the political imagination to include a sense that people and their institutions needed to coordinate and govern the world economy.

The First World War was a shock to every aspect of Free Trade's distributional magic. Internationally, the idea that commerce would foster peace and establish a world order free of political power was bankrupt. Radical Cobdenites had dreamt of taking politics out of international relations. New internationalists wanted to put it back, with the help of supra-national organizations. Domestically, too, the war revealed flaws in the distributional ideal. Free Trade, it became clear, had failed to inoculate Britain against cartels and combines. In the context of profiteering, scarcities, and fluctuations, fairness came to mean stable access and fair prices, not cheapness. The rise of the welfare state completed this handover in distributional justice from Free Trade to social democratic institutions. Of course, it is possible to combine a liberal trade policy with a welfare state, but the expansion of pensions, unemployment benefits, and other social services inevitably meant that free trade lost much of its importance as a weapon against poverty and hunger. State benefits came to matter more than cheap imports.

The current debate about globalization can be understood as another stage in the erosion of free trade's distributional appeal. What was once a democratic utopia has turned into dystopia. The dispersal of power is now associated with a loss of sovereignty and the uprooting of local democracy, leaving people at the mercy of unaccountable international corporations and organizations. There are some anarcho-capitalists and libertarians, in think tanks like the Future of Freedom Foundation and the Cobden Centre, who continue to be inspired by the old model and wish to roll back all forms of state intervention and abolish the WTO and international organizations altogether. Outside these small circles, there is little confidence that commerce can be left to itself to steer global integration. In fact, some of the current debate looks toward systems of coordination, just as disillusioned Free Traders did after the First World War. The idea that economic globalization has outpaced political globalization, given renewed prominence by Joseph Stiglitz, had been the point of departure for new internationalists ninety years ago. Similarly, the idea that commerce should be coordinated fairly according to human need can be traced back to progressive politics in the inter-war years and abortive plans for a world food board. We tend to think of ourselves as children of the cold war, but when it comes to globalization we remain the heirs of an earlier generation.

The democratic appeal of Free Trade has been a major theme of this book. Amongst many democratic statesmen and political scientists today, this pairing is presumed to be a natural cause and effect: democracies produce freer trade.[14] This is only to be expected, the argument goes, because democracies make for greater transparency and accountability. Politicians want to be elected. Their electorates benefit from freer trade. So in a democracy, politicians find it much harder to introduce high tariffs that benefit a small vested interest.

This argument is reasonable at a certain abstract level but it is not sufficiently subtle or wide-ranging to be of much use as a tool of historical interpretation. On aggregate, democracies might trade more than autocracies. That still leaves us with rather big differences between democracies. The data supporting the theory is about the 1970s–90s, when the average tariff rate for less-developed countries fell by 60 per cent.[15] This was a distinctive era of advancing democratization and neoliberalism, prompted by internal as well as external forces; the WTO and the IMF are not as all-powerful as critics sometimes claim and governments often chose to lower tariffs for internal reasons.[16]

Twenty years is a short chapter in the history of democracy. In the modern world, democracies have adopted vastly different trade policies, and changed them periodically. The United States' turn to freer trade (14 per cent on manufactured imports in 1950, below 5 per cent in 1990) is quite recent. In the late nineteenth century, the great republic levied tariffs of almost 50 per cent on manufactured goods, higher than those in tsarist Russia or imperial Germany. Britain had 0 per cent and combined Free Trade with Empire. In 1931, the United States had higher tariff walls than fascist Italy.[17] In Britain, universal suffrage was followed by the introduction of tariffs. The 1920s demonstrated that democratic conditions do not prevent politicians and publics from turning away from liberal policies to all kinds of trade regulation. In any case, tariff levels alone are only part of the story. There has been a veritable explosion of non-tariff barriers, such as quotas, anti-dumping policies, export subsidies, product and hygienic standards. If contemporary democracies have seen a decline in formal tariff barriers, they have also seen a rise in these less transparent handicaps and incentives, more easily hidden away from voters.[18] According to the World Bank, average anti-dumping duties are seven to ten times higher than tariffs in industrial countries.[19]

There may be other ways of thinking about the relationship between democracy and Free Trade. Political scientists, this book suggests, may have been looking through the wrong end of the lens. Instead of using political institutions as a starting point and analysing how political regimes affect trade policy, we should also ask how popular attitudes to trade leave their mark on political culture. Free Trade mattered to Britons before the First World War because it was seen to promote democracy, peace, and social justice. Free Trade was a democratic ticket for the excluded. Free Trade was cause, not effect. It shaped democratic culture, rather than just being a policy outcome of democratic institutions.

The democratic culture of Free Trade past also casts a fresh light on the present popular critique. The current movements for trade justice and fair trade tap into a strong moral conscience. Critics may fault them for a weak grasp of economics, but, in the public eye, they are the virtuous. As anyone who has attended public debates between supporters and critics of trade liberalization can attest, the law of comparative advantage does not even dent the moral armour of a fair-trade-minded audience. The renewed ethical interest in trade should be applauded, but it has also promoted a morally lopsided view of modern history. In this view, the 'moral economy' of traditional societies, epitomized by a fair price and mutual regard, was crushed by liberal economics and a capitalist system of markets, profits, and freedom of exchange. Customary morals were replaced by modern markets. Free Trade demoralized economic life. For current supporters, fair trade promises the coming of a new moral economy.[20] This is a deeply flawed view of modernity and morality. It is dubious to set up a dichotomy between traditional moral communities and modern commercial systems. Many peasant societies combine profit-motives and moral sympathy. Nor do commerce and caring have to be mutually exclusive.[21] Instead of extinguishing morality, popular Free Trade spoke in a rich ethical vocabulary of justice, fairness, and peace.

The citizen-consumer, a central figure in the *Free Trade Nation*, also casts doubts on a second, related view of globalization. Amongst fair trade and trade justice movements, trade liberalization is blamed on rich corporations and international organizations, like the IMF and the World Bank. Frequent icons are the dollar-waving tycoon or the rich capitalist pig.[22] Free trade is an economic instrument of the rich, Fair Trade the social and moral weapon of the people. Historically, this is not how globalization has developed. It has not just been driven forward by states and corporations, forcing citizens and consumers to react. Citizen-consumers were integral to the success of Free Trade before the First World War. Free Trade had people power, with deep roots in civil society. If consumers and social movements in the North today are demanding trade justice or seeking moral renewal in a cup of fair-trade coffee, therefore, they are not just up against multinationals or neo-liberal economists. They are also confronting a global trade system that an earlier generation of consumers and progressives helped build. The moral view of the world according to fair trade has a historical blind spot. Morally energized civic-minded consumers opted for Free Trade in the past. Modern history, in other words, is not a sharp break from morality to materialism. There were always alternative moral tracks running through it. What changed in the British case was that people switched moral tracks, first onto a democratic track of Free Trade, then, after the First World War, onto one of trade coordination and regulation.

History is not a good predictor, nor can it compete with economic models and decide which policy is best, but it is useful for broadening our point of view. It helps us to step back and recognize that what looks familiar or self-evident to us today may have had quite different meanings in the past.

It can shake up our moral certainties. For people currently concerned about what trade is doing to our lives and to the world, this book has one final lesson. To buy a particular product as a sign of concern for distant producers is not a progressive prerogative. Consumer power has been a vehicle of emancipatory causes in the modern period, from anti-slavery boycotts to shopper leagues fighting sweatshops. But it also had a forgotten conservative, imperialist twin. The extraordinary spread of 'caring at a distance' via moral consumerism in the last couple of decades did not come out of a historical vacuum. In addition to drawing on Christian ideas and networks, it also entered a field already prepared by an equally sizable imperial consumerism, with thousands of Conservative housewives urging their fellow Britons to buy Empire goods and express their concern and solidarity with their imperial cousins far away. To us their imperialist outlook is disturbing, but they had little doubt about the moral superiority of their cause.

The changing historical meanings of free trade and fair trade should remind us that, whichever side we currently champion, our own moral positions and the future consequences of our actions may be more ambivalent than we can see if we just look at the here and now. One protagonist in our story who was especially attuned to the influence of past ideas on politics was John Maynard Keynes. 'A study of the history of opinion is a necessary preliminary to the emancipation of the mind', Keynes wrote in 1926. 'I do not know which makes a man more conservative—to know nothing but the present, or nothing but the past.' In this book I have tried to bring to life the big battle over Free Trade in an earlier era of globalization and to make it speak to our own. This earlier battle involved many of the same groups and issues still debated today—about the costs and benefits of openness, the relation between trade and justice, and the place of civil society and democratic institutions in a global economy.

Unlike Keynes, I have been less interested in great thinkers or economic theorists than in the flow of popular ideas and assumptions about the economy. There is an economy in the mind, but it is not the purified model of the market and rational choice that economists have constructed. In the past few decades, a group of economists and psychologists have themselves begun to subject this model to revision, stressing that rationality can be 'bounded', that choice can be 'myopic', and that people can feel more intensely about losses than about gains.[23] These are welcome amendments but they ultimately continue to look at human societies through the lens of methodological individualism. They project models onto human societies, rather than exploring the beliefs, practices, and relations specific to different cultures over time. Some sociologists have argued that 'the economy' is a construct created by liberal economists.[24] We should not exaggerate the power of economists. All people have an economy in the mind, but few live and think according to a distinct individualist model of calculating costs and benefits.

In this book, I have tried to unfold the economy in the mind of Britons a hundred years ago—how it got there, how it was connected to ideas about political life, ethics, and national identity, and how these connections were loosened and rearranged over time. How people understand the economy is always interwoven with ideas about power, social order, and morality, and in this way, the economy in the mind is not only a mirror of economic realities outside it. By influencing how people behave, organize, mobilize, or withdraw from public life, it helps to shape the world in which we live.

Notes

INTRODUCTION

1. *Daily News*, 6 June 1904, pp. 7–8.
2. B. Russell, 'The Tariff Controversy', *The Edinburgh Review* 199 (1904); see *The Collected Papers of Bertrand Russell, vol. 7, Contemplation and Action, 1902–1914*, ed. R. A. Rempel (London, 1985), pp. 190 ff; Russell to Lucy Donnelly, 29 July 1903, in C. Moorehead, *Bertrand Russell: A Life* (London, 1992), p. 141.
3. A. O. Hirschman, *The Passions and the Interests: Political Arguments for Capitalism before its Triumph* (Princeton, 1977); R. F. Teichgraeber, *Free Trade and Moral Philosophy: Rethinking the Sources of Adam Smith's Wealth of Nations* (Durham, 1986); I. Hont, *Jealousy of Trade: International Competition and the Nation-State in Historical Perspective* (Cambridge, Mass., 2005).
4. P. A. Pickering and A. Tyrrell, *The People's Bread: A History of the Anti-Corn Law League* (London, 2000); B. Hilton, *Age of Atonement: The Influence of Evangelicalism on Social and Economic Thought, 1785–1865* (Oxford, 2006); A. Howe, *Free Trade and Liberal England 1846–1946* (Oxford, 1997). For a focus on institutional openings, see now C. Schonhardt-Bailey, *From the Corn Laws to Free Trade: Interests, Ideas, and Institutions in Historical Perspective* (Cambridge, Mass., 2006).
5. For synthetic overviews and further reading, see the essays by Anthony Howe and Frank Trentmann in D. Winch and P. O'Brien (eds), *The Political Economy of British Historical Experience, 1688–1914* (Oxford, 2002), pp. 192–242; B. Hilton, *Corn, Cash, Commerce: The Economic Policies of the Tory Governments 1815–1830* (Oxford, 1977); N. McCord, *The Anti-Corn Law League, 1838–1846* (London, 1958); P. Ayçoberry, 'Freihandelsbewegungen in Deutschland und Frankreich in den 1840er und 1850er Jahren', In *Liberalismus im 19. Jahrhundert: Deutschland im europäischen Vergleich*, ed. D. Langewiesche (Göttingen, 1988), pp. 296–304; W. Kaiser, 'Cultural Transfer of Free Trade at the World Exhibitions, 1851–1862', *The Journal of Modern History*, 77/3 (2005); pp. 563–90. A. Howe and S. Morgan (eds), *Rethinking Nineteenth-Century Liberalism: Richard Cobden Bicentenary Essays* (Aldershot, 2006); P. T. Marsh, *Bargaining on Europe: Britain and the First Common Market, 1860–1892* (New Haven and London, 1999).

6. P. Bairoch, *Commerce extérieur et développement économique de l'Europe au XIXe siècle* (Paris, 1976); K. D. Barkin, *The Controversy over German Industrialization 1890–1902* (Chicago, 1970); R. G. Möller, 'Peasants and Tariffs in the Kaiserreich: How Backwards were the *Bauern*'. *Agricultural History* 55 (1981), pp. 370–84; H. Rosenberg, 'Political and Social Consequences of the Great Depression of 1873–1896 in Central Europe', in *Imperial Germany*, ed. J. J. Sheehan (New York, 1976).

7. See J. M. Hobson, *The Wealth of States: A Comparative Sociology of International Economic and Political Change* (Cambridge, 1997).

8. E. Rothschild, *Economic Sentiments: Adam Smith, Condorcet, and the Enlightenment* (Cambridge, Mass., 2002), esp. pp. 72–86; G. Stedman Jones, *An End to Poverty? A Historical Debate* (London, 2004), pp. 16–63.

9. Hilton, *Age of Atonement*; Stedman Jones, *An End to Poverty?*

10. B. Hilton, *A Mad, Bad, and Dangerous People? England 1783–1846* (Oxford, 2006), pp. 543–58.

11. Pickering and Tyrrell, *People's Bread*, esp. chs 4 and 7.

12. League of Nations, *Tariff Level Indices* (Geneva, 1927), p. 15.

13. A. Nicholls and C. Opal (eds), *Fair Trade: Market-driven Ethical Consumption* (London, 2005); M. Barrat Brown, *Fair Trade* (London, 1993).

14. T. Harford, *The Undercover Economist* (London, 2006). *The Economist*, 7 Dec. 2006.

15. J. E. Stiglitz and A. Charlton, *Fair Trade for All: How Trade can Promote Development* (Oxford, 2005). See also Consumers International, *Consumer Charter for Trade* (2003), and *Asia Pacific Consumer*, 33/3 (2003).

16. Bairoch, *Economics and World History*, ch. 4; A. K. Rose, 'Do We Really Know That the WTO Increases Trade?', *American Economic Review*, 94/1 (March 2004), pp. 98–114; O. Accominotti and M. Flandreau, 'Does Bilateralism Promote Trade? Nineteenth Century Liberalization Revisited', Centre for Economic Policy Research discussion paper no. 5423 (Jan. 2006). See also S. Pollard, 'Free Trade, Protectionism, and the World Economy', in M. H. Geyer and J. Paulmann (eds), *The Mechanics of Internationalism: Culture, Society, and Politics from the 1840s to the First World War* (Oxford, 2001), p. 44.

17. Howe, *Free Trade and Liberal England*.

18. E. H. H. Green, *The Crisis of Conservatism: The Politics, Economics and the Ideology of the British Conservative Party, 1880–1914* (London and New York, 1995); R. A. Rempel, *Unionists Divided: Arthur Balfour, Joseph Chamberlain and the Unionist Free Traders* (Newton Abbot and Hamden, Conn., 1972); A. Gollin, *Balfour's Burden: Arthur Balfour and Imperial Preference* (London, 1965); P. Williamson, *National Crisis and National Government: British Politics, the Economy and Empire, 1926–1932* (Cambridge, 1992); R. C. Self, *Tories and Tariffs: The Conservative Party and the Politics of Tariff Reform, 1922–1932* (London, 1986).

19. S. A. Aaronson, *Trade and the American Dream* (Lexington, Ky., 1996), p. 7.

20. S. D. Krasner, 'State Power and the Structure of International Trade', *World Politics*, 28 (1976), p. 317. See also C. Kindleberger, *The World in Depression, 1929–39* (London, 1973) and R. Gilpin, *The Political Economy of International Relations* (Princeton, 1987).

21. Counterfactual calculations suggest that unilateral Free Trade was suboptimal; see D. Irwin, 'Welfare Effects of British Free Trade: Debate and Evidence from the 1840s', *Journal of Political Economy* 96 (1988), 1142–64; D. Mc-Closkey, *Enterprise and Trade in Victorian Britain: Essays in Historical Economics* (London, 1981), pp. 155–72.

22. Marsh, *Bargaining on Europe*; see also P. O'Brien and G. Pigman. 'Free Trade, British Hegemony and the International Economic Order in the Nineteenth-Century', *Review of International Studies* 18 (1992), 89–113; A. L. Friedberg, *The Weary Titan: Britain and the Experience of Relative Decline, 1895–1905* (Princeton, 1988); Hobson, *Wealth of States*.

23. P. J. Cain and A. G. Hopkins, 'Gentlemanly Capitalism and British Expansion Overseas. II. New Imperialism, 1850–1945', *Economic History Review* 45 (1987), 1–26, and their *British Imperialism: Innovation and Expansion 1688–1914* (London, 1993).

24. A. C. Howe, 'Free Trade and the City of London, 1820–1870', *History*, 77/251 (1992), pp. 391–410; F. Trentmann, 'The Transformation of Fiscal Reform: Reciprocity, Modernization, and the Fiscal Debate within the Business Community in Early Twentieth-Century Britain', *Historical Journal*, 39/4 (1996), pp. 1005–48; W. Mock, *Imperiale Herrschaft und nationales Interesse: 'Constructive Imperialism' oder Freihandel in Grossbritannien vor dem Ersten Weltkrieg* (Stuttgart, 1982), esp. pp. 393–7; A. J. Marrison, *British Business and Protection, 1903–32* (Oxford, 1996); M. J. Daunton, ' "Gentlemanly Capitalism and British Industry 1820–1914" ' *Past and Present* 122 (1989), pp. 119–58. Similarly, on the continent, agricultural politics did not follow clear-cut economic interests; see R. Aldenhoff-Hübinger, *Agrarpolitik und Protektionismus: Deutschland und Frankreich im Vergleich 1879–1914* (Göttingen, 2002).

25. P. Gourevitch, *Politics in Hard Times: Comparative Responses to International Economic Crises* (Ithaca, NY, 1986).

26. Marshall Library (Cambridge), Marshall Papers, Misc. I, 14 April 1911.

27. F. Trentmann, 'Political Culture and Political Economy', *Review of International Political Economy*, 5/2 (1998), pp. 217–51; M. Bevir, *The Logic of the History of Ideas* (Cambridge, 1999); M. Bevir and F. Trentmann (eds), *Markets in Historical Contexts: Ideas and Politics in the Modern World* (Cambridge, 2004); G. Hodgson, *How Economics Forgot History* (London, 2001); H. Berghoff and J. Vogel (eds), *Wirtschaftsgeschichte als Kulturgeschichte: Dimensionen eines Perspektivenwechsels* (Frankfurt and New York, 2004); M. Daunton, *Trusting Leviathan: The Politics of Taxation in Britain, 1799–1914* (Cambridge, 2001), pp. 8–15.

28. D. A. Irwin, *Against the Tide: An Intellectual History of Free Trade* (Princeton, 1996).

29. D. A. Irwin, 'The Political Economy of Free Trade: Voting in the British General Election of 1906', *Journal of Law and Economics* 37 (1994), 75–108. For a critique, see my 'Political Culture and Political Economy'.

30. It thus retrieves human agency, something that has just as easily been lost in post-structuralist accounts of discourse as in economistic accounts which view behaviour as the inexorable product of material forces.

31. R. McKibbin, 'Why was there no Marxism in Great Britain?', in R. McKibbin, *The Ideologies of Class: Social Relations in Britain 1880–1950* (Oxford, 1994), pp. 31–2.

32. E. F. Biagini, *Liberty, Retrenchment and Reform: Popular Liberalism in the Age of Gladstone, 1860–1880* (Cambridge, 1992), ch. 2; H. C. G. Matthew, 'Disraeli, Gladstone and the Politics of mid-Victorian budgets', *Historical Journal* 22 (1979); McKibbin, 'Why was there no Marxism in Great Britain?', pp. 1–41.

33. W.W. Rostow, *The World Economy: History and Prospect* (London, 1978), p.166.

34. D. Tanner, *Political Change and the Labour Party, 1900–1918* (Cambridge, 1990), pp. 99–129.

35. F. Trentmann, 'The Modern Genealogy of the Consumer: Meanings, Knowledge, and Identities', in J. Brewer and F. Trentmann (eds), *Consuming Cultures, Global Perspectives: Historical Trajectories, Transnational Exchanges* (Oxford and New York, 2006), pp. 19–69.

36. National-Liberals bemoaned the narrow, particularist perspective of consumers, a ' "*Nurkonsumentenstandpunkt*" ', cit. in C. Nonn, *Verbraucherprotest und Parteiensystem im wilhelminischen Deutschland* (Düsseldorf, 1996), pp. 76–8.

37. D. M. Fox, *The Discovery of Abundance: Simon N. Patten and the Transformation of Social Theory* (Ithaca, NY, 1967), esp. pp. 29, 56–7.

38. P. L. Maclachlan, *Consumer Politics in Postwar Japan: The Institutional Boundaries of Citizen Activism* (New York, 2002); pp. 58–84; S. Garon and P. L. Maclachlan (eds), *The Ambivalent Consumer: Questioning Consumption in East Asia and the West* (Ithaca, NY, 2006).

39. M. J. Sandel, *Democracy's Discontent: America in Search of a Public Philosophy* (Cambridge, Mass., 1996); T. W. Adorno and M. Horkheimer, *Dialectic of Enlightenment* (New York, 1972; orig. 1944); J. Habermas, *The Structural Transformation of the Public Sphere* (Cambridge, Mass., 1989; 1962); D. Marquand, *Decline of the Public* (Cambridge, 2004).

40. M. Davis, *Late Victorian Holocausts: El Niño Famines and the Making of the Third World* (London, 2001).

41. C. Hall, *Civilising Subjects: Metropole and Colony in the English Imagination 1830–1867* (Oxford, 2002); F. Cooper and A. L. Stoler, *Tensions of Empire: Colonial Cultures in a Bourgeois World* (Berkeley and Los Angeles, 1997).

42. A. Krueger, 'Willful Ignorance: The Struggle to Convince the Free Trade Skeptics,' Geneva, 18 May 2004, www.imf.org/external/np/speeches/2004/051804a.htm.

43. See, for example, L. Rockwell, of the Mises Institute, 'Stop the WTO', *Free Market* (Feb. 1994) and 'The Coming of US Fascism' (2001), www. LewRockwell.com. *Eigentümlich Frei*, 4/17 (Sept. 2001), pp. 4–19.

PROLOGUE I

1. *The Times*, 16 March 1903, p. 12.
2. I. Little, T. Scitovsky, and M. Scott, *Industry and Trade in Some Developing Countries* (Oxford, 1970), table 5.1, pp. 162–3; League of Nations, *Tariff Level Indices* (Geneva, 1927), p. 15; P. Bairoch, *Economics and World History: Myths and Paradoxes* (Chicago, 1993), pp. 24, 26, 138. These are nominal tariff rates—effective rates in many instances were often more than twice as high.
3. J. Wigley, in *The Liberal Agent*, 5/32 (April 1903), pp. 167–8; T. R. Buchanan to Arthur Elliot, 4 Oct. 1903, Elliot Papers, National Library of Scotland, Edinburgh, MS 19493.
4. H. Gladstone to A. Hudson, 30 Dec. 1903, Gladstone Papers, British Library, London, MS 46021.
5. *Daily News*, 16 Dec. 1903, p. 8.
6. Goschen to John St Loe Strachey 18 June 1903; Strachey Papers, House of Lords Record Office, London, MS 7/4/5.
7. E. W. Hamilton, diary, 17 Dec. 1903, Hamilton Papers, British Library, MS 48,681.
8. *Italo Svevo's London Writings*, ed. J. Gatt-Rutter and B. Moloney (Market Harborough, 2003), pp. 201–2.

I. FREE TRADE STORIES

1. 'Free Trade For the Isle of the Sea' by W. Handley, to the tune of 'Red, White and Blue', *The Liberal Agent*, 7/37 (July 1904), pp. 56–7.
2. *Daily News*, 27 July 1903, p. 4.
3. National Archives (NA), T 168/54, 'The Conditions and Effects of "Dumping"' (7 July 1903), 6.
4. Free Trade Union, *A Message from the Forties: A Free Trade Masque* (n.d. 1909).
5. *The Times*, 11 June 1909, 12 e.
6. *South Wales Daily Post*, 15 Jan. 1910, p. 6.
7. J. Clapham, *Free Trade and Steel, 1850–1886* (1932; Cambridge, 1952), p. 460.
8. NA 30/60/39, 'Memorandum with Statistical Tables and Charts prepared by the Board of Trade on Changes in the Cost of Clothing' (Oct. 1904), p. 8.
9. NA, T 168/93, 'Extract from Memorandum by the principal of the Statistical Office, reviewing the Customs Revenue for the year 1902/3', pp. 45–6.
10. M. Bulmer, K. Bales, and K. Kish Sklar (eds), *The Social Survey in Historical Perspective* (Cambridge, 1991).

11. Even 65% in some heavy industries in the north, as an investigation by the United States Department of Labor revealed, see L. H. Lees, 'Getting and Spending: The Family Budgets of English Industrial Workers in 1890', in J. M. Merriman (ed.), *Consciousness and Class Experience in Nineteenth-Century Europe* (New York, 1979), pp. 169–86. See also I. Gazeley, 'The Cost of Living for Urban Workers in Late Victorian and Edwardian Britain', *Economic History Review*, 42/(2) (1989), pp. 207–21; D. J. Oddy, 'Working-Class Diets in Late Nineteenth-Century Britain', *Economic History Review*, 23 (1970), pp. 314–23.

12. A. L. Bowley, *Wages and Incomes in the United Kingdom since 1860* (Cambridge, 1937); C. H. Feinstein, 'What Really Happened to Real Wages? Trends in Wages, Prices, and Productivity in the United Kingdom, 1880–1913', *Economic History Review*, 43 (1990), pp. 329–55.

13. NA 30/60/39, 'Bread Supply in Time of War', p. 15.

14. C. Petersen, *Bread and the British Economy, c. 1770–1870* (Aldershot, 1995).

15. J. Vernon, *Hunger: A Modern History* (Cambridge, Mass., 2007).

16. Campbell-Bannerman papers, British Library, London, MS 41,220, Lewis Harcourt to Campbell-Bannerman, 25 Nov. 1903.

17. Campbell-Bannerman MS 41,225, Campbell-Bannerman to Ripon 19 Oct. 1903.

18. F. G. Bettany, 'The Free Trade Poet: a Reminder', *New Liberal Review*, 6/32 (Sept. 1903), pp. 201–7.

19. Harcourt papers, Bodleian Library, Oxford, MS 657, William to Lewis Harcourt, 28 and 29 June 1903.

20. *New Liberal Review*, 5/30 (1903), p. 815.

21. *Summary of Federation News*, Women's Liberal Federation (WLF), Feb. 1905, p. 12. Elliot Papers, MS 19549, 'Fiscal Proposals of the Tariff Reform League', speech by Hamilton at Lincoln, 20 Oct., 1905, p. 5. Chiozza Money, *100 Points for Free Trade* was sold in cheap copies for one penny by the Free Trade Union.

22. A. Somerville, *Free Trade and the League: A Biographic History of the Pioneers of Freedom of Opinion, Commercial Enterprise and Civilisation, in Britain: From the Times of Serfdom to the Age of Free Trade in Manufactures, Food and Navigation* (Manchester, 1853).

23. Cobden Club, Leaflet no. XLII, *'The Good Old Times' by an Aston Voter for the Last Half Century* (1885); *A History of the Cobden Club*, written by Members of the Club (London, 1939), p. 39. See also A. C. Howe, 'Towards the "Hungry Forties": Free Trade in Britain, c. 1880–1906' in *Citizenship and Community: Liberals, Radicals and Collective Identities in the British Isles 1865–1931*, ed. E. Biagini (Cambridge, 1996), pp. 193–218.

24. *Summary of Federation News*, WLF, Dec. 1904, p. 12; *Daily News*, 8 Nov. 1904, p. 4; J. Cobden Unwin (ed.), *The Hungry Forties: Life under the Bread Tax* (London, 1904), pp. 20, 24.

25. Cobden Unwin, *Hungry Forties*, pp. 65, 95, 120–1.

26. Ibid. p. 136.

27. *The Liberal Agent*, 5/32 (April 1903), p. 184.

28. Clapham, *Free Trade and Steel*, pp. 498 ff.; 560 ff.; N. F. R. Crafts, *British Economic Growth During the Industrial Revolution* (Oxford, 1985); W. H. Chaloner, *The Hungry Forties* (London, 1957). Studies of height suggest a pretty continuous decline of nutritional standards from the late eighteenth century all the way into the 1860s; see R. Floud, A. Gregory, and K. Wachter, *Height, Health and History: Nutritional Status in the United Kingdom, 1750–1980* (Cambridge, 1990).

29. Quoted in B. Hilton, *The Age of Atonement: The Influence of Evangelicalism on Social and Economic Thought, 1795–1865* (Oxford, 1988), p. 109.

30. W. Cunningham, *The Case Against Free Trade* (London, 1911), pp. 56–63.

31. *Hungry Forties*, pp. 252, 257, 265, 274.

32. E. F. Biagini, *Liberty, Retrenchment and Reform: Popular Liberalism in the Age of Gladstone, 1860–1880* (Cambridge, 1992); P. Joyce, *Democratic Subjects: The Self and the Social in Nineteenth-Century England* (Cambridge, 1994), pp. 190–204.

33. J. Campbell, *An Examination of the Corn and Provision Laws, from their First Enactment to the Present Period* (Manchester, n.d. [c. 1842]), repr. in *Chartist and Anti-Chartist Pamphlets*, ed. D. Thompson (New York and London, 1986), p. 62; G. Stedman Jones, *Languages of Class: Studies in English Working Class History, 1832–1982* (Cambridge, 1983).

34. *Report*, The Cobden Club 1911 & 1912, p. 16; Cobden and Unwin Papers, West Sussex Record Office, Chichester, MS 1190, annual general meeting of the Cobden Club (28 April 1913).

35. For example, at Reigate on 23 Oct. 1905, in a 'warmly applauded lecture' by Mrs Freeman Thomas at Central Hall, *Summary of Federation News*, Nov. 1905, p. 12.

36. *Summary of Federation News*: Jan. 1905, p.15 (Horsted Keynes WLA, national school, 25 Nov. 1904, 'one of the largest audiences ever seen there'); Dec. 1905, p. 20 (Oxted and District WLA); Feb. 1910, p. 21 (South Portland).

37. Free Trade Union, 'England Under Protection' (leaflet no. 95, 18 Nov. 1907); see also the popular 1903 leaflet the 'Good Old Days' (1903).

38. *Reynolds's Newspaper*, 31 Jan. 1904, p. 7; *Daily News*, 1 July 1903; Richard Robbins (born 1817), *Westminster Gazette*, 8 June 1903, and widely reprinted as the leaflet 'Food and Wages' (Liberal Publication Department, no. 1945), and in the *Liberal Monthly*, Sept. 1907, p. 107. See also *The Liberal Agent* (April 1903), p. 184 and October 1904, p. 105; and P. Lynch, *The Liberal Party in Rural England 1885–1910* (Oxford, 2001), pp. 186–7.

39. J. W. Welsford, *The Reign of Terror: An Experiment in Free Trade Socialism. Illustrated by 45 Reproductions of Lantern Slides, Photographed from Contemporary Engravings, etc.* (1909), pp. 1–2, 19.

40. W. Cunningham, *Political Economy, Treated as an Empirical Science* (Cambridge, 1887); *The Rise and Decline of the Free Trade Movement* (Cambridge, 2nd edn

1905); W. J. Ashley, *The Tariff Problem* (London, 1903); W. J. Welsford, *The Strength of Nations: An Argument from History* (London, 1907) and *The Strength of England: A Politico-Economic History of England From Saxon Times to The Reign of Charles the First* (London, 1910).

41. British Library of Political and Economic Science (BLPES), Coll. Misc. 519, no. 85.

42. See L. Nead, 'Paintings, Films and Fast Cars: A Case Study of Hubert von Herkomer', *Art History*, 252 (2002), pp. 240–55.

43. BLPES, Coll. Misc. 519, no. 82.

44. *Reynolds's*, 10 Jan. 1904, p. 5.

45. Ibid. 12 June 1904, p. 4; Dollman's painting is now in the Art Gallery in Salford.

46. E. P. Thompson, *The Making of the English Working Class* (1963; Harmondsworth, 1984), p. 70.

47. National Liberal Federation, *Annual Report and Speeches* (1908), p. 69; see also *Liberal Monthly*, 1907 p. 59; H. Bell, *Who Pays for Protection* (Cambridge, 1908).

48. F. Davis in *Daily Chronicle*, 26 Nov. 1910, p. 5.

49. *Hungry Forties*, p. 54.

50. See above, pp. 33–4.

51. *Illustrated London News*, 22 Jan. 1910, p. 135.

52. D. L. Schacter, *Searching for Memory: The Brain, the Mind, and the Past* (New York, 1996).

53. R. G. Moeller, 'Peasants and Tariffs in the Kaiserreich: How Backwards were the *Bauern*', *Agricultural History* 55 (1981), pp. 370–84.

54. Bonar Law papers, House of Lords Record Office, London, 41/M/14, 'Answers to Circulars on Colonial Preference', n.d. The seat had been uncontested in the January 1906 general election but Liberals won with a small majority in April 1906. As Pelling notes, this rural 'constituency only became marginal in 1910, and this may have been due to the attraction of Tariff Reform to the Leiston engineering workers, who were reported to be "doubtful" on the eve of polling'; H. Pelling, *Social Geography of British Elections, 1885–1910* (London, 1967), p. 101.

55. G. D. H. Cole, *A Century of Co-operation* (London, 1947), pp. 371–2.

56. P. Gurney, *Co-operative Culture and the Politics of Consumption in England, 1870–1930* (Manchester, 1996), p. 20.

57. R. Nash, 'The Co-operative Housewife', in *Labour and Protection*, ed. H. W. Massingham (London, 1903), pp. 182–3.

58. Co-operative Union Archives, Manchester, Committee of the Co-operative Congress, minutes 23 Aug. 1902. Seventy of the WCG's 293 branches protested, Women's Cooperative Guild, *Annual Report* (1902), pp. 11–12.

59. *Report of the 36th Annual Co-operative Congress* (1904), pp. 330–1.

60. *Co-operative News*, 20 March 1880.

61. Herbert Gladstone MS 46,061, Welby to H. Gladstone, 10 Jan. 1904.

62. Holyoake Papers, Manchester, no. 2805.

63. Ibid. 2919; Thomas Potter to Holyoake, 6 March 1884; 2934, Morley to Holyoake, 6 May 1884; Donald Murray to Holyoake, 10 Jan. 1893.

64. *Rochdale Observer*, 4 Dec. 1897, p. 8.

65. Holyoake, 'In the Days of Protection', in *Labour and Protection*, ed. Massingham (London, 1903), and reprinted in *Reynolds's Newspaper*, 29 Nov. 1903, p. 3; Holyoake Papers, Massingham to Holyoake, 15 July 1903.

66. R. J. Morris, 'Clubs, Societies, and Associations', in *The Cambridge Social History of Britain, 1750–1950*, Vol. 3, ed. F. M. L. Thompson (Cambridge, 1990), pp. 416–17.

67. Holyoake, 'In the Days of Protection', p. 112.

68. At a demonstration of the Free Trade Union at Queen's Hall on 28 Feb. 1908, London, Lloyd George Papers, B/5/2/8.

69. G. H. Wood 'Social Movements and Reforms of the Nineteenth Century', *The Co-operative Annual*, 14/8 (Aug. 1903), p. 4; A. Clarke, *'The Men Who Fought For Us' in the 'Hungry Forties'* (Manchester, 1914), pp. 5, 11, 280.

70. Quoted in *Bolton Co-operative Record*, 14/12 (Dec. 1903), p. 27. See also *Songs and Dialogues for the use at Annual Festivals and Other Meetings of Societies*, Central Cooperative Board (Manchester, 1887), pp. 41 ff.

71. Mrs Bury at the annual conference of the Women's National Liberal Association (WNLA), at Holborn Restaurant, 7–8 June 1904, quoted in *The Quarterly Leaflet of the Women's National Liberal Association*, no. 36 (June 1904), pp. 5–6.

72. *Manchester and Salford Cooperative Herald*, Dec. 1903, p. 199. Women's Cooperative Guild, *21st Annual Report* (1904), p. 11.

73. Nash, 'Co-operative Housewife', pp. 203–4 and 195.

74. L. T. Hobhouse, *The Labour Movement* (London, 1893), pp. 60–86 and S. Collini, *Liberalism and Sociology: L. T. Hobhouse and Political Argument in England, 1880–1914* (Cambridge, 1979), pp. 61–78. See also S.-G. Schnorr, *Liberalismus zwischen 19. und 20. Jahrhundert: Reformulierung liberaler politischer Theorie in Deutschland und England am Beispiel von Friedrich Naumann und Leonard T. Hobhouse* (Baden-Baden, 1990); S. den Otter, *British Idealism and Social Explanation: A Study in Late Victorian Social Thought* (Oxford, 1996).

75. BLPES, Coll. Misc. 519, no. 25.

76. See George Thompson's praise of ladies' speaking on behalf of the poor, *Manchester Times*, 18 Dec. 1941, p. 2; A. Tyrrell, 'Woman's Mission' and Pressure Group Politics in Britain (1825–60), *Bulletin of John Rylands University Library*, 63 (1980), pp. 194–230; S. Morgan, 'Domestic Economy and Political Agitation: Women and the Anti-Corn Law League, 1839–46', in K. Gleadle and S. Richardson (eds), *Women in British Politics, 1760–1860: The Power of the Petticoat* (Basingstoke, 2000), pp. 115–33.

77. Women's Liberal Federation, *17th Annual Report* (1904), p. 19.

78. *Westminster Gazette*, 20 July 1903.

79. As Liberal women from Liverpool put it at a meeting at City Hall, 21 March 1904, *Quarterly Leaflet of WNLA*, 35 (Apr. 1904).

80. Ibid. no. 56 (July 1909), p. 10.

81. *Summary of Federation News*, WLF, Feb. 1910, p. 21.

82. Victoria and Albert Museum, Poster collection, E. 179-1968/Y60/37 by an anonymous artist.

83. *Awake Britannia! A short sketch dealing with Tariff Reform*, by Lesley Wright (n.d., 1908); a play that originated with the Eddisbury (Cheshire) Women's Unionist Association. See also *'What Free Trade Did for Bill'*, by Gertrude Jennings, in Cornwall Record Office, Wrangham Papers, X392/147.

84. J. Lawrence, *Speaking for the People: Party, Language and Popular Politics in England, 1867–1914* (Cambridge, 1998).

85. BLPES, Coll. Misc. 519, no. 61.

86. 'Free Trade Doctrine—Under Tariff Reform', *Tariff Reform at a Glance* (London, 1905).

87. 'To the Working Men of England', *Tariff Reform Illustrated* (1904), pp. 43–4.

88. *The League*, 12 April 1845, cit. in Morgan, 'Domestic Economy', pp. 122–3.

89. University of Bristol Special Collections, DM 1045.

90. *Quarterly Leaflet of WNLA*, no. 36 (June 1904), p. 5.

91. *Saturday Night: A Dream of Tariff Reform* (London, 1909), written by Alice Parsons of Cheltenham and C. H. Jones, the Liberal agent for Camberwell; a 'clever and entertaining' play and 'much appreciated' by audiences like those at York, after speeches and songs, *Quarterly Leaflet of WNLA*, no. 58 (1910), p. 28.

92. *Reynolds's*, 2 Aug. 1903, p. 4.

93. As Mrs Tomkinson, the wife of a west Cheshire MP put it, *The Quarterly Leaflet of WNLA*, no. 32 (July 1903), p. 8.

94. Thomas Lough, 'The Workman's Cupboard', in *Labour and Protection*, ed. Massingham, p. 151.

95. *Set of Leaflets*, Liberal Publication Department (1903), no. 1862.

96. James quoted in S. Koven, *Slumming: Sexual and Social Politics in Victorian London* (Princeton, NJ, 2004), p. 5.

97. *Daily Graphic*, 15 Dec. 1909, p. 7.

98. J. H. Yoxhall, 'Daily Bread', in *New Liberal Review*, 7/37 (Feb. 1904), p. 57.

99. Mrs Elizabeth Eade, born 1895 (no. 38, p. 49); P. Thompson, and T. Lummis, Family Life and Work Experience Before 1918, 1870–1973 [computer file]. 5th Edition. Colchester, Essex: UK Data Archive [distributor], April 2005. SN: 2000. (With special thanks to Elizabeth Bishop for her assistance.)

100. For such a link, see Campbell-Bannerman MS 41,227, Shaw Lefevre to Campbell-Bannerman, 1 Feb. 1904; for a critique, see Percy Ashley's memo 'The Price of Corn and the Extent of Pauperism, (n.d., 1903) to A. J. Balfour, Balfour MS 49,780.

101. *The Times*, 21 Oct. 1910, 23b.

102. In possession of the author.

103. Strachey Papers S/5/5/12, Dicey to Strachey, 29 Sept. 1909.

104. Elliot papers 19552, Circular of Cambridge University Free Trade Association (Aug. 1904), which included Maitland, Pigou, and G. M. Trevelyan.

105. *The Times*, 15 Aug. 1903, 4b.

106. *Quarterly Leaflet of WNLA*, no. 36 (June 1904), p. 5.

107. M. Ostrogorski, *Democracy and the Organization of Political Parties: Volume I, England* ([1902] New York, 1964), pp. 291, 299.

108. G. Wallas, *Human Nature in Politics* (London, 1908).

109. Burns papers, British Library, MS 46,327, 14 Oct. 1909.

110. Robert Cecil papers, British Library, MS 51157, confidential memo by Hugh Cecil, 10 Jan. 1915.

111. Keynes papers, King's College, Cambridge, Box 1/29, Keynes spoke at the Cambridge Union Society, 24 Jan. 1905.

112. Hamilton MS 48,628, Robert Spencer to Hamilton, 8 Oct. 1906.

113. Campbell-Bannerman MS 52,517, Campbell-Bannerman to Bryce 29 Oct. 1900.

114. 'What a cheerful thought for New Year's Eve', Campbell-Bannerman to Bryce, 31 Dec. 1903, Campbell-Bannerman MS 41, 211.

115. Campbell-Bannerman MS 41,227, Shaw Lefevre to Campbell-Bannerman, 3 Jan. 1910.

116. *Daily News*, 6 June 1904.

117. NA 30/60/44, 'Memorandum' by Blain (Treasury), 1903. See also M. Daunton, *Trusting Leviathan: The Politics of Taxation in Britain, 1799–1914* (Cambridge, 2001).

118. Hamilton MS 48,679, diary 20 April 1902.

119. A. J. Balfour, *Economic Notes on Insular Free Trade* (London, 1903).

120. Balfour MS 49,780, 'Mr. Chamberlain's scheme of Preferential and Protective Duties', memo by G. L. Ryder, 4 July 1903. NA, T 168/93, Hamilton papers, 'The Basis of the Proposed Silk Duties', memo by Pittar, 25 March 1904.

121. NA 30/60/44, Gerald Balfour 'Methods of Fiscal Reform' (confidential), 6 Jan. 1904, p. 7.

122. Balfour MS 49,729, Lansdowne to Sandars, 24 Jan. 1907.

123. Balfour MS 49,831, A. J. Balfour to Gerald Balfour, 10 Nov. 1905.

124. Campbell-Bannerman MS 41,237, Campbell-Bannerman to A. Crowe, 10 May 1902.

125. *Daily News*, 8 Jan. 1904.

126. Ibid., 19 Dec. 1903, p. 10.

127. H. Washington, *Our Surtax and the Poor* (Ottawa, 1905), pp. 10–11.

128. Lloyd George Papers A 11/2/39: 16 Nov. 1903, at Woodside, Aberdeen.

129. Robert Cecil MS 51,194, 'Conservative Policy' (1911).

130. *Anti-Bread Tax Circular*, 5 May 1841. Similarly Lloyd George at Bradford, *Yorkshire Daily Observer*, 3 March 1904.

131. *Aberdeen Free Press*, 14 Nov. 1903.

132. E. P. Thompson, 'The Moral Economy of the English Crowd in the Eighteenth Century', *Past and Present*, 50 (1971), pp. 76–136; Vernon, *Hunger*.

133. Lloyd George Papers A/12/2/49, reported in *Perthshire Courier*, 29 Nov. 1904.

134. Hobson on 'Capitalism in U.S.A.', 1 July 1903, *Minutes of the Rainbow Circle, 1894–1924*, ed. M. Freeden, Camden Fourth Series Vol. 38 (London 1989), pp. 114–15; Hobson at the International Free Trade Congress, cit. *The Times*, 6 Aug. 1908, p. 6.

135. W. E. Dowding, *Two Great Tariff Trials of 1912* (London n.d. 1912), p. 27; J. M. Robertson, *The Battle for Free Trade* (London, 1923), p. 30; F. W. Hirst, *Monopolies, Trusts and Kartells* (London, 1905).

136. 1906 election in Rochdale, see *Alexander Gordon Cummins Harvey: A Memoir*, ed. F. W. Hirst (London, 1926), p. 62.

137. Free Trade Union, 19 March 1909, no. 124; Arthur Chamberlain interview with the *Manchester Guardian*, 8 Sept. 1903.

138. Strachey Papers S7/7/5 (Albert) Earl Grey to Strachey, 8 Feb. 1906.

139. Hugh Bell, 'The Iron and Steel Trade', in *British Industries under Free Trade*, ed. Harold Cox (London, 1904), p. 282. When Bell died in 1931 he left £260,000.

140. Pierce quoted in *The Case Against Protection*, summarized by E. Cozens Cooke (London, 1909), pp. 72–4; *The Times*, 5 Sept. 1908, 8b; [Lord Eversley], *Tariff Makers: Their Aims and Methods* (London, 1909), pp. 80–1.

141. Strachey Papers S/7/7/14, Strachey to Earl Grey, 4 March 1909.

142. *The Reformers' Year Book* (1906), p. 5.

143. *Manchester Guardian*, 20 July 1911.

144. *Hansard*, 4s, 102: 724–30 (7 Feb. 1902).

145. Spender MS 46,391, Cromer to J. A. Spender, 2 May 1908.

146. Elliot MS 19550, Address by the Earl of Cromer to the Unionist Free Trade Club, 29 June 1909. See also Robert Cecil Papers 51,159, Robert Cecil to Northcliffe, 3 Aug. 1909; Robert Cecil Papers 51,158, F. W. Lambton (Earl of Durham) to Robert Cecil, n.d. [July 1907].

147. *Fortnightly Review* (1911), p. 791.

148. Strachey Papers S/4/3/6, Strachey to Hugh Cecil, 30 Oct. 1909.

149. Strachey Papers S/5/5/16, Dicey to Strachey, 14 March 1910.

150. Strachey Papers S/4/14/14, Cox to Strachey, 19 Sept. 1922, 23 Nov. 1922, 5 Dec. 1922.

151. R. A. Rempel, *Unionists Divided: Arthur Balfour, Joseph Chamberlain and the Unionist Free Traders* (Newton Abbot, 1972).

152. *Liberal Monthly*, Apr. 1910, p. 11.

153. W. Thompson, *An Inquiry into the Principles of the Distribution of Wealth* (1824), quoted in M. Hilton 'The Legacy of Luxury: Moralities of Consumption Since the Eighteenth Century', *Journal of Consumer Culture*, 4/1 (2004), p. 104.

154. E. D. Rappaport, *Shopping for Pleasure: Women and the Making of London's West End* (Princeton, 2000); L. Nead, *Victorian Babylon: People, Streets and Images in Nineteenth-Century London* (New Haven and London, 2000); P. Bailey, *Popular Culture and Performance in the Victorian City* (Cambridge, 1998).

155. F. Trentmann (ed.), *The Making of the Consumer: Knowledge, Power and Identity in the Modern World* (Oxford and New York, 2005); M. Daunton and M. Hilton (eds), *The Politics of Consumption: Material Culture and Citizenship in Europe and America* (Oxford, 2001); C. Sussman, *Consuming Anxieties: Consumer Protest, Gender and British Slavery, 1713–1833* (Stanford, Calif., 2000).

156. F. Bastiat, *Sophismes Économiques* (Paris, 1846). Bastiat's *What is Seen and What is not Seen: or, Political Economy in One Lesson* appeared in newspapers and book form in 1859. In 1886 the fifth people's edition was published of his *Essays on Political Economy*. Famously, Bastiat's last recorded words on his deathbed in 1850 were ' "We must learn to look at everything from the point of view of the consumer." '

157. *The Gladstone Diaries*, ed. H. C. G. Matthew, vol. X (Oxford, 1990), 30 June 1883, p. 467.

158. See, for example, Liberal women's advice to canvassers, *Summary of Federation News*, Dec. 1905, p. 8.

159. Nonn, *Verbraucherprotest*. See also M.-E. Chessel, 'Women and the Ethics of Consumption in France at the Turn of Twentieth Century', in Trentmann, *Making of the Consumer*, pp. 81–98.

160. Hamilton diary, 48,679, 20 April 1902.

161. NA, T 168/52, Hamilton, 'The Question of New Taxation Discussed', 13 Dec. 1901. NA 30/60/44, Blain's Memorandum, n.d. but summer 1903.

162. Balfour MS 49,780, 'Note on the agreement in Treasury letter' by Ryder, 19 Feb. 1902; Balfour MS 49,779, Hewins, 'The Fallacy of regarding the fiscal controversy as a revival of the controversy of Free Trade v. Protection', 18 Feb. 1907.

163. As some contemporaries pointed out, F. W. Kolthammer, *Some Notes on the Incidence of Taxation on the Working-Class Family* (London, 1913).

164. Marshall MS (1911–12), formerly Box 6 (12), 'Leading features of protective duties'.

165. See the discussion below, pp. 154–61.

166. NA, T 168/54, 'The Conditions and Effects of "Dumping" ', 7 July 1903; L. G. Chiozza-Money, 'Through Preference to ... Protection' (Free Trade Union, Aug. 1903), 'The Dumping Bogey', ch. 13; Trentmann, 'Transformation of Fiscal Reform', pp. 1025–9.

167. *Quarterly Leaflet of WNLA*, no. 56 (July 1909), p. 10.

168. H. Cox, 'The Basis of Free Trade', p. 26, reprinted in the *Westminster Gazette*'s popular edition, *Westminster Popular*, no. 19 (1903).

169. Mond in *British Industries under Free Trade* (1904), ed. Cox, p. 222.

170. 22 March 1910, *Free Trader*, p. 135.

171. L. Maxse, 'Cobden and Cobdenism', in *The National Review*, vol. 43 (March–Aug. 1904), p. 865.

172. Report of the Annual Meeting of the National Reform Union, 12 March 1902 (in Harcourt MS 106–13), quoted at p. 23.

173. W. S. Churchill, *For Free Trade* (London, 1906), p. 61.

174. Lawrence, *Speaking for the People*, p. 106–7.

175. *Glasgow Evening News*, 26 Dec. 1903, p. 2.

176. *South Wales Daily News*, 15 Jan. 1910, p. 3.

177. Campbell-Bannerman MS 41, 211, Campbell-Bannerman to Bryce, 7 Dec. 1903.

178. J. A. Hobson, *Work and Wealth: A Human Valuation* (London, 1914), pp. 133–4.

179. Hobson, *Work and Wealth*, pp. 155 ff.

180. J. A. Hobson, *Evolution of Modern Capitalism* (1897 edn), pp. 380 and 368 ff. for the following.

181. J. A. Hobson, *The New Protectionism* (London, 1916), pp. 6–7.

182. Mark Sykes to Bonar Law, 17 Dec. 1912, Bonar Law MS 28/1/48.

2. BREAD AND CIRCUSES

1. A. Mond, introduction to W. E. Downing, *Two Great Tariff Trials of 1912* (London, n.d. 1912), p. 4.

2. *The Times*, 21 Jan. 1910, p. 10.

3. *The Free Trader*, 15 Jan. 1910, p. 34.

4. For this and the following: *The South Bucks Free Press, Wycombe, Maidenhead, and Marlow Journal*, 28 Jan. 1910, pp. 2–4, 4 Feb. 1910, p. 5.; *The Times*, 22 Jan. 1910, p. 7; *Daily Mail*, 22 Jan. 1910, p. 7; *The Daily Telegraph*, 24 Jan. 1910, p. 14.

5. *The South Bucks Free Press*, 28 Jan. 1910, p. 3–4, 4 Feb. 1910, p. 6, 11 Feb. 1910, p. 2; *Daily Telegraph*, 21 Jan. 1910, p. 8.

6. *The Droitwich Guardian*, 5, 12, 19 Feb. 1910.

7. D. A. Irwin, *Against the Tide: An Intellectual History of Free Trade* (Princeton, NJ, 1996); J. Bhagwati, *Protectionism* (Cambridge, Mass., 1989).

8. H. C. G. Matthew, 'Rhetoric and Politics in Great Britain, 1860–1950', in P. J. Waller (ed.) *Politics and Social Change in Modern Britain: Essays Presented to A. F. Thompson* (Brighton, 1987), pp. 34–58. As Peter Clarke has shrewdly observed: 'Intolerance at elections was the contempt of the strong for the weak, and pleas for fair play and free speech were advertisements of weakness', *Lancashire and the New Liberalism* (Cambridge, 1971), p. 143.

9. Hawtrey Papers, Churchill College, Cambridge, HTRY 6/5/1 (1913).

10. A. Fitzroy, *Memoirs*, Vol. I (London, 1925), 31 July 1903, p. 144.

11. *Labour Gazette*, Jan. 1912. Unemployment in the engineering trades was 11.6% in 1909.

12. J. Rose, *The Intellectual Life of the British Working Classes* (New Haven, CT, 2002), ch. 10.

13. *The Liberal Agent*, 34 (Oct. 1903), p. 104. *Sheffield Daily Telegraph*, 12 Jan. 1910, p. 5. One enterprising supporter even proposed loaf-shaped gas balloons, an idea not taken up by the National Liberal Federation; J. A. Spender, *Sir Robert Hudson: A Memoir* (London, 1930), p. 74.

14. Petersen, *Bread and the British Economy*, pp. 30–1.

15. Pickering and Tyrrell, *The People's Bread*, pp. 9, 140, 201–2.

16. University of Bristol Special Collections, DM 1877.

17. Political postcard, private collection.

18. NA, COPY 1/227 (2), 1905. With thanks to Hugh Alexander at the National Archives.

19. *Illustrated London News*, 20 Jan. 1906, p. 90.

20. *Daily Chronicle*, 29 Nov. 1910, p. 3.

21. 'Fiscal Economy', Valentine series; private collection.

22. Conservative party postcard, no. 72 P.C.; private collection. See also Tariff Reformers' use of the royal crown and monogram alongside the two loaves in their posters, recalled by Francis W. Soutter, *Fights for Freedom: The Story of My Life* (London, 1925), pp. 39 ff.

23. 'International Exchange', National Film and Television Archive (London), 602401A; D. Gifford, 'Fitz: The Old Man of the Screen', in *All Our Yesterdays: 90 Years of British Cinema*, ed. C. Barr (London, 1986), p. 314; thanks to Luke McKernan and Simon Brown for information on Fitzhamon.

24. *Tariff Reform Illustrated* (London, 1904), pp. 4, 18.

25. *The People*, Topical Cartoons, by Harry Furniss; private collection. A. Opyrchal, *Harry Furniss 1854–1925: Confessions of a Caricaturist* (National Portrait Gallery, 1983).

26. Huskinson had initially developed this image in the winter of 1907–8 showing Campbell-Bannerman; *The Liberal Monthly*, Feb. 1908, p. 22.

27. For a view that food prices were a non-ideological issue which enabled Conservatives to win more rural votes, see P. Lynch, *The Liberal Party in Rural England 1885–1910* (Oxford, 2001), pp. 12, 191.

28. Harcourt MS 668, Lewis Harcourt to William Harcourt, 13 Dec. 1903.

29. *Manchester Guardian*, 25 July 1903; see also W. H. Dawson, 'An Object-Lesson from Germany', in *Labour and Protection* (1903), ed. Massingham, pp. 288–9.

30. BLPES, Coll. Misc. 246.

31. Free Trade Union, *General Leaflets*, no. 154, 11 March 1909; *The Free Trader*, 15 Feb. 1910, pp. 77, 80; Free Trade Union, *Tales of the Tariff Trippers: An Exposure of the Tariff Reform Tours in Germany* (London, 1910), pp. 12, 55; W. E. Downing, *Two Great Tariff Trials of 1912* (1912), pp. 56–7. *Illustrated London News*, 22 Jan. 1910, p. 125; *The Times*, 23 Nov. 1912, p. 9–10. For a picture of a French horsemeat butcher, see Free Trade Union, *Special Election Leaflets, Illustrated* (London, 1909), no. 300.

32. *The Times*, 21 Jan. 1910, p. 10.

33. *Daily Mail*, 4 Jan. 1910, p. 8.

34. *Daily Record and Mail*, 15 Jan. 1910, p. 7; *The Free Trader*, 17 Nov. 1910, p. 19; *Somerset and Wilts Journal*, 4 Nov. 1910, p. 5.

35. 'The Humour of It. A Personal Narrative of a Tripper', by Edward Baker, in Free Trade Union, *Tales of the Tariff Trippers* (London, 1910), p. 18; M. Oldroyd, *A Tariff Reform Trip* (London, 1909).

36. *Tariff-ridden Germany: A Visit of Enquiry by J. Ramsay MacDonald, M.P. Reprinted from and published by the Daily News* (London, 1910), pp. 5–6.

37. Bonar Law at Anerley, *The Times* 11 Jan. 1910, 10 d.

38. *Daily Telegraph*, 18 Jan. 1910, p. 7 and 6 Jan. 1910, p. 4; *South Wales Daily Post*, 15 Jan. 1910, p. 3 (reporting *The Lancet*); *Daily Mail*, 12 Jan. 1910, p. 7; *Sheffield Daily Telegraph*, 21 Jan. 1910, p. 5.

39. *Cost of Living in German Towns: Report of an Inquiry by the Board of Trade into Working Class Rents, Housing and Retail Prices*, Cd. 4032 (1908), pp. 379, 437–8. See also the Tariff Reformer J. Ellis Barker in *South Wales Daily Post*, 11 Jan. 1910, p. 6 and *Daily Telegraph*, 7 Jan. 1910, p. 15. W. J. Ashley, *The Progress of the German Working Classes in the Last Quarter of a Century* (London, 1904), pp. 155–61; T. Lindenberger, 'Die Fleischrevolte am Wedding' and C. Nonn, 'Fleischteuerungsprotest und Parteipolitik im Rheinland und im Reich 1905–14', in M. Gailus and H. Volkmann (eds), *Der Kampf um das Tägliche Brot: Nahrungsmangel, Versorgungspolitik und Protest, 1770–1990* (Opladen, 1994), pp. 282–304, 305–15; U. Spiekermann, 'Das Andere verdauen: Begegnungen von Ernährungskulturen', in U. Spiekermann and G. U. Schönberger (eds), *Ernährung in Grenzsituationen* (Berlin, 2002), p. 93.

40. Tariff Commission Papers, TC8 2/18 B 289, R. C. Baynes to P. Hughes, 31 Dec. 1909.

41. C. Lansbury, *The Old Brown Dog: Women, Workers, and Vivisection in Edwardian England* (Madison, 1985); H. Ritvo, *The Platypus and the Mermaid and other Figments of the Classifying Imagination* (Cambridge, Mass., 1997).

42. As John Burns noted in the Commons, citing the medical officer of health for the London County Council, *Hansard*, 5s, 16: 870 (11 April 1910).

43. NA, BT 55/39, I. & S. 2, parts 4–5, 11 Jan. 1917.

44. Free Trade Union, *Leaflets* (London, 1907–10), no. 156 (16 March 1909), citing J. B. Wilson, who had defected from the Batley deputation to Germany. See also *Daily News*, 12 June 1905.

45. K. O. Morgan, 'Lloyd George and Germany', *The Historical Journal*, 39/3 (1996), pp. 755–66.

46. *Western Daily Mercury*, 10 Jan. 1910.

47. He continued: 'an attempt was now being made to show that black bread and horseflesh were very wholesome. (Laughter). Their opponents were preparing the people for Protection already. (Cheers.)', at Wolverhampton, *The Times,* 13 Jan. 1910, p. 8. To some in the City, the radical campaign was

'ridiculous' and reinforced a dislike of Lloyd George. Leopold Rothschild found Lloyd George particularly 'offensive about German sausages' and had little doubt that 'taken as a whole the English food is worse prepared certainly than the French or German'. Rothschild Archives (London), RAL XI/130A/4, 13 Jan. 1910.

48. Lloyd George Papers, A/13/1/4, 30 Jan. 1905. See also *North Wales Observer*, 2 Oct. 1903.

49. *The Free Trader* explained it away as Campbell-Bannerman having misread Booth, 17 Nov. 1910, p. 23.

50. *The Free Trader*, July 1910, pp. 188 ff., and Aug. 1910, p. 236.

51. The Tariff Reformer Rowland Hunt won with a majority of 970; the vacancy was caused by the death of the Liberal Unionist MP R. J. Moore, who had been unopposed in the previous elections. For Liberal reactions, *The Liberal Agent*, Jan. 1904, no. 35, p. 130; Herbert Gladstone MS 46,021, 30 Dec. 1903.

52. *The Standard*, 29 March 1910, p. 5.

53. *The Free Trader*, 15 Feb. 1910, p. 75.

54. *Liberal Year Book for 1911* (London, 1911), p. 18; National Liberal Federation, *Annual Report and Speeches* (1910), pp. 17–18.

55. Gladstone to Robert Hudson, 2 Jan. 1904, Herbert Gladstone MS 46,021.

56. *Daily News*, 19 Dec. 1903, p. 10; Sheridan Jones to Churchill, 29 Dec. 1903, Churchill Papers, Char 2/10. He later changed the name to the Free Trade Protection Association; Herbert Gladstone MS 46,485, diary entry 8 March 1904. See also correspondence between Una Birch and Arthur Elliot, 1, 2, 4 Jan. 1904 and Madeleine Elliot to Una Birch 28 Dec. 1905; Elliot MSS 19,493 and 19,494.

57. Herbert Gladstone to Campbell-Bannerman, 1 June 1903, Campbell-Bannerman MS 41,216. Harold Cox to Gladstone, 14 Dec. 1903, Herbert Gladstone MS 46,061; Lord Welby to Gladstone, 15 Dec. 1903 and 10 June 1904, Herbert Gladstone MS 46,061.

58. L.T. Hobhouse to Gladstone n.d. [July 1903] and Gladstone to J. B. Robinson, 23 July 1903, Herbert Gladstone MS 46,060; Hobhouse to Gladstone, 30 Nov. 1903, Herbert Gladstone MS 46,061.

59. Hobhouse to Gladstone, 30 Oct. 1903, Herbert Gladstone MS 46,061.

60. Pearson Papers, Science Museum Library, London, Ledgers 5/2 and 5/3, Cashbook 5/4 and 5/5; Lewis Harcourt to Gladstone, 24 July 1903, Herbert Gladstone MS 45,997; John Brunner to Gladstone, 19 Dec. 1905, Herbert Gladstone MS 46,063.

61. Wallace Carter, 'Tariff Reform Campaign', encl. in Wallace Carter to Robert Cecil, 5 March 1908, Robert Cecil MS 51158.

62. *The Free Trader*, 15 Feb. 1910, p. 65.

63. Churchill Papers, Char 2/43, 2/44, 2/53, 2/54, 2/61.

64. Wallace Carter, 'Tariff Reform Campaign', Robert Cecil MS 51,158.

65. *Stirling Saturday Observer*, 22 Jan. 1910, p. 5. See also *The Free Trader*, 15 Jan. 1910, p. 34.

66. Churchill Papers, Char 2/54, Caird to Churchill, 15 Feb. 1911, and, similarly, 6 Jan. 1911.

67. Churchill Papers, Char 2/44, Carter to Caird, 28 June 1910. Bonar Law MS 18/7/196 for the accounts given by chartered accountants in 1911. See also F. Coetzee, *For Party or Country: Nationalism and the Dilemmas of Popular Conservatism in Edwardian England* (Oxford, 1990), pp. 144–5.

68. Churchill Papers, Char 2/54, Report to Winston Churchill, Jan. 1911. *The Free Trader*, 15 Feb. 1910, p. 65; *The Times*, 7 April 1911, p. 6; K. Grant, 'Christian Critics of Empire: Missionaries, Lantern Lectures and the Congo Reform Campaign in Britain', *Journal of Imperial and Commonwealth History*, 29/2 (2001), pp. 22–58; Pickering and Tyrrell, *People's Bread*, pp. 20, 199.

69. Churchill Papers, Char 2/54, Wallace Carter, National Free Trade Lectures, Report to Winston Churchill, Jan. 1911, pp. 5–7.

70. *The Free Trader*, June 1910, pp. 172 ff., July 1910, pp. 203 ff., Aug. 1910, 234–5.

71. Soutter, *Fights for Freedom*, p. 106.

72. *Summary of Federation News*, IV, no 8, 10 Feb. 1906, p. 5.

73. University of Bristol Special Collections, 24th Annual Report of the Executive Committee of the Women's Liberal Federation (9 May 1911), p. 13.

74. *The Free Trader*, Aug. 1910, p. 235.

75. Soutter, *Fights for Freedom*, p. 108.

76. *Summary of Federation News*, IV, no 8, 10 Feb. 1906, p. 10.

77. *Quarterly Leaflet of WNLA*, July 1903, p. 11.

78. Ibid. Aug. 1910, p. 17.

79. *The Free Trader*, May 1910, p.133, and June 1910, p.174.

80. Ibid., May 1910, p. 133.

81. Ibid. 15 Sept. 1910, p. 23, and 19 Jan. 1911, p. 24.

82. Churchill Papers, Char 2/54, Crawshay-Williams to Churchill, 10 Aug. 1911.

83. Rose, *Intellectual Life of the British Working Classes*, p. 274.

84. *The Lancaster Guardian*, 27 Aug. 1910, p. 5.

85. Churchill Papers, Char 2/44, Wallace Carter to Churchill, 11 April 1910.

86. Caird liked the idea so much that he wanted to see the seaside lecture campaign doubled, Churchill Papers, Char 2/44, Caird to Churchill on 19 Aug. 1910.

87. *A Liberal Chronicle: Journals and Papers of J. A. Pease, 1st Lord Gainford, 1908–1910*, eds. C. Hazlehurst and C. Woodland (London, 1993), pp. 32, 248.

88. Data based on Churchill Papers, Char 2/44, Wallace Carter to Churchill, 13 July 1910, 'Seaside Campaign', and *The Free Trader*, 15 Sept. 1910, pp. 27–9, 20 Oct. 1910, pp. 30–1. The map offers a conservative estimate of audiences' size; references to 'more than a hundred meetings', for example, have been counted and mapped as one hundred.

89. *The Lancaster Guardian*, 27 Aug. 1910, pp. 5–6; *The Free Trader*, 20 Oct. 1910, p. 31.

90. *The Lancaster Guardian*, 27 Aug. 1910, p. 5.
91. Churchill Papers, Char 2/44, Wallace Carter to Churchill, 11 April 1910.
92. *The Free Trader*, 20 Oct. 1910, p. 29, and 15 Sept. 1910 p. 28. The 160 meetings in Blackpool and the Isle of Man had an estimated audience of 103,500, or well over 600 people per meeting; Churchill Papers, Char 2/44, Wallace Carter to Churchill, 24 April 1910.
93. *The Free Trader*, 20 Oct. 1910, p. 29.
94. Wallas, quoted in *The Liberal Agent*, 12 (Jan. 1910), pp. 139, 142, 146.
95. *The Liberal Agent*, 13/63 (Jan. 1911), pp. 122 ff.
96. *The Free Trader*, 20 Oct. 1910, p. 30.
97. Ibid. 15 Sept. 1910, p. 28, and 20 Oct. 1910, p. 28.
98. *The Lancaster Guardian*, 27 Aug. 1910, p. 6.
99. *The Free Trader*, 15 Sept. 1910, p. 28.
100. Ibid., 20 Oct. 1910, p. 29.
101. *The Lancaster Guardian*, 27 Aug. 1910, p. 5. See also Crawshay-Williams to Churchill, 10 Aug. 1911, Churchill Papers, Char 2/54.
102. J. Vernon, *Politics and the People: A Study in English Political Culture, c. 1815–1867* (Cambridge, 1993).
103. G. E. Harrison in *The Liberal Agent*, 12/60 (April 1910), pp. 179 ff. For the continued importance of open meetings, disruption and physical clashes, see now also J. Lawrence, 'The Transformation of British Public Politics after the First World War', *Past and Present*, 190 (2006), pp. 185–216.
104. J. C. Skinner in *The Liberal Agent* 11/56 (April 1909), p. 142. See further Kathryn Rix, 'The party agent and English electoral culture, 1880–1906' (unpubl. Ph.D. thesis, University of Cambridge, 2001).
105. *The Liberal Agent* 11/56 (April 1909), pp. 155–9.
106. *Daily Mail*, 5 Jan. 1910.
107. People's History Museum, Manchester, Tariff Reform League, Pamphlet Series, n.d. [c.1908–9], p. 23.
108. A.W. Coats, 'Political Economy and the Tariff Reform Campaign of 1903', *Journal of Law and Economics* 11 (April 1968), pp. 181–229.
109. *The Times*, 10 March 1909, p. 12 c.
110. Soutter, *Fights for Freedom*, p. 29; T. Palmer Newbould, *Pages From a Life of Strife, Being Some Recollections of William Henry Chadwick* (London, 1910).
111. *Daily Record and Mail*, 15 Jan. 1910, p. 7. See also the 82 year-old Ralph Ashton's recollections on the horrors of the 1840s, *Daily Chronicle*, 6 Dec. 1910, p. 6.
112. Alfred Henry (no. 63), born 1890, p. 20; UK Data Archive, Thompson and Lummis, Family Life and Work Experience Before 1918.
113. Churchill Papers, Char 2/44, Wallace Carter to Churchill, n.d., March 1910, second memo on Lecture Scheme, and the report in Char 2/44, Wallace Carter to Churchill, 13 July 1910.

114. *The Free Trader*, Aug. 1910, p. 232. Mr Osborn gave lectures on 'What I saw in Protectionist Germany', Char 2/44, report for July, in Wallace Carter to Churchill, 2 Aug. 1910.

115. For the horse-drawn van, see K. Rix, ' "Go out into the Highways and the Hedges" ', the Diary of Michael Sykes, *Parliamentary History*, 20/2 (2001), pp. 209–31.

116. *Daily Telegraph*, 4 Jan. 1910, p. 11.

117. Ibid., 14 Jan. 1910, p. 12.

118. Ibid., 4 Jan. 1910, p. 11; 5 Jan. 1910, p. 11; 6 Jan. 1910, p. 12; 7 Jan. 1910, p. 11.

119. Churchill Papers, Char 2/44, Churchill to Caird 28 March 1910 and Wallace Carter to Churchill, 21 March 1910.

120. *Daily Telegraph*, 6 Jan. 1910, p. 11.

121. *Leeds Mercury*, 15 Jan. 1910, p. 6. *The Free Trader*, 15 Feb. 1910, pp. 79–80.

122. Churchill Papers, Char 2/44, Wallace Carter to Churchill, 21 March 1910; Caird to Churchill, 30 March 1910; Churchill to Caird, 28 March 1910. For the January 1910 election, Caird had provided funds specifically to cover all urban centres with Free Trade posters, amounting to an enormous total of 264,000 double crown units, 'an awful lot of money to spend on fireworks' Churchill told Asquith on 21 December 1909, but necessary to win the battle of 'mural literature'; Char 2/43.

123. *Leeds Mercury*, 14 Jan. 1910, p. 3.

124. *The Liberal Monthly*, July 1908, p. 11; Free Trade Union leaflet no. 111 'Look Before You Leap!'

125. *Report of an enquiry by the Board of Trade into working class rents, housing and retail prices, together with the rates of wages in certain occupations in the principal industrial towns of the United States of America (1911)*, Cd. 5609, lxxxviii.

126. *Leaflets Issued by the Free Trade Union* (London, 1907–10), 'What Does Protection Mean in America?'; these images were reprinted in many provincial newspapers, e.g. *The Cambria Daily Leader*, 8 Jan. 1910, p. 7.

127. Churchill Papers, Char 2/54, Dowding's memo to Wallace Carter, 27 April 1911.

128. The most recent discussion is Kaiser, 'Free Trade at World Exhibitions'. See also P. H. Hoffenberg, *An Empire on Display: English, Indian, and Australian Exhibitions from the Crystal Palace to the Great War* (Berkeley, CA, 2001).

129. Churchill Papers, Char 2/44, Wallace Carter to Churchill, 21 March 1910; *The Liberal Monthly*, May 1909; p. 6.

130. *Daily Telegraph*, 13 Jan. 1910, p. 5; Churchill Papers, Char 2/54, Report to Churchill, Jan. 1911, p. 40.

131. Churchill Papers, Char 2/54, 'Extracts From Letters Respecting the National Free Trade Exhibition', p. 37, encl. in report to Churchill, Jan. 1911.

132. A few entertainments mixed cinematograph pictures with songs, such as the Tariff Reform shows by Mr and Mrs Pyne, *The Optical Lantern and Cinematograph Journal*, vol. I (March 1905), p. 98.

133. *The Optical Lantern and Cinematograph Journal*, March 1906, p. 91, and Dec. 1906, p. 31.

134. *Summary of Federation News*, Nov. 1903, p. 11.

135. *The Liberal Agent* 32 (April 1903), p. 185.

136. Churchill Papers, Char 2/54, report to Churchill, Jan. 1911, p. 31.

137. V. Toulmin and S. Popple, *Visual Delights: Essays on the Popular and Projected Image in the 19th Century* (Trowbridge, 2000); L. Nead, 'Velocities of the Image c. 1900', *Art History*, 27/5 (2004), pp. 745–69.

138. M. Pugh, *The Tories and the People*, 1880–1935 (Oxford, 1985), pp. 90–1.

139. *The Liberal Agent*, 5/32 (April 1903), p. 182.

140. Ibid., Oct. 1903 no. 34, pp. 79–82.

141. *The Liberal Monthly*, Nov. 1909, p. 11; *Picture Politics*, Dec. 1910, p. 16.

142. Rivers in *The Liberal Agent* 11/56 (April 1909), p. 150. Agents, like Rivers, often worked the lantern to accompany female speakers, for example, in the national school at Horsted Keynes, where he showed Gould's 'amusing' slides to 'one of the largest audiences ever seen there', *Summary of Federation News*, Jan. 1905, p. 15.

143. *The Liberal Agent*, 5/32 (April 1903), p. 183.

144. L. Tickner, *The Spectacle of Women: Imagery of the Suffrage Campaign, 1907–1914* (London, 1987), ch. 2–3.

145. *The Liberal Agent*, 5/33 (July 1903), p. 79.

146. Churchill interview with *The Free Trader*, May 1910, p. 120.

147. *The Free Trader*, 15 Jan. 1910, p. 34; Carter to Churchill n.d. [March 1910], in Char 23/44; also Char 2/54, p. 31.

148. *Quarterly Leaflet of WNLA*, Jan. 1905, p. 20 (Hoole and Newton). *Summary of Federation News*, Oct. 1903, p. 11 (Huddersfield); Feb. 1905, p. 15 (Royston).

149. Churchill Papers, Char 2/44, Churchill to Caird, 22 Feb. 1910.

150. *The Free Trader*, 15 Feb. 1910, p. 80; see also p. 77 for a van in Sunderland.

151. Churchill Papers, Char 2/54, encl. in final report, Jan. 1911.

152. T. Russell (ed.), *Advertising and Publicity* (London, 1911), p. 26; before becoming president of the society of advertisement consultants, Russell had been the advertising manager of *The Times*.

153. *The Liberal Agent*, 7/39 (Jan. 1905), pp. 128–32.

154. Ibid., 36 (April 1904), p. 202, and 61 (July 1910), pp. 24 ff; *Daily Mail*, 4 Jan. 1910 p. 10; Clarke, *Lancashire and the New Liberalism*, pp. 131 ff; N. Blewett, *The Peers, the Parties and the People: The General Elections of 1910* (London, 1972), pp. 312 ff.

155. W. S. Rogers, *A Book of the Poster, Illustrated with Examples of the Work of the Principal Poster Artists of the World* (London, 1901), pp. 8, 40.

156. *Daily Graphic*, 17 Dec. 1909, p. 3.

157. J. Hassall, 'Posters', in Russell, (ed.), *Advertising and Publicity* (London, 1911), p. 118, emphases in original.

158. Greaster Manchester County Record Office, Doc. Phography Archive, Ref. 802/155b.

159. *Tariff Reform League Leaflets*, 'A Lesson in "Free Trade." '; *The Times*, 1 March 1909, p. 12. See also *The Advertising World*, Nov. 1911, p. 584; with thanks to Stefan Schwarzkopf for this reference.

160. *The Cambria Daily Leader*, 13 Jan. 1910.

161. House of Commons, 23 Feb. 1910.

162. *Daily Chronicle*, 22 Nov. 1910, p. 7, reproducing the image from *Truth*'s Christmas special.

163. Churchill Papers, Char 2/54, from message of the agent in Cambridge.

164. *Daily Record and Mail*, 5 Jan. 1910, p. 7.

165. *The Free Trader*, 15 Feb. 1910, pp. 84–5.

166. *Western Daily Mercury*, 4 Jan. 1910, p. 6.

167. *The Liberal Monthly*, Dec. 1910, p. 3.

168. *The Liberal Agent*, 13/63 (Jan. 1911), p. 127. For a case in Glasgow, see *Evening Citizen*, 26 Nov. 1910, p. 9.

169. *The Kinematograph and Lantern Weekly*, 2 April 1908, p. 357.

170. *Daily Chronicle*, 7 Dec. 1910, p. 5.

171. *The Optical Lantern and Cintematograph Journal*, 2 (Feb. 1906), p. 68.

172. Churchill Papers, Char 2/54, Carter report to Churchill. F. W. S. Craig, *British Parliamentary Election Results, 1885–1918* (London, 1974), pp. 99, 279, 380. H. Pelling, *Social Geography of British Elections, 1885–1910* (London, 1967), pp. 65, 113.

173. Churchill Papers, Char 2/54, Carter report to Churchill, Jan. 1911, p. 18.

174. J. Fraser, 'Propaganda on the Picture Postcard', in *Oxford Art Journal*, 3 (1980), pp. 39–54; R. Carline, *Pictures in the Post* (London, 1971), pp. 92–3; Tickner, *Spectacle of Women*, p. 50.

175. 'BB' to Miss S. C. Evans, Tenby [Dyfed], 10 May 1906; in possession of the author.

3. Uneasy Globalizers

1. At Birmingham, *The Times*, 17 May 1902, p. 12.

2. W. S. Churchill, *For Free Trade: A Collection of Speeches* (London, 1906), pp. 72–3.

3. National Liberal Federation, *Annual Report and Speeches* (1909), p. 96.

4. *Justice*, 4 June 1904, p. 1.

5. P. Snowden, 'An Imperial Zollverein', *The Platform*, no.103, 20 June 1903, repr. in *I.L.P. News*.

6. R. J. S. Hoffman, *Great Britain and the German Trade Rivalry 1875–1914* (Philadelphia, 1933); B. H. Brown, *The Tariff Reform Movement in Great Britain,*

1881–1895 (New York, 1943); P. M. Kennedy, *The Rise of Anglo-German Antagonism, 1860–1914* (London, 1980).

7. W. Mock, *Imperiale Herrschaft und nationales Interesse: 'Constructive Imperialism' oder Freihandel in Grossbritannien vor dem Ersten Weltkrieg* (Stuttgart, 1982), p. 52.

8. Ibid.; E. H. H. Green, *The Crisis of Conservatism: The Politics, Economics and Ideology of the British Conservative Party, 1880–1914* (London, 1995).

9. *Mr. Chamberlain's Speeches* (New York, 1914), ed. C. W. Boyd, p. 134.

10. Ibid., p. 137.

11. Salisbury had to acknowledge in 1891 that they had been unable to find out 'the species of reasoning' behind these pledges, cit. in H. Birchenough, 'England's Opportunity: Germany or Canada', *The Nineteenth Century*, 245 (July 1897), p. 4.

12. E. H. H. Green, 'The Political Economy of Empire, 1880–1914', in *The Oxford History of the British Empire: The Nineteenth Century*, ed. Andrew Porter (Oxford, 1999), p. 363.

13. An exception was wool textiles, which jumped from $6 million in 1897 to $10 million in 1901. Overall, the share of goods from Britain declined, in spite of preference, from 26% in 1900 to 21% of Canada's imports; Edward Porritt, *Sixty Years of Protection in Canada, 1846–1907* (London, 1908), ch. 6; S. B. Saul, *Studies in British Overseas Trade 1870–1914* (Liverpool, 1960), pp. 182–3.

14. E. E. Williams, 'The Sacrifice of Canada', *The National Review*, 36 (Sept. 1900), 430–9.

15. Birchenough, 'England's Opportunity', p. 5; compare H. Birchenough, 'Do Foreign Annexations Injure British Trade?', *Nineteenth Century*, 41 (1897), pp. 993–1004.

16. NA, FO 83/1803, 8–9 May 1901.

17. Birchenough, 'England's Opportunity', pp. 4, 7.

18. John Gallagher and Ronald Robinson, 'The Imperialism of Free Trade', *Economic History Review*, 2nd ser., 6 (1953), pp. 1–15.

19. R. J. Moore, 'Imperialism and "Free Trade" Policy in India, 1853–4', *The Economic History Review*, 17/1 (1964), pp. 135–45.

20. D. Todd, 'John Bowring and the Global Dissemination of Free Trade', *Historical Journal*, 51/2 (2008), 373–397.

21. Gallagher and Robinson, 'Imperialism of Free Trade', p. 11.

22. D. C. M. Platt, 'Further Objections to an "Imperialism of Free Trade", 1830–1860', *Economic History Review*, 2nd ser., 26 (1973), pp. 77–91.

23. V. de Grazia, *Irresistible Empire: America's Advance through 20th-Century Europe* (Cambridge, Mass., 2005).

24. D. C. M. Platt, *Finance, Trade, and Politics in British Foreign Policy, 1815–1914* (Oxford, 1968), pp. 89 ff. See also O'Brien and Pigman, 'Free Trade, British Hegemony and the International Economic Order'.

25. NA, FO 371/257, 'Memorandum on the Present State of British Relations with France and Germany', 1 Jan. 1907, pp. 10–13.
26. D. N. McCloskey, *Enterprise and Trade in Victorian Britain: Essays in Historical Economics* (London, 1981), ch. 8; D. A. Irwin, 'Welfare Effects of British Free Trade: Debate and Evidence from the 1840s', *Journal of Political Economy* 96 (1988), pp. 1142–64.
27. P. T. Marsh, *Bargaining on Europe: Britain and the First Common Market, 1860–1892* (New Haven, CT, 1999).
28. NA, CO 323/486, CO 41125, 12 Nov. 1903.
29. NA, FO 881/7426, 'Questions in the Commercial Department', 12 Nov. 1900.
30. Ibid.
31. NA, T 168/54, Blain memorandum, Sept. 1903.
32. 'Questions in the Commercial Department', pp. 1–2.
33. NA T 1/9779A/1178: Pittar memo, 16 Jan. 1901, encl. in undersecretary of state for foreign affairs to secretary of Treasury, 9 Jan. 1902.
34. NA 30/60/36, Lansdowne, cabinet memo, 6 March 1903, p. 3.
35. NA 30/60/36, cabinet memo, 6 March 1903, p. 4.
36. NA, BT 12/45, Hopwood to Foreign Office, 18 July 1903.
37. Britain was also excluded from the advantages granted by the United States in preferential agreements with France, Germany, and Italy.
38. NA, BT 12/45, Llewellyn Smith to Foreign Office, 2 Feb. 1904.
39. NA, FO 811/8566, 'Memorandum respecting the Negotiation of Tariff Treaties with Foreign Powers', 19 Oct. 1903.
40. NA, T1/10569A, interdepartmental conference at Board of Trade, 11 Dec. 1905.
41. NA, T1/10569A, Hamilton to Asquith, 9 Feb. 1906.
42. H. Llewellyn Smith, *The Board of Trade* (London, 1928), pp. 68–9.
43. NA, BT 12/42, Bateman to ACC 11 April 1900, and Bateman to Foreign Office, 1 May 1900.
44. NA, CO 323/475, CIC report and ACC memorial of 4 Oct. 1901; NA, FO 881/7937, Board of Trade to Foreign Office, 8 July 1901, and Herbert Hughes 7 Feb. 1901. See also Edwin P. Jones (secretary of the Swansea Chamber) 22 Jan. 1901. FO 881/8132, E. H. Middlebrook (sec. of the Morley Chamber), to Lansdowne 30 Jan. 1902.
45. NA, FO 192/167, 'Report of the commercial intelligence committee: report to the board of trade on the new Swiss and Roumanian, and the proposed new Dutch customs tariffs', 28 July 1904.
46. NA, CO 323/475, 'Summary of Replies' (CIC report), pp. 3, 22.
47. *The Chamber of Commerce Journal*, 22/108 (April 1903), p. 86.
48. NA, BT 12/45, John Brennan and John Kinning to Llewellyn Smith, 2 Feb. 1904.
49. M. Daunton, ' "Gentlemanly Capitalism" and British Industry 1820–1914', *Past and Present* 122 (1989), pp. 119–58; A. C. Howe, 'Free Trade and the City

of London, c.1820–1870', *History* 77 (1992), pp. 391–410; F. Trentmann, 'The Transformation of Fiscal Reform: Reciprocity, Modernization, and the Fiscal Debate within the Business Community in Early Twentieth-Century Britain', *Historical Journal*, 39/4 (1996), pp. 1005–48; A. J. Marrison, *British Business and Protection, 1903–32* (Oxford, 1996). For an older view, see P. J. Cain and A. G. Hopkins, 'Gentlemanly Capitalism and British Expansion Overseas. II. New Imperialism, 1850–1945', *Economic History Review* 45 (1987), pp. 1–26.

50. NA, CO 323/477, W. H. Cooke (Chamber of Shipping) to FO, 31 May 1902.

51. P. Clarke, 'The End of Laissez Faire and the Politics of Cotton', *Historical Journal* 15 (1972), pp. 493–512. One such cotton manufacturer who supported fiscal reform as a way of responding to dumping and the loss of markets was Baynes from Blackburn; see *Rossendale Free Press*, 17 June 1905.

52. *Chamber of Commerce Journal*, 22/108 (April 1903), p. 80.

53. London Chamber of Commerce Archives, MS 16,459, III, 1, council minutes, 8 Oct. 1903.

54. Joseph Chamberlain to Austen Chamberlain, 12 Nov. 1904, in Julian Amery, *The Life of Joseph Chamberlain*, Vol. 4, *1901–1903* (London, 1951), p. 644.

55. Gollin, *Balfour's Burden*.

56. NA 30/60/36, Foreign Office memo on 'Retaliation', 22 May 1901. 'Memorandum prepared in the Board of Trade for the Cabinet', section VII: 'The export policy of trusts in certain foreign countries', in Austen Chamberlain Papers, Birmingham, AC 17/2/6.

57. NA 30/60/44, Gerald Balfour 'Methods of Fiscal Reform', confidential, 6 Jan. 1904.

58. This dual aim would not have been easy to achieve, because Free Trade had left the state without the necessary statistical knowledge. Customs data recorded the type of goods, not where they came from. This suited the purpose of raising revenue but limited the scope for retaliation.

59. NA, CO 323/485, Lascelles to Lansdowne, 23 April 1903.

60. *Hansard*, 4s, 123: 878 (15 June 1903).

61. NA, CO 323/486, Lansdowne to Lascelles, 21 Oct. 1903.

62. NA 30/60/44, Lansdowne memo, 5 Nov. 1903.

63. Bundesarchiv Potsdam, 09.01.AA/9350, Metternich memo to Bülow, 24 Nov. 1903.

64. NA 30/60/44, Gerald Balfour, 'Notes on Lord Lansdowne's Memorandum of 4 November 1903'.

65. Ph. G. Chalmin, 'The Important Trends in Sugar Diplomacy before 1914', in B. Albert and A. Graves (eds), *Crisis and Change in the International Sugar Economy, 1860–1914* (Norwich and Edinburgh: ISC Press, 1984), pp. 9–19.

66. S. Mintz, *Sweetness and Power: The Place of Sugar in Modern History* (New York, 1985), p. 195.

67. Board of Trade, Return 'showing...the Estimated Production of Cane and Beet Sugar...; the Total Consumption and Consumption Per Head...', Aug. 1907, in *Parliamentary Papers*, no. 334, lxxxi; part IV, British colonial exports of sugar.

68. Board of Trade, Return 'Estimated Production of Cane and Beet Sugar...; the Total Consumption and Consumption Per Head' in *Parliamentary Papers*, no. 334, lxxxi; part II, part III.

69. G. Martineau in *Both Sides of the Sugar Convention* (London, 1907), p. 1. For the battle outside Europe, see B. Orlove, 'Meat and Strength: The Moral Economy of a Chilean Food Riot', *Cultural Authropology* 12/2 (1997), pp. 234–68.

70. Avebury MS, Add. 49667, Northbrook to Avebury, 15 Feb. 1900; Howe, *Free Trade and Liberal England*, pp. 206 ff.

71. NA, FO 881/7426 Bergne memo, 12 Nov. 1900, p. 17. India even kept up its countervailing duties after Austria-Hungary had stopped its bounties, NA, CO 323/486.

72. NA, T1/9994, p. 3; Gerald Balfour in *Hansard*, 4s, 126/587–98 (28 July 1903). See also F. S. Lyons, *Internationalism in Europe, 1815–1914* (Leyden, 1963), pp. 103–10.

73. NA 30/60/38, 7775–94, correspondence between Lansdowne, Phipps, and Plunkett, 10, 14, 21 Feb. 1902; 'Sugar Convention Bill', Gerald Balfour, Feb. 1903; *International Convention Relative to Bounties on Sugar, signed at Brussels, 5 March 1902*, Cd.1535.

74. See H. Fountain's memo to the President of the Board of Trade (n.d., 1912), 'The Sugar Convention and the question of the proposed withdrawal therefrom', in Asquith Papers, MS 93, and also the untitled memo in MS 93, ff. 112–18.

75. S. Ziegler, *Die Zuckerproduktion der Welt und ihre Statistik* (Magdeburg, 1912), table 21.

76. NA 30/60/41, Llewellyn Smith, 'The Rise in the Price of Sugar', memo for cabinet, 13 Dec. 1904, p. 2.

77. 6 Dec. 1904 speech at Bramley, see his notes in Herbert Gladstone, MS 46,112.

78. Robson (South Shields), in *Hansard*, 4s, 126: 751 (29 July 1903).

79. Women's Liberal Federation, Annual Meeting of the Council, on 12–14 May 1903; Halifax, Yorkshire, 13 May 1903, p. 9. See also *Summary of Federation News*, WLF, January 1905, pp. 6–11.

80. 'The Sugar Convention', *Set of Leaflets on Preferential Tariffs and Current Political Questions* (1903), no. 1916, Liberal Publication Department.

81. *The Brussels Convention and Free Trade, Speeches Delivered by Earl Spencer and Sir H. Campbell-Bannerman, at a Cobden Club Banquet, on Nov. 28th, 1902* (London, 1903), pp. 27, 31.

82. S. De Jastrzebski, 'The Sugar Convention and the Sugar Tax', in *Both Sides of the Sugar Convention* (London, 1907), p. 11.

83. NA 30/60/44, Gerald Balfour's notes on 'Suggestions for a Unionist Fiscal Policy' (March 1904), point 4.

84. Strachey to Welby, 29 June 1908, Strachey Papers, S/6/2/31.

85. T. Gibson Bowles, letter to *The Times*, 13 July 1908, p. 3.

86. *The Times*, 15 July 1908, p. 14. See also Gibson Bowles in *Hansard*, 4s, 183: 245 (30 Jan. 1908); *The Times*, 4 July 1908, p. 11 and 16 July 1908, p. 12. Free Trade MPs formed a committee to fight the sugar convention with J. M. Robertson as honorary secretary; *The Times*, 22 July 1908, p. 14.

87. H. C. G. Matthew, *The Liberal Imperialists: The Ideas and Politics of a Post-Gladstonian Élite* (Oxford, 1973).

88. NA 30/60/44, Giffen, 'Commercial Union between the United Kingdom and the Colonies', 9 Feb. 1891, with additional remarks July 1894. Giffen letter to *The Times*, 17 June 1902.

89. For colonial reactions, see Amery, *Chamberlain*, pp. 329 ff.; Porritt, *Protection in Canada*; Mock, *Imperiale Herrschaft*, pp. 325–50, and Howe, *Free Trade and Liberal England*, pp. 240 ff.

90. W. Laurier to Bonar Law, 25 Oct. 1911, Bonar Law Papers 18/7/201.

91. *Annual Register* (1903), p. 207.

92. 'Brief Memorandum prepared in the Board of Trade on the future wheat production and exportation of the North West of Canada', n.d. [1903], NA 30/60/44.

93. See A. Offer, 'Costs and Benefits, Prosperity, and Security, 1870–1914', in *Oxford History of the British Empire: The Nineteenth Century*, pp. 690–711; M. Edelstein, *Overseas Investment in the Age of High Imperialism* (New York, 1982); P. O'Brien, 'The Costs and Benefits of British Imperialism 1846–1914', *Past and Present*, 120 (1980), pp. 163–200.

94. Howe, *Free Trade and Liberal England*, pp. 56–63.

95. L. Colley, *Britons: Forging the Nation 1707–1837* (New Haven, CT, 1992), pp. 31 ff.; S. Pincus, *Protestantism and Patriotism: Ideologies and the Making of English Foreign Policy, 1650–1668* (Cambridge, 1996); B. Hilton, *The Age of Atonement: The Influence of Evangelicalism on Social and Economic Thought, 1785–1865* (Oxford, 1988); R. F. Spall, 'Free Trade, Foreign Relations, and the Anti-Corn-Law League', *The International History Review*, 10/3 (1988), pp. 345–516.

96. E. Baines, *On the Moral Influence of Free Trade* ….(London, 1830), p. 49.

97. *Report of the Conference of Ministers of all Denominations on the Corn Laws* (Manchester, 1841), reprinted in A. Kadish (ed.), *The Corn Laws*, 6 vols. (1996), *IV*, p. 173.

98. Lloyd George at a great demonstration at Aberdeen, 13 Nov. 1903, Lloyd George Papers, A/11/2. The last line is from Cardinal Newman's 'Less Kindly Light'. For early Victorian views, see pp. 5–6 above.

99. Hall, *Civilising Subjects*.

100. Churchill, *For Free Trade*, pp. 72–3.

101. Undated, handwritten MS [c. 1904–5], Robert Cecil MS 51194.

102. 'Memorandum on Proposals to remit the extra duties on wine imported from the colonies ... ', Bateman, 28 April 1899, NA 30/60/44, p. 10.

103. 'Colonial Preference', *Leaflets Issued by the Free Trade Union* (London, 1907–10), 22 Feb. 1909 (no. 91).

104. Burns Diary 46323, 17 Feb. 1905.

105. Salisbury to Gerald Balfour, 8 Jan. 1904, NA 30/60/44.

106. Bodleian Library, Oxford, Zimmern MS 136, 'United Britain, a Study in XXth-century Imperialism' n.d., [1905]; MS 136, 'The Seven Deadly Sins of Tariff Reform', (n.d., 1905?).

107. Keynes Papers, Box 1./29, Nov. 1903.

108. L. Mallet to Strachey, 7 Nov. 1899, Strachey S/15/1/19.

109. 'Memorandum on Preferential Trade Arrangements with the Colonies', Gerald Balfour, June 1902 for cabinet', NA 30/60/36, p. 3.

110. *Set of Leaflets on Preferential Tariffs* (Oct. 1903), Liberal Publication Department, no. 1970; Rosebery had given the speech at Sheffield, 13 Oct. 1903.

111. K. Grant, *A Civilised Savagery: Britain and the New Slaveries in Africa, 1884–1926* (New York, 2005), pp. 32–7.

112. Davis, *Late Victorian Holocausts*.

113. Duties were also *ad valorem* instead of specific.

114. *Lord George Hamilton's Resignation: A speech by the Rt. Hon. Lord G. Hamilton, M.P., at Ealing, 22 October 1903* (1903), published by the Unionist Free Food League.

115. *Summary of Federation News*, WLF, March 1904, pp. 12–13.

116. W. A. S. Hewins, *Tariff Reform in Relation to Cotton* (London, 1909).

117. H. Taylor, *Tariff Reform and the Cotton Trade: A Lancashire Man's Reply to Mr. Hewins' Manchester Address* (n.d., 1909), pp. 1, 5; first published in the *Bolton Evening News*, 23 July 1909.

118. 'Patriotism and Empire', (1912?), Robert Cecil MS 51194.

119. What Churchill called 'vulgar brag', *For Free Trade*, p. 27.

120. M. Taylor (ed.), *The European Diaries of Richard Cobden, 1846–1849* (Aldershot, 1994).

121. J. A. Hobson, *Imperialism: A Study* (London, 1902) and 'The Approaching Abandonment of Free Trade', *The Fortnightly Review*, 71 (1902), 434–44.

122. Hobson, *Imperialism*, p. 86.

123. F. Trentmann, 'The Strange Death of Free Trade: The Erosion of 'Liberal Consensus' in Great Britain, c.1903–32' in *Citizenship and Community: Liberals, Radicals and Collective Identities in the British Isles, 1865–1931*, ed. E. Biagini (Cambridge, 1996), pp. 219–50.

124. Hobson, 'Free Trade and Foreign Policy', *The Contemporary Review*, 74 (1898), p. 177.

125. Hobson, *Imperialism*, p. 32, and pp. 86–7 for below; see also Hobson, 'Free Trade and Foreign Policy', pp. 167–80.

126. L. Courtney, 'What is the Advantage of Foreign Trade?', *The Nineteenth Century*, 53 (May 1903), pp. 806, 811.
127. Hobson, *Imperialism*, p. 337.
128. Hobson, *International Trade*, pp. 140–1.
129. As Peter Cain has argued, 'J. A. Hobson, Cobdenism, and the Radical Theory of Economic Imperialism', *Economic History Review*, 31/4 (1978), and in *Hobson and Imperialism: Radicalism, New Liberalism and Finance 1887–1938* (Oxford, 2002). But compare, P. Clarke, 'Hobson, Free Trade, and Imperialism', *Economic History Review*, 31/2 (1984); Long, *Towards a New Liberal Internationalism*, pp. 112–15; A. J. F. Lee, 'A Study of The Social and Economic Thought of J. A. Hobson', unpubl. London Ph.D. thesis, 1970, ch. 8.
130. Hobson, 'Ethics of Tariff Issue', *The British Friend*, 12/10 (Oct. 1903), pp. 282–4. See also 'The Inner Meaning of Protectionism', *The Contemporary Review*, 84 (1903).
131. *The Times*, 5 Aug. 1908, p. 8.
132. Courtney of Penwith, *Peace or War?* (London, 2nd edn, 1910), repr. from *The Contemporary Review*, p. 25.
133. P. Laity, *The British Peace Movement 1870–1914* (Oxford, 2002), pp. 136–7.
134. Hobson, *Imperialism*, part II, ch. iv.
135. N. Angell, *The Great Illusion: A Study of the Relation of Military Power in Nations to their Economic and Social Advantage* (London, 1911 3rd rev. edn), first published as *Europe's Optical Illusion* in 1909.
136. N. Angell, *Patriotism Under Three Flags: A Plea for Rationalism in Politics* (1903); *After All: The Autobiography of Norman Angell* (London, 1951), pp. 86–107.
137. N. Angell, *The Foundations of International Polity* (London, 1914), Appendix B., p. 220.
138. H. S. Weinroth, 'Norman Angell and The Great Illusion', *Historical Journal*, 17 (1974). See also A. J. A. Morris, *Radicalism Against War: The Advocacy of Peace and Retrenchment* (London, 1972).
139. F. Leventhal, *The Last Dissenter: H. N. Brailsford and His World* (Oxford, 1958), p. 108–13; Laity, *Peace Movement*, pp. 191–3.
140. Angell, *Great Illusion*, p. 383.
141. *Clarion*, 29 May 1903; similarly, Clynes, the president of the Federation of Lancashire Trades Councils, *Clarion*, 3 July 1903.
142. *Dictionary of Labour Biography*, 6 (1982), p. 140; *Labour Leader*, 3 Dec. 1909. Moll to Johnson, 18 Nov. 1909, ILP 4 Box 22, British Library of Political and Economic Science, London; K. D. Brown, 'The Trade Union Tariff Reform Association, 1904–1913', *Journal of British Studies* 9 (1970), pp. 141–53.
143. F. Bealey and H. Pelling, *Labour and Politics 1900–1906* (London, 1958), p. 207.
144. *Labour Leader*, 10 Oct. 1903, p. 321.
145. [H. H. Champion] *The Facts about the Unemployed* (London, 1886), p.12.
146. M. Brodie, *The Politics of the Poor: The East End of London 1885–1914* (Oxford, 2004), pp. 40–1.

147. Trades Union Congress, 1898 Report.

148. *Justice*, 14 May 1904, p. 8.

149. J. Paton, *Proletarian Pilgrimage: An Autobiography* (London, 1935), p.185. See also N.E.C. minutes, 3 Feb. 1904, People's History Museum, Manchester.

150. *Labour Leader*, 13 Jan. 1905, p. 487.

151. Ibid., 10 Oct. 1903.

152. Snowden, 'An Imperial Zollverein'.

153. Snowden, *Chamberlain Bubble*, p. 16, which sold 40,000 copies in its first year, and Snowden in *Labour Leader*, 24 Nov. 1905, p. 408.

154. D. Tanner, 'The Development of British Socialism, 1900–1918', *Parliamentary History*, 16/1 (1997), pp. 48–66; F. Trentmann, 'Wealth versus Welfare: The British Left Between Free Trade and National Political Economy Before The First World War', *Historical Research*, 70/171 (1997), pp. 70–98.

155. Snowden, *Chamberlain Bubble*, p.16. Compare Snowden, 'An Imperial Zollverein' with Peter Kropotkin, *Fields, Factories and Workshops* (London, 1901 ed.), p. 4; for Kropotkin's influence, see also *Reynolds*, 27 Sept. 1903, p. 5; 24 July 1904, p. 2; Hardie, *Serfdom to Socialism*, pp. 35, 113–14.

156. Ramsay MacDonald, *Labour and the Empire* (London, 1907), p. 92.

157. *Justice*, 14 Nov. 1903, p. 1.

158. R. B. Suthers, *John Bull and Doctor Free Trade* [1908] p. 9.

159. MacDonald, *Zollverein*, p. 163.

160. S. and B. Webb, *Industrial Democracy* (London, 2nd edn 1902), p. 865.

161. Shaw to Webb, 17 Nov. 1904, cit. in Bealey and Pelling, *Labour and Politics*, p. 171.

162. *The Diary of Beatrice Webb*, ed. N. and J. MacKenzie, II (London, 1983), 15 June 1903.

163. Keir Hardie, *Labour Leader*, 10 Oct. 1903, p. 323.

164. *ILP conference report 1911*. Hardie in *Hamburger Echo*, 5 Nov. 1910.

165. *Justice*, 20 Feb. 1904, p.1.

166. C. Cross, *Philip Snowden* (London, 1966), pp. 129–30.

167. Hardie, *Labour Leader*, 17 Oct. 1903, p. 341.

168. M. Huberman, 'A Ticket To Trade: Belgian Workers and Globalization Before 1914', *Economic History Review* (forthcoming).

169. R. Fletcher, *Revisionism and Empire:Socialist Imperialism in Germany 1897–1914* (London, 1984); Nonn, *Verbraucherprotest*; C. Torp, *Die Herausforderung der Globalisierung: Wirtschaft und Politik in Deutschland, 1860–1914* (Göttingen, 2005), pp. 245–51.

PROLOGUE II

1. *Cobden Club Report of 1913* (London, 1914), p. 7.

2. A view explicitly made in *Cobden Club Report of 1909* (London, 1910), p. 13.

4. Consumers Divided

1. *The Co-operative News*, 14 Jan. 1918.
2. *The National Food Journal*, 10 March 1920, p. 29.
3. *Home and Politics*, July 1925, p. 2.
4. *Co-operative News*, 27 Sept. 1919, pp. 1, 4; *Daily News*, 22 Sept. 1919, p. 1; *Daily Herald*, 22 Sept. 1919, pp.1–2; *Reynolds's*, 28 Sept. 1919, p. 2.
5. B. J. Davis, *Home Fires Burning: Food, Politics, and Everyday Life in World War I Berlin* (Chapel Hill, NC, 2000); A. Offer, 'Blockade and the Strategy of Starvation', in R. Chickering and S. Förster (eds), *Great War, Total War: Combat and Mobilisation on the Western Front, 1914–1918* (Cambridge, 2000), pp. 169–88.
6. For this argument, see my earlier 'Bread, Milk and Democracy: Consumption and Citizenship in Twentieth-Century Britain' in M. Daunton and M. Hilton (eds), *The Politics of Consumption: Material Culture and Citizenship in Europe and America* (Oxford, 2001), pp. 129–63, and subsequently, M. Hilton, *Consumerism in Twentieth-Century Britain* (Cambridge, 2003), esp. ch. 2.
7. People's History Museum (PHM), Manchester, WNC 4/1/22 and WNC/Add/21/12. See also R. Harrison, 'The War Emergency Workers' National Committee, 1914–1920', in A. Briggs and J. Saville (eds), *Essays in Labour History, 1886–1923* (London, 1971), pp. 211–59.
8. B. Williams, May 1915, cit. in Harrison, 'War Emergency Workers' National Committee', p. 232.
9. *National Food Journal*, 27 Nov. 1918, table II, pp. 164.
10. Ibid., 13 March 1918, p. 345 and 10 Oct. 1917, p. 36; *The Times*, 12 May 1917, p. 7.
11. Mikuláš Teich, 'Science and Food During the Great War: Britain and Germany', in H. Kamminga and A. Cunningham (eds), *The Science and Culture of Nutrition, 1840–1940* (Amsterdam, 1995), p. 227.
12. H. G. Corner, of the London Telephone Service, in Nov. 1917, cit. in D. J. Oddy, *From Plain Fare to Fusion Food: British Diet from the 1890s to the 1990s* (Woodbridge, Suffolk, 2003), p. 82.
13. PHM, WNC/ADD/9/37, Aug. 1916.
14. PHM, WNC/5/1/2/5, National Convention on The National Food Supply, Dec. 1917.
15. *Reynolds's*, 13 Jan. 1918, p. 3 (for Brighton); B. Waites, 'The Government of the Home Front and the "Moral Economy" of the Working Class', in P. Liddle (ed.), *Home Fires and Foreign Fields: British Social and Military Experience in the First World War* (London, 1985), pp. 186–9; H. Weinroth, 'Labour Unrest and the Food Question in Great Britain, 1914–1918,' *Europa*, I/2 (Spring 1978), 140–6; M. Barnett, *British Food Policy During the First World War* (London, 1985), pp. 135–42, although her idea that the consumer as a social force did not exist before the war is mistaken.

16. PHM, WNC/7/2/33, 'Treachery!', n.d.

17. P. Gurney, *Co-operative Culture and the Politics of Consumption in England, c. 1870–1930* (Manchester, 1996), pp. 208–25.

18. W. Beveridge, *British Food Control* (London, 1928), p. 335.

19. PHM, WNC/7/2, poster, n.d.

20. Beveridge Papers, BLPES, XIV/4, 'Memorandum by the Food Controller', 4 Aug. 1919.

21. *National Food Journal*, 12 Sept. 1917, pp. 1, 3.

22. Ibid. 26 Sept. 1917, p. 32; 13 Feb. 1918; 8 May 1918, p. 44. See also Barnett, *Food Policy*, pp. 125 ff.

23. *National Food Journal*, 10 Oct. 1917, p. 37; for Rhondda, 12 Sept. 1917, p. 6.

24. PHM, WNC 5/4/14.ii, J. S. Middleton, the secretary of the WEWNC, to J. R. Clynes, 28 Jan. 1918.

25. PHM, WNC 5/4, Williams to executive council, 10 Jan. 1918; *Co-operative News*, 16 Feb. 1918, p. 137.

26. PHM, WNC 5/4, Phillips to Clynes, 27 Jan. 1918 and Middleton to Clynes, 28 Jan. 1918; *National Food Journal*, 26 Dec. 1917, p. 171.

27. Beveridge, *British Food Control*, Table VI, p. 207.

28. *Co-operative News*, 19 Jan. 1918, p. 46; 26 Jan. 1918, pp. 66, 77.

29. PHM, CC 94/3, 'Report on the Constitution and Work of the Consumers' Council'.

30. B. Williams, 'The Famine of 1918', *Co-operative News*, 5 Jan. 1918, pp. 4–5.

31. T. Bonzon and B. Davis, 'Feeding the Cities', in J. Winter and J.-L. Robert (eds), *Capital Cities at War: Paris, London, Berlin 1914–1919* (Cambridge, 1997), pp. 315–20; T. de Nijs, 'Food Provision and Food Retailing in The Hague, 1914–1930', in F. Trentmann and F. Just, *Food and Conflict in Europe in the Age of the Two World Wars* (Basingstoke, 2006), pp. 74–6.

32. *The Statist*, 29 June 1918, p. 1136.

33. PHM, CC/Mil/46, Report on Action Taken Towards the Control and Distribution of Milk, 6 Jan. 1919; *National Food Journal*, 15 Oct. 1919, pp. 514–15.

34. *Yorkshire Observer*, 13 Dec. 1916.

35. PHM, CC/Mil/90, 'Details in regard to the milk supply of the City of New York', Feb. 1919, by Wilfred Buckley. For Victorian patterns, see John Burnett, *Plenty and Want: a Social History of Diet in England from 1815 to the Present Day* (London, 1966), pp. 121–43, 165. According to D. J. Oddy, workers increased their weekly consumption of milk in the thirty years before the war from 1.4 to 1.8 pints per head, 'A Nutritional Analysis of Historical Evidence: The Working-Class Diet, 1880–1914', in *The Making of the Modern British Diet*, ed. D. Oddy and D. Miller (London, 1976), p. 216.

36. Major Hunt in *Hansard*, 5s, 98: 844 (24 Oct. 1917); *National Food Journal*, Vol. I, no. 4, p. 65; 14 Nov. 1917, p. 77; 12 Dec. 1917, p. 143; *Glasgow Herald*, 5 Nov. 1919.

37. PHM, CC/CP/126, Stuart Bunning at the Consumers' Council conference, 19 Feb. 1920.

38. PHM, CC/Mil/43, reports by inspectors, Sept. 1918; CC/Mil/54, Nottingham medical officer of health to Consumers' Council, Jan. 1919.

39. PHM, CC/Mil/23, Consumers' Council Milk Sub-Committee to Waldorf Astor, 3 May 1918. There were some continuities in personnel and expertise; before joining the Consumers' Council C. T. Cramp had served on the Astor Committee.

40. PHM, CC/Mil/7/1, Ministry of Food, Report on Action Taken Towards the Control and Distribution of Milk, early 1919.

41. *Co-operative News*, 8 Nov. 1919, p. 12; 15 Nov. 1919, p. 12; 27 Dec. 1919, p. 8.

42. PHM, CC/Mil/163, Ronald Caws to Marion Phillips, 22 Dec. 1919; WCG *36th Annual Report* (1918–19), p. 15.

43. PHM, CC/MIL/143, *Exeter Express and Echo*, 9 Sept. 1919.

44. PHM, CC/CP 67, Summary of Food Commissioners' Reports, 17 Dec. 1919.

45. Lieut.-Colonel Thorne on 10 Nov. 1919, *Hansard*, 5s, 121: 32–3. See also the Women's Cooperative Guild in the Midlands, *Co-operative News*, 13 Dec. 1919, p. 13.

46. PHM, CC/PP/56, Memorandum from the Reforms Sub-Committee, The Consumers' Council, For the Information of Organised Bodies of Consumers, 21 April 1920.

47. *National Food Journal*, 23 Jan. 1918, p. 226.

48. Ibid., 25 Sept. 1918, p. 27.

49. *Co-operative News*, 13 April 1918, p. 227.

50. Ibid., 3 Aug. 1918, p. 526.

51. PHM, WNC 17/4, London Food Vigilance Committee, 'Milk. A Challenge to Labour', n.d., c. Nov. 1917, emphasis in original.

52. PHM, CC/CP/81. *National Food Journal*, 11 Sept. 1918.

53. BLPES, Coll. Misc 92, Beveridge Collection, 26, Memorandum on Combines and Trusts, 18 May 1920 by W. Cowper; J. B. Jefferys, *Retail Trading in Britain, 1850–1950* (Cambridge, 1954), pp. 227–8.

54. *Daily News*, 11 June 1919, p. 1; PHM, CC/REF/70, minutes of reforms sub-committee, 5 Dec. 1919 (Marion Phillips). See also Phillips in *Reynolds's*, 19 May 1918, p. 2.

55. *Co-operative News*, 27 Aug. 1918, p. 550.

56. Ibid., 22 Feb. 1919, p. 125.

57. Ibid., 19 July 1919, p. 1.

58. PHM, CC/Gen/135i, Address by McCurdy, 16 July 1919.

59. *National Food Journal*, 12 Nov. 1919, p. 545.

60. PHM, CC/CP.126, 19 Feb. 1920, Report of proceedings.

61. *Co-operative News*, 22 Feb. 1919, p. 134.

62. Women's Co-operative Guild, *The Milk We Want* (London, 1925), p. 6; Jefferys, *Retail Trading*, pp. 58, 236–8.

63. M. Llewelyn Davies, *Women as Organised Consumers* (Manchester, 1921), pp. 1, 3.

64. A. H. Enfield, *The Place of Co-operation in the New Social Order* (London, 1920), p. 11.

65. *The Times*, 8 May 1920, p. 17.

66. *The Statist*, 29 June 1918, p. 1136. See also Hilton, *Consumerism in Twentieth-Century Britain*, pp. 66 ff.

67. PHM, CC/CP 30, 13 Nov. 1919.

68. PHM, CC/CP 196, 20 May 1920.

69. PHM, CC/Ref/90, note by Mr. Uthwatt. *The Co-operative News*, 20 Dec. 1919, p. 2.

70. For this and the following: PHM, CC/CP.126, 19 Feb. 1920, Report of proceedings.

71. Oddy, *Plain Fare to Fusion Food*, p. 91; for a more optimistic view, J. M. Winter, 'The Impact of the First World War on Civilian Health in Britain', *Economic History Review*, 2nd ser., 30/3 (August 1977), 487–507.

72. M. Weatherall, 'Bread and Newspapers' in Kamminga and Cunningham (eds), *The Science and Culture of Nutrition, 1840–1940*, p. 198.

73. E. J. T. Collins, ' "The Consumer Revolution" and the Growth of Factory Foods', in Oddy and Miller, *Making of the British Diet*, pp. 26–43.

74. PHM, CC/Gen/30, memorandum from Local Government Board and correspondence, 4 Apr. 1918.

75. BLPES, Coll. Misc. 92, XX/4, Food War Committee, Royal Society, Report on the Digestibility of Breads, March 1918, pp. 4, 34–5.

76. F. Ranson, *Food Values*, n.d. [1926], and *Food Purity* (1926).

77. *National Food Journal*, 8 May 1918, p. 442.

78. Housewives' evidence to the Commission was distributed in a popular edition, *Why Your Food Costs More* (London, 1925), quoted at p. 27.

79. *Co-operative News*, 6 Dec. 1930, p. 12.

80. E. Ross, *Love and Toil* (Oxford, 1993), p. 218.

81. PHM, CC/PP/41, Ministry of Health, 'Use of Milk' pamphlet 1, Oct. 1920.

82. K. Waddington, *The Bovine Scourge: Meat, Tuberculosis and Public Health, 1850–1914* (Woodbridge, 2006), p. 159.

83. Ibid.; J. Phillips and M. French, 'Adulteration and Food Law, 1899–1939', *Twentieth-Century British History*, 9 (1998), pp. 350–69; P. J. Atkins, 'White Poison? The Social Consequences of Milk Consumption, 1850–1930', *Social History of Medicine*, 5 (1992), pp. 202–27; A. Stanziani, 'Alimentation et santé sous la IIIe République (1870–1914)', in A. Chatriot, M.-E. Chessel, and M. Hilton (eds), *Au Nom du Consommateur: Consommation et politique en Europe et aux États-Unis au XX Siècle* (Paris, 2004), pp. 135–49; H. Reif and R. Pomp, 'Milchproduktion und Milchvermarktung im Ruhrgebiet, 1870–1930', *Jahrbuch für Wirtschaftsgeschichte*, 1 (1996), 77–107.

84. Women's Cooperative Guild, *Maternity: Letters From Working-Women* (London, 1915); G. Scott, *Feminism and the Politics of Working Women: The Women's Co-operative Guild, 1880s to the Second World War* (London, 1998), p. 119.

85. PHM, CC/Mil/26, The National Clean Milk Society, Report of Investigation, 1918.

86. *The Times*, 13 April 1916, p. 5.

87. PHM, CC/Mil/43/122, A Short Talk to Mothers on Milk, June 1919; for the 19th London Labour Conference, 22 July 1920, CC/Mil/43/166; *The Times*, 9 May 1919, p. 14, and 21 April 1920, p. 10.

88. PHM, CC/Mil/54 and 80: letters by G. Sutherland Thomson, 19 March 1919 and by P. Boobbyer, medical officer of Health, Nottingham, Jan. 1919.

89. PHM, CC/Mil/79, Edinburgh Women's Citizen Association, 18 March 1919.

90. *The Milk We Want* (1925).

91. PHM, CC/PP/41, Ministry of Health, Pamphlet on the Use of Milk, Oct. 1920.

92. *Reynolds's Newspaper*, 19 May 1918, p. 2.

93. BLPES, Coll. Misc. 370, leaflet no. 203 (1927).

94. John Hurt, 'Feeding the Hungry Schoolchild in the First Half of the Twentieth Century', in Oddy and Miller, *Diet and Health in Modern Britain*, pp. 178–206; Charles Webster, 'Government Policy and School Meals and Welfare Foods, 1939–70', in Smith, *Nutrition in Britain*, pp. 190–213; P. J. Atkins, 'Fattening Children or Fattening Farmers? School Milk in Britain, 1921–1941', *Economic History Review*, 58/1 (2005), pp. 57–78; J. Vernon, 'The Ethics of Hunger and the Assembly of Society: The Techno-Politics of the School Meal in Modern Britain', *American Historical Review*, 110/3 (2005), pp. 693–725.

95. PHM, CC/PP/41, Ministry of Health, Pamphlet on the Use of Milk, Oct. 1920.

96. *The Milk Industry*, Apr. 1925, pp. 81–2; May 1925, p. 65; Nov. 1928, p. 79; A. Jenkins, 'Modest Beginnings', in A. Jenkins (ed.) *Drinka Pinta: The Story of Milk and the Industry that Serves it* (London, 1970), pp. 80–107; *The Times*, 6 Nov. 1928, p. 11.

97. C. Cook, *The Age of Alignment: Electoral Politics in Britain, 1922–29* (London, 1975); Cowling, *Impact of Labour*, pp. 275–330.

98. F. W. Hirst, 'Free Trade—its Annus Mirabilis', *Contemporary Review*, 126 (1924), 153–61.

99. *Sheffield Daily Independent*, 23 Nov. 1923, p. 7 and 30 Nov. 1923, p. 5.

100. *The Evening News* (Glasgow), 26 Nov. 1923, p. 7; *Paisley Daily Express*, 5 Dec. 1923.

101. *Paisley Daily Express*, 1 Dec. 1923.

102. C. M. M. McDonald, *The Radical Thread: Political Change in Scotland; Paisley Politics, 1885–1924* (East Linton, 2000), pp. 247–54.

103. T. Henderson in *Co-operative News*, 24 Nov. 1923, p. 12, and *Co-operative News*, 8 Dec. 1923, p. 12.

104. *Co-operative News*, 1 Dec. 1923, p. 13.

105. *The Times*, 13 April 1923, p. 7.

106. *The Sheffield Forward*, Dec. 1923, no. 32, p. 1. See, similarly, Arthur Ponsonby in Sheffield, *Reynolds's Newspaper*, 2 Dec. 1923, p. 2.

107. J. Jones in *Hansard*, 5s, 168: 46 (13 Nov. 1923).

108. *Co-operative News*, 17 Nov. 1923, p. 12. The election song 'Peace, peace, peace among the nations' followed the tune of the Edwardian 'Stamp, stamp, stamp, upon Protection', *Co-operative News*, 8 Dec. 1923, p. 2.

109. *Co-operative News*, 24 Nov. 1923, p. 9.

110. Ibid., election supplement, 24 Nov. 1923, p. 1.

111. McKibbin, *Ideologies of Class*, pp. 259–93.

112. *Why Your Food Costs More: Extracts from the Evidence of Housewives and Points from the Findings and Recommendations of the Royal Commission on Food Prices* (London, 1925).

113. C. Addison, *The Nation and Its Food* (London, 1929). For further discussion, see Ch. 6 below, and Hilton, *Consumerism in Twentieth-Century Britain*, pp. 117–24.

114. P. Graves, *Labour Women: Women in British Working-Class Politics 1918–39* (Cambridge, 1994); Scott, *Feminism*.

115. 'Up the Housewives!', *The Labour Woman*, 1 Sept. 1929, p. 132; 'Deal Gently with the Profiteers!', *The Labour Woman*, 1 Dec. 1929, p. 193.

116. J. Stephen, *Flapdoodle about 'Flappers'* (1928), p. 4.

117. *The Labour Woman*, 1 June 1925, pp. 91–4; *Report of the Eighth National Conference of Labour Women*, 1927, pp. 57 ff.; *Report of the Tenth National Conference of Labour Women*, 1929, pp. 46 ff.; A. Dollan, *Don't Misuse Your Power* (London, 1928).

118. I. Zweiniger-Bargielowska, *Austerity in Britain: Rationing, Controls, and Consumption, 1939–1955* (Oxford, 2000).

119. *The Times*, 13 Jan. 1911, p. 10; 18 Jan. 1911, p. 6; 10 Feb. 1911, p. 6; 27 March 1911, p. 7.

120. Imperial War Museum (London), Women at Work Collection, British Women's Patriotic League, *7th Annual Report* (1915), p. 3; *8th Annual Report* (1916), p. 8. For the Edwardian context, see J. Bush, *Edwardian Ladies and Imperial Power* (Leicester, 2000).

121. Annual meeting, *The Times*, 23 March 1926, p. 22.

122. *Primrose League Gazette*, March 1929, p. 12; these stamps could be obtained at the Army and Navy Stores.

123. Empire Marketing Board, *Annual Report* (1929), p. 25; *Annual Report* (1932), p. 108. See also S. Constantine, ' "Bringing the Empire Alive": The Empire Marketing Board and Imperial Propaganda, 1926–33', in J. M. MacKenzie (ed.), *Imperialism and Popular Culture* (Marchester, 1986), pp. 192–231;

D. Judd, *Empire: The British Imperial Experience, from 1765 to the Present* (London, 1996), pp. 273–86.

124. M. Pugh, *Women and the Women's Movement in Britain, 1914–1999* (Houndmills, 2000), pp. 125, 140; D. Jarvis, 'Mrs. Maggs and Betty: The Conservative Appeal to Women Voters in the 1920s', *Twentieth Century British History*, 5/2 (1994), pp. 129–52.

125. *Home and Politics*, Oct. 1924, p. 23.

126. *The Times*, 12 April 1926, p. 9.

127. *Home and Politics*, May 1924, p.10.

128. Ibid., May 1925, p. 14.

129. Ibid., Oct. 1926, p. 16.

130. Ibid., Aug. 1926, p.16.

131. *Walthamstow and Leyton Guardian*, 18 Nov. 1927, p. 15 and 22 Nov. 1927, p. 13.

132. F. Trentmann, 'Before "Fair Trade": Empire, Free Trade, and the Moral Economies of Food in the Modern World', in *Environment and Planning D: Society and Space*, 25/6 (2007), pp. 1079–1102.

133. *Home and Politics*, Aug. 1924, pp. 7f, emphasis in original.

134. Empire Marketing Board, *Annual Report* (May 1928 to May 1929, London) pp. 24–5.

135. *Home and Politics*, Dec. 1924, p. 8.

136. Ibid., Oct. 1924, p. 14.

137. Ibid., June 1925, p. 4, quoting Haden Guest, a heterodox imperial Labour MP, and his recent exposures of fruit packing in Turkey. See also *Weekly Mail and Cardiff Times*, 3 Nov. 1928, p. 6.

138. *Walthamstow and Leyton Guardian*, 18 Nov. 1927, p. 15.

139. R. Self, 'Treasury Control and the Empire Marketing Board: The Rise and Fall of Non-Tariff Preference in Britain', *Twentieth Century British History*, 5/2 (1994), pp. 153–82.

140. K. Gerth, *China Made: Consumer Culture and the Creation of the Nation* (Cambridge, Mass., 2003); L. Trivedi, 'Visually Mapping the "Nation": Swadeshi Politics in Nationalist India, 1920–30', *Journal of Asian Studies*, 62/1 (2003), pp. 11–41.

141. *Home and Politics*, Sept. 1927, p. 7.

142. Ibid., Sept. 1927, p. 7, and see also June 1925, p. 4 and Aug. 1926, p. 19.

143. Ibid., Sept. 1924, p. 4 and also Nov. 1924, p. 10 and June 1925, p. 9.

144. *The Times*, 13 May 1929, p. 10.

145. Ibid., 10 May 1929, p. 13.

146. M. Jacobs, ' "How About Some Meat": The Office of Price Administration, Consumption Politics, and State Building from the Bottom up, 1941–1946', *The Journal of American History*, 84/3 (1997), pp. 910–41.

147. H. Hope, Conservative MP for Forfar, in *Hansard*, 5s, 191: 70–2 (2 Feb. 1926).

148. Amery at the third annual Advertising Convention, *The Times*, 20 July 1927, p. 11; 18 July 1927, p. 15; and at the annual meeting of the Incorporated Society of British Advertisers, *The Times*, 12 June 1929, p. 10. For the imperial outlook of advertisers, see S. Schwarzkopf's forthcoming Ph.D. thesis at Birkbeck on the formation of the advertising profession, ch. 4.

5. VISIBLE HANDS

1. Adam Smith, *The Wealth of Nations* (1776), book IV, ch. II, p. 487, E. Cannan edition (1904).
2. Robertson, Liberal MP, House of Commons, 8 Aug. 1918.
3. 'Education To-day', *The Spectator*, 23 Nov. 1929, pp. 757–8.
4. 'Report on a Conference held at Balliol College, Oxford, September 28–30 to consider Inter-allied Economic Problems and their relation to the war and during the Transition Period', Zimmern Papers, Bodleian, Oxford, MS 80–1.
5. P. Clarke, *Liberals and Social Democrats* (Cambridge, 1978); M. Freeden, *Liberalism Divided: A Study in British Political Thought 1914–1939* (Oxford, 1986); M. Bentley, *The Liberal Mind 1914–1929* (Cambridge, 1977).
6. *Manchester Guardian*, 13 July 1916.
7. *The Scotsman*, 1 July 1916.
8. *Morning Post*, 6 Aug. 1915.
9. *Morning Post*, 16 Dec. 1915; *Chamber of Commerce Journal* 35/261–8 (Jan.–Aug. 1916), and no 272 (Dec. 1916); The British Chamber of Commerce Paris, Report presented by the Board of Directors for the Year 1916 (1916), pp. 30–8; A. Redford, *Manchester Merchants and Foreign Trade* (Manchester, 1956), pp. 203 ff. For Hewins, A. Marrison, *British Business and Protection, 1903–32* (Oxford, 1996), pp. 236–41.
10. C. P. Scott Papers, MS 50,908, J. Young to Scott, 26 Feb. 1916.
11. *Hansard*, 5s, 77: 671–2 (23 Dec. 1915).
12. G.-H. Soutou, *L'or et le sang: les buts de guerre économiques de la Première Guerre mondiale* (Paris, 1989), pp. 234–44. See also H.-I. Schmidt, 'Wirtschaftliche Kriegsziele Englands und Interallierte Kooperation', *Militärgeschichtliche Mitteilungen*, 1 (1981), pp. 37–54.
13. NA, BT 55–8, 'Post-Bellum Tariff Policy and British Commercial Treaties', Aug. 1916, p. 9.
14. Runicman to P. Ashley 16 April 1916, Runciman papers, Newcastle University, Special Collections, MS 143.
15. Runciman papers MS 143, 'Notes of a Conference at Paris on 6th May between the President of the Board of Trade and the French Minister of Commerce on the Programme for the Economic Conferences of the Allies', 10 May 1916.
16. Llewellyn Smith to Runicman, 7 June 1916, Runciman papers, MS 143.

17. Asquith Papers, Bodleian Library, MS 30, 'Memorandum on the Paris Economic Conference' by the Board of Trade, 30 June 1916. See also Llewellyn Smith's evidence to the Balfour of Burleigh Committee, 14 Sep. 1916, in NA, BT 55/10.

18. Balfour of Burleigh, Memorandum of Fiscal Policy, 5 Jan. 1917, p. 4, NA, BT 55/8.

19. NA, Cab 23/2, 3 April 1917. See further J. Turner, *British Politics and the Great War* (New Haven, CT, 1992), pp. 350–1.

20. Wilson had already ruled out any kind of special economic alliance in his 'Five Particulars' in September 1918. See R. E. Bunselmeyer, *The Cost of War, 1914–1919: British Economic War Aims and the Origin of Reparation* (Hamden, Conn., 1975), p. 81.

21. *Hansard*, 5s, 82: 1674 (18 May 1916).

22. *Hansard*, 5s, 85: 380 (2 Aug. 1916).

23. Edward Carson in *Hansard*, 5s, 85: 342–7 (2 Aug. 1916).

24. *Manchester Guardian*, 6 July 1916; *The Times*, 7 July 1916, p. 9 g; *Daily News*, 27 July 1916.

25. *Hansard*, 5s, 85: 348–58 (2 Aug. 1916).

26. *Hansard*, 5s, 85: 379–89 (2 Aug. 1916).

27. *The U.D.C.*, 1/2 (Dec. 1915), p. 13.

28. Other active speakers were F. J. Shaw, of the Cobden Club, Buxton and Labour's Egerton P. Ward; Morel Papers, BLPES, *The U.D.C.*, 2/1 (Nov. 1916), p. 10 and no. 4 (Feb. 1917), p. 48; Hobson, 'Political Economy from Paris', *The U.D.C.* 1/9 (July 1916), pp. 97–8; *The U.D.C.* 1/10–12 (Aug.–Oct. 1916). For the UDC, and the Quaker conference in support of Free Trade, see M. Swartz, *The Union of Democratic Control in British Politics During the First World War* (Oxford, 1971), esp. p. 93.

29. Fourth Annual Meeting of the General Council of the UDC, Report, 1917–18 (London, 1918), p. 2, in War Reserve Collection, University Library, Cambridge.

30. Hugh Bell, 'Trade after the War', *The Accountant's Magazine*, 21 (Feb. 1917), pp. 55–66, and (March 1917), pp. 98–126.

31. F. W. Hirst, 'Economic Programmes after the War', *Atlantic Monthly*, 119 (Feb. 1917), pp. 243–6.

32. J. M. Robertson, *Fiscal Policy after the Wars* (Cobden Club: London, 1916), p. 17.

33. J. M. Robertson, 'Trade after the War', *The Accountant's Magazine*, 21 (May 1917), quoted at pp. 208, 210, 222.

34. F. J. Shaw, 'Women and the New Protectionism', in *WLF News*, 1 March 1917, p. 5.

35. *WLA Federation News*, annual report, 1 June 1917, pp. 20–1; *31st Annual Report of the Executive Committee of the Women's Liberal Federation* (March 1918), pp. 11, 18.

36. *31st Annual Report ... of the Women's Liberal Federation* (March 1918), p. 36.

37. Beauchamp to McKenna 27 Jan. 1919, Runciman papers, MS 177.

38. C. Mallet to Runciman 22 May 1921, Runciman papers, MS 190.

39. Letter by W. R. Doxford, 18 Sep. 1928, Runciman papers, MS 215.

40. Cobden and Unwin Papers, West Sussex Record Office, MS 1997, Cobden Club subscription book 1921–50.

41. Buckmaster to Runciman, 31 May 1920, Runciman papers MS 185.

42. *Common Sense*, 17 March 1917, pp. 161–2.

43. Gordon C. Harvey to Walter Runciman, 20 July 1919, Runciman papers, MS 177.

44. *Hansard* 85: 364–79, 2 Aug. 1916.

45. Robertson, 'Trade after the War', p. 221. See also Robertson in the House of Commons, *Hansard* 109: 1621–4, 8 Aug. 1918.

46. G. Lowes Dickinson, *Economic War After the War*, UDC pamphlet no. 19a. (Aug. 1916); *The Autobiography of G. Lowes Dickinson and other Unpublished Writings*, ed. D. Proctor (London, 1973).

47. Hobson, 'Economic War', *The U.D.C.*, 2/13 (Nov. 1917), p. 154.

48. E. D. Morel, *The African Problem and the Peace Settlement*, UDC pamphlet no. 22a (July 1917).

49. Dickinson, *Economic War After the War*, p. 13.

50. Loreburn to C. P. Scott, 13 April 1919, C. P. Scott papers, MS 50, 909.

51. 'Conference at Oxford, September 1918', Zimmern Papers MS 80–1.

52. Ibid.

53. 'Post-Armistice Policy', repr. In J. A. Salter, *Allied Shipping Control: An Experiment in International Administration* (Oxford, 1921), doc. 14, p. 329, and see also pp. 220–1.

54. A. Zimmern, *The Prospects of Democracy and other Essays* (London, 1929), pp. 18, 218–19.

55. Salter, *Allied Shipping Control*, p. 246.

56. Ibid., p. 252.

57. Ibid., p. 280.

58. Lloyd, 'Towards an International Policy', *The Nation and Athenaeum*, 11 Nov. 1922, p. 226.

59. Salter, *Allied Shipping Control*, p. 255.

60. A. Zimmern, 'Capitalism and International Relations', originally given at a conference of working-class organizations convened by Ruskin College in Birmingham, 21–2 Sept. 1917, repr. in *Nationality and Government: With other War-time Essays* (London, 1918), pp. 278–97, cit. at p. 285.

61. Zimmern, 'Capitalism and International Relations', p. 293.

62. Brailsford, 'Foundations of Internationalism', *The English Review*, 27 (July 1918), pp. 87–101.

63. J. M. Keynes, *The Economic Consequences of the Peace* (London, 1919), p. 249.

64. L. S. Woolf, *International Economic Policy*, Labour party pamphlet, 1919.

65. E. F. Wise, 'International Food Control', 20 June 1919, BLPES, Lloyd Papers, 3/2.

66. League of Nations Archive (Geneva), 10/R 305, 10/3494: E. M. H. Lloyd memo to Secretary General 23 March 1920.

67. E. Barker, *Political Thought in England: From Herbert Spencer to the Present Day* (London, 1915), p. 238.

68. *Minutes of the Rainbow Circle, 1894–1924*, ed. M. Freeden (London, 1989), 10 May 1915, p. 249.

69. Greenwood, 'International Economic Relations', in: A. J. Grant, A. Greenwood, J. D. I. Hughes, P. H. Kerr, and F. F. Urquhart, *An Introduction to the Study of International Relations* (London, 1916), cit. at pp. 102–3.

70. Greenwood, 'International Economic Relations', p. 110.

71. [A. Zimmern], 'Economic Nationalism', 'A European Retrospect', 'A Colonial Retrospect', 'Internationalism and Economic Relations in the Transition Period': *The Athenaeum*, Nov. 1917, pp. 560–2; Jan. 1918, pp. 13–17, Feb. 1918, pp. 74–7; Dec. 1918. Greenwood was the author of 'Internationalism versus Nationalism', *The Athenaeum*, Aug. 1918, pp. 335–6.

72. J. A. Hobson, *Richard Cobden: The International Man* (London, 1919); W. H. Dawson, *Richard Cobden and Foreign Policy* (London, 1926). See also S. Berger, 'William Harbutt Dawson: The Career and Politics of an Historian of Germany', *English Historical Review*, 116/1 (2001), pp. 76–113.

73. Hobson, *Cobden*, p. 11.

74. Most recently, P. Cain, *Hobson and Imperialism: Radicalism, New Liberalism and Finance 1887–1938* (Oxford, 2002), esp. pp. 237 ff., but cf. Long, *Towards a New Liberal Internationalism*.

75. [A. Greenwood], 'Cobden, Internationalism, and Democracy', *The Athenaeum*, 4639 (March 1919), pp. 91–2.

76. *Journal of Political Economy*, 28/3 (March 1920), p. 260.

77. *Journal of the Royal Institute of International Affairs*, 6/2 (March 1927), pp. 116–17.

78. *The Economic Journal*, 37/146 (June 1927), pp. 308–10.

79. *The Nation and Athenaeum*, 40/11 (Dec. 1926), p. 424.

80. Ibid., 41/4 (Apr. 1927), pp. 102–3.

81. See pp. 313–15 below.

82. E. M. H. Lloyd, *Stabilisation: An Economic Policy for Producers and Consumers* (London, 1923), p. 18.

83. Ibid., pp. 12, 22.

84. Ibid., p. 114.

85. BLPES, Lloyd papers, 4/4: Memorandum on State Monopoly on Wheat and Flour as a Means of Stabilising Prices, June 1925.

86. League of Nations, *Commercial Policy in the Inter-war Period: International Proposals and National Policies* (Geneva, 1942); League, C.E.C.P. 97, W. T. Page, Memorandum on European Bargaining Tariffs, Geneva, 1927.

87. H. James, *The End of Globalization: Lessons from the Great Depression* (Cambridge, Mass., 2002), pp. 108–9; Z. Steiner, *The Lights that Failed: European International History 1919–1933* (Oxford, 2005), pp. 446 ff.
88. League of Nations Archive, 10/402/28790. *Looking Forward*, Oct. 1921, pp. 87–90.
89. 'My Memoirs by Sir George Paish', MS (1951), BLPES, LSE Coll. Misc. 621/1.
90. League of Nations Archive, 1927 conference materials, V. 3, 20 May 1927 (Walter Layton).
91. League of Nations, procès verbaux, E/PC/1st Session/P.V.2. (1), 22 March 1928.
92. D. Serruys, 'Les Traités de Commerce', *La Revue Contemporaine*, 1 March 1923, pp. 264–70; new internationalists picked up on this, see Zimmern, 'Fiscal Policy', pp. 251–2, and his letter to the *Times*, 6 Dec. 1923.
93. Daniel Serruys, cit. in R. Boyce, *British Capitalism at the Crossroads, 1919–32* (Cambridge, 1987), p. 132, and ch. 4 more generally. Serruys was director of the treaty department of the French Ministry of Commerce. For the differences between Serruys and Chapman, the British negotiator, see League of Nations Archive, 10C/R 2737, 3255, 22 March 1928 and 23 May 1928. See also the note by Brunet and Schüller on the work of the League's economic committee, 8 Jan. 1930, 10C/R 2735.
94. 'Report of the Conference', 23 May 1927, repr. in *The Economic Consequences of the League: The World Economic Conference, with an Introduction by Sir Arthur Salter* (London, 1928), Appendix II, p. 194.
95. League of Nations archive, C.E.C.P. 95, Paul de Rousiers, 'Cartels and Trusts and their Development', memo for the preparatory committee of the 1927 conference. Roussiers was a professor at the Ecole des Sciences politiques, Paris. See also Julius Hirsch, 'National and International Monopolies from the Point of View of Labour, the Consuming Public and Rationalisation', C.E.C.P. 99—Hirsch was a former German minister. D. H. MacGregor, the Oxford professor of political economy, offered a more sceptical note in C.E.C.P. 93.
96. BLPES, Lloyd Papers, 7/5 'Control of Meat Imports', n.d.
97. Salter, 'Economic Policy: The Way to Peace and Prosperity', in *The Problems of Peace: Lectures Delivered at the Geneva Institute of International Relations at the Palais des Nations, August 1927* (London, 1928), p. 365.
98. League of Nations archive, 10/S 132: 295/15, Loveday papers on economic conference; 'Aide Memoire' and 'Notes from conservation between Sir Arthur Salter, Mr. Loveday, M. Stoppani and M. Jacobson, on May 1st 1927'. See also League, C.E.C.P. 24, E. Grossmann, 'Methods of Economic Rapprochement', Zurich, 15 Sep. 1926. For the corporate politics of these industrial agreements, see Maier, *Recasting Bourgeois Europe*, and Boyce, *British Capitalism*.

99. League of Nations Archive, 10/59284/53332, proposals by A. Pugh, 14 May 1927, and S.C.E.9, Memorandum on Economic Tendencies Capable of Affecting the Peace of the World, by the Labour Party and the T.U.C.

100. Salter, *Recovery: The Second Effort* (New York, 1932), p. 237; Salter, *The Framework of an Ordered Society* (Cambridge, 1933), lecture one.

101. League of Nations archive, Salter papers, 10/S 132, 308 a, Lovejoy, 'The Measurement of Tariff Levels', 28 May 1929.

102. D. J. Markwell, 'Sir Alfred Zimmern Revisited: Fifty Years On', *Review of International Studies*, 12 (1986), pp. 279–92, quoted at p. 280. See also P. Rich, 'Alfred Zimmern's Cautious Idealism', in D. Long and P. Wilson (eds), *Thinkers of the Twenty Years' Crisis: Inter-War Idealism Reassessed* (Oxford, 1995), pp. 79–99, and now J. Morefield, *Covenants Without Swords: Idealist Liberalism and the Spirit of Empire* (Princeton, 2005); O. Murray, 'Ancient History, 1872–1914', in M. G. Brock and M. C. Curthoys (eds), *The History of the University of Oxford, VII, Part 2* (Oxford, 2000), pp. 333–60.

103. A. J. Toynbee, *Acquaintances* (London, 1967), pp. 49–61.

104. L. Mumford, *Sketches from Life* (New York, 1982), p. 395.

105. A. Zimmern, 'Economic Nationalism', *The Athenaeum* (Nov. 1917), p. 560.

106. Zimmern Papers, MS 134, draft of 'The Charter in the minds of men'.

107. A. Zimmern, *Europe in Convalescence* (London, 1922), pp. 191–2.

108. Zimmern, 'Capitalism and International Relations', p. 284.

109. For the idealist legacy and Zimmern's similarities with T. H. Green's thought, see now Morefield, *Covenant Without Swords*, esp. pp. 56–95. See also J. Harris, 'Political Thought and the Welfare State'; J. Harris, 'Platonism, Positivism and Progressivism', in *Citizenship and Community*, ed. Biagini, pp. 343–60; S. den Otter, *British Idealism and Social Explanation: A Study in Late Victorian Thought* (Oxford, 1996); F. M. Turner, *The Greek Heritage in Victorian Britain* (New Haven, 1981).

110. A. Zimmern, 'Progress in Government' (1916), in *Nationality and Government*, p. 151.

111. A. Zimmern, 'German Culture and the British Commonwealth', first published in R. W. Seton-Watson, J. Dover Wilson, Alfred E. Zimmern, and Arthur Greenwood, *The War and Democracy* (London, 1914), repr. in *Nationality and Government*, pp. 1–31, quoted at p. 22. For the general climate, see S. Wallace, *Images of Germany: British Academics 1914–1918* (Edinburgh, 1988), chs 9, 10.

112. Zimmern, 'German Culture', p. 13, emphases in original. Turner's view that 'Zimmern upheld politics as a matter primarily of administration and the meeting of practical material needs to insure a life of quality' is debatable (Turner, *Greek Heritage*, p. 262).

113. A. Zimmern, 'True and False Nationalism', address to the inter-denominational conference of social service unions at Swanwick, 28 June 1915, repr. in *Nationality and Government,* p. 66.

114. B. Russell, 'National Independence and Internationalism', *Atlantic Monthly*, vol. 119 (May 1917), p. 627.

115. G. Varouxakis, *Mill on Nationality* (London, 2002). For critiques of Mill, see W. Kymlicka (ed.), *The Rights of Minority Cultures* (Oxford, 1995) and B. Parekh 'Decolonizing Liberalism', in A. Shtromas (ed.), *The End of 'Isms'?: Reflections on the Fate of Ideological Politics after Communism's Collapse* (Oxford, 1994).

116. J. R. Seeley, *The Expansion of England* (London, 1883), p. 158; D. Bell, 'From Ancient to Modern in Victorian Imperial Thought', *Historical Journal*, 49/3 (2006), 735–59.

117. Zimmern, 'True and False Nationalism', p. 77.

118. A rare recognition of Zimmern in the recent debate about nationality has been W. Kymlicka, *Multicultural Citizenship: A Liberal Theory of Minority Rights* (Oxford, 1995), though he perhaps over-emphasizes the importance of minority rights to Zimmern.

119. A. Zimmern, 'Nationality and Government' in *Nationality and Government*, p. 53. See now also G. Sluga, *The Nation, Psychology and International Politics* (Basingstoke, 2006), ch. 3.

120. Zimmern, 'True and False Nationalism', p. 76.

121. For an excellent recent close reading of these two thinkers, see Morefield, *Covenant Without Swords*, p. 106 ff., though it underestimates Zimmern's break with the inherited Free Trade vision.

122. Zimmern, 'True and False Nationalism', p. 81.

123. Ibid., p. 76.

124. A. Zimmern, *Third British Empire* (London, 2nd edn, 1927), p. 70.

125. A. Zimmern, 'Great Britain, the Dominions, and the League of Nations' (1928), in *L'Année Politique française et étrangère*, 1928, repr. in *Prospects of Democracy*, p. 301.

126. Zimmern Papers, MS 83, League of Nations Union Sub-Committee on Economic Problems, 26 Nov. 1918.

127. Zimmern, 'Fiscal Policy and International Relations', p. 245. See also B. Russell, 'National Independence and Internationalism', p. 625.

128. Zimmern, 'Fiscal Policy', p. 241. See also Salter, *Allied Shipping Control*, p. 247.

129. Zimmern, 'The British Commonwealth and the League of Nations', in *Problems of Peace* (London 1928), p. 299.

130. A. Zimmern, 'The Prospects of Democracy', in *Prospects of Democracy*, an address delivered on 8 November 1927 at Chatham House, that originally appeared in *Journal of Royal Institute of International Affairs* (May 1928), p. 12. See also Ernest Barker's paper to the League of Nations Society, 'The Power of a League of Nations', 1918, in Zimmern papers MS 83.

131. B. Metzger, 'Towards an International Human Rights Regime during the Inter-war years' in K. Grant, P. Levine and F. Trentmann (eds), *Beyond*

Sovereignty: Britain, Empire and Transnationalism, c.1880–1950, (Basingstoke, 2007), pp. 54–79.

132. A. Zimmern, *Public Opinion and International Affairs* (Manchester, 1931), p. 9.

6. LOSING INTEREST

1. In his introductory statement at the preliminary meetings of the Committee, National Archives (NA), BT 55/8.
2. F. D. Moore of Richard Moore & Sons & F. D. Moore & Co., Bradford, 5 Oct. 1916, to the textile industries committee, NA, BT 55/119.
3. J. Wheatley, *Socialise the National Income!* (Independent Labour Party, 1927).
4. Milton S. Sharp to the Committee on Textile Industries, 7 July 1916, NA, BT 55/117, at 19.
5. Mr Makower, NA, BT 55/115, 18 Sep. 1916, p. 9.
6. Britain's industrial decline and the contribution of the return to gold to it have attracted controversy ever since Keynes concluded at the time that it added 10% to British prices. Keynes' figures probably exaggerated the effect. See D. Moggridge, *The Return to Gold, 1925* (Cambridge, 1969), and K. G. P. Matthews' two articles on 'Was Sterling Overvalued in 1925?', *Economic History Review,* 2nd ser., 39/4 (1986), pp. 572–87 and 42/1 (1989), pp. 90–6. See also the shrewd observations by B. Eichengreen, 'The British Economy between the Wars', in R. Floud and P. Johnson, *The Cambridge Economic History of Modern Britain, II: Economic Maturity, 1860–1939* (Cambridge, 2004), esp. pp. 324–32. For particular industries, see N. K. Buxton and D. H. Aldcroft (eds), *British Industry Between the Wars* (London, 1979); S. Pollard, *The Development of the British Economy, 1914–80* (London, 3rd edn 1983), pp. 51–107; and now S. Bowden and D. M. Higgins, 'British Industry in the Interwar Years', in Floud and Johnson, *Economic Maturity,* pp. 374–402.
7. Memo by H. J. Skelton, 27 Sept. 1916, NA, BT 55/38, 8.
8. Milton S. Sharp, 7 July 1916, NA, BT 55/117, at p. 7.
9. Committee on Commercial and Industrial Policy, *Interim Report on Certain Essential Industries* (1918), cd. 9032; *Interim Report on the Importation of Goods from the Present Enemy Countries after the War* (1918), cd. 9033; *Final Report,* cd. 9035 (1918). For the Board of Trade committees, see NA, BT 55/20–4, BT 55/38–41, BT 55/112–21, and the respective 1918 *Reports of the Departmental Committee Appointed to Consider the Position of: the Iron and Steel Trades After the War,* cd. 9071; *the Textile Trades After the War,* cd. 9070; *the Engineering Trades After the War,* cd. 9073; *the Shipping and Shipbuilding Industries After the War,* cd. 9092; *the Electrical Trades After the War,* cd. 9072 (all London, 1918). See also Marrison, *British Business,* pp. 241–55, and Trentmann, 'Transformation of Fiscal Reform', *Historical Journal,* 39 (1996), pp. 1032–48.
10. Minutes of 25 July 1916, NA, BT 55/8.
11. Balfour of Burleigh, 18 Jan. 1917, NA, BT 55/8.

12. Lennox Lee, 5 July 1916, and Herbert W. Lee, 6 July 1916, NA, BT 55/117.
13. William Priestley, 20 Oct. 1916, NA, BT 55/120, at 17.
14. Mark Oldroyd, 17 Oct. 1916, NA, BT 55/119, at 14.
15. 7 June 1917 and 2 Aug. 1917, NA, BT 55/8.
16. J. E. Shaw, 19 Oct. 1916, NA, BT 55/120, at 18. See also Duncan Law, 20 Oct. 1916, NA, BT 55/120.
17. R. Edwards, 22 Nov. 1916, NA, BT 55/120, at 17.
18. C. Cochrane, 30 Nov. 1916, NA, BT 55/39.
19. W. Watson, 3 Oct. 1916, NA, BT 55/119.
20. T. W. Alsop, 12 Oct. 1916, NA, BT 55/38, at 56.
21. Wire Netting Association, memo of 2 Nov. 1916, NA, BT 55/38.
22. William Pearce, 7 June 1917, in NA, BT 55/13.
23. 'Summary of Miscellaneous Suggestions submitted to the Committee', revised Oct. 1917, in NA, BT 55/9.
24. Alfred Herbert, 27 July 1916, NA, BT 55/22, at 5 and 16.
25. J. E. Corby, 31 Oct. 1916, NA, BT 55/120, at 10–11.
26. Herbert, 27 July 1916, NA, BT 55/22, at 6.
27. R. Edwards, 22 Nov. 1916, NA, BT 55/120.
28. Preliminary Report on British Magneto Industry by Lieut. Commander W. A. Bristow, 8 Dec. 1916, NA, BT 55/12.
29. Advance Report by the Engineering Industries Committee on Wolfram Ore and Tungsten from the Point of View of National Safety, 20 Oct. 1916, in NA, BT 55/8.
30. Arthur Balfour, 'Statement for Board of Trade regarding the Tungsten Situation', 6 Nov. 1916, in NA, BT 55/12.
31. Evidence of the Magneto Industry to the Balfour of Burleigh Committee, 29 Nov. 1916, NA, BT 55/12.
32. For example, George Allen of Walker, Allen & Sons, manufacturers of coloured woven goods, who were shareholders in British Dyes but unimpressed by its progress; 6 July 1916, in NA, BT 55/117.
33. Peter Rylands, 25 Aug. 1916, NA, BT 55/38.
34. Cited in L. F. Haber, *The Chemical Industry 1900–1930: International Growth and Technological Change* (Oxford, 1971), p. 56.
35. See Bristow's Report, 8 Dec. 1916, NA, BT 55/12.
36. B. Ellinger, 21 June 1916, NA, BT 55/116.
37. Reply by the Minority of the Inquiry, Hugh Bell, John E. Davison, and James Gavin, 31 Oct. 1916, NA, BT 55–8. The Liverpool merchant and Liberal MP Archibald Williamson was another rare sceptic, 7 June 1917, NA, BT 55/13.
38. *Morning Post*, 20 July 1916.
39. Alfred Booth and Archibald Denny, 12 July 1917, in NA, BT 55/11, at 4; Harold Dixon, 15 Dec. 1916, NA BT 55/113; Charles Henry, 7 June 1917, NA, BT 55/13.

40. Peter Rylands, 2 Nov. 1916, in NA, BT 55/38 with appendix for the industry agreement of 20 Feb. 1906, which excluded Holland and Scandinavia.

41. F. List, *Das Nationale System der Politischen Ökonomie* [1841]. 2nd edn (Jena, 1920); R. Szporluk, *Communism and Nationalism: Karl Marx versus Friedrich List* (Oxford, 1988).

42. J. H. Pearce, 'Strictly confidential. Statement re German Steel Syndicate', 20 Oct. 1916 and evidence 2 Nov. 1916, NA, BT 55/38. See also H. J. Skelton, 27 and 28 Sep., and 11 Oct. 1916, NA, BT 55/38, and C. Copland Perry, 'A Report on ... the Stahlwerksverband', NA, BT 55/24.

43. Tariff Commission, I, *Iron and Steel* (London, 1904), para. 407, Per Pro The Bromford Iron Co., see BLPES, TC 4 16/3.

44. W. H. Mitchell, Tariff Commission, II, 2 *Woollen Industry* (London, 1905), no. 31, para. 1609, and also I, *Iron and Steel*, para. 57.

45. J. H. Pearce, 2 Nov. 1916, NA, BT, 55/38.

46. Clarendon Hyde, cross-examining Frederick Best of the steelmaker Thomas Firth & Sons, 1 Dec. 1916, NA, BT 55/23, at 22.

47. H. Birchenough, 7 June 1917, NA, BT 55/13.

48. J. Harworth, F.B.I. district secretary, Manchester F.B.I. committee minutes, 5 June 1917, Warwick Modern Records Centre, 200/F/1/1/210.

49. H. Pilling, 8 Sep. 1916, NA, BT 55/22.

50. P. Ashley to Balfour of Burleigh, 12–13 July 1917, NA, BT 55/12.

51. G. Chauvin, 19 Oct. 1916, NA, BT 55/20, at 35, 57.

52. H. J. Skelton, 28 Sep. 1916, in NA, BT 55/38, at 6–7.

53. C. S. Maier, *In Search of Stability* (Cambridge, 1987), chs. 1 and 3, and most recently his *Among Empires: American Ascendancy and Its Predecessors* (Cambridge, Mass. 2006), 191–228. Tariffs, of course, were only one (and a blunt) tool for creating the stability required by a productivist settlement.

54. Summary of Information Furnished by the War Trade Intelligence Department, 30 Aug. 1916, NA, BT 55/8.

55. Memo by Board of Customs and Excise on the Administration of Anti-Dumping Laws, 6 Sep. 1917, NA, BT 55/9.

56. 'Stenographic Report of Deputation of Representatives of the Federation of Master Cotton Spinners ... ', 5 July 1922, p. 16, NA, Cab 24, C.P. 4087.

57. R. K. Snyder, *The Tariff Problem in Great Britain, 1918–23* (Stanford, 1944), pp. 100 ff.; K. O. Morgan, *Consensus and Disunity: The Lloyd George Coalition Government, 1918–22* (Oxford, 1979), pp. 333–4.

58. Cabinet Committee on Safeguarding of Industries Bill 1921, 19 Feb. 1921, NA, Cab 27/140. E. S. Montagu, 'Safeguarding of Industries Bill', 5 March 1921, Cab 24, C.P. 2676.

59. NA, Cab 27/127: Note by the First Lord of the Admiralty (Amery), 27 Feb. 1923, C.P. No. 129 (23); Memorandum by the President of the Board of Trade, C.P. 126 (23); Committee on Safeguarding of Industries Act, Report by the Lord President of the Council (Salisbury), 4 March 1923, C.P. 138 (23).

60. Compare J. Turner (ed.), *Businessmen and Politics: Studies of Business Activity in British Politics, 1900–45* (London, 1984) and F. Trentmann, 'Transformation of Fiscal Reform' with the thesis by K. Middlemas, *Politics in Industrial Society: The Experience of the British System Since 1911* (London, 1979). See also C. Maier, *Recasting Bourgeois Europe: Stabilization in France, Germany, and Italy in the Decade After World War I* (London, 1975).

61. Marrison, *British Business*, pp. 294–323.

62. A. Balfour, 7 June 1917, NA, BT 55/13.

63. J. Turner, 'The British Commonwealth Union and the General Election of 1918', *English Historical Review* 93 (1978), 528–59.

64. Minutes of meeting, 8 Nov. 1923, Hannon Papers, House of Lords Records Office, H 13/3.

65. M. Sharp, 7 July 1916, NA, BT 55/117.

66. L. B. Atkinson, 12 July 1916, NA, BT 55/20, at 50.

67. Evidence on 4 May 1916, NA, BT 55/22, and 'Memorandum of the Recommendations made by the British Engineers' Association', 4 May 1916, NA, BT 55/24, at 5–6.

68. Marrison, *British Business*, pp. 256–93, 443–6 for detailed discussion.

69. Safeguarding of Industries Act, Part II: Fabric Gloves Committee's Report, memo by Ashley, Jan. 1922, and note by Mr Eddison, 1 Feb. 1922, NA, BT 198, B.T.C. 862.

70. 11 Oct. 1916, NA, BT 55/38.

71. Beveridge, *British Food Control*, Table XVIII, p. 359.

72. *Labour and the New Social Order* (1918), pp. 16, 20.

73. Labour Party, *Report of the Nineteenth Annual Conference* (1919), p. 148.

74. Brougham Villiers [F. J. Shaw], *Tariffs and the Worker* (London, 1919).

75. E. Whetham, *The Agrarian History of England and Wales, III: 1914–39* (Cambridge, 1978), pp. 103, 172 ff.

76. *Hansard*, 5s., 176: 2110 (30 July 1924). NA, Cab 23/48, 9 July 1924.

77. 'Sugar Beet', cabinet memo by N. Buxton, 30 May 1924, NA, Cab 24/167, C.P. 325 (24). See also Buxton's speech at the annual meeting of the British Sugar Beet Society, *The Times*, 10 Apr. 1924, p. 16.

78. 'Sugar Beet Subsidy', cabinet memo by Addison, Minister of Agriculture 26 Jan. 1931, NA, Cab 24/219, C.P. 17 (31).

79. *British General Election Manifestos, 1900–74*, ed. F. W. S. Craig (London, 1975), p. 47.

80. D. Howell, *MacDonald's Party: Labour Identities and Crisis, 1922–1931* (Oxford, 2002), pp. 234–308.

81. *Report of the Annual Conference of the Independent Labour Party*, 1923, p. 89, and pp. 120–1. See further, D. Howell, *A Lost Left: Three Studies in Socialism and Nationalism* (Chicago, 1986), part III.

82. E. Hunter, *Socialism at Work*, ILP Study Courses No. 3 (1921), pp. 14–16.

83. C. R. Attlee, *Economic History*, ILP Study Courses No. 4 (1923), p. 22.

84. 'The Loaf and the Plough: the Problem of British Farming', *New Leader*, 19 Oct. 1923, p. 9.

85. *Report of the Annual Conference of the Independent Labour Party*, 1924, pp. 75, 131.

86. H. N. Brailsford, J. A. Hobson, A. Creech Jones, and E. F. Wise, *The Living Wage* (1926), pp. 2, 13, 18, 29, 42; F. M. Leventhal, *The Last Dissenter: H. N. Brailsford and his World* (Oxford, 1985), esp. pp. 188–95.

87. 'Markets and Dominions', *New Leader*, 12 Oct. 1923, p. 2.

88. Lloyd papers, BLPES, 7/5. Lloyd was also the author of the ILP pamphlet 'The Socialisation of Banking and Credit. By "Realist"' (1923), see Fenner Brockway to Lloyd, 9 and 29 Oct. 1923, Lloyd papers 7/9.

89. *Labour's Road to Power, The Policy of the Living Income*, ILP tract 104 (1926), p. 13. See also A. Fenner Brockway, *Socialism—with Speed!* (1928).

90. MacDonald to Hobson, 8 Oct. 1926, cit. D. Marquand, *Ramsay MacDonald* (London, 1977), p. 455.

91. *Socialism and the Empire* (1926), report of the ILP Empire Policy Committee, which included Leonard Woolf, C. R. Buxton, and Harold Laski.

92. *Report of the Eighth National Conference of Labour Women*, May 1927 (1927), p. 57. See also *Report of the Tenth National Conference of Labour Women*, Apr. 1929 (1929), pp. 46 ff.

93. *The Collected Writings of John Maynard Keynes*, IX (Cambridge, 1972), p. 282.

94. P. Clarke, *The Keynesian Revolution in the Making, 1924–1936* (Oxford, 1988), p. 43.

95. NA, Cab 23/48, 5 Aug. 1924, Cab 47 (24)2; Cab 21/285, The Proposed Dyestuffs Agreement, memo by S. Webb, 22 July 1924; S. Webb to R. McKenna, 7 Aug. 1924, Midlands Bank Archive, 192.010.

96. The Export Credits Guarantee Scheme. Note by the Department of Overseas Trade, 17 June 1929, NA, Cab 27/389, D.U.(29)7.

97. Safeguarding of Industries Act (Part I), Board of Trade memo, 5 July 1922, p. 5, NA, Cab 27/178.

98. *Hansard*, 5s, 183: 65–7 (28 April 1925). By the late 1920s, the safeguarding duties brought in another £1.5 million per year.

99. M. Daunton, *Just Taxes: The Politics of Taxation in Britain, 1914–1979* (Cambridge, 2002).

100. *Yorkshire Evening Post*, 6 Dec. 1923, p. 10; see also 1 Dec. 1923, p. 8.

101. At the meeting of the advisory council to the Board of Trade's Department of Commerce, on 5 Oct. 1927, NA, BT 197, minutes of 73rd meeting.

102. 'Safeguarding of Industries, Application from the Iron and Steel Industry', cabinet memo by Cunliffe-Lister, 15 June 1925, NA, Cab 24/173, CP 292.

103. 'Iron and Steel Industry: Summary of Evidence and of Memoranda submitted to the Committee of Civil Research', 16 Nov. 1925, pp. 11–12, NA, Cab 24/175, C.P. 482; S. Tolliday, 'Tariffs and Steel 1916–34: The Politics of Industrial Decline', in Turner, *Businessmen and Politics*, pp. 50–75.

104. 'Safeguarding of Industries', memo by Cunliffe-Lister, 6 Oct. 1925, p. 3, NA, Cab 24/174, C.P. 417.

105. Eichengreen, 'British Economy between the Wars'.

106. O. Mosley and J. Strachey, *Revolution by Reason* (London, 1925), p. 27.

107. Empire Industries Association Parliamentary Committee, 22 Sep. 1925, 1 Feb. 1926, 19 April 1926, Modern Records Centre, University of Warwick, MSS 221/1/2/1. L. Haden Guest, *The Labour Party and the Empire* (London, 1926).

108. 3 Dec. 1925, in Iron and Steel Trades Confederation papers, MSS 36/F30, Modern Records Centre, Warwick.

109. 'Empire Preference or Free Trade—Which?' in *The People's Year Book and Annual of the English and Scottish Wholesale Societies 1925* (Manchester, 1925), pp. 146–53.

110. J. B. Priestley, *English Journey* (London, 1934), pp. 158, 160.

111. NA, BT 197, 26 Sep. 1923; a referendum by the *Yorkshire Evening Argus* produced 345 votes in favour of safeguarding and 91 against. In 1925, 86 per cent of Bradford manufacturers as well as most merchants demanded safeguarding, Report of the Worsted Committee, Modern Records Centre, Warwick, 126/EB/WC/1, February 1926.

112. 'Safeguarding of Industries: Report of the Woollen and Worsted Committee', memo by Cunliffe-Lister, 2 May 1929, NA, Cab 24/203, C. P. 137. BT 197/5, 2 Nov. 1927, 'Mr. Aykroyd's Memorandum on the Position of Trade in the Textile Industry in the West Riding of Yorkshire', Committee on Industry and Trade (Balfour Committee), III: *Survey of the Textile Industries* (1928).

113. *Hansard*, 5s, 213: 1392 (Cunliffe-Lister 21 Feb. 1928); *Hansard*, 5s, 219: 1365 (Steel-Maitland 4 July 1928).

114. 'Memorandum on Safeguarding of Industries' by the Labour Party Research and Information Department, Modern Records Centre, Warwick, MSS 36/P56, July 1928.

115. J. S. Foreman-Peck, 'Tariff Protection and Economics of Scale: The British Motor Industry before 1939', *Oxford Economic Papers*, 31/2 (July 1979), 237–57; M. Miller and R. A. Church, 'Motor Manufacturing', in Buxton and Aldcroft, *British Industry between the Wars*, pp. 179–215.

116. NA, BT 198/15, B.T.C. 1340, 24 Feb. 1927.

117. F. W. Hirst, *Safeguarding and Protection* (London, 1926), p. 52.

118. Modern Records Centre, Warwick, 221/1/4/1, Empire Industries Association Finance Committee; 200/F/1/1/74; 221/1/2/1, EIA Parliamentary Committee. Empire Industries Association, *Annual Report*, 1928.

119. A. Mond, *Industry and Politics* (London, 1927), p. 9.

120. For the following: NA, BT 55/23, Dudley Docker, representing the Federation of British Industires, 15 Dec. 1916, p. 4. NA, Cab 24/9; 'Imperial Trade Relations', memo by Mond, G.T. 385 (1917). Cab 24/139; 'Notes on a Further Political Programme', memo by Mond, 5 Oct. 1922.

121. Haber, *Chemical Industry*, pp. 291–300.

122. *Collected Writings of Keynes*, XIX, Part 2 (London 1981), p. 735.

123. *Britain's Industrial Future, being the Report of the Liberal Industrial Inquiry* (London, 1928), pp. 57–8. R. Skidelsky, *John Maynard Keynes, II: The*

Economist as Saviour (London, 1992), pp. 264 ff.; Clarke, *Keynesian Revolution*, pp. 81 ff.

124. *Collected Writings of Keynes, XIX*, Part 1 (London, 1981), p. 409, para. 16,563.
125. *Britain's Industrial Future*, pp. 45–6.
126. Keynes to *The Economist*, 26 March 1929, *Collected Writings of Keynes, XIX*, Part 2, p. 803.
127. N. Dimsdale and N. Horsewood, 'Fiscal Policy and Employment in Interwar Britain', *Oxford Economic Papers*, 47/3 (July 1995), 369–96.
128. *The Young Liberal Bulletin* (Dec. 1924).
129. *Free Trade Union: Imperial Preference, an address delivered at the Trocadero, London, 28 October 1926, by Walter Runciman* (London, 1926), in Runciman papers, Newcastle University Special Collections, MS 209.
130. A. Bowley and J. Stamp, *The National Income 1924: A Comparative Study of the Income of the United Kingdom in 1911 and 1924* (Oxford, 1927).
131. 1 Jan. 1927, House of Lords Records Office, Stansgate papers, ST/85/1.
132. E. Benn to W. Runciman, 14 Dec. 1928, Runciman papers MS 221.
133. Walter Runciman to Lord Merston, 14 Feb. 1929, Runciman papers MS 221.

7. FINAL DAYS

1. D. Abel, *A History of British Tariffs, 1923–42* (London, 1945); T. Rooth, *British Protectionism and the International Economy: Overseas Commercial Policy in the 1930s* (Cambridge, 1993).
2. *Hansard*, 261: 279–97 (4 Feb. 1932).
3. F. W. Hirst diary 21 Nov. 1931 and 29 Aug. 1932, cit. in Hirst, *The Formation, History and Aims of the Liberal Free Trade Committee, 1931–46* (Heyshott, 1947), pp. 13, 23, with thanks to Philip Williamson for sharing this privately printed source with me.
4. P. Williamson, *National Crisis and National Government: British Politics, the Economy and Empire, 1926–1932* (Cambridge, 1992); B. Eichengreen, 'Sterling and the Tariff, 1929–32', *Princeton Studies in International Finance* 48 (Princeton, 1981); R. Bassett, *Nineteen Thirty-one: Political Crisis* (London, 1958); S. Ball, *Baldwin and the Conservative Party: The Crisis of 1929–1931* (New Haven, 1988).
5. From £729 million in 1929 to £422 million in the twelve months ending September 1931. This partly reflected the fall in prices by 35 per cent, but even measured in 1931 prices, the collapse of British exports is astounding: from £614 million in 1929 to just over £400 million; NA, Cab 27/467, C. P. 25 (32), Report of the Cabinet Committee on the Balance of Trade, 19 Jan. 1932.
6. Shipbuilding Employers' Federation report to the Advisory Committee to the Department of Overseas Trade, NA, BT 90/13, minutes 28 May 1930.

7. See Neville Chamberlain's account of 30 Jan. 1932, in Chamberlain papers, NC 8/18/1. NA, Cab 27/467, B.T. (31), Cabinet Committee on the Balance of Trade, minutes of 8 Jan. 1932.

8. NA, Cab 27/467, B.T. (31), 1st meeting on 16 Dec. 1931.

9. Sir Walter Raine, the deputy-president, *The Times*, 6 Oct. 1928, p. 6.

10. 3 June 1930, cit. Marrison, *British Business*, p. 397.

11. Marrison, *British Business*, pp. 414–26.

12. *Commonwealth Trade: A New Policy* (1930), pp. 6–7. The memo had originally been prepared in May 1930. See also Milne-Bailey's memo of 15 July 1930, in TUC Archives, T 217, 935.1.

13. 12 June 1930, Citrine Papers, BLPES, London, 1/7, World Tour 1930, II; see also 15 June 1930.

14. R. Nugent to W. Mullins, 17 Dec. 1930, FBI industrial policy committee, Modern Records Centre, Warwick, 200/F/3/S1/13/1.

15. *The Times*, 4 July 1930, p. 10.

16. Tolliday, *Business, Banking and Politics*.

17. *The Times*, 16 July 1930, p. 9.

18. Schuster at Lincoln, *The Times*, 24 Oct. 1930, p. 11; Martin on 6 Nov. 1930 in his inaugural address as President of the Institute of Bankers, *The Bankers' Magazine* (Dec. 1930), pp. 851–2.

19. Abel, *Benn*, p. 68.

20. *The Times*, 4 March 1931, p. 14.

21. For this and the below, see Keynes' memorandum to the Committee of Economists of the Economic Advisory Council, 21 Sept. 1930, *Collected Writings of Keynes*, XIII (London, 1973), cit. pp. 184–5, 191, 199. See further Skidelsky, *Keynes*, II, pp. 363–78 and B. Eichengreen, 'Keynes and Protection', *Journal of Economic History*, 44 (1984), pp. 363–73.

22. Notes of Discussion, 28 Feb. 1930, Macmillan Committee, *Collected Writings of Keynes*, XX (London, 1981), p. 117.

23. Keynes' memo to the EAC, *Collected Writings of Keynes*, XIII, (London, 1973), p. 193.

24. Keynes, 'Proposals for a Revenue Tariff', *New Statesman and Nation*, 7 March 1931, repr. in *Collected Writings of Keynes*, IX (*Essays in Persuasion*), pp. 231–8.

25. W. Beveridge (ed.), *Tariffs: The Case Examined* (London, 1931).

26. Alfred Beesley to Edwin Cannan, 2 March 1932, Cannan papers 1032, BLPES.

27. *Evening Standard*, 16 March 1931.

28. A. Bullock, *The Life and Times of Ernest Bevin, I* (London, 1960), pp. 417–47. Citrine, too, was moving towards a revenue tariff, see G. Locock to J. Lithgow, 20 Feb. 1931, in Nugent Papers, Modern Records Centre, Warwick, 200/F/3/D1/9.

29. *TUC Report, 1930*, p. 283.

30. MacDonald diary entry for 19 Aug. 1931, MacDonald papers, NA, MS 1753.

31. Williamson, *National Crisis*, pp. 285–343; Marquand, *Ramsay Macdonald*; Skidelsky, *Second Labour Government*; Snowden, *Autobiography*, II.

32. Lansbury, 'Unemployment Policy', 22 Nov. 1930, NA, Cab 27/435, C. P. 390 (30).

33. R. R. Enfield, 'Import Boards', pp. 30–1, NA, Cab 27/417, paper no. 14.

34. Addison memo, 'Statutory Quota of British Wheat in Flour', 5 May 1930, NA, Cab 24/211, C.P. 143. See also the cabinet discussion of 15 April 1931, Cab 23/66, Cab 22(31)–8, p.12.

35. *Manchester Guardian*, 14 July 1930. See also Lloyd's 'Notes on the Wheat Position and the Idea of an Import Board', n.d., c. mid-1930, and his memo to the Committee on Agricultural Policy, 15 March 1930 (CAP 30, no. 16), Lloyd papers 4/4.

36. *Hansard*, 241: 1402f (16 July 1930). See also Wise's address to cooperators, *Co-operative News*, 22 Feb. 1930, p. 6.

37. For this view, Thorpe, *British General Election*, p. 145.

38. *Co-operative News*, 28 Nov. 1931, p. 4. See also 'The Foolish Fetish of Cheapness', *The People's Weekly*, 11 Oct. 1930, p. 10.

39. *Co-operative News*, 11 April 1931, p. 10.

40. Ibid., 12 April 1930, p. 1, 28 Feb. 1931, p. 1.

41. Ibid., 28 Nov. 1931 p. 4.

42. *Report of the 31st Annual Conference*, p. 199.

43. Craig, *British Election Manifestos*, p. 90.

44. Thorpe, Table 10.1, p. 220.

45. *Co-operative News*, 15 Aug. 1931, p. 13, 24 Oct. 1931, pp. 2–3.

46. Ibid., 18 Oct. 1930, p. 12.

47. Co-operative Party, *Britain Reborn, Buy British*, no. 4 (Manchester, 1932); *The Times*, 23 Feb. 1932, p. 9; 23 Nov. 1933, p. 8.

48. The formal split between Samuelites and Simonites eliminated any remaining chances of revival, see D. Dutton, '1932: A Neglected Date in the History of the Decline of the British Liberal Party', *Twentieth Century British History*, 14/1 (2003), pp. 43–60.

49. FBI Fiscal Policy Enquiry Committee, minutes 19 June 1931, FBI papers, 200/F1/1/74.

50. Hirst diary, 15 Oct. 1931, Hirst, *Liberal Free Trade Committee*, p. 11.

51. Correspondence between Mrs Hirst and Villard, 7 May, 2 and 10 June 1931, Houghton Library, Harvard College, Cambridge Mass., bMSAm 1323.

52. Dunford House, Sussex, guestbook.

53. 'A Memorandum of Recent Experiences, by E. G. Brunker,' 14 Nov. 1930, in Runicman papers MS 225.

54. Hirst diary, 19 Feb. 1932, Hirst, *Liberal Free Trade Committee*, p. 20.

55. FBI Fiscal Policy Enquiry Committee, minutes 12 Nov. 1931, 19 June 1931, FBI papers, 200/F1/1/74. Marrison, *British Business*, pp. 418–19.

56. Frederick Leith Ross, the government's chief economic adviser, in 1935 attributed 60% to cheap money, 30% to the tariff, and a mere 10% to

Ottawa; 10A/R 4406, Leith Ross to P. Stoppani at the League of Nations, 9 May 1935, League Archives, 10A/R 4406; S. Howson, *Domestic Monetary Management in Britain, 1919–38* (Cambridge, 1975). A more positive view is M. Kitson and S. Solomou, *Protectionism and Economic Revival: the British Inter-war Economy* (Cambridge, 1990), but see Eichengreen's concise diagnosis in 'British economy', pp. 330–42. For Ottawa, see Rooth, *Protectionism*.

57. e.g. at a speech in Norwich, 8 March 1935, Runciman papers MS 215, and already at the cabinet committee on the balance on trade, NA, Cab 27/467, B.T. (31), minutes of 8 Jan. 1932.

58. 'Pros and Cons of Tariffs', 25 Nov. 1932, repr. in *Collected Writings of Keynes* (London 1982), XXI, quoted at pp. 206–7.

59. *Report of the National Conference of Labour Women*, 1932, p. 83.

60. M. D. Stocks, *Doctor Scholefield: An Incident of the Hungry Forties* (Manchester, 1936).

61. *League of Nations, Commercial Policy in the Interwar Period: International Proposals and National Policies* (Geneva, 1942); F. Trentmann, 'Coping with Shortage: The Problem of Food Security and Global Visions of Coordination, c. 1890s–1950', in *Food and Conflict in Europe in the Age of the Two World Wars*, ed. F. Trentmann and F. Just (Basingstoke, 2006), pp. 13–48.

62. Rappard gave the 8th Cobden lecture in 1936: *The Common Menace of Economic and Military Armaments* (London, 1936). For these networks, see R. Cockett, *Thinking the Unthinkable: Think-Tanks and the Economic Counter-Revolution, 1931–83* (London, 1994).

63. Hirst, *Liberal Free Trade Committee*, pp. 28–32.

64. Abel, *Free Trade Challenge*, pp. 17–18; *The Free Trader*, 30 (Dec. 1945), p. 10. Alexander's papers in BLPES, Coll. Misc. 565.

EPILOGUE

1. *Eigentümlich frei*, 4/17 (Sep. 2001), pp. 4, 10–12; http://www.local.attac.org/attac40/article.php3?id_article=62.

2. http://www.oxfam.org/en/programs/campaigns/maketradefair/navigation_page.2005-11-22.6064108504.

3. I have traced this advancing amnesia at greater length in 'The Resurrection and Decomposition of Cobden in Britain and the West: an Essay in the Politics of Reputation', in A. Howe and S. Morgan (eds), *Rethinking Nineteenth-Century Liberalism* (Aldershot, 2006), pp. 264–88.

4. 13 Dec. 2005, at http://www.wdm.org.uk/news/presrel/current/freetrade.htm.

5. *The Guardian*, 26 Sept. 2005, p. 8; *New Statesman*, 31 Oct. 2005, p. xvi. See also *The Independent*, 19 Feb. 2003, p. 7; *The Guardian*, 18 Sept. 2004, p. 14.

6. A. Maddison, *The World Economy: A Milennial Perspective* (OECD, 2001), Table F-5, p. 363.

7. These figures are more modest than earlier estimates in 2001 and 2003, see D. van der Mensbrugghe, 'Estimating the Benefits of Trade Reform: Why Numbers Change', in R. Newfarmer, *Trade, Doha, and Development* (Washington D.C/World Bank, 2006), pp. 59–75.

8. See esp. M. Wolf, *Why Globalization Works* (New Haven, CT, 2004), pp. 109 ff., pp. 138–219; J. Bhagwati, *In Defense of Globalization* (Oxford, 2004), pp. 51–72. See also P. Legrain, *Open World: The Truth About Globalisation* (London, 2002). World Bank, *Global Monitoring Report 2007* (Washington DC, 2007), pp. 39–65.

9. See further Newfarmer, *Trade, Doha, and Development*.

10. J. Stiglitz, *Making Globalization Work: The Next Steps to Global Justice* (London, 2006).

11. James, *End of Globalisation*, pp. 101–67.

12. B. S. Bernanke, 'Global Economic Integration: What's New and What's Not?', 25 Aug. 2006, 13th annual economic symposium, Jackson Hole, Wyoming, http://www.federalreserve.gov/boarddocs/speeches/2006/2006 0825/default.htm.

13. A. Baker, 'Why Is Trade Reform so Popular in Latin America? A Consumption-Based Theory of Trade Policy Preferences', *World Politics*, 55/3 (2003), pp. 423–55; M. Murillo, *Labour Unions, Partisan Coalitions and Market Reform in Latin America* (New York, 2001).

14. H. Bliss and B. Russett, 'Democratic Trading Partners: The Liberal Connection, 1962–89', *Journal of Politics*, 60/4 (1998), pp. 1126–47; E. Mansfield, H. V. Milner, B. P. Rosendorff, 'Free To Trade: Democracies, Autocracies, and International Trade', *American Political Science Review*, 94/2 (2000), pp. 305–21.

15. H. V. Milner and K. Kubota, 'Why the Move to Free Trade? Democracy and Trade Policy in the Developing Countries', *International Organization* 59 (2005), pp. 107–43.

16. Bhagwati, *In Defense of Globalization*. A more critical view of the IMF and World Bank is J. E. Stiglitz, *Globalization and Its Discontents* (London, 2002). See also D. Harvey, *A Brief History of Neoliberalism* (Oxford, 2005), esp. pp. 87–119.

17. P. Bairoch, 'European Trade Policy, 1815–1914', in *Cambridge Economic History of Europe*, ed. P. Mathias and S. Pollard, VIII (Cambridge, 1989), pp. 1–160; H. Liepmann, *Tariff Levels and the Economic Unity of Europe* (London, 1938).

18. D. Y. Kono, 'Optimal Obfuscation: Democracy and Trade Policy Transparency', *American Political Science Review*, 110/3 (2006), pp. 369–84.

19. And five times higher in developing countries, see World Bank, *Global Monitoring Report 2005* (Washington DC, 2005).

20. The idea that the new liberal political economy of Adam Smith 'entailed a demoralising of the theory of trade and consumption', was given its iconic

status by E. P. Thompson in his seminal article on 'The Moral Economy of the English Crowd in the Eighteenth Century', *Past and Present* 50 (1971), pp. 76–136. A second major influence was Karl Polanyi's, *The Great Transformation*. See the Guide to Further Reading for critiques.

21. D. N. McCloskey, *The Bourgeois Virtues: Ethics for an Age of Commerce* (Chicago, 2006). P. R. Greenough, 'Indulgence and Abundance as Asian Peasant Values: A Bengali Case in Point', *Journal of Asian Studies*, 42/4 (1983), pp. 831–50. See also V. A. Zelizer, *The Purchase of Intimacy* (Princeton, NJ, 2005).

22. e.g., Intermon Oxfam's posters 'El Comercio Trabaja a Favor de Los Ricos', at the Barcelona Fair Trade week, May 2005. *The Guardian*, 18 Sept. 2004, p. 14.

23. H. Simon, *Models of Man, Social and Rational: Mathematical Essays on Rational Human Behavior in a Social Setting* (New York, 1957); D. Kahneman and A. Tversky (eds), *Choices, Values, and Frames* (Cambridge, 2000); A. Offer, *The Challenge of Affluence: Self-Control and Well-Being in the United States and Britain since 1950* (Oxford, 2006).

24. M. Callon (ed.), *The Laws of the Markets* (London, 1998).

Guide to Further Reading

The following Guide is meant to give readers some principal points of entry into the larger literature. A fuller seventy-five page list of the main archival collections, printed sources, and scholarly books and articles can be found at http://www.bbk.ac.uk/hca/staff/franktrentmann/Free TradeNation. The endnotes for each chapter also give citations. I have tried to trace Free Trade across different genres of sources, from visual materials to the private collections of politicians, from popular leaflets to cabinet papers, and from the thoughts of businessmen and consumers to the ideas of public intellectuals. These have been all too frequently studied in separate compartments and branches of history. This can provide depth and detail but also runs the risk of obscuring the interplay and connections between different spheres of life. Inevitably, the separation of archives, libraries, and source materials does violence to the constant braiding and unbraiding of people's lives that is history. In the research for this book I have tried to read across the various fields to follow the flow of the debate and show as best as I can how people understood and connected economy and politics over time.

The best overview of Britain in the twentieth century is Peter Clarke's thought-provoking *Hope and Glory* (London, 1996). For the social and economic transformation of Britain between the Great Exhibition in 1851 and the Festival of Britain in 1951, readers are now fortunate to have Martin Daunton's magisterial *Wealth and Welfare* (Oxford, 2007), which arrived as this book was going to press.

In the writing of history, and British history in particular, the last two decades have seen a widening gulf between politics and the economy. This estrangement resulted in no small part from two opposing intellectual fashions. One group of historians followed a 'linguistic turn', drawing on postmodernism. The most sustained application is Patrick Joyce's *Democratic Subjects* (Cambridge, 1994); the essays in *Re-reading the Constitution* (Cambridge, 1996), edited by James Vernon, are the most wide-ranging. These cultural histories had the benefit of opening up the realm of politics to the narrative construction of power and identities in stories and discourse. The material world was marginalized. The linguistic turn has generated much theoretical debate; the problems with the use of 'discourse' are clearly brought out by Mark Bevir, *The Logic of the History of Ideas* (Cambridge, 1999), which looks to 'beliefs' instead.

A second group, meanwhile, has taken a more positivist turn, applying economic models and statistical regressions to the past. For our period, the fruits of this approach are brought together in the second volume of the new *Cambridge Economic History of Modern Britain* (Cambridge, 2003), edited by Roderick Floud and Paul Johnson. 'Cliometric' history's statistical rigour allows it to clarify complex aggregate problems, such as the costs and benefits of Free Trade and Empire. But it has also led to an abstraction of the economy, disconnected from what people did, felt, and thought in the past. For all their ideological differences, liberal economics and postmodernism were part of the same momentum that pulled the economy apart from politics and culture. Deirdre McCloskey is a rare case of someone who straddled both approaches, first with seminal contributions to the former, especially in *Enterprise and Trade in Victorian Britain* (London, 1981), before emphasizing the role of *Knowledge and Persuasion in Economics* (Cambridge, 1994). Otherwise these camps have produced two incommensurable languages. They rarely talk to each other. This is a pity. The 'economy' and 'politics' are artificial abstractions, not reflections of some natural reality. The past does not come separated in these neat containers. In this book I have sought to repair some of these broken connections, by starting not with an abstract model but with how the economic and political ideas and practices of people in the past were woven together, stretched, loosened, and newly intertwined.

The intellectual origins of Free Trade in the seventeenth and eighteenth centuries have attracted a large literature. Albert Hirschman's essay *The Passions and the Interests* (Princeton, 1977) remains a model of clarity and argument, showing how commerce came to be appreciated for its virtuous, softening *douceur*. Richard Teichgraeber's *'Free Trade' and Moral Philosophy*

(Durham, NC, 1986) takes the story up to Adam Smith, Emma Rothschild in her illuminating *Economic Sentiments* (Cambridge Mass., 2001) all the way to Condorcet and the French Revolution. The tensions between the commercial model and economic nationalism are the focus of Istvan Hont's *Jealousy of Trade* (Cambridge, Mass., 2005). Gareth Stedman Jones' thought-provoking *An End to Poverty?* (London, 2005) looks at how freedom of trade became truncated and lost its social democratic vision during the revolutionary and Napoleonic wars. The subsequent takeover of the idea by Tory Liberals and its central place in evangelical religion can be followed in Boyd Hilton's seminal *Corn, Cash and Commerce* (Oxford, 1977) and *The Age of Atonement* (Oxford, 1988).

In *Against the Tide* (Princeton, 1996), Douglas Irwin gives an economist's account of how the idea of Free Trade fought off intellectual critics time and again, becoming a more rigorous and refined theory in the process. What counts as a strong and useful theory, of course, depends on what it is wanted for and who is asking. For all its analytical beauty, admired by liberal economists to this day, the ideas of Smith and Ricardo often came second best in the modern world, overpowered by the theories of Karl Marx and Friedrich List, a story well told by Roman Szporluk in *Communism and Nationalism* (New York, 1988). Even in Britain, liberals were not the only thinkers in town, as Anna Gambles shows in her study of conservative economic discourse, *Protection and Politics* (Woodbridge, 1999). International trade theory does not stand still. There are many guides to recent developments but few are as accessible and authoritative as Paul Krugman's *Rethinking International Trade* (Cambridge, Mass., 1990) and *Pop Internationalism* (Cambridge, Mass., 1996) or Jagdish Bhagwati's *Protectionism* (Cambridge, Mass., 1989).

Britain's repeal of the Corn Laws in 1846 occupies a pivotal place in the literature—perhaps too much so. In part, this is because Cobden and followers heralded it as a historical watershed at the time, in part because the lobbying activities of the Anti-Corn Law League have given political scientists a convenient test case for models of collective action. Both of these claims should be viewed with a dose of caution. Norman McCord's *The Anti-Corn Law League* (London, 1958) remains the standard history. Paul Pickering and Alex Tyrrell's *The People's Bread* (London, 2000) offers a more rounded view of the League, especially good on the role of women, but can also be read to reveal its social and regional limits. John Morley's *Life of Richard Cobden* (London, 1881) remains the classic biography; a more recent one is Nicholas Edsall's *Richard Cobden: Independent Radical* (Cambridge, Mass., 1986). The latest political scientist to turn to Repeal is Cheryl Schonhardt-Bailey, *From the Corn Laws to Free Trade* (Cambridge, Mass., 2006), who attempts the perhaps impossible task of isolating interests from ideas and institutional factors. Many of the key terms and questions were first outlined by E. E. Schattschneider in his *Politics, Pressure and the Tariff* (New York, 1935), a study of the revision of the 1929–30 US tariff.

The relationship between trade, interest groups, and political coalitions is the focus of two influential accounts in political science and international relations, Peter Gourevitch's *Politics in Hard Times* (Ithaca, NY, 1986) and Ronald Rogowski's *Commerce and Coalitions* (Princeton, 1989). These are best read alongside recent historical works that show how agriculture, finance, and industry were internally far more divided than these models recognize. A more complex picture of agrarian interests emerges from Rita Aldenhoff-Hübinger, *Agrarpolitik und Protektionismus: Deutschland und Frankreich im Vergleich 1879–1914* (Göttingen, 2002). I have discussed conceptual as well as empirical problems in 'Political Culture and Political Economy', in *Review of International Political Economy*, vol. 5 (1998).

Free Trade needs to be placed in a European and global setting. We have several useful starting points. The essays in *The Political Economy of British Historical Experience, 1688–1914* (Oxford, 2002), edited by Donald Winch and Patrick O'Brien, chart how the British model took shape in a competitive transnational mode of observation, critique, and emulation. Readers interested in the rise and fall of Cobden's international influence can now turn to the essays assembled by Tony Howe and Simon Morgan in *Rethinking Nineteenth-Century Liberalism* (Aldershot, 2006), which, in spite of its title, also traces the decline of his public reputation in the twentieth century, increasingly limited to libertarian and neo-conservative think-tanks. European trade policies are discussed by Paul Bairoch, *Commerce extérieur et développement économique de l'Europe au XIXe siècle* (Paris, 1976) and in his *Economics and World History* (New York, 1993) which exposes the connection between liberal policies and economic growth as a myth.

That Free Trade was not all about peaceful and benign exchange but also about force and domination was the thesis Ronald Robinson and John Gallagher put forth in their classic article on the 'Imperialism of Free Trade' published in *The Economic History Review* in 1953; the term had originally been put into circulation by protectionist historical economists like William Cunningham half a century earlier. The rise of the United

States into a superpower gave it fresh salience, and it has been debated ever since. Bernard Semmel's *The Rise of Free Trade Imperialism* followed in 1970 (London, 1970). See also D. C. M. Platt, *Latin America and British Trade* (London, 1972), and on India: Peter Harnetty, *Imperialism and Free Trade* (Vancouver, 1972); Basudev Chatterji, *Trade, Tariffs, and Empire* (Oxford, 1992). P. J. Cain and A. G. Hopkins gave this debate a new direction with their thesis of 'gentlemanly capitalism' in which the City and Empire walk hand in hand; see their *British Imperialism, 1688–1914* (London, 1993) and *Gentlemanly Capitalism and Imperial Expansion*, edited by Raymond Dumett (London, 1999). Thanks to them the place of finance in imperialism is now clearly recognized, although it is unnecessary to view City and Industry as rival blocks or milieus. David Kynaston's four volumes will transport readers into *The City of London* (London, 1994–2001).

The strongest indictment of Free Trade is Mike Davis' enormously controversial *Late Victorian Holocausts* (London, 2001) where Britain's Free Trade Empire plays the role of murderous accomplice in the great drought in India in the late 1870s. To what degree Free Trade was always coercive and whether a different trade system might have prevented mass starvation are open to question, but that it is debated is thanks to Davis' original weaving together of political economy and global and environmental history. With *The Birth of the Modern World* (Oxford, 2004) Chris Bayly has written a model global history that, too, places 1846 in a longer history of globalization. At the same time as pointing to the imperial force of Free Trade, especially in the Middle East and in China, Bayly highlights the very limited, fragile integration of world trade by the mid-nineteenth century. How deeply the Empire suffused British society is a matter of controversy. Bernard Porter's provocative *Absent-Minded Imperialists* (Oxford, 2004) finds little evidence of imperial culture, but this is partly a result of where and how he was looking to measure cultural influences. For the opposite view, see, for example, Catherine Hall, *Civilising Subjects* (Oxford, 2002). As far as Free Trade is concerned the issue is not one of imperial presence or absence but of competing visions of empire. The differences between the British and the American Empire are discussed in Bernard Porter's *Empire and Superempire* (New Haven, CT, 2006). Reading Victoria de Grazia's *Irresistible Empire* (Cambridge, Mass., 2005) on the American 'market empire' is stimulating in this context, for Cobdenites never managed to construct a similar expansionist network of state support, cultural agencies, and business.

In *Bargaining on Europe* (New Haven, CT, 1999), Peter Marsh follows the European trade network sparked by Cobden and Chevalier's treaty in 1860, and how it was hollowed out in the next generation, a process which he blames squarely on Britain's unilateral stance of waiting on the sidelines for France to drive forward the process of commercial integration. The late nineteenth century revealed the limited power of the Free Trade Empire to force open world markets. How Free Trade helped transform the Victorian British state from a fiscal-military state into a more neutral, consensual regime is discussed in Martin Daunton's *Trusting Leviathan* (Cambridge, 2001) and is a running thread in Richard Price's *British Society, 1680–1880* (Cambridge, 1999). The British state's response to relative decline and tariff proposals is examined by Aaron Friedberg in *The Weary Titan* (Princeton, 1988), with obvious parallels with American decline in mind. Rival states, by contrast, discovered tariffs as a way of financing social and military projects, factors highlighted by John Hobson in *The Wealth of States* (Cambridge, 1997). For the United States, see David Lake, *Power, Protection and Free Trade* (Ithaca, NY, 1988).

In their coverage of the battle between Free Trade and Tariff Reform before the First World War, most researchers have flocked to one side, the Conservative party and protectionist pressure groups, in spite of the fact that what really needs explaining in the British case is the peculiar mobilization and defence of Free Trade. This has left the literature lopsided. The fiscal controversy becomes a game of shadow boxing, rather than an interactive, dynamic fight, especially at the level of everyday politics and communication. Ewen Green's *The Crisis of Conservatism* (London, 1995) is the most wide-ranging and stimulating, although the 'radical' or modernizing aspects of Tariff Reform can be exaggerated. In addition there are Bernard Semmel, *Imperialism and Social Reform* (London, 1960), Alan Sykes, *Tariff Reform in British Politics* (Oxford, 1979), Wolfgang Mock, *Imperiale Herrschaft und nationales Interesse* (Stuttgart, 1982); Frans Coetzee, *For Party or Country* (Oxford, 1990); Alfred Gollin, *Balfour's Burden* (London, 1965); and Richard Rempel, *Unionists Divided* (Newton Abbot, 1972). To get a taste of the distinct flavour of 'Cakes and Ale' popular Conservatism, readers can turn to Jon Lawrence, *Speaking for the People* (Cambridge, 1998). Peter Marsh brings out the businessman inside the politician in his biography of *Joseph Chamberlain* (New Haven, 1994). Readers with more time may also benefit from dipping into the more partisan six-volume biography begun by J. L. Garvin, the fervent Tariff Reform editor of *The*

Observer, in the late 1920s and only completed by Julian Amery in the 1960s (London, 1932–69). Robert Self picks up the story of tariff reform after the First World War in *Tories and Tariffs* (London, 1986).

By contrast, historians, and social scientists more generally, have found it difficult to engage with the changing meaning and position of Free Trade in society and politics. Liberal-minded writers have invoked its natural superiority. Critics have demonized it as laissez-faire individualism. This made it hard to appreciate that Free Trade was not some unchanging substance that had entered British bones in 1846 but a historically evolving set of beliefs, communities, and politics that, to survive, could not just rest on the laurels of Cobden and Peel but needed to adapt and innovate. The most thorough study of how Free Trade established its hold on power after 1846 is Anthony Howe's *Free Trade and Liberal England* (Oxford, 1998), which especially offers an important account of how what had been a radical set of policies became a governing tool of a ruling elite. The centrality of Free Trade to popular Gladstonian liberalism is brought out in Eugenio Biagini's *Liberty, Retrenchment and Reform* (Cambridge, 1992).

Many historians of Edwardian liberalism were writing under the shadow of the welfare state and inspired by hopes for a progressive alliance. Inevitably, this articulated itself in a preoccupation with the genesis of social democracy, in particular the history of social reform, the relationship between Liberals and Labour, and the decline of the Liberal party. Free Trade was always acknowledged as part of liberal culture, but writers' intellectual curiosity and political energy lay elsewhere—by the 1960s–70s Free Trade was firmly associated with free market conservatives and opposition to the European community. There are many insights in Peter Clarke's classic trilogy, *Lancashire and the New Liberalism* (Cambridge, 1971), *Liberals and Social Democrats* (Cambridge, 1978), and *The Keynesian Revolution in the Making* (Oxford, 1988). In *Liberalism and Sociology* (Cambridge, 1979), Stefan Collini unfolds the new liberal thought of Hobhouse, who, in addition to being a leading sociologist was secretary of the Free Trade Union. Michael Freeden offers an analytical approach in *The New Liberalism* (Oxford, 1978).

Inquiries into the radical continuities between Liberalism and Labour set off a fruitful debate, not least for identifying divergence as much as convergence; see *Currents of Radicalism* (Cambridge, 1991), edited by Eugenio Biagini and Alastair Reid, and the follow-up *Citzenship and Community* (Cambridge, 1996), compiled by Biagini. To understand the rise of Labour, see Duncan Tanner, *Political Change and the Labour Party,*

1900–1918 (Cambridge, 1990); Ross McKibbin's *The Evolution of the Labour Party* (Oxford, 1974) and his *Ideologies of Class* (Oxford, 1994); and Alastair Reid's history of trade unions, *United We Stand* (London, 2004).

The literature on the First World War is vast. Paul Kennedy's *The Rise of Anglo-German Antagonism* (London, 1980) remains invaluable. The best overall account now is David Stevenson, *Cataclysm* (New York, 2004). On the imperial and domestic politics of food, see Avner Offer, *The First World War: An Agrarian Interpretation* (Oxford, 1989) and Margaret Barnett, *British Food Policy During the First World War* (London, 1985). For the impact on the state, see Kathleen Burk (ed.), *War and the State* (London, 1982), for politics, see John Turner, *British Politics and the Great War* (New Haven, 1992); John Grigg, *Lloyd George: War Leader, 1916–18* (London, 2002); and Michael Bentley, *The Liberal Mind, 1914–29* (Cambridge, 1977).

Accounts of post-war politics have been strongest at the level of parties, leaders, and governments: Kenneth O. Morgan, *Consensus and Disunity* (Oxford, 1979) on the Lloyd George coalition; John Campbell, *Lloyd George: The Goat in the Wilderness, 1922–31* (London, 1977); Maurice Cowling, *The Impact of Labour* (Cambridge, 1971); Trevor Wilson, *The Downfall of the Liberal Party* (London, 1966); Chris Cook, *The Age of Alignment* (Toronto, 1975); David Howell's *MacDonald's Party* (Oxford, 2002) and David Marquand, *Ramsay MacDonald* (London, 1977); Stuart Ball, *Baldwin and the Conservative Party* (London, 1988) and Philip Williamson, *Stanley Baldwin* (Cambridge, 1999); Andrew Thorpe, *The British General Election of 1931* (Oxford, 1991). How political manoeuvres, rather than business pressure, created the 'crisis' and national government of 1931 is revealed in Philip Williamson, *National Crisis and National Government* (Cambridge, 1992).

Economic diplomacy and tensions between City and Industry are followed in Robert Boyce, *British Capitalism at the Crossroads* (Cambridge, 1987). Businessmen's fiscal views are discussed in fine detail in Andrew Marrison's *British Business and Protection* (Oxford, 1996). In *Politics in Industrial Society* (London, 1979), Keith Middlemas came closest to presenting a British version of corporatism, a model with considerable political as well as intellectual pull at that time. Since then, there has been scepticism, see John Turner (ed.), *Businessmen and Politics* (London, 1984). Richard Davenport Hines, *Dudley Docker* (Cambridge, 1984) paints a wonderfully vivid and important picture of a leading businessman and 'trade warrior' in action.

Since the 1980s, a rediscovery of civil society and an interest in consumption has stimulated new questions and approaches. Instead of a focus on parties and the state, civil society turned attention to social movements and visions of social self-organization. John Keane's collection *Civil Society and the State* (London, 1988) set off a wave of new ideas. The controversial history of the concept can be traced in the *Civil Society* reader (New York, 2005) which John Hall and I put together. Historians have put the concept to different uses, see the essays in Jose Harris (ed.), *Civil Society in British History* (Oxford, 2003), my own collection *Paradoxes of Civil Society* (Oxford, 2003, 2nd edn), Nancy Bermeo and Philip Nord (eds), *Civil Society Before Democracy* (Lanham Md., 2000), and Stefan-Ludwig Hoffmann, *Civil Society* (Basingstoke, 2006). An excellent case study of associational life in nineteenth-century Leeds is R. J. Morris, *Class, Sect, and Party* (Manchester, 1990). Though not framed in terms of civil society, see also Peter Gurney, *Co-operative Culture and the Politics of Consumption in England* (Manchester, 1996); Gillian Scott's study of the Women's Cooperative Guild, *Feminism and the Politics of Working Women* (London, 1998); and Martin Pugh, *Women and the Women's Movement in Britain, 1914–59* (Basingstoke, 1992).

The renewed interest in consumers and in civil society should be seen in tandem. The work of American historians has been especially helpful in highlighting the affinities as well as tensions between consumption and citizenship: Lizabeth Cohen, *A Consumer's Republic* (New York, 2003); Meg Jacob, *Pocketbook Politics* (Princeton, NJ, 2005). See also Erika Rappaport, *Shopping for Pleasure* (Princeton, NJ, 2000); *Getting and Spending* (Cambridge, 1998), edited by Susan Strasser, Charles McGovern, and Matthias Judt; Martin Daunton and Matthew Hilton (eds) *The Politics of Consumption* (Oxford, 2001); Matthew Hilton, *Consumerism in Britain* (Cambridge, 2004); and *The Making of the Consumer* (Oxford, 2006), which I edited. The Free Trade citizen-consumer was always only an ideal. In reality, citizenship and public life was carved up in different class-based consuming cultures, expertly reconstructed and brought to life by Ross McKibbin, *Classes and Cultures* (Oxford, 1998). See further the essays John Brewer and I assembled in *Consuming Cultures, Global Perspectives* (Oxford, 2006).

For internationalism, see Peter Cain, *Hobson and Imperialism* (Oxford, 2002); David Long, *Towards a New Liberal Internationalism* (Cambridge, 1996); David Laity, *The British Peace Movement* (Oxford, 2001); Martin Ceadel, *Semi-Detached Idealists* (Oxford, 2000); David Long and Peter

Wilson (eds), *Thinkers of the Twenty Years' Crisis* (Oxford, 1995); Fred Leventhal, *The Last Dissenter* (Oxford, 1985) on H. N. Brailsford; Chrisine Bolt, *Sisterhood Questioned?* (London, 2004). We also now have an excellent reading of Zimmern, Murray, and idealist liberalism, thanks to Jeanne Morefield, *Covenants Without Swords* (Princeton, 2005). See also Glenda Sluga, *Nation, Psychology, and International Politics, 1870–1919* (Basingstoke, 2006) and Peter Mandler, *The English National Character* (New Haven, CT, 2006). For public intellectuals in Britain (they do exist), see Stefan Collini, *Absent Minds* (Oxford, 2006).

Our understanding of economic knowledge and policy is overshadowed by the towering figure of Keynes. Robert Skidelsky's monumental three-volume biography *John Maynard Keynes* (London, 1983–2002) sees him breaking with new liberalism. In *The Keynesian Revolution in the Making*, Peter Clarke describes a more on-going evolution of new liberal ideas (Cambridge, 1988). See also Peter A. Hall (ed.), *The Political Power of Economic Ideas* (Princeton, 1989); Mary Furner and Barry Supple (eds), *The State and Economic Knowledge* (Cambridge, 1990); Daniel Ritschel, *The Politics of Planning* (Oxford, 1997); Richard Toye, *The Labour Party and the Planned Economy* (Woodbridge, 2003). For the hibernation and resurgence of free market ideas in the second half of the twentieth century, see Richard Cockett, *Thinking the Unthinkable* (London, 1994).

How we should think about morals and markets has been a subject of prolonged debate. Recent social scientists, associated with Actor-Network-Theory, have rightly stressed that 'the economy' is an analytical abstraction and warned against projecting it onto reality as if human relations corresponded to it. But to apply this insight to then focus on how economists and accountants order the world in economic categories, as Michel Callon notably has done in the collection *The Laws of the Markets* (Oxford, 1997), is only of limited use. Instead, as this book tries to do, we should start with how people understand the economic world, and trace the moral, political, and cultural associations that sustain their views, and their rearrangement over time.

Some writers and commentators continue to view modern history in terms of a sharp caesura, a shift in the nineteenth century from a 'moral economy' to one of liberal markets and selfish consumerism. E. P. Thompson's 'Moral Economy of the English Crowd in the Eighteenth Century', originally published in *Past and Present* in 1971, and Karl Polanyi's *The Great Transformation* (Boston, 1944) had a profound influence on an earlier generation of historians and social scientists. The idea remains popular with current Fair Traders looking for a 'remoralization' of the economy but has largely lost its academic credentials. Markets and morals, money and affection, are not mutually exclusive but continue to overlap in our world, in private and public lives. Adam Smith understood this. A stimulating account by a recent sociologist is Viviana Zelizer, *The Purchase of Intimacy* (Princeton, NJ, 2005); Deirdre McCloskey, *The Bourgeois Virtues* (Chicago, 2006) offers an idiosyncratic mix of personal stories, economics, and ethics by a renowned economic historian.

For the world depression in 1929–31 and international relations in the inter-war years, see Harold James, *The End of Globalization* (Cambridge Mass., 2001); Zara Steiner, *The Lights that Failed* (Oxford, 2005). For the gold standard and the monetary factors behind Britain's adoption of the general tariff, see Barry Eichengreen's *Golden Fetters* (Oxford, 1992) and *Sterling and the Tariff* (Princeton, 1981). Tariff bargaining is analysed in depth by Tim Rooth, *British Protectionism and the International Economy* (Cambridge, 1993), who finds few gains; see also Forrest Capie, *Depression and Protectionism* (London, 1983). Michael Kitson and Solomos Solomou are more optimistic in *Protectionism and Economic Revival* (Cambridge, 1990)—too much so, according to commentators like Eichengreen who stress how the tariff was like a cushion, retarding rationalization.

For trade policy, international organizations, and the world economy after the Second World War see Harold James, *The Roman Predicament: How the Rules of International Order Create the Politics of Empire* (Princeton, NJ, 2006); Charles Maier, *Among Empires: American Ascendancy and Its Predecessors* (Cambridge, Mass., 2006); Robert Gilpin, *The Political Economy of International Relations* (Princeton, 1987); Anne Krueger, *Trade Policies and Developing Nations* (Washington DC, 1995).

In the contemporary debate about globalization, the one book that probably did most to capture and reinforce popular critiques was Naomi Klein's attack on global corporations and branding in *No Logo* (New York, 1999). An introduction to Fair Trade is Alex Nicholls and Charlotte Opal, *Fair Trade* (London, 2005). There are now several popular books by economists who make the case for trade liberalization: Martin Wolf, *Why Globalisation Works* (New Haven, 2004); Jagdish Bhagwati, *In Defense of Globalization* (Oxford, 2004); Philippe Legrain, *Open World* (London, 2002). Joseph Stiglitz, the Nobel-prize winning Columbia economist and former chief economist at the World Bank, has occupied a singularly important role in mediating between the extremes of globalization critics and liberal economists, defending the gains from greater free trade but also calling for government intervention and more transparent, better coordinated international organizations, themes explored in his best-selling *Globalisation and Its Discontents* (London, 2002) and *Making Globalisation Work* (London, 2006).

Index